Contents

Practical Deep Learning for Computer Vision with Python

First Edition

David Landup

Publisher Information

Practical Deep Learning for Computer Vision with Python

by David Landup

Published by StackAbuse

StackAbuse books are created and meant to be purchased for educational purposes. Online editions for most titles are available at www.stackabuse.com. For more information, visit the website or contact us at support@stackabuse.com.

Cover Design and Illustrator: Jovana Ninković

September 2022: First Edition

Revision History of the First Edition:

2022-09-15: First Release

2022-10-10: Second Release

1 Preface

1.1 Who This Book is For?

We are interfacing with deep learning and the applications of deep learning algorithms every day. With the technology shifting away from only the "cool kids" to practically everyone - there's a huge influx of researchers from various domains, as well as software engineers in the field.

This book is dedicated to everyone with a basic understanding of machine learning and deep learning, to orient themselves towards or initially step into computer vision - an exciting field in which deep learning has been making strides recently. The book will primarily be using Keras - the official high-level API for TensorFlow, with some PyTorch in later lessons.

While prerequisite knowledge of Keras isn't strictly required, it will undoubtedly help. I won't be explaining what an activation function is, how cross-entropy works or what weights and biases are. There are amazing resources covering these topics, ranging from free blogs to paid books - and covering these topics would inherently steer the focus of the book in a different direction than it's intended to be set in. The book is written to be beginner-friendly, with layers to be extracted through multiple reads. Not everything is likely to "stick" after the first read, so intermediate users will find useful information on critical thinking, advanced techniques, new tools (many are covered and used interchangeably instead of reusing the same pipeline), and optimization techniques. The last lesson covers how we can achieve 90% parameter reduction and 50% training time reduction while maintaining validation accuracy, for example.

I've decided to use Keras for the vast majority of the book because it's proven de-facto to be the best framework for relaying high-level concepts into actionable code that delivers results, without drowning you in the technical details. On the other hand, you can dig deeper and access lower levels of the API when required. While TensorFlow, the back-end typically used with Keras, isn't as highly regarded by the deep learning community, it's still the leading framework powering the majority of production applications, and provides a great ecosystem besides the framework itself. You don't need to interface with TensorFlow's lower-level API if you don't want to, if you use Keras. Additionally, TensorFlow gets a worse reputation than it should have, due to the tech debt present from earlier days and versions, which is rapidly being changed.

Lessons that utilize PyTorch are located later in the book in a situation where deviating from the TensorFlow ecosystem benefits us more than it doesn't, such as for object detection. A good engineer can switch tools, and while it's tempting to stay in a single ecosystem, you shouldn't base your experience and knowledge on the quirks of a single framework - but rather, focus on building skills and understanding of concepts through different lenses.

While writing the book I've focused on covering both the technical, intuitive and practical side of concepts, demystifying them and making them approachable.

The name of the book starts with *"Practical..."*. Many think that this mainly means having lots and lots of code and not much theory. Skipping important *theory of application* leads to bad science and bad models for production. Throughout the book I'll be detouring to cover various techniques, tools and concepts and then implement them practically. It's my humble opinion that practicality requires an explained basis, as to why you're practically doing something and how it can help you. I tried making the book practical with a focus on making you *able* to implement things practically. This includes a lot of breaks in which we ask ourselves *"Ok, but why?"* after code samples.

This also includes okay-but-not-ideal practices in the beginning, identifying their weaknesses, and correcting them later on. This builds foundations much stronger than just going with the better practice from the get-go, since many times, the differences aren't too aparent from a quick glance. These small differences are what makes ML research irreproducible and production systems fail silently. They're understandable to make, and easy to slip into your workflow. **Let's work them out** lesson by lesson.

Things don't always work - you should know why you're trying them out. I want this book to not only teach you the techical side of Computer Vision, but also *how to be a Computer Vision engineer.*

1.1.0.1 For the Researcher: I hope that this effort pays off in the sense that professionals coming from different fields don't struggle with finding their way through the landscape of deep learning in the context of computer vision, and can apply the correct methodologies required for reproducible scientific rigor. In my time navigating research papers - there are clear issues with applying deep learning to solve current problems. From leaking testing data into training data, to incorrectly applying transfer learning, to misusing the backbone architectures and preventing them to work well, to utilizing old and deprecated technologies that are objectively out of date - modern research could significantly be improved by providing a guiding hand that helps researchers navigate the landscape and avoid common pitfalls. **These mistakes are understandable.** Re-orienting from a lifetime of life sciences to applying computer vision to a problem you're passionate about is **difficult**. Addressing this requires building resources that equip researchers with the required know-how to shine in computer vision as much as they shine in their respective fields. This book tries to do exactly that.

1.1.0.2 For the Software Engineer: I used to be a software engineer before diving into machine and deep learning. It's a vastly different experience. Many call deep learning *"Software 2.0"* - a term coined by Andrej Karpathy, one of the major names in deep learning and computer vision. While some raise disputes about the naming convention - the fact of the matter is that it's fundamentally different than what a classical software engineer is used to. Software is about precisely writing down a sequence of steps for a machine to take to achieve a goal. This is both the beauty and bane of software - if it works, it works exactly and only because you wrote it to work. If it doesn't work, it doesn't work exactly and only because you wrote it to not work (usually accidentally). With Software 2.0, instead of explicitly writing instructions, we write the container for those instructions, and let it figure out a way to reach some desired behavior.

At many junctions and problems I tried to solve using software, it was extremely difficult to come up with instructions, and for some problems, it was downright impossible. Imbuing software with machine and deep learning models allows our solutions to problems to also include something extra - something that's beyond our own expertise. When I wanted to help solve an unrealistic bubble in the real estate market by providing accurate appraisals free of charge for all users of the website - I knew that I would never be able to code the rules of what makes the price of some real estate. It was both beyond my expertise, and beyond my physical capabilities. In the end, I built a machine learning system that outperformed local agencies in appraisals and imbued my software with this ability. As a software engineer - you can **empower your code** with machine and deep learning.

1.1.0.3 For the Student: Every fresh graduate that lands an internship gets to realize the gap between traditional academic knowledge and production code. It's usually a process in which you get hit with a hard case of an impostor syndrome, fear and self-doubt. While these feelings are unnecessary, they're understandable, as you're suddenly surrounded by a wall of proprietary solutions, frameworks and tools nobody told you about before and nuanced uses of paradigms you might be familiar with. Thankfully, this state is easily dispelled through practice, mentorship and simply getting familiar with the *tools*, in most cases. I hope that this book helps you get ahold of the reins in the deep learning ecosystem for computer vision, covering various tools, utilities, repositories and ideas that you can keep in the back of your head. Keep at it, slow and steady. Incremental improvement is an amazing thing!

1.1.0.4 For the Data Enthusiast: You don't have to be a professional, or even a professional in training, to appreciate data and hierarchical abstraction. Python is a high-level programming language, and easy to get a hold of even if you haven't worked with it before. Without any experience in computer science, software engineering, mathematics or data science, the road will definitely be more difficult, though. Many issues you might run into won't necessarily be tied to the language or ecosystem itself - setting up a development environment, handling versions of dependencies, finding fixes for issues, etc. are more likely to be a show stopper for you than learning the syntax of a `for` loop. For example, debugging is natural for software engineers, but is commonly being put off by practitioners who step into ML/DL without an SE background.

Even so, delegating your environment to free online machines (such as Google Colab or Kaggle) removes a lot of the issues associated with your local environment! They're useful for novices as much as for advanced practicioners. They offer free and paid versions, and really helped make both research and sharing results much easier, especially for those without an SE background.

You might also be a philosopher or ethicist looking to break into data or AI ethics. This is an important and growing field. Computer vision systems (as have other machine learning systems) have faced their criticisms in the past in regards to ethically questionable biases. Only when we realize that we have problems can we start fixing them - and we need more people assessing the work of data scientists and helping to root out bias. Having a surface-level understanding of these systems might be sufficient for some analysis - but having a more in-depth understanding (even if you don't intend on **building** some yourself) can help you assess systems and aid in improving them.

1.2 Do I Need Expensive Equipment?

No. It's great if you have it, but it's not necessary. Having a tower build with 4 graphics cards won't make you a good deep learning engineer nor researcher - it'll just make the algorithms run faster.

Some datasets, to be fair, are possible but simply impractical to run on slower systems, and computer vision is generally best done with a GPU. If you don't have access to one *at all* - you can always use cloud-based providers. **They're free**. Platforms like Kaggle and Google Colab, at the time of writing, provide you with a weekly quota (in hours) of free GPUs you can use. You just connect to their cloud-based service, and run your notebooks. Even if you have a GPU, chances are that theirs are going to be better than yours. The selection of GPUs and access changes through time, so to stay up to date with their offerings, it's best if you visit the websites yourself.

Other providers do exist as well - and they typically offer a subscription that nets you access to better resources and/or have a payment model where you pay for each minute/hour you use their resources for. I purposefully won't mention or explicitly endorse any paid product for obvious reasons in the book though, a quick Google search can find the competitive services.

Without a doubt - services like these substantially help democratize knowledge and access to resources, making research from any part of the world, from the comfort of your home very possible and plausible. You can get cutting-edge performance models within a reasonable timeframe, on a lot of the tasks you decide to dedicate your time to, with these services.

1.3 How the Course is Structured

The book is structured through *Guides* and *Guided Projects*.

Guides serve as an introduction to a topic, such as the following introduction and guide to *Convolutional Neural Networks*, and assume no prior knowledge in the narrow field but can assume prior knowledge of prerequisites (such as at least basic understanding of loss functions and activation functions for example).

Guided Projects are self-contained and serve to bridge the gap between the cleanly formatted theory and practice and put you knee-deep into the burning problems and questions in the field. With Guided Projects, we presume only the knowledge of the narrower field that you could gain from following the lessons in the book. For the digital version of this material: You can enroll into Guided Projects as individual mini-courses, though, you gain access to all relevant Guided Projects by enrolling "Practical Deep Learning for Computer Vision with Python". All of the content from the online version is ported into the physical version.

Once we've finished reviewing *how* they're built, we'll assess *why* we'd want to build them. Theory is theory and practice is practice. Any theory will necessarily be a bit behind the curve - it takes time to produce resources like books and courses, and it's not easy to "just update them".

> *Guided Projects* are our attempt at making our courses stay relevant through the years of research and advancement. Theory doesn't change as fast. The application of that theory does.

In the following lesson, we'll jump into *Convolutional Neural Networks* - how they work, what they're made of and how to build them, followed by an overview of some of the modern architectures. This is quickly followed by a real project with imperfect data, a lesson on critical thinking, important techniques and further projects.

1.4 Source Code and Notebooks

The source code of this book is made public and freely available on GitHub[1], throughout various Jupyter Notebooks that encapsulate all of the Guided Projects in the book. This GitHub repository is meant to serve as a central place to hold all of the source code, track issues and changes and host a community of people looking to apply Computer Vision to their field.

As APIs change and new practices are put into place, I'll be updating the repository. I've executed and tested all code samples in the book and they work at the time of publishing.

If you're having issues with some code samples, there's a chance that an API change occurred, so check the repository. Some URLs were shortened in the book due to rendering issues, and they'll be present in the repository.

[1] https://github.com/DavidLandup0/dl4cv

1.5 Contact

If you want to contact the author (questions, issues, remarks, other feedback, sharing your own work), please don't hesitate to send an email to *david@stackabuse.com*!

2 Introduction to Computer Vision

2.1 The Role of Vision

Take a moment to look around you. There's *stuff* all around you! If you're sitting at a desk, you're likely in front of a monitor, and a keyboard - and maybe a hot (or cold) beverage of choice in a mug. If you're in public transport, there are pipes, shoes, people, seats.

> How long did it take for you to infer what these objects are and how laborious was the process?

When you look down at your coffee mug, you're not at all surprised by the object in front of you. You've been able to do that since you were much younger than you are now. If you can *read* this - you've already trained yourself in visual pattern recognition, and context recognition, stringing together words in a sentence to form a coherent message. Way before you can read, even as a baby, you can distinguish between a cat and a dog, as well as between a bird and a whale. Whether you're aware of the *labels* we've assigned to them ("dog", "chien", "собака", "Hund", etc.) doesn't change the fact that the features that make up a dog are different from the features that make up a whale.

> Vision is one of the dominant senses in humans.

Other senses, and more particularly, our *perception* of our surroundings depends on vision. *"Seeing is believing"* is a very common quote, implying that something doesn't *exist* if we can't see it. Naturally, we can't deny the existence of gravity or electrical forces because we just can't see them, and the quote is outdated. Additionally, when you *see* something while under the influence of psychodelics - it doesn't necessarily mean that it exists outside of and regardless of your own subjective experience. While arguments could be made against the semantics of the quote, such as that we see the *effects* of gravity, and therefore, we need to *see to believe*, the role of *sight* is integral to our perception of the world around us.

2.2 How Do We See?

Note This section is meant for a wider public. It will condense some neuroscience and computer science research and concepts into a digestible format, omitting some technical details and simplifying the vast fields, in order to paint a picture that you can turn into a foundation. The point is to give you a framework of thought that's useful to use when thinking about vision and perception, and to help scope what it exactly is that we're trying to solve with computer vision.

It's fairly well known *how our eyes work* and how the signal gets to our visual cortex, that makes sense of it. Modeling the eye, we made extremely powerful and complex cameras, which work in much the same way.

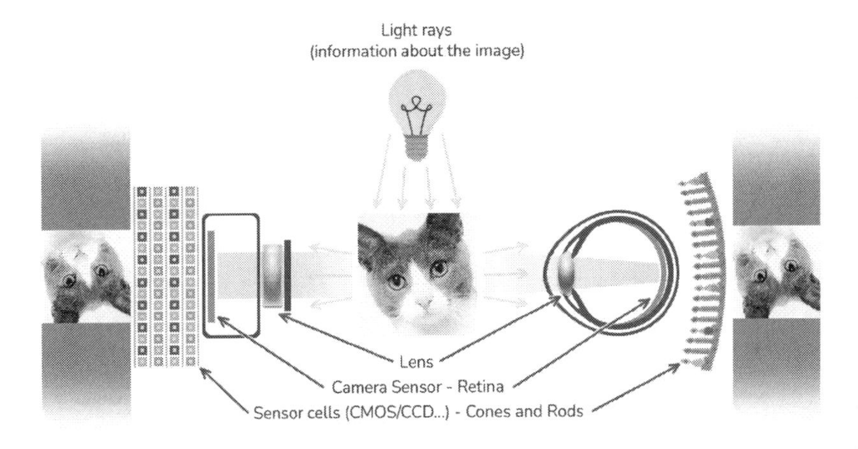

Figure 1:

While eyes have *cones* and *rods* that react to the different frequencies of visible light, cameras have arrays of light-responsive sensors (known as photodiodes) that do the same. Cameras are, quite literally, mechanical eyes and work using the same principles as our organs!

Though, where things become somewhat unclear is *after* that. How are these "images" represented in our brains and how do we exactly make sense of them. In recent years, amazing advancements have been made into the theory of the visual cortex (and the neocortex in general), but there's still a lot left to be discovered. In computers, images are represented as sets of binary digits, which can be decoded into a set of RGB values that are to be displayed on a screen. This is partly due to the way sensors and monitors work - recording spatial intensity of light on the sensors and displaying that same information on a monitor.

> There is no solidified scientific consensus on perception and consciousness, yet, there are useful frameworks of thought.

There are many promising theories and advances are being made with each passing year, but we still lack a unified theory of how information entering your eyes gives rise to your experience. However, tremendous strides have been made and some mechanisms of the brain have been understood well. *How we perceive information* can be decoupled from *how we process information*, and we know a thing or two about how the visual cortex uses the signals that come from our eyes, and some guesses as to how it can be decoded into our perception.

To solve computer vision, we need to solve vision (information processing and perception). That's no small task. While simplified, it helps to think of vision as a two-stage process - **encoding** and **decoding**. This concept is also one of the key concepts in computer science, and a driving factor behind various neural network architectures and systems, some of which will be covered later in the book.

Encoding is useful for *understanding*, as it captures the salient information in a signal and reshapes it into something more useful (whatever useful may mean for a certain goal).

Decoding is useful for *explaining*, as it takes the salient encoded information and turns it either into an approximation of the original signal, or any reshaped form of it.

In the context of deep learning, this concept is applicable in various fields. Some of these (that concern us for this book are:

- **Natural Language Processing (NLP)** - encoder networks are great at understanding sentences, while decoder networks are great at generation.
- **Computer Vision (CV)** - encoding visual information is usually done via neural networks we call *Convolutional Neural Networks (CNNs or ConvNets for short).* Encoder-decoder architectures can be used for generative neural networks that project meaningful signals into images. We'll create an encoder-decoder network to describe images using text later in the book.

In the context of computer science, the concept is applicable to such a wide variety of applications that you're relying on encoding-decoding systems probably every second of your life.

> The information we capture (encode) is different from what we perceive (decode).

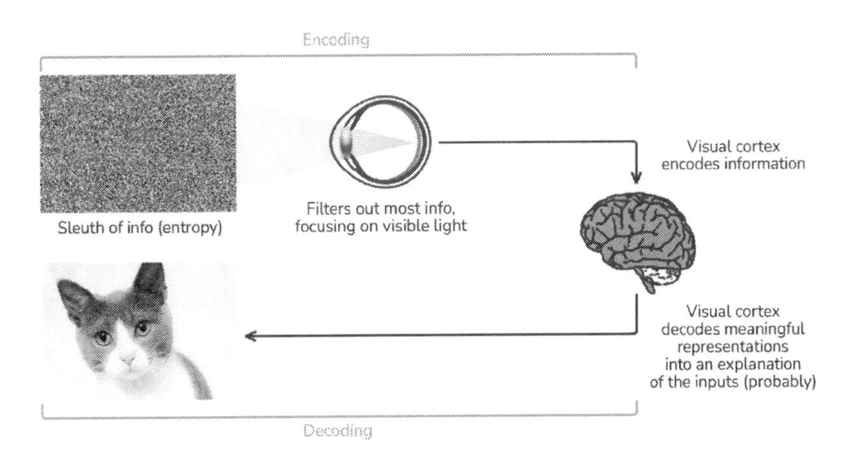

Figure 2:

If you choose to represent the state of the world around you as information - there's a sleuth of it. Electromagnetic waves of various frequencies fly around (and through you) at any given moment. Barring all other properties and constituent elements of physics - your eyes filter out only a small portion of the EMS (electromagnetic spectrum) known to us as *visible light*. The photon that bumps onto a cat and enters your eye isn't qualitatively different from the photon that hit the wall, or a dog. They're informationally decoupled from the object they bumped into. Yet, when it enters your eye, which activates the optic nerve (which again, transfers information in the form of an electric sigal, not the photon itself), and into the visual area of the cerebral cortex (commonly shortened to the visual cortex) - meaningful representations of that information are encoded, even through several layers of abstraction in serialization.

What happens after this is debatable but an increasing number of neuroscientists believe that the brain makes a Bayesian best guess at what explains the incoming signal, and project that prediction into the "3D world" that we see. This *inside-out* rather than the *outside-in* model might be unintuitive for some, but it explains much of the phenomena we couldn't explain otherwise. Some, such as Anil Seth, a professor of Cognitive and Computational Neuroscience at the University of Sussex, go as far as to call our perception **controlled hallucinations**. While the name might make it sound more esoteric than it really is - the idea is that what we perceive is just what we project as prediction of what the world must be to explain the inputs, in a controlled manner. This would be useful evolutionarily, since that allowed us to escape predators, undersand scenes around us, coordinate ourselves, etc.

> The inside-out model also allows us to frame computer vision in a different light. Those only concerned with encoding intuitively think of vision as an outside-in process since you obtain information from the 'outside' and make conclusions 'inside'. Vision is more than that.

Whether this theory is right or not doesn't change the fact that thinking in this framework helps scope computer vision. We typically use images obtained through cameras (mechanical eyes), use neural networks to encode information (one part of the visual cortex) and another neural network to decode that information (whether it's to decode it into a class, for classification of images, a caption for the image, a segmentation mask, bounding boxes for objects, or back into another representation of the image):

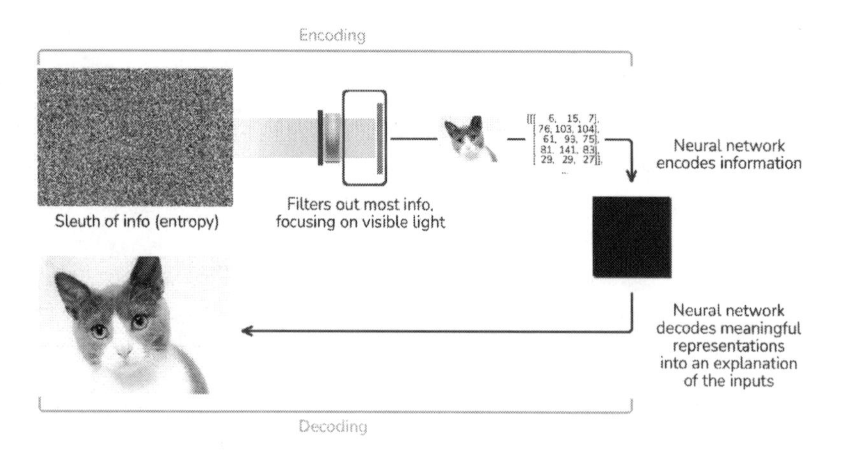

Figure 3:

We'll be building deep learning systems that classify images, feed into decoders to generate text, detect objects and their locations, semantically segment images, and so on in the book. Throughout all of these, the concept of encoding information will be always present, while the way we decode it differs based on your task:

- Classification
- Object detection
- Caption generation
- Segmentation
- Pose Estimation
- Image generation
- etc...

We'll form a more in-depth view into what these entail later in this lesson.

We've figured out the encoding part further than the decoding part so far, both with deep learning and with neuroscience. Some of the latest emerging advancements are concerned in large part with decoding (VAEs, GANs, diffusion models, etc.).

The first big advancement in utilizing deep learning for computer vision came when Kunihiko Fukushima modeled the way (the encoding part of) the visual cortex works computationally, back in 1979, dubbed the Neocognitron. We're still riding on the avalanche started by that paper but we've also (recently) started exploring some other models on feature extraction.

We'll come back to the Neocognitron later.

2.3 Computer Vision and Deep Learning

This segways us into Computer Vision! Computer Vision is a very large field, with a plethora of sub-fields. It was a notoriously difficult field to make advances in, *especially* before deep learning. Computer vision is difficult, and exciting.

> How do you automate the process of object detection, classification, segmentation, etc.?

Humans are exceedingly good at spatial awareness even when standing still. You're aware of whether an object is closer or further away from you, as well as where it's located in respect to other objects. How do you exactly code this? Even if you had all the time in the world to make a rule-based system in which a straight line, with another straight line, that has a curvature on the side is a "mug" - you'd have a hard time thinking of all the possibilities and edge cases. In computer vision - rule-based systems were ruled out fairly quickly as a concept.

> As often, we reasoned by analogy. We found what works well and tried modeling it.

From 1958[2] to 1968[3], David H. Hubel and Torsten N. Wiesel performed experiments with cats and monkeys, examining how their visual cortex works. Amongst other findings, their experiments reported that for both cats and monkeys, neurons in the visual cortex have a *small local receptive field*.

This underlies how our neurons encode visual input. *Some neurons* fire *some of the time*, on certain small features. Some neurons only fired at straight lines, while some fired only at curved lines. Throughout the experiments, they noticed that some neurons have a larger receptive field, and that these neurons typically reacted to more complex patterns, which were *created by* the more simple patterns that some other neurons fire for. These were, at the time, dubbed *"simple cells"* and *"complex cells"* in absence of a better term.

> While the visual cortex isn't as simple and clear cut as "Neuron 1 fires only on horizontal lines, and should thus be named the horizontal neuron" - this discovery was crucial.

The visual cortex, like much of the rest of the neocortex, works with **hierarchies**, low-level features (straight or curved lines) feed into higher-level features (edges), which feed into higher-level features, until you know how to discern a cat from a dog or a whale, or the letter "A" from the digit "4" even though their constituent features are shared.

[2] https://www.ncbi.nlm.nih.gov/pmc/articles/PMC1363130/
[3] https://www.ncbi.nlm.nih.gov/pmc/articles/PMC1359523/

Figure 4:

This was something to go from! And in 1979 Kunihiko Fukushima published the *"Neocognitron: A Self-organizing Neural Network Model for a Mechanism of Pattern Recognition Unaffected by Shift in Position"*[4]. The architecture built on top of the idea of S-Cells (simple cells) and C-Cells (complex cells), where simple cells feed into complex cells, creating a hierarchy. It was a self-organizing system, into which you'd feed representative images. This was a precursor to modern **Convolutional Neural Networks (CNNs)**, which have proliferated and advanced the field from recognizing basic shapes and patterns to superhuman ability in recognizing objects and localizing them in images and even live videos.

What was started by Fukushima was extended by Yann LeCunn, one of the "godfathers" of AI, in 1998 via *"Gradient-Based Learning Applied to Document Recognition"*[5], in which raw input is passed through a *feature extractor* and the resulting feature vector is passed through a *trainable classifier module* that determines the class of the input.

> If you've worked with CNNs before - this will sound very familiar.

At this point, it's worth taking a step back and realizing that CNNs, like all models, are just models of how the visual cortex works. Just as a digital calculator and an analog calculator can both give the same results - the way they work towards that goal is inherently different. They're not a miniature visual cortex. They're a miniature visual-cortex inspired architecture, that yieds similar performance.

[4]https://www.rctn.org/bruno/public/papers/Fukushima1980.pdf
[5]http://yann.lecun.com/exdb/publis/pdf/lecun-01a.pdf

2.4 Alternatives to CNNs?

In general, there are two schools of thought:

- We should reason by analogy
- We should reason from first principles

Both methods work, most of the time. When it's unclear from which principles to go from, we might as well reason by analogy to establish a field, and then re-think the process from the ground up with newfound first principles. This is also exactly what happened with computer vision.

Our first attempts at solving computer vision was trying to directly model the visual cortex. Recently, a totally different architecture has been proposed, built on ***the Attention Mechanism***, and the architecture is known as a **Transformer**. It was proposed in 2017 by the Google Brain and Google Research teams in *"Attention Is All You Need"*[6]. A lot of attention is being shown to the promise of the new architecture and the field is divided - it's very unclear which type of architecture holds the *most* potential down the line.

Ironically - *Vision Transformers* took cues from the hierarchical architectures of CNNs, which propelled them upwards in leaderboards! Before that - they weren't very flexible.

For a while, it seemed that transformers are taking the lead and on a website such as PapersWithCode[7], you can see an up-to-date leaderboard of models and the architectures they're built on. In 2022, at the point in time in which transformers were at the top of the leaderboard, *ConvNeXt*, a *"ConvNet for the 2020s"*[8], was released, humbly reminding everyone that there's still much to discover, such as porting ideas of transformers to CNNs (closing the loop of 'inspiration').

Recently - people have been making combinations of CNNs *and* Transformers! Nobody knows what the future holds, but it's exciting. It's a great idea to keep track of the leaderboard from time to time - it changes very frequently!

[6] https://arxiv.org/abs/1706.03762
[7] https://paperswithcode.com/sota/image-classification-on-imagenet
[8] https://arxiv.org/abs/2201.03545

2.5 Computer Vision Tasks and Applications

Computer Vision is a vast field and can be applied to a wide variety of problems. We can automate a lot of actions we take such as pulling a level, clicking a button, sounding an alarm, etc. but it used to be very hard to automate the decision process that lead to those actions.

Clicking a button is simple! Recognizing a bear near the campsite, for which you'll want to sound an alarm, didn't use to be really simple for computers. While many "box" computer vision into mainly image classification (which factually is a big part of it, in different flavors), it's much *much* more than just that. A general rule of thumb is:

> Can you see that something is different from something else?

If yes - you can apply computer vision to it. If not - you can still *probably* apply computer vision to it. A popular example is sound! If you join a competition to recognize the sounds of animals, such as birds - you'll find that it's easier to convert the sound into a soundwave or better yet - a spectrogram, and classify them using computer vision, instead of analyzing patterns in the sound sequences themselves.

Here's an example from a Kaggle Notebook[9] written by Shreya, for the BirdCLEF competition:

[9]https://www.kaggle.com/code/shreyasajal/birdclef-librosa-audio-feature-extraction

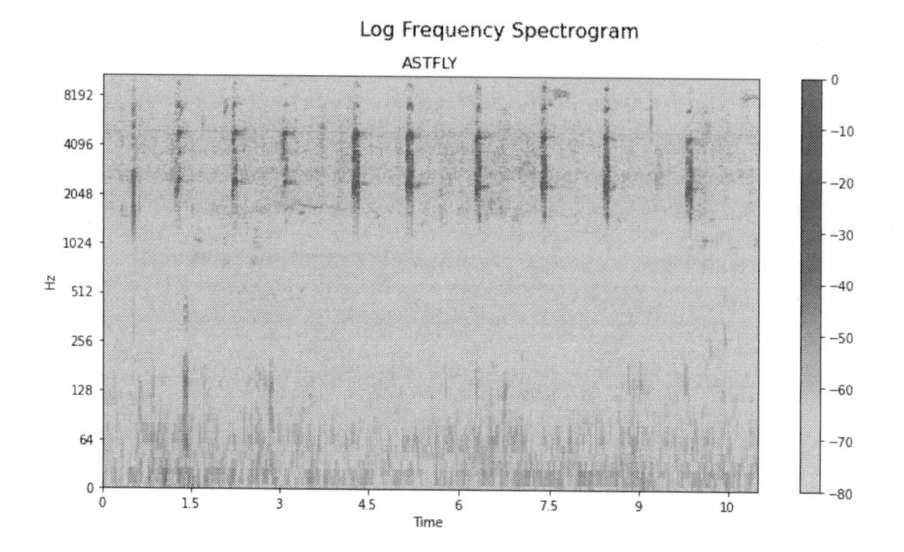

Figure 5: Shreya's Visualization of bird sounds as a spectrogram

This is what an Ash-throated Flycatcher's ("astfly") sounds *look like*! Depending on the type of spectrogram you use, the images can very clearly delineate one species of bird from another. A similar technique was used by Ray Kurzweil's company that tried tackling understanding human speech **back in the 1980s**. They realized that it's easier to plot the frequencies wavelengths and classify phonemes based on those frequencies, rather than analyzing sequences with manually-coded expert systems from that time. In *"How to Create a Mind"*, Kurzweil reflects on the technique:

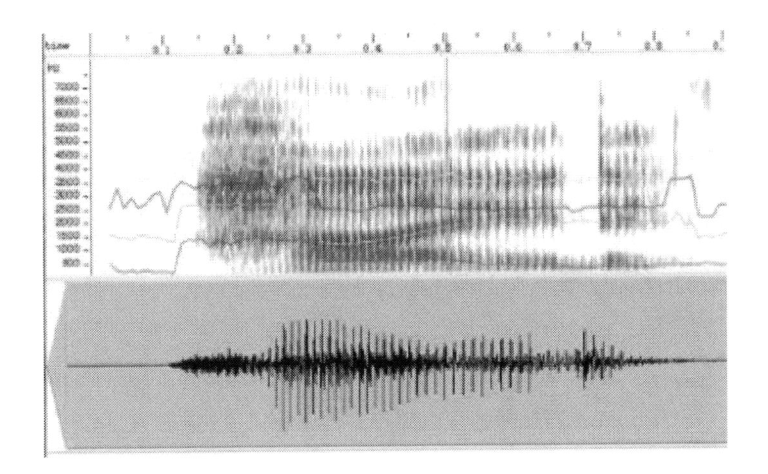

Figure 6: A spectrogram of a person saying the word 'hide', as taken from Ray Kurzweil's book - "How to Create a Mind"

Computer vision can also be applied to unlikely domains such as *malware detection*, as proved by a number of researchers such as Mahmoud Kalash, Mrigank Rochan et al. in their paper titled *"Malware Classification with Deep Convolutional Neural Networks"*[10], Joshua Saxe et al. in their paper titled *"Deep neural network based malware detection using two dimensional binary program features"*[11], etc. If you turn malware binary into 8-bit binary vectors, and then turn those binary vectors into RGB - you can plot images of the source code. Now, these images don't really mean much to us, but distinct patterns occur in malware that don't appear in regular software.

[10]https://ieeexplore.ieee.org/abstract/document/8328749
[11]https://ieeexplore.ieee.org/abstract/document/7413680

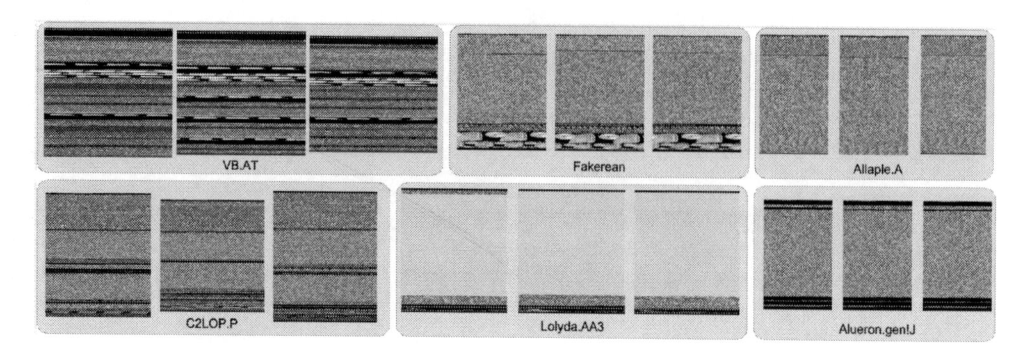

Figure 7: Figure from "Malware classification with deep convolutional neural networks" by Mahmoud Kalash, Mrigank Rochan, et al.

Kalash and Rochan report a 98.52% and 99.97% accuracy, while many of the other papers report 95%+ accuracy rates on the relevant malware detection benchmarks.

Data visualization is an art in and of itself - and you can plot just about anything if you have data for it. If you can plot it, you can probably apply computer vision to it. In a sense, computer vision can be applied to practically all data - not just images. Images are just pixel intensity data anyway, so the fact that we can apply computer vision to images already itself is built on the fact that we can apply it to data in general. Let's take a look at some popular tasks and applications of computer vision!

2.5.1 Optical Character Recognition

Optical character recognition was one of the first applications of computer vision! It held promise of digitalizing old issues of newspapers, books, and other literature in the process of switching from physical and analog devices to digital. Additionally, a good omni-font optical character recognition tool could help automate reading.

While there were attempts in 1913 to create a reading machine by Dr. Edmund Fournier d'Albe - the machine ultimately was only able to read a word a minute and could only recognize a few letters with a very specific font. In 1974, Ray Kurzweil's company developed an omni-font OCR machine, that used to read text out loud, and dubbed it the "Kurzweil Reading Machine". It read 150 words per minute, while the average human could read 250.

At the time - this was a revolutionary invention, the size of an entire table. Now, you can quickly download OCR applications that decode images to text, in practically all languages in the world and offer translation services on the spot. Google Translate can even read text from your camera in real-time, and *replace* the text on the screen with an augmented, translated version. This works the best on street signs, which have a solid background (which can easily be extended over the original text) and by placing the recognized and translated text over it:

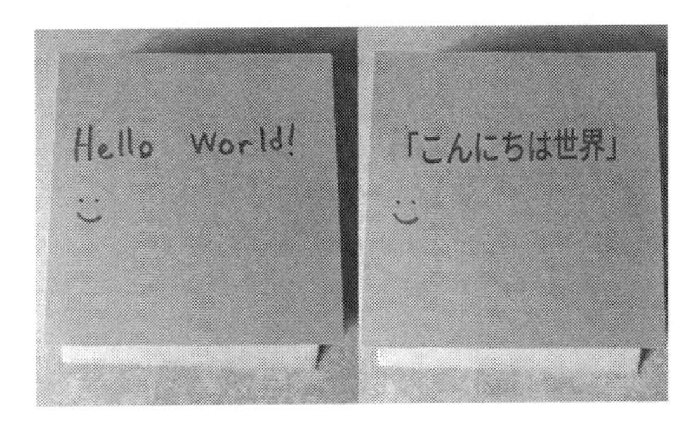

Figure 8: Real-Time OCR via Google Translate, translating from English to Japanese

It worked! "こんにちは世界" is correct, and it fully understood what I wrote! Applications like these have major implications for travel, human communication and understanding. While this is a hybrid application between computer vision *and* natural language processing, you have to understand what's in front of you to be able to translate it.

2.5.2 Image Classification

Image classification is the staple task and a very wide blanket. Image classification can be further applied onto various domains:

- Medical Diagnosis
- Manufacturing defect detection
- Alarm systems (burglar detection)
- Malware detection
- etc.

In medical diagnosis, classifiers can learn to distinguish between images containing cancerous and non-cancerous cells, diabetes from retinopathy images, pneumonia from X-rays, etc. In manufacturing, classifiers can identify defective products, such as bottles without caps, broken toys, health convention violations, etc. Coupled with CCTV cameras, alarm systems can recognize the presence of a human after working hours, or even to distinguish a burglar from an employee and sound an alarm.

One major limitation of *image classification* is the implication that an **image** belongs to a class:

Figure 9:

In each of these images, there's more going on then a single label! Typically, we intuitively know that **something in an image** belongs to a class, not the entirety of the image. Although an image classifier can be very powerful and find patterns that divide classes, for more realistic applications, we'll want to *localize* objects, and perhaps even predict multiple labels for these objects. For example, a shirt can be a blue, yellow, green, black, or any of various other colors. It can also be a long-sleeve shirt or a short-sleeve shirt. It can have X and Y or M and N. Predicting multiple applicable (non-exclusive) labels is known as multi-label image classification (as opposed to single-label classification) and the technique broadened the application of the type of system.

Additionally, you can classify an image to a label, and then localize what made the prediction go off. This is known as "classification + localization". However - in more advanced systems, we perform object recognition/detection, not classification.

2.5.3 Object and Face Detection

Object detection includes recognizing and classifying an object in an image, regardless of the rest of the image. For example, you can classify an entire image as a "mug" if there's a mug in it. Or, you can classify a mug as a "mug" within an image. The latter is much more accurate and realistic!

Now, this may sound like classification + localization with extra steps, but it isn't. We're not classifying an *image* and localizing what made the prediction go off. We're detecting an *object* within an image.

Figure 10:

We'll cover YOLOv5, Detectron2, etc. in more depth in a later lesson, and train our own object detection network!

More and more, object detection is being applied to recognize objects from input. This can be corals at the bottom of the sea from a live feed camera (helping marine biologists preserve endangered species), pothole detection (helping humans and cars avoid them), weapon detection (helping keep venues safe), pedestrian detection (helping keep urban planning and traffic safe), etc.

Image classification is not being replaced by object detection - they're used for different tasks. Image classification ***used*** to be used for the tasks object detection is now better at, but this a branching of tasks - you'll train both classifiers and detectors as a computer vision engineer. Image classification is easier to explain and implement, so it's typically the first technique to be covered in most learning resources.

In a similar vein - face recognition technology is essentially object detection! First, the system has to detect a face, its position in the image, and then compare the embeddings of the image to a recorded set of embeddings belonging to an individual. Meta's face recognition algorithms used to offer to tag people automatically in images, but the feature was removed due to privacy concerns of a single company having access to billions of annotated images that can be quickly and easily linked to individuals. Naturally, the privacy concerns haven't only been raised against Meta - any form of identifying information is generally subject to privacy concerns.

Gallery applications on phones can detect and recognize selfies of you and your friends, creating folders that you can easily access. Face recognition can be used to perform visual identification (say, an employee's access to a certain part of a building), for law enforcement (could be a bit Orwellian, perhaps), and a plethora of other applications.

2.5.4 Image Segmentation

When you take a look in front of yourself and see an object - you're also aware of where it starts and where it ends. You're aware of the boundaries that define an instance of some object, and that when a "mug" ends, there might be some empty space until a "notebook" object, and that they're both resting on a "table".

This is segmentation! You're segmenting a mug from a notebook. Segmentation comes in a couple of flavors:

- Semantic segmentation
- Instance segmentation
- Panoptic segmentation (combination of Semantic and Instance segmentation)

Semantic segmentation involves segmenting which pixels belong to which class in an image. Instance segmentation involves segmenting which instances belong to which class in an image. The difference is similar to the difference between image classification and object detection. With semantic segmentation - it doesn't matter which chair is which, all that's important is that something belongs to the "chair" class. Instance segmentation will note the qualitative difference between each instance of a "chair". "This chair" and "that chair" aren't the same chair, even though they're next to each other.

You can think of image classification, classification + localization, object detection, semantic segmentation and instance segmentation as *levels* of microscopy you want to apply to an image. Segmentation is, in a sense, pixel-level classification while image classification classifies an entire image (and all of the pixels) from something (potentially) in the center of the image.

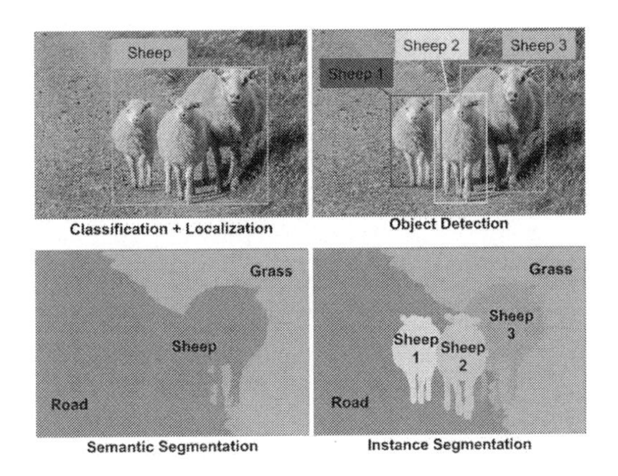

Figure 11:

Later in the book we'll be building an areal drone semantic segmentation model:

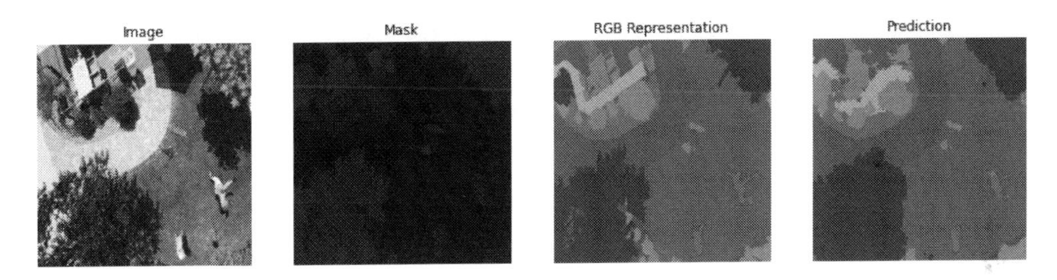

Figure 12:

2.5.5 Pose Estimation

People move in predictable ways. If something's predictable, you can bet that someone's trying to make a model that predicts or estimates some value regarding it. Whether you want to predict someone's pose slightly in the future, or whether you want to quantify their presence - pose estimation is the process of estimating spatial locations of key body joints such as elbows, heads, knees, feet and hands.

Xbox and PlayStation used pose estimation for their Kinect and EyeToy products (both of which are now, sadly, retired) which allowed the consoles to track the movement of players and augment them into games. If you've had the chance to play with some of these, it's probably an experience you'll remember - at least I know I'll remember mine.

Pose estimation can be used to totally remove expensive tracking equipment for film-making and 3D movement tracking (although it's not quite there yet). If you no longer need to have a tracking suit to create CGI movies - recreating scenes in 3D will be significantly easier! Metaverse-type worlds where your movement is translated directly into the Euclidean space of another world will become more accessible (requiring just a simple camera worth a few dollars). In recent years, a whole new genre of entertainment online arose - VTubers (Virtual YouTubers) who use pose estimation from webcams to translate their movement onto virtual bodies (typically 2D) as a replacement for their own presence on streams. Personal identity and expression while retaining privacy can be redefined with such technology.

Finally, pose estimation can be transfered to robotics. It's conceivable that we could attempt training robots to perform human-like movements through training data of our own movement (quantified through pose estimation) or manually control them through our own movement, similar to how we'd control 3D models in a virtually augmented world.

Figure 13: TensorFlow's MoveNet Overview:
https://www.tensorflow.org/lite/examples/pose_estimation/overview

If you own the physical copy of this book you can view the Gif here[12].

[12]https://www.tensorflow.org/lite/examples/pose_estimation/overview

Figure 14: Keypoint detection with Detectron2, Lesson 9

2.5.6 Motion Analysis

Motion analysis builds upon object detection, motion detection, tracking and pose estimation. In human brains, the cerebellum performs adaptive prediction of movement[13], and it's pretty effortless for us. A ball falling downward will reach our hand in an approximately predictable manner. A soccer player uses this knowledge to kick a ball into the goal, and a goalkeeper uses this same knowledge to predict where the ball will be in a short while and will try to intercept it.

It's oftentimes understated how important this prediction ability is! Motion analysis, in a sense, a blanket term for multiple abilities that make such predictions possible.

[13] https://www.ncbi.nlm.nih.gov/pmc/articles/PMC5477675/

2.5.7 Image Restoration and De-noising

Physical images suffer more than digital ones through time, but both physical images and digital ones can degrade if not protected properly. Hard drives can become faulty, electromagnetic waves can introduce noise, and physical images can oxidize, fade out, and get exposed to environments unfriendly to the printing paper.

Computer vision can be applied to restore, colorize and de-noise images! Typically, motion blur, noise, issues with camera focus, and physical damage to scanned images can be fairly successfuly removed. There are many papers dealing with image restoration (PapersWithCode task page[14]), and the results are getting better by the day - here are the results of *"Learning Deep CNN Denoiser Prior for Image Restoration"* by Kai Zhang et al.:

Figure 15: "Learning Deep CNN Denoiser Prior for Image Restoration" by Kai Zhang, Wangment Zuo, Shuhang Gu and Lei Zhang

Figure 16: "Learning Deep CNN Denoiser Prior for Image Restoration" by Kai Zhang, Wangment Zuo, Shuhang Gu and Lei Zhang

[14]https://paperswithcode.com/task/image-restoration

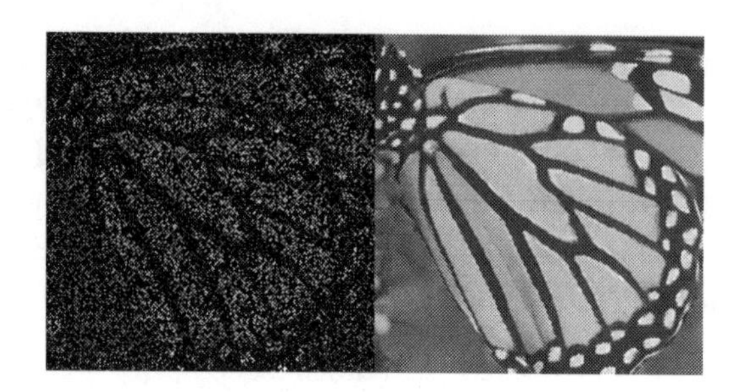

Figure 17: "Learning Deep CNN Denoiser Prior for Image Restoration" by Kai Zhang, Wangment Zuo, Shuhang Gu and Lei Zhang

Soon enough, the movie scenes in which the secret intelligence agents *"pause, rewind, enhance"* a blurry image to a full HD one might not be too far away from reality!

2.5.8 Scene Reconstruction

Scene reconstruction is a fairly new and extremely exciting application of computer vision! We can construct a scene in our minds, given an image. When talking with someone, you know that they're not a flat, 2D piece of paper, and that if you were to circle around them, there's the back of their head. You're effectively constructing a 3D model of the world around you all the time - so, can we do this with code?

Turns out, we can. At least to a degree as of writing. Typically, this includes taking images from a couple of angles, from which a 3D structure of an object can be inferred. Then, a 3D mapping can be created. Some of the most amazing visuals were created by the Google Research team, and can be found at nerf-w[15].

Research has also been conducted in limiting the input to a single angle (single viewpoint), and while the methods are still new, they're promising.

[15]https://nerf-w.github.io/

2.5.9 Image Captioning, Image Generation, Visual Questions and Generative Models

Increasingly, vision is being combined with language. Another task relatively easy for us but (which used to be) hard for computers is image captioning. Given an image, you could describe what's going on if the image has enough context - can computers? Other than image captioning, given a description, we can imagine an image - can computers? If I ask you to describe a certain part of an image, or answer a question regarding its contents, you could - can computers?

This involves more than just vision - it involves a lot of context from natual language processing as well as a deep visual understanding. Up until recently, this was a far-fetched task, but with each passing year, there's rapid progress in this field, with some amazing results being released in 2022, as of writing.

For instance, DAMO Academy and the Alibaba Group released *"Unifying Architectures, Tasks, and Modalities Through a Simple Sequence-To-Sequence Learning Framework"*[16], in which their model (OFA) handles these exact tasks! It's got a ResNet backbone for computer vision (popular CNN architecture, covered in detail and used later in the book and unifies it with other deep learning architectures to generate text and images based on the task at hand:

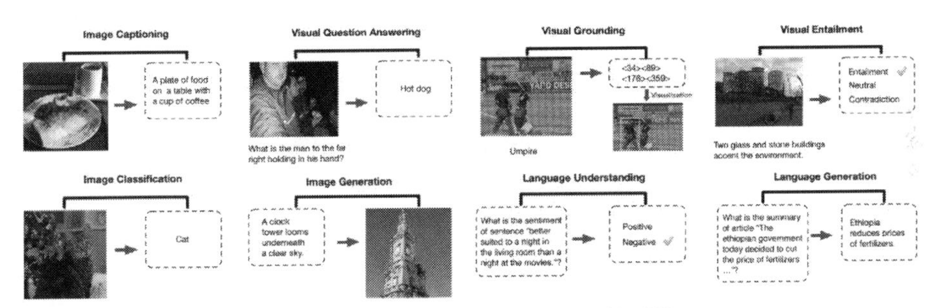

Figure 1: Examples of various tasks supported by OFA.

Figure 18: "Unifying Architectures, Tasks, and Modalities Through a Simple Sequence-To-Sequence Learning Framework"

[16]https://arxiv.org/abs/2202.03052

Needless to say - this is an exceedingly difficult goal, and reviewing the work in a compact manner doesn't do justice to the effort and scope of their work. Text-to-image conversion (which is really, a Sequence-to-Sequence conversion) has gotten a lot of attention in the recent years and months! A great example is the viral *"Dream"* application, developed by WOMBO. It allowed users to input seed text, from which lucid images were created. A user could pick between several "styles" to go from, such as "vibrant", "fantasy", "steampunk", "psychic", etc. Within seconds, with a real-time view of the patterns being brushed on the screen, a user would be prompted with a synthetically generated image, from the text they've input.

The code isn't open source, so we can only speculate how the team achieved this, but it appears as if they've performed *Neural Style Transfer* (transferring the style of an image to another one, typically used to convert images to another style, such as turning a regular photo into a Klimt-esque image), mixed with a text-to-image generator. What gave the application popularity is how mysterious and deeply *beautiful* the generated images were. They stirred emotions - fear, happiness, inquisitiveness, wonder. Truly, that's what art is about, isn't it?

Here are a few images, generate from the same prompt - "robot dreaming of electric sheep". While none of these feature a robot with a sleeping bubble with images of electric sheep, you can clearly see that both the "robot" and "sheep" patterns appear throughout several styles:

Figure 19: Images generated by the Dream Application

There's something deeply beautiful about these images, even though they could be touted as simple pattern recall with a bit of style. There's beauty in patterns, and pattern recall. We'll take a look at a great example of another type of image generation later, known as the *Deep Dream* algorithm, which embeds prior belief of patterns into an image, resulting in hallucinogenic views, and implement it.

Aleksa Gordić, a DeepMind research engineer, implemented the Deep Dream algorithm[17] and has produced some of the most beautiful images I've ever seen with it:

Figure 20: Results of Aleksa Gordić's Implementation of Deep Dream

We'll be doing our own implementation as well:

Figure 21:

We won't dwindle too much on the details of the implementation or how it works now - that's for a later lesson! If you're new to this - there's a bit of walking to do before running. Don't worry though, the road is pretty well-made and maintained!

Recently DALL · E 2, created by OpenAI has been making waves. It was released

[17]https://github.com/gordicaleksa/pytorch-deepdream

alongside *"Hierarchical Text-Conditional Image Generation with CLIP Latents"*[18] and can create extremely well-crafted images from textual description. On their website (openai.com/dall-e-2), you can use their interactive demonstration to generate a few images by simply pointing and clicking:

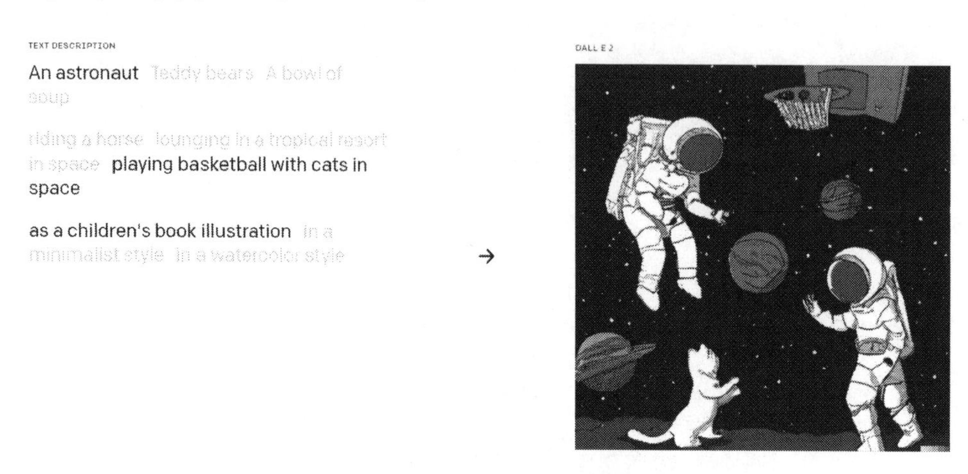

Figure 22:

Under the hood, it encodes the prompt you supply, and the encoding is mapped to an image encoding and added to an image of noise (random pixels), which is then used by a decoder to generate an image. One of the most interesting things about the generated images is that they're very plausible! While you probably won't see an astronaut riding a horse in space, it positions astronauts in the position they would be in if they were to ride a horse. If you request an image of fruit with hands - they're positioned in such a way to resemble what most would imagine fruits with hands looking like. This doesn't always work though.

Update 1: Since writing this lesson initially, Google released Imagen and Parti - two state-of-the-art caption-to-image models, just weeks apart. Shortly after that, StabilityAI released Stable Diffusion - a caption-to-image model that leverages the idea of diffusion models, like DALL · E 2. Diffusion models, put shortly, learn to de-noise input, from gaussian noise to an image, step by step. Stable Diffusion, like Imagen and DALL · E 2, use a *Contrastive Language–Image Pre-training (CLIP)* network as the text

[18]https://arxiv.org/abs/2204.06125

encoder, that outputs a latent representation of the input prompt.

Since the release, Twitter feeds are *full* of images generated by DALL · E 2, Stable Diffusion and comparisons of the results for the same prompts.

Update 2: In August of 2022, StabilityAI released the source code for Stable Diffusion, and hosted both an inference API and a `diffusers` library on HuggingFace - a machine learning platform, community, model zoo and organization. The `diffusers` API is beautifully simple, in true HuggingFace fashion, and you can download and run it with as little as:

```
1 $ pip install diffusers==0.2.4 transformers scipy ftfy
```

```
1 from diffusers import StableDiffusionPipeline
2
3 # Get your token at https://huggingface.co/settings/tokens
4 pipe =
      StableDiffusionPipeline.from_pretrained("CompVis/stable-diffusion-v1-4",
      use_auth_token=YOUR_TOKEN)
5 pipe.to("cuda")
6
7 prompt = "a photograph of an astronaut riding a horse"
8 image = pipe(prompt)["sample"][0]
```

Due to the obvious potential misuse of high-resolution, photorealistic image generation for arbitrary prompts - you'll have to sign up on HuggingFace and generate an access token to use the `StableDiffusionPipeline`. A great notebook to start with is hosted on Google Colab by HuggingFace[19]!

Text-to-image generation is pretty "hot" right now, and the second half of 2022 is defined with new research that boggles the mind. Exciting to see if anything new will be released by the end of 2022, and what the upcoming years will bring!

Note: Whenever a model is released with closed access, either to protect IP for a commercial product or for safety reasons - someone, somewhere, will implement an approximation of it and release it in the wild. An instance of this can also be seen with DALL · E 2 and Imagen, which are both closed for the wide public. Craiyon, formerly

[19]https : / / colab.research.google.com / github / huggingface / notebooks / blob / main / diffusers / stable_diffusion.ipynb

known as DALL-E mini was quick to provide a mini-DALL · E implementation for the masses. Similarly, the `diffusers` library at HuggingFace is meant to democratize diffusion models for the public. Open source work is underapreciated, but propells the world forward by distributing knowledge, and thus, the power to act to everyone. You can learn more about diffusion models and the `diffusers` library in another HuggingFace Google Colab[20]. If someone from HuggingFace is reading this - you rock! <3

Update 3: Merely two weeks after this book was initially published in September 2022 - KerasCV, covered in a more detail later, has incorporated Stable Diffusion. SD was implemented in TensorFlow/Keras by Divam Gupta[21], a research engineer at Meta VR labs and the creator of Liner.AI. Just days layer, it was incorporated into KerasCV, which as of September 2022 provides the fastest, most efficient and simplest pipeline for stable diffusion:

```
import keras_cv
from tensorflow import keras

# AMP for faster inference
keras.mixed_precision.set_global_policy("mixed_float16")
# XLA on
model = keras_cv.models.StableDiffusion(jit_compile=True, img_width=512,
    img_height=512)
# Generate images
images = model.text_to_image("photorealistic cute bunny teaching deep
    learning for computer vision", batch_size=3)
```

The only thing left is to plot them:

```
def plot_images(images):
    plt.figure(figsize=(20, 20))
    for i in range(len(images)):
        ax = plt.subplot(1, len(images), i + 1)
        plt.imshow(images[i])
        plt.axis("off")

plot_images(images)
```

[20] https : / / colab.research.google.com / github / huggingface / notebooks / blob / main / diffusers / diffusers_intro.ipynb

[21] https://github.com/divamgupta/stable-diffusion-tensorflow

Figure 23:

The ported implementation[22] itself is only a few hundred lines long - 350 for the model and 100 for generation. It might be a bit difficult following it if you're not versed in CV yet, though. Since a good portion of the required knowledge will be covered - you should be able to read it without much issues by the end of the book.

If you're running the code on Google Colab, remember to install KerasCV and update TensorFlow/cuDNN:

```
1 ! pip install keras_cv
2 ! pip install --upgrade tensorflow-gpu
3 ! apt install --allow-change-held-packages libcudnn8=8.1.0.77-1+cuda11.2
```

It's hardly possible to encapsulate the entire landscape of research and development in a single lesson, especially for a very volatile field like this. Yet - the list of tasks above is a fairly comprehensive list of some of the main applications of computer vision that you'll be encountering.

2.6 Classic Computer Vision Datasets

There are various datasets you could start playing with! Some are standardized as classic benchmarks, while some are simply popular with practicioners. There are too many to count and counting datasets would be like counting people. A 2-image dataset is a dataset! This is neither meant to be a "list of computer vision datasets", but simply includes *some* of the noteworthy or fun ones oftentimes used online.

[22]https://github.com/keras-team/keras-cv/tree/master/keras_cv/models/generative/stable_diffusion

2.6.1 Dogs vs. Cats

Dogs vs. Cats[23] is oftentimes used for teaching purposes, and can typically be fit very easily to a practically 100% accuracy.

2.6.2 Hot Dog - Not Hot Dog

Hot Dog - Not Hot Dog[24] is a joke binary classification dataset, inspired by a TV show, that lets you train a classifier to classify hot dogs and *not* hot dogs (everything else). Everything is either a hot dog, or isn't!

2.6.3 CIFAR10 and CIFAR100

CIFAR10 and CIFAR100[25] are two datasets created by researchers from the Canadian Institute For Advanced Research. Both datasets have 60k images, 32x32 in size (fairly small). CIFAR10 has ten classes (airplane, automobile, bird, cat, deer, dog, frog, horse, ship, truck), while CIFAR100 has 100 classes. The 100 classes are organized into 20 *coarse* labels such as "food containers" each of which contains *fine classes* such as "bottles", "bowls", "cans", "cups" and "plates".

The datasets use as a *great* starting point! CIFAR10 is not too hard to fit, since the features that make a horse are fairly different from the ones making up a frog. It's not too hard to get a decent accuracy for it even for beginners who are just starting out. CIFAR100 is much harder to fit (making you rethink your architecture and look for ways to understand it better), in part due to the fact that it has 10 times the classes of CIFAR10 and the same number of images, making the leap from 6k per class to only 600 per class. Additionally, if you're doing fine-label prediction, the distinction between a cup or a can isn't too obvious. We'll talk more about these two datasets and train a classifier for each in the next lesson.

[23] https://www.kaggle.com/c/dogs-vs-cats
[24] https://www.kaggle.com/datasets/dansbecker/hot-dog-not-hot-dog
[25] https://www.cs.toronto.edu/~kriz/cifar.html

2.6.4 ImageNet

ImageNet[26] is the current *flagship* for computer vision training and evaluation. It used to be the largest and most realistic datasets we had, but much larger datasets exist today, including datasets with billions of images. Some datasets are locked to company employees, while some are fully public. ImageNet is one of the largest public datasets, with 1000 classes, spanning over 14.2M images in *real sizes* which, in addition, vary between images. They're not all uniformly sized.

Most models are trained and evaluated on and for ImageNet, and most research papers use it as the benchmark. If you make a breakthrough model - this is where you'll test it! It's worth noting just how huge of a dataset it is. 14.2M images might not *sound* like a lot, but as soon as you start working on computer vision problems, you'll realize that you're extremely lucky if you have a hundred thousand images (and that it's also already a difficult number to deal with computationally), and just lucky to have 10k. Whenever you're dealing with a pre-trained network in computer vision, you'll typically be able to load in ImageNet weights and transfer this knowledge to other datasets. We'll dive into transfer learning soon enough, in a later lesson, so we won't focus on that now. It's worth noting upfront that Transfer Learning is another large part of why computer vision has advanced so much in the past years and some luminaries consider Transfer Learning to be one of (if not) the most important topic to cover in educational resources.

2.6.5 Imagenette

Imagenette[27] is a subset of ImageNet. Jeremy Howard, the author of Fast.ai, created Imagenette so that he could test out prototypes of new networks faster. Training on ImageNet takes a lot of time, and his personal advice on making sure that tests can be made within a couple of minutes for quick validation couldn't be applied to such a huge dataset. Making experimentation and validation faster, and democratizing datasets like this is a huge part of why AI researchers have been able to advance the field so rapidly in the years leading up to now.

[26] https://www.image-net.org/

[27] https://github.com/fastai/imagenette

2.6.6 MS Coco

MS Coco[28]: Common Objects in Context is a fairly large dataset of, well, objects in context. Context is really important for any machine learning system, and computer vision in particular. COCO has 330k images, 200K of which are labelled (labeling is extremely expensive). If labeled, images, have bounding boxes for one or multiple objects in the image, 5 captions per image and the dataset features 1.5M object instances. While CIFAR10, CIFAR100 and ImageNet are aimed at classification (whether an image belongs to a class) - COCO can be used for various other applications such as object detection, caption generation and instance segmentation.

The landscape changes through time. The best way to stay on top of the datasets you can use to train your models is to search for them. There's enough to go around, and it's oftentimes best to find a dataset in a specific niche you're interested in. For instance, you might be interested in applying computer vision to medical diagnosis (we'll cover an entire end-to-end project for breast cancer diagnosis later), self-driving cars, pose estimation for translating human movement into 3D, art generation, etc.

Depending on the specific thing you want to build - there's likely a dataset out there, ready for you to tackle it. Some of them won't be pretty - they'll be full of misshapen data, broken or too few images or most importantly - they might lack labels or even have wrong labels, etc. This is currently one of the biggest hurdles to get over. Finding a good way to get *labelled* data is hard, and some are switching to unsupervised methods in an attempt to circumvent the issue. As of writing, MS COCO takes ~50GB of storage space.

2.6.7 MNIST

The MNIST hand-written digits[29] and Fashion-MNIST[30] datasets are very well known, and simple datasets. They're mainly used for educational purposes, and originally created a long time ago while CNNs were still in their infancy.

[28] https://cocodataset.org/#home
[29] http://yann.lecun.com/exdb/mnist/
[30] https://github.com/zalandoresearch/fashion-mnist

2.6.8 Google's Open Images

The Open Images[31] dataset is a 9M image dataset with almost 16M bounding boxes on 600 categories, 2.8M instance segmentation masks on 350 categories, 3.3M relationship annotations for 1.5K relationships, 700k localized narratives and 60M image-level labels on 20k categories. This amount of meta-data allows us to create a wide variety of computer vision applications!

In sheer scale, it's comparable to ImageNet, but like MS COCO it provides bounding boxes, relationship annotations, instance segmentation, etc. Oh, and it's 565GB in size if you decide to download it locally.

2.7 Searching for Datasets

Having a list of some popular datasets is great. But - how do you search for them? You'll be doing a lot of searching, curation and creation in the future, so having at least a broad idea of places that offer high quality datasets is a great starting place!

Other than the platforms highlighted in this section - Google is your best friend.

2.7.1 Kaggle

Kaggle is one of the world's largest Data Science/ML platforms in the world, with a thriving community. It offers over 50k datasets (in all domains of Data Science), typically created by regular users but also research teams, companies and institutes.

Kaggle is also known for holding competitions with very decent prizes, depending on the budgets of the companies and teams that approach them. This way - eager data scientists can work on the burning unsolved problems in the world, without strings attached, gain rewards for their work, and companies/research teams can crowd-source solutions to problems that can help the world (or increase profits).

At any given point, you'll find several competitions on Kaggle that last for a few months with prize pools reaching $50-75k (though, most give you "knowledge" and "swag"), and thousands upon thousands of teams enrolling and competing to produce the best models from medicine and medical diagnosis, to stock exchange predictions, image matching,

[31] https://storage.googleapis.com/openimages/web/index.html

identifying near-extinct species of animals and preserving them to identifying and localizing plants and animals from satellite images.

Kaggle has a CLI that allows you to programatically download datasets (helping automate Data Science pipelines) and provides users with an environment in which to run notebooks free of charge, with a weekly quota for free GPU usage (the number of hours depends on the availability). It's more than safe to say that Kaggle plays an important part in the proliferation, democratization and advancement of Data Science all around the world.

We'll be working with Kaggle CLI and Kaggle datasets later in the book.

2.7.2 HuggingFace

HuggingFace is a primarily NLP-based community, with some computer vision datasets. However, as noted in earlier sections, computer vision is being combined with NLP in an increasing rate. For visual question answering, image captioning, and similar tasks - you'll probably want to at least peruse HuggingFace.

While offering a "modest" 4.5K datasets as of writing, HuggingFace is gaining more and more traction and attention from the community, and it's worth having it on your radar for the days to come.

A large part of HuggingFace's philosophy is democratization of knowledge, and it's a lovely community to be in, with open source implementations and models based on cutting-edge research, and trained for weeks of months on clusters of GPUs for the public.

2.7.3 TensorFlow Datasets

TensorFlow Datasets is a collection and corpora of datasets, curated and ready for training. All of the datasets from the module are standardized, so you don't have to bother with different preprocessing steps for every single dataset you're testing your models out on. While it may sound just like a simple convenience, rather than a game-changer - if you train a lot of models, the time it takes to do overhead work gets beyond annoying. The library provides access to datasets from MNIST to Google Open Images (11MB - 565GB), spanning several categories such as Audio, D4rl, Graphs,

Image, Image Classification, Object Detection, Question Answering, Ranking, Rlds, Robomimic, Robotics, Text, Time Series, Text Simplification, Vision Language, Video, Translate, etc.

As of 2022, 278 datasets are available and *community* datasets are supported, with over 700 HuggingFace datasets and the Kubric dataset generator. If you're building a *general* intelligent system, there's a very good chance there's a public dataset there. For all other purposes - you can download public datasets and work with them, with custom pre-processing steps. Kaggle, HuggingFace and academic repositories are popular choices.

Another amazing feature is that datasets coming from TensorFlow Datasets are optimized. They're packed into a `tf.data.Dataset` object, with which you can maximize the performance of your network through pre-fetching, automated optimization (on the back of TensorFlow), easy transformations on the entirety of the dataset, etc. and you can "peel away" the TensorFlow-specific functionality to expose the underlying NumPy arrays which can generically be applied to other frameworks as well.

We'll be working with TensorFlow datasets as well later in the book.

2.7.4 Google Research and Cloud Datasets

Google's own datasets can be found at research.google/tools/datasets[32], alongside other tools and services. There's "only" slightly above 100 datasets as of writing, but these aren't small datasets, and indluce behemoths such as Google Open Images, Covid-19 Open Data, YouTube-8M, Google Landmarks, etc.

2.7.5 DatasetSearch

Quite literally the "Google" of datasets, created by Google and accessible under datasets.research.google.com[33]! It searches for datasets from a wide variety of repositories, including Kaggle, academic institutions, and even finds the associated scholarly articles published regarding a found dataset.

[32] https://research.google/tools/datasets/
[33] https://datasetsearch.research.google.com/

This isn't a curated list - it's a search engine for datasets mentioned in other places with extra useful metadata such as the license, authors, context, content explanation, date of upload, website it's hosted on, etc.

2.8 Useful Tools

When just starting out, you don't really need a lot of tools. When you're starting out with pottery - having some clay, water and a flat surface is quite enough. Though, as you practice, you'll likely naturally want to get some tools - a wire to separate your creation from the surface, carving tools for details, a spinning wheel, etc.

For beginners, using a lot of tools can be overwhelming, and most skip them in lieu of trying things out. This is fine, but it's worth keeping some tools in mind for later use when you feel the need for them. Some of these are fairly mandatory, like the use of OpenCV or Pillow, though, you'll only really *need* a few methods, and anything above that is great but not necessary.

2.8.1 KerasCV

Currently, KerasCV[34] is under construction. It's a horizontal add-on to Keras, specifically meant to enable making industry-grade computer vision applications easier.

It'll feature new layers, metrics, losses and data augmentation building blocks that are too specialized for general Keras, but very applicable and can be broadly used in Computer Vision tasks. While it's still only under construction - it's on the radar of many, including myself. When it gets released, this book will be updated.

In the meantime, the book will dedicate a lesson to KerasCV and the new layers currently built into the beta version. A lesson on KerasCV is included.

2.8.2 OpenCV and Pillow

Originally created by Intel, OpenCV is a real-time computer vision library with support for a wide variety of computer vision tasks. While it is an entire self-contained

[34]https://github.com/keras-team/keras-cv

ecosystem - practicioners can decide to use it for image loading and processing, before feeding them into their own applications, frameworks and models. OpenCV is highly performant and established in the computer vision community, with ports to multiple languages. It contains *many* modules[35] that span from core functionalities such as reading and writing images/processing them to clustering and search in multi-dimensional spaces, a deep learning module, segmentation methods, feature detection, specialized matrix operations, etc. You can do Computer Vision in OpenCV exclusively if you want to.

On the other hand, you have Pillow! Pillow is a fork of PIL (Python Image Library) and is used for image processing. It's not a computer vision library - it's an image processing library. The API is simple and expressive, and it's a very widely used library in the community.

There's no competition between OpenCV and Pillow - they're different libraries used for different tasks. A portion of OpenCV overlaps with Pillow (image processing), but that's about it. Choosing between OpenCV and Pillow is more akin to choosing between a foldable knife and a swiss army knife. Both of them can cut stuff, but one of them also has a bottle opener, a can opener, and might even have a fork hidden inside! If you're just cutting, both will do the job just fine.

Throughout the book we'll mainly be performing just image processing, so going with either Pillow or OpenCV makes sense. I personally prefer using OpenCV because because of the more low-level API, but if you're new to this, Pillow has a more forgiving learning curve (and is less complicated) and the results you'll get are pretty much the exact same anyway.

There are a couple of small different implementation details to note, such as that OpenCV natively uses the BGR format, not the RGB format (which most others use). Most libraries will detect this and load the images in just fine so to the eye, there is no difference. Though, when you try to infer a class from an image, it'll most likely be totally wrong, since the different format produces different results.

Both APIs are simple and similar, but Pillow's API is simpler and less verbose. In most cases, the OpenCV API calls the central module to which you provide objects for processing:

```
1 img = cv2.resize(img, (width, height))
```

[35] https://docs.opencv.org/4.x/

While for Pillow, you call the methods on the objects themselves:

```
img = img.resize((width, height))
```

Both libraries can read resources, transorm images, change formats, translate, flip, rotate and all the other good stuff you'd like to do. A good analogy is that OpenCV is to Computer Vision what Scikit-Learn is to Machine Learning. A well-rounded, all-around applicable library with strong traditional foundations and wrappers/support for new approaches, such as neural networks.

2.8.3 TensorFlow Debugger (tfdbg)

Debugging TensorFlow models isn't fun. Debugging itself is never fun - but there's a special place in my heart for debugging TensorFlow models. It can't be overstated how much high-level APIs (such as Keras) with selective customization of the underlying components made development easier, more accessible and more elegant.

You'll naturally be much less likely to introduce bugs into your code with Keras, since a lot of the not-easy-to-write implementations are optimized and bug-free through it, but you'll eventually probably work with the lower-level API either in a search of more control, or out of necessity. At that point - using the TensorFlow Debugger (tfdbg) will help you keep your peripherals safe from yourself in a gust of frustration. Patience is a virtue for debugging.

2.8.4 LRFinder

A learning rate finder, popularized by Jeremy Howard of Fast.ai, is a nifty tool for finding an optimal starting learning rate! We'll cover a the relevant portion of the original research paper, concept behind it and an implementation for the tool with Keras later in the book.

2.8.5 TensorFlow Datasets (tfds)

`tfds` is a module that allows you to access, download and extract data from the TensorFlow Datasets repository. We'll work with it later in the book.

2.8.6 Know-Your-Data (TF KYD)

TensorFlow's GUI tool - Know Your Data[36], which is still in beta (as of writing), aims to answer important questions on data corruption (broken images, bad labels, etc.), data sensitivity (does your data contain sensitive content), data gaps (obvious lack of samples), data balance, etc.

A lot of these can help with avoiding bias and data skew - arguably one of the most important things to do when working on projects that can have an impact on other humans.

2.8.7 EthicalML

Not a tool, but a GitHub repository - EthicalML[37] is a repository that acts as a list of open source tools and libraries that can act as a bounding landscape for you. It's run by the Institute for Ethical AI and Machine Learning.

From explainability tools to data pipelines and ETL, commercial platforms, serialization and versioning, etc., you can really get a good feel for production ML, MLOps (Machine Learning + DevOps), and links to sign up to some great newsletters such as the *Machine Learning Engineer Newsletter*, lead by Alejandro Saucedo. They send out some really good stuff!

[36] https://knowyourdata-tfds.withgoogle.com/
[37] https://github.com/EthicalML/awesome-production-machine-learning

3 Guide to Convolutional Neural Networks

3.1 What are Convolutional Neural Networks?

We've had a short introduction to CNNs as a concept in the previous lesson, so let's dive into them in a bit more detail here. *Convolutional Neural Networks* (CNNs) are, as mentioned earlier, a type of Deep Artificial Neural Networks (ANNs). The name arises from their use of *convolutional layers* which perform *feature extraction* - more on them a bit later.

Note: Convolutional layers, and the convolution operation are at the core of CNNs and it's worth taking out a bit of time to *really* understand what's going on there.

Again, like with most other learning networks, CNNs aim to mimic the human brain (currently best-known learning algorithm) - and in this case, the visual perception that humans have. With the expansion of the neocortex, humans (and other mammals, but to a lesser degree) were able to start noticing intricate abstract patterns in the world around them. This higher-level abstraction is what, down the line, allowed us to make out symbols and give them meaning - giving birth to *art, culture and language.*

These things are hard to mimic, in large part because they're hard to explain. If you ask a musician or artist to explain their notes or strokes with a brush - more often than not, you'll receive an answer along the lines of:

> "It's hard to explain. It felt right.

Machine Learning algorithms have recently been proving that this intuition is replicable with highly sophisticated statistical reasoning, and that we genuinely can teach machines to be creative - generating art and music. This is a very wide topic, and a topic best left for another time.

CNNs are commonly used to analyze and solve problems in the field of Computer Vision, and employ a few tactics that allow them to do this in a much more efficient manner than many other approaches. Some of these tactics were, as usual, inspired by the cortical connections of neurons and the way they fire, in the visual cortex, when provided with visual stimuli. Though, they can be applied to other fields as well, and have recently been extensively used in *Graph-based reasoning*.

Graph Convolutional Neural Networks have recently been used in fields such as computational biology and drug discovery, where convolutional neural networks are employed on graph-like structures such as molecules. Everything can be a graph, and graphs are all around us in nature! From building blocks of life such as molecules to busy streets of New York city. *Graph Neural Networks* are their own field, and we won't be diving into them much. Our focus is on using CNNs for *Computer Vision*.

Due to underlying principles of data storage (binary data), we can *technically* represent *everything* as a sequence of `0`s and `1`s, even if it's not an efficient way to represent something. Neural Networks *excel* at understanding and extracting features and patterns in these sequences, similar to how *humans* excel at extracting patterns from the physical world around us.

Images are made from large sequences of pixels - which inherently have a numerical nature. Each pixel contains three channels (physically, *"triads"*) - RGB, each of which has a value ranging from `0..256`, in most cases. This gives us the standard 16.7M colors on the screens that we're used to seeing all around us.

The problem is - images contain a huge amount of data. How much? As noted by *Dr. Mike Pound of the University of Nottingham,* in a video released by *Computerphile*[38], it's remarkable how much data we can store in mediums such as images without having anyone notice it.

The image on the left is a raw image, while the image on the right contains hidden data within itself:

[38]https://www.youtube.com/watch?v=TWEXCYQKyDc

Figure 24: Steganographic image vs Original Image by Dr. Mike Pound and Computerphile

How much data? The *entire works of William Shakespeare*. 39 plays, 154 sonnets and 3 poems. *"Hamlet"* alone has over 30,000 words. All of this was embedded simply by changing the two last (least) significant bits of a 8-bit per channel image. We don't perceive much of a difference between these images, due to the already varying intensities of colors and shapes.

In general, most real images have way more data than what we could reasonably train Densely-Connected Neural Networks on. They're high dimensional, comprising of a seriously large input space, for which, an even larger amount of dense neurons would be required to model. Even if we could find a way to combat the issue of overfitting such high-dimensional data - the computational power required to do so would be prohibitively large. We're used to 4K images, but even with smaller numbers, such as 50x50 pixel images - the number of connections would skyrocket. The 2500 input pixels, with say 1000 input neurons would result in 2.5M connections and thus trainable parameters **in the first layer**. You can almost smell the coal burning in the power plants providing us with the power to train that network.

> If a 1.5kg (3 pound) wetware brain can do so much with an estimated 15W of power, densely-connected ANNs probably aren't the solution.

One of the key problems regarding Computer Vision was to reduce the amount of data that needs to be processed, while increasing the number of extracted features that can then be used to classify and recognize patterns in an image.

> This is where Convolutional Neural Networks kick in.

3.2 The Basic Architecture of a CNN

Before feeding the data for classification - we'll have to reduce the amount of information that's being fed. Amazingly enough, this doesn't mean ***manual pre-processing***, nor techniques such as Principal Component Analysis[39], Linear Discriminant Analysis[40] or other forms of dimensionality reduction[41]. We leave the hard work of optimization to the Neural Network itself!

The architecture of CNNs is generally composed of 3 distinct types of layers:

- **Convolutional Layers**
- **Pooling Layers**
- **Fully-Connected Layers**

Generally speaking - convolutional layers are interlaced with pooling layers, and this symbiosis can be seen as *one unit* of a CNN, while the fully-connected layers can be seen as a separate unit on top of the first one. The convolutional (and pooling) layers are known to be *feature extractors* and extract the features that make a class what it is. The fully-connected layers are, essentially, an entire MLP on top of the feature extractors, and act as a classifier.

[39] https://stackabuse.com/implementing-pca-in-python-with-scikit-learn/
[40] https://stackabuse.com/implementing-lda-in-python-with-scikit-learn/
[41] https://stackabuse.com/dimensionality-reduction-in-python-with-scikit-learn/

> To that end - a CNN is really, a network of feature extractors and a classifier network on top of it.

There are more nuances and variations than this - but this is the gist of it so let's start there.

A beautiful and great example of hierarchical representations can be seen in *"Convolutional Deep Belief Networks for Scalable Unsupervised Learning of Hierarchical Representations"*[42] by Lee et. al. While they've used a different NN topology (Deep Belief Networks, known as DBNs) which are used for *hierarchical generation* (totally different task), the concept of low-level layers learning simple representations, and high-level layers learning complex representations is beautifully visualized:

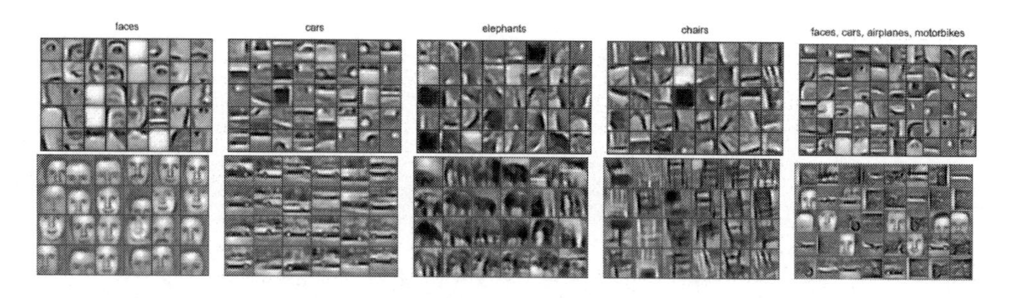

Figure 25: "Convolutional Deep Belief Networks for Scalable Unsupervised Learning of Hierarchical Representations"_ by Lee et. al.

You can clearly see earlier layers initially learn the constituent elements of objects, such as tyres and straight lines for cars, and eyes/noses for human faces. The features between cars, elephants and chairs aren't too different as well! Once you go up in the complexity hierarchy, you get entire representations. In the case of faces, they might prove to be a bit of nightmare fuel, though.

Note: ***It's okay if you don't get everything from the first go.*** What's important is for you to get an *intuitive feeling* for what these layers do. That's more than enough to go ahead and

[42]http://robotics.stanford.edu/~ang/papers/icml09-ConvolutionalDeepBeliefNetworks.pdf

build CNNs. In each explanation, we'll build an intuitive reference, and then go into the details. If you don't *deeply understand* the details now - feel free to re-read them later, once you get your hands on training a simple CNN.

3.3 The Convolutional Layer

The fundamental building block of any CNN is a *Convolutional Layer*. Before diving into how they work on the fundamental level - it helps to have a scope of what their *point* is in a network.

> Convolutional Layers perform **feature extraction** and result in **feature maps**. Feature extraction is achieved through **convolution**, and repetitive convolutions across an entire image result in a feature map.

Note: A feature map is (typically) a 3D tensor (width x height x depth). More on them later.

In the proceeding sections, we'll go into what all of this really entails, building on top of a basic intuition into the nitty-gritties.

Let's take a look at the input and output of a *convolutional layer* before diving into how this input is transformed into an output. Don't mind the code for now if you don't understand it already, this is mainly for illustrative purposes:

```
1 # Creating a convolutional layer - each of these parameters will be
      explained later
2 conv = keras.layers.Conv2D(filters=1,
3                   strides=5,
4                   padding = 'same',
5                   kernel_size=5)
6
7 # Imports to fetch, process and display an image
```

```
8  import urllib.request
9  import matplotlib.pyplot as plt
10 import cv2
11
12 # Public domain image
13 url =
       'https://upload.wikimedia.org/wikipedia/commons/0/02/Black_bear_large.jpg'
14 urllib.request.urlretrieve(url, 'bear.jpg')
15
16 input_image = cv2.imread('bear.jpg')
17 input_image = cv2.resize(input_image, (200, 200))
18 plt.imshow(input_image)
```

Figure 26:

Once we have the image loaded in, as a NumPy array, let's prepare it for the convolutional layer and pass it through, visualizing the result:

```
1 # OpenCV loads images in BGR format, and the image is of 'int' dtype
2 def preprocess_img(img):
3     img = cv2.cvtColor(img, cv2.COLOR_BGR2RGB).astype('float32')
```

```
4       # CNNs expect a (batch_size, height, width, depth) input, so we're adding
5       # a batch dimension for the one image we're passing in
6       return np.expand_dims(img, 0)
7
8   input_image = preprocess_img(input_image)
9
10  # Pass the image through the convolutional layer
11  convolved = conv(input_image)
12  plt.imshow(convolved_filters[0, :, :, 0])
```

This results in a *feature map*:

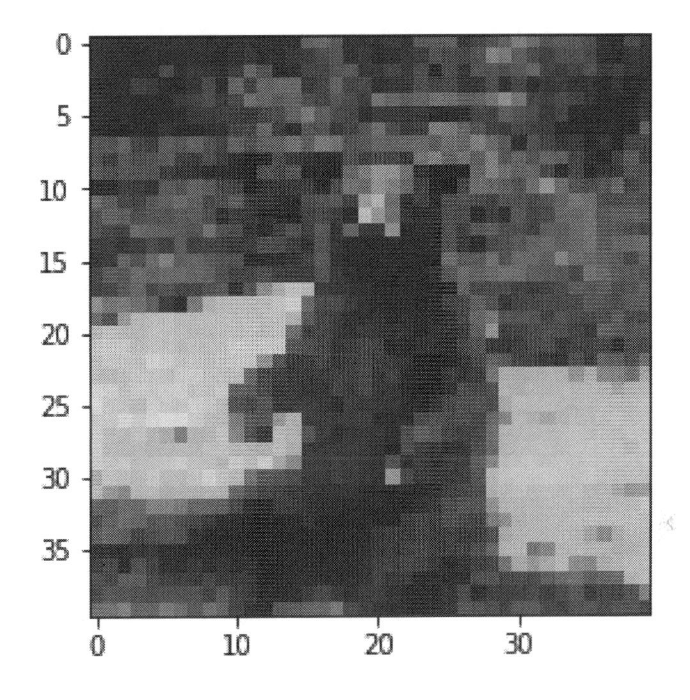

Figure 27:

What does this really mean, and how does this happen? Let's take a moment to appreciate the process that just took place, on a more granular level, right before building a network with several of these layers.

3.3.1 Convolutions - From Mathematics to Images

So, what's a *convolution*? A convolution, in mathematical terms, is an operation between two functions that results in a third function. This resulting function describes how the first affects the other. The term was appropriated from mathematics, like many in computer science are. And as usual - it's changed to a degree.

Note: If you have formal education in mathematics or even electrical engineering (convolutions are used in signal processing), you might have a different idea of what convolutions are. Bear in mind that in the realm of deep learning, *convolution* is what you'd refer to as *cross-correlation*.

> A convolution, in layman's terms, in the context of Deep Learning, is the multiplication of of two matrices. One matrix is a **filter/kernel** (a set of a neuron's weights) that we slide over the image, and the other matrix is the part of the image covered by the filter.

Each convolution results in a new layer, with the shape of:

$$((Width - KernelSize + 4 * PaddingSize)/StrideSize) + 1$$

We'll talk about kernel sizes, padding and stride later:

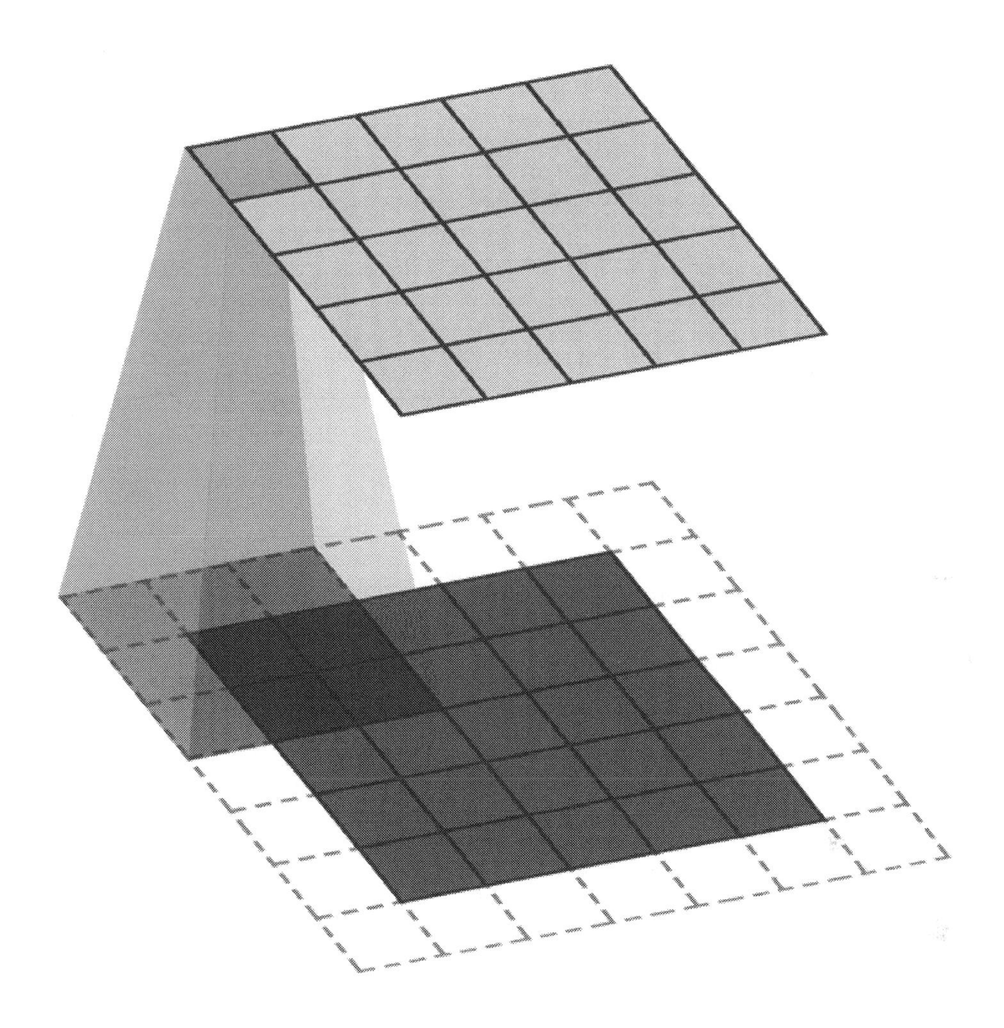

Figure 28:

The filter/kernel is smaller than the input image - and typically, *much smaller*. The idea behind using a small filter that repeatedly performs convolutions on the image is integral to why CNNs are so versatile, and they're a reflection of the small receptive field of each neuron in the visual cortex, as discovered by David H. Hubel and Torsten N.

> Each filter can pick up a feature. When applied on a patch of the image, it results in a vector of values. Some of the underlying features might be diminished while others are enhanced.

In a sense, a *filter* allows us to find the same pattern, even if it's scattered throughout an image, since it proceeds sliding over the image, amplifying the data only on the features it's fit for. It'll react to a horizontal line in the top of the image just as well as in the bottom of the image.

When explaining how filters work - it's worth taking a look at how they were manually defined, back when we didn't delegate this job to machines. Here's a filter for horizontal lines:

```
1 matrix([[0, 0, 0],
2         [1, 1, 1],
3         [0, 0, 0]])
```

However, since these are the *weights* of a *neuron*, which are **trainable** - we don't have to attempt creating them by hand. We can have the network *learn* the filters it needs to use to get a high accuracy!

If a neuron relies on this filter to provide it with input values - it'll react only to horizontal lines (multiplying them by 1, resulting in them staying as they are), and ignore the rest (multiplying them with 0). That neuron would pick up only horizontal lines and activate for those.

Again, a filter is just a set of weights of a neuron. This means that we're *reusing the weights between many neurons*. This is also known as weight-sharing. Weight-sharing allows us to detect *many* patterns, with less computational complexity and less energy:

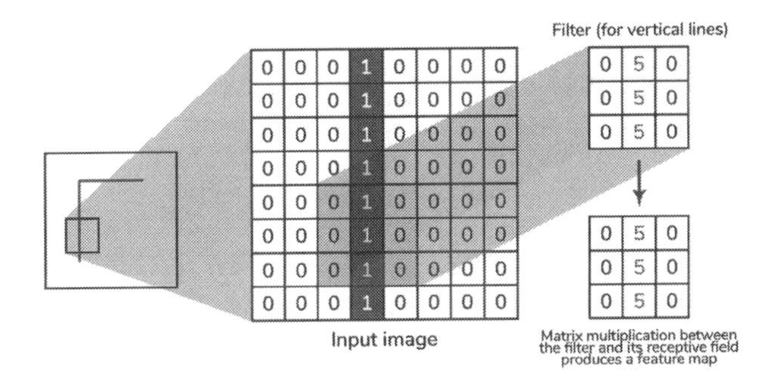

Figure 29:

Once a filter has been passed over the entire image, its activations are saved as a *feature map* of that filter.

This filter, that amplified vertical lines, allows us to detect vertical lines in any image now. Many different filters are passed over the same image, each producing a different feature map. Through these feature maps, a network can learn what features make a dog or a whale.

Note: Being able to detect the same pattern, regardless of its position in the image, is known as *translation invariance*. This is where CNNs crush Densely-Connected Neural Networks, which learn **global patterns**, rather than **local patterns**. Because of this, you can train CNNs for a shorter period of time, on fewer data points, and achieve better generalization abilities.

Translational invariance isn't the only reason why CNNs excel at this task. They use this **knowledge hierarchically**, like the visual cortex does. Low-level features are combined to produce higher level features. The first convolutional layers will typically learn about edges and curves. The final convolutional layers will, depending on the dataset you're working with, for instance will be able to learn distinctions between types of dog snouts. The higher-level layers build on *top* of the lower level layers, and only on the ones relevant in building a higher-level representation.

> A layer that recognises plus signs could be a higher-level layer, that inherits feature maps from layers the recognize horizontal lines and vertical lines. However, it won't connect to any layers for recognizing, say, curved edges, since there are no curved edges in a plus sign.

A popular analogy is imagining a flashlight, and a piece of paper with some patterns on it. If you were in the dark, and shone the flashlight right behind the piece of paper, you'd be able to see a small portion of the patterns, right in front of the light. For a more acurate analogy, this would be a UV flashlight, that reacts only to a portion of the ink, amplifying and accentuating a certain feature of the ink. You'd have to use a different UV light to get the second type of feature, and so on.

The filter size is very customizable here - and changing the size will also change the receptive field, which in turn affects the calculations that build the feature map. A common filter size is 3x3, though, this isn't a set rule. Another common size if 5x5. For larger images, you can use larger filter sizes, but this mainly depends on what types of features you want to pick up. You can both get too detailed and too general here.

> Convolutions can be done on 1 dimension, 2 dimensions or 3 dimensions.

Images are typically represented with *depth*, not just *height* and *width*. The *depth* of most images is 3 - its RGB values. Each channel of a pixel is a layer in this image depth. Greyscale images have a single channel, and thus, are 1 layer in depth.

Depending on the images you're applying filters to, you'll perform convolutions on 1 dimension, 2 dimensions or 3 dimensions. While *depthwise separable convolutions* do exist - we'll save those for a later lesson, once all of this sinks in through practical examples and visualizations.

So *really*, the size of the filter illustrated before wasn't 3x3 - it was 3x3x3:

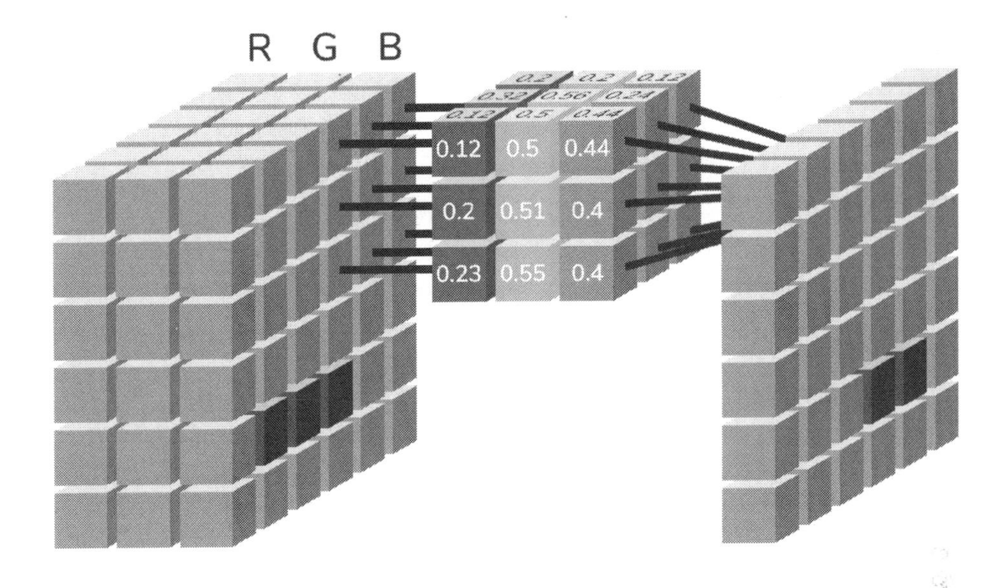

Figure 30:

To recap and summarize:

- Filters are neuron weights, and are trainable.
- Filters slide over images, performing matrix multiplication between the filter and the patch of the image "below it". This operation is known as a *convolution.*
- Through many convolutions, which amplify features a filter was "made to" find, we produce a *feature map.*
- Feature maps are stacked on top of each other in the hierarchy of layers, where lower-level layers capture simpler patterns and higher-level layers capture more complex patterns made from the lower-level ones.

How do filters slide over an image and how big are these steps? The *step size* that filters take is known as a *filter stride.*

3.3.2 Filter Stride

So far, in the illustrations, we've moved the filter by *1 pixel* in each step. Since the filter is 3 pixels wide and tall, 2 of the pixels in each convolution are essentially reused. Having a

1-pixel step is known as having a *stride* of *1*.

As usual, there's no one best size for the stride. It's *commonly* set to *2*, since it works for a wide variety of applications, so if you can't make any assumptions on a good stride size for your specific task - a sensible default is *2*.

Having a larger stride also means, in effect, shrinking the images, since you're taking larger steps and convolving the input underneath the filter (capturing less data). For instance, here's the same bear image from before, with strides of 1 to 5:

```
conv_images = []

for i in range(1, 6):
    conv = keras.layers.Conv2D(filters=1,
                strides=i,
                padding = 'same',
                kernel_size=5)

    convolved = conv(input_image)
    conv_images.append(convolved)

fig, ax = plt.subplots(nrows=1, ncols=5, figsize=(16, 6))
for i, img in enumerate(conv_images):
    ax[i].imshow(img[0, :, :, 0])
```

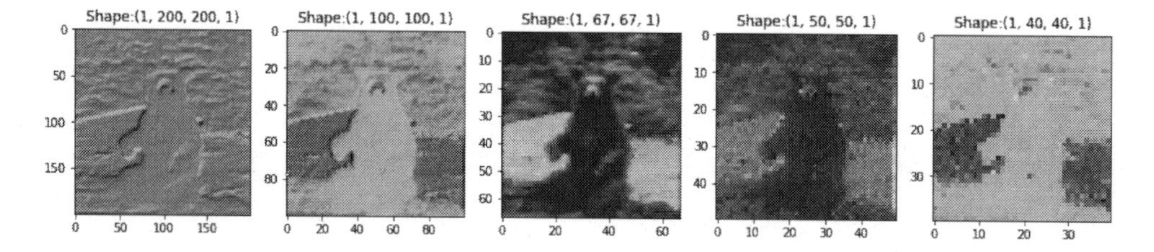

Figure 31:

The first image, with a stride of 1 retains the 200x200 size, while the final one, with a stride of 5 has a size of 40x40. Additionally, you can see how each layer learned something different, annotated by the brightness of the pixels (larger values are brighter, and larger values are produced when a feature is favored by a filter). Since the filter weights start out as random, you'll have different results on each run. The first layer learned about the color of the grass behind the bear. The second layer learned about horizontal/diagonal edges (you can see the diagonal line in the back, and the underside of the bear's hand). The third filter learned about the color of the bear and the forest behind it, etc.

The larger the stride, the more "ground" is covered in each step, and thus, the faster the computation. The lower the stride, the longer it takes to extract features. It's not only about speed - it's about knowledge representations, since a portion of each matrix in a convolution is likely present in another convolution.

As a matter of fact - what about central pixels? In the illustration we've used earlier, the central 4 pixels have, in fact, been present in *every single convolution (all receptive fields)* since no matter how you move the filter across the image, they'll be present in the corner.

This assigns a disproportional weight to the pixels in the center of the image, and that clearly poses a problem in terms of generalization. While you won't work with images *this small* and a filter of this size, the problem of central information taking the spot is present even with larger images. Moreover, the edges don't nearly get the same amount of attention, since the top left pixel is present in only one convolution!

> This gives center-features higher prevalence over features farther away from it. How do we battle this?

3.3.3 Filter Padding

To equalize the importance of features between the center and the edges, we use *padding*. There are two types of padding we typically use:

- "Same" padding
- "Valid" padding

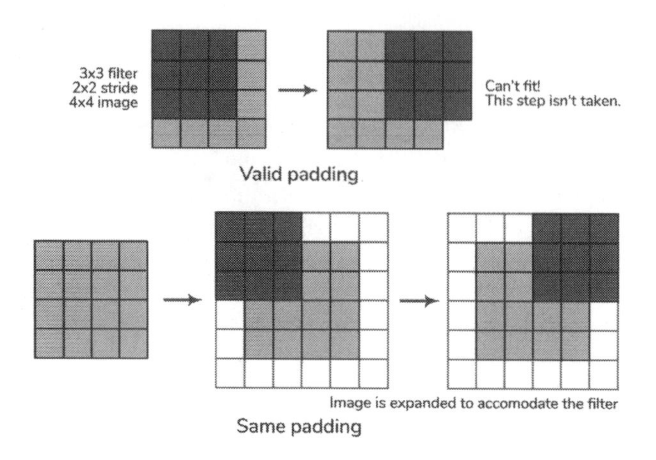

Figure 32:

If the padding is "same", if necessary, a convolutional layer will add zeros around the input. Everything multiplied by 0, is naturally, 0, making the additions have 0 informational value. The amount to be added depends on the input image and the stride size.

If the padding is "valid", the input is *trimmed* to fit into the given number of steps of the filter. For instance, if the filter has a *stride* of *3* and size of `3x3x3` and the input image is 10x10 - only the first 9 pixels of the 10x10 image (in width) can fit into the steps the filter takes. The final column of pixels will be pruned away.

> In a similar way, if you're frosting a cake - you can either add more frosting to make it more even, or trim the cake on the sides and use less frosting.

Through padding, we added more value to the edges of the image, while taking away the unbalanced value from the center. This ultimately shifts the resulting calculation, and typically results in a more accurate feature map.

3.3.4 Effects of the Filter Size, Stride and Padding on Feature Maps

All of these affect the *feature map* - the filter size, the stride size, the depth of the images and padding. How? Let's take a look at the previous example of how a feature map looks like. Now that we've got a good idea of what the parameters of a Convolutional Layer are, we can play around with them and visualize the results.

Since the padding doesn't make much of a visual difference, we'll mainly play around with the size of the filters (kernels) and stride:

```
conv_images_kernel_size = []

for i in range(1, 6):
    conv = keras.layers.Conv2D(filters=1,
                strides=1,
                padding = 'same',
                kernel_size=i)

    convolved = conv(input_image)
    conv_images_kernel_size.append(convolved)

conv_images_stride_size = []

for i in range(1, 6):
    conv = keras.layers.Conv2D(filters=1,
                strides=i,
                padding = 'same',
                kernel_size=5)

    convolved = conv(input_image)
    conv_images_stride_size.append(convolved)

fig, ax = plt.subplots(nrows=1, ncols=5, figsize=(16, 4))
fig.suptitle('Effect of Filter Size', fontsize=16)
for i, img in enumerate(conv_images_kernel_size):
    ax[i].imshow(img[0, :, :, 0])

fig, ax = plt.subplots(nrows=1, ncols=5, figsize=(16, 4))
fig.suptitle('Effect of Stride Size', fontsize=16)
for i, img in enumerate(conv_images_stride_size):
    ax[i].imshow(img[0, :, :, 0])
```

This results in:

Effect of Stride Size

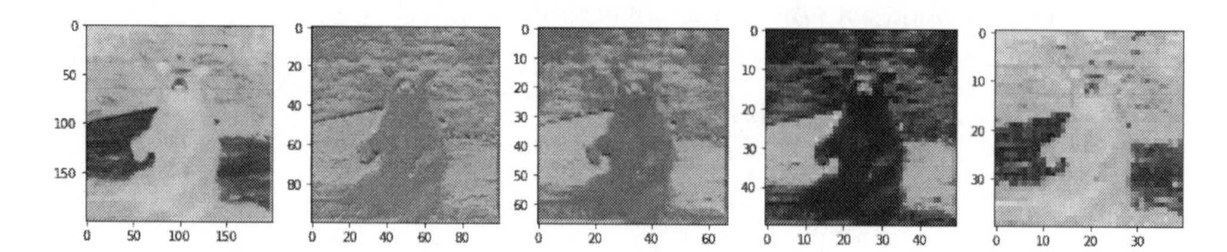

With a larger filter size - images are a bit smoother. Some of the fine-grained details you can see in the first image aren't that present in the last one. With a larger stride-size, more parts of the image are "glossed over" and the feature maps are smaller.

Convolving already convolved feature maps allows us to extract meaningful patterns and information from images. This segways us into the next type of layer, typically present after a few stacked convolutional layers - the *pooling layers*.

3.4 Pooling Layer

Pooling layers are simple, but important. In a similar way to how convolutional layers slide over images and create parts of feature maps, pooling layers slide over images and *pool* them. Pooling refers to taking the maximum value (or mean) of a receptive field, resulting in subsampling of the image, and in effect, making it smaller.

Pooling layers make images smaller to reduce the computational load and make training faster, however, they also reduce the number of parameters that a network needs to tune, by reducing the number of pixels in an image. This makes the networks generalize better (by making it harder to overfit), even if they decide to use smaller strides to capture more information.

Note: By pruning data away, and aggregating it based on *macro* features, rather than *micro* features, we make a tradeoff between attention to detail and generalization ability. Two images, that are very similar, when passed through a pooling layer, may create the same output. This in effect makes the network totally blind to the micro features that were pruned away. In most cases, this is a good tradeoff, since we want the network to know that a snout, even if moved a bit - is still a snout. Though, in some particular cases, and especially in ones where *invariance* isn't sought after, excessive pooling (or any at all) might hurt the model's accuracy. In some of the Guided Projects accompanying this book we'll see this in action.

Pooling layers aggregate data, and the two most common forms of aggregation are *max-pooling* and *mean-pooling*:

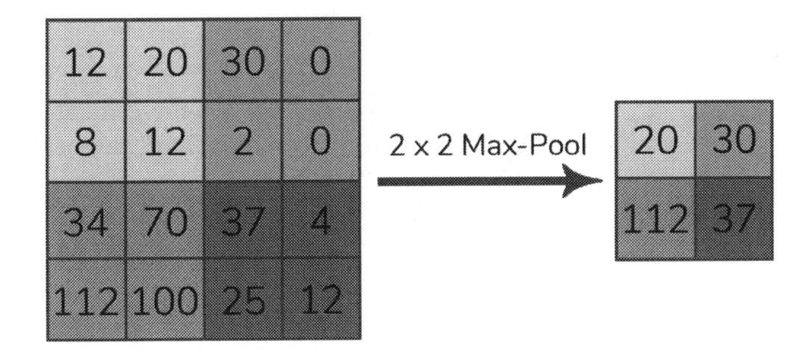

Figure 33:

In a *2x2* max pooling layer, such as this one - the maximum value of each 2x2 filter is used and put into the smaller feature map. In a 2x2 mean pooling layer, the mean value of them would be taken instead.

With a stride of 2, it'll make the image 4 times smaller - choosing one out of every 4 pixels - making a result half of the width, and half of the height:

```
pooling = keras.layers.MaxPooling2D(2)
result = pooling(input_image)

plt.imshow(result[0, :, :, 0])
```

Figure 34:

Finally, this leads us to the final typical building block of CNN classifiers - the fully-connected layer.

3.5 Fully-Connected Layer

The fully-connected layer is sometimes known as the *classification head* or *classification top*. Once an image has been convolved and pooled multiple times - only its defining features are left, in the shape of a small map that's totally illegible to humans.

These maps converge to a similar vector if the images were similar to begin with. This is where a fully-connected, MLP-style network can help! Let's recap - MLPs learn global patterns, while CNNs learn local patterns, due to the fact they're modelled similar to the visual cortex with small receptive fields. Once flattened, we're again learning global patterns from these flattened vectors. Doesn't this defeat the purpose?

Well, a face consists of local patterns, such as eyes and noses, and global patterns, such as the fact that most people have two eyes, and a nose in between. The context of where things go is well-modelled by the fully-connected classification top (and can be modelled by high-level convolutional layers as well). There are alternatives to this architecture, such as the fully-convolutional architecture, which also do well.

Depending on how intricate the patterns are, you can use anywhere between a single fully connected layer and a large number of them with most modern networks reducing the number of layers. Depending on the classification task, the final layer will contain the same number of neurons as there are classes, and you'll use an appropriate activation function for them:

- Sigmoid for binary tasks
- Softmax for multi-class tasks

Before being fed into a dense classifier, we used to flatten maps into long vectors. How do we flatten the feature maps? Keras offers a pretty handy `keras.layers.Flatten()` layer, which accepts the feature maps and flattens them into a 1D tensor, ready to be fed into an MLP. It's worth noting that you should take the number of convolutions, stride size and number of pooling layers into consideration when flattening. The smaller the feature maps are in the end, the less training parameters there'll be after flattening. The tremendous reduction in computational cost given to us by convolutional and pooling layers can be partially undone with an unwise positioning of a flattening layer. Additionally, if you reduce the feature maps down too much, there won't be much to learn from, as even the macro features will blend in. In the recent years, we've been moving away from flattening layers, and usually opt out for a much better alternative. More on that in the next and upcoming lessons.

3.6 Combining Layers

When you combine the layers we've covered so far, you get something along these lines:

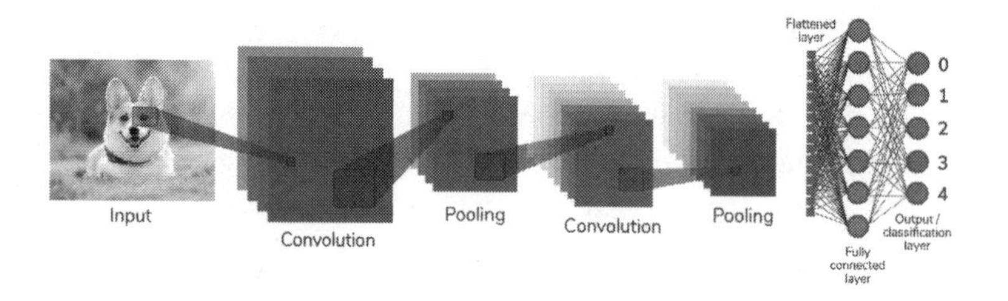

Figure 35:

Features start out being generic, getting closer and closer to domain knowledge up the hierarchy. Most of the *domain knowledge* is located in the top of the model, in the fully-connected layer. Beneath it, we've got the feature extractor. Keep this in mind for the upcoming project!

This is a *classic* CNN, and you'll see illustrations similar to this one very frequently in your future work with computer vision. Most other architectures are built on top of this conceptual idea, and tweak it either slightly or substantially.

Note: Again, terminology can be fuzzy. Arguably, this is a CNN + MLP combination, not just a CNN, even though we colloquially call it a CNN. To be technically correct - this can be called a *CNN Classifier,* since a *CNN base/feature extractor* is used to extract features, and an MLP is used to classify these features into classes. In a similar vein, a CNN base can be topped with other architectures. Notably, if you feed the output features of a CNN into an RNN or Transformer, alongside tokenized sentences - you can teach a network to generate descriptions of images. We'll implement this in a guided project later. It's important to remember that a CNN is technically just the feature extractor, for which you can put various "tops" on.

For reference, here's the proposed architecture of LeNet-5 - the network that spiked the interest in CNNs, written by Yann LeCunn, back in 1998. It can't be overstated how important the release of that paper was in 1998, and the breakthrough can be easily surmised as:

```
lenet5 = keras.Sequential([
    keras.layers.Conv2D(6, (5,5), padding = 'same', input_shape=[28, 28, 1],
        activation = 'tanh'),
    keras.layers.AveragePooling2D((2,2)),

    keras.layers.Conv2D(16, (5,5), padding = 'same', activation = 'tanh'),
    keras.layers.AveragePooling2D((2,2)),

    keras.layers.Conv2D(120, (5,5), padding = 'same', activation = 'tanh'),
    keras.layers.Flatten(),
    keras.layers.Dense(84, activation = 'tanh'),
    # LeCunn used Radial Basis Function, which isn't built into Keras
    # Modern networks use 'softmax', so we'll use that instead to
    # avoid having to define a custom activation function for now
    keras.layers.Dense(10, activation = 'softmax')
])
```

`tanh` is not really used as often anymore as an activation function, and `relu` is the new "default". It would've amped the accuracy up in this architecture significantly too. Additionally, since AlexNet in 2012 (which won the yearly computer vision competition that year), we've started generally stacking multiple convolutional layers on top of each other *before* any pooling.

We additionally can use `Dropout` layers, as well as `BatchNormalization` layers as we usually would with other types of networks. Dropout remains a great technique to force robustness into a model's weights, though, `BatchNormalization` *can* perform oddly with CNNs if you don't use it right, and it's typically placed before any dropout if it's present, and after an activation function layer through which an image has been passed through.

This architecture is severily outdated, yet, it started a movement that we're still exploring to this day. It was written for the MNIST hand-written digits dataset, and subsequently used in banks to recognize the written digits and automate laborious copying by hand.

Let's load the dataset in and train this network on it - and I promise, this is the first and last time we use the MNIST hand-written digits dataset in the book. I'd much rather lead you through some *real* projects instead of focusing on this set:

```
# Compile network with categorical crossentropy loss to classify 10 digits
# Adam is a more modern optimizer LeCunn didn't use at the time
lenet5.compile(loss = 'sparse_categorical_crossentropy', optimizer = 'adam',
    metrics=['accuracy'])

# Load data
(x_train, y_train), (x_test, y_test) = keras.datasets.mnist.load_data()
# Reshape to single-channel (28, 28, 1)
```

```
x_train = x_train.reshape((x_train.shape[0], 28, 28, 1))
x_test = x_test.reshape((x_test.shape[0], 28, 28, 1))

fig, ax = plt.subplots(1, 10, figsize=(10,2))
for i in range(10):
    ax[i].imshow(x_train[i])
    ax[i].axis('off')
    plt.subplots_adjust(wspace=1)

plt.show()
```

This results in a series of numbers, 28x28 in size:

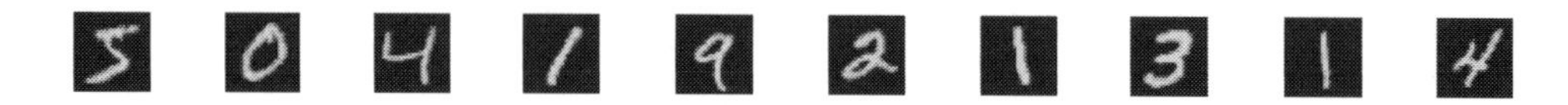

Figure 36:

Let's fit a model to learn to classify these:

```
# Fit model
history = lenet5.fit(x_train, y_train, epochs=5)
```

Within 5 epochs and a few seconds per epoch, we get a breakthrough for 1998:

```
Epoch 1/5
1875/1875 [==============================] - 7s 4ms/step - loss: 0.1419 -
    accuracy: 0.9578
Epoch 2/5
1875/1875 [==============================] - 7s 4ms/step - loss: 0.0997 -
    accuracy: 0.9698
Epoch 3/5
1875/1875 [==============================] - 7s 4ms/step - loss: 0.0993 -
    accuracy: 0.9689
Epoch 4/5
1875/1875 [==============================] - 7s 4ms/step - loss: 0.0952 -
    accuracy: 0.9708
Epoch 5/5
1875/1875 [==============================] - 7s 4ms/step - loss: 0.0883 -
    accuracy: 0.9726
```

This model is evaluated at:

```
lenet5.evaluate(x_test, y_test)
# 313/313 [==============================] - 1s 2ms/step - loss: 0.0817 -
    accuracy: 0.9737
```

And, let's visualize some of the predictions:

```
fig, ax = plt.subplots(1, 10, figsize=(10,2))
for i in range(10):
    # Obtain an image
    img = x_test[i]
    # Predict image - remember, CNN expects a (batch, height, width, depth)
        input
    # so we expand by the first dimension to make a batch of one image
    pred = lenet5.predict(np.expand_dims(img, 0))

    ax[i].imshow(img)
    # softmax outputs a probability for every class
    # such as (0.8, 0.1, 0.0, 0.0, etc.) so we obtain the highest
        probability class
    # and set it as the title (most confident prediction)
    ax[i].set_title(f"Pred:\n {np.argmax(pred)}")
    ax[i].axis('off')
    plt.subplots_adjust(wspace=1)

plt.show()
```

This results in an easily verifiable:

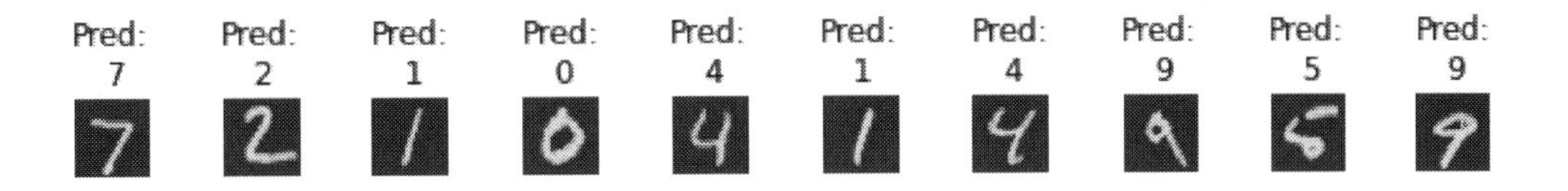

Figure 37:

If we were to *just* switch out `'tanh'` with `'relu'` - the acuracy would've gotten up to 99% in the same 5 epochs:

```
Epoch 5/5
1875/1875 [==============================] - 7s 4ms/step - loss: 0.0292 -
    accuracy: 0.9912
```

Armed with this knowledge, let's jump into a small project, that's not as easy to fit even nowadays - there's no point in building a network around a dataset that we can fit with 99-100% confidence, since real world applications are far from that. We'll define our own CNN for it, using modern practices and techniques, using the basic building blocks outlined in the lesson so far.

In later lessons, we'll explore some of the more advanced building blocks used in cutting-edge architectures, as well as the architectures themselves. First, we'll use them as black-box building blocks, and then dive into what makes each of them uniquely performant and ingenious in their own right.

Time to put the theory into practice! If it didn't all fit into place already, there's a good chance it will now that you can build and see the results. If not - don't worry! Once the practical application is finished, try revisiting the initial explanations in the lesson. Many people have an "a-ha" moment after practicing with CNNs an then re-reading the introductory parts.

Note: With high-level APIs such as Keras that do the heavy lifting, it's easy to forget how things work under the hood, and it's worth revisiting them in the initial phases of learning (as well as some time down the line). If you haven't had any exposition to some of the terminology used here, it might take you a bit of time to get things to click. It's easy to conect the dots looking backwards, but not so much looking forwards. This is how discoveries are made!

---

4 Guided Project: Building Your First Convolutional Neural Network With Keras

Time to put the theory into practice! If it didn't all fit into place already, there's a good chance it will now that you can build and see the results. If not - don't worry! Once the practical application is finished, try revisiting the initial explanations in the lesson. Many people have an "a-ha" moment after practicing with CNNs an then re-reading the introductory parts.

Note: With high-level APIs such as Keras that do the heavy lifting, it's easy to forget how things work under the hood, and it's worth revisiting them in the initial phases of learning (as well as some time down the line). If you haven't had any exposition to some of the terminology used here, it might take you a bit of time to get things to click. It's easy to conect the dots looking backwards, but not so much looking forwards. This is how discoveries are made!

4.1 The Intel Image Classification Dataset - Importing and Exploration

Let's try working with the *Intel Image Classification*[43] dataset. It's a great dataset to go further from, since it's not super easy to get a high accuracy from the get-go. Additionally, there are some features that are easy to mix up for a network, which will serve as a great introduction into *model evaluation* and how you can learn about what makes it trip up and misclassify an image.

The dataset consists of 14k images for training and 3k for testing, sized at 150x150, with 6 classes: "buildings", "forest", "glacier", "mountain", "sea" and "street". As you could assume from the classes, it mainly consists of images of natural scenes (as much as buildings can be natural).

[43]https://www.kaggle.com/datasets/puneet6060/intel-image-classification

> It may sound like this should be a walk in the park, like the Dogs vs. Cats classification is. However, consider the classes again. A mountain oftentimes contains a forest on it. A glacier is in the sea and there are buildings all around on streets! These classes, although, seemingly totally different, are fairly intertwined.

Note: This phenomena is known as *co-occurrence*. Some things are generally present with other things in images. A network might learn a *co-occurring feature* as *part of a class,* whereas, it might not be. Learning a co-occurring feature and assuming a class is similar to mixing up **correlation** with **causation**, and it's a major fallacy that results in a bias that can easily go unnoticed because of its very nature. Correctly identifying and evaluating wrong predictions as well as visualizing what networks learn is a great way to spot and remove this bias.

Co-occurrence is present in any sort of data - and most notably images and text. For instance, imagine we're trying to classify boats and cars. Boats are typically located in water while car's aren't (unless you're James Bond). The network can learn the intricacies of what makes a boat a boat - or it can go the easy way and learn that whatever's on the huge blue patch of water is a boat. It's a single, super simple feature - "if lots of blue on image blue: boat", and it would lead to a high level of accuracy faster than actually learning what a boat is. This happens commonly in image classification, where a stray object can become the defining feature, rather than the one we're envisioning. Really, the image has lots of objects - a boat, a sailor, the sea, the sun, etc. We label the images as "boat" or "car" because we're focusing on a specific object. We'll talk about object recognition and recognizing both the class and position of multiple objects on an image in a later project.

In *"Practical Deep Learning for Cloud, Mobile & Edge"*, written by Anirudh, Siddha and Meher, and published by O'Reilly - the authors note an interesting story to warn of co-occurrence. The story outlies how the military tried training a classifier to identify camouflaged tanks in forests, and got a near-100% accuracy! Turns out - the images of tanks in forests were taken on the same shady day, while images of just forests were taken on a sunny day. The network, apparently, learned to distinguish the shade of the sky as "tank" or "no tank", and proved to be useless in practice.

> Whether this actually happened or not doesn't really matter. There's probably a thousand unsung stories of networks failing due to mistaking correlation for truth, and co-occurrence is a major part of that. Even more commonly - there are thousands of models that work well, but not for the reason you might think. This is dangerous, as a change in the environment can suddenly break it, and due to a long history of great performance, you can believe that it's still doing well.

Note: You can download the associated Jupyter Notebook with all of the source code here[44].

With this in mind, let's get to loading the data! First of all, let's download the dataset. You can either download it manually on its Kaggle page, by clicking the *"Download"* button and extracting the folder inside. Alternatively, you can download it using Kaggle's CLI[45]:

```
$ kaggle datasets download -d puneet6060/intel-image-classification
```

The `kaggle datasets download` command allows you to easily download datasets from the platform, and you can get the command for downloading any dataset by selecting *"Copy API command"* under the three dots next to *"Download"*. The dataset has 363MB, so it shouldn't take too long to download. Once it is, it'll be zipped, so let's extract it:

```
import os
import zipfile

if not os.path.exists('./intel-image-classification/'):
    with zipfile.ZipFile("intel-image-classification.zip","r") as zip_ref:
        zip_ref.extractall("intel-image-classification")
```

We're extracting the contents into a directory named `intel-image-classification`. Let's quickly check whether that worked well:

[44]https://s3.amazonaws.com/s3.stackabuse.com/media/guided+projects/_Deep+Learning+for+Computer+Vision+in+Python+-+Lesson+3%2C+Building+Your+First+Convolutional+Neural+Network+With+Keras.ipynb

[45]https://www.kaggle.com/docs/api

```
for filename in os.listdir('intel-image-classification'):
    print(filename)
```

```
seg_pred
seg_test
seg_train
```

We have segments for training, testing and prediction! The prediction segment isn't always present with public datasets, and is only present here since this dataset used to be a competition a few years back. The prediction segment was used to validate the final models and pick a winner - not the test set. We'll ignore the prediction set for now.

Generally, public datasets can be lumped together (raw data), split into a training and testing set or even split into a training, testing *and* validation set. You'll always want to have a validation set separate from the testing set, so since we're missing one, we'll create it from the training set, to abide by the rules of the now-finished competition.

First off - it's laborious to write `./intel-image-classification` over and over again. Let's create a `config` dictionary to hold some of the commonly used paths and potential configurations. Additionally, the dataset has 6 classes - `'buildings', 'forest', 'glacier', 'mountain', 'sea', 'street'`, but the classes in the dataset are labeled numerically - `0, 1, 2, 3, 4, 5`. For our own leisure, we'll want to have a list of classnames that we can reference. The great thing about numerical labels - we can access the corresponding textual label given the numerical one, acting as its index!

Let's make a configuration dictionary:

```
ROOT_PATH = 'intel-image-classification'

config = {
    # The dataset is weirdly formatted to have a nested directory
    # with the same name
    'TRAIN_PATH': os.path.join(ROOT_PATH, 'seg_train', 'seg_train'),
    'TEST_PATH': os.path.join(ROOT_PATH, 'seg_test', 'seg_test'),
    'VALID_PATH': os.path.join(ROOT_PATH, 'seg_pred', 'seg_pred'),
    'BATCH_SIZE' : 16,
    'IMG_SIZE' : 224
}

# Classname for nicer reading
classnames=['buildings', 'forest', 'glacier', 'mountain', 'sea', 'street']
```

Great! Let's list the directories in the train segment and their length:

```
for dirname in os.listdir(config['TRAIN_PATH']):
    print(f"Path: \'{dirname}\', Length:
        {len(os.listdir(config['TRAIN_PATH']+dirname))}")
```

This results in:

```
Path: 'buildings', Length: 2191
Path: 'forest', Length: 2271
Path: 'glacier', Length: 2404
Path: 'mountain', Length: 2512
Path: 'sea', Length: 2274
Path: 'street', Length: 2382
```

6 classes, roughly equally distributed. It's *great* to have roughly equal distributions for machine learning (since most algorithms perform better on roughly equal distributions), though, not all datasets are like that. In a later project, we'll see what a heavy imbalance means, how to fix it and whether we want to fix it. Let's not burden ourselves too much with those implications for now.

Let's take a look at the number of images in the training and testing folders as well:

```
training_images_sum = 0
for filename in os.listdir(config['TRAIN_PATH']):
    training_images_sum=training_images_sum+
        len(os.listdir(config['TRAIN_PATH']+filename))
print(f'Number of training examples: {training_images_sum}')
# Number of training examples: 14034

testing_images_sum = 0
for filename in os.listdir(config['TEST_PATH']):
    testing_images_sum=testing_images_sum+
        len(os.listdir(config['TEST_PATH']+filename))
print(f'Number of testing examples: {testing_images_sum}')
# Number of testing examples: 3000
```

14 thousand images isn't a *huge* amount - some datasets count into the millions. However, it's quite enough for a lot of classifiers, depending on how different the classes are.

4.2 Exploratory Data Analysis

Let's define a `display_images()` function that accepts a classname that we want to inspect and the segment/subset of the data (training or testing, for instance) and displays a grid of images from that class and subset:

```
1 def display_images(class_name, subset):
2     if subset == 'train':
3         directory = f"{config['TRAIN_PATH']+class_name}"
4     else:
5         directory = f"{config['TEST_PATH']+class_name}"
6 
7     fig = plt.figure(figsize=(10, 10))
8 
9     for index, img_path in enumerate(os.listdir(directory)[:25]):
10         img = plt.imread(f'{directory}/{img_path}')
11         ax = fig.add_subplot(5, 5, index+1)
12         ax.imshow(img)
13         ax.axis('off')
14 
15     plt.tight_layout()
16     plt.show()
```

The function makes a 5x5 grid of images, removing the spines to make them look nicer and allows us to inspect the classes within different subsets:

```
1 display_images('buildings','train')
```

Figure 38:

There's a greyscale image in the beginning (models trained only on colored images can "forget" most of their knowledge if they then classify a greyscale image, so having some during training is a great idea), followed by a bird's view of a city (or more like Spiderman's view) and a close-up of what appears to be a skylight of a building. Another image shows a large part of the sky with buildings on the sides and one of the images shows a small adorable red house with a street in front of it. The first image from the left, on the fifth row shows a building behind palm trees and plastic barricades. The building isn't even in the focus! There's quite a bit of variance here. The fact that there's variance implies two things:

- We can build a robust model to detect buildings
- We're going to have a harder time building a robust model to detect buildings

Let's take a look at images of streets:

```
display_images('street','train')
```

Figure 39:

The first image shows more buildings than streets. The third image as well! It's 90% building, 10% street! The fourth image contains a greyscale image of a police officer covering a portion of the street. The first image in the second row looks much more like a *"buildings"* image than a street image. In fact, the cute red house and this image intuitively belong to the same class! The image in the center of the plot really highlights how variant this category is. There's barely any street on it!

If you were to forget which classes you plotted from - how many images do you think you'd get right here? I'd most likely "misclassify" 5 of these images as buildings, since almost no street is present in those. That's 75% in accuracy!

> Can our model figure out a better predictor of what makes a street?

Let's find out. Time to load the data in and preprocess it.

4.3 Data Preprocessing

There's a multitude of ways you can load images from the disk. A general pipeline would be to identify the paths, iterate over the images, load them in alongside their label, and put them in a set:

```
1  from glob import glob
2
3  def read_images(train_path, test_path, valid_path):
4      # All directories you want to load in
5      paths = [train_path, test_path, valid_path]
6      # Which sets are to be returned
7      sets = []
8
9      for path in paths:
10         images = []
11         labels = []
12         print(f'Loading images from: {path}')
13         data = glob(f'{path}/*/*', recursive=True)
14         for img_path in data:
15             # Get label from pathname
16             label = img_path.split('\\')[1]
17             # Turn label into numerical value (0..5)
18             # because the network will expect numbers
19             numerical_label = classnames.index(label)
20             # Read the image and convert to RGB format (OpenCV reads in BGR
                   by default)
21             # This is crucial, since the images *look* the same to us but
                   the numbers
22             # are totally switched for the network
23             img = cv2.imread(img_path)
24             img = cv2.cvtColor(img, cv2.COLOR_BGR2RGB)
25             # Resize if it's in the wrong size for any reason
26             img = cv2.resize(img, (150, 150))
27             # Append labels and images
28             labels.append(numerical_label)
29             images.append(img)
```

```
30          # Convert lists into NumPy arrays
31          images = np.array(images, dtype = 'float32')
32          labels = np.array(labels, dtype = 'float32')
33          # Normalize images from `0..255` to `0..1` to save on computational
34          # resources during training
35          images=images/255
36          # Add set to `sets`
37          sets.append((images, labels))
38      return sets
39
40  # Load tuples of training, testing, and pred sets
41  (x_train, y_train), (x_test, y_test), _ = read_images(config['TRAIN_PATH'],
        config['TEST_PATH'], config['VALID_PATH'])
```

You'd then simply call:

```
1 # Define and compile
2 model = ...
3 model.fit(x_train, y_train, epochs=50)
```

This pipeline works well - loading data in and preprocessing it depending on your architecture (format, size, normalization, etc). However, even this relatively small dataset can easily eat up gigabytes in RAM if you load it into memory fully. If you've got a strong machine, this isn't an issue. If you don't - you can use free cloud-based services such as Kaggle Notebooks or Google Colab, which have loads of RAM. Though, this is unscalable and doesn't make much sense since it ties datasets to hardware.

Alternatively - you can run this code locally by utilizing a nifty trick and loading the data in batches! These batches are typically 16-32 images in size (though, you can go arbitrarily high, which isn't recommended for good convergence nor your RAM). Loading data in batches can easily be done using Keras' `ImageDataGenerator` class, which, flows from a directory or Pandas `DataFrame` or NumPy array, loading smaller batches into memory at a given step.

`ImageDataGenerator` additionally allows us to perform *Data Augmentation* and preprocessing steps to fully automate the process for any given input. Data augmentation warrants a section of its own, and we'll dive into it in a moment.

Another important feature of `ImageDataGenerator` is that each generator keeps track of the *filenames* and *classes* of the data being produced by a generator, which will play a crucial role *later* in the guide, when we perform Principal Component Analysis and t-SNE to analyze what the model has learned. If we don't use generators, we'd have to keep track of these ourselves, which is much messier. The abstraction away from the nitty-gritties helps flatten the learning curve and get you up and running faster.

The `ImageDataGenerator` class is part of the `preprocessing` module for images and can be imported as:

```
from tensorflow.keras.preprocessing.image import ImageDataGenerator

# Intantiate data generators
train_datagen = ImageDataGenerator()
test_datagen = ImageDataGenerator()
```

These generators can then flow from directories with a given structure:

```
class_1
  - sample0.png
  - sample1.png
  - sample2.png
class_0
  - sample0.png
  - sample1.png
  - sample2.png
```

Many datasets are formatted like this, and Keras can be smart about slightly different structures and correctly identify classes and instances. Our dataset is formatted like this as well! We can, without any further preprocessing, load these in. In a later project, we'll take a look at what to do if a dataset doesn't follow this format and how to load, resize and otherwise preprocess data while putting it into the appropriate folders for this structure, automatically. In the meantime, you can `flow_from_directory()`:

```
# Seed set for reproducibility
train_generator = train_datagen.flow_from_directory(config['TRAIN_PATH'],
                                                    target_size=(150,150),
                                                    batch_size=32,
                                                    class_mode = 'categorical',
                                                    subset = 'training',
                                                    seed=2)

valid_generator = train_datagen.flow_from_directory(config['TRAIN_PATH'],
                                                     target_size=(150,150),
                                                     batch_size=32,
                                                     class_mode =
                                                         'categorical',
                                                     subset = 'validation',
                                                     seed=2)

test_generator = test_datagen.flow_from_directory(config['TEST_PATH'],
                                                  target_size=(150,150),
                                                  batch_size=32,
                                                  # Important - confusion
                                                      matrices can get messed
                                                      up with
                                                  # the ImageDataGenerator
```

```
                                  class if the images are
                                  shuffled.
21                              # Since it's just the test
                                  set, we don't lose
                                  anything from not
22                              # shuffling
23                              shuffle=False,
24                              class_mode = 'categorical',
25                              seed=2)
```

```
1 Found 11230 images belonging to 6 classes.
2 Found 2804 images belonging to 6 classes.
3 Found 3000 images belonging to 6 classes.
```

Most of these arguments are optional with reasonable defaults. The `class_mode` can be `'binary'` or `'categorical'`, and reflects the number of classes we'll use. The `batch_size` is typically set to 16-32, and it's generally not advised to go higher. Higher batch sizes can make for unstable training with worse overall convergence. A model can start overfitting on a minibatch and get delusional, resulting in not-so-great performance for that batch. Then, it'll overcompensate in the next. Like an inexperienced driver overcompensating for turns during their first snowstorm, which ultimately leads to them not controlling the car - large minibatches are generally not a good idea.

In an agreeing response to a great paper exploring the effect of minibatch size on Stochastic Gradient Descent, *"Revisiting Small Batch Training for Deep Neural Networks"*[46], Yann LeCun tweeted:

> *"Training with large minibatches is bad for your health. More importantly, it's bad for your test error. Friends dont let friends use minibatches larger than 32."*

Note: Time-series regression doesn't suffer from minibatch sizes in the same way, and larger minibatches can lead to better performance there, due to the nature of the networks used for that task.

Before deciding whether we want to perform any further preprocessing or augmentation in the data generators - let's first take a detour and assess data augmentation itself.

[46]https://arxiv.org/abs/1804.07612

4.4 Data Augmentation - Curse or Salvation?

So, what's data augmentation? It's fairly simple - applying transformations to images, in such a way as to not change the nature of the image, resulting in an artificially expanded set for training. Conceptually, you can imagine it as:

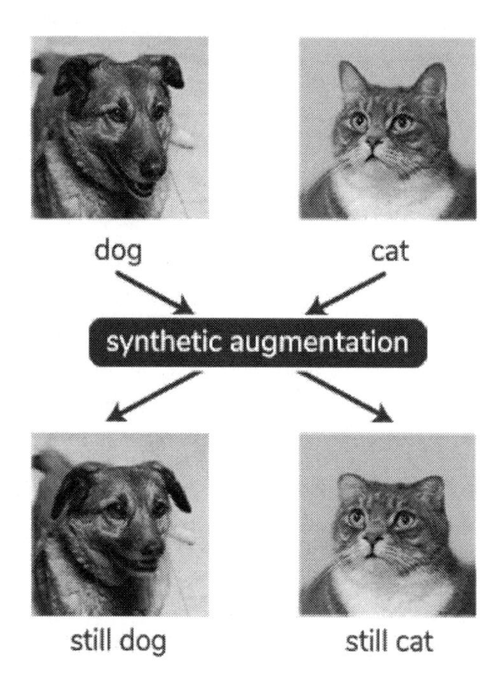

Figure 40:

Though, in reality, it's nowhere near as intricate as this - it's usually flipping images, rotating them, slight color changes, moving them from the center, zooming, etc. You can perform 10 transforms on the same image, producing 10 different images! Effectively, data augmentation *replaces* your original set (many believe it just augments/adds to the original one, which is in part due to the name), with multiple copies of it with slight variations. Suddenly, a 10k image training set can become a 100k image training set.

Naturally, you don't want to overdo it, and at one point, you don't really gain any new variance and your model starts overfitting, so it's not a magical potion to take to expand sets arbitrarily. It's not a replacement for a larger dataset - but it does help with increasing variance of the data and thus the robustness of the model. Some regard data augmentation as a *"magic tool"* (not in the sense that it's mystical, but that it helps with generalization as if it's magical) and in online circles, you'll generally hear statements such as:

> "The Magic of Data Augmentation" "Data Augmentation to the rescue"

Though, data augmentation *also* implies something else. Yes, it's a great way to help a network generalize, by making it learn that a cat is still a cat even if it's slightly rotated. This only makes sense! We wouldn't want a model to forget what a cat is because it's rotated a bit. This might seem like we're giving the model context but don't forget - **machine learning models don't have context** (in the same way that humans do), and data augmentation doesn't help them get it. It, in fact, helps them **become blind to it**. If we show fives images of a cat to a model, slightly altered, and say it's a cat - it'll generalize better that all five images contain a cat:

```
1 import urllib.request
2 import cv2
3
4 # Public domain image
5 url = 'https://upload.wikimedia.org/wikipedia/commons/1/15/Greycat.jpg'
6 urllib.request.urlretrieve(url, 'cat.jpg')
7 cat_image = cv2.imread('cat.jpg')
8
9 cat_image_expanded = np.expand_dims(cat_image, axis=0)
10
11 # Perform transformations and augmentation
12 cat_datagen = ImageDataGenerator(rescale=1./255,
13         rotation_range=20,
14         zoom_range=0.15,
15         width_shift_range=0.2,
16         height_shift_range=0.2,
17         shear_range=0.15,
18         horizontal_flip=True,
19         fill_mode = "nearest")
20 # Flow from the image (NumPy array)
21 cat_generator = cat_datagen.flow(cat_image_expanded, batch_size=25)
22
23 fig, ax = plt.subplots(nrows=1, ncols=5, figsize=(15,5))
24 for i in range(5):
25     image = next(cat_generator)[0]
26     ax[i].imshow(image)
27     ax[i].axis('off')
```

Figure 41:

It'll learn that even if the image is skewed, flipped or otherwise altered, it's a cat. However - it's won't learn that *it's a cat in different positions*, it'll learn that *it's a cat*. Yes, it's a cat, that's true. *But*, it's a cat *in a slightly different position*. This might sound like just a nuance, but the importance of nuances like this can't be overstated if we're to reach *real* computer vision or real intelligent systems. We're boosting the model's invariance to the position of objects in an image (which is one of the features of CNNs that made them as powerful as they are), but *too much invariance* becomes *blindness* to features, rather than generalization. Or rather - it could be called *overgeneralization*.

Here, other than helping the model generalize better - we're making it blind to cat translations and positions. We're telling it that all of these images are **the same thing**. As humans, we're aware that these images are not the same, yet, that they *represent* the same image. We think within the context of this image, instead of taking the label at face value. This sort of context is currently out of reach for engineers to code into models, and it'll likely be for a while. The downside of blindness to context *generally* isn't a deal-breaker, and we benefit more from gaining higher accuracy in this tradeoff. However, it's worth remembering this fact, since for the future of computer vision, we'll want to find a way to encode *context* into images as well. Context is probably one of the most important, currently unsurmountable hurdle we want to pass for *real* intelligence in these systems.

For now - data augmentation works wonderfully - it helps expand sets (which are expensive to label), increase invariance and help models generalize better. We just need to keep in mind that this step isn't one that'll be there forever, since it doesn't align us with the ultimate goal.

To that end, Yann LeCun describes data augmentation as a *"necessary evil"* that works great, but isn't something that'll take us to the end of the road.

Going back to our own data generators for the Intel Images, let's add a few arguments:

```
from tensorflow.keras.preprocessing.image import ImageDataGenerator

train_datagen = ImageDataGenerator(rescale=1./255,
        rotation_range=20,
        zoom_range=0.15,
        width_shift_range=0.2,
        height_shift_range=0.2,
        shear_range=0.15,
        horizontal_flip=True,
        fill_mode = "nearest",
        validation_split=0.2)

test_datagen = ImageDataGenerator(rescale=1./255)
```

We've rescaled the images to `0..1`, which is the first step in this new pipeline. We then define the rotation, zoom, width and height shift ranges, allow the images to be flipped horizontally, and fill any gaps that might be caused by these translations, with the *"nearest"* strategy (finding the nearest pixels and expanding them). You can pass lots of other arguments here for more granular control over augmentation, and you can additionally pass in any arbitrary function that returns an image as a preprocessing step which works both *with* other transformations or alone:

```
def preprocess_img(img):
    # Flip, rotate, normalize, yadda yadda...
    return img

train_datagen = ImageDataGenerator(preprocessing_function=preprocess_img)
```

Since we want to have a *validation set* as well, a `validation_split` argument allows us to separate a validation set from a training set, by setting the `subset` argument of a generator:

```
train_generator = train_datagen.flow_from_directory(config['TRAIN_PATH'],
                                                    target_size=(150,150),
                                                    batch_size=32,
                                                    class_mode = 'categorical',
                                                    subset = 'training',
                                                    seed=2)

valid_generator = train_datagen.flow_from_directory(config['TRAIN_PATH'],
                                                     target_size=(150,150),
                                                     batch_size=32,
                                                     class_mode =
                                                          'categorical',
                                                     subset = 'validation',
                                                     seed=2)

test_generator = test_datagen.flow_from_directory(config['TEST_PATH'],
                                                  target_size=(150,150),
```

```
17                                                  batch_size=32,
18                                                  shuffle=False,
19                                                  class_mode = 'categorical',
20                                                  seed=2)
```

```
1 Found 11230 images belonging to 6 classes.
2 Found 2804 images belonging to 6 classes.
3 Found 3000 images belonging to 6 classes.
```

The `train_generator` yields batches of 32 images, with their contents and labels, so we can fit a model just by calling:

```
1 model.fit(train_generator, ...)
```

The `valid_generator` will be used for `validation_data` during fitting, and `test_generator` will be used for testing the performance. We're done with preprocessing and loading! The `ImageDataGenerator` instances yield batches when called upon as iterators:

```
1 # Return type is a tuple of (images, labels)
2 batch = next(train_generator)
3
4 images = batch[0]
5 labels = batch[1]
6
7 images.shape # (32, 150, 150, 3)
8 labels.shape # (32, 6)
```

The batch consists of 32 images, 150x150 in size, and 3 in depth (RGB values), while the `labels` consists of 32 one-hot encoded labels corresponding to the 6 classes in the dataset. Our data's loaded in and ready to be trained on. Now - it's time to define a model.

4.5 Defining a Convolutional Neural Network and Training

4.5.1 Model Definition

So - we've been acquainted with the building blocks of CNNs in the previous lesson. How do we put them into good use and how do you choose which layers to put where? There are some conventions to follow, though, all of them can be tweaked or changed depending on your specific dataset, and the best way to find a good architecture for your own model is to experiment.

You'll also find conflicting information, such as, whether the filter size should be small or large in the beginning. Some argue that filter sizes should start out large to prune away the unimportant data and reduce computational costs, while the images are still on the larger end, making the models focus on the more salient features from the get-go. Some argue that smaller filter sizes should be used to capture as much local information as possible and then make them larger to capture more global features (following the idea of the visual cortex hierarchy). Some keep the filter sizes the same throughout the entire architecture!

> So, what's the right approach when it comes to filter sizes? Generally, I've personally found that starting out with smaller filter sizes and keeping them the same size after pooling works well, since the same filter size is then proportionally bigger in the next convolutional block, capturing more global patterns. Though, the best way to find filter sizes is to experiment.

It's generally agreed upon that you're likely to want to start out with shallow but wide layers, followed by deeper and narrower layers later on. This is reflected in the number of filters you use, which is typically increased through the number of layers (more filters stacked on top of each other means "deeper"), while the representations shrink through pooling and convolutions ("narrower").

> So, what's the right approach when it comes to depth per layer? Yeah, you generally want to have a shallow-to-deep model. Though, experiment. You might just come up with a new paradigm!

How many layers should you use? Start with an educated guess, or by "feeling". If it doesn't generalize well - add more layers. Once it starts overfitting, simplify the architecture and add regularization layers such as `Dropout` and `BatchNormalization` (or don't, it's not a crime). You won't always be able to overfit the dataset! This can mean a plethora of things, but it's not a bad idea to take a look at whether the data is clean and the labels are correct. A sufficiently large model will overfit if the underlying data is *fittable*. In a later lesson, we'll come back to overfitting and reassess whether it's a foe or a friend in this endeavor.

All in all - historically, networks applied convolutional layers to input images (multiple of them, called a "block"), and then downsized the images through pooling after each block (average or more commonly, max pooling) and increased the number of filters applied through the blocks. This proved to be a pretty good strategy for creating powerful classifiers! Modern architectures include some other ingenious ideas to boost performance, scale better and require fewer parameters to fit a dataset. We'll take a detailed look at modern architectures in a later lesson. For your first CNN - you'll do great even without these tweaks.

A good strategy for designing networks is to get inspiration from other architectures! There's nothing stopping you from taking a look at what others have done, and going from there. Reasoning by analogy isn't without its merit, though, trying to build something fully from scratch and first principles has its own merit too. Here, we'll build a CNN conceptually similar to VGG16 - a couple of convolutional layers, followed by an activation function each, and a max pooling layer. The two convolutional layers and max pooling layer comprise a single *block* that repeats throughout the architecture, with an increasing number of filters in each. Once the feature maps are sufficiently small for a classifier to learn from them - we'll `Flatten()` the feature maps and add a feed-forward neural network on top:

```
1 model = keras.models.Sequential([
2     # 64 filters, with a size of `3x3`
3     keras.layers.Conv2D(64, (3, 3), activation = 'relu', padding = 'same',
          input_shape=[150, 150, 3]),
4     # You can also simply add one dimension for the size, it'll be
          symetrical `(3)`
5     keras.layers.Conv2D(64, 3, activation = 'relu', padding = 'same'),
6     keras.layers.MaxPooling2D((2, 2), (2, 2)),
7     keras.layers.BatchNormalization(),
8
9     keras.layers.Conv2D(128, 3, activation = 'relu', padding = 'same'),
10    keras.layers.Conv2D(128, 3, activation = 'relu', padding = 'same'),
11    # Same goes for MaxPooling `(2, 2)` is equal to `(2, 2), (2, 2)`
12    keras.layers.MaxPooling2D(2, 2),
13    keras.layers.BatchNormalization(),
14
15    keras.layers.Conv2D(256, 3, activation = 'relu', padding = 'same'),
16    keras.layers.Conv2D(256, 3, activation = 'relu', padding = 'same'),
17    keras.layers.MaxPooling2D(2, 2),
18    keras.layers.BatchNormalization(),
19
20    keras.layers.Flatten(),
21    keras.layers.Dense(64, activation = 'relu'),
22    keras.layers.BatchNormalization(),
23    keras.layers.Dropout(0.3, seed=2),
24    keras.layers.Dense(6, activation = 'softmax')
25 ])
```

Here, we choose a filter size of `3x3`, for an input size of `150x150` images. The network should be able to pick out relatively small features that make these images what they are. We're following a simple rule - two convolutional layers, each with a `'relu'` activation, and `'same'` padding, followed by a `MaxPooling` layer that cuts the representation down in half. Since we have 3 max pooling layers, the final maps before being flattened will be of shape `(18, 18)`, and you can go significatly smaller than this. We're not doing that for easier visualization later.

That's small enough to fit well with a dense top (and should ideally be smaller)! Be careful of the number of dense layers in the classifier top. The number of parameters can easily explode here and more parameters oftentimes means that the model will not only partially overfit the training set compared to the testing set, but also poorly fit the dataset overall. Typically, if you have more than a single dense layer - you'll start out with a larger number of neurons and progress downward to the number of classes - 6 in this case.

Since we're classifying the probability of each class in an image (confidence of the network that the image to each class), we use a `'softmax'` activation in the final layer.

After each convolutional block - we have a `BatchNormalization()` layer to normalize the result of the previous block before it gets fed into the next block. Sometimes, `BatchNormalization()` is put *before* max pooling, though, in my personal experience, it tends to work better when put *after* max pooling.

4.5.2 Compiling the Model

We can compile the network now, define the loss function, the optimizer, and the metrics we'll want to keep an eye out for:

```
1 model.compile(loss = "categorical_crossentropy",
2               optimizer = keras.optimizers.Adam(),
3               metrics=['accuracy',
4                        keras.metrics.TopKCategoricalAccuracy(k=2)])
```

Since we're using a `'categorical'` class mode (2D one-hot encoded labels) when loading images in - we'll use `'categorical_crossentropy'` as the loss function. If we were to use a `'sparse'` class mode (1D integer labels, such as `0..6`) when loading images in, we'd have used `'sparse_categorical_crossentropy'`. They use the same loss function under the hood, just the representation of classes is different.

Adam is a great default optimizer to try out! It performs well for most tasks, so during hyperparameter tuning, you could try out other optimizers. Finally - for the metrics, we won't only rely on accuracy. As we've seen before, some classes seriously overlap. In many instances of streets, we could've assumed that the class was actually a building, and we'd have been wrong. However, if someone asked us to figure out what it could be if it's *not* the first choice - we'd probably be *very accurate* in assessing the classes.

> "Yeah, this looks like a street class, but it could also be a building class since there's a bunch of buildings on the screen."

That's what *Top-K Categorical Accuracy* is - where *K* is some number we're taking into consideration. For classifiers that work with a large number of classes and which have to make nuanced decisions - scoring by accuracy is simply unfair. I wouldn't say that I don't know what a street or a building are - but the 75% accuracy I got from the images earlier would imply a shaky knowledge of what these are! *Accuracy* as a metric, is essentially, *Top-1 Categorical Accuracy* and it's pretty difficult to get that score very high for complex problems. Most of the papers you'll read on complex image classification will have some level of Top-K accuracy besides Top-1 accuracy, depending on the number of classes in the dataset. If it's 1000 classes, like with ImageNet - people commonly also calculate a Top-5 accuracy score besides the Top-1 accuracy score.

In our case, if we had a Top-6 accuracy score for *6 classes* - even if our model had absolutely no clue about what was going on, it'd have a 100% accuracy score. We'll want to keep *K* of a Top-K accuracy minimal, which in our case is 2. Even with `k=2`, the score is likely to be fairly high given the small number of classes we have, but it will be a decent proxy for how well the model has learned the difference between classes. Let's take a look at the summary of the model!

```
1 model.summary()
```

```
1 Model: "sequential"
2 _________________________
3 Layer (type)                 Output Shape              Param #
4 =====================
5 conv2d (Conv2D)              (None, 150, 150, 64)      1792
6 _________________________
7 conv2d_1 (Conv2D)            (None, 150, 150, 64)      36928
8 _________________________
9 max_pooling2d (MaxPooling2D) (None, 75, 75, 64)        0
10 _________________________
11 conv2d_2 (Conv2D)            (None, 75, 75, 128)       73856
```

```
12 _________________________________________________________________
13 conv2d_3 (Conv2D)            (None, 75, 75, 128)       147584
14 _________________________________________________________________
15 max_pooling2d_1 (MaxPooling2 (None, 37, 37, 128)       0
16 _________________________________________________________________
17 conv2d_4 (Conv2D)            (None, 37, 37, 256)       295168
18 _________________________________________________________________
19 conv2d_5 (Conv2D)            (None, 37, 37, 256)       590080
20 _________________________________________________________________
21 max_pooling2d_2 (MaxPooling2 (None, 18, 18, 256)       0
22 _________________________________________________________________
23 flatten (Flatten)            (None, 82944)             0
24 _________________________________________________________________
25 dense (Dense)                (None, 64)                5308480
26 _________________________________________________________________
27 batch_normalization (BatchNo (None, 64)                256
28 _________________________________________________________________
29 dropout (Dropout)            (None, 64)                0
30 _________________________________________________________________
31 dense_1 (Dense)              (None, 6)                 390
32 =================================================================
33 Total params: 6,454,534
34 Trainable params: 6,454,406
35 Non-trainable params: 128
36 _________________________________________________________________
```

You can clearly see how the max pooling layers downsize the image from 150 to 75, to 37 and then 18. Additionally, you can see the number of filters grow from 64 to 128 and 256 in these steps in parallel, as we've increased them as well. The feature maps are pretty small near the end. The smaller the representation is, the more dense the information is. There is a sweet spot where you have almost all of the salient features in a map, at which point, downsizing more always results in losing more information than you'd want. The bad news is - there's no real way to know what this point is, especially since it heavily depends on your input data. A common general final feature map size is 7x7. Experiment!

Once the feature maps are flattened - we've got a feature vector of ***82944*** features. Yikes. Once that gets paired up to a Dense layer of 64 neurons, the number of trainable parameters skyrockets by 5.3M, and to the 6.4M total mark in the end. This isn't a small network nor a particularly efficient one. This could be avoided by making the network deeper, employing some other techniques developed through the years such as skip connections, depthwise separable convolutions, etc. but we'll leave that for a later lesson in which we'll do a deep dive into the defining architectures of the field and implement many of them from scratch.

Keep in mind that some of the more powerful networks being used in the industry can easily reach up to several hundred millions parameters. The "base" networks, which are typically smaller, consist of a few million, but recently, architecture design is shifting towards networks that don't only do well when smaller - but towards models that can also scale well. VGG19 has 143M parameters! Our architecture is inspired by the VGG architecture, so it's no surprise that we've got 6.4M. In fact, if you just made our model deeper - that's the essence of VGG. This *type* of architecture is slowly being phased out, and even though they're still (unfortunately) relevant today, we'll want to be a bit more conscious about the number of parameters going forward. VGG used to be a leader in terms of performance, at the cost of a huge network. Now, they perform fairly well, but are being outperformed by smaller networks. In a later lesson, we'll be exploring these techniques and build better models, with fewer parameters.

In this project, we'll see what these 83k features really encode, visualizing them through *Principal Component Analysis (PCA)* and *t-Distributed Stochastic Neighbor Embeddings (t-SNE)*.

Note: VGG models have quite a large number of parameters due to their nature - and architectures like ResNet, EfficientNet, etc. have done great work in reducing that number. The Curse of Dimensionality is very true and Occam's Razor is potentially one of the most important principles in science, and having a larger model isn't always better. EfficientNetB0 has a very modest 5.3M parameters (compared to some other architectures) and delivers state-of-the-art performance. That's much more impressive than a model with the same level of performance, but with 100M parameters!

4.5.3 Finding a Learning Rate

One of the most important hyperparameters to set is the `learning_rate` of the optimizer you're using. So, how to choose it? Again - most optimizers have sensible defaults that work well for lots of problems. Though, this oftentimes leads to unoptimized performance even if it's good. Choosing the right learning rate can mean better generalization, faster convergence and fewer computational resources used!

Traditionally, you'd try one learning rate, followed by another one (larger or smaller), and so on until you find a good one. Typically - `1e-2, 1e-3, 1e-4, 1e-5`, etc. Though, say `1e-4` has great performance! What if you'd get better performance with `1.01e-4`? How granular do you want to get with testing? You can always add a decimal and get a new learning rate.

So - how do you figure out which learning rate to use? Note that this isn't a question of *how you should change the learning rate* during training. This refers to the initial learning rate. In the beginning, you want to maximize the change in loss (with a slope pointing to the minimum). This tends to be a higher learning rate, though, you can go too high even here, and make it difficult to reduce it to a more sustainable number. Let's recap, once you start, there are various methods of updating the learning rate during training to optimize the learning process such as linear decay, exponential decay or any other non-linear function to make the decay (reduction) of the learning rate more optimized. Alternatively - you can leave it all to Keras and only update the learning rate if need be, through the `ReduceLROnPlateau()` callback, which, depending on its `patience`, will reduce the learning rate only when required. This is a pretty simple rule and it works surprisingly well! Though, it can be outperformed by other techniques as well. Keras offers a `LearningRateScheduler` class, to which you can pass *any function* that returns the learning rate, on each epoch, and use that function as your custom learning rate scheduler.

> If there were a hands-down winner - everyone would be using it. There is none. Experimentation is your friend, once again!

In 2015., Leslie N. Smith released *"Cyclical Learning Rates for Training Neural Networks"*[47]. The author argues that the method completely dismisses the need to manually search for a learning rate, by making it *cyclical*, instead of monotonically decreasing it. The cycle would consist of two learning rates, one lower and one higher - the higher learning rate would help the network jump out of saddle points (in which gradients are pretty small, but the model hasn't converged at an approximately optimal position yet), and the lower learning rate would help fine-tune it to a global optimum. Three strategies were proposed:

- Triangular
- Triangular 2

[47] https://arxiv.org/abs/1506.01186

- Exponential range

In the first - the learning rate just oscillates between two rates through time. In the second, the amplitude of the triangles created by the cycle between the two learning rates is decreased in half on each step. In the third, the amplitude is decreased exponentially. The idea is supposed to make training faster and more robust, and reading the paper is a heart-felt suggestion. Though - now we have to find *two* learning rates, not just one! The author proposed an automated approach to finding these two rates. Building on top of this method, Jeremy Howard, the author of fast.ai created the famous `lr_find()` method for each `Learner` (network) and popularized the approach through the highly accessible API of fast.ai, bringing it to the masses. It's used to find the optimal starting learning rate, given a network, and to minimize the manual guesswork that goes into it. The method starts with a really low learning rate, and steps towards a really high learning rate in each iteration (typically set at a ludicrous number, such as `1` or `10`) where we know the loss will explode upwards.

If you record and plot the loss at each iteration - you have a loss curve where you can clearly identify at which learning rate the loss was the lowest! **You don't want to pick where it's lowest**. This will typically be an unstably high learning rate, such as `1e-1`. You want to pick the point in which the slope of the loss is the steepest towards the minimum - i.e. when the network is learning the fastest. You can identify this visually, or more precisely, through code (using derivatives) and start from there. Leslie suggests using the Cyclical Learning Rate method to update the rate, though really, you're free to use any method that works well for you.

Now - the method was written for fast.ai - not Keras. However, kind open source contributors have written ports for Keras, inspired by the original paper and Jeremy's implementation!

For instance, you can use Surmenok's implementation, which can also be found on GitHub[48]. The class is *a bit* outdated, and uses calls such as `fit_generator()` rather than just `fit()` (which works with generators by default now), but it works! Alternatively, Adrian Rosebrock adapted an implementation of the method from ktrain[49], and it works in much the same way Sumenok's implementation does, but it lacks methods to calculate derivatives and thus, to plot the change in loss. To address this, I've taken the liberty of

[48]https://github.com/surmenok/keras_lr_finder
[49]https://github.com/amaiya/ktrain

combining their implementations into a single file that you can get on GitHub[50], linking to the original implementations.

4.5.4 Training the Model

Let's start out with just base-Keras, utilize the `ReduceLROnPlateau()` callback with the default learning rate of Adam, and then benchmark it against finding the learning rate and updating it with a function. To make experimentation with learning rates easier and to avoid having to rewrite the same model definition code multiple times - let's wrap our model-building and compilation in a method:

```
def build_model():
    model = keras.models.Sequential([
        keras.layers.Conv2D(64, 3, activation = 'relu', padding = 'same',
            input_shape=[150, 150, 3]),
        keras.layers.Conv2D(64, 3, activation = 'relu', padding = 'same'),
        keras.layers.MaxPooling2D((2, 2), (2, 2)),
        keras.layers.BatchNormalization(),

        keras.layers.Conv2D(128, 3, activation = 'relu', padding = 'same'),
        keras.layers.Conv2D(128, 3, activation = 'relu', padding = 'same'),
        keras.layers.MaxPooling2D((2, 2), (2, 2)),
        keras.layers.BatchNormalization(),

        keras.layers.Conv2D(256, 3, activation = 'relu', padding = 'same'),
        keras.layers.Conv2D(256, 3, activation = 'relu', padding = 'same'),
        keras.layers.MaxPooling2D((2, 2), (2, 2)),
        keras.layers.BatchNormalization(),

        keras.layers.Flatten(),
        keras.layers.Dense(64, activation = 'relu'),
        keras.layers.BatchNormalization(),
        keras.layers.Dropout(0.3, seed=2),
        keras.layers.Dense(6, activation = 'softmax')
    ])

    model.compile(loss = "categorical_crossentropy",
                  optimizer = keras.optimizers.Adam(),
                  metrics=['accuracy',
                           keras.metrics.TopKCategoricalAccuracy(k=2)])

    return model
```

[50] https://github.com/DavidLandup0/keras-lrfinder

4.5.4.1 Base-Keras Let's instantiate the model, add a couple of callbacks and train it. An epoch should take ~1min on a decent GPU (I ran it on a GTX 1660 Super), though, it should take less than that on services such as Google Colab and Kaggle when using a GPU (downwards to 40s each). In the previous lesson in the book - we dealt with a network that took less than a second to run an epoch! This is normal. We defined a decently sized network, and we're feeding it decently sized images (150x150) compared to last time. Since it might take up to an hour to train this network - take a hot or cold beverage of your choice, and kick your feet up. You can read a book in this time as well or revisit the last lesson in the book to check whether some of the theory clicks better now! Or maybe even wash the dishes you've been putting off for the past week. There are plenty of things to do while networks train, and I've found it to be a great time to do exercise or walk outside. Since I like sitting, it also incentivizes me to run long tests only when I'm fairly sure they can work, and to focus on quick tests rather than long ones to validate ideas.

Let's build a model and train it:

```
model_basek = build_model()

callbacks = [
    tf.keras.callbacks.ModelCheckpoint(filepath =
        'intel-classification_reduceonplateau.h5', save_best_only=True),
    tf.keras.callbacks.ReduceLROnPlateau()
]

# train_generator yields a batch of images and labels
history_base = model_basek.fit(train_generator,
                    validation_data = valid_generator,
                    callbacks = callbacks,
                    epochs = 50)
```

```
Epoch 1/50
351/351 [==============================] - 70s 182ms/step - loss: 1.1321 -
    accuracy: 0.5724 - top_k_categorical_accuracy: 0.7965 - val_loss: 3.0933
    - val_accuracy: 0.2746 - val_top_k_categorical_accuracy: 0.4650
...
Epoch 50/50
351/351 [==============================] - 58s 165ms/step - loss: 0.1743 -
    accuracy: 0.9409 - top_k_categorical_accuracy: 0.9918 - val_loss: 0.2634
    - val_accuracy: 0.9087 - val_top_k_categorical_accuracy: 0.9832
```

Note: The first epoch typically takes longer to run, since this is the first time Keras is seeing this data and there's a bunch of initialization overhead. As soon as the second epoch - a lot of it will be cached and accessed much more quickly.

The model achieved a 90.8% accuracy on the validation set, and our Top-2 Accuracy is as high as 98.3%! The model appears to have fit the data very successfully. You should never expect a 100% accuracy. Labels can be wrong, models can be deluded and more importantly - humans don't have a 100% accuracy on most computer vision datasets. For instance, it was tested how humans fare on the ImageNet dataset in *"ImageNet Large Scale Visual Recognition Challenge"*[51] by Russakovsky et al. in 2014. They concluded that, optimistically, a human annotator has around 2.4% error rate, when measured against Top-5 accuracy. In other words, 97.6% Top-5 accuracy. As of writing, according to *PapersWithCode.com*, there are about 20 different computer vision models that outperform that number, the top one holding a 99.02% Top-5 Accuracy.

> Computer Vision systems are already at superhuman level, for a lot of tasks.

There isn't a study concerning human accuracy for the Intel Image Classification dataset. Though - there's nothing stopping *you* from testing it yourself! There are 3000 images in the test set. Take out some time during the day to annotate them yourself, check your accuracy, and then compare it to the model's. Consider that you've had years and years of your life for training, and have context, while machine learning models don't. It was trained for less than an hour! If you don't feel like doing it manually - Andrej Karpathy wrote an application[52] to assess human accuracy on the ImageNet dataset. You'll be represented with various images, and with all labels. Once you choose five of them, you can see the answers and the answers of a computer vision algorithm. Don't worry - it doesn't cheat by taking a look at your answers. It's likely better than you.

4.5.4.2 LRFinder and Exponential Decay Before we go into the evaluation of a model - we do have something to go from in terms of a performance benchmark. Let's try finding a suitable starting learning rate with a more custom exponential decay. Download the `LearningRateFinder` script from GitHub and insert it into your Jupyter Notebook environment. Then, you can import and start the search through:

[51] https://arxiv.org/abs/1409.0575
[52] https://cs.stanford.edu/people/karpathy/ilsvrc/

```
from keraslrfinder import LearningRateFinder

model_lrfind = build_model()
# Length of the training data, divided by the batch number, yielding steps
    per epoch
# train_generator.classes returns *all labels*, not their unique values
steps_per_epoch = np.ceil((len(train_generator.classes)/float(32)))
# Instantiate lr_finder for the model
lr_finder = LearningRateFinder(model_lrfind)
# Find the optimal starting learning rate
lr_finder.find(train_generator, startLR=1e-10, endLR=10, epochs=3,
    stepsPerEpoch=steps_per_epoch)
```

Typically, you'll run the fit for 3-5 epochs:

```
Epoch 1/3
351/351 [==============================] - 48s 133ms/step - loss: 2.4664 -
    accuracy: 0.1880 - top_k_categorical_accuracy: 0.3728
Epoch 2/3
351/351 [==============================] - 48s 135ms/step - loss: 1.5865 -
    accuracy: 0.4464 - top_k_categorical_accuracy: 0.6649
Epoch 3/3
351/351 [==============================] - 37s 104ms/step - loss: 20.3708 -
    accuracy: 0.4555 - top_k_categorical_accuracy: 0.7046
```

And now, you can plot the loss as a function of the learning rate:

```
lr_finder.plot_loss()
```

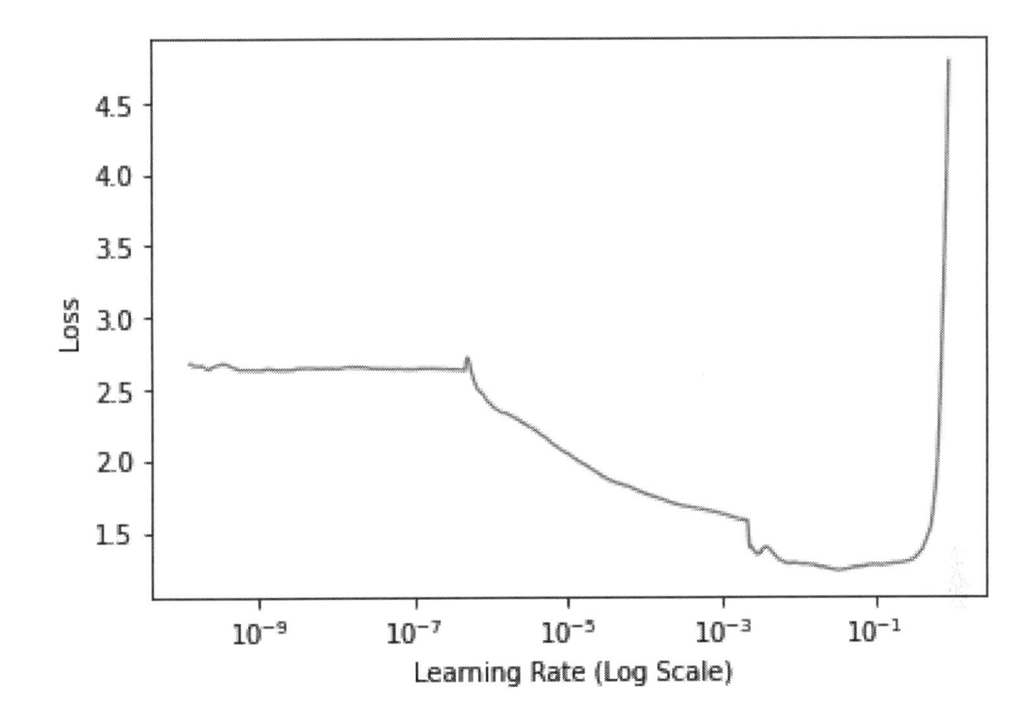

Figure 42:

This is a fairly smoothed plot of the loss - it's much more rocky than that. Let's plot the change in loss over time:

```
lr_finder.plot_loss_change(sma=1)
```

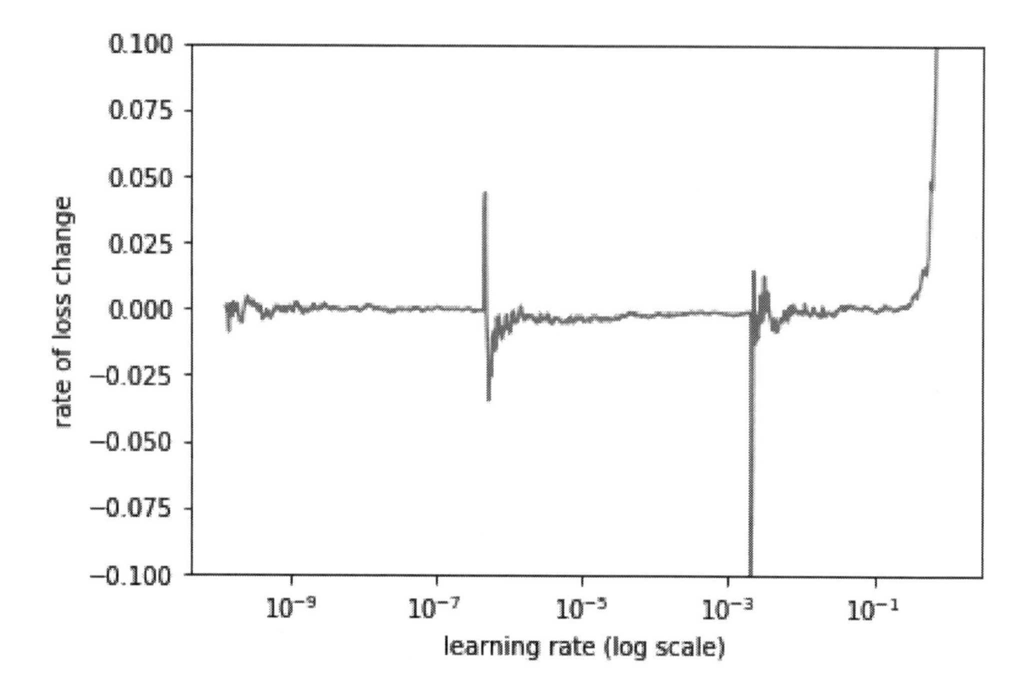

Figure 43:

The biggest drops in the loss was at:

```
lr_finder.get_best_lr(sma=1) # 0.002154435
```

Note: Always verify the number against the plot and use the same smoothing as applied to the previous plot, given the smoothing applied *during the process of calculating derivatives*. If you smooth too much, the `get_best_lr()` function may return an unexpected result.

Finally, let's define a learning rate scheduler, given the best starting learning rate, and have it decay by some factor each 5 epochs (`5*steps_per_epoch` steps):

```
lr_schedule = tf.keras.optimizers.schedules.ExponentialDecay(
    lr_finder.get_best_lr(sma=1),
    decay_steps=5*steps_per_epoch,
    decay_rate=0.83,
    staircase=True)

model_lr = build_model()
model_lr.compile(loss = "categorical_crossentropy",
              optimizer = keras.optimizers.Adam(learning_rate=lr_schedule),
              metrics=['accuracy',
                       keras.metrics.TopKCategoricalAccuracy(k=2)])

callbacks = [
    tf.keras.callbacks.ModelCheckpoint(filepath =
        'intel-classification_lrfinderandschedule.h5', save_best_only=True),
]

history_lr = model_lr.fit(train_generator,
                    validation_data = valid_generator,
                    callbacks = callbacks,
                    epochs = 50)
```

```
Epoch 1/50
351/351 [==============================] - 58s 164ms/step - loss: 1.1780 -
    accuracy: 0.5425 - top_k_categorical_accuracy: 0.7794 - val_loss: 1.1701
    - val_accuracy: 0.5467 - val_top_k_categorical_accuracy: 0.7675
...
Epoch 50/50
351/351 [==============================] - 58s 164ms/step - loss: 0.1897 -
    accuracy: 0.9320 - top_k_categorical_accuracy: 0.9919 - val_loss: 0.2956
    - val_accuracy: 0.8994 - val_top_k_categorical_accuracy: 0.9807
```

The final numbers are pretty similar. It looks like the second model overfit slightly more, but we'll really only want to make conclusions after evaluating them. It's time to evaluate your model (with or without your own annotations). There's a basic-level evaluation that you can do - plotting learning curves, evaluating using metrics and plotting a confusion matrix. This is the bare minimum you'll want to do to get any idea of its performance. However - there's much more you can do, and it's generally not stressed enough how important it is to do *error analysis*:

- Where was the model wrong?
- What *made it* predict wrong?
- What was the model's attention on/What features influenced the model's prediction?
- What do the learned features look like? Can we separate them into distinct classes?
- How close are the features that make *Class N* to the features that make *Class M*?

You don't need to know these to asses the accuracy level of your model. You need these to *know your model.*

Evaluating models is an extremely important aspect of building them. Sure - the *training* part is more exciting, and seeing the loss go down is a thrilling, almost addictive feeling. Though, it's all an illusion if you don't perform good evaluation! You can't just look at the training accuracy and conclude the development process. You can't also just look at the validation score and conclude it. You can't just look at the *test accuracy* and conclude it. Evaluation is much more than that.

Naturally, the degree of importance of evaluation depends on the domain as well. This book is intended for people of various backgrounds - both specialists and generalists. If you're a specialist in a field, and looking to include computer vision to improve a pipeline, you'll know best what it means to have an incorrect prediction for your own domain. Some instances of high-risk predictions include, really, anything that can affect another living being in a tangible way. If you're building an automated rocket docking system which relies on computer vision - if the rocket doesn't dock well, it can fall over and explode. If you're building an Orwellian surveillance system (which I kind of hope you aren't) - you'll probably want to make sure you don't send tickets to innocent people, letting the perpetrators go without any repercussions. If you're building a system for police cars to perform Optical Character Recognition on all adjacent vehicles and check if they're all registered and issue fees for those who're driving unregistered vehicles - you want to make sure you don't send a ticket to the wrong person because your system mistook an 'O' for a '0'. If you're building a medical system to classify a disease and match patients to a possible treatment, you don't want to misdiagnose them and give them potentially life-threatening treatment. If you're classifying the cuisine of a dish from an image - you won't hurt anyone if you label a baguette as an authentic German bread, though, your food classification app might not get the best reviews.

All of these instances highlight a different degree of importance in the confidence of the model. *You* know best what it would mean if things went wrong. Assume they will, a priori. Assess what might happen in the worst case. Then - evaluate your model and weigh the promises and perils of implementing it in production.

4.6 Evaluating a Model - The Basics

Evaluating models can be streamlined through a couple of simple methods that yield stats that you can reference later. If you've ever read a research paper - you've heard of a model's accuracy, weighted accuracy, recall (sensitivity), specificity, or precision. Keep in mind how misleading these numbers can be. In a later project, when we learn to classify Breast Cancer as malignant or benign, we'll deal with all of these metrics extensively, realizing how illusory they can be even *together*, not just as individual metrics.

While this is a handy way of assessing the promise of a model - just getting a classification report isn't enough. It's a great start though!

4.6.1 Learning Curves

We'll want to visualize the progress of learning through time first. It helps to see the road we took to the goal, not just the goal:

```
1 acc, val_acc = history_basek.history['binary_accuracy'],
      history_basek.history['val_binary_accuracy']
2 loss, val_loss = history_basek.history['loss'],
      history_basek.history['val_loss']
3 fig, ax = plt.subplots(1, 2, figsize=(16, 4))
4 fig.suptitle('CNN Classifier Learning Curves', fontsize=18)
5
6 ax[0].plot(acc, label = 'Accuracy')
7 ax[0].plot(val_acc, label = 'Validation Accuracy')
8 ax[0].grid(axis = 'y', linestyle = '--')
9
10 ax[1].plot(loss, label = 'Loss')
11 ax[1].plot(val_loss, label = 'Validation Loss')
12 ax[1].grid(axis = 'y', linestyle = '--')
13
14 ax[0].legend()
15 ax[1].legend()
16 plt.show()
```

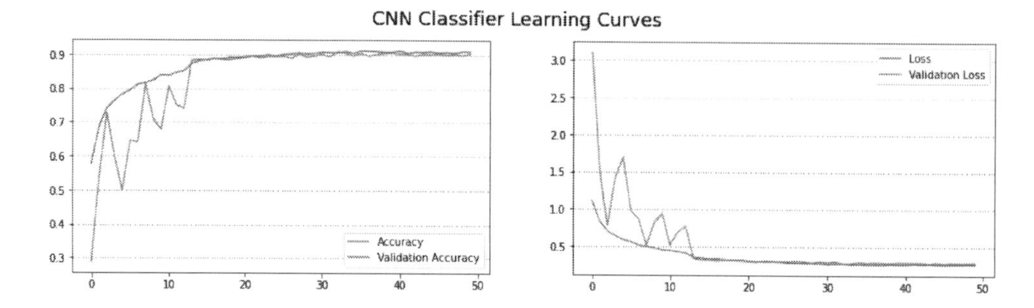

Figure 44:

You can see when the learning rate reduction occurs, given the more sudden rise/drop in accuracy/loss on epochs 37 and 49. This can also be validated by plotting the learning rate through time:

```
lr = history.history['accuracy'], history.history['val_accuracy']
fig, ax = plt.subplots(figsize=(8, 4))

ax.plot(lr, label = 'Learning Rate')
ax.grid(axis = 'y', linestyle = '--')
ax.legend()

plt.show()
```

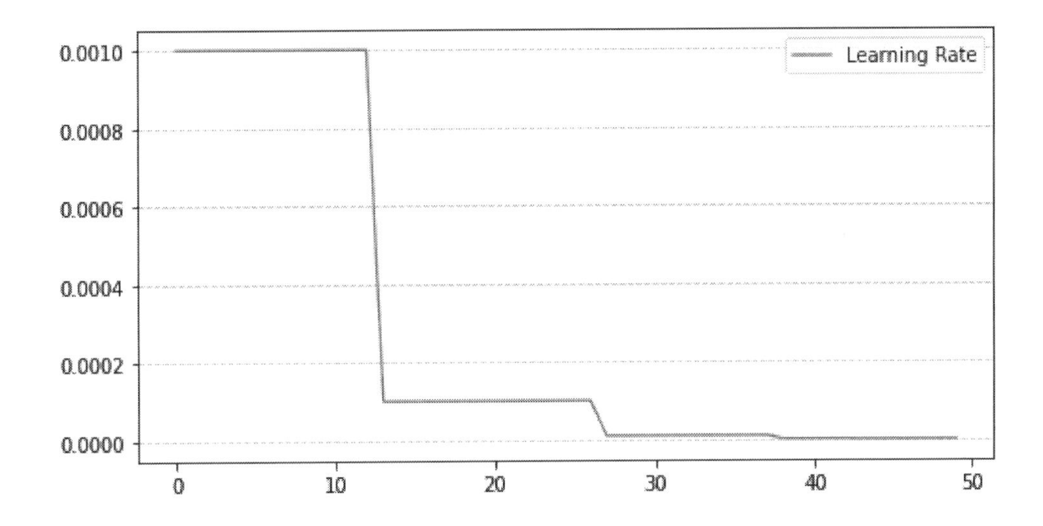

Figure 45:

The same can be done for the other model (though, since we're using a `LearningRateScheduler`, there is no `"lr"` property of the history):

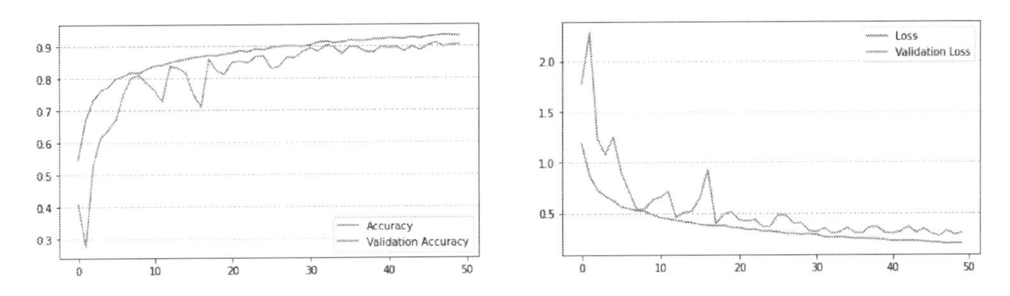

Figure 46:

The training, although yielding an ever so slightly lower accuracy, was more stable in the beginning, but didn't settle later. Both models initially had a learning rate that was set too high, resulting in pretty rocky training. Through time, as they decreased, the training got more stable. In the former case, it got stable later during the training process, while in the latter case, it was stabilized much earlier but failed to really converge. It appears as if both of the models could've gotten better through more training, since the curves haven't plateaued fully. So far - we'll be more likely to choose the first model, given its stability throughout training.

4.6.2 Metric Evaluation

Next - let's go ahead and perform the basic metric evaluation. By invoking the `evaluate()` method - we test against the metrics defined during training:

```
model_basek.evaluate(test_generator)
model_lr.evaluate(test_generator)
```

```
94/94 [==============================] - 4s 42ms/step - loss: 0.2764 -
     accuracy: 0.9040 - top_k_categorical_accuracy: 0.9820
94/94 [==============================] - 4s 42ms/step - loss: 0.3232 -
     accuracy: 0.8963 - top_k_categorical_accuracy: 0.9793
```

The first model is performing slightly better. It's worth noting that with such slight differences, you can't *really* say one is better than the other. If the testing set was different, it might've been the other way around.

`scikit-learn` has a really handy method - `classification_report()` that tests against general classification metrics, such as recall, F1 and precision. Since our predictions are each a list of 6 probabilities for each class, we'll want to get the most probable class alongside the `test_generator.classes` for the report:

```
from sklearn import metrics

y_pred1 = model_basek.predict(test_generator)
y_pred2 = model_lr.predict(test_generator)

print('Base-Keras' + metrics.classification_report(test_generator.classes,
     np.argmax(y_pred1, axis=1)))
print('LRFinder ' + metrics.classification_report(test_generator.classes,
     np.argmax(y_pred2, axis=1)))
```

```
Base-Keras          precision    recall  f1-score   support

           0        0.87      0.92      0.89       437
           1        0.97      0.98      0.98       474
           2        0.89      0.85      0.87       553
           3        0.87      0.83      0.85       525
           4        0.90      0.95      0.93       510
           5        0.92      0.90      0.91       501

```

```
10      accuracy                          0.90      3000
11     macro avg       0.90      0.91      0.90      3000
12  weighted avg       0.90      0.90      0.90      3000
13
14 LRFinder        precision    recall  f1-score   support
15
16             0       0.83      0.95      0.89       437
17             1       0.98      0.97      0.97       474
18             2       0.92      0.80      0.86       553
19             3       0.85      0.86      0.86       525
20             4       0.87      0.95      0.91       510
21             5       0.95      0.86      0.90       501
22
23      accuracy                          0.90      3000
24     macro avg       0.90      0.90      0.90      3000
25  weighted avg       0.90      0.90      0.90      3000
```

The weighted average is practically the same, and the macro average is only slightly different for the base model. Both of these models look promising - but with such a small difference in performance, we'll want to go with the more stable one. Let's reload the model and reference it as a `model` variable for further evaluation:

```
1 model = keras.models.load_model('intel-classification_reduceonplateau.h5')
```

4.6.3 Confusion Matrix

A really common way to assess the model's performance, and the first stepping stone into *wrong predictions* is a confusion matrix. Confusion matrices are one of the standard and basic ways to assess the abilities of a classifier! Confusion matrices plot the true values against the predicted values for each class. This results in a tabular matrix of confidence and confusion!

You can clearly see which class has been predicted right, and which has been predicted as some other class, including the number of predictions:

```
 1 from sklearn.metrics import confusion_matrix
 2 import seaborn as sns
 3
 4 # Predict classes
 5 y_preds = model.predict(test_generator)
 6 # Compute matrix for the most confident guesses
 7 matrix = confusion_matrix(test_generator.classes, y_preds.argmax(axis=1))
 8
 9 # Plot on heatmap
10 fig, ax = plt.subplots()
11 sns.heatmap(matrix, ax=ax, fmt = 'g', annot=True)
```

```
12
13 # Stylize heatmap
14 ax.set_xlabel('Predicted labels')
15 ax.set_ylabel('True labels')
16 ax.set_title('Confusion Matrix');
17 ax.xaxis.set_ticklabels(classnames)
18 ax.yaxis.set_ticklabels(classnames)
```

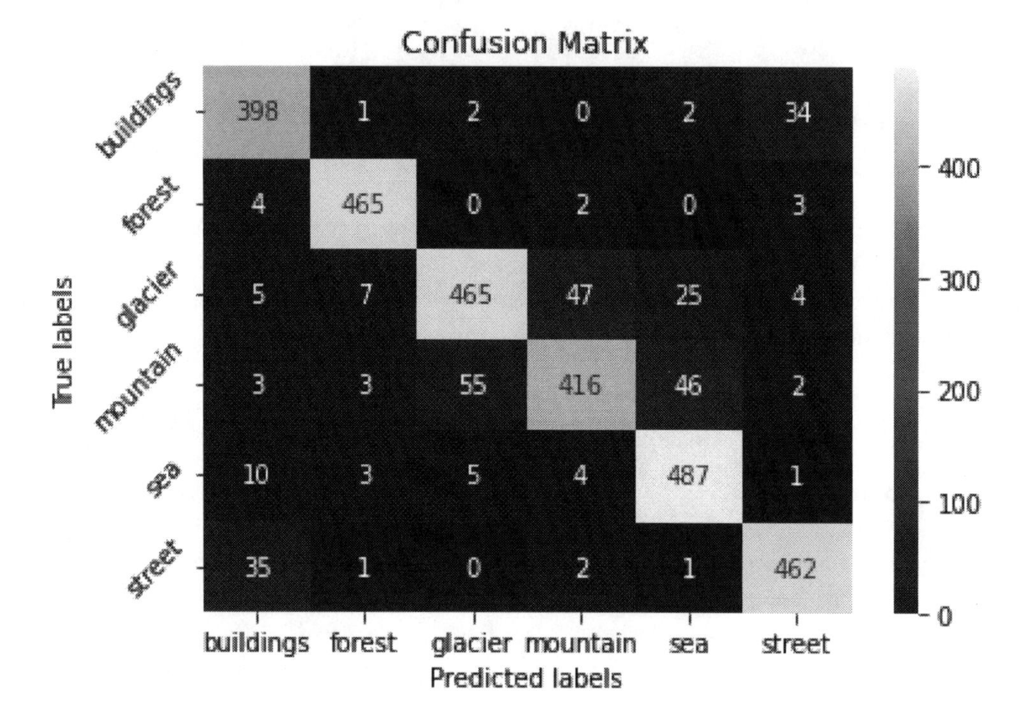

Figure 47:

The model confused some instances of "glacier" with "mountain" (snowy tops?), as well as instances of class "buildings" with "street". It's worth noting that "sea" was predicted as "mountain" multiple times, but not the other way around - this means that a model probably picked up a strong feature of the "mountain" class, which it confuses with something else present in seas.

We do remember the huge overlap between these classes such as "buildings" images containing more streets than buildings, so issues like these are to be expected. There's little confusion other than buildings/streets, and mountains/glaciers. With lots of classes, confusion matrices can get really hard to read, unfortunately. The colors help here!

4.6.4 Plotting Predictions

Finally, let's plot some predictions from the test set. We'll plot the images, predicted and actual labels, assessing what we see manually for at least a bit of insight into what the model has learned.

Note: You'll want to shuffle the test generator before predicting, lest the batch contains the same class for all inputs.

```
test_generator = test_datagen.flow_from_directory(config['TEST_PATH'],
                                                  target_size=(150,150),
                                                  batch_size=32,
                                                  shuffle=True,
                                                  class_mode = 'categorical',
                                                  seed=2)
```

Now, let's get the next batch and predict their labels, plotting them with the actual and predicted labels:

```
batch = next(test_generator)

images = batch[0]
labels = batch[1]

for index, image in enumerate(images):
    # Plot
    ax = fig.add_subplot(6, 6, index+1)
    plt.imshow(image)
    # Inference
    image = np.expand_dims(image, 0)
    pred = model.predict(image)
    pred = np.squeeze(pred)
    # Display relevant info
```

```
15     ax.set_title(f'Actual: {labels[index]} \n Pred: {classnames[pred]}',
           fontsize=16)
16
17 plt.tight_layout()
18 plt.show()
```

Figure 48:

All predictions but two are correct! The only incorrect ones are for a building being predicted as a street and vice versa. In the first occurrence, the mistake is pretty reasonable. In the other occurrence, it's much more clearly a building than a street. Speaking of these two wrong predictions - why did the model guess wrong here? Let's first go ahead and identify all of the *wrong* predictions and then try to figure out why they happen.

4.7 Evaluating a Model Like a Pro

There's much more to evaluating a model over metric evaluation and predicting a batch and checking manually. These are the numbers you'd put out to signify how great your model is, if you were to write a publication - however, it's still a black box system in which we have no clue as to why the street before was classified as a building and vice versa. We do know that there's an overlap, but what has the model learned to make it misclassify in a relatively obvious image like the one above?

Note: Before going further, let's unshuffle the test set again. I know - it's tedious, and I wish there were a shorter way to do this, but there isn't. Some of the visualizations down the line we'll make are affected by the order of data.

```
1 test_generator = test_datagen.flow_from_directory(config['TEST_PATH'],
2                                                     target_size=(150,150),
3                                                     batch_size=32,
4                                                     shuffle=False,
5                                                     class_mode = 'categorical',
6                                                     seed=2)
7
8 y_preds = model.predict(test_generator)
```

4.7.1 Identifying Wrong Predictions

Let's start out by identifying the wrong predictions. The `test_generator.classes` property is a NumPy array of the classes - one class for each instance. It's the length of our test set (3000) and can be used to directly compare against the most confident predictions in our `y_preds`:

```
test_generator.classes
# array([0, 0, 0, ..., 5, 5, 5])
y_pred_classes = np.argmax(y_preds, axis=1)
y_pred_classes
# array([0, 0, 0, ..., 4, 0, 5])

test_generator.classes != y_pred_classes
# array([False, False, False, ...,  True,  True, False])
```

In this snippet, we can see that the first 3 predictions are right, but that in the last three - there's some turmoil. You can turn these two sets of array into a boolean mask and search for the indices of the wrong predictions. Whenever a class from `test_generator.classes` doesn't match a class from `y_pred_classes` - `True` is returned, and this identifies the instance from which we can get the index:

```
wrong_preds_indices = np.where(test_generator.classes != y_pred_classes)
wrong_preds_indices[0][:10]
# array([ 5, 23, 25, 30, 31, 38, 67, 79, 86, 88], dtype=int64)
```

Once we have the indices - we can find the paths of the misclassified images, through `test_generator.filenames` which returns a list of filenames that the `ImageDataGenerator` reads from:

```
wrong_pred_paths = np.take(test_generator.filenames, wrong_preds_indices[0])
wrong_pred_paths
```

```
array(['buildings\\20074.jpg', 'buildings\\20250.jpg',
       'buildings\\20294.jpg', 'buildings\\20374.jpg',
       ...
```

We've identified the incorrectly classified images! Let's load them in, their true labels and predictions:

```
import cv2

miss_imgs = []
actual_labels = []
preds = []

for wrong_pred_path in wrong_pred_paths:
    img = cv2.imread(config['TEST_PATH']+wrong_pred_path)
    img = cv2.resize(img, (150,150))
    img = cv2.cvtColor(img, cv2.COLOR_BGR2RGB)
    img = img/255
```

```
12
13      miss_imgs.append(img)
14      pred = model2.predict(np.expand_dims(img, 0))
15      preds.append(np.argmax(pred))
16      actual_labels.append(wrong_pred_path.split('\\')[0])
```

There isn't a lot of them, so we can plot a large portion of them in a single plot (100 images) and still be able to see for ourselves what's going on. We'll plot the index as well so it's easier to pick out a specific image if we want to inspect it further:

```
1 subset = miss_imgs[:100]
2 fig = plt.figure(figsize=(20, 20))
3
4 for index, img in enumerate(subset):
5     ax = fig.add_subplot(10, 10, index+1)
6     ax.imshow(img)
7     ax.set_title(f'Actual: {actual_labels[index]} \n Pred:
          {classnames[preds[index]]}, \n {index}', fontsize=16)
8     ax.axis('off')
9
10 plt.tight_layout()
11 plt.show()
```

Figure 49:

- On index 3, we can see that the image of sky was classified as a street. The image is taken between two buildings. Has the model learned that streets are found between buildings? It's a good approximation, since we probably didn't have images of highways in the dataset. This is, well, co-occurrence. Buildings co-occur with streets, in a fairly recognizable format (streets are typically between buildings) so even if the image actually points to the sky - the position of the buildings fooled the model. This is already a good sign of why our model's mixed up some streets and buildings!

- On index 7, the trees in the front made it think it's a forest, disregarding the building in the back.
- On index 9, we see the exact same issue with buildings and streets.
- On indices 10, 13 and 17 - these are arguably streets, not buildings. I'd tend to agree with the model here.
- On index 19 - this looks more like a forest than a building as well. Siding with the model.
- On indices 40 and 41 - the first image does look like a mountain to me, and the second one is definitely a mountain! Are the labels wrong?

Wait, something's off here. What's with label 44? And... 45? There's a guitarist at index 49 and a truck at index 51! Index 52 is labeled as a glacier, by *having a sign with the word "glacier"* on top of a mountain. These are clearly wrong labels. For a lot of these - the model's predictions actually seem to be more correct than the original labels. For some, the images simply don't belong to the actual classes, and for some - to be fair, our model got them wrong.

Let's take a closer look at some of these:

```
1 subset_series = pd.Series(subset)
2 actual_labels_series = pd.Series(actual_labels)
3 preds_series = pd.Series(preds)
4
5 example_indices = [2, 3, 6, 7, 8, 9, 10, 11, 26, 29, 30, 36, 44, 45, 49, 51,
      75, 79, 90, 99]
6
7 example_imgs = subset_series[example_indices]
8 example_labels = actual_labels_series[example_indices]
9 example_preds = preds_series[example_indices]
10
11 example_imgs = list(example_imgs)
12 example_labels = list(example_labels)
13 example_preds = list(example_preds)
14
15 fig = plt.figure(figsize=(20, 5))
16
17 for index, img in enumerate(example_imgs):
18     ax = fig.add_subplot(2, 10, index+1)
19     ax.imshow(img)
```

```
20      ax.set_title(f'Actual: {example_labels[index]} \n Pred:
            {classnames[example_preds[index]]}')
21      ax.axis('off')
22
23  plt.show()
```

These highlight some of the co-occurrence issues we've talked about before and highlight some of the wrong labels. A building was classified as the sea because of the blue sky mixed with teal-colored glass. Because we performed augmentation - images of the sea with the horizon were likely skewed, so the model wasn't given a chance to correlate the horizon with the sea:

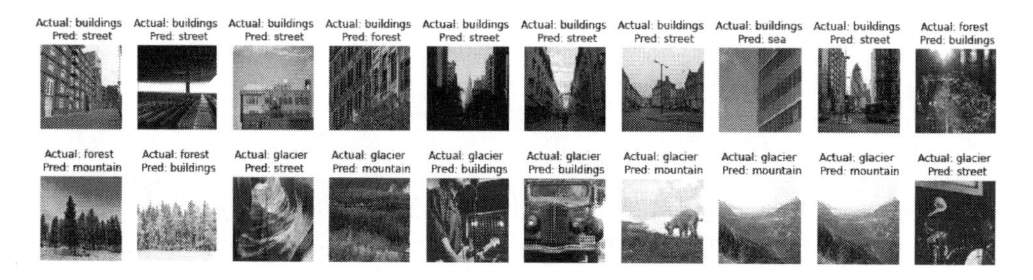

Figure 50:

Our model proved to be very capable on this dataset, though, not fully. There are some plain wrong predictions, but it was also (by chance) able to identify some of the wrongly-labeled images. We could actually use the model to *fix the dataset*. This is best done supervised, by a human, since otherwise we'd alter the dataset to fit the model, which is a huge red flag. There are ~170 wrong predictions, which wouldn't take too long to go through manually and fix. Images of guitarists, canyons and trucks can go to the recycle bin, while images of goats on mountain tops and mountains can go to their correct folder.

> Real world data is dirty. It's improperly labelled, messy, and otherwise oftentimes requires processing. Labelling data takes time, and thus, is expensive. This is one of the biggest hurdles in machine learning today, which is why unsupervised methods are increasingly being proposed as a way to skip this issue entirely.

4.7.2 What Makes Predictions Wrong - Visualizing Attention of a CNN

So - for the *actual wrong* predictions, why were they wrong? With the strides made by the *Interpretable AI* movement - we're seeing more and more work being put into analyzing why vision systems make decisions. Every so often, you'll find new research papers that explain vision models. Some models are trained to annotate decisions with words, while some are trained to annotate regions of images.

While we still can't get a message such as:

> This image was classified because of co-occurrence between buildings and their positions to streets.

We can get a pretty good idea with open-source tools today. One of the most popular techniques used for this is *Gradient-Weighted Class Activation Mapping*[53], colloquially known as *GradCam*. It's an integral part of the `keras-vis` and `tf-keras-vis` packages (both created by the same author(s)).

4.7.3 tf-keras-vis and GradCam++

`keras-vis` (GitHub[54]), now migrated to `tf-keras-vis` (GitHub[55]) since Keras became the official high-level API of TensorFlow, implements several very useful techniques that can be used to debug and identify what convolutional neural networks learn. As of writing, they support:

- Activation maximization
- Saliency maps
- Class activation maps

These are amazing tools, implemented from amazing papers. You can find and read them all on the GitHub page linked above. Going too far into `tf-keras-vis` would make us go on a large tangent, so we won't dive into the library itself, but rather, focus on a more specific use case for now. We're interested in the *"attention"* of our CNN - in other

[53]https://arxiv.org/abs/1610.02391
[54]https://github.com/raghakot/keras-vis
[55]https://github.com/keisen/tf-keras-vis

words, which parts of an image excite the neurons that fire for a given class. We'll be working with the smaller subset of images from before:

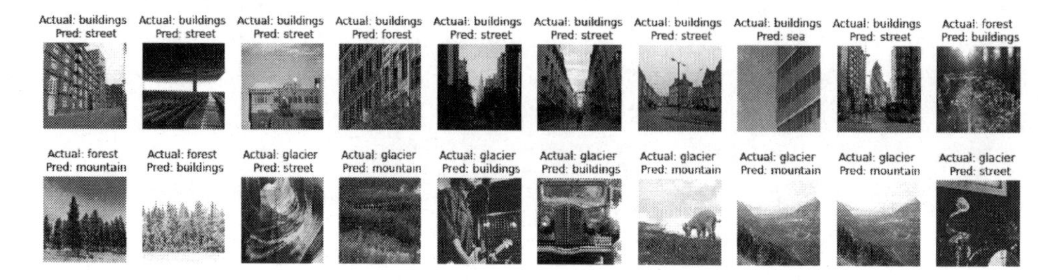

Figure 51:

This is known as making a *Class Activation Map*, and `tf-keras-vis` implements several well-known algorithms for this. We'll be using GradCam++[56], an improved version of the original GradCam. Let's install `tf-keras-vis`:

```
1 $ pip install tf-keras-vis
```

The official documentation[57] of the library has some great examples and is a great starting point! Their explanations do assume you've read the relevant papers, though. The class is pretty easy to use - we'll instantiate a `GradcamPlusPlus`, providing it with our `model` that's ready to infer, and run images through that object. Note that we're using SoftMax as the activation function - which doesn't work really well with GradCam++ unfortunately. Thankfully, `tf-keras-vis` allows us to replace the function with a linear one, which works great with GradCam++, using a single argument:

```
1 # Import relevant modules
2 from matplotlib import cm
3 from tf_keras_vis.gradcam_plus_plus import GradcamPlusPlus
4 from tf_keras_vis.utils.model_modifiers import ReplaceToLinear
5 from tf_keras_vis.utils.scores import CategoricalScore
6
7 # Instantiate GradCamPlusPlus with our model, and a replaced activation
      function
8 gradcam = GradcamPlusPlus(model,
9                           model_modifier=ReplaceToLinear(),
10                          # Cloning so the replacement isn't done in-place
                                 (replaced on a clone of the model)
```

[56]https://arxiv.org/abs/1710.11063

[57]https://keisen.github.io/tf-keras-vis-docs/examples/attentions.html#GradCAM++

```
11                              clone=True)
12
13 fig = plt.figure(figsize=(20, 5))
14
15 # For each image, plot it, calculate the class activation map
16 # and overlay the map over the image for reference
17 for index, img in enumerate(example_imgs):
18     ax = fig.add_subplot(2, 10, index+1)
19
20     # You have to create a score function or instantiate CategoricalScore
           corresponding to our classes
21     # Note that if you're using the CategoricalScore class, you pass in the
           *indices* of the classes
22     # starting at `0`, so we have 6 labels, with label indices going up to 5
23     cam = gradcam(CategoricalScore(5), img)
24     heatmap = np.uint8(cm.jet(cam[0])[..., :3] * 255)
25
26     ax.imshow(img)
27     ax.imshow(heatmap, cmap = 'jet', alpha=0.4)
28     ax.set_title(f'Actual: {example_labels[index]} \n Pred:
           {classnames[example_preds[index]]}')
29     ax.axis('off')
30
31 plt.tight_layout()
32 plt.show()
```

It helps to plot a smaller number of images for better viewing, though, you can also extend them on your screen. Seeing the several buildings being classified as streets now makes more sense. The model has learned that the *edges* of buildings define a street. After all, this is where a street begins! This isn't far from our earlier hypothesis of the model assuming that whatever is between buildings is a street. After all, it has to know the boundaries of the buildings to know that there's there are two buildings, between which, whatever a "street" is lies. This is really noticeable on images 6 and 7, where the streets are inferred from the roots of the buildings and the top edges. We do see some windows creeping in as well - a nasty side effect of co-occurrence.

The sea-building was classified as a sea due to the straight line and all the blue. The mountains are classified based on the shape of the outlines of the mountains. You can clearly see that trees and grass also light up on mountains as well. For the images that were mislabeled - we see odd activations all over the place. The model is able to pick up features such as lines and curvature, but isn't able to map it to the correct label since no correct label exists:

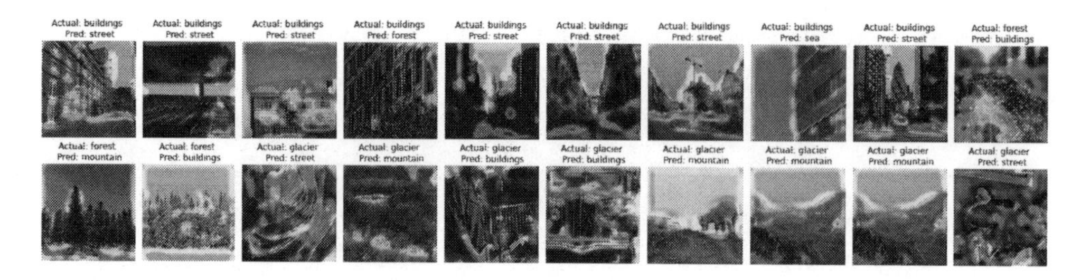

Figure 52:

Arguably, the features of the truck are closest to a building so it's not like the model was just randomly guessing. `tf-keras-vis` is a great library, and it's encouraged to play around more with it. You can produce other types of visualizations for further study of your model! This is a great homework exercise. You can find examples in their documentation. Instead, let's focus on another aspect of visualizing learned features.

4.7.4 Learned Feature Analysis - Principal Component Analysis and t-SNE

We can go one step further with visualization. François Chollet, the author of Keras, describes himself as a visual **thinker**:

> *"I think visual analogies and motion are a fundamental building block of the mind. [...] You often express your thoughts by visualizing concepts in 2D space."*

Features are vectors. Vectors can have many dimensions. These dimensions can specify a some point in some space, that clearly defines this feature. You can think of this as the **space of knowledge** - more technically, it's known as **feature space** and when its dimensions are reduced, most refer to it as ***latent space*** (also known as embedding space or latent feature space). We're bad at thinking beyond 3 dimensions, though, features can go into the hundreds, and tens of thousands of dimensions. Our model produces an 83k-feature vector after flattening, from which our dense classifier network learns to discern features.

So, can we visualize this space somehow? Well, no. As long as it's still in 83k dimensions. However, we can visualize it as long as it's within 2 or 3 dimensions! Dimensionality

Reduction is an art and science in and of itself, and it's oftentimes used for visualizing high-dimensional vectors, besides reducing the dimensionality a model needs to learn from. Various techniques for reducing the dimensionality exist, some of which include:

- Principal Component Analysis (PCA)
- Linear Discriminant Analysis (LDA)
- Autoencoders
- Random Projections (not really used commonly anymore)
- t-Distributed Stochastic Neighbor Embeddings (t-SNE)

From these, PCA is one of the most popular techniques, and t-SNE is a much newer technique used to cluster like-points together in Euclidean space. High-dimensional data suffers from the Curse of Dimensionality - most points in really high-dimensional space end up having a similar Euclidian distance from the center, similar to how the "shell" of an atom is formed around the nucleus, with a void in-between. This makes it really difficult for t-SNE to work well, so we typically apply some other linear dimensionality reduction technique, such as PCA before t-SNE to reduce the dimensions to a much more manageable scale. As a rule of thumb, t-SNE doesn't work well with over 50 dimensions, so you'll want to reduce the dimensions before trying to feed data into the algorithm. PCA is really good at preserving the relationships between data, even with smaller dimensions, so condensing our 83k-dimensional vector into a 2 or 3-dimensional vector will preserve *enough* relationship information for us to still be able to form a coherent image of where these knowledge representations are in Euclidean space!

Naturally, we'd lose a lot of variance by condensing so much, so you wouldn't want to *learn* from these components - this is only done for visualization. Why? It helps to see where knowledge representations sit compared to other representations, since this helps validate what the model's learned. Similar embeddings (feature vectors) will sit close to each other in Euclidean space, while different representations will sit far away from each other.

Fun Fact: In effect, similar images will be clumped together. You can make a recommender system with this! Or, in a similar way - reverse image search. Once a model's learned to distinguish between images using their features well, you can find the nearest neighbors of an image in Euclidean space, and return them as "Similar Images". This is how Google Reverse Image Search, CelebsLikeMe and Pinterest essentially work! There's a bit more to consider here, such as optimizing the model for similarity search, rather than classification (by offloading more to convolutional layers, which then encode domain knowledge within the features, rather than having the densely connected network encode domain knowledge). This idea can be translated to any other similarity search - Spotify learns to find music based on a similar technique, YouTube learns to recommend similar videos, etc.

Other than model validation and similarity search - it's plain amazing to imagine the reduction operation, where you can point to a **point in Euclidean space** and identify a knowledge representation!

So how do we do this? We could work with the classifier top (which is much more linear and has much clearer lines between classes), though, what we're really interested in is the feature maps created by the convolutional blocks, which encode the *real* knowledge representations, while the classifier only learns to pick from these representations, and which contribute to a class being what it is.

Let's expose the convolutional base of our model, by adding all of the layers except for the classifier top into a new network - `feature_extractor`:

```
1 feature_extractor = keras.Sequential()
2
3 # Last 5 layers are the classifier top
4 for layer in model2.layers[:-5]:
5     feature_extractor.add(layer)
6
7 feature_extractor.summary()
```

This will yield a new network:

```
1 Model: "sequential"
2 _______________________
3 Layer (type)                 Output Shape              Param #
4 =====================
5 conv2d (Conv2D)              (None, 150, 150, 64)      1792
6 _______________________
7 conv2d_1 (Conv2D)            (None, 150, 150, 64)      36928
```

```
8 ________________________
9 max_pooling2d (MaxPooling2D) (None, 75, 75, 64)        0
10 ________________________
11 conv2d_2 (Conv2D)            (None, 75, 75, 128)       73856
12 ________________________
13 conv2d_3 (Conv2D)            (None, 75, 75, 128)       147584
14 ________________________
15 max_pooling2d_1 (MaxPooling2 (None, 37, 37, 128)       0
16 ________________________
17 conv2d_4 (Conv2D)            (None, 37, 37, 256)       295168
18 ________________________
19 conv2d_5 (Conv2D)            (None, 37, 37, 256)       590080
20 ________________________
21 max_pooling2d_2 (MaxPooling2 (None, 18, 18, 256)       0
22 ========================
23 Total params: 1,145,408
24 Trainable params: 1,145,408
25 Non-trainable params: 0
26 ________________________
```

The final output of the max pooling layer would, in our regular model, be flattened and put through the densely-connected network:

```
1 features = feature_extractor.predict(test_generator)
2 features.shape
3 # (3000, 18, 18, 256)
```

The max pooling layer extracts 18x18 feature maps from the 3000 images. Let's flatten them now, since PCA expect 2D input (flattened from higher dimensions):

```
1 features = features.reshape(len(features), -1)
2 features.shape
3 # (3000, 82944)
```

We could've left the `Flatten()` layer and skipped this part, true. Though, not all architectures use a flattening layer! If you don't - you'll want to flatten the features manually. If you do - you can leave the flattening layer there and skip this step.

Once flattened, let's just save our the filenames and classes from the `test_generator` before going further. The filenames will allow us to fetch and plot the images again, and the classes will help us color the features once plotted in 2D:

```
1 filenames = test_generator.filenames
2 class_ids = test_generator.classes
```

Finally, let's make use of `scikit-learn` to perform Principal Component Analysis:

```
1 from sklearn.decomposition import PCA
```

```
2 pca = PCA(n_components=2)
3
4 features_pca = pca.fit_transform(features)
5 f_pca_component1 = features_pca[:,0]
6 f_pca_component2 = features_pca[:,1]
```

We've got two principal components now! We'll plot a scatter plot on the same figure for each class, containing only the principal component markers from the corresponding classname:

```
1 plt.subplots(figsize=(10,10))
2
3 for class_id, classname in enumerate(classnames):
4     # Plot all principal components for the given classname and ID, labeling
        by classname
5     plt.scatter(f_pca_component1[class_ids == class_id],
6                 f_pca_component2[class_ids == class_id],
7                 label = classname,
8                 alpha=0.4)
9
10 plt.legend(prop={"size": 15})
11 plt.title("PCA")
12 plt.show()
```

Depending on what your model's learned, you'll get something along these lines:

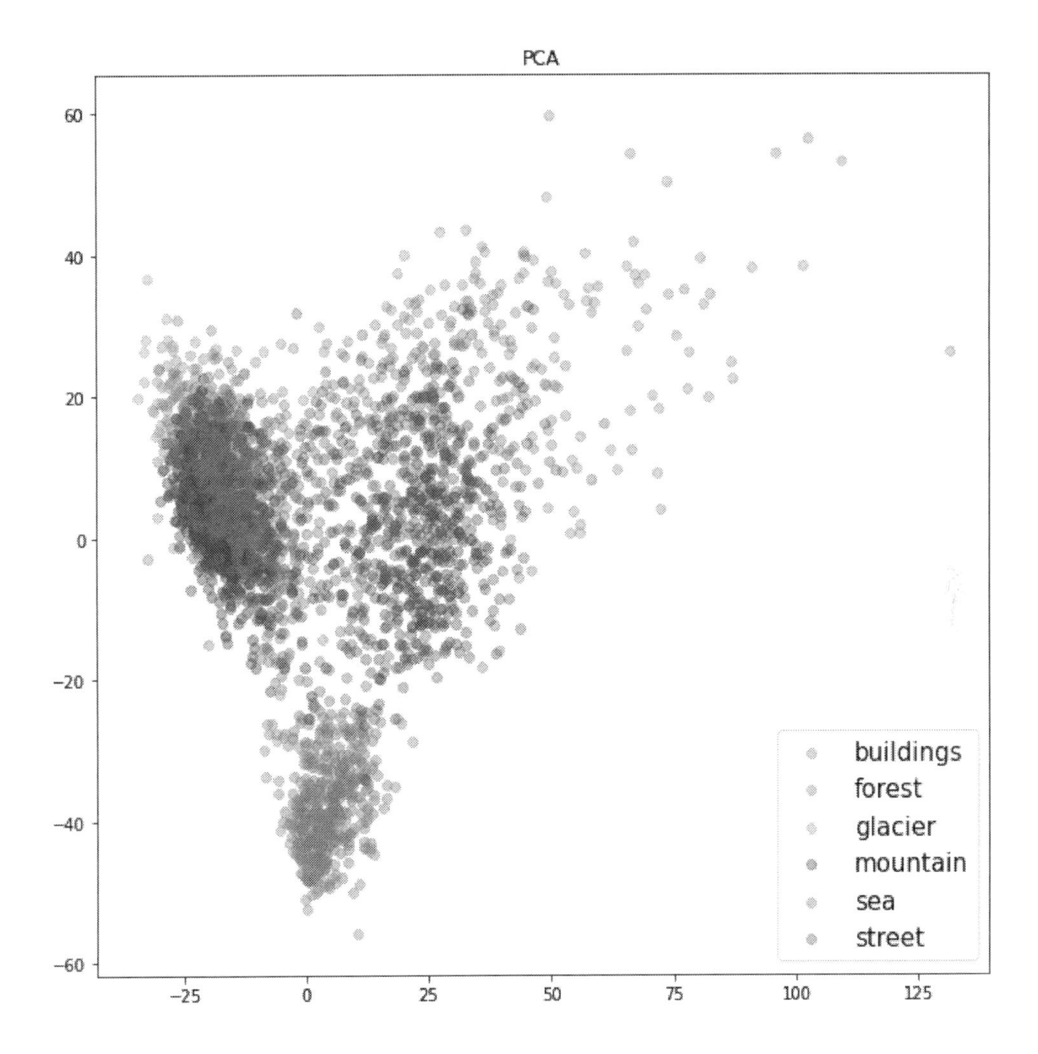

Figure 53:

The classes are delineated, though, not all of them. For instance, we can see that glacier, mountain and sea images have features in common. Buildings are scattered around with streets and forests are somewhat lonely and tightly clustered at the bottom. Plotting in 2D can make us forget that although this projection shows glaciers, mountains and seas together - if we were to plot in 3D, it's conceivable that the classes would be separated vertically, and that we're enjoying a top-down projection.

This is, in fact, what you'd see if you were to perform PCA to 3 components and plot them:

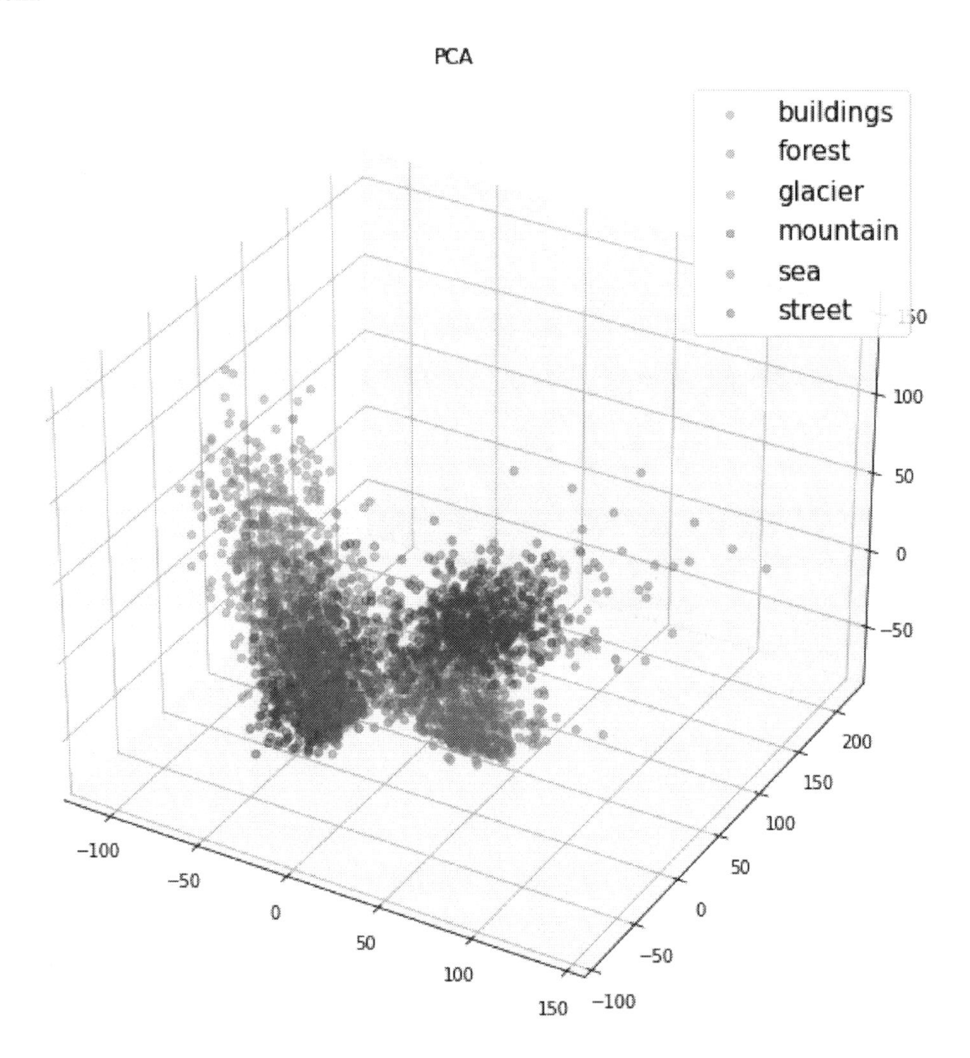

Figure 54:

Suddenly - they don't look as connected! We'll be doing t-SNE with the features represented in 2D. Let's import `TSNE` from `scikit-learn`, and fit it on our `features_pca`. We'll want two components in the end as well, just as with PCA. The `perplexity` and `n_iter` are variables to play around with, and learning how to interpret and intuitively *feel* these is beyond the scope of this lesson. However, websites like Distill offer a *great* interactive playground for t-SNE[58]!

Once t-SNE is performed, we'll plot the results and add a color bar for easier navigation:

```
from sklearn.manifold import TSNE
tsne_results = TSNE(n_components=2,
                    verbose=1,
                    perplexity=75,
                    n_iter=1000,
                    random_state=2,
                    metric = 'euclidean').fit_transform(features_pca)

fig, ax = plt.subplots(figsize=(16, 8))

scatter_plot = ax.scatter(tsne_results[:, 0],
                          tsne_results[:, 1],
                          c=class_ids,
                          cmap = 'coolwarm')
plt.colorbar(scatter_plot)
plt.show()
```

[58]https://distill.pub/2016/misread-tsne/

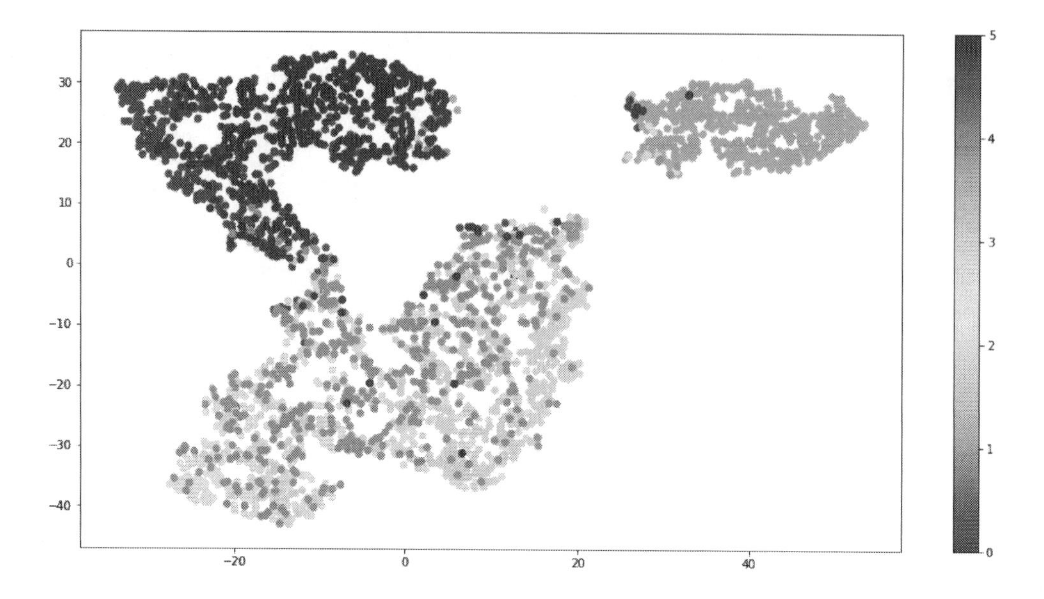

Figure 55:

Again - we're losing some of the relationship between data points through a top-down projection, so the overlapping classes are likely to have a more clearly defined separation in 3D. We can see that forests are comfortably situated away from the rest of the classes, with a couple of outliers erring towards buildings (either mislabeled data, or images of buildings behind trees). There's a huge overlap between seas and glaciers (because glaciers are... floating in seas) and the snowy mountain tops share some relationship to the icy glaciers.

While this view gives us a really clear idea of class positions in Euclidean space - we'd do much better in terms of interpretation if we were to see the appropriate images as the scatter plot markers. Thankfully - using Matplotlib's `OffsetImage` and `AnnotationBbox` - and calling on the image paths from `test_generator.filenames`, we can plot the images instead of markers:

```
1 from matplotlib.offsetbox import OffsetImage, AnnotationBbox
2
3 def plot_images_in_2d(x, y, image_paths, axis=None, zoom=1):
4     axis = plt.gca()
5     for xi, yi, image_path in zip(x, y, image_paths):
6         image = cv2.imread(config['TEST_PATH']+image_path)
```

```
7          image = cv2.resize(image, (100, 100))
8          image = cv2.cvtColor(image, cv2.COLOR_BGR2RGB)
9          img = OffsetImage(image, zoom=zoom)
10         anno_box = AnnotationBbox(img, (xi, yi),
11                                   xycoords = 'data',
12                                   frameon=False)
13         # Adds annotation box (image) to the axis
14         # *Note:* requires updating data limits and autoscaling
15         axis.add_artist(anno_box)
16     axis.update_datalim(np.column_stack([x, y]))
17     axis.autoscale()
18 
19 def show_tsne(x, y, filenames):
20     fig, axis = plt.subplots(figsize=(20, 20))
21     plot_images_in_2d(x, y, filenames, zoom=0.25, axis=axis)
22     plt.show()
```

Now, let's call the method and visualize the landscape of knowledge representations, in a format much more interpretable to humans:

```
1 show_tsne(tsne_results[:, 0], tsne_results[:, 1], filenames)
```

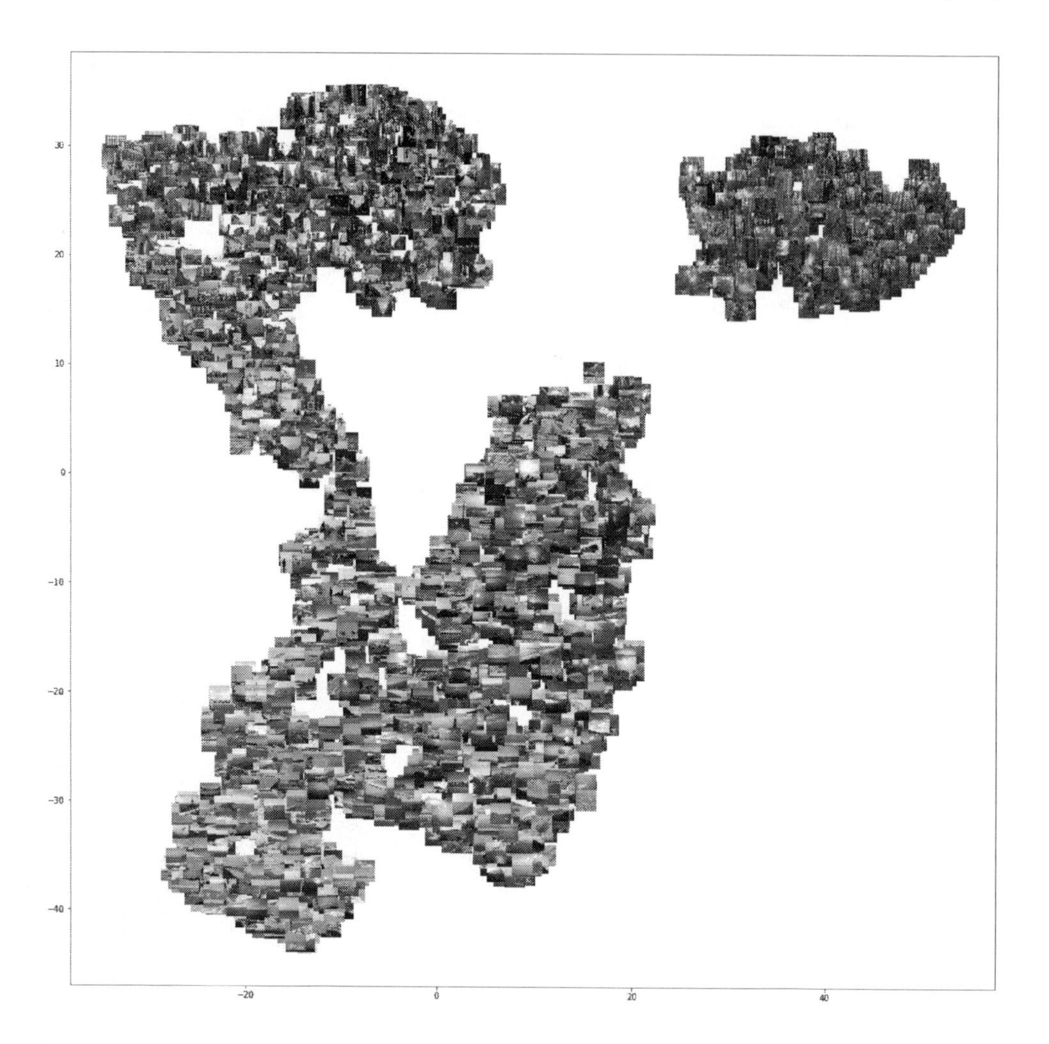

Figure 56:

You can clearly see images clustered together by similarity and sort of "blurred lines" between certain classes. There's a slow transition from glaciers to the sea, and a street bridge towards buildings. There are some building images with trees that are clustered as forests, but they're clearly closer to the buildings than the rest of the forest images. t-SNE is a beautiful algorithm and visualizing the learned features of a network really gets you a mile further in understanding it.

Additionally - this is what your classifier top learns to classify from! Now, it learns to classify from a much higher-dimensional space, but you can conceptually imagine it as this (or in 3D). Now, the task of classifying these images with a simple MLP on the top doesn't sound really daunting. It can infer the class of an image based on where it's located in the 83k-dimensional latent space. We're feeding these embeddings into the MLP and teaching it to classify them based on their location.

Imagining a CNN in this light - a dance between a convolutional base that transforms input images and clusters them together in latent space, and a classifier top that builds on that knowledge gives you insight into how a traditional "black-box" system operates. Really, it's a beautiful symbiosis and there's little "black-boxing" happening here. The way in which images are convolved and turned into embeddings that we simplified and visualized is covered in detail in the previous lesson of the book and the way in which positions of these images can be correlated with classes is very intuitive.

> Demistyfication through dissection is the first step in your road to mastery.

4.8 Home Excercise

Flattening isn't really being used that often for classification tops anymore. Global Average Pooling is - which condenses all of the feature maps into a single one, pooling all of the relevant information into a single map that can be easily understood by a single dense classification layer instead of multiple layers.

Instead of flattening a feature map like `(7, 7, 32)` into a vector of length `1536` and training one or multiple layers to discern patterns from this long vector: we can condense it into a `(7, 7)` vector and classify directly from there. Here's a small excercise for you!

Replace the `Flatten()` layer with a `GlobalAveragePooling()` layer, and add a single `Dense` layer on top for classification. Re-train this network and note the difference in the parameter count and training curves. In the following lessons, you'll learn a lot more about CNN architectures and recent trends in model development.

5 Overfitting Is Your Friend, Not Your Foe

> It's true, nobody wants **overfitting** end models, just like nobody wants **underfitting** end models.

Overfit models perform great on training data, but can't generalize well to new instances. What you end up with is a model that's approaching a fully hard-coded model tailored to a specific dataset.

Underfit models can't generalize to new data, but they can't model the original training set either.

The **right model** is one that fits the data in such a way that it performs well predicting values in the training, validation and test set, as well as new instances.

5.1 Overfitting vs. Data Scientists

Battling overfitting is given a spotlight because it's more illusory, and more tempting for a rookie to create overfit models when they start with their Machine Learning journey. Throughout books, blog posts and courses, a common scenario is given:

> "This model has a **100% accuracy rate**! It's perfect! Or not. Actually, it just badly overfits the dataset, and when testing it on new instances, it performs with **just** X%, which is equal to random guessing."

After these sections, entire book and book chapters are dedicated to **battling overfitting** and how to avoid it. The word itself became stigmatized as a *generally bad thing*. And this is where the general conception arises:

> "I must avoid overfitting at all costs."

It's given much more spotlight than underfitting, which is equally as "bad". It's worth noting that "bad" is an arbitrary term, and none of these conditions are inherently "good" or "bad". Some may claim that overfit models are technically more *useful*, because they at least perform well on *some data* while underfit models perform well on *no data*, but the illusion of success is a good candidate for outweighing this benefit.

For reference, let's consult *Google Trends* and the *Google Ngram Viewer*. Google Trends display trends of search data, while the Google Ngram Viewer counts number of occurences of *n-grams* (sequences of *n* items, such as words) in literature, parsing through a vast number of books through the ages:

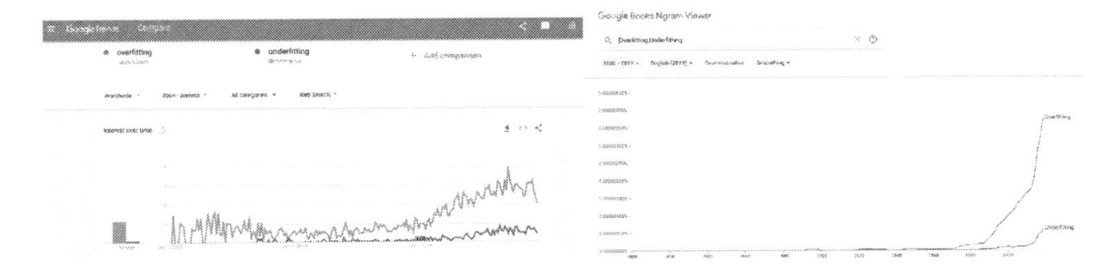

Figure 57:

Everybody talks about overfitting and mostly in the context of avoiding it - which oftentimes leads people to a general notion that it's **inherently a bad thing**.

This is *true*, to a *degree*. Yes - you don't want the end model to overfit badly, otherwise, it's practically useless. But you don't arrive at the end model right away - you tweak it numerous times, with various hyperparameters. During this process is where you **shouldn't mind seeing overfitting happening** - it's a ***good sign***, though, **not a good result**.

5.2 How Overfitting Isn' t as Bad as It' s Made Out to Be

> A model and architecture that has the ability to overfit, is more likely to have the ability to generalize well to new instances, if you simplify it (and/or tweak the data).

-

If a model *can* overfit, it has enough *entropic capacity* to extract features (in a meaningful and non-meaningful way) from data. From there, it's either that the model has more than required entropic capacity (complexity/power) or that the data itself isn't enough (very common case).

The reverse statement can also be true, but more rarely. If a given model or architecture underfits, you can try tweaking the model to see if it picks up certain features, but the type of model might just be plain wrong for the task and you won't be able to fit the data with it no matter what you do. Some models just get stuck at some level of accuracy, as they simply can't extract enough features to distinguish between certain classes, or predict values.

In **cooking** - a reverse analogy can be created. It's better to undersalt the stew early on, as you can always add salt later to taste, but it's hard to take it away once already put in.

In **Machine Learning** - it's the opposite. It's better to have a model overfit, then simplify it, change hyperparameters, augment the data, etc. to make it generalize well, but it's harder (in practical settings) to do the opposite. Avoiding overfitting *before* it happens might very well keep you away from finding the right model and/or architecture for a longer period of time.

In practice, and in some of the most fascinating use cases of Machine Learning, and Deep Learning, you'll be working on datasets that you'll be having trouble overfitting. These will be datasets that you'll routinely be underfitting, without the ability of finding models and architectures that can generalize well and extract features.

It's also worth noting the difference between what I call **true overfitting** and **partial overfitting**. A model that overfits a dataset, and achieves 60% accuracy on the training set, with only 40% on the validation and test sets is overfitting a part of the data. However, it's not **truly overfitting** in the sense of eclipsing the entire dataset, and achieving a near 100% (false) accuracy rate, while its validation and test sets sit low at, say, ~40%.

A model that partially overfits isn't one that'll be able to generalize well with simplification, as it doesn't have *enough* entropic capacity to truly (over)fit. Once it does, my argument applies, though it doesn't guarantee success, as clarified in the proceeding sections.

5.3 Case Study - Friendly Overfitting Argument

The MNIST handwritten digits dataset[59], compiled by Yann LeCun is one of the classical benchmark datasets used for training classification models. LeCun is widely

[59]http://yann.lecun.com/exdb/mnist/

considered one of the founding fathers of deep learning and I've quoted him multiple times in the book lessons with hidden gems of expertise he's shared - with contributions to the field that most can't put under their belt, and the MNIST handwritten digits dataset was one of the first major benchmarks used for the early stages of Convolutional Neural Networks. It was used to prove the potential of the jab at computer vision, and as mentioned earlier, we're still riding the wave started by that effort.

> It's also the most overused dataset, potentially ever.

Nothing wrong with the dataset itself - it's actually pretty good, but finding example upon example on the same dataset online is just plain boring. It has use in the introductory parts, where the simplicity can help lower the barrier to entry, though, at one point - **we overfit ourselves** looking at it. How much? Here's my attempt at listing the first ten MNIST digits from the top of my head:

```
1 5, 0, 4, 1, 9, 2, 2, 4, 3
```

How did I do? Let's take a look:

```
 1 from tensorflow import keras
 2 import numpy as np
 3 import matplotlib.pyplot as plt
 4
 5 # Import and normalize the images, splitting out a validation set
 6 (X_train_full, Y_train_full), (X_test, Y_test) =
       keras.datasets.mnist.load_data()
 7
 8 X_valid, X_train = X_train_full[:5000]/255.0, X_train_full[5000:]/255.0
 9 Y_valid, Y_train = Y_train_full[:5000], Y_train_full[5000:]
10
11 X_test = X_test/255.0
12
13 # Print out the first ten digits
14 fig, ax = plt.subplots(1, 10, figsize=(10,2))
15 for i in range(10):
16     ax[i].imshow(X_train_full[i])
17     ax[i].axis('off')
18     plt.subplots_adjust(wspace=1)
19
20 plt.show()
```

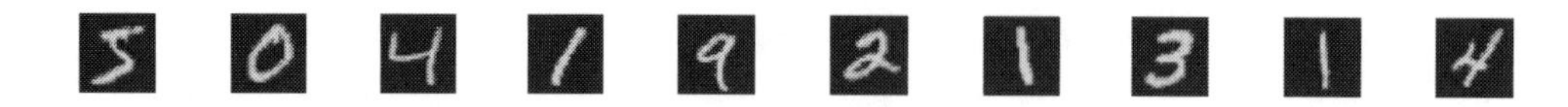

Figure 58:

Almost there.

> I'll use this chance to make a public plea to all content creators and educators to not overuse this dataset beyond the introductory parts, where the simplicity of the dataset can be used to lower the barrier to entry. *Please*.

What's wrong with simplicity? I am not trying to be contrarian, nor belittle novices in the field. Overusing the MNIST dataset, in my opinion, can do more harm than good to novices. The fact of the matter is - this dataset makes it hard to build a model that underfits. It's just too simple - and even a fairly small Multilayer Perceptron (MLP) classifier built with an intuitive number of layers and neurons per layer can easily reach upwards of 98% accuracy on the training, testing and validation set. Here's a Jupyter Notebook[60] of a simple MLP achieving ~98% accuracy on both the training, validation and testing sets, which I spun up with sensible defaults.

> I haven't even bothered to try tuning it to perform better than the initial setup.

How can you make the impact and ingenuity of CNNs apparent and make it feel *tangible* on this dataset? For advanced practitioners, it's easy to forget how confusing "basic" terminology and "intuition" can be when you're new to a field. It's a genuinely difficult thing to do. To this end, advanced practitioners typically turn to simple datasets for educational purposes to make it easier for someone to grasp the concepts and slowly build from there upwards. However, it's hard to highlight other important concepts on a dataset such as this one:

- Co-occurrence (no such thing here)
- Incorrect labels, data cleaning (no incorrect labels, no need for data cleaning)
- Data augmentation (you don't need it at all)

[60] https://github.com/StackAbuse/friendly-overfitting-argument/blob/main/Friendly-Ovetfitting-Argument.ipynb

- The need for *understanding* models, not just evaluating by metrics (works well, why bother)
- Transfer Learning (you don't need it at all)

The distinction is almost like the distinction between being able to drive a car by pressing on pedals and steering, and being able to point to a part in the mechanism and know what it does. Not everybody wants to know how a Doppelkupplungsgetriebe works, and you don't need to in order to drive a car! I don't want to teach you how to be a mechanic and how to fix the part if it fails. I do want you to know at least *rudimentarily* how it works, since if something does go awry, you don't just helplessly lift your feet from the pedals and hope for the best.

The first step is **demystifying** - a Doppelkupplungsgetriebe is a dual-clutch transmission. If you speak some German, you might've known that even if you're not into cars. Making a dual-clutch transmission is no easy task, but understanding that a regular transmission works as a set of levers to move something forward isn't difficult. Building on this simple concept, and *somehow* putting two transmissions together - you get an amazing feat of engineering!

Terminology is there to standardize the language used by practitioners all over the world. If you're new, good luck getting up to speed with everything! With interdisciplinary fields, there's a bunch of conflicting terminology as well. Same concepts have multiple names, and some names refer to different things based on your background. I've used a cheap trick, using a long German word to shroud the concept of levers. Only 1.75% of the human population speaks German, so there's a high probability that you haven't seen this compounded word or its constituent elements before. I've *abstracted the concept* behind a word, making it easier to distance yourself from the inner workings. The MNIST dataset enables you to *abstract the workings* of a neural network and be content with it, whatever it does and however it does that. Only by being exposed to some of the concepts above can you get to build *real* computer vision systems, and it's better done sooner than later, even if the ramp to climb is slightly higher.

Building a 99% accurate classifier from the get-go can give the illusion of true understanding. While it's philosophically debatable, in my subjective opinion, the illusion of true understanding is more dangerous than not - it's fine if you don't yet quite get concept X and Y, as long as you're aware that these are hills that you can get over later, but without knowing they're there at all, you'll have a harder time navigating yourself. The point isn't to belittle you if you don't truly grasp things, but to enable you to build your understanding by providing a landscape of concepts you'll eventually encounter. It takes time to have everything to sink in. Take it slow.

5.3.1 The CIFAR10 and CIFAR100 Datasets

Let's use a dataset that's more complicated than MNIST handwritten digits, and which makes a simple MLP underfit but which is simple enough to let a decently-sized CNN to truly overfit on it. A good candidate is the *CIFAR dataset*[61].

> There's a 10 classes of images in CIFAR10, and 100 in CIFAR100. Additionally, the CIFAR100 dataset has 20 families of *similar* classes, which means the network additionally has to learn the minute differences between similar, but different classes. These are known as "**fine labels**" (100) and "**coarse labels**" (20) and predicting these is equal to predicting the specific class, or just the family it belongs to.

For instance, here's a superclass (coarse label) and it's subclasses (fine labels):

Superclass

Subclasses

food containers

bottles, bowls, cans, cups, plates

A cup is a cylinder, similar to a soda can, and some bottles may be too. Since these low-level features are relatively similar, it's easy to chuck them all into the *"food container"* category, but higher-level abstraction is required to properly guess whether something is a *"cup"* or a *"can"*.

What makes this job even harder is that CIFAR10 has 6000 images per class, while CIFAR100 has 600 images per class, giving the network less images to learn the ever so subtle differences from. Cups without handles exist, and cans without ridges do too. From a profile - it might not be too easy to tell them apart.

[61] https://www.cs.toronto.edu/~kriz/cifar.html

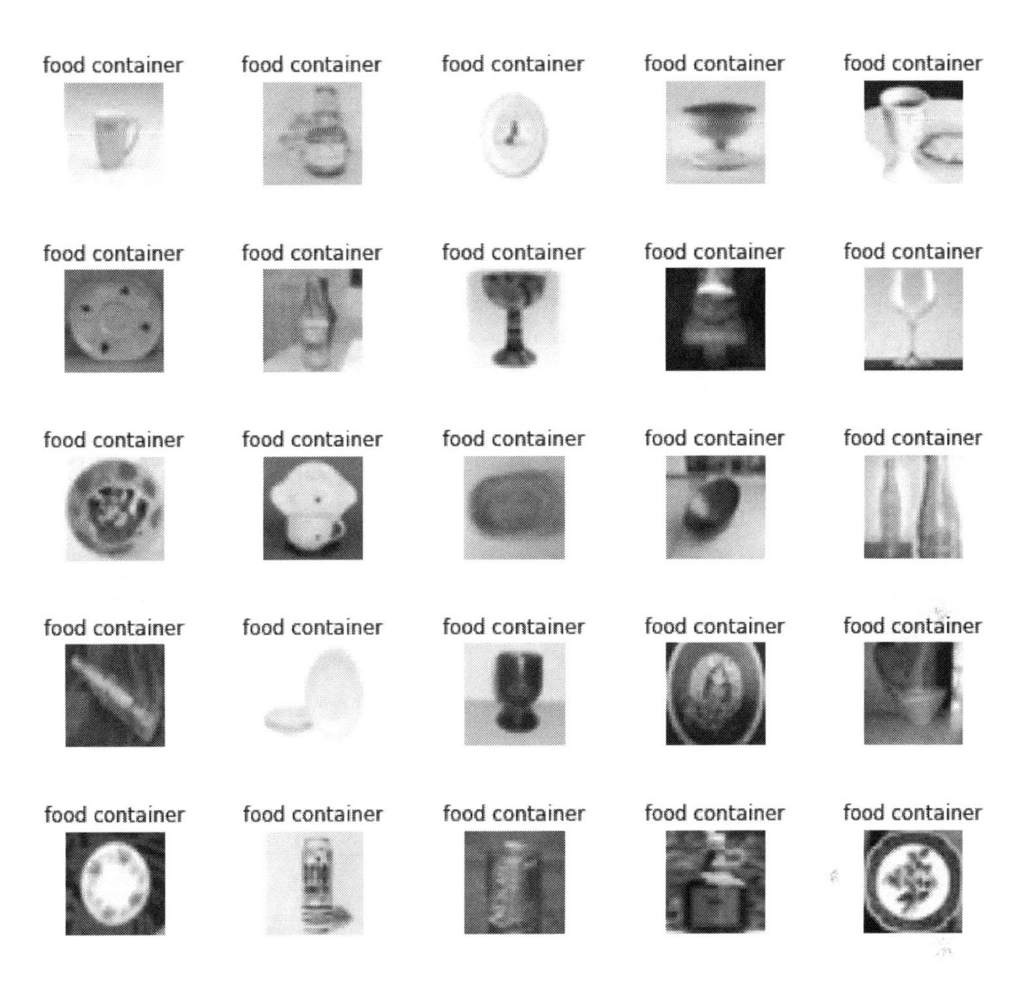

Figure 59:

This is where, say, an MLP simply doesn't have the abstraction power to learn, and it's doomed to fail, horribly underfitting - due to learning only global patterns. Again, Convolutional Neural Networks took hints from neuroscience and the hierarchical pattern recognition that the brain performs which generalizes knowledge much better - a major benefit being translational invariance (it doesn't care where or how the object is positioned in the image). These networks are able to extract features like this, and excel at the task. So much so that they oftentimes overfit badly and can't be used as is in the end - where we typically sacrifice some accuracy for the sake of generalization ability.

Let's train two different network architectures on the CIFAR10 and CIFAR100 dataset as an illustration of my point.

> This is also where we'll be able to see how even when a network overfits, it's no guarantee that the network itself will definitely generalize well if simplified - it might not be able to generalize if simplified, though there is a tendency. The network might be **right**, but the **data** might not be enough.

In the case of CIFAR100 - just 500 images for training (and 100 for testing) per class is not enough for a simple CNN to *really* generalize well on the entire 100 classes, and we'll have to perform data augmentation to help it along. Even with data augmentation, we might not get a highly accurate network as there's just so much you can do to the data. If the same architecture performs well on CIFAR10, but not CIFAR100 - it means it simply can't distinguish from some of the more fine-grained details that make the difference between cylindrical objects that we call a "cup", "can" and "bottle", for instance.

> The vast majority[a] of advanced network architectures that achieve a high accuracy on the CIFAR100 dataset perform data augmentation or otherwise expand the training set.
>
> [a]https://paperswithcode.com/sota/image-classification-on-cifar-100

Most of them *have to*, and that's not a sign of bad engineering. In fact - the fact that we can expand these datasets and help networks generalize better is a sign of engineering ingenuity. What's been said about Data Augmentation before still stands - it's not the road to the end. Though, a temporary solution that gets the job done until we have a radically different approach to learning algorithms doesn't invalidate the idea!

Additionally, I'd invite any human to try and guess what these are, if they're convinced that image classification isn't too hard with images as small as 32x32:

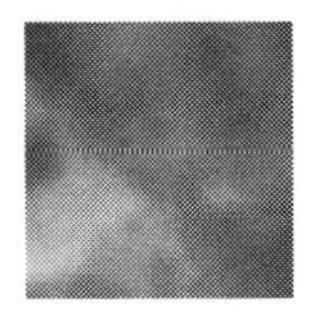 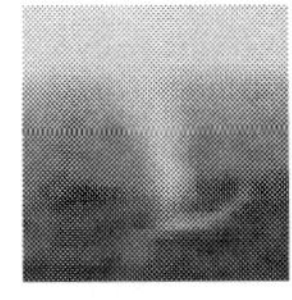 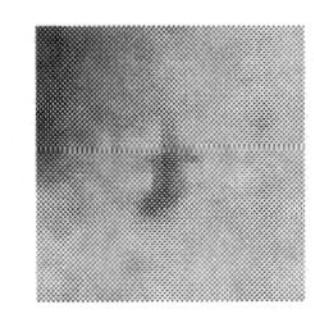 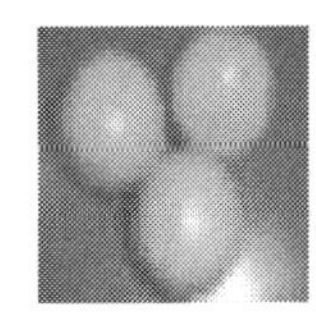  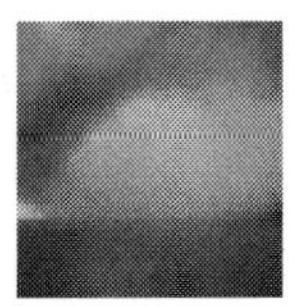

Figure 60:

Is *Image 4* a few oranges? Ping pong balls? Egg yolks? Well, probably not egg yolks, but that requires prior knowledge on what "eggs" are and whether you're likely to find yolks sitting on the table, which a network won't have. Consider the amount of prior knowledge you may have regarding the world and how much it affects what you see.

5.3.2 Importing the Data

But first off, let's load it in, separate the data into a training, testing and validation set, normalizing the image values to `0..1`:

```
1 from tensorflow import keras
2 import numpy as np
3 import matplotlib.pyplot as plt
4
5 (X_train_cifar10, Y_train_cifar10), (X_test_cifar10, Y_test_cifar10) =
      keras.datasets.cifar10.load_data()
6
7 print(X_train_cifar10.shape)
8 print(Y_train_cifar10.shape)
9
10 X_valid_cifar10, X_train_cifar10 = X_train_cifar10[:5000]/255.0,
      X_train_cifar10[5000:]/255.0
11 Y_valid_cifar10, Y_train_cifar10 = Y_train_cifar10[:5000],
      Y_train_cifar10[5000:]
12
13 X_test_cifar10 = X_test_cifar10/255.0
```

Then, let's visualize some of the images in the dataset to get an idea of what we're up against:

```
1 fig, ax = plt.subplots(5, 5, figsize=(10, 10))
2 ax = ax.ravel()
3
4 # Labels come as numbers of [0..9], so here are the class names for humans
5 class_names = ['Airplane', 'Automobile', 'Bird', 'Cat', 'Deer', 'Dog',
      'Frog', 'Horse', 'Ship', 'Truck']
```

```
6
7  for i in range(25):
8      ax[i].imshow(X_train_cifar10[i])
9      ax[i].set_title(class_names[Y_train_cifar10[i][0]])
10     ax[i].axis('off')
11     plt.subplots_adjust(wspace=1)
12
13 plt.show()
```

Figure 61:

5.3.3 Underfitting Multilayer Perceptron

Pretty much no matter what we do, the MLP won't perform that well. It'll definitely reach some level of accuracy based on the raw sequences of information coming in - but this number is capped and probably won't be too high. The network will start overfitting at one point, learning the concrete sequences of data denoting images, but will still have low accuracy on the training set even when overfitting, which is the prime time to stop training it, since it simply can't fit the data well.

Let's add in an `EarlyStopping` callback to avoid running the network beyond the point of common sense, and set the `epochs` to a number beyond what we'll run it for (so `EarlyStopping` can kick in). We'll use the Sequential API to add a couple of layers with `BatchNormalization` and a bit of `Dropout`. They help with generalization and we want to at least *try* to get this model to learn something.

The main hyperparameters we can tweak here are the number of layers, their sizes, activation functions, kernel initializers and dropout rates, and here's a "decently" performing setup:

```
checkpoint = keras.callbacks.ModelCheckpoint("simple_dense.h5",
    save_best_only=True)
early_stopping = keras.callbacks.EarlyStopping(patience=10,
    restore_best_weights=True)
reduceLr = keras.callbacks.ReduceLROnPlateau()

model = keras.Sequential([
  keras.layers.Flatten(input_shape=[32, 32, 3]),
  keras.layers.BatchNormalization(),
  keras.layers.Dense(75),

  keras.layers.Dense(50, activation = 'elu'),
  keras.layers.BatchNormalization(),
  keras.layers.Dropout(0.1),

  keras.layers.Dense(50, activation = 'elu'),
  keras.layers.BatchNormalization(),
  keras.layers.Dropout(0.1),

  keras.layers.Dense(10, activation = 'softmax')
])

model.compile(loss = "sparse_categorical_crossentropy",
              optimizer = keras.optimizers.Adam(),
              metrics=["accuracy"])

history = model.fit(X_train_cifar10,
                    Y_train_cifar10,
```

```
27                    epochs=60,
28                    validation_data=(X_valid_cifar10, Y_valid_cifar10),
29                    callbacks=[checkpoint, early_stopping, reduceLr])
```

Let's see if the starting hypothesis is true - it'll start out learning and generalizing to some extent but will end up having low accuracy on both the training set as well as the testing and validation set, resulting in an overall low accuracy.

For CIFAR10, the network performs "okay"-ish:

```
1 Epoch 1/60
2 1407/1407 [==============================] - 8s 6ms/step - loss: 1.8187 -
     accuracy: 0.3524 - val_loss: 1.5867 - val_accuracy: 0.4346
3 ...
4 Epoch 36/60
5 1407/1407 [==============================] - 8s 5ms/step - loss: 1.2868 -
     accuracy: 0.5415 - val_loss: 1.3413 - val_accuracy: 0.5216
```

Let's take a look at the history of its learning:

```
1 pd.DataFrame(history.history).plot()
2 plt.show()
3
4 model.evaluate(X_test_cifar10, Y_test_cifar10)
5 # 313/313 [==============================] - 1s 2ms/step - loss: 1.3264 -
     accuracy: 0.5255
```

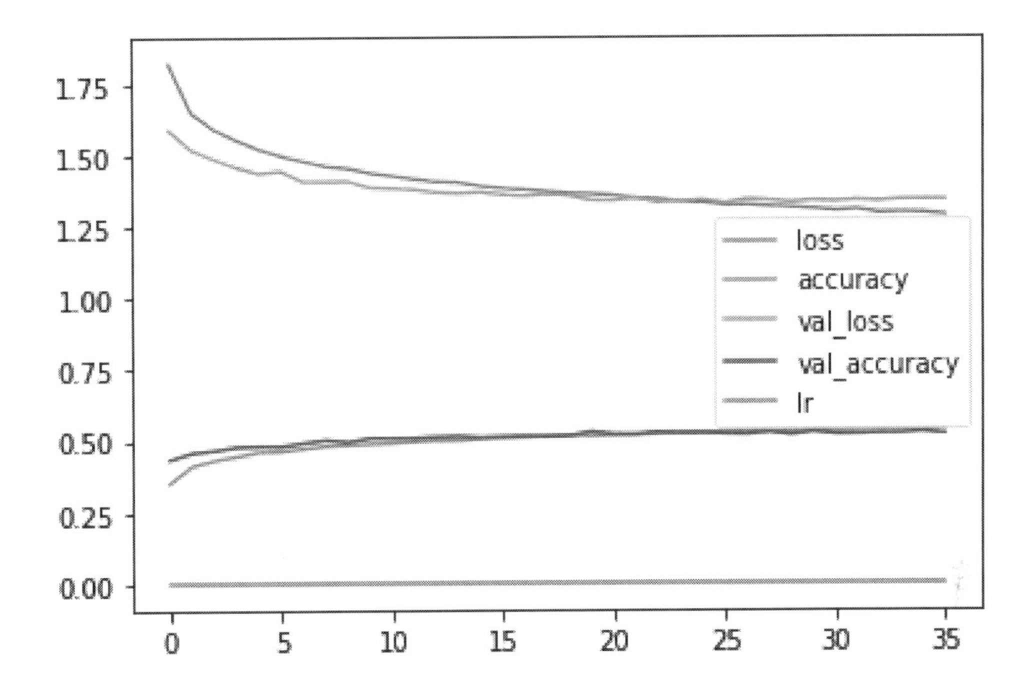

Figure 62:

The overall accuracy gets up to ~52% and the network gets here pretty quickly and starts plateauing. 50% of images being correctly classified sounds like tossing a coin, but remember that there are 10 classes here, so if it were randomly guessing, it'd on average guess a single image out of ten so this is much better than tossing a coin, yet still far away from a practically useful system. Let's switch to the CIFAR100 dataset, which also necessitates a network with at least a tiny bit more power, as there are less training instances per class, as well as a vastly higher number of classes:

```
1 checkpoint = keras.callbacks.ModelCheckpoint("bigger_dense.h5",
      save_best_only=True)
2 early_stopping = keras.callbacks.EarlyStopping(patience=10,
      restore_best_weights=True)
3 reduceLr = keras.callbacks.ReduceLROnPlateau()
4
5 # Modify the model
6 model1 = keras.Sequential([
7   keras.layers.Flatten(input_shape=[32, 32, 3]),
8   keras.layers.BatchNormalization(),
```

```
9     keras.layers.Dense(256, activation = 'relu', kernel_initializer =
          "he_normal"),
10
11    keras.layers.Dense(128, activation = 'relu'),
12    keras.layers.BatchNormalization(),
13    keras.layers.Dropout(0.1),
14
15    keras.layers.Dense(100, activation = 'softmax')
16 ])
17
18
19 model1.compile(loss = "sparse_categorical_crossentropy",
20               optimizer = keras.optimizers.Adam(),
21               metrics=["accuracy"])
22
23 history = model1.fit(X_train_cifar100,
24                      Y_train_cifar100,
25                      epochs=50,
26                      validation_data=(X_valid_cifar100, Y_valid_cifar100),
27                      callbacks=[checkpoint, early_stopping, reduceLr])
```

The network performs fairly badly:

```
1 Epoch 1/50
2 1407/1407 [==============================] - 6s 4ms/step - loss: 3.8801 -
      accuracy: 0.1186 - val_loss: 3.5474 - val_accuracy: 0.1686
3 ...
4 Epoch 15/50
5 1407/1407 [==============================] - 6s 4ms/step - loss: 2.4661 -
      accuracy: 0.3692 - val_loss: 3.1840 - val_accuracy: 0.2626
```

And let's plot the history of its progress, as well as evaluate it on the testing set (which will likely perform as well as the validation set):

```
1 pd.DataFrame(history.history).plot()
2 plt.show()
3
4 model1.evaluate(X_test_cifar100, Y_test_cifar100)
5 # 313/313 [==============================] - 1s 2ms/step - loss: 3.0887 -
      accuracy: 0.2670
```

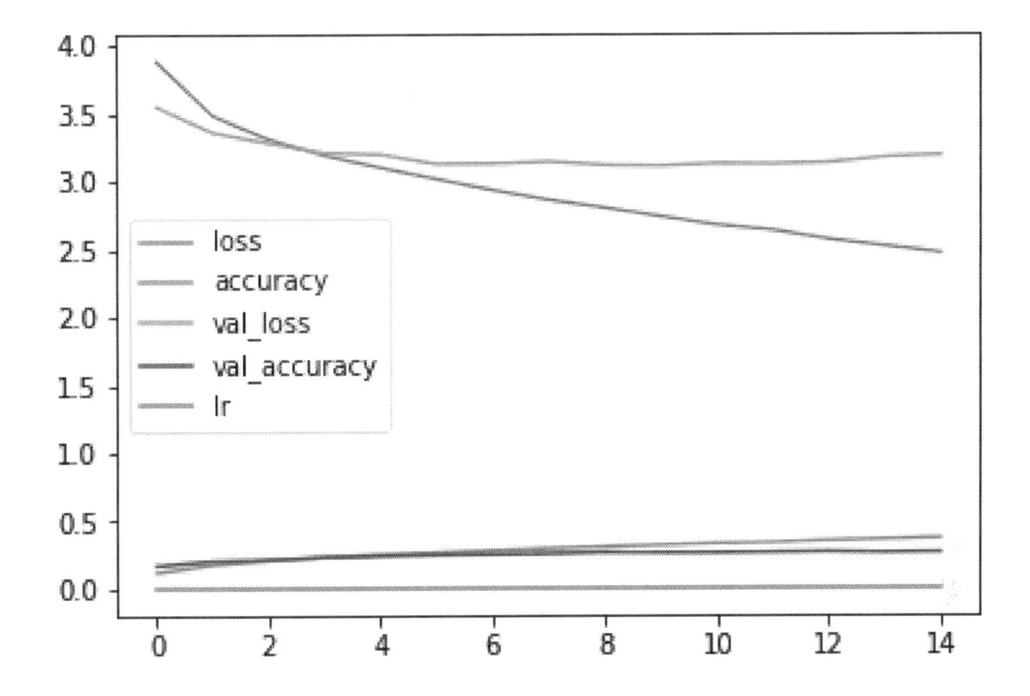

Figure 63:

As expected, the network wasn't able to grasp the data well. It ended up having an overfit accuracy of 37%, and an actual accuracy of 27%. The accuracy capped at 37% - it wasn't *really* able to overfit the dataset, even if it overfit some parts of it that it was able to discern given the limited architecture. This model doesn't have the necessary entropic capacity required for it to truly overfit for the sake of my argument. This form of overfitting is just the plain inability of a network to learn much.

This model and its architecture simply isn't well suited for this task - and while we could technically get it to (over)fit more, it'll still have issues on the long-run. For instance, let's turn it into a bigger network, which would theoretically let it recognize more complex patterns:

```
1 model2 = keras.Sequential([
2   keras.layers.Flatten(input_shape=[32, 32, 3]),
3   keras.layers.BatchNormalization(),
4   keras.layers.Dense(512, activation = 'relu', kernel_initializer =
        "he_normal"),
```

```
5
6    keras.layers.Dense(256, activation = 'relu'),
7    keras.layers.BatchNormalization(),
8    keras.layers.Dropout(0.1),
9
10   keras.layers.Dense(128, activation = 'relu'),
11   keras.layers.BatchNormalization(),
12   keras.layers.Dropout(0.1),
13
14   keras.layers.Dense(100, activation = 'softmax')
15 ])
```

Though, this doesn't do much better at all:

```
1 Epoch 24/150
2 1407/1407 [==============================] - 28s 20ms/step - loss: 2.1202 -
      accuracy: 0.4507 - val_loss: 3.2796 - val_accuracy: 0.2528
```

It's much more complex (density explodes), yet it simply cannot extract much more:

```
1 model1.summary()
2 model2.summary()
```

```
1 Model: "sequential_17"
2 ...
3 Total params: 845,284
4 Trainable params: 838,884
5 Non-trainable params: 6,400
6 _________________________
7 Model: "sequential_18"
8 ...
9 Total params: 1,764,324
10 Trainable params: 1,757,412
11 Non-trainable params: 6,912
```

5.3.4 Overfitting Convolutional Neural Network on CIFAR10

Now, let's try doing something different. Switching to a CNN will significantly help with extracting features from the dataset, thereby allowing the model to *truly* overfit, reaching much higher (illusory) accuracy. We'll kick out the `EarlyStopping` callback to let it do its thing. Additionally, we won't be using `Dropout` layers, and instead try to force the network to learn the features through more layers rather than by distributing the features more evenly.

Note: Outside of the context of trying to prove the argument, this would be horrible advice. This is opposite of what you'd want to do by the end. Dropout helps networks generalize better, by forcing the non-dropped neurons to pick up the slack and thus distributing the knowledge more equally. Forcing the network to learn through more layers it more likely to lead to an overfit model for all practical purposes.

The reason I'm purposefully doing this is to allow the network to horribly overfit as a **sign of it's ability to actually discern features, before simplifying it and adding** `Dropout` **to really allow it to generalize.** If it reaches high (illusory) accuracy, it can extract much more than the MLP model, which means we can start simplifying it. Let's once again use the Sequential API to build a CNN on the CIFAR10 dataset:

```
1 checkpoint =
      keras.callbacks.ModelCheckpoint("overcomplicated_cnn_cifar10.h5",
      save_best_only=True)
2 early_stopping = keras.callbacks.EarlyStopping(patience=10,
      restore_best_weights=True)
3 reduceLr = keras.callbacks.ReduceLROnPlateau()
4
5 model = keras.models.Sequential([
6     keras.layers.Conv2D(64, 3, activation = 'relu', padding = 'same',
          input_shape=[32, 32, 3]),
7     keras.layers.Conv2D(64, 3, activation = 'relu', padding = 'same'),
8     keras.layers.MaxPooling2D(2),
9     keras.layers.BatchNormalization(),
10
11    keras.layers.Conv2D(128, 2, activation = 'relu', padding = 'same'),
12    keras.layers.Conv2D(128, 2, activation = 'relu', padding = 'same'),
13    keras.layers.MaxPooling2D(2),
14    keras.layers.BatchNormalization(),
15
16    keras.layers.Conv2D(256, 3, activation = 'relu', padding = 'same'),
17    keras.layers.Conv2D(256, 3, activation = 'relu', padding = 'same'),
18    keras.layers.MaxPooling2D(2),
19    keras.layers.BatchNormalization(),
20
21    keras.layers.Conv2D(512, 3, activation = 'relu', padding = 'same'),
22    keras.layers.Conv2D(512, 3, activation = 'relu', padding = 'same'),
23    keras.layers.BatchNormalization(),
24
25    keras.layers.Flatten(),
26    keras.layers.Dense(64, activation = 'relu'),
27    keras.layers.Dense(10, activation = 'softmax')
28 ])
29
```

```
30 model.compile(loss = "sparse_categorical_crossentropy",
31               optimizer = keras.optimizers.Adam(),
32               metrics=["accuracy"])
33
34 model.summary()
```

It's got a solid 5M parameters:

```
1 ...
2 =====================
3 Total params: 5,091,338
4 Trainable params: 5,089,418
5 Non-trainable params: 1,920
6 _____________________
```

Let's fit the model:

```
1 history = model.fit(X_train_cifar10,
2                     Y_train_cifar10,
3                     epochs=50,
4                     batch_size=32,
5                     validation_data=(X_valid_cifar10, Y_valid_cifar10),
6                     callbacks=[checkpoint])
```

Awesome, it overfit pretty quickly! Within just a few epochs, it started overfitting the data, and by epoch 31, it got up to 99%, with a much lower validation accuracy:

```
1 Epoch 1/50
2 1407/1407 [==============================] - 26s 17ms/step - loss: 2.2679 -
      accuracy: 0.2344 - val_loss: 2.0906 - val_accuracy: 0.2748
3 ...
4 Epoch 50/50
5 1407/1407 [==============================] - 25s 18ms/step - loss: 0.0320 -
      accuracy: 0.9921 - val_loss: 1.2880 - val_accuracy: 0.7950
```

Since there are only 10 output classes, even though we tried overfitting it *a lot* by creating an unnecessarily big CNN, the validation accuracy is still fairly high - around 79%. It performs equally on the testing set:

```
1 pd.DataFrame(history.history).plot()
2 plt.show()
3
4 model.evaluate(X_test_cifar10, Y_test_cifar10)
5 # 313/313 [==============================] - 2s 6ms/step - loss: 1.3350 -
      accuracy: 0.7958
```

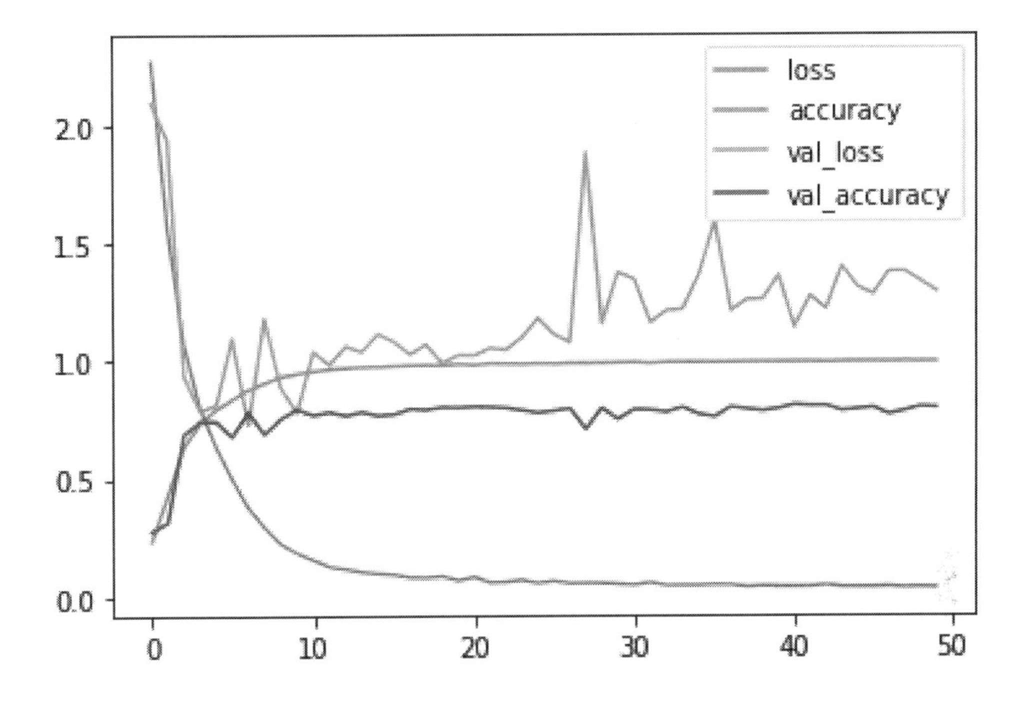

Figure 64:

5.3.5 Simplifying the Convolutional Neural Network on CIFAR10

Now, let's simplify it to see how it'll fare with a more reasonable architecture. We'll add in `Dropout` to help with the generalization:

```
1 checkpoint = keras.callbacks.ModelCheckpoint("simplified_cnn_cifar10.h5",
      save_best_only=True)
2 early_stopping = keras.callbacks.EarlyStopping(patience=25,
      restore_best_weights=True)
3
4 model = keras.models.Sequential([
5     keras.layers.Conv2D(32, 3, activation = 'relu', padding = 'same',
          input_shape=[32, 32, 3]),
6     keras.layers.Conv2D(32, 3, activation = 'relu', padding = 'same'),
7     keras.layers.MaxPooling2D(2),
8     keras.layers.BatchNormalization(),
9     keras.layers.Dropout(0.4),
10
11    keras.layers.Conv2D(64, 2, activation = 'relu', padding = 'same'),
```

```
    keras.layers.Conv2D(64, 2, activation = 'relu', padding = 'same'),
    keras.layers.MaxPooling2D(2),
    keras.layers.BatchNormalization(),
    keras.layers.Dropout(0.2),

    keras.layers.Conv2D(128, 3, activation = 'relu', padding = 'same'),
    keras.layers.Conv2D(128, 3, activation = 'relu', padding = 'same'),
    keras.layers.MaxPooling2D(2),
    keras.layers.BatchNormalization(),
    keras.layers.Dropout(0.2),

    keras.layers.Conv2D(256, 3, activation = 'relu', padding = 'same'),
    keras.layers.Conv2D(256, 3, activation = 'relu', padding = 'same'),
    keras.layers.MaxPooling2D(2),
    keras.layers.BatchNormalization(),
    keras.layers.Dropout(0.2),

    keras.layers.Flatten(),
    keras.layers.Dense(32, activation = 'relu'),
    keras.layers.BatchNormalization(),
    keras.layers.Dropout(0.3),
    keras.layers.Dense(10, activation = 'softmax')
])

model.compile(loss = "sparse_categorical_crossentropy",
              optimizer = keras.optimizers.Adam(decay=0.0015),
              metrics=["accuracy"])

model.summary()
```

We've dropped the blocks with 512 filters, and lowered the number of neurons in the fully connected layer - and the number of trainable parameters has plummeted:

```
...
======================
Total params: 1,176,714
Trainable params: 1,175,690
Non-trainable params: 1,024
______________________
```

Let's train the network now:

```
history = model.fit(X_train_cifar10,
                    Y_train_cifar10,
                    epochs=100,
                    batch_size=32,
                    validation_data=(X_valid_cifar10, Y_valid_cifar10),
                    callbacks=[checkpoint, early_stopping])
```

How does it perform?

```
Epoch 1/100
```

```
1407/1407 [==============================] - 16s 11ms/step - loss: 1.6067 -
    accuracy: 0.4297 - val_loss: 1.2940 - val_accuracy: 0.5420
...
Epoch 43/100
1407/1407 [==============================] - 16s 11ms/step - loss: 0.1579 -
    accuracy: 0.9474 - val_loss: 0.6138 - val_accuracy: 0.8324
```

The learning curves look much better, and it got to a higher level of accuracy. Most importantly - it got there *faster* on each epoch (15s vs 25s), and it took fewer epochs (just 8) to get to an 80% accuracy:

```
pd.DataFrame(history.history).plot()
plt.show()

model.evaluate(X_test_cifar10, Y_test_cifar10)
# 313/313 [==============================] - 1s 4ms/step - loss: 0.5734 -
    accuracy: 0.8187
```

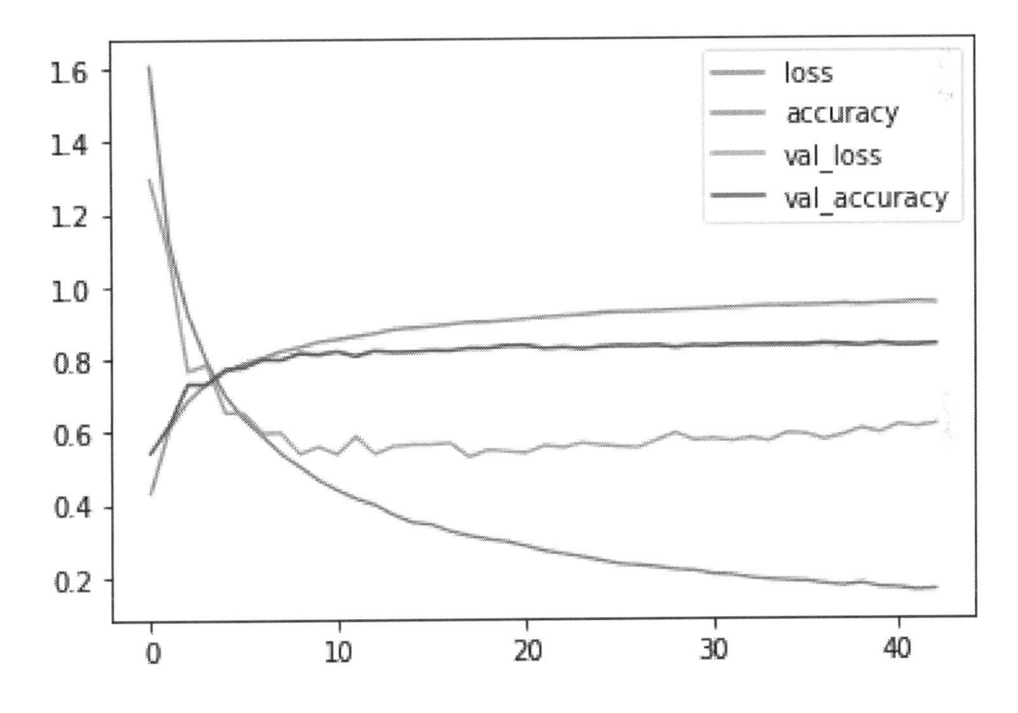

Figure 65:

The smaller network was faster to converge, and converged better! Let's take a look at some of the predictions:

```
y_preds = model.predict(X_test_cifar10)
# 10-class probabilities
print(y_preds[1]) # [3.6550809e-05 6.1900028e-05 ... ]
# Get index of class
print(np.argmax(y_preds[1])) # 8

fig, ax = plt.subplots(6, 6, figsize=(10, 10))
ax = ax.ravel()

for i in range(0, 36):
    ax[i].imshow(X_test_cifar10[i])
    ax[i].set_title(f"Actual: {class_names[Y_test_cifar10[i][0]]} \nPred:
        {class_names[np.argmax(y_preds[i])]}")
    ax[i].axis('off')
    plt.subplots_adjust(wspace=1)

plt.show()
```

Figure 66:

The main misclassifications are two images in this small set - a dog was misclassified as a deer (respectable enough), but a closeup of an emu bird was classified as a cat (funny enough so we'll let it slide).

5.3.6 Overfitting Convolutional Neural Network on CIFAR100

What happens when we go for the CIFAR100 dataset?

```
checkpoint =
    keras.callbacks.ModelCheckpoint("overcomplicated_cnn_model_cifar100.h5",
    save_best_only=True)
early_stopping = keras.callbacks.EarlyStopping(patience=10,
    restore_best_weights=True)

model = keras.models.Sequential([
    keras.layers.Conv2D(32, 3, activation = 'relu', kernel_initializer =
        "he_normal", kernel_regularizer=keras.regularizers.l2(l=0.01),
        padding = 'same', input_shape=[32, 32, 3]),
    keras.layers.Conv2D(32, 3, activation = 'relu', padding = 'same'),
    keras.layers.MaxPooling2D(2),
    keras.layers.BatchNormalization(),

    keras.layers.Conv2D(64, 2, activation = 'relu', padding = 'same'),
    keras.layers.Conv2D(64, 2, activation = 'relu', padding = 'same'),
    keras.layers.MaxPooling2D(2),
    keras.layers.BatchNormalization(),

    keras.layers.Conv2D(128, 3, activation = 'relu', padding = 'same'),
    keras.layers.Conv2D(128, 3, activation = 'relu', padding = 'same'),
    keras.layers.MaxPooling2D(2),
    keras.layers.BatchNormalization(),

    keras.layers.Conv2D(256, 3, activation = 'relu', padding = 'same'),
    keras.layers.Conv2D(256, 3, activation = 'relu', padding = 'same'),
    keras.layers.BatchNormalization(),

    keras.layers.Conv2D(512, 3, activation = 'relu', padding = 'same'),
    keras.layers.Conv2D(512, 3, activation = 'relu', padding = 'same'),
    keras.layers.BatchNormalization(),

    keras.layers.Conv2D(1024, 3, activation = 'relu', padding = 'same'),
    keras.layers.Conv2D(1024, 3, activation = 'relu', padding = 'same'),
    keras.layers.BatchNormalization(),

    keras.layers.Flatten(),
    keras.layers.Dense(256, activation = 'relu'),
    keras.layers.BatchNormalization(),
    keras.layers.Dense(128, activation = 'relu'),
    keras.layers.BatchNormalization(),

    keras.layers.Dense(100, activation = 'softmax')
])

model.compile(loss = "sparse_categorical_crossentropy",
              optimizer = keras.optimizers.Adam(decay=0.0015),
              metrics=["accuracy"])

model.summary()
```

This network has a *whopping 23M* paramters:

```
...
=====================
Total params: 23,089,284
Trainable params: 23,084,484
Non-trainable params: 4,800
_____________________
```

Let's train it for 50 epochs and take a look at the results:

```
history = model.fit(X_train_cifar100, Y_train_cifar100,
                    epochs=50,
                    batch_size=32,
                    validation_data=(X_valid_cifar100, Y_valid_cifar100),
                    callbacks=[checkpoint])
```

It took about a minute per epoch, and ended up being totally overfit with a fairly low validation accuracy:

```
Epoch 1/50
1407/1407 [==============================] - 65s 45ms/step - loss: 4.4327 -
    accuracy: 0.0741 - val_loss: 4.0984 - val_accuracy: 0.1038
...
Epoch 50/50
1407/1407 [==============================] - 61s 44ms/step - loss: 0.1467 -
    accuracy: 0.9961 - val_loss: 4.6064 - val_accuracy: 0.3634
```

Let's simplify the model real quick to get it to generalize better!

5.3.7 Simplifying the Convolutional Neural Network on CIFAR100

And this is where it becomes clear that the ability to overfit doesn't **guarantee** that the model could generalize really well (but it still will oftentimes generalize better) when simplified. In the case of CIFAR100, there aren't many training instances per class, and this will make learning a lot harder. Let's try it out:

```
checkpoint = keras.callbacks.ModelCheckpoint("simplified_cnn_model2.h5",
    save_best_only=True)
early_stopping = keras.callbacks.EarlyStopping(patience=10,
    restore_best_weights=True)

model = keras.models.Sequential([
    keras.layers.Conv2D(64, 3, activation = 'relu', padding = 'same',
        input_shape=[32, 32, 3]),
    keras.layers.Conv2D(64, 3, activation = 'relu', padding = 'same'),
    keras.layers.MaxPooling2D(2),
    keras.layers.BatchNormalization(),
    keras.layers.Dropout(0.4),
```

```
10
11      keras.layers.Conv2D(128, 2, activation = 'relu', padding = 'same'),
12      keras.layers.Conv2D(128, 2, activation = 'relu', padding = 'same'),
13      keras.layers.MaxPooling2D(2),
14      keras.layers.BatchNormalization(),
15      keras.layers.Dropout(0.2),
16
17      keras.layers.Conv2D(256, 3, activation = 'relu', padding = 'same'),
18      keras.layers.Conv2D(256, 3, activation = 'relu', padding = 'same'),
19      keras.layers.MaxPooling2D(2),
20      keras.layers.BatchNormalization(),
21      keras.layers.Dropout(0.2),
22
23      keras.layers.Flatten(),
24      keras.layers.Dense(64, activation = 'relu'),
25      keras.layers.BatchNormalization(),
26      keras.layers.Dropout(0.3),
27      keras.layers.Dense(100, activation = 'softmax')
28  ])
29
30
31  model.compile(loss = "sparse_categorical_crossentropy",
32                optimizer = keras.optimizers.Adam(decay=0.0015),
33                metrics=["accuracy"])
34
35  model.summary()
```

This network has a mere 1.3M parameters compared to the previous one - can it fit the data any better? Keep the 36% validation accuracy in mind as we go further. The network itself is pretty similar to the one we've had for CIFAR10 - though, the first block has more filters, and we have more neurons in the dense layer to hopefully get a bit more nuance out of the images:

```
1 ...
2 =====================
3 Total params: 1,293,284
4 Trainable params: 1,292,260
5 Non-trainable params: 1,024
6 _____________________
```

The model ultimately gets to a 53% validation accuracy:

```
1 Epoch 1/150
2 1407/1407 [==============================] - 19s 13ms/step - loss: 4.4462 -
      accuracy: 0.1092 - val_loss: 3.7245 - val_accuracy: 0.1810
3 ...
4 Epoch 81/150
5 1407/1407 [==============================] - 19s 13ms/step - loss: 1.3214 -
      accuracy: 0.6465 - val_loss: 1.8335 - val_accuracy: 0.5324
```

The test set yields a similar number:

```
1 model.evaluate(X_test_cifar100, Y_test_cifar100)
2 # 313/313 [==============================] - 1s 5ms/step - loss: 1.7554 -
      accuracy: 0.5486
```

It's plateauing and can't really get to generalize the data super well. The same type of model had high accuracy on the CIFAR10 dataset, which has the same input shape and similar images in the dataset. It appears that the model can be reasonably accurate with the general shapes, but not the distinction between fine shapes. Alternatively - it might be just right, but it doesn't have enough training data. We can't *really* know this until we try training it on more data (which we don't really have with CIFAR100).

What's important is that the simpler model performs better than the more complicated one in terms of validation accuracy and training speed - so the more complex CNN didn't get any additional detail-recognition capabilities from all the extra parameters. Here, the problem likely lies in the fact that there are only 500 training images per class, which really isn't enough, and given how blurred the images are, some features that it could pick up are blurred to oblivion and thus become unimportant and undefining. In the more complex network, this leads to overfitting, because there's not enough diversity - when simplified to avoid overfitting, this causes underfitting as again, there's no diversity.

> This is why the vast majority of the papers mentioned before, and the vast majority of networks augment the data of the CIFAR100 dataset.

It's genuinely not a dataset for which it's easy to get high accuracy on, even though it's fairly pristine (right labels, uniform images, etc.), and a simple CNN like we're building probably won't cut it for *super* high accuracy. Just remember the number of quite specific classes, how uninformative some of the images are, and *just how much prior knowledge humans have to discern between these.*

Let's do our best by augmenting a few images and artificially replacing the training data with an expanded set, to at least try to get a higher accuracy.

> If you'd like to take a look at the landscape of these models, PapersWithCode[a] has done a beautiful compilation of papers, source code and results.
>
> [a]https://paperswithcode.com/sota/image-classification-on-cifar-100

5.3.8 Data Augmentation with Keras' ImageDataGenerator Class

Will data augmentation help? Usually, it does, but with a *serious* lack of training data like we're facing, there's just so much you can do with random rotations, flipping, cropping, etc. Other augmentation techniques exist, that make for more robust systems, especially in cases like these. They'll be covered later.

If an architecture can't generalize well on a dataset, you'll likely boost it via data augmentation, but it probably won't be a whole lot. A much better approach to boosting a classifier like this is to utilize the amazing benefits of *Transfer Learning*, alongside (or instead of) data augmentation. We'll cover Transfer Learning in the next lesson.

That being said, let's use Keras' `ImageDataGenerator` class to try and generate some new training data with random changes, in hopes of improving the model's accuracy. Given the constant random variations in the data, the model is less likely to overfit on the same number of epochs, as the variations make it keep adjusting to "new" data. Let's convert the labels of the dataset to categorical values:

```
1 Y_train_cifar100 = keras.utils.to_categorical(Y_train_cifar100, 100)
2 Y_valid_cifar100 = keras.utils.to_categorical(Y_valid_cifar100, 100)
3 Y_test_cifar100 = keras.utils.to_categorical(Y_test_cifar100, 100)
```

Note: The `ImageDataGenerator`'s `flow()` method can flow from NumPy arrays, such as our labels. However, you can't manually set a `class_mode` such as with `flow_from_dataframe()` and `flow_from_directory()`. Our class mode is a *sparse* class mode (integers from `0`, `99`, denoting a class). The `flow()` method automatically treats them as `categorical` (one-hot encoded), *even if they're not*.

Once the labels have been formatted, let's instantiate our data generators, going fairly easy on the augmentations, since the images are really small and even small distortions might change their meaning:

```
1 train_datagen = ImageDataGenerator(width_shift_range=0.1,
      height_shift_range=0.1, horizontal_flip=True)
```

```
2 valid_datagen = ImageDataGenerator()
3 test_datagen = ImageDataGenerator()
4
5 train_generator = train_datagen.flow(X_train_cifar100, Y_train_cifar100,
      batch_size=32)
6 valid_generator = valid_datagen.flow(X_valid_cifar100, Y_valid_cifar100,
      batch_size=32)
7 test_generator = test_datagen.flow(X_test_cifar100, Y_test_cifar100,
      batch_size=32)
```

Finally, let's define a model and run it for, say, 150 epochs:

```
1 checkpoint = keras.callbacks.ModelCheckpoint("augmented_cnn_model2.h5",
      save_best_only=True)
2 early_stopping = keras.callbacks.EarlyStopping(patience=25,
      restore_best_weights=True)
3 reduceLr = keras.callbacks.ReduceLROnPlateau()
4
5 model = keras.models.Sequential([
6     keras.layers.Conv2D(64, 3, activation = 'relu', padding = 'same',
          input_shape=[32, 32, 3]),
7     keras.layers.Conv2D(64, 3, activation = 'relu', padding = 'same'),
8     keras.layers.MaxPooling2D(2),
9     keras.layers.BatchNormalization(),
10    keras.layers.Dropout(0.2),
11
12    keras.layers.Conv2D(128, 2, activation = 'relu', padding = 'same'),
13    keras.layers.Conv2D(128, 2, activation = 'relu', padding = 'same'),
14    keras.layers.MaxPooling2D(2),
15    keras.layers.BatchNormalization(),
16    keras.layers.Dropout(0.2),
17
18    keras.layers.Conv2D(256, 3, activation = 'relu', padding = 'same'),
19    keras.layers.Conv2D(256, 3, activation = 'relu', padding = 'same'),
20    keras.layers.MaxPooling2D(2),
21    keras.layers.BatchNormalization(),
22    keras.layers.Dropout(0.2),
23
24    keras.layers.Flatten(),
25    keras.layers.Dense(64, activation = 'relu'),
26    keras.layers.BatchNormalization(),
27    keras.layers.Dropout(0.3),
28    keras.layers.Dense(100, activation = 'softmax')
29 ])
30
31 # Remember, not `sparse_categorical_crossentropy`, we've re-formatted the
      labels
32 model.compile(loss = "categorical_crossentropy",
33               optimizer = keras.optimizers.Adam(),
34               metrics=["accuracy",
                     keras.metrics.TopKCategoricalAccuracy(k=3)])
35
36 history = model.fit(train_generator,
37                     epochs=150,
```

```
38                      validation_data=valid_generator,
39                      callbacks=[checkpoint, early_stopping, reduceLr])
```

```
1 Epoch 1/150
2 1407/1407 [==============================] - 19s 13ms/step - loss: 3.8945 -
     accuracy: 0.1109 - top_k_categorical_accuracy: 0.2332 - val_loss: 3.2462
     - val_accuracy: 0.2130 - val_top_k_categorical_accuracy: 0.3974
3 ...
4 Epoch 96/150
5 1407/1407 [==============================] - 18s 13ms/step - loss: 0.8162 -
     accuracy: 0.7542 - top_k_categorical_accuracy: 0.9128 - val_loss: 1.2793
     - val_accuracy: 0.6612 - val_top_k_categorical_accuracy: 0.8406
```

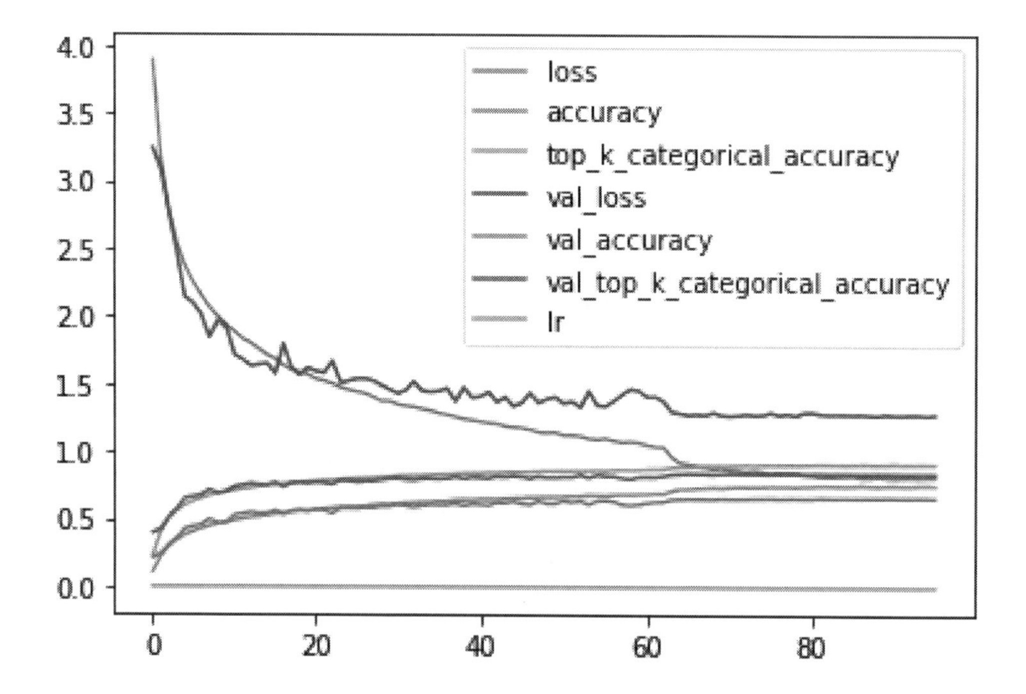

Figure 67:

The model is performing with 66% on Top-1 Accuracy and 84% in terms of Top-3 Accuracy on the validation set, and there's not a lot of overfitting going on. This network simply can't learn and fit the data with really accuracy, even though variations off it do have the entropic capacity to overfit the data. However, it's worth noting that it significantly outperforms the bigger network.

```
model.evaluate(test_generator)
# 313/313 [==============================] - 1s 4ms/step - loss: 1.2476 -
    accuracy: 0.6698 - top_k_categorical_accuracy: 0.8434
```

Just like with CIFAR10, it helps to have the class names separated out as strings rather than integer labels. This both helps us discern how big mistakes are (such as confusing a `maple_tree` with an `oak_tree`, or a `sweet_peper` with a `table`), but it also simply makes much more sense to us to be able to read what something is. Unfortunately, Keras doesn't provide class names besides the integer classes. Fortunately, this is something TensorFlow Datasets (`tfds`) does provide!

We'll use TensorFlow Datasets in the next lesson, and have an introduction to the module at the same time. Let's separate out a list of `classnames`, which you can also obtain through the downloadable Jupyter Notebook or the book s GitHub repository:

```
classnames = ['apple', 'aquarium_fish', 'baby', 'bear', 'beaver',
              'bed', 'bee', 'beetle', 'bicycle', 'bottle',
              'bowl', 'boy', 'bridge', 'bus', 'butterfly',
              'camel', 'can', 'castle', 'caterpillar', 'cattle',
              'chair', 'chimpanzee', 'clock', 'cloud', 'cockroach',
              'couch', 'crab', 'crocodile', 'cup', 'dinosaur',
              'dolphin', 'elephant', 'flatfish', 'forest', 'fox',
              'girl', 'hamster', 'house', 'kangaroo', 'computer_keyboard',
              'lamp', 'lawn_mower', 'leopard', 'lion', 'lizard',
              'lobster', 'man', 'maple_tree', 'motorcycle', 'mountain',
              'mouse', 'mushroom', 'oak_tree', 'orange', 'orchid',
              'otter', 'palm_tree', 'pear', 'pickup_truck', 'pine_tree',
              'plain', 'plate', 'poppy', 'porcupine', 'possum',
              'rabbit', 'raccoon', 'ray', 'road', 'rocket',
              'rose', 'sea', 'seal', 'shark', 'shrew',
              'skunk', 'skyscraper', 'snail', 'snake', 'spider',
              'squirrel', 'streetcar', 'sunflower', 'sweet_pepper', 'table',
              'tank', 'telephone', 'television', 'tiger', 'tractor',
              'train', 'trout', 'tulip', 'turtle', 'wardrobe',
              'whale', 'willow_tree', 'wolf', 'woman', 'worm',]
```

With the label class names separated out, let's fetch a batch, predict the values and plot them with the actual and predicted labels:

```
batch = next(test_generator)
images = batch[0]
labels = batch[1]

fig = plt.figure(figsize=(10, 10))

for index, image in enumerate(images):
```

```
8     ax = fig.add_subplot(6, 6, index+1)
9     plt.imshow(image)
10
11    image = np.expand_dims(image, 0)
12    pred = model.predict(image)
13    pred = np.squeeze(pred)
14
15    label = np.argmax(labels[index])
16    pred_index = np.argmax(pred)
17
18    ax.set_title(f'Actual: {classnames[label]} \n Pred:
          {classnames[pred_index]}')
19    ax.axis('off')
20
21 plt.tight_layout()
22 plt.show()
```

Figure 68:

Some of these misclassifications are pretty understandable. I have no clue what the second image from the right, in the penultimate row is. Kind of looks like a hedgehog, or maybe a porcupine? Apparently - it's a caterpillar. The shark with the open mouth was classified as a ray, probably because the shape of the shark's head resembles that of a ray. A small brown blob, supposedly a "bear" was classified as a skunk, etc. To be fully fair to the classifier - images as small as these are really confusing.

Is there anything we can do to boost performance? Certainly, a 66% Top-1 Accuracy doesn't scream *"computer vision outperforms humans regularly"*. There are a few things we can do to address performance and boost it. First of all - we'll want to ditch the current architecture, and move to a more robust one, with higher generalization capabilities. Second of all - instead of altering the training images and training from scratch, we can harness the amazing benefits of Transfer Learning and transfer some knowledge from other domains to this one. Third of all - we'll want to perform hyperparameter tuning, and tweak better candidates to squeeze out the best of them.

In the next lesson - we'll be covering Transfer Learning, boosting the accuracy to 80%, and get acquainted with TensorFlow Datasets, one of the best ways to get a hold of standardized datasets, with all the necessary metadata (such as label names, which you'd otherwise have to find online manually), and optimized for being trained on.

5.4 Conclusion

Overfitting isn't inherently a bad thing - it's just *a thing*. No, you don't want overfit end-models, but it shouldn't be treated as the plague and can even be a good sign that a model could perform better given more data and a simplification step. If a model can totally overfit the data, with a near-100% accuracy, it's very likely to be able to fit it at least decently when simplified.

New models are being released and benchmarked against community-accepted datasets frequently, and keeping up with all of them is getting harder.

> Most of these models are open source, and you can implement them yourself as well.

This means that the average enthusiast can load in and play around with the cutting edge models in their home, on very average machines, not only to gain a deeper understanding and appreciation of the craft, but also to contribute to the scientific discourse and publish their own improvements whenever they're made.

> In this lesson, you'll learn how to use pre-trained, cutting edge Deep Learning models for Image Classification and repurpose them for your own specific application. This way, you're leveraging their high performance, ingenious architectures and

> someone else's training time - while applying these models to your own domain!

6 Image Classification with Transfer Learning - Creating Cutting Edge CNN Models

6.1 Transfer Learning for Computer Vision and Convolutional Neural Networks

Knowledge and *knowledge representations* are very universal. A computer vision model trained on one dataset learns to recognize patterns that might be very prevalent in many other datasets.

Notably, in *"Deep Learning for the Life Sciences"*, by Bharath Ramsundar, Peter Eastman, Patrick Walters and Vijay Pande, it's noted that:

> "There have been multiple studies looking into the use of recommendation system algorithms for use in molecular binding prediction. Machine learning architectures used in one field tend to carry over to other fields, so it's important to retain the flexibility needed for innovative work."

For instance, straight and curved lines, which are typically learned at a lower level of a CNN hierarchy are bound to be present in practically all datasets. Some high-level features, such as the ones that distinguish a bee from an ant are going to be represented and learned much higher in the hierarchy:

Figure 69:

The "fine line" between these is what you can reuse! Depending on the level of similarity between your dataset and the one a model's been pre-trained on, you may be able to reuse a small or large portion of it.

> A model that classifies human-made structures (trained on a dataset such as the Places365) and a model that classifies general images (trained on a dataset such as ImageNet) are bound to have **some** shared patterns, although, not a lot.

You might want to train a model to distinguish, say, *buses* and *cars* for a self-driving car's vision system. You may also reasonably choose to use a very performant architecture that has proven to work well on datasets similar to yours. Then, the long process of training begins, and you end up having a performant model of your own!

However, if another model is likely to have similar representations on lower *and* higher levels of abstraction, there's no need to re-train a model from scratch. You may decide to use some of the already pre-trained weights, which are just as applicable to your own application of the model as they were applicable to the creator of the original architecture. You'd be **transferring** some of the knowledge from an already existing model to a new one, and this is known as ***Transfer Learning***. The importance and versatility of transfer learning is, in my opinion, understated. It's oftentimes put to the side, or briefly mentioned at the end of lessons and lectures, and it's oftentimes the last concept covered when learning about CNNs.

Whenever you're reading about the application of computer vision to a specific problem - chances are, it's transfer learning in the background. If you spend your afternoons like me reading research papers in various fields (that I have barely any knowledge in), you'll notice how commonly transfer learning is used, even when not mentioned by that name. It's so prevalent that it's practically *assumed* that transfer learning is used. With pre-loaded models and transferred knowledge - almost *anyone* can utilize the power of deep learning to further a field.

- Doctors can use computer vision models to diagnose images (X-ray, histology, retinoscopy, etc.)
- Cities can use computer vision to detect pedestrians and cars on streets and adapt traffic lights to optimize the flow of transportation
- Malls can use computer vision to detect parking occupancy
- Marine biologists can use computer vision to detect endangered coral reefs

(TensorFlow's Great Barrier Reef competition[62])

- Manufacturers can use computer vision to detect defects in production lines (such as missing pills in medicine)
- News outlets can use computer vision to digitize old newspaper issues
- Agricultural plants can use computer vision to detect crop yields and health (and insects/other pests)

From optimizing workflows and investments to saving human lives - computer vision is *very* applicable. Though - read through the list again. Who are the people using these technologies? Doctors, biologists, farmers, city planners. They might not have a extensive computer/data science background or powerful hardware required to train large networks, but they can see benefits from those networks even if they're not optimized. Through democratized models, they don't need a data science background. Through free and cheap cloud training providers and pre-trained networks, they don't need powerful hardware.

> Training with pre-built architectures and downloadable weights has become so streamlined that a kid with a slow internet connection and barely working computer can create more accurate models than top-of-the-line equipment and professionals could a decade or two ago.

The benefit of transfer learning isn't limited to shortening training. If you don't have a lot of data, a network won't be able to learn some of the distinctions early on. If you train it extensively on one dataset, and then transfer to another one, *a lot of the representations are already learned* and it can be fine-tuned on the new dataset. In the case of CIFAR100 we've worked with in the last lesson - many of the images can be found (in larger sizes) in datasets like ImageNet, and a lot could've been transferred with a pretrained model. This would, in effect, be what data augmentation saught to be - expanding the dataset (albeit, indirectly), with instances of data from another dataset. While you don't *really* expand the new dataset, the knowledge encoded in the model being fine-tuned is transfered between them.

The closer the dataset of a pre-trained model is to your own, the more you can transfer. The more you can transfer, the more of your own time and computation you can save. It's worth remembering that training neural networks does have a carbon footprint, so you're not only saving time!

[62]https://www.kaggle.com/c/tensorflow-great-barrier-reef

Typically, transfer learning is done by loading a pre-trained model, and **freezing** its layers. In many cases, you can just cut off the **classification layer** (the final layers, or, *head/densly-connected layer*) and just re-train the a new top, while keeping all of the other abstraction layers intact. This is paramount to using the convolutional base as a feature extractor, and you just re-train the classifier which contains all of the domain knowledge (the convolutional blocks are much more generic). In other cases, you may decide to re-train several layers in the convolutional hierarchy alongside the top, and this is typically done when the datasets contain sufficiently different data points that re-training multiple layers is warranted. You may also decide to re-train the entirety of the model to fine-tune all of the layers.

These two approaches can be summarized as:

- Using the Convolutional Network as a Feature Extractor
- Fine-Tuning the Convolutional Network

In the former, you use the underlying model as a fixed feature extractor, and just train a dense network on top to discern between these features. In the latter, you fine-tune the entire (or portion of the) convolutional network, if it doesn't already have representative feature maps for some other more specific dataset, while also relying on the already trained feature maps and just updating them to also fit your own needs.

Here's a visual representation of how Transfer Learning works:

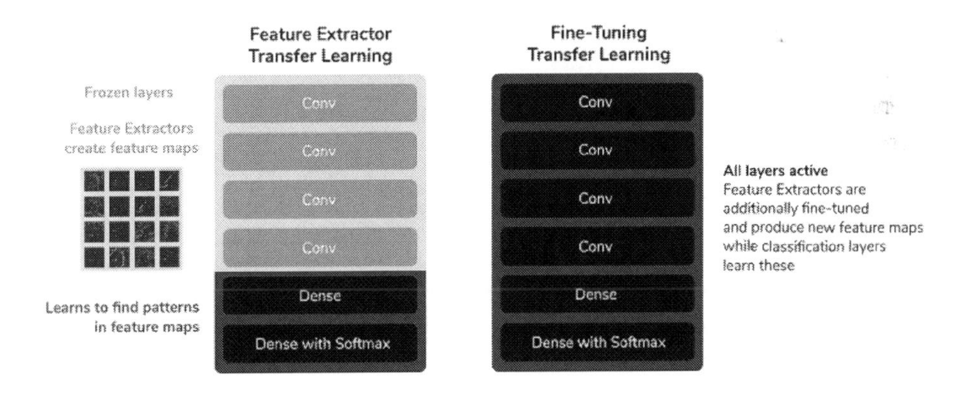

Figure 70:

6.2 Established and Cutting Edge Image Classification Models

Many models exist out there, and for well-known datasets, you're likely to find hundreds of well-performing models published in online repositories and papers. A good holistic view of models trained on the ImageNet dataset can be seen at PapersWithCode[63].

Some of the well-known published architectures that have subsequently been ported into many Deep Learning frameworks include:

- *EfficientNet*
- *SENet*
- *Inception* and *Xception*
- *ResNet*
- *VGGNet*

Note: Being well-known doesn't mean that an architecture is going to perform at the state of the art. For example, you probably don't want to use VGGNet for transfer learning, because newer, more robust, more efficient architectures have been ported and pre-trained.

The list of models on PapersWithCode is constantly being updated, and you shouldn't hang up on the position of these models there. Many of the new models that take the top places are actually based on the ones outlined in the list above.

Unfortunately, some of the newest models aren't ported as pre-trained models within frameworks such as Tensorflow and PyTorch, though, the teams are pretty dilligent in porting them with pre-trained weights. It's not like you'll be losing out on *a lot* of the performance, so going with any of the well-established ones isn't really bad at all.

[63]https://paperswithcode.com/sota/image-classification-on-imagenet

6.3 Transfer Learning with Keras - Adapting Existing Models

With Keras, the pre-trained models are available under the `tensorflow.keras.applications` module. Each model has its own sub-module and class. When loading a model in, you can set a couple of optional arguments to control how the models are being loaded.

Note: You can find the ported models at Keras.io[64], but the list doesn't include the newest and experimental models. For a more up-to-date list, visit TensorFlow's Docs[65].

For instance, the `weights` argument, if present, defines which pre-trained weights are to be used. If omitted, only the architecture (untrained network) will be loaded in. If you supply an `'imagenet'` argument - a pre-trained network will be returned for that dataset. Alternatively, you can provide a path to a file with the weights you want to load in (as long as it's the exact same architecture).

Additionally, since you'll most likely be removing the top layer(s) for Transfer Learning, the `include_top` argument is used to define whether the top layer(s) should be present or not!

```
1 import tensorflow.keras.applications as models
2
3 # 98 MB
4 resnet = models.resnet50.ResNet50(weights = 'imagenet', include_top=False)
5 # 528MB
6 vgg16 = models.vgg16.VGG16(weights = 'imagenet', include_top=False)
7 # 23MB
8 nnm = models.NASNetMobile(weights = 'imagenet', include_top=False)
9 # etc...
```

---

[64]https://keras.io/api/applications/
[65]https://www.tensorflow.org/api_docs/python/tf/keras/applications?version=nightly

Note: If you've never loaded pre-trained models before, they'll be downloaded over an internet connection. This may take anywhere between a few seconds and a couple of minutes, depending on your internet speed and the size of the models. The size of pre-trained models spans from as little as *14MB* (typically lower for *Mobile* models) to as high as *549MB*.

EfficientNet is a family of networks that are quite performant, scalable and, well, efficient. They were made with reducing learnable parameters in mind, so they only have 4M parameters to train. Consider that VGG19, for instance, has 139M. On a home setup, this also helps with training times significantly!

Let's load in one of the members of the EfficientNet family - EfficientNetB0:

```
1 effnet = keras.applications.EfficientNetB0(weights = 'imagenet',
      include_top=False)
2 effnet.summary()
```

This results in:

```
 1 Model: "efficientnetb0"
 2 _________________________________________________________________
 3  Layer (type)                    Output Shape         Param #     Connected to
 4 =================================================================
 5  input_2 (InputLayer)            [(None, None, None,  0           []
 6                                   3)]
 7
 8  rescaling_1 (Rescaling)         (None, None, None,   0
       ['input_2[0][0]']
 9                                  3)
10
11 ...
12 ...
13
14  block7a_project_bn (BatchNorma  (None, None, None,   1280
       ['block7a_project_conv[0][0]']
15  lization)                       320)
16
17  top_conv (Conv2D)               (None, None, None,   409600
       ['block7a_project_bn[0][0]']
18                                  1280)
19
20  top_bn (BatchNormalization)     (None, None, None,   5120
       ['top_conv[0][0]']
21                                  1280)
22
```

```
23  top_activation (Activation)     (None, None, None,    0
        ['top_bn[0][0]']
24                                  1280)
25
26 =========================================================
27 Total params: 4,049,571
28 Trainable params: 4,007,548
29 Non-trainable params: 42,023
30 _________________________________________________________
```

On the other hand, if we were to load in EfficientNetB0 with the top included, we'd also have a few new layers at the end, that were trained to classify the data for ImageNet. This is the top of the model that we'll be training ourselves for our own application:

```
1 effnet = keras.applications.EfficientNetB0(weights = 'imagenet',
      include_top=True)
2 effnet.summary()
```

This would include the final top layers, with a `Dense` classifier in the end:

```
1 Model: "efficientnetb0"
2 _________________________________________________________
3  Layer (type)                    Output Shape          Param #     Connected to
4 =========================================================
5  input_1 (InputLayer)            [(None, 224, 224, 3  0           []
6                                  )]
7
8  rescaling (Rescaling)           (None, 224, 224, 3)  0
        ['input_1[0][0]']
9
10 ...
11 ...
12
13 block7a_project_bn (BatchNorma  (None, 7, 7, 320)   1280
       ['block7a_project_conv[0][0]']
14  lization)
15
16  top_conv (Conv2D)              (None, 7, 7, 1280)   409600
        ['block7a_project_bn[0][0]']
17
18  top_bn (BatchNormalization)    (None, 7, 7, 1280)   5120
        ['top_conv[0][0]']
19
20  top_activation (Activation)    (None, 7, 7, 1280)   0
        ['top_bn[0][0]']
21
22  avg_pool (GlobalAveragePooling  (None, 1280)        0
        ['top_activation[0][0]']
23  2D)
24
25  top_dropout (Dropout)          (None, 1280)         0
        ['avg_pool[0][0]']
```

```
26
27  predictions (Dense)             (None, 1000)          1281000
        ['top_dropout[0][0]']
28
29 ====================================================
30 Total params: 5,330,571
31 Trainable params: 5,288,548
32 Non-trainable params: 42,023
33 ____________________________________________________
```

Their names start with `top_` to annotate the fact that they belong to the top classifier.

Note: This structure may change through time. In an earlier version of Keras, the `top_conv`, `top_bn` and `top_activation` **weren't** loaded in if the `include_top` argument was set to `False`, while in the newest version, they do (and their names still have the `top_` prefix, making it a bit more confusing. **Always** check what the "top" is in a model, before defining your own, whether it's inspired by the original implementation or not.

We won't be using the top layers, as we'll be adding our own top to the EfficientNet model and re-training only the ones we add on top (before fine-tuning the convolutional base). It is worth noting what the architecture is originally using for the top, though! They seem to be using a `GlobalAveragePooling2D` and `Dropout` before the final `Dense` classification layer. These tops are typically optimized for networks, so it's wise to reuse the structure at least for the baseline.

6.3.1 Preprocessing Input for Pre-trained Models

Note: Data preprocessing plays a crucial role in model training, and most models will have different preprocessing pipelines. You don't have to perform guesswork here! Where applicable, a model comes with its own `preprocess_input()` function.

The `preprocess_input()` function applies the same preprocessing steps to the input as they were applied during training. You can import the function from the respective module of the model, if a model resides in its own module. For instance, ResNets have their own `preprocess_input` function:

```
1 from keras.applications.resnet50 import preprocess_input
```

That being said, loading in a model, preprocessing input for it and predicting a result in Keras is as easy as:

```
1 import tensorflow.keras.applications as models
2 from keras.applications.resnet50 import preprocess_input
3
4 resnet50 = models.ResNet50(weights = 'imagenet', include_top=True)
5
6 img = # get data
7 img = preprocess_input(img)
8 pred = resnet50.predict(img)
```

Note: Not all models have a dedicated `preprocess_input()` function, because the preprocessing is *done within the model itself*. For instance, EfficientNet that we'll be using doesn't have its own dedicated preprocessing function, since the preprocessing layers within the model take care of that. This is becoming more and more common.

That's it! Now, since the `pred` array doesn't really contain human-readable data, you can also import the `decode_predictions()` function alongside the `preprocess_input()` function from a module. Alternatively, you can import the generic `decode_predictions()` function that also applies to models that don't have their dedicated modules:

```
1 from keras.applications.model_name import preprocess_input,
      decode_predictions
2 # OR
3 from keras.applications.imagenet_utils import decode_predictions
4 # ...
5 print(decode_predictions(pred))
```

Tying this together, let's get an image of a black bear via `urllib`, save that file into a target size suitable for EfficientNet (the input layer expects a shape of `(batch_size, 224, 224, 3)`) and classify it with the pre-trained model:

```
1 from tensorflow import keras
2 from keras.applications.family_name import preprocess_input,
      decode_predictions
3 from tensorflow.keras.preprocessing import image
4
5 import urllib.request
6 import matplotlib.pyplot as plt
7 import numpy as np
8
9 # Public domain image
10 url =
      'https://upload.wikimedia.org/wikipedia/commons/0/02/Black_bear_large.jpg'
11 urllib.request.urlretrieve(url, 'bear.jpg')
12
13 # Load image and resize (doesn't keep aspect ratio)
14 img = image.load_img('bear.jpg', target_size=(224, 224))
15 # Turn to array of shape (224, 224, 3)
16 img = image.img_to_array(img)
17 # Expand array into (1, 224, 224, 3)
18 img = np.expand_dims(img, 0)
19 # Preprocess for models that have specific preprocess_input() function
20 # img_preprocessed = preprocess_input(img)
21
22 # Load model and run prediction
23 effnet = keras.applications.EfficientNetB0(weights = 'imagenet',
      include_top=True)
24 pred = effnet.predict(img)
25 print(decode_predictions(pred))
```

We got the image from a URL, however - you can fetch the image from a mobile device, a REST API call, or any other source and classify it. Really - using a pre-trained classifier is as easy as importing it, feeding an image into it and decoding the results. You can serve a computer vision model to an end-user with only a few lines of code! This results in:

```
1 [[
2 ('n02133161', 'American_black_bear', 0.6024658),
3 ('n02132136', 'brown_bear', 0.1457715),
4 ('n02134418', 'sloth_bear', 0.09819221),
5 ('n02510455', 'giant_panda', 0.0069221947),
6 ('n02509815', 'lesser_panda', 0.005077324)
7 ]]
```

It's fairly certain that the image is an image of an American Black Bear, which is right! When preprocessed with a preprocessing function, the image may change significantly. For instance, ResNet's preprocessing function would change the color of the bear's fur:

Figure 71:

It looks a lot more brown now! If we were to feed this image into EfficientNet, it'd think it's a *brown bear*:

```
[[
('n02132136', 'brown_bear', 0.7152758),
('n02133161', 'American_black_bear', 0.15667434),
('n02134418', 'sloth_bear', 0.012813852),
('n02134084', 'ice_bear', 0.0067828503), ('n02117135', 'hyena', 0.0050422684)
]]
```

It's important not to mix and match preprocessing functions between models. For instance, ResNet learns that what we see as *brown* is called *black*, since the color got changed through preprocessing, and it only ever saw what we call "brown" with the label "black". Now, it wasn't trained to classify colors - but it was trained to classify between a black bear and a brown bear, and the colors are definitely mixed.

> Is this a good thing or a bad thing?

Depends on who you ask. John Locke, one of the most influential philosophers of all time classified properties of objects into *primary* and *secondary* qualities and made a clear distinction between them. Primary qualities are those that exist independent of an observer. A book is a book and it has a size, irrespective of how I see it. That's a primary quality. Secondary qualities are those that depend on an observer (color, taste, smell), etc.

and these are quite subjective. From an early age, many people have asked themselves whether "my yellow" is the same as "your yellow". We might see different colors but were thaught to call it "yellow". This doesn't change the fact that a *yellow book* is a *book*!

Regardless of whether it's *true* or not, it's *conceivable* that we all see the world in a slightly different way. There is no clear reason why that would stop us from communicating, building and understanding the world, especially since we can assign numerical, ubiqutous values to explain the sources of subjective experience. This isn't "yellow" - it's an electromagnetic wave with a wavelength of around 600nm. Your red and green receptors in the eye react to it and you "see yellow"! Nowadays, we can describe *secondary qualities*, such as *color* as non-disputable properties as well. It is true that it's easier to provide a raw image into a model, have the *model* do the preprocessing (like EfficientNet does) rather than having a separate function, since you then don't have to think about the preprocessing as much. However - it's not objectively better or worse that ResNet "mixes up" colors. As a matter of fact, this diversity in knowledge can actually lead to some beautiful visualizations down the line. We'll see what that entails in another lesson when we cover the **DeepDream algorithm**.

Awesome! The model works. Now, let's add a new top to it and re-train the top to perform classification for something outside of the ImageNet set.

6.3.2 Adding a New Top to a Pre-trained Model

When performing transfer learning, you'll typically be loading models without tops, or remove them manually:

```
1 # Load without top
2 # When adding new layers, we also need to define the input_shape
3 effnet_base = keras.applications.EfficientNetB0(weights = 'imagenet',
4                                                 include_top=False,
5                                                 input_shape=((224, 224, 3)))
6
7 # Or load the full model
8 full_effnet = keras.applications.EfficientNetB0(weights = 'imagenet',
9                                                   include_top=True,
10                                                  input_shape=((224, 224, 3)))
11
12 # And then remove X layers from the top
13 trimmed_effnet = keras.Model(inputs=full_effnet.input,
       outputs=full_effnet.layers[-3].output)
```

We'll be going with the first option since it's more convenient. Depending on whether you'd like to fine-tune the convolutional blocks or not - you'll either freeze or won't freeze them. Say we want to use the underlying pre-trained feature maps and freeze the layers so that we only re-train the new classification layers at the top:

```
effnet_base.trainable = False
```

You don't need to iterate through the model and set each layer to be `trainable` or not, though you can. If you'd like to turn off the first `n` layers, and allow some higher-level feature maps to be fine-tuned, but leave the lower-level ones untouched, you can:

```
for layer in effnet_base.layers[:-2]:
    layer.trainable = False
```

Here, we've set all layers in the base model to be untrainable, except for the last two. If we check the model, there are only ~2.5K trainable parameters now:

```
effnet_base.summary()
```

```
# ...
================================================
Total params: 4,049,571
Trainable params: 2,560
Non-trainable params: 4,047,011
________________________________________________
```

Now, let's define a `Sequential` model that'll be put on top of this `effnet_base`. Fortunately, chaining models in Keras is as easy as making a new model and putting it on top of another one! You can leverage the Functional API and just chain a few new layers on top of a model.

Let's add a `GlobalAveragePooling2D` layer, some `Dropout` and a dense classification layer:

```
gap = keras.layers.GlobalAveragePooling2D()(effnet_base.output,
    training=False)
do = keras.layers.Dropout(0.2)(gap)
output = keras.layers.Dense(100, activation = 'softmax')(do)

new_model = keras.Model(inputs=effnet_base.input, outputs=output)
```

Note: When adding the layers of the EfficientNet, we set the `training` to `False`. This puts the network in *inference mode* instead of *training mode* and it's a different parameter than the `trainable` we've set to `False` earlier. Weight trainability (`trainable`) is different from mode (`training`) for all layers except `BatchNormalization`. This is a crucial step if you wish to unfreeze layers later on as inference mode for `BatchNormalization` will carry over. *BatchNormalization* computes moving statistics. When unfrozen, it'll start applying updates to parameters again, and will "undo" the training done before fine-tuning. Since TF 2.0, setting the model's `trainable` as `False` also turns `training` to `False` but only for `BatchNormalization` layers.

Alternatively, you can use the Sequential API and call the `add()` method multiple times, or pass it in in the list of layers:

```
new_model = keras.Sequential([
    effnet_base,
    keras.layers.GlobalAveragePooling2D(),
    keras.layers.Dropout(0.2),
    keras.layers.Dense(100, activation = 'softmax')
])

new_model.layers[0].trainable = False
```

This adds the entire model as a layer itself, so it's treated as one entity:

```
Layer: 0, Trainable: False # Entire EfficientNet model
Layer: 1, Trainable: True
Layer: 2, Trainable: True
...
```

If a model is sequential, you can simply add it as:

```
new_model = keras.Sequential()
new_model.add(base_network.output) # Add unwrapped layers
new_model.add(...layer)
...
```

Though, this fails for non-sequential models. It's advised to use the Functional API for applications like these, since the Sequential API doesn't offer the required flexibility and not all models are sequential (as a matter of fact, since TF 2.4.0, all pre-trained models are functional). Additionally, you can't easily put the base network into inference mode - there's no `training` argument. The fact that the entire EfficientNet model is a black-box layer doesn't help us work easily with it, so the minor convenience of the Sequential API doesn't really benefit us much, and has several cons.

Back to our model - there are 100 output neurons for the CIFAR100 classes, with a softmax activation. Let's take a look at the trainable layers in the network:

```
for index, layer in enumerate(new_model.layers):
    print("Layer: {}, Trainable: {}".format(index, layer.trainable))
```

This results in:

```
Layer: 0, Trainable: False
Layer: 1, Trainable: False
Layer: 2, Trainable: False
...
Layer: 235, Trainable: False
Layer: 236, Trainable: False
Layer: 237, Trainable: True
Layer: 238, Trainable: True
Layer: 239, Trainable: True
Layer: 240, Trainable: True
Layer: 241, Trainable: True
```

Awesome! Let's load in the dataset, preprocess it and re-train the classification layers on it. We'll be using the same CIFAR100 dataset from the last lesson, since it proved to be a difficult one to train a CNN on. The lack of data and limitations of data augmentation made it difficult to create a powerful classifier. Let's see if we can employ transfer learning to help us!

6.4 TensorFlow Datasets

We'll be working with the *CIFAR100 dataset*[66], again. Though, this time around, we won't be loading it as a bare NumPy array from Keras. We'll be working with TensorFlow Datasets!

Keras' `datasets` module contains a few datasets, but these are mainly meant for benchmarking and learning and aren't too useful beyond that point. We can use `tensorflow_datasets` to get access to a much larger corpora of datasets! Additionally, all of the datasets from the module are standardized, so you don't have to bother with different preprocessing steps for every single dataset you're testing your models out on. While it may sound just like a simple convenience, rather than a game-changer - if you train a lot of models, the time it takes to do overhead work gets beyond annoying. The

[66] https://www.tensorflow.org/datasets/catalog/cifar100

library provides access to datasets from MNIST to Google Open Images (11MB - 565GB), spanning several categories:

- Audio
- D4rl
- Graphs
- Image
- Image Classification
- Object Detection
- Question Answering
- Ranking
- Rlds
- Robomimic
- Robotics
- Text
- Time Series
- Text Simplification
- Vision Language
- Video
- Translate
- etc...

And the list is growing! As of 2022, there are 278 datasets available, the names of which you can obtain via `tfds.list_builders()`. Additionally, TensorFlow Datasets supports *community* datasets, with over 700 HuggingFace datasets and the Kubric dataset generator. If you're building a *general* intelligent system, there's a very good chance there's a public dataset there. For all other purposes - you can download public datasets and work with them, with custom pre-processing steps. Kaggle, HuggingFace and academic repositories are popular choices.

Additionally, in a similar effort, TensorFlow released an amazing GUI tool - Know Your Data[67], which is still in beta (as of writing) and aims to answer important questions on data corruption (broken images, bad labels, etc.), data sensitivity (does your data contain sensitive content), data gaps (obvious lack of samples), data balance, etc.

A lot of these can help with avoiding bias and data skew - arguably one of the most

[67]https://knowyourdata-tfds.withgoogle.com/

important things to do when working on projects that can have an impact on other humans.

Another amazing feature is that datasets coming from TensorFlow Datasets are `tf.data.Dataset` objects, with which you can maximize the performance of your network through pre-fetching, automated optimization, easy transformations, etc.

Note: If you're not a fan of proprietary classes, such as `Dataset` - you can convert it back into a simple NumPy array for framework-agnosticism. It's advised to work with `tf.data.Dataset`s though.

The module can be installed through:

```
1 $ pip install tensorflow_datasets
```

Once installed, you can access the list of available datasets via:

```
1 print(tfds.list_builders())
2 print(f'Number of Datasets: {len(tfds.list_builders())}')
```

```
1 ['abstract_reasoning', 'accentdb', 'aeslc', 'aflw2k3d', ...]
2 Number of Datasets: 278
```

Though, you're more likely to use the relevant web pages on the TensorFlow Datasets website, which offers more information, sample images, etc. rather than this list. To load a dataset, you can use the `load()` function:

```
1 dataset, info = tfds.load("cifar100", as_supervised=True, with_info=True)
2 class_names = info.features["label"].names
3 n_classes = info.features["label"].num_classes
4 print('Class names:', class_names)
5 print('Num of classes:', n_classes)
```

Datasets can be imported as unsupervised or supervised, and with or without additional information, such as the label names and the number of classes. In the code snippet above, we've loaded in `"cifar100"` as a supervised dataset (with labels) and information:

```
Class names: ['apple', 'aquarium_fish', 'baby', ...]
Num of classes: 100
```

The `info.features["label"].names` list can come in handy! It's a list of human-readable labels that correspond to the numerical labels in the dataset. We don't have to find a list manually online or type it out this way!

6.4.1 Train, Test and Validation Splits with TensorFlow Datasets

One of the optional arguments you can pass into the `load()` function is the `split` argument. The new *Split API* allows you to define which *splits* of the dataset you want to split out. By default, for this dataset, it only supports a `'train'` and `'test'` split - these are the "official" splits for *this dataset*. There's no `valid` split.

Note: Each dataset has an *"official"* split. Some only have the 'train' split, some have a 'train' and 'test' split and some even include a 'validation' split. This is the *intended* split and only if a dataset supports a split, can you use that split's string alias. If a dataset contains only a 'train' split, you can split that training data into a train/test/valid set without issues.

These correspond to the `tfds.Split.TRAIN` and `tfds.Split.TEST` and `tfds.Split.VALIDATION` enums, which used to be exposed through the API in an earlier version.

You can really slice a `Dataset` into any arbitrary number of sets, though, we typically do three - `train_set`, `test_set`, `valid_set`:

```
(test_set, valid_set, train_set), info = tfds.load("cifar100",
                                        split=["test", "train[0%:20%]",
                                            "train[20%:]"],
                                        as_supervised=True,
                                            with_info=True)

class_names = info.features["label"].names
```

```
6 n_classes = info.features["label"].num_classes
7 print(f'Class names: {class_names[:10]}...', ) # ['apple', 'aquarium_fish',
      'baby', 'bear', 'beaver', 'bed', 'bee', 'beetle', 'bicycle', 'bottle']...
8 print('Num of classes:', n_classes) # Num of classes: 100
9
10 print("Train set size:", len(train_set)) # Train set size: 40000
11 print("Test set size:", len(test_set)) # Test set size: 10000
12 print("Valid set size:", len(valid_set)) # Valid set size: 10000
```

We've taken `'test'` split and extracted it into the `test_set`. The slice between 0% and 20% of the `'train'` split is assigned to the `valid_set` and everything beyond 25% is the `train_set`. This is validated through the sizes of the sets themselves as well.

Instead of percentages, you can use absolute values or a mix of percentage and absolute values:

```
1 # Absolute value split
2 test_set, valid_set, train_set = tfds.load("cifar100",
3                                            split=["test", "train[0:10000]",
                                                  "train[10000:]"],
4                                            as_supervised=True)
5
6 print("Train set size:", len(train_set)) # Train set size: 40000
7 print("Test set size:", len(test_set)) # Test set size: 10000
8 print("Valid set size:", len(valid_set)) # Valid set size: 10000
9
10
11 # Mixed notation split
12 # 5000 - 50% (25000) left unassigned
13 test_set, valid_set, train_set = tfds.load("cifar100",
14                                            split=["test[:2500]", # First
                                                  2500 of 'test' are assigned
                                                  to `test_set`
15                                            "train[0:10000]",    # 0-10000 of
                                                  'train' are assigned to
                                                  `valid_set`
16                                            "train[50%:]"],        # 50% -
                                                  100% of 'train' (25000)
                                                  assigned to `train_set`
17                                            as_supervised=True)
```

You can additionally do a *union* of sets, which is less commonly used, as sets are interleaved then:

```
1 train_and_test, half_of_train_and_test = tfds.load("cifar100",
2                                 split=['train+test', 'train[:50%]+test'],
3                                 as_supervised=True)
4
5 print("Train+test: ", len(train_and_test))                # Train+test:  60000
6 print("Train[:50%]+test: ", len(half_of_train_and_test)) # Train[:50%]+test:
      35000
```

These two sets are now heavily interleaved.

6.4.2 Even Splits for N Sets

Again, you can create any arbitrary number of splits, just by adding more splits to the split list:

```
split=["train[:10%]", "train[10%:20%]", "train[20%:30%]", "train[30%:40%]",
    ...]
```

However, if you're creating many splits, especially if they're even - the strings you'll be passing in are very predictable. This can be automated by creating a list of strings, with a given equal interval (such as 10%) instead. For exactly this purpose, the `tfds.even_splits()` function generates a list of strings, given a prefix string and the desired number of splits:

```
import tensorflow_datasets as tfds

s1, s2, s3, s4, s5 = tfds.even_splits('train', n=5)
# Each of these elements is just a string
split_list = [s1, s2, s3, s4, s5]
print(f"Type: {type(s1)}, contents: '{s1}'")
# Type: <class 'str'>, contents: 'train[0%:20%]'

for split in split_list:
    test_set = tfds.load("cifar100",
                                split=split,
                                as_supervised=True)
    print(f"Test set length for Split {split}: ", len(test_set))
```

This results in:

```
Test set length for Split train[0%:20%]: 10000
Test set length for Split train[20%:40%]: 10000
Test set length for Split train[40%:60%]: 10000
Test set length for Split train[60%:80%]: 10000
Test set length for Split train[80%:100%]: 10000
```

Alternatively, you can pass in the entire `split_list` as the `split` argument itself, to construct several split datasets outside of a loop:

```
ts1, ts2, ts3, ts4, ts5 = tfds.load("cifar100",
                                split=split_list,
```

```
3                          as_supervised=True)
```

6.4.3 Loading CIFAR100 and Data Augmentation

With a working understanding of `tfds` under your belt - let's load the CIFAR100 dataset in:

```
1 import tensorflow_datasets as tfds
2 import tensorflow as tf
3
4 (test_set, valid_set, train_set), info = tfds.load("cifar100",
5                                         split=["test", "train[0%:20%]",
                                               "train[20%:]"],
6                                         as_supervised=True,
                                               with_info=True)
7
8 class_names = info.features["label"].names
9 n_classes = info.features["label"].num_classes
10 print(f'Class names: {class_names[:10]}...', ) # ['apple', 'aquarium_fish',
      'baby', 'bear', 'beaver', 'bed', 'bee', 'beetle', 'bicycle', 'bottle']...
11 print('Num of classes:', n_classes) # Num of classes: 100
12
13 print("Train set size:", len(train_set)) # Train set size: 40000
14 print("Test set size:", len(test_set)) # Test set size: 10000
15 print("Valid set size:", len(valid_set)) # Valid set size: 10000
```

Let's take note of a couple of relevant variables in a `config` dictionary:

```
1 config = {
2     'TRAIN_SIZE' : len(train_set),
3     'BATCH_SIZE' : 32
4 }
```

Now, the CIFAR100 images are significantly different from the ImageNet images! Namely, CIFAR100 images are just 32x32, while our EfficientNet model expects 224x224 images. We'll want to resize the images in any case. We might also want to apply some transformation functions on duplicate images to artificially expand the sample size per class since the dataset doesn't have enough of them. With `ImageDataGenerator`, we've seen that you have a very loose degree of freedom when it comes to augmentation, and the process is highly automated. When dealing with TensorFlow Datasets, in order to get to use every little bit of optimization they provide - you'll typically use `tf.image` operations to translate, rotate, etc. images in the `preprocess_image()` function.

Instead of a dedicated `preprocess_image()` function, you can simply chain several `map()` calls with lambda functions, but this approach is significantly less readable and isn't recommended for any larger number of operations. It's better to define functions and call them instead of using lambdas.

The downside is - `tf.image` is fairly rudimentary. Unlike Keras' rich(er) operations, there are surprisingly enough only a few that can be used for random augmentation, and they offer a smaller degree of freedom. This is in part because `tf.image` isn't meant to be used for augmentation as much as for general image operations. We'll talk more about Keras augmentations and external libraries later.

Note: A great alternative, making your model more preprocessing-agnostic is to embed preprocessing layers into the model, such as `keras.layers.RandomFlip()` and `keras.layers.RandomRotation(0.2)`.

Let's define a preprocessing function for each image and its associated label:

```
1 def preprocess(image, label):
2     resized_image = tf.image.resize(image, [224, 224])
3     img = tf.image.random_flip_left_right(resized_image)
4     img = tf.image.random_brightness(img, 0.4)
5     # Preprocess image with model-specific function if it has one
6     # processed_image = preprocess_input(resized_image)
7     return img, label
```

Additionally, since we don't want to perform any random transformations to the validation and testing sets, let's define a separate function for those:

```
1 def preprocess_test_valid(image, label):
2     resized_image = tf.image.resize(image, [224, 224])
3     # Preprocess image with model-specific function if it has one
4     # processed_image = preprocess_input(resized_image)
5     return resized_image, label
```

And finally, we'll want to apply this function to each image in the sets! This is easily done via the `map()` function. Since the input into the network also expects batches (`(batch_size, 224, 224, 3)` instead of `(224, 224, 3)`) - we'll also `batch()` the datasets after mapping:

```
train_set =
    train_set.map(preprocess).batch(32).repeat().prefetch(tf.data.AUTOTUNE)
test_set =
    test_set.map(preprocess_test_valid).batch(32).prefetch(tf.data.AUTOTUNE)
valid_set =
    valid_set.map(preprocess_test_valid).batch(32).prefetch(tf.data.AUTOTUNE)
```

In this example, we're using `tf.data` - the built-in module for creating data pipelines and optimizing their usage. It's not to be confused with `tfds`, which is just a library for *fetching* datasets, while `tf.data` does the heavy lifting on the hardware. The `prefetch()` function is optional but helps with efficiency and the `tf.data.AUTOTUNE` call lets TensorFlow optimize how to perform prefetching. As the model is training on a single batch, the `prefetch()` function pre-fetches the next batch so it's not waited upon when the training step is finished. Similarly enough, you could use functions like `cache()` and `interleave()` to further optimize IO and data extraction, though, these aren't to be used blindly. If used at an incorrect place or time, they're likely to make your pipelines *slower*! We'll dedicate a lesson to optimizing data pipelines later. For now - let's just `prefetch()`.

We have a `repeat()` call on the `train_set`, which isn't present in other sets. This is analogous to the `ImageDataGenerator` class, which produces an infinite number of training samples, with random transformations. On each request, the `preprocess_image()` function we wrote will randomly transform the incoming images, so we have a fresh steady stream of slightly altered data. We don't want to do this for the testing and validation sets, other than making the images the same size and applying the common pre-processing step if there is one (EfficientNetB0 doesn't have an external preprocessing function).

Note: Test-time augmentation is a thing too.

Let's quickly take a look at some of the images from any of the sets:

```
fig = plt.figure(figsize=(10, 10))

```

```
3 i = 1
4 for entry in test_set.take(25):
5
6     sample_image = np.squeeze(entry[0].numpy()[0])
7     sample_label = class_names[entry[1].numpy()[0]]
8     ax = fig.add_subplot(5, 5, i)
9
10    ax.imshow(np.array(sample_image, np.int32))
11    ax.set_title(f"Class: {sample_label}")
12    ax.axis('off')
13    i = i+1
14
15 plt.tight_layout()
16 plt.show()
```

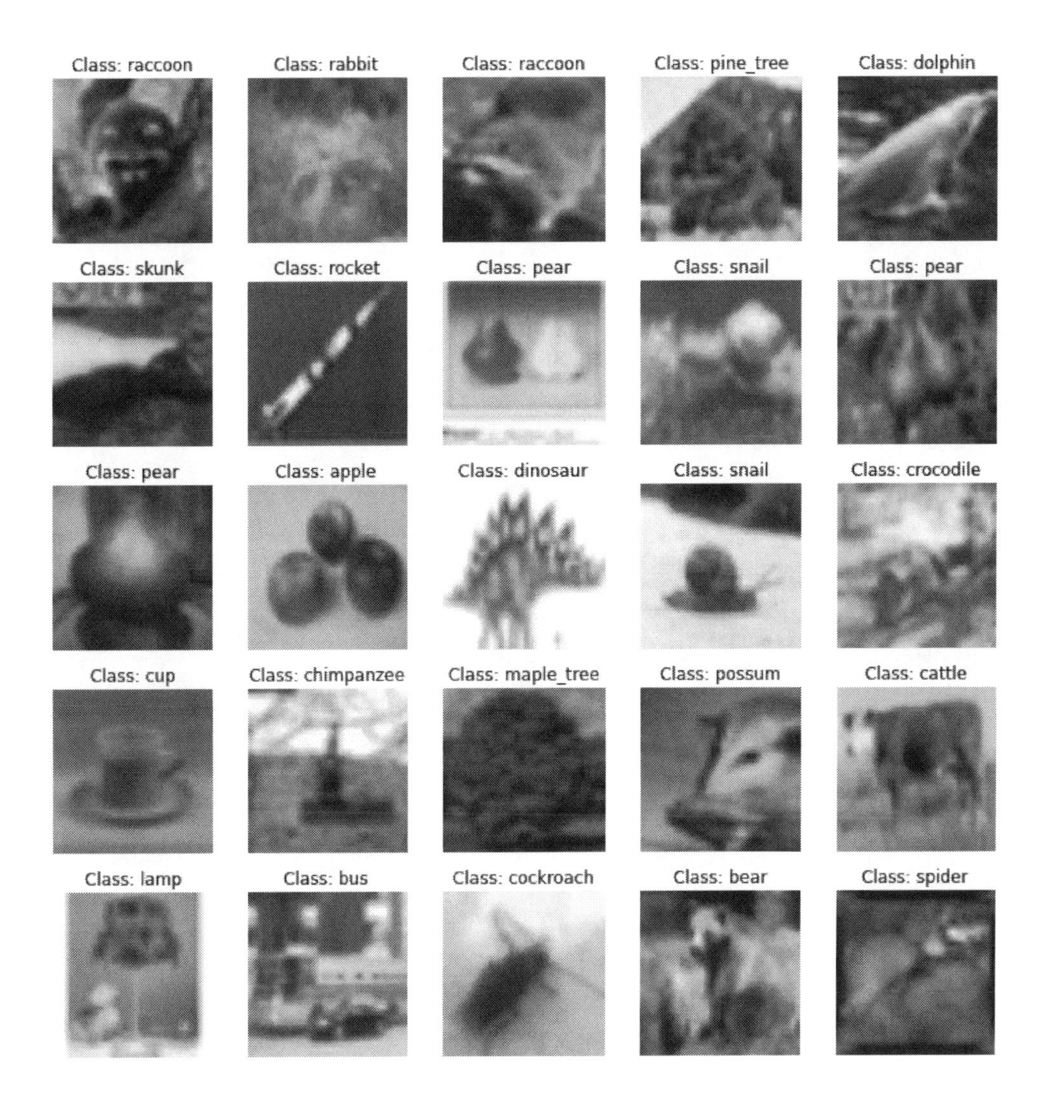

Figure 72:

6.5 Training a Model with Transfer Learning

With the data loaded, preprocessed and split into adequate sets - we can finally train the model on it.

Since we're doing sparse classification, a `sparse_categorical_crossentropy` loss should work well, and the `Adam` optimizer is a reasonable default optimizer. Let's compile the model, and train it on a few epochs. It's worth remembering that most of the layers in the network are frozen! We're only training the new classifier on top of the extracted feature maps.

Only once we train the top layers, we may decide to *unfreeze* the feature extraction layers, and let them fine-tune a bit more. This step is optional but allows you to *really* squeeze out the best of a model, but naturally takes more resources to do. A good rule of thumb is to try and compare the datasets and guesstimate which levels of the hierarchy you can re-use without re-training, to avoid re-training some of the levels that might be redundant to re-train if your machine can't computationally handle it.

It's actually surprising how well ImageNet weights transfer to *most* datasets, even if they don't appear to have any remote connection to the domain. We'll especially see this in the next Guided Project on breast cancer classification from histology images. Another good rule of thumb is to always use transfer learning when you can.

Let's compile the network and check its structure:

```
1 checkpoint = keras.callbacks.ModelCheckpoint(filepath =
      'effnet_transfer_learning.h5', save_best_only=True)
2
3 new_model.compile(loss = "sparse_categorical_crossentropy",
4                   optimizer = keras.optimizers.Adam(),
5                   metrics=["accuracy",
                        keras.metrics.SparseTopKCategoricalAccuracy(k=3)])
6
7 new_model.summary()
```

This is a great time to validate whether you've correctly frozen the layers:

```
1 ...
2 =================================================================
3 Total params: 4,177,671
4 Trainable params: 128,100
5 Non-trainable params: 4,049,571
6 _________________________________________________________________
```

Only 128k trainable parameters! Naturally, it'll take longer to train this network than a 128k network, since there's a lot more going on - the entirety of the network is there, just not all of it is trainable. It'll take less time than training the entire network, though. Let's train the new network (really, only the top of it) for 10 epochs:

```
history = new_model.fit(train_set,
                        epochs=10,
                        steps_per_epoch =
                            config['TRAIN_SIZE']/config['BATCH_SIZE'],
                        callbacks=[checkpoint],
                        validation_data=valid_set)
```

Since the `train_set` is infinite, we'll want to define the `steps_per_epoch`. This may take some time and is ideally done on a GPU. Depending on how large the model is, and the dataset being fed into it. If you don't have access to a GPU, it's advised to run this code on any of the cloud providers that give you access to a free GPU, such as Google Colab, Kaggle Notebooks, etc. Each epoch can take anywhere from 60 seconds on stronger GPUs to 10 minutes, on weaker ones.

This is the point in which you sit back and go grab a coffee (or tea)! After 10 epochs, the train and validation accuracy are looking good:

```
Epoch 1/10
1250/1250[==============================] - 97s 76ms/step - loss: 1.9179 -
    accuracy: 0.5196 - sparse_top_k_categorical_accuracy: 0.7216 - val_loss:
    1.3436 - val_accuracy: 0.6324 - val_sparse_top_k_categorical_accuracy:
    0.8225
...
Epoch 10/10
1250/1250[==============================] - 86s 74ms/step - loss: 0.8610 -
    accuracy: 0.7481 - sparse_top_k_categorical_accuracy: 0.9015 - val_loss:
    1.0820 - val_accuracy: 0.6935 - val_sparse_top_k_categorical_accuracy:
    0.8651
```

It has a 69% validation accuracy, and an 86% Top-3 validation accuracy. These are far from the potential of the network though - the classification top has probably done all it could with the feature extractors as they are now. Let's take a look at the learning curves!

6.5.1 Evaluating Before Fine-Tuning

Let's first test this model out, before trying to unfreeze all of the layers. We'll perform some basic evaluation - metric, learning curves and a confusion matrix. Let's start with the metrics:

```
new_model.evaluate(test_set)
# 157/157 [==============================] - 10s 65ms/step - loss: 1.0806 -
    accuracy: 0.6884 - sparse_top_k_categorical_accuracy: 0.8718
```

~69% on the testing set, and close to the accuracy on the validation set. It has a pretty decent 87% Top-3 accuracy. Looks like our model is generalizing well, but there's still room for improvement. Let's take a look at the learning curves:

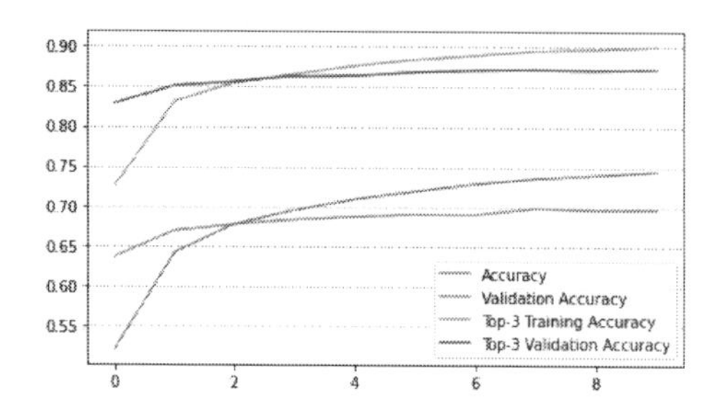

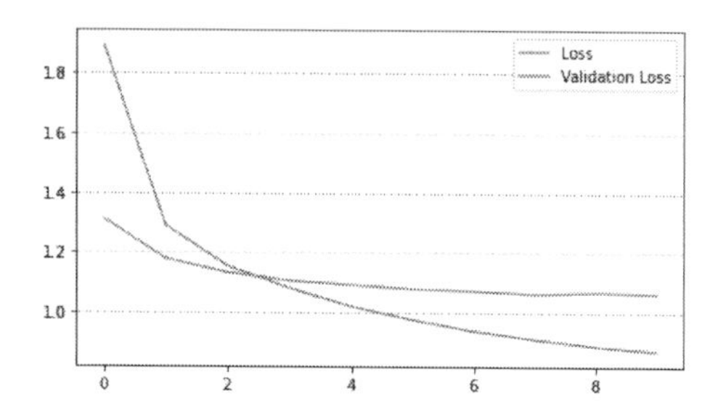

Figure 73:

The training curves are to be expected - they're pretty short since we only trained for 10 epochs, but they've quickly plateaued, so we probably wouldn't have gotten much better performance with more epochs.

Let's predict the test set and extract the labels from it to produce a classification report and confusion matrix:

```
y_pred = new_model.predict(test_set)
labels = tf.concat([y for x, y in test_set], axis=0)
```

Since we have 100 classes - both the classification report and confusion matrix are going to be *very large* and hardly readable:

```
from sklearn import metrics
print(metrics.classification_report(labels, np.argmax(y_pred, axis=1)))
```

```
        precision    recall  f1-score   support

   0         0.89      0.89      0.89        55
   1         0.76      0.78      0.77        49
   2         0.45      0.64      0.53        45
   3         0.45      0.58      0.50        52
...
```

We only have around 50 images per class in the testing set, but we can't really get more than that. It's clear that some classes are better-learned than other classes, such as 0 having significantly higher recall and precision than, say, class 3.

This is actually surprising, since class `0` is `apple` and `3` is `bear`! ImageNet has images of bears, and even classifies different types of bears, so you'd expect the network to generalize to bears well, transfering the knowledge from ImageNet. If anything - this speaks about how much of a "prescription" this network effectively has, given how small the images are.

Let's plot the confusion matrix:

```
from sklearn.metrics import confusion_matrix
import seaborn as sns

matrix = confusion_matrix(labels, y_pred.argmax(axis=1))

# Plot on heatmap
fig, ax = plt.subplots(figsize=(15, 15))
sns.heatmap(matrix, ax=ax, fmt = 'g')

# Stylize heatmap
ax.set_xlabel('Predicted labels')
ax.set_ylabel('True labels')
ax.set_title('Confusion Matrix')

# Set ticks
ax.xaxis.set_ticks(np.arange(0, 100, 1))
ax.yaxis.set_ticks(np.arange(0, 100, 1))
ax.xaxis.set_ticklabels(class_names, rotation=90, fontsize=8)
ax.yaxis.set_ticklabels(class_names, rotation=0, fontsize=8)
```

This results in:

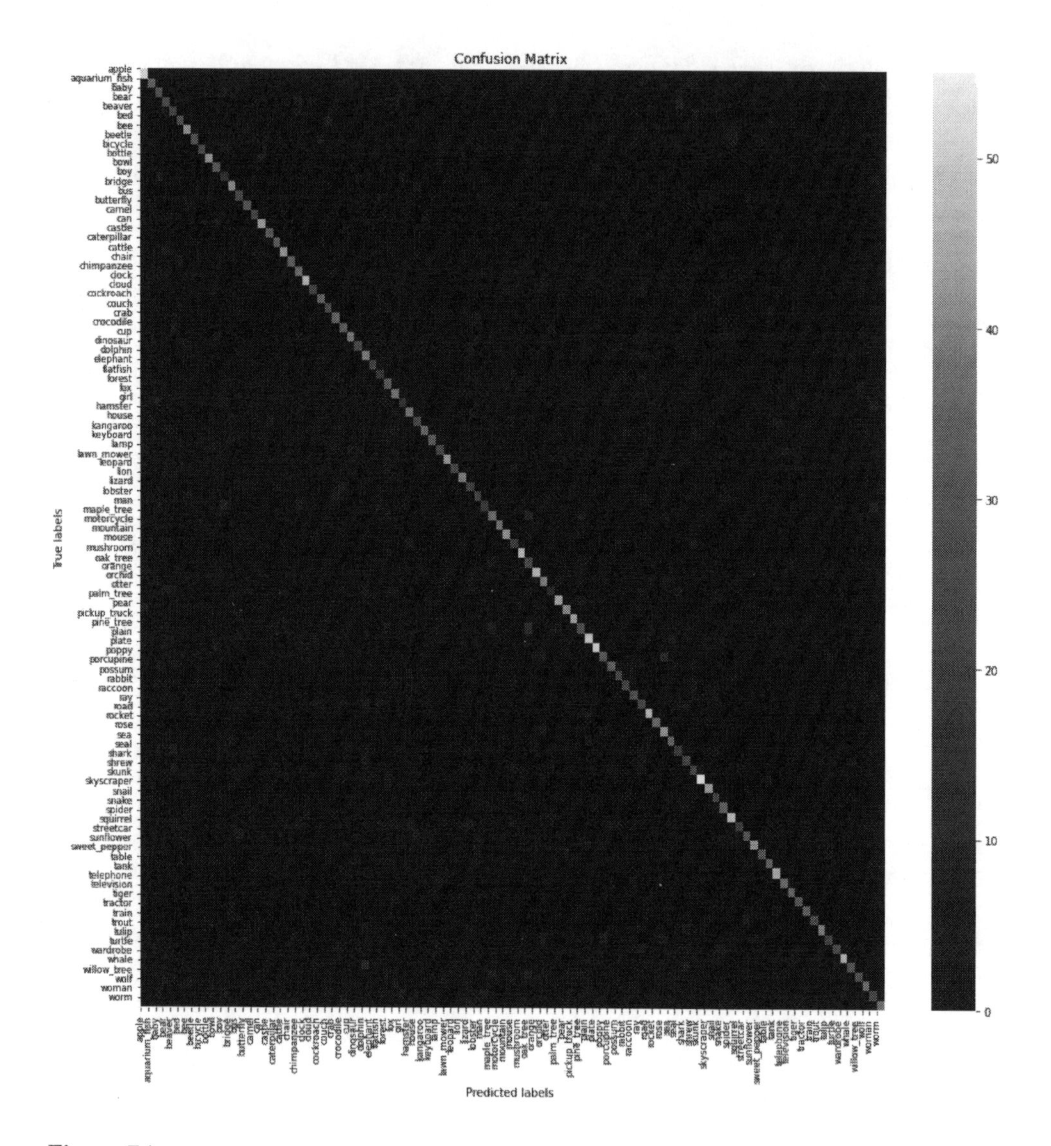

Figure 74:

Again - the confusion matrix is pretty large, since we have 100 classes. Though, for the most part, it looks like it's actually generalizing to classses well, albeit, not ideal.

Can we fine-tune this network further? We've replaced and re-trained the top layers concerned with classification of feature maps, but the feature maps themselves might not be ideal! While they are *pretty good*, these images are simply different from ImageNet, so it's worth taking the time to update the feature extraction layers as well. Let's try unfreezing the convolutional layers and fine-tuning them as well.

6.5.2 Unfreezing Layers - Fine-Tuning a Network Trained with Transfer Learning

Once you've finished re-training the top layers, you can close the deal and be happy with your model. For instance, suppose you got a 95% accuracy - you seriously don't need to go further. However, why not?

If you can squeeze out an additional 1% in accuracy, it might not sound like a lot, but consider the other end of the trade. If your model has a 95% accuracy on 100 samples, it misclassified 5 samples. If you up that to 96% accuracy, it misclassified 4 samples.

> The 1% of accuracy translates to a 25% decrease in false classifications.

Whatever you can further squeeze out of your model can actually make a significant difference on the number of incorrect classifications. Again, the images in CIFAR100 are *much* smaller than ImageNet images, and it's almost as if someone with great eyesight suddenly gained a huge prescription and only saw the world through blurry eyes. The feature maps *have to* be at least somewhat different!

Let's save the model into a file so we don't lose the progress, and unfreeze/fine-tune a loaded copy, so we don't accidentally mess up the weights on the original one:

```
1 new_model.save('effnet_transfer_learning.h5')
2 loaded_model = keras.models.load_model('effnet_transfer_learning.h5')
```

Now, we can fiddle around and change the `loaded_model` without impacting `new_model`. To start out, we'll want to change the `loaded_model` from inference mode back to training mode - i.e. *unfreeze the layers* so that they're trainable again.

Note: Again, if a network uses `BatchNormalization` (and most do), you'll want to keep them frozen while fine-tuning a network. Since we're not freezing the entire base network anymore, we'll just freeze the `BatchNormalization` layers instead and allow other layers to be altered.

Let's turn off the `BatchNormalization` layers so our training doesn't go down the drain:

```
for layer in loaded_model.layers:
    if isinstance(layer, keras.layers.BatchNormalization):
        layer.trainable = False
    else:
        layer.trainable = True

for index, layer in enumerate(loaded_model.layers):
    print("Layer: {}, Trainable: {}".format(index, layer.trainable))
```

Let's check if that worked:

```
Layer: 0, Trainable: True
Layer: 1, Trainable: True
Layer: 2, Trainable: True
Layer: 3, Trainable: True
Layer: 4, Trainable: True
Layer: 5, Trainable: False
Layer: 6, Trainable: True
Layer: 7, Trainable: True
Layer: 8, Trainable: False
...
```

Awesome! Before we can do anything with the model, to "solidify" the trainability, we have to recompile it. This time around, we'll be using a smaller `learning_rate`, since we don't want to *train* the network, but rather just fine-tune what's already there:

```
checkpoint = keras.callbacks.ModelCheckpoint(filepath =
    'effnet_transfer_learning_finetuned.h5', save_best_only=True)

# Recompile after turning to trainable
loaded_model.compile(loss = "sparse_categorical_crossentropy",
                  optimizer = keras.optimizers.Adam(learning_rate=3e-6,
                      decay=(1e-6)),
                  metrics=["accuracy",
                      keras.metrics.SparseTopKCategoricalAccuracy(k=3)])

history = loaded_model.fit(train_set,
                        epochs=15,
                        steps_per_epoch =
                            config['TRAIN_SIZE']/config['BATCH_SIZE'],
                        callbacks=[checkpoint],
                        validation_data=valid_set)
```

Again, this may take some time - so sip on another beverage of your choice (stay hydrated) while this runs in the background. The fine-tuning time heavily depends on the architecture you chose to go with but most of the cutting-edge architectures will take some time on a home-grade setup.

Once it finishes, it should reach up to around 80% in accuracy and around 93% on Top-3 accuracy on the validation set:

```
1 Epoch 1/15
2 1250/1250[==============================] - 384s 322ms/step - loss: 0.6567 -
      accuracy: 0.8024 - sparse_top_k_categorical_accuracy: 0.9356 - val_loss:
      0.8687 - val_accuracy: 0.7520 - val_sparse_top_k_categorical_accuracy:
      0.9069
3 ...
4 Epoch 15/15
5 1250/1250[==============================] - 377s 322ms/step - loss: 0.3858 -
      accuracy: 0.8790 - sparse_top_k_categorical_accuracy: 0.9715 - val_loss:
      0.7071 - val_accuracy: 0.7971 - val_sparse_top_k_categorical_accuracy:
      0.9331
```

Additionally, if you take a look at the learning curves, they appear to have not plateaued, and we could've probably increased the performance of the model further if we were just to train it for longer:

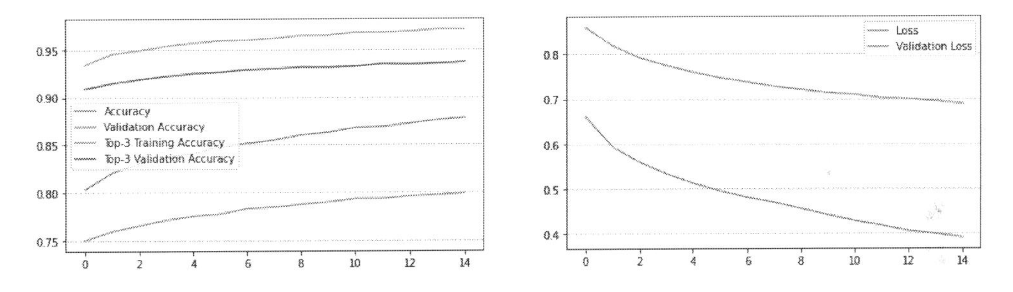

Figure 75:

Note: We probably could've seen further performance increases through further training. Note that training for longer, naturally, takes time. While comparatively low to many other architectures and datasets, a 100 epochs on this dataset took over 10h to train on a home GPU. It's understandable if you're antsy about waiting this long, but unfortunately, 10h isn't even too long to wait for a network to train.

Let's evaluate it and visualize some of the predictions:

```
loaded_model.evaluate(test_set)
# 157/157 [==============================] - 10s 61ms/step - loss: 0.7041 -
    accuracy: 0.7920 - sparse_top_k_categorical_accuracy: 0.9336
```

```
fig = plt.figure(figsize=(10, 10))

i = 1
for entry in test_set.take(25):
    # Predict, get the raw Numpy prediction probabilities
    # Reshape entry to the model's expected input shape
    pred = np.argmax(loaded_model.predict(entry[0].numpy()[0].reshape(1,
        224, 224, 3)))

    # Get sample image as numpy array
    sample_image = entry[0].numpy()[0]
    # Get associated label
    sample_label = class_names[entry[1].numpy()[0]]
    # Get human label based on the prediction
    prediction_label = class_names[pred]
    ax = fig.add_subplot(5, 5, i)
    # Plot image and sample_label alongside prediction_label
    ax.imshow(np.array(sample_image, np.int32))
    ax.set_title(f"Actual: {sample_label}\nPred: {prediction_label}")
    ax.axis('off')
    i = i+1

plt.tight_layout()
plt.show()
```

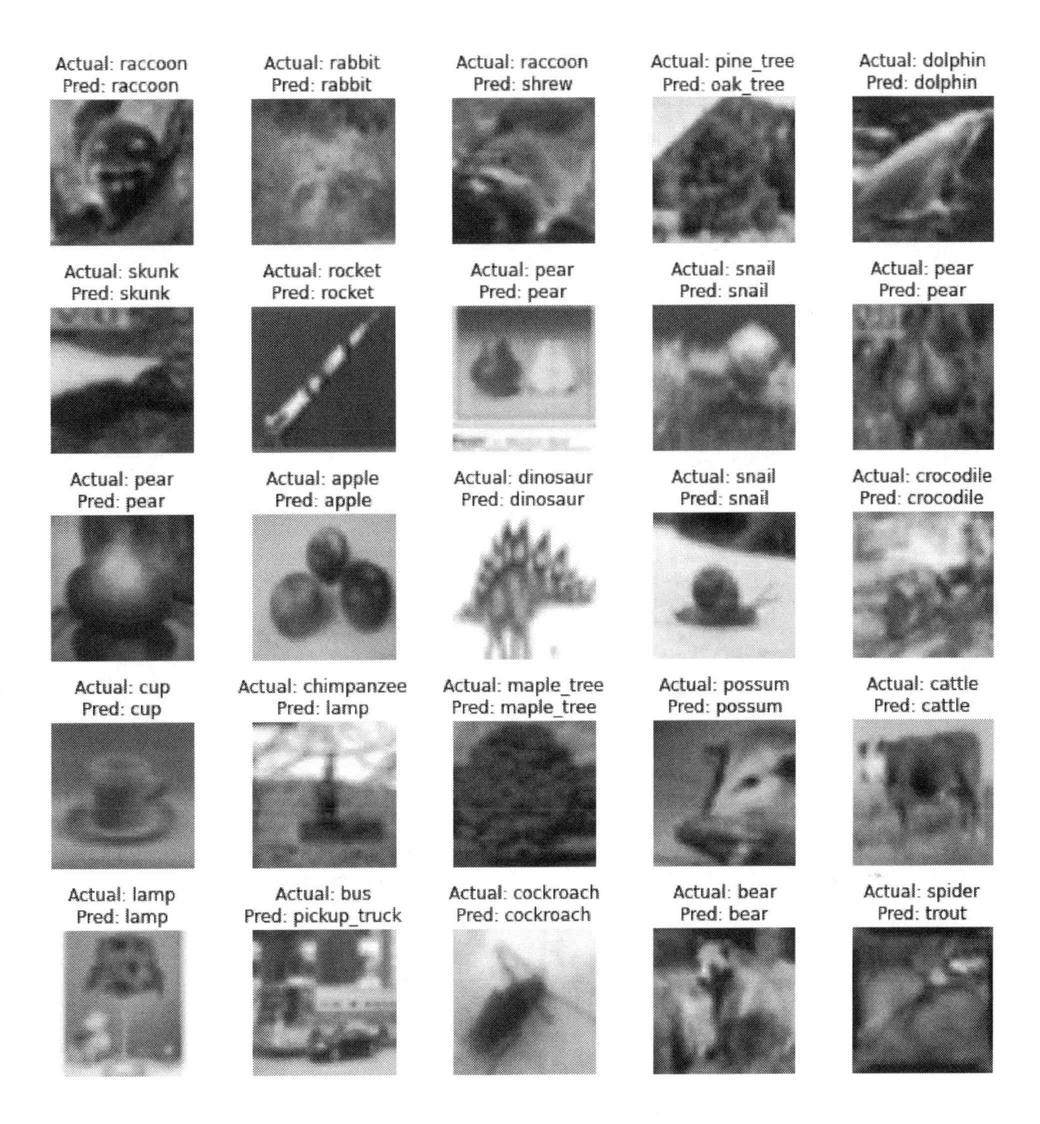

Figure 76:

A couple of misclassifications, as you'd expect of an 80% accurate model. A raccoon was classified as a shrew which is a mole-like animal (not *too far* from the truth). A chimpanzee was classified as a lamp (I'd have classified it as a beer bottle). A bus was classified as a pickup truck. This one is curious - as the blue stripe on the bus makes it appear a bit like a pickup truck. It looks like the model understood the blue stripe as the end of the bed of a pickup truck, instead of recognizing the grey top as part of the bus. Finally, a spider was classified as a trout, which is a very different class, but the image is so blurred and small that It's totally understandable.

Our previous model, a custom one, built and trained on this dataset had a 66% Top-1 accuracy, which means we've **decreased the error-rate by** 39% (from 33 per 100 images to 20 per 100 images).

If you want to obtain the Top-K predictions (not just the most probable one), instead of using `argmax()` you can utilize TensorFlow's `top_k()` method:

```
1 pred = loaded_model.predict(np.expand_dims(img, 0))
2 top_probas, top_indices = tf.nn.top_k(pred, k=k)
3
4 print(top_probas)  # tf.Tensor([[0.900319   0.07157221 0.00889194]],
      shape=(1, 3), dtype=float32)
5 print(top_indices) # tf.Tensor([[66 88 21]], shape=(1, 3), dtype=int32)
```

If you'd like to display this information alongside the input and the predictions - you could plot the input image, next to a bar chart of the confidence of the network:

```
 1 for entry in test_set.take(1):
 2     img = entry[0][0].numpy().astype('int')
 3     label = entry[1][1]
 4
 5     # Predict and get top-k classes
 6     pred = loaded_model.predict(np.expand_dims(img, 0))
 7     top_probas, top_indices = tf.nn.top_k(pred, k=3)
 8     # Convert to NumPy, squeeze and convert to list for ease of plotting
 9     top_probas = top_probas.numpy().squeeze().tolist()
10     # Turn indices into classes
11     pred_classes = []
12     for index in top_indices.numpy().squeeze():
13         pred_classes.append(class_names[index])
14
15     fig, ax = plt.subplots(1, 2, figsize=(16, 4))
16     ax[0].imshow(img)
17     ax[0].axis('off')
18     ax[1].bar(pred_classes, top_probas)
19
20 plt.tight_layout()
```

Here, the network is pretty confident that the image is an image of a raccoon. There's a bit of a tiger and a chimpanzee there, but the probabilities are really low:

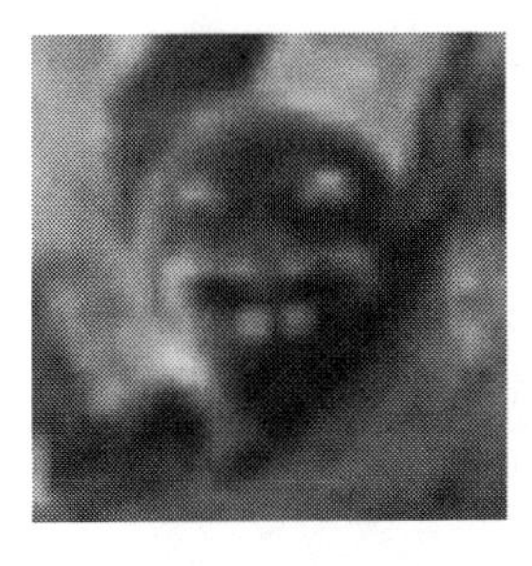

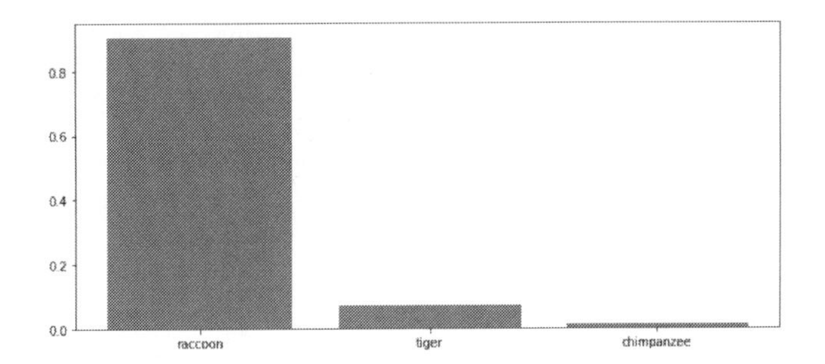

Figure 77:

What about the spider-trout from before?

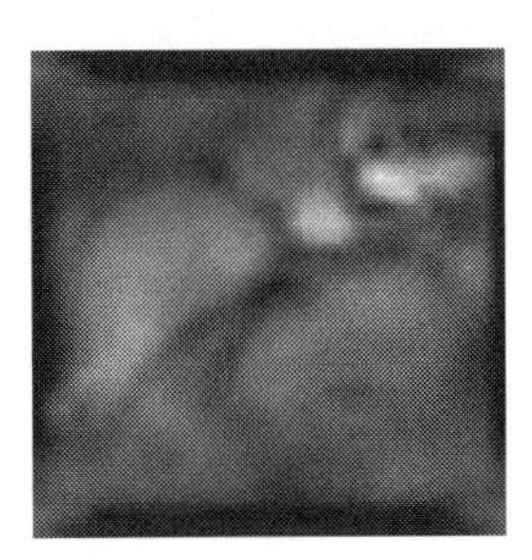

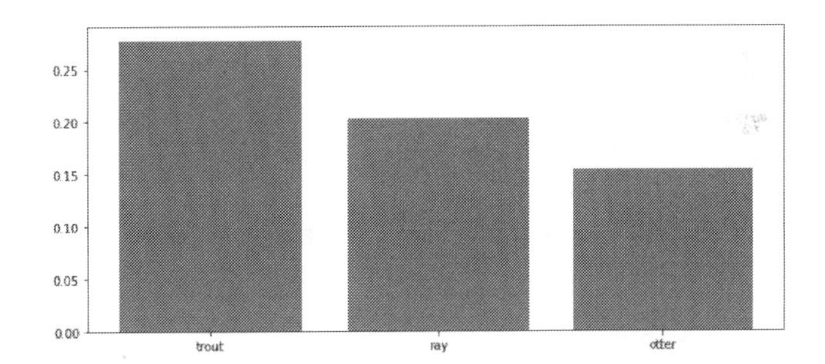

Figure 78:

The network is fairly lost here - all of the probabilities are low, and none of them are right. If you take the top probability at face value and return that class, it sounds like the model was seriously wrong, but when you inspect its confidence, its "line of reasoning" can become a lot clearer. Generally, and especially when returning results to an end-user, you'll want to display the confidence of the model, and potentially other Top-K classes and their probabilities, if the highest probability isn't too high.

For instance, if the top probability is below, say, 50% - you could return multiple classes and their probabilities, such as in the second input image. If the model is fairly certain, you could return just the top class and its probability.

Finally, let's take a look at the confusion matrix compared to the previous one:

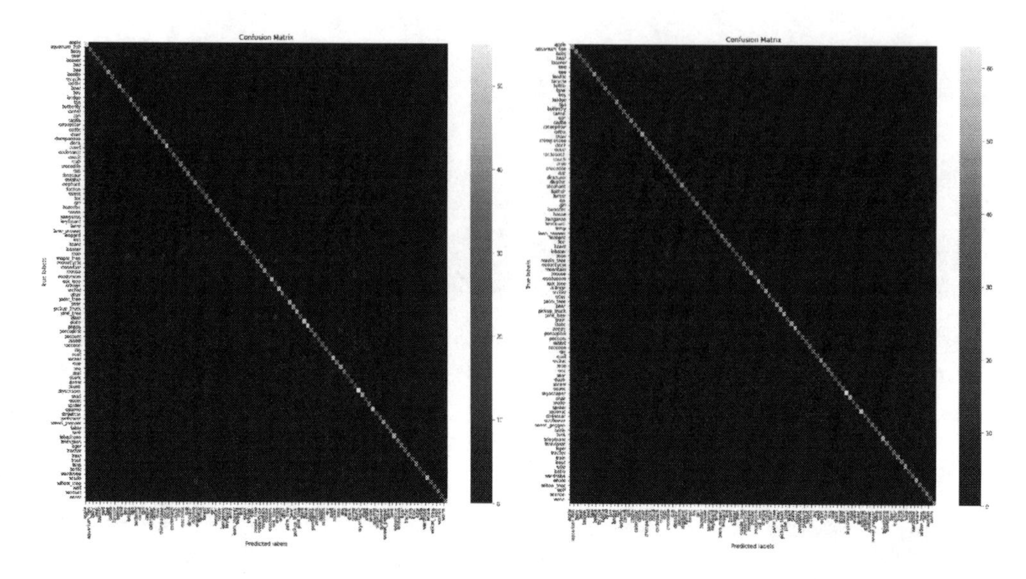

Figure 79:

While it's still not perfect - it's looking much cleaner!

6.6 Conclusion

Transfer learning is the process of transferring already learned knowledge representations from one model to another, when applicable. This concludes the lesson on transfer learning for Image Classification with Keras and Tensorflow. We've started out with taking a look at what transfer learning is and how knowledge representations can be shared between models and architectures.

Then, we've taken a look at some of the most popular and cutting edge models for Image Classification released publically, and piggy-backed on one of them - EfficientNet - to help us in classifying some of our own data. We've taken a look at how to load and examine pre-trained models, how to work with their layers, predict with them and decode the results, as well as how to define your own layers and intertwine them with the existing architecture.

This lesson introduced TensorFlow Datasets, the benefits of using the module and the basics of working with it. Finally, we've loaded and preprocessed a dataset, and trained our new classification top layers on it, before unfreezing the layers and fine-tuning it further through several additional epochs.

In this lesson, we'll be diving into a hands-on project, from start to finish, contemplating what the challenge is, what the reward would be for solving it. Specifically, we'll be classifying *benign* and *malignant* **Invasive Ductal Carcinoma** from histopathology images. If you're unfamiliar with this terminology - no need to worry, it's covered in the guided project.

We'll start out by performing *Domain Research*, and getting familiar with the domain we're trying to solve a problem in. We'll then proceed with *Exploratory Data Analysis*, and begin the standard Machine Learning Workflow. For this guide, we'll both be building a CNN from scratch, as well as use pre-defined architectures (such as the **EfficientNet** family, or **ResNet** family). Once we benchmark the most promising baseline model - we'll perform hyperparameter tuning, and evaluate the model.

7 Guided Project - Breast Cancer Classification with Keras

In this lesson, we'll be diving into a hands-on project, from start to finish, contemplating what the challenge is, what the reward would be for solving it. Specifically, we'll be classifying *benign* and *malignant* **Invasive Ductal Carcinoma** from histopathology images. If you're unfamiliar with this terminology - no need to worry, it's covered in the guided project.

We'll start out by performing *Domain Research*, and getting familiar with the domain we're trying to solve a problem in. We'll then proceed with *Exploratory Data Analysis*, and begin the standard Machine Learning Workflow. For this guide, we'll both be building a CNN from scratch, as well as use pre-defined architectures (such as the **EfficientNet** family, or **ResNet** family). Once we benchmark the most promising baseline model - we'll perform hyperparameter tuning, and evaluate the model.

7.1 Machine Learning in Medicine

Machine Learning has been increasingly employed in medicine, and is helping save lives from a wide variety of medical conditions. The application of Machine Learning in Medicine is vast, and an extremely complex topic in and of itself, but some of the major areas include:

- **Precision Medicine** (Tailoring medicine to individuals)
- **Medical Imaging Diagnosis** (Diagnosing conditions based on images, etc.)
- **Drug Discovery** (Generating structures such as proteins or drug-like molecules, bioactivity prediction, etc.)

> Precision Medicine is a movement that focuses on personalized, precise medicine, which naturally builds upon robust datasets, unique to the individuals receiving treatment.

Instead of a one-size-fits-all approach, which has been employed so far, Precision Medicine aims to tailor treatment to an individual based on their lifestyle, environment and genetics. Naturally, Precision Medicine is *built* on top of robust datasets, generated from the ever-increasing list of gadgets and devices we can use to monitor health.

> **Medical Imaging Diagnosis** is a field which is helping automate and even improve the accuracy of diagnosis based on medical imagery.

Figuring out whether someone's afflicted with a given ailment is difficult. It takes years of practice, intuition and experience to diagnose with a relative level of certainty whether someone's afflicted with a condition or not based on medical imagery. Automating this process has *significant* implications for the speed of diagnosis - and the faster someone can get diagnosed, the faster they can receive treatment. In some cases, this time can be of the essence.

> **Drug Discovery** is a field in which we utilize Machine Learning methods, as well as computational aids to search the landscape of chemical compounds, and predict their properties in an environment as complex as the human body.

Drug Discovery with Machine Learning is a new, up-and-coming field, with major financial and temporal implications. Designing a drug can take years if not decades, and *in-vitro/in-vivo* studies take place in *real time*, under varying conditions. Delegating any of these tasks can create an environment in which we can perform rapid drug design, and provide remedies to new conditions faster than ever.

> As a Machine Learning practitioner, **you** can help make a difference.

In this guided project, we'll be working within the field of ***Medical Imaging Diagnosis***, tackling the classification of one of the major groups of cancer - **breast cancer**.

7.2 Challenge/Problem Statement

Let's take a moment to define the problem we're trying to solve:

> Cancer is oftentimes physically noticable in tissue and can be more easily treatable when detected early. **Histology** studies tissues, and **Pathology** studies diseases. **Histopathology** studies diseases in tissues! Pathologists examine images of tissue (histology images), and come up with a verdict. Cancer kills up to 10M people every year[a] and is one of the leading causes of death globally. Alongside lung, colon and stomach cancer - breast cancer kills 700.000 people every year. Certain areas might not have the equipment or schooling necessary to make diagnosis a swift

> procedure, so patients might have to travel to get diagnosed, prolonging the period in which they can't receive treatment.
>
> [a]https://ourworldindata.org/cancer#deaths-from-cancer

In a sense, pathologists are performing classification (*positive,* or *negative*) based on patterns and occurrences in the images (visual features). This is a long and laborious process, and requires experience.

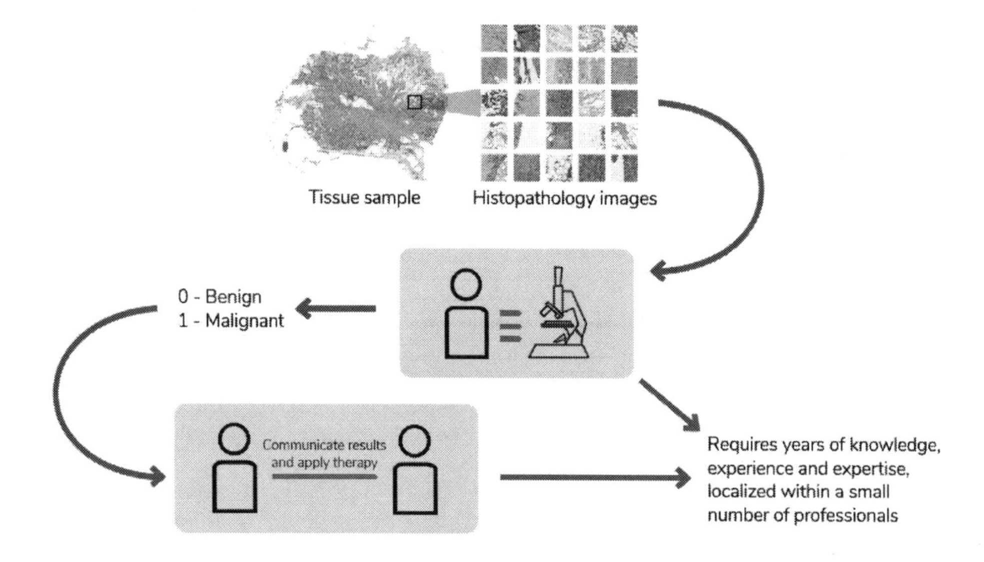

Figure 80:

7.3 Reward for Solving the Problem

> Fast, accurate and early diagnosis improves the probability of survival. Machine Learning models can be deployed globally or locally, and can process large sums of data in a fraction of the time it takes humans. On various occassions - it's been proven that Machine Learning models, when trained right, can distinguish features better than humans, and can perform image classification to a higher degree of accuracy, even without much context, and/or low image resolution.

According to Cleveland Clinic[68]:

> Invasive ductal carcinoma is quite curable, especially when detected and treated early. The five-year survival rate for localized invasive ductal carcinoma is high —nearly 100% when treated early on. If the cancer has spread to other tissues in the region, the five-year survival rate is 86%. If the cancer has metastasized to distant areas of your body, the five-year survival rate is 28%.

A quick calculation shows that early detection can save up to 400.000 lives annually. There's a large incentive to provide global, accessible, accurate and swift diagnosis tools, especially in regions where expertise is hard to obtain and come by. With automation-prone tasks out of the way, doctors can focus on what they're the best at - administering medicine, observing the effects and steering the procedure to help patients.

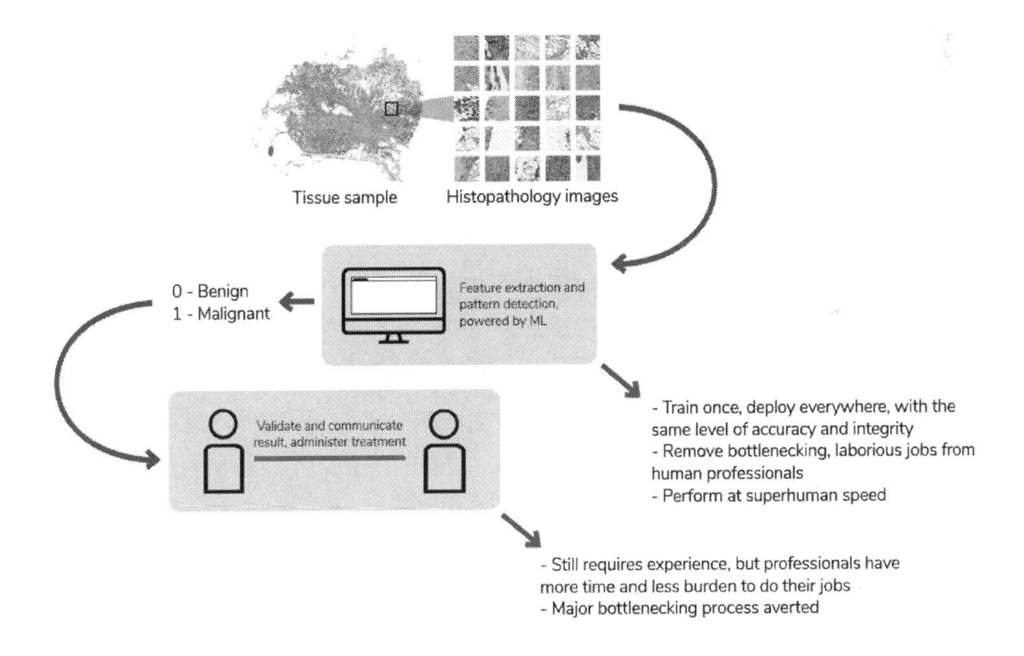

Figure 81:

[68]https://my.clevelandclinic.org/

7.4 Domain Research and Exposition

Let's take a moment to get familiar with the domain. When trying to solve a problem in *any* domain, you have to have at least rudimentary knowledge of what you're trying to solve, why you're trying to solve it, and what the data means in the context of the domain. Without knowing anything about the domain - it's hard to tell whether a model is really working or not. As a rule of thumb - it's best to consult with someone in the field, and get their input, especially in the later stages of model development.

Though - to get started, you'll typically be on your own, so being able to quickly get a grasp of some of the basic concepts is crucial!

Invasive Ductal Carcinoma (IDC) is by far the most common breast cancer subtype, accounting for 80% of the cases. By tackling this one subtype alone, we can address 80% of the cases.

Tumors are bundles of cells that aren't supposed to bundle, and grow into solid lumps. Tumors can be benign (non-cancerous) and confied to a particular region and might not cause any problems. They could grow and cause problems through sheer size, though. If a tumor starts growing *outside* of the confounds of the group of cells - it becomes malignant (cancerous). Cancer can invade local tissue or metastasize and attack further tissue. There's much more to be said about tumors and cancer, including subtypes and its degrees, but the dataset we're working with simply classifies images as *non-cancerous* (benign) and *cancerous* (malignant).

For this specific dataset, there's surprisingly little medical knowledge you *need* to have in order to build a capable classifier. This is in large part due to the fact that it took hundreds of years of cummulative scientific knowledge on behalf of doctors of medicine to label and prepare datasets from which we can infer knowledge. It is on their experience and expertise that we're able to build models for feature extraction and classification, with high degrees of accuracy and integrity.

To a Machine Learning engineer - this task *almost* boils down to regular image classification! However, there are certain implications that come with this dataset, that are scarcely present in other datasets you might've worked with before. We'll specifically focus on *making educated guesses* in a later section, while contemplating class imbalance, augmentation, cost-sensitive learning, etc.

That being said - let's jump into the data!

7.5 Loading the Data

We'll start out by downloading the dataset and loading it in. We'll be working with the Breast Histopathology Images[69] dataset. It contains 198738 **IDC(-)** image patches and 78786 **IDC(+)** image patches.

- IDC(-) refers to *benign* cases
- IDC(+) refers to *malignant* cases

Note: IDC(-) in this dataset implies that the patient doesn't have *Invasive Ductal Carcinoma*. It implies that they have a *benign* case or normal tissue, rather than a *malignant* case. Besides IDC, another condition exists - ***Non-Invasive Ductal Carcinoma*** also known as ***Ductal carcinoma in situ (DCIS)***.

The dataset comes from a 2016 study - *"Deep learning for digital pathology image analysis: A comprehensive tutorial with selected use cases"*[70] by *Andrew Janowczyk* and *Anant Madabhushi*. Their study focused on several tasks, one of which was IDC clasification, for which they had an *F-score* of *0.7648* on 50k testing patches.

The dataset we're working with is derived from 279 patients, each of which has a unique ID. Each patient has a dedicated folder, named by their ID, with two subfolders - `0` and `1`. The folder named `0` consists of images of *benign tissue samples* (those without IDC markers). The folder named `1` consists of images of *malignant tissue samples* (those containing IDC markers).

You can download the dataset using Kaggle's CLI:

```
1 $ kaggle datasets download -d paultimothymooney/breast-histopathology-images
```

---

[69]https://www.kaggle.com/paultimothymooney/breast-histopathology-images
[70]https://pubmed.ncbi.nlm.nih.gov/27563488/

Note: Using the `kaggle datasets` command neccessitates that you've exported a `kaggle.json` authentication file from your Kaggle profile and have it under `~/.kaggle/`.

If you haven't already, download it, create a `~/.kaggle` directory and copy/`chmod` the file from the folder in which it's originally located:

```
1 $ mkdir ~/.kaggle
2 $ cp kaggle.json ~/.kaggle/
3 $ chmod 600 ~/.kaggle/kaggle.json
```

This is the `C:\Users\username\.kaggle` directory on Windows.

Histopathology images are large, and very small features and markers are present, which is why the images were brokend down into *patches*, 50x50 pixels in size. Each patient, therefore, has many *image patches*, that together would comprise entire images.

Each patch has a distinct name format - `uxXyYclassC.png`, where `u` is the patient's ID, `x` is the X-coordinate from which the patch was extracted, `y` is the Y-coordinate from which the patch was extracted and the `class` is either `0` or `1`, denoting whether IDC markers are present or not in that patch.

The coordinates were given so that whole images can be reconstructed from the patches, but also so that we can *color the patches* in the whole images, which is fairly standard procedure in pathology. We'll be doing this in the EDA section shortly as well!

That all being said - let's extract the downloaded zip into `breast-histopathology-images`:

```
1 $ unzip breast-histopathology-images.zip -d breast-histopathology-images
```

Note: When downloaded, the `.zip` file contains 279 folders - one for each patient. Additionally, another folder is present, which contains these same 279 folders again. This, by all means, appears to be a mistake, so feel free to delete the extra last folder after extraction.

Great! We can now get into examining this data with Python. Let's start by creating a `config` dictionary like last time:

```
config = {
    'ROOT_PATH' : 'breast-histopathology-images',
    'IMG_SIZE' : 200,
    'BATCH_SIZE' : 8
}
```

```
data = os.listdir(config['ROOT_PATH'])
len(data)
# 279
```

Indeed, there are 279 folders, denoting 279 patient IDs:

```
data[:10]
```

Let's take a look at the first 10:

```
['10253',
 '10254',
 '10255',
 '10256',
 '10257',
 '10258',
 '10259',
 '10260',
 '10261',
 '10262']
```

Within each of these folders, there's a `0` and `1` folder:

```
patient_10253 = os.listdir(os.path.join(config['ROOT_PATH'], '10253'))
# ['0', '1']
```

And within each of them, a number of images:

```
patient_10253_0 = os.listdir(os.path.join(config['ROOT_PATH'], '10253', '0'))
patient_10253_1 = os.listdir(os.path.join(config['ROOT_PATH'], '10253', '1'))

print(patient_10253_0[:5])
# ['10253_idx5_x1001_y1001_class0.png', '10253_idx5_x1001_y1051_class0.png',
    '10253_idx5_x1001_y1101_class0.png',
    '10253_idx5_x1001_y1151_class0.png', '10253_idx5_x1001_y1201_class0.png']
print(patient_10253_1[:5])
```

```
7 # ['10253_idx5_x501_y351_class1.png', '10253_idx5_x501_y401_class1.png',
      '10253_idx5_x551_y301_class1.png', '10253_idx5_x551_y351_class1.png',
      '10253_idx5_x551_y401_class1.png']
```

The filenames are on the longer end, but contain really valuable data! Working with lists isn't really ideal, so let's get the data only for the first patient, and store it in a couple of `DataFrame`s instead, combining them together into a single one:

```
1 df_0 = pd.DataFrame()
2
3 for path in patient_10253_0:
4     split = path.split('_')
5     # Extract elements 2 and 3, substringing the first char
6     x_coord = split[2][1:]
7     y_coord = split[3][1:]
8     idc_class = 0
9
10    data = {"path": os.path.join(config['ROOT_PATH'], '10253', '0', path),
11            "x_coord": x_coord,
12            "y_coord": y_coord,
13            "idc_class": idc_class}
14
15    df_0 = df_0.append(data, ignore_index=True)
16
17
18 print(df_0)
19
20 df_1 = pd.DataFrame()
21
22 for path in patient_10253_1:
23     split = path.split('_')
24     # Extract elements 2 and 3, substringing the first char
25     x_coord = split[2][1:]
26     y_coord = split[3][1:]
27     idc_class = 1
28     # Hardcoded path for now, we'll address this later
29     data = {"path": os.path.join(config['ROOT_PATH'], '10253', '1', path),
30             "x_coord": x_coord,
31             "y_coord": y_coord,
32             "idc_class": idc_class}
33
34     df_1 = df_1.append(data, ignore_index=True)
35
36
37 # Combine dataframes
38 df = df_0.append(df_1).reset_index()
39 # Convert the coordinates to integers, from objects
40 df['x_coord'] = df['x_coord'].astype('int')
41 df['y_coord'] = df['y_coord'].astype('int')
```

This dataframe now consists of:

	idc_class	path	x_coord	y_coord
0	0.0	./breast-histopathology-images/10253/0/10253_i...	1001	1001
1	0.0	./breast-histopathology-images/10253/0/10253_i...	1001	1051
2	0.0	./breast-histopathology-images/10253/0/10253_i...	1001	1101
3	0.0	./breast-histopathology-images/10253/0/10253_i...	1001	1151
4	0.0	./breast-histopathology-images/10253/0/10253_i...	1001	1201
...	...	...	...	...
544	1.0	./breast-histopathology-images/10253/1/10253_i...	851	601
545	1.0	./breast-histopathology-images/10253/1/10253_i...	851	651
546	1.0	./breast-histopathology-images/10253/1/10253_i...	851	701
547	1.0	./breast-histopathology-images/10253/1/10253_i...	851	751
548	1.0	./breast-histopathology-images/10253/1/10253_i...	901	351

549 rows × 4 columns

Figure 82:

Great, we've got patch paths (meaning, we can get the images for each one), the `x_coord` and `y_coord` for each patch (meaning, we know where it is in the image) and the `idc_class` for that specific patch! Using this data, we can reconstruct the original whole images, and even go as far as to mark the IDC positive sections in them, with a different color as if with a highlighter.

7.6 Exploratory Data Analysis (EDA)

Before reconstructing the images, let's try creating a scatter plot with this data, setting the `c` (color) to correspond to the `idc_class`, giving us an *outline* of the IDC positive areas compared to the negative ones, knowing full well that the coordinates are really just the *starts* of the patches (top-left corner):

```
fig, ax = plt.subplots(figsize=(8, 8))
```

```
2 ax.scatter(x = df['x_coord'], y=df['y_coord'], c=df['idc_class'], cmap =
      'coolwarm')
3 plt.show()
```

This results in a pretty indicative image:

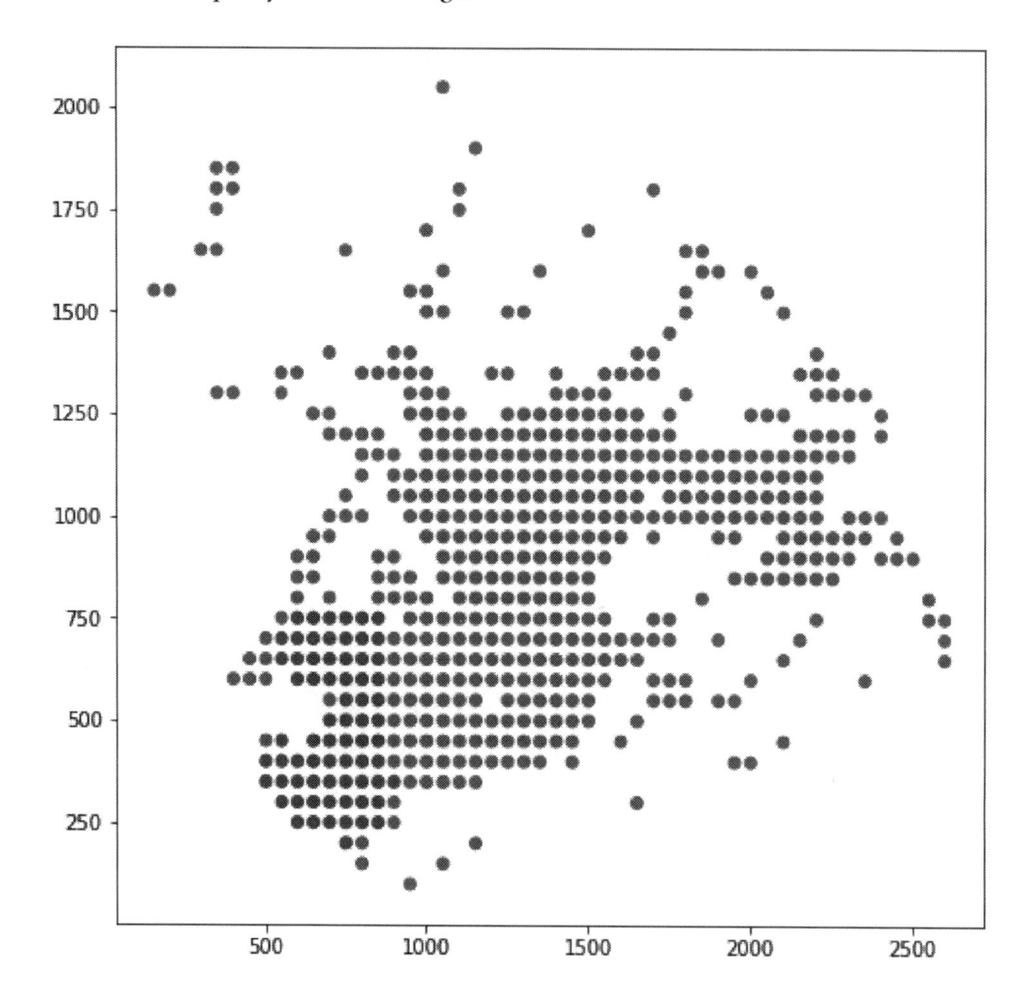

Figure 83:

It looks like some patches are missing! The Kaggle page doesn't mention this, but generally, data points are typically missing either due to being pruned away during processing of the raw data, or because of an instrument misfire, causing the data point to lose informative value.

We should still be fine without some of these patches though. Let's go ahead and try reconstructing this image, plotting an appropriate *patch*, instead of a scatter plot marker. Since we're dealing with a decent list of patches, and having to deal with many `Axes` instances can be pretty tiring - let's create a *grid* of "patches" (stand-ins) and a *mask* for the IDC positive patches, that can be colored in a different color and "stamped on" the underlying image. This method was inspired by Kaggle Grandmaster Laura Fink![71]

The grid and mask will both start out with stand-in values, ideally in white. White is represented as all RGB channels, with values at 255, so we can make a white grid and mask with:

```
1 grid = 255*np.ones(shape = (100, 100, 3)).astype(np.uint8)
2 mask = 255*np.ones(shape = (100, 100, 3)).astype(np.uint8)
```

These will now both essentially be:

```
1 array([[[255, 255, 255],
2         [255, 255, 255],
3         [255, 255, 255],
4         ...,
5         [255, 255, 255],
6         [255, 255, 255],
7         [255, 255, 255]],
8         ...
```

And of shape:

```
1 print(grid.shape) # (100, 100, 3)
```

If we were to visualize these as images - there wouldn't be much going on - these are all white pixels. Let's use our `x_coord` and `y_coord`'s maximum values as the wrapper as to how many pixels should be in the image (shape of the grid and mask), and for each image in the `DataFrame`, get its `x_coord` and `y_coord`, set its boundary (`_coord+50`) and imprint the pixel values of the images *onto* the grid:

```
1 max_x = df['x_coord'].max()
2 max_y = df['y_coord'].max()
3
4 # Shape of (2101, 2651, 3)
```

[71]https://www.kaggle.com/allunia

```
5 # A placeholder for each pixel, with 3 color options and max values for each
      channel (RGB)
6 grid = 255*np.ones(shape = (max_y + 50, max_x + 50, 3)).astype(np.uint8)
7 mask = 255*np.ones(shape = (max_y + 50, max_x + 50, 3)).astype(np.uint8)
8
9 for i in range(len(df)):
10         # Get image and label
11         image = cv2.imread(df['path'][i])
12         idc_class = df['idc_class'][i]
13
14         # Extract X and Y coordinates
15         x_coord = df['x_coord'][i]
16         y_coord = df['y_coord'][i]
17         # Add 50 pixels to find ending boundary for each image
18         x_end = x_coord + 50
19         y_end = y_coord + 50
20
21         # Assign image pixel values to placeholder 255 values
22         """
23         Image is something along the lines of:
24         [[[206 164 226]
25           [196 154 224]
26           [211 175 225]
27           ...
28           [237 221 240]
29           [214 184 232]
30           [235 213 243]],
31           ...
32         """
33         # `grid` will then contain each patch's image values encoded into
               the grid
34         grid[y_coord:y_end, x_coord:x_end] = image
35
36         # If `idc_class` is `1`, change the RED channel of the `mask` to 255
               (intense red)
37         # and other channels to `0` (remove color info, leaving just red)
38         if idc_class == 1:
39             mask[y_coord:y_end, x_coord:x_end, :1] = 255
40             mask[y_coord:y_end, x_coord:x_end, 1:] = 0
```

Finally, we can show the grid and the mask on top of it:

```
1 plt.figure(figsize=(12, 12))
2 plt.imshow(grid)
3 plt.imshow(mask, alpha=0.1)
4 plt.show()
```

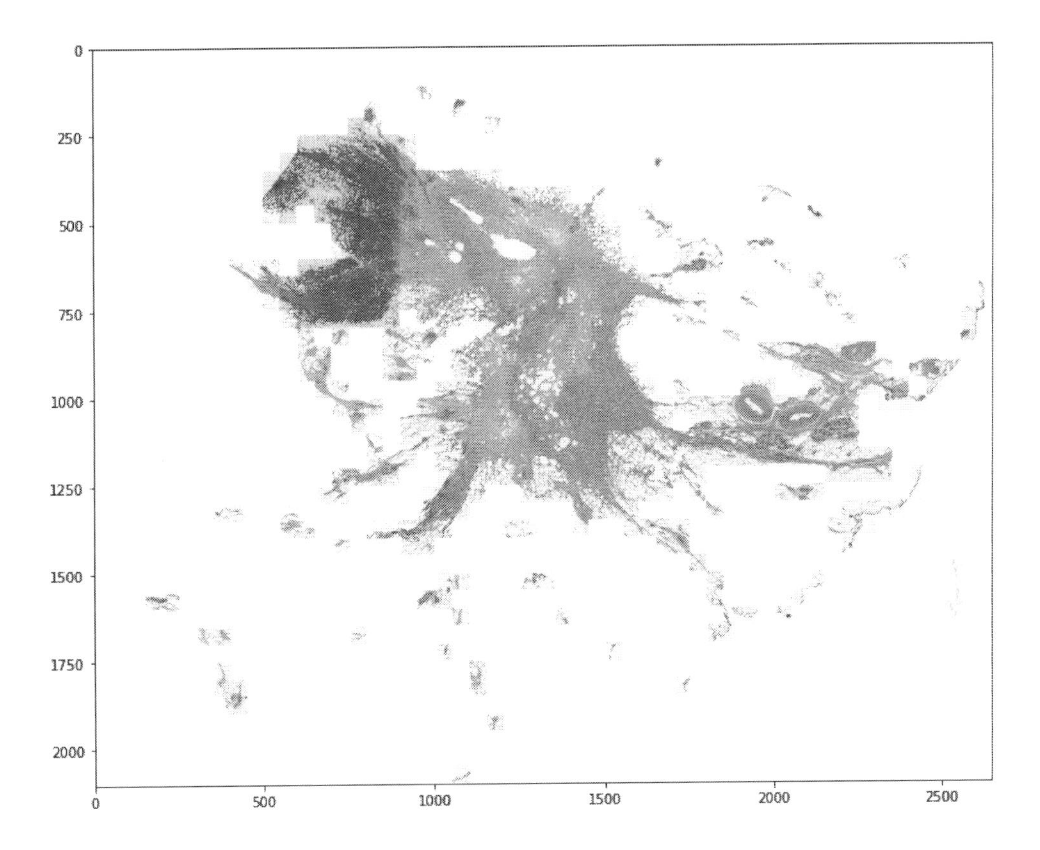

Figure 84:

Let's load in more data, creating a `DataFrame` consisting of information of *all* of the patches, the patient IDs, their IDC classes, etc. and plot summary statistics that'll help us get a general view of the dataset:

```
from glob import glob
data = glob(os.path.join(config['ROOT_PATH'], '*', '*', '*'), recursive=True)
print(len(data))
# 277524

def get_all_dfs():
    dfs = []

    for index, path in enumerate(data):
        split = path.split('_')
        # Extract elements 2 and 3, substringing the first char
```

```
12          patient_id = split[0].split('\\')[1]
13          x_coord = split[2][1:]
14          y_coord = split[3][1:]
15          idc_class = split[4][-5]
16
17          df_data = {"patient_id": patient_id,
18                     "x_coord": x_coord,
19                     "y_coord": y_coord,
20                     "idc_class": idc_class,
21                     "path": path}
22          df = pd.DataFrame()
23          dfs.append(df.append(df_data, ignore_index=True))
24          print(f'Finished appending {index}/{len(data)}', end = '\r')
25
26          df_all = pd.concat(dfs).reset_index(drop=True)
27          df_all['x_coord'] = df_all['x_coord'].astype('int')
28          df_all['y_coord'] = df_all['y_coord'].astype('int')
29          df_all['idc_class'] = df_all['idc_class'].astype('int')
30      return df_all
31
32  df_all = get_all_dfs()
```

Note: This piece of code takes a bit to execute, since we're creating a fairly large `DataFrame`. We won't be using the dataframes after inspecting them, though.

Let's start out with a count plot of the `idc_class`:

```
1 import seaborn as sns
2 sns.countplot(x = 'idc_class', data=df_all)
```

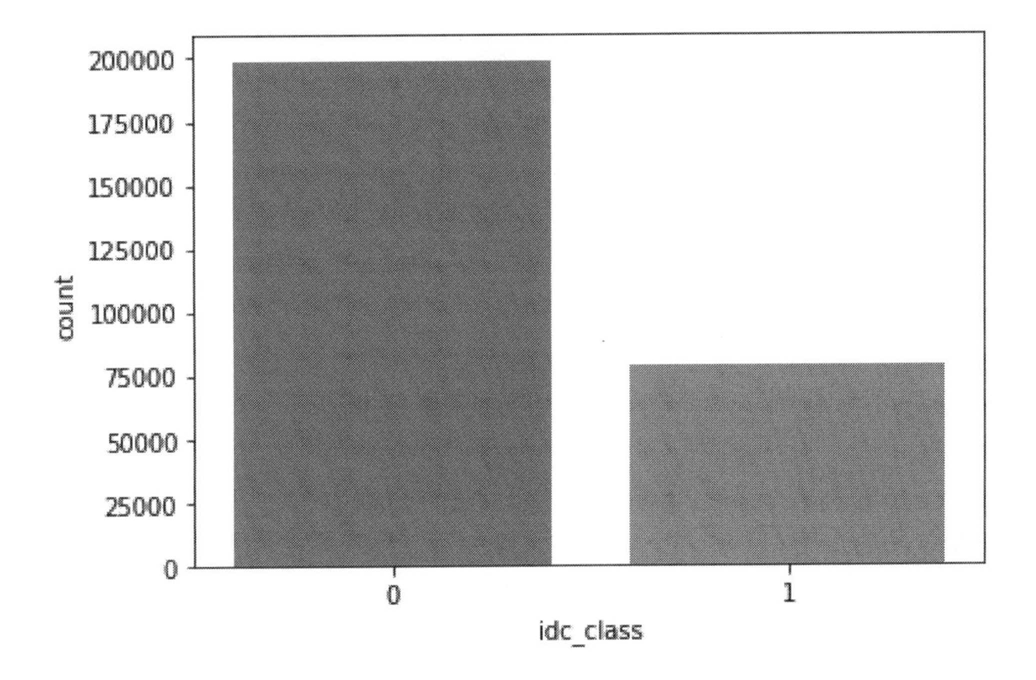

Figure 85:

There's a pretty big imbalance between the classes. This'll make generalization harder, since focusing on the dominant class might prove to be favorable with certain architectures. We'll contemplate class imbalance and its implications in detail in the next lesson, during data preprocessing.

Let's take a look at the frequency of images per patient - are they evenly spread out?

```
df_all['patient_id'].value_counts()
```

Some patients have *way more* data than others and the amount of data per patient is diverse!

```
13693    2395
16550    2302
10288    2278
10308    2278
9323     2216
          ...
16895     151
```

```
8 9175        118
9 8957        111
10 9262        94
11 16534       63
```

This won't necessarily make training and learning from these patches harder - we'll train a system to diagnose IDC by *patch*, not by an entire image. Though, it would make it a bit harder if we wanted to run a test for *all patients* and highlight the regions in the tissue that's rated as IDC positive, since not all patients have whole images that can be used for annotations.

Let's plot the whole images for some of the patients from the top of the list:

```
patient_ids = ['13693', '16550', '10288', '10308', '9323']

for patient_id in patient_ids:
    df = df_all.loc[df_all['patient_id'] ==
        patient_id].reset_index(drop=True)
    max_x = df['x_coord'].max()
    max_y = df['y_coord'].max()

    grid = 255*np.ones(shape = (max_y + 50, max_x + 50, 3)).astype(np.uint8)
    mask = 255*np.ones(shape = (max_y + 50, max_x + 50, 3)).astype(np.uint8)

    for i in range(len(df)):
        # Get image and label
        image = cv2.imread(df['path'][i])
        # Image shape might not be 50x50, in which case, it's a broken patch
        # and we don't want to load it in
        if(image.shape==(50, 50, 3)):
            idc_class = df['idc_class'][i]
            x_coord = df['x_coord'][i]
            y_coord = df['y_coord'][i]
            x_end = x_coord + 50
            y_end = y_coord + 50

            grid[y_coord:y_end, x_coord:x_end] = image

            if idc_class == 1:
                mask[y_coord:y_end, x_coord:x_end, :1] = 255
                mask[y_coord:y_end, x_coord:x_end, 1:] = 0

    plt.figure(figsize=(8, 8))
    plt.suptitle(f'Patient ID: {patient_id}')
    plt.imshow(grid)
    plt.imshow(mask, alpha=0.2)
    plt.show()
```

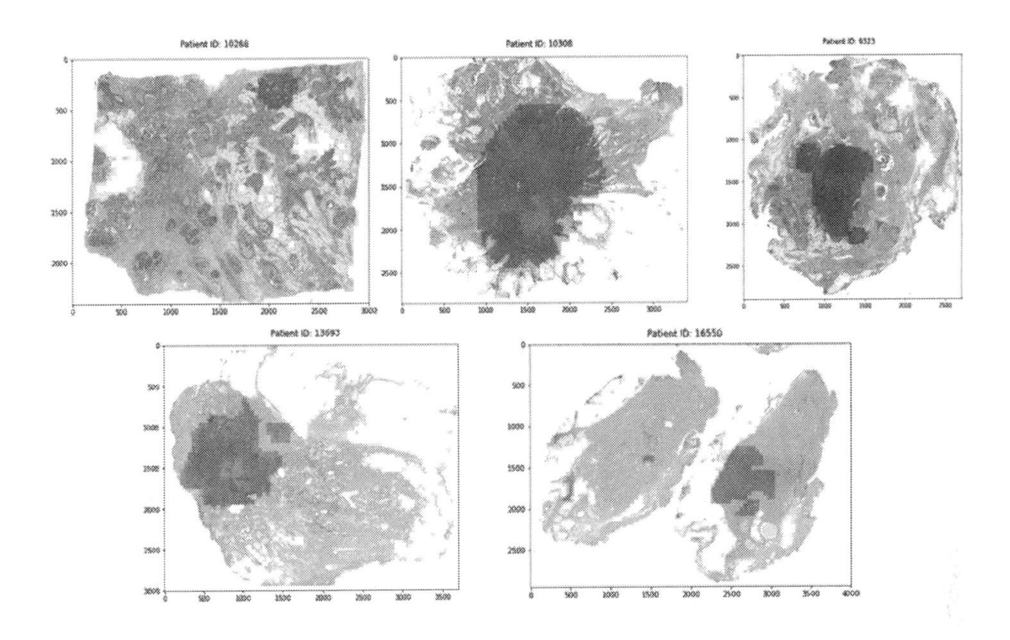

Figure 86:

Some slides have small areas covered by the mask, such as with *patient 10288,* though some have a fairly large area, such as *patient 10308.* Let's see if we can train a classifier to figure out *why* certain patches are IDC positive and which aren't.

7.7 Machine Learning Workflow

We've done Exploratory Data Analysis and got familiar with the dataset we're working with. Now - it's time to hop into the standard Machine Learning Workflow, starting with preprocessing data.

7.7.1 Data Preprocessing

We've worked with `DataFrame`s so far, though, this was all without images - we only stored their paths in case we want to retrieve and plot them. One way to load images is to simply iterate through the data and load them in:

```
import cv2

x = []
y = []

# Loading in 1000 images
for i in data[:1000]:
    if i.endswith('.png'):
        label=i[-5]
        img = cv2.imread(i)
        # Transformation steps, such as resizing
        img = cv2.resize(img,(200,200))
        x.append(img)
        y.append(label)
```

`x` and `y` are Python lists - which are very efficient at appending data at the cost of higher memory usage. Let's convert them to NumPy arrays, split them into a training and testing set, and call the garbage collection module to clear `x` and `y` from memory since we won't be using them anymore:

```
# Reduce from float32 for memory footprint
x = np.array(x, dtype = 'float16')
y = np.array(y, dtype = 'float16')

from sklearn.model_selection import train_test_split
x_train,x_test,y_train,y_test=train_test_split(x,y, shuffle=True,
    test_size=0.3)

import gc
x = None
y = None
gc.collect()
```

```
x_train.shape
# (700, 200, 200, 3)
```

This is the *general* process for converting images to NumPy arrays, but there's an issue here. We have 277k images. For images of size 50x50 - this could probably fit into a home system with 256GB of RAM into memory, but even though it can, it's just plain inefficient. There's no need to strain a machine with all of the images being loaded into memory at once, and 50x50 images are *fairly small*, making it harder to extract meaningful feature maps from them.

On a more home-like machine, with 32-64GB of RAM, you could fit up to 25k images of 100x100 size, of 10k of 200x200 into memory, yet this is inefficient as well.

This can be solved with an `ImageDataGenerator`, as earlier. We can stream data directly from our disk, loading batches into the memory and seamlessly providing the next batch during training (optionally, applying transformations to achieve data augmentation) instead. This can scale down to machines with as little as a single gigabyte of memory, if need be! There's a better alternative to `ImageDataGenerator`, though, and we'll be using it. Even though we'll use the alternative, we might want to reorganise the data to make it a bit simpler to work with, and in the meantime, make it compatible with `ImageDataGenerator` as well.

Our data is formatted as:

```
patient_1
  - class0.png
  - class1.png
  - class1.png
  - class0.png
patient_2
  - class0.png
  - class1.png
  - class1.png
  - class0.png
...
```

While a much more intuitive format for loading the processing the data is:

```
class_1
  - sample0.png
  - sample1.png
  - sample2.png
class_0
  - sample0.png
  - sample1.png
  - sample2.png
```

If we were to use Keras' `ImageDataGenerator` class here - it could treat each patient as a class, and assume that we're trying to classify the *patient* based on the images within the directories. Even for the alternative, it'd make it easier to have dedicated `train`, `test` and `valid` directories, with `class_1` and `class_2` subdirectories each.

We should instead be having a `1` and `0` directory, with images of IDC(+) and IDC(-) respectively. Let's write a script that creates a *truncated* dataset, and reformats the directories to the format Keras would love to work with.

Note: We're creating a truncated dataset to test out the models on smaller sets for efficiency's sake. You're free to use the entirety of the dataset, but be prepared to wait *a long time* before you can benchmark them. Once the benchmarking is done on smaller datasets, we can load in the entirety of the images.

```
from sklearn.model_selection import train_test_split

if not os.path.exists('./hist_images_small/'):
    print('Making folders for hist_images_small')
    os.mkdir('./hist_images_small/')

    os.mkdir('./hist_images_small/train/')
    os.mkdir('./hist_images_small/test/')
    os.mkdir('./hist_images_small/valid/')

    os.mkdir('./hist_images_small/train/0/')
    os.mkdir('./hist_images_small/train/1/')
    os.mkdir('./hist_images_small/test/0/')
    os.mkdir('./hist_images_small/test/1/')

    os.mkdir('./hist_images_small/valid/0/')
    os.mkdir('./hist_images_small/valid/1/')
```

Now, let's iterate over the length of the dataset, in large steps, and use the steps as the starting and ending indices for our `data` list, loading the associated images in, reshaping them, and saving them in the appropriate folder:

```
# enumerate() to get `batch_num`, starting at 1
# range() starting at 1000 and incrementing in steps of 1000 towards the
    fifth of the length of the dataset
# we're loading in only a 10th of the data
for batch_num, indices in enumerate(range(1000, int(len(data)/10), 1000), 1):
    x = []
    y = []

    # Load in `indices-1000` to `indices`
    # 0:1000, 1000:2000, 2000:3000, etc.
    for i in data[indices-1000:indices]:
        if i.endswith('.png'):
            label=i[-5]
            img = cv2.imread(i)
            x.append(img)
            y.append(label)

    # Create NumPy Arrays from Python lists
    x = np.array(x, dtype = 'float16')
    y = np.array(y, dtype = 'float16')

```

```
21      print(f'Processing batch {batch_num}, with images from {indices-1000} to
            {indices}')
22
23      # Perform train-test split
24      x_train, x_test, y_train, y_test = train_test_split(x,y, shuffle=True,
            test_size=0.4, stratify=y)
25
26      # For each image in `x_train` - save it, including the associated
            batch_number and sample in the appropriate directory
27      for index, img in enumerate(X_train):
28          idc_class = y_train[index]
29          path = os.path.join('hist_images_small', 'train', str(idc_class),
                f'batch_{batch_num}_sample_{index}.png')
30          cv2.imwrite(path, img.astype('int'))
31
32      for index, img in enumerate(X_test):
33          if index%2 == 0:
34              idc_class = y_test[index]
35              path = os.path.join('hist_images_small', 'test', str(idc_class),
                    f'batch_{batch_num}_sample_{index}.png')
36              cv2.imwrite(path, img.astype('int'))
37     else:
38         idc_class = y_test[index]
39         path = os.path.join('hist_images_small', 'valid', str(idc_class),
               f'batch_{batch_num}_sample_{index}.png')
40         cv2.imwrite(path, img.astype('int'))
```

The test size is 40%, since we have a lot of data to work with to make a capable classifier, annd having a larger testing and validation set is important to truly evaluate it. We can afford a large support for our metrics! The 40% will be split evenly between a test and validation set.

The step size of 1000 is arbitrary. It can be as low as 1 or as high as 50000. Running this shouldn't take too long, and maps all of the images in the original directories onto a new format, with processed images:

```
1 Processing batch 1, with images from 0 to 1000
2 Processing batch 2, with images from 1000 to 2000
3 ...
4 Processing batch 54, with images from 53000 to 54000
5 Processing batch 55, with images from 54000 to 55000
```

With the images in place - we can create a dataset from them. So far, we did that with the `ImageDataGenerator` class, which was a Python generator. It made our previous project simpler and easier to run, but using generators isn't advised in this day and age. As an alternative, we'll be using `tf.data` - the official TensorFlow module for handling data and creating powerful data pipelines for training models.

The central class is `tf.data.Dataset`, and we can create them from several sources - but the most common and simplest way is to make them `from_tensor_slices()` and process them:

```
dataset = tf.data.Dataset.from_tensor_slices((features,
    labels)).map(process_fn)
```

The features can really be anything - but they're typically some raw information on the features you actually want the dataset to have. In our case, it can be a list of image paths, and the `process_fn()` can turn those paths into Tensors representing images. As a matter of fact - this is exactly what we'll be doing!

To make things easier, we'll also extract the labels from the filenames into a list, so we'll have a list for image paths and a list for their labels:

```
train_paths_small = glob(os.path.join('hist_images_small', 'train', '*',
    '*'), recursive=True)
test_paths_small = glob(os.path.join('hist_images_small', 'test', '*', '*'),
    recursive=True)
valid_paths_small = glob(os.path.join('hist_images_small', 'valid', '*',
    '*'), recursive=True)
```

```
def get_labels(pathlist):
    labels = []
    for path in pathlist:
        labels.append(int(path.split(os.sep)[2]))
    labels = np.array(labels)
    return labels

train_labels_small = get_labels(train_paths_small)
test_labels_small = get_labels(test_paths_small)
valid_labels_small = get_labels(valid_paths_small)
```

Our `train_paths` and `train_labels` will together form a `train_set`, and so on. Let's inspect the number of images we're dealing with:

```
print(len(train_paths_small)) # 16085
print(len(test_paths_small))  # 5370
print(len(test_paths_small))  # 5370
```

And they consist of:

```
train_paths_small[:5]
```

```
['hist_images_small/train/0/batch_137_sample_223.png',
 'hist_images_small/train/0/batch_25_sample_592.png',
 'hist_images_small/train/0/batch_99_sample_482.png',
```

```
'hist_images_small/train/0/batch_253_sample_491.png',
'hist_images_small/train/0/batch_5_sample_38.png']
```

```
train_labels_small[:5] # array([0, 0, 0, 0, 0])
```

With our labels and paths ready - let's create a `Dataset` from them, then map each entry with the `preprocess` function nwhich turns that path into a Tensor representing the image that a CNN can learn from:

```
def preprocess(image_path, label):
    img = tf.io.read_file(image_path)
    img = tf.image.decode_jpeg(img)
    img = tf.image.resize(img, size=[config['IMG_SIZE'], config['IMG_SIZE']])
    img = tf.cast(img, tf.float32)
    label = tf.cast(label, tf.float32)

    return img, label

def create_dataset(images, labels):
    dataset = tf.data.Dataset.from_tensor_slices((images,
        labels)).shuffle(len(images))
    dataset = dataset.map(preprocess)
    dataset = dataset.batch(config['BATCH_SIZE'], drop_remainder=True)
    dataset = dataset.prefetch(tf.data.AUTOTUNE)
    return dataset
```

It's important to shuffle our dataset, as (almost) always. With these methods, we can create `Dataset` instances:

```
train_set_small = create_dataset(train_paths_small, train_labels_small)
test_set_small = create_dataset(test_paths_small, test_labels_small)
valid_set_small = create_dataset(valid_paths_small, valid_labels_small)
```

Let's visualize a batch:

```
for img_batch, label_batch in valid_set_small.take(1):
    fig = plt.figure(figsize=(10,10))
    for i in range(len(img_batch)):
        ax = fig.add_subplot(4,4,i+1)
        ax.imshow(img_batch[i].numpy().astype('int'))
        ax.set_title(label_batch[i].numpy())
plt.tight_layout()
```

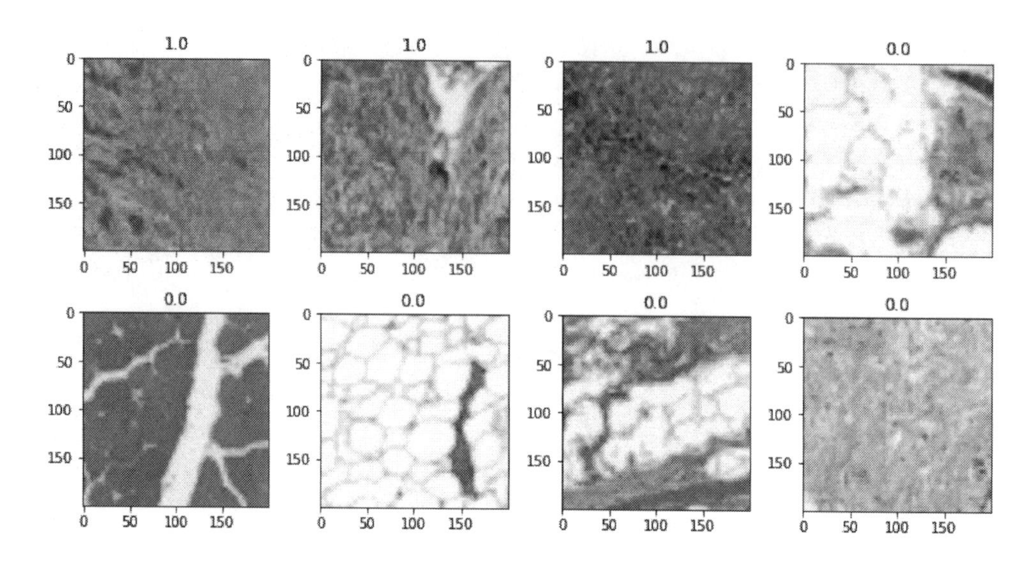

Figure 87:

Now, before we continue, let's address a glaring problem - class imbalance.

7.7.1.1 Class Imbalance - Issue or Not? Here, we run into the *potential* issue of class imbalance. There's an imbalance between the number of IDC(+) and IDC(-) samples. Most Machine Learning algorithms perform best when there's a *roughly* equal number of samples, and this stands *especially* for binary classification such as we're trying to do. If one class is oversampled, a classifier can learn to mainly predict that class, regardless of any features that come in.

> It's worth noting that it's ideal for this balance between classes to exist **naturally**.

Given the fact that negative samples are much more numerous than positive ones - our test set will also have a lot of negative samples. Since there's 277524 samples in total, 198738 of which are negative - that's ~71% class `0` samples.

> If our model misclassifies **every single positive** (class `1`) **sample**, it'll still get 71%

> in accuracy, if it gets the other classifications right. In other words, if it outputs a constant *0* for every input, it'll still get 71% accuracy.

That obviously defeats the purpose of the classifier. Intuitively, we'll want to get rid of this imbalance, but let's also explore some other implications of altering the balance of the classes.

- What is the "real" distribution of classes?
- What makes the difference between classes?
- What makes the network predict wrong?

These are crucial questions to ask, and depend on the dataset you're working with. Based on the answers, trying to fix class imbalance **will either make or break your model**, and sometimes you just have to live with the imbalance.

Let's answer these questions for our own dataset first:

> "What is the real distribution of classes"

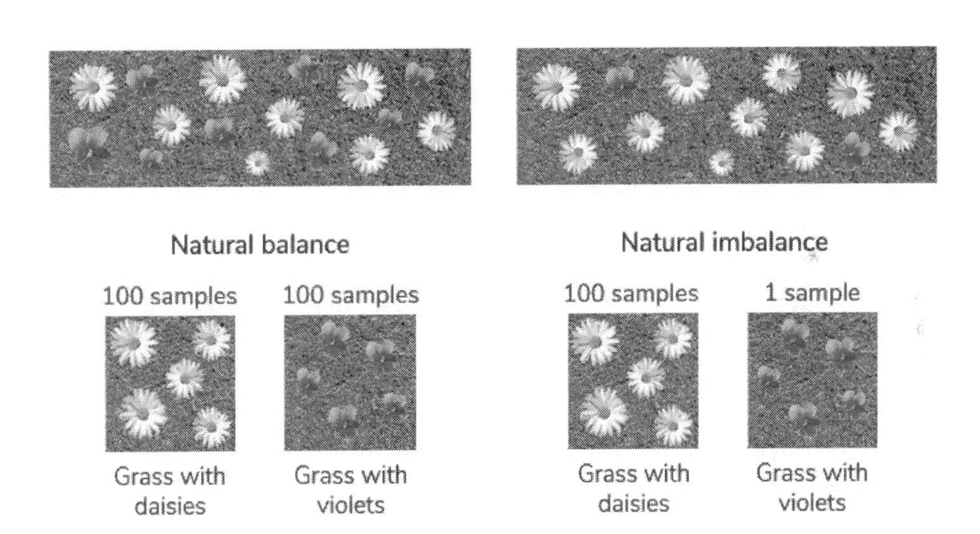

Figure 88:

If we have a garden, with an equal amount of daisies and violets - it's natural to train a classifier to pay equal attention to them, through a binary classification learning algorithm. If violets are *really rare* - sure, each *sample* will have a few violets, just like each sample might have a few daisies - but a model may completely ignore violets knowing full well it'll get a 99% accuracy by classifying everything as daisies! From that perspective, violets are outliers, and outliers don't make for great generalization ability changers.

In other words - what proportion of tissue shows markers for IDC? Well, as we've seen in the EDA section - not a lot. The proportion of IDC(+) to IDC(-) is low, so having more class `0` samples is natural for the network to train on. If we were to force that proportion to reach 1:1 - we'd be training the network to become *super sensitive* and misfire sensitively on one of the sides.

This is, in fact, the exact thing we'd see if we were to force a 50/50 split between the classes on this specific model and dataset. Here's a count plot of the classes of the *output* and the count plot of the classes in the `test_set` the outputs tried predicting for, when the training dataset was altered by the **Synthetic Minority Oversampling Technique** (SMOTE), but was evaluated by a natural distribution in the test set:

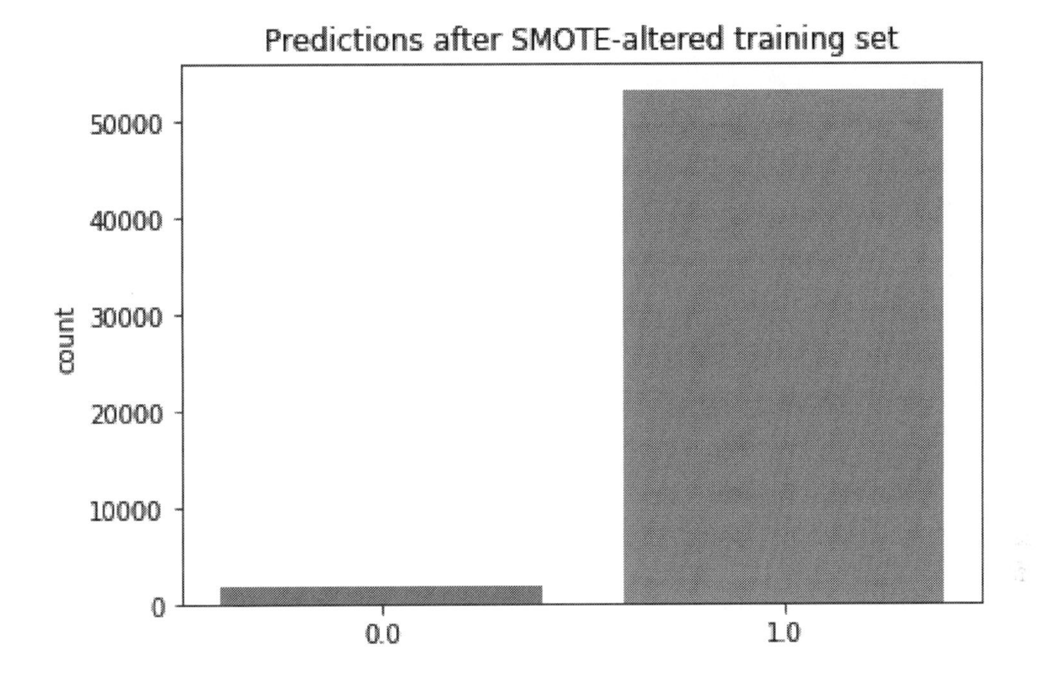

Figure 89:

The network almost always goes for `1`, even though the training data was enhanced to have a 50/50 split of classes, because it was deluded as to which classes are *really* present. The natural proportion of class `1` and class `0` isn't 50/50, and by forcing the proportion, we hurt the model. If it were conceivable that both classes can be naturally equally present - this would be much less likely to occur.

In my tests - trying to fix the class imbalance hurt the model.

> "What makes the difference between classes?"

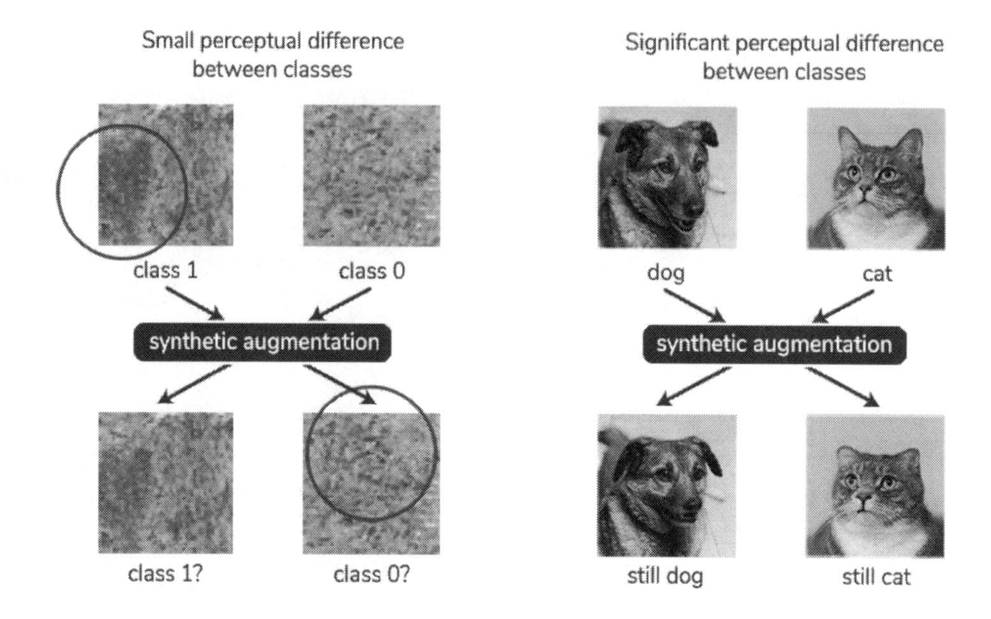

Figure 90:

What makes the difference between IDC(-) and IDC(+)? Well, I don't know. I'm not a pathologist. Though, to the untrained eye, which the network also is - there doesn't seem to be much of a difference. It's the subtle cues and hints that *seem* to make the difference between the classes. Any method of equalizing the class imbalance that creates *synthetic* data for one of the classes will typically alter the new inputs to prevent major overfitting on the duplicate entries.

If subtle cues are what makes the difference between IDC(-) and IDC(+) - most synthetic generation resamplers will end up totally wrecking the network's knowledge of what's going on. On the other hand, if we were classifying a "dogs vs cats" classifier and had a class imbalance - slightly altering the dog images won't change a dog to a cat!

In the illustration above - the length of the cat's ears doesn't change it into a dog, nor does shortening the dog's snout change it into a cat. However, if (for the sake of argument), something like a darker patch of tissue could be a signifier for IDC - what happens if an IDC(-) sample gets a random darker patch due to a random synthetic augmentation process?

This was a conceptual example - synthetic augmentation processes don't exactly work like this. They're much more prone to introducing random noise, and pooling, instead of coherently making ears or snouts shorter. However - on grainy, 50x50 images, changing a few pixels around can have dramatic effect. Whatever we do with the data - we don't want to *alter* it. Rotating images, moving them around, etc. *should* be fine!

> "What makes the network predict wrong?"

This question is tied to the previous one. What makes the network predict wrong is the inability to discern between the classes. If this inability stems from the fact that the classes are very *similar*, then increasing the number of one class can also amplify the number of images that teach the network to predict wrongly. If this inability stems from the fact that the classes are very different, and the network can't discern between them - it's probably a case of a lack of entropic capacity.

> All of that is to say - we're likely to **hurt** the generalization abilities of our model, on this dataset, if we try fixing the class imbalance.

Here, we make an educated guess and won't try fixing the imbalance, as it's more likely to hurt us than to help us.

7.7.1.2 How to Balance Imbalanced Sets? While we're already at the topic of class imbalance and fixing it - let's at least take a moment to appreciate how it is done, when it should be done. For multi-class models (binary classification suffers more from "fixing" imbalance), and especially ones that aren't this sensitive, fixing class imbalance will very likely help a ton.

Note that none of the code in this section will not make it to the final model's inputs and that this is a purely hypothetical scenario for cases in which you might *want to* perform balancing. Libraries like Scikit-Learn doesn't have any built-in methods or modules for balancing imbalanced datasets. However, third-party solutions do exist, and they play well with Scikit-Learn!

We'll be using the `imblearn` (Imbalanced Learn)[72] module, which offers a wide variety of re-sampling techniques to battle strong imbalance.

In general, when you have strong imbalance - you can either:

[72]https://github.com/scikit-learn-contrib/imbalanced-learn

- Ignore it (if fixing would cause more issues, such as our case)
- Undersample the strong class (in our case, undersampling the IDC(-) samples)
- Oversample the weak class (in our case, oversampling the IDC(+) samples)
- Combine undersampling and oversampling (undersample IDC(-) and oversample IDC(+))
- Ensemble balanced sets

Commonly, you won't have enough samples in *both* classes, so undersampling might pose an issue since the more numerous set is being trimmed down to the less numerous set. In those cases, you'll prefer to either combine undersampling and oversampling, or straight up oversample the weaker class.

Undersampling can be as easy as slicing off a part of the dataset, using the slice notation of NumPy arrays (though, this would require you to have an array either sorted, or different arrays for your classes):

```
1 strong_class = strong_class[:x]
```

There are much more sophisticated methods of achieving undersampling, and it's worth taking a look at the `imblearn` module's GitHub page for those.

Note: Like most of Scikit-Learn's `fit_()` methods, `imblearn`'s methods also take in 2D arrays. For instance, if our `x_train` is a 4D array - `(length, 200, 200, 3)`. If we wanted to balance it, we'd have to reshape it back to a 2D array, fit it with the samplers, and then shape it back.

```
1 # Calculate desired shape
2 X_train_shape = x_train.shape[1] * x_train.shape[2] * x_train.shape[3]
3 # Flatten X into a 2D array
4 X_flattened = x_train.reshape(x_train.shape[0], X_train_shape)
```

Once we're done resampling - we'd reshape the result back to our 4D array! Oversampling also has various approaches, a popular one being *Synthetic Minority Over-sampling Technique (SMOTE)*:

```
from imblearn.over_sampling import SMOTE
x_train, y_train = SMOTE(random_state=42).fit_resample(X_flattened, y_train)
```

An alternative to oversampling would be to undersample:

```
from imblearn.under_sampling import RandomUnderSampler
x_train, y_train =
    RandomUnderSampler(random_state=42).fit_resample(X_flattened, y_train)
```

The `RandomUnderSampler` separates the `x_train` and `y_train` into classes, and undersamples the more numerous one, randomly. You don't have to either sort the data into classes or separate them into two sets! Once the `fit_resample()` is called, we can perform a count plot to check how many instances per class there are.

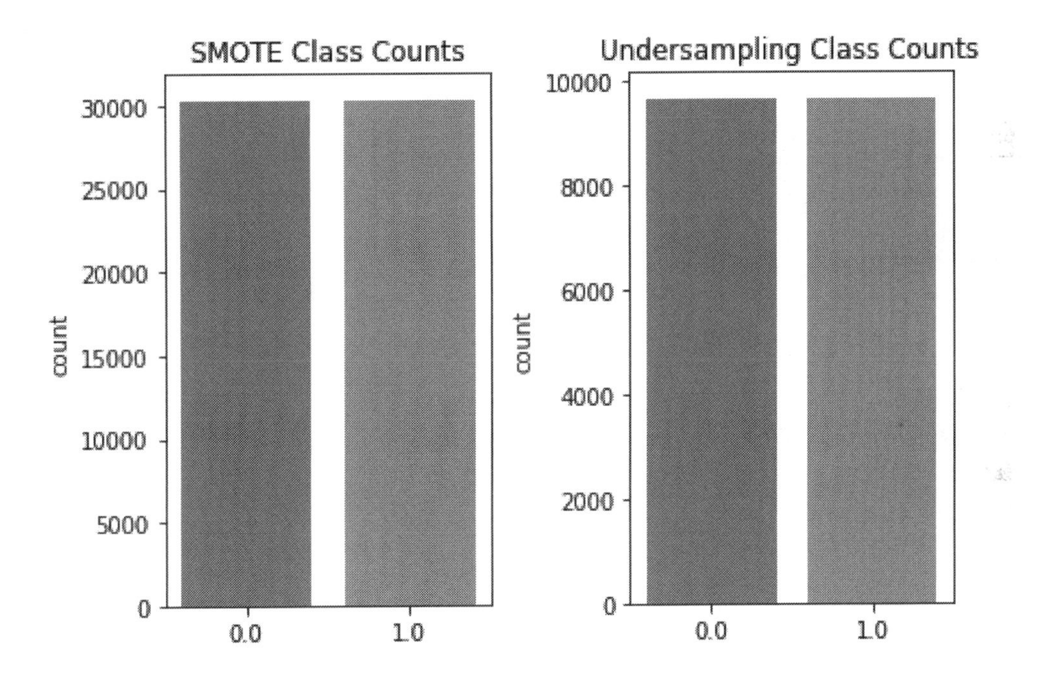

Figure 91:

Finally, we'd want to reshape `x_train` back to the original shape:

```
x_train = x_train.reshape(len(x_train), 200, 200, 3)
```

Note: The `RandomUnderSampler class`, while undersampling, also sorts the inputs. Our hypothetical `x_train` would have half of its samples consisting of consecutive `0`s followed by another half of its samples consisting of `1`. We'd want to shuffle `x_train, y_train, x_test, y_test` before using them any further.

```
from sklearn.utils import shuffle

x_train, y_train = shuffle(x_train, y_train)
x_test, y_test = shuffle(x_test, y_test)
```

7.7.1.3 Imbalance Implications and Hypotheses - Making Educated Guesses

Since we've decided to not balance the classes - we do have to consider some things. For instance - accuracy is likely to be a bad metric for network performance, because 71% accuracy is a *given* considering the imbalance.

> We'll want to use metrics besides accuracy when we fit the model, since accuracy isn't going to be a good proxy for performance.

In cases such as these - **recall** is a great metric to keep in mind, since it's calculated by dividing true positives by the number of relevant examples (how correct the model is at figuring out true positives). Additionally **precision** is the ratio between true positives and *all* positives. The **AUC** (Area Under Curve) is a good measure of how well the model discerns between classes, so a high AUC score is a good *indication* as to how well a model could perform, but is far from sacrosanct.

It'll be harder to steer the network in accurately representing IDC(+) instances in its internal knowledge representations, since there's a larger incentive in pushing out `0` predictions for most inputs. In other words - the *recall-precision balance* will be a tough one.

You might retort that F1 is based on the the harmonic mean between recall and precision - and it is. It's a great metric to keep in mind here, and we will. Since Keras doesn't have a built-in F1 Score metric, we'll define our own F1 metric later on. For the baseline model

- there's no need to, and we'll take a look at precision and recall individually, as their mean can be manipulated by each of them individually.

Ideally - we'd find a loss function to align with F1, but there is no such loss function built-in. Binary Crossentropy is what's used when we're performing binary classification, typically.

> Binary Crossentropy has an issue with imbalanced datasets.

This makes our job here much harder, since the most widely used loss function for binary classification doesn't work very well for our dataset. Additionally, since we'll eventually want to maximize the F1 score (a tall order) - how do we maximize F1?

> Which loss function maximizes F1?

Well, Binary Crossentropy does well with F1, but can fail with heavy imbalance if we do nothing. We'll be performing cost-sensitive learnig later to combat this. Many are tempted to turn to the function calculating F1 and to use that instead as a loss function, but it's non-differentiable, meaning, you can't calculate gradients for it, and gradients are necessary for Gradient Descent to optimize it.

$$F1 = (2 Precision Recall)/(Precision + Recall)$$

We can tweak the function to turn it into a differentiable calculation, making it a possible loss function for our model - and we will. In the *Hyperparameter Tuning* section, we'll define a custom *F1 Metric* and *F1 Loss* to see if that helps to any degree, keeping an open mind to the option that it doesn't help.

Intuitively, it *should*, but it doesn't have to be the case. On datasets that have a hard-to-achieve F1 score, the tug-of-war between precision and recall might not settle favorably for us. It's probable that one will generally degrade the other, and that we won't be able to get *both* of them to a very high number.

Considering the fact that the loss function we'll be using isn't fully aligned with the key metric we want to keep track of, F1 is likely to bounce up and down during training - it's optimizing for *binary accuracy* which we've already concluded is a poor metric for an honest performance of the model, and isn't aligned with F1.

Learning from imbalanced classes is an active area of research, and a big hurdle in the field of machine learing. While some solutions do exist - such as synthetically sampling, undersampling, etc., we've cut them off as viable solutions due to the nature of our specific dataset.

> Spoiler Alert: Neither defining F1 as a metric, nor a tweaked differentiable F1 loss helps here, so we won't be using it from the get-go.

One final thing we can employ is ***weighted/cost-sensitive learning***. We can give more weight to one class, rather than another, during training, and while this weight can be consulted about with professionals from the domain - a good rule of thumb is to start with the *inverse proportion* of the *natural proportion* of classes in the dataset. In our case, we've got ~3.4 IDC(-) samples for every 1 IDC(+) sample. It turned out to be a bit too high in experiments, so I've lowered it to 3.

Let's quickly define a dictionary, `class_weights` that we can pass into the `fit()` method later on:

```
1 # Assigning a higher weight to the positive class (IDC(+) samples)
2 class_weights = {0:1, 1:3}
```

Feel free to play with this number!

Note: An alternative to cost-sensitive learning is to simply tweak the treshold for classification. Since we're doing binary classification - the default treshold for figuring out which class a prediction belongs to is 0.5. If the result of the `sigmoid` activation is above 0.5 - it belongs to class 1 and vice versa. The authors of the original paper turned the treshold down to 0.29, reflecting the undersampling of the classes. Though, this doesn't "beat in" the innate value difference into the model.

7.7.2 Model Definition - CNN from Scratch

Let's start out by defining a custom CNN architecture! After benchmarking it, we'll try out some other well-known architectures, such as the ResNet and EfficientNet families.

In the end, we can create a baseline model comparison, and choose which model to fine-tune in the end.

The model definition will start with *Keras Preprocessing Layers*, which include layers for flipping, zooming, rotation, etc. They can effectively do most of the augmentations we used to do with `ImageDataGenerator`, but are *part of the model*! We'll come back to them in more detail in the next lesson, so let's not distract ourselves with them too much here:

```
model = keras.models.Sequential([
    keras.layers.InputLayer(input_shape=[config['IMG_SIZE'],
        config['IMG_SIZE'], 3]),
    keras.layers.RandomRotation(0.2),
    keras.layers.RandomZoom(0.15),
    keras.layers.RandomFlip("horizontal"),

    keras.layers.Conv2D(32, 3, activation = 'relu', padding = 'same',),
    keras.layers.Conv2D(32, 3, activation = 'relu', padding = 'same'),
    keras.layers.MaxPooling2D(2),
    keras.layers.BatchNormalization(),

    keras.layers.Conv2D(64, 2, activation = 'relu', padding = 'same'),
    keras.layers.Conv2D(64, 2, activation = 'relu', padding = 'same'),
    keras.layers.MaxPooling2D(2),
    keras.layers.BatchNormalization(),

    keras.layers.Conv2D(128, 3, activation = 'relu', padding = 'same'),
    keras.layers.Conv2D(128, 3, activation = 'relu', padding = 'same'),
    keras.layers.MaxPooling2D(2),
    keras.layers.BatchNormalization(),

    keras.layers.Conv2D(256, 3, activation = 'relu', padding = 'same'),
    keras.layers.Conv2D(256, 3, activation = 'relu', padding = 'same'),
    keras.layers.MaxPooling2D(2),
    keras.layers.BatchNormalization(),

    keras.layers.Conv2D(512, 3, activation = 'relu', padding = 'same'),
    keras.layers.Conv2D(512, 3, activation = 'relu', padding = 'same'),
    keras.layers.MaxPooling2D(2),
    keras.layers.BatchNormalization(),

    keras.layers.Flatten(),
    keras.layers.Dense(32, activation = 'relu'),
    keras.layers.BatchNormalization(),
    keras.layers.Dropout(0.4),
    keras.layers.Dense(1, activation = 'sigmoid')
])
```

The architecture is conceptually very similar to the VGG16 architecture, and progressively "shrinks down" the input representation through several convolutional and max pooling layers. This is also a pretty typical architecture for CNNs from mid-2010s, but is outdated compared to newer architectures (covered in lesson 7).

We're using a `sigmoid` activation function because we're performing binary classification and want to see the confidence of the network in the classification. Whether it's `0.51` or `0.99`, `0.23` or `0.0`. We'll ultimately have to round these to the nearest integer but it'll help to know how *confident* the network is in the final binary label.

Note: We're using one output neuron here, but could've just as well used two. Whether the network gives us a categorical prediction between two classes (benign or malignant) with a given probability, or a binary prediction towards one class (malignant) with a certain probability, exactly and only *because* one excludes the other, the label for the other can be inferred from the first. 5% probability that the input image is of a malignant IDC (class 1) means that the network is 95% confident that it is benign (class 0) and vice versa. The choice between `1` or `2` output neurons for binary classification makes the difference in regards to which Loss Function we'll use, but nothing more than that.

Since we only have 1 output neuron - we'll be using the `"binary_crossentropy"` loss function. If we were having 2 output classes, naturally, we'd choose something such as the `"categorical_crossentropy"` or `"sparse_categorical_crossentropy"` functions. `"adam"` is a sensible default optimizer, so we'll use that. Since binary accuracy isn't the best metric given the class imbalance - we'll also keep track of precision, recall and AUC:

```
1 model.summary()
2
3 model.compile(loss = "binary_crossentropy",
4               optimizer = 'adam',
5               metrics=[
6                   keras.metrics.BinaryAccuracy(),
7                   keras.metrics.Precision(),
8                   keras.metrics.Recall(),
9                   keras.metrics.AUC()
10              ])
```

```
1 ...
2 =====================
```

```
3 Total params: 5,275,489
4 Trainable params: 5,273,441
5 Non-trainable params: 2,048
6 _________________________
```

We've got a decently sized network with 5.2M trainable parameters. Let's see what it can do! We'll define `EarlyStopping`, `ModelCheckpoint` callbacks. Since it's not a particularly small (but also not a particularly large) network, we'll want to stop it if it doesn't improve through time:

```
1 callbacks = [
2     tf.keras.callbacks.EarlyStopping(patience=5),
3     tf.keras.callbacks.ModelCheckpoint(filepath = 'breast_cancer_custom.h5',
        save_best_only=True)
4 ]
5
6 history = model.fit(train_set_small,
7                     validation_data = valid_set_small,
8                     callbacks = callbacks,
9                     epochs = 15,
10                    class_weight = class_weights)
```

The `class_weights` is a hyperparameter to tune, and plays an important role here. After 8 epochs, the training is halted:

```
1 Epoch 1/15
2 2020/2020 [==============================] - 135s 65ms/step - loss: 0.7632 -
      binary_accuracy: 0.7530 - precision: 0.4821 - recall: 0.7942 - auc:
      0.8298 - val_loss: 0.5842 - val_binary_accuracy: 0.7868 - val_precision:
      0.8104 - val_recall: 0.1337 - val_auc: 0.8489
3 ...
4 Epoch 15/15
5 2020/2020 [==============================] - 130s 64ms/step - loss: 0.6044 -
      binary_accuracy: 0.8184 - precision: 0.5751 - recall: 0.8493 - auc:
      0.8924 - val_loss: 0.4232 - val_binary_accuracy: 0.8250 - val_precision:
      0.5953 - val_recall: 0.8250 - val_auc: 0.8956
```

The loss was pretty rocky, going up and down (unstable training), and this translates to recall and precision being rocky during training. Again, the loss function we've used isn't perfectly aligned with them, so that's to be expected at least to a degree - but the recall is *really* rocky, while precision is somewhat stable. That doesn't signal well.

Let's evaluate the baseline model:

```
1 # Load the best saved model, not necesarily the last
2 model = keras.models.load_model('breast_cancer_custom.h5')
3
4 # To hold true and predicted labels
```

```
5  y_pred = np.array([])
6  y_true_small = np.array([])
7  count = 0
8
9  # Shuffling a set means shuffling it during inference too.
10 # We can't just stack and re-use the `y_true_small` array unfortunately.
11 # We'll have to iterate, predict and store ground truth every time.
12 for x, y in test_set_small:
13     print(f'Evaluating batch {count}/{len(test_set_small)}', end = '\r')
14     count += 1
15     y_pred = np.concatenate([y_pred, model(x).numpy().flatten()])
16     y_true_small = np.concatenate([y_true_small, y.numpy()])
17
18 # Plot confusion matrix
19 sns.heatmap(confusion_matrix(y_true_small, np.round(y_pred)), annot=True,
       fmt = 'g')
20 plt.show()
21 # Print classification report
22 print(sklearn.metrics.classification_report(y_true_small, np.round(y_pred)))
```

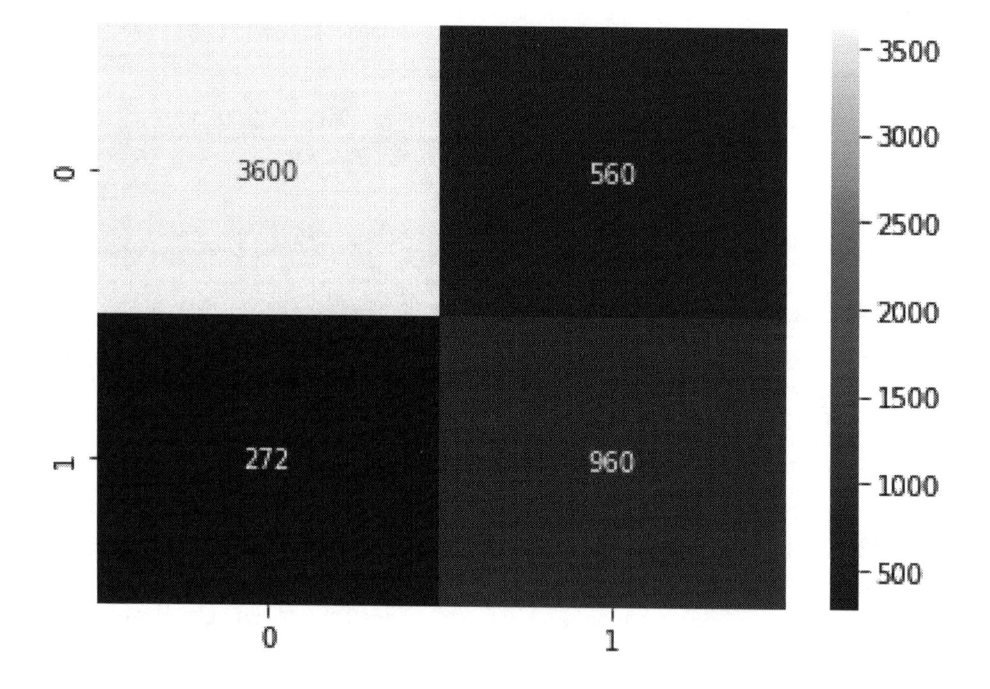

Figure 92:

```
1               precision    recall  f1-score   support
2
3         0.0       0.93      0.87      0.90      4160
4         1.0       0.63      0.78      0.70      1232
5
6    accuracy                           0.85      5392
7   macro avg       0.78      0.82      0.80      5392
8 weighted avg      0.86      0.85      0.85      5392
```

Not bad! A 0.9 F1 for class `0` and 0.7 F1 for class `1`. The latter is evidently being harder to learn about with a lower precision and recall. This will serve as a good baseline. Let's try some other models out.

7.7.3 Model Definition - EfficientNetV2S Base

With the custom CNN baseline checked, let's see if we can utilize some of the pre-existing architectures to boost the performance. These architectures have specialized building blocks and will typically perform better than a solution as simple as the one laid out in the previous section. Keras comes with a bunch of built-in models, both pre-trained and empty!

Let's load in `EfficientNetV2BM`, an architecture of Google's EfficientNet family. You might intuitively conclude that the weights that come with ImageNet aren't too relevant here. Those are great for animals (bunch of animals in ImageNet), manmade objects, etc. There are a lot of high-level features embedded into ImageNet weights and the images we're dealing with have lines (straight, diagonal and curved) and circles for the large part.

> "These features are relatively low in the complexity hierarchy, so we wouldn't be able to transfer much of the knowledge representations from ImageNet" - many would retort.

And many would miss out on some of the amazing benefits of Transfer Learning through this. Not only are these levels transferable - they're, as a matter of fact, surprisingly relevant to our own dataset. Using pre-trained weights, and then fine-tuning the network on our own dataset not only increased the overall accuracy/recall/precision of the model, but it also stabilized the training!

There's a serious lack of pre-trained models in Medical Image Diagnosis, and given how relevant ImageNet can be - releasing more pre-trained models online might help the field grow faster.

Note: Using EfficientNetV2M as a feature extractor, naturally, won't work really well, unless you **only** freeze some of the lower levels (only the starting ones). On the other hand, fine-tuning the entirety of the network from the get-go is a great example of transferring general knowledge to this dataset.

The applicability and importance of Transfer Learning seems to be underestimated. In our example, it doesn't intuitively seem like ImageNet is too relevant for transferring knowledge - but it actually is. If you are to argue differently - try using EfficientNet with and without pre-trained weights on this dataset and compare them.

Getting back to the point - the EfficientNet family, spanning from B0 to B7 is an efficiently-scaling, highly-performant family of models. Alongside some other architectures, it's consistently ranked in the top performant models in most benchmarks. Additionally, recently, the second version of the family has been published, and the second version is meant to be used as `V2S`, `V2M` and `V2L`, with `V2B0..V2B3` as legacy models for comparison with older variants. We'll cover them in more detail in upcoming chapters.

Before we get into them on a more technical level, let's have some fun and build something useful with them:

```
1 model2 = keras.models.Sequential([
2     keras.layers.InputLayer(input_shape=[config['IMG_SIZE'],
          config['IMG_SIZE'], 3]),
3     keras.layers.RandomRotation(0.2),
4     keras.layers.RandomZoom(0.15),
5     keras.layers.RandomFlip("horizontal"),
6     keras.applications.EfficientNetV2S(weights =
          'imagenet',include_top=False),
7     keras.layers.GlobalAveragePooling2D(),
8     keras.layers.Dropout(0.3),
9     keras.layers.Dense(1, activation = 'sigmoid')
10 ])
11
12 model2.summary()
```

Note that there's no `Flatten()` layer! More on that in the next lesson. We've added the entirety of the network as a single layer, instead of exposing the building layers through `EfficientNetV2BS.output`. The only difference this makes is whether the `summary()` prints out a long, convoluted block or a shorter one:

```
...

====================
Total params: 20,332,641
Trainable params: 20,178,769
Non-trainable params: 153,872
______________________
```

Awesome, let's train the network! It's got ~20M trainable parameters, significantly more than our own solution. The great thing about EfficientNet networks is that they're, well, efficient! This one won't take 4 times the training time it took for our custom CNN. If your machine runs out of memory, try `EfficientNetV2B0` or running the code on Google Colab/Kaggle.

The same metrics and callbacks will be useful this time around as well:

```
callbacks = [
    tf.keras.callbacks.EarlyStopping(patience=5),
    tf.keras.callbacks.ModelCheckpoint(filepath =
        'breast_cancer_effnetv2s.h5', save_best_only=True),
]

model2.compile(loss = "binary_crossentropy",
               optimizer = 'adam',
               metrics=[
                   keras.metrics.BinaryAccuracy(),
                   keras.metrics.Precision(),
                   keras.metrics.Recall(),
                   keras.metrics.AUC()
               ])

history2 = model2.fit(train_set_small,
                      validation_data = valid_set_small,
                      callbacks = callbacks,
                      epochs = 15,
                      class_weight = class_weights)
```

```
Epoch 1/15
2020/2020 [==============================] - 448s 215ms/step - loss: 0.6542
    - binary_accuracy: 0.7968 - precision_1: 0.5423 - recall_1: 0.8218 -
    auc_1: 0.8760 - val_loss: 0.4105 - val_binary_accuracy: 0.8096 -
    val_precision_1: 0.5597 - val_recall_1: 0.9248 - val_auc_1: 0.9274
...
Epoch 9/15
```

```
5 2020/2020 [==============================] - 431s 214ms/step - loss: 0.4935
     - binary_accuracy: 0.8540 - precision_1: 0.6341 - recall_1: 0.8832 -
     auc_1: 0.9275 - val_loss: 0.3369 - val_binary_accuracy: 0.8520 -
     val_precision_1: 0.6364 - val_recall_1: 0.8805 - val_auc_1: 0.9333
```

The EfficientNet was much more stable during training, and didn't bounce around as much as our own network did. This is, in a way, indication that it was able to learn some distinctive features between the classes.

Let's evaluate it:

```
 1 model2 = keras.models.load_model('breast_cancer_effnetv2s.h5')
 2 
 3 y_pred = np.array([])
 4 y_true_small = np.array([])
 5 count = 0
 6 
 7 for x, y in test_set_small:
 8     print(f'Evaluating batch {count}/{len(test_set_small)}', end = '\r')
 9     count += 1
10     y_pred = np.concatenate([y_pred, model2(x).numpy().flatten()])
11     y_true_small = np.concatenate([y_true_small, y.numpy()])
12 
13 sns.heatmap(confusion_matrix(y_true_small, np.round(y_pred)), annot=True,
     fmt = 'g')
14 plt.show()
15 
16 print(sklearn.metrics.classification_report(y_true_small, np.round(y_pred)))
```

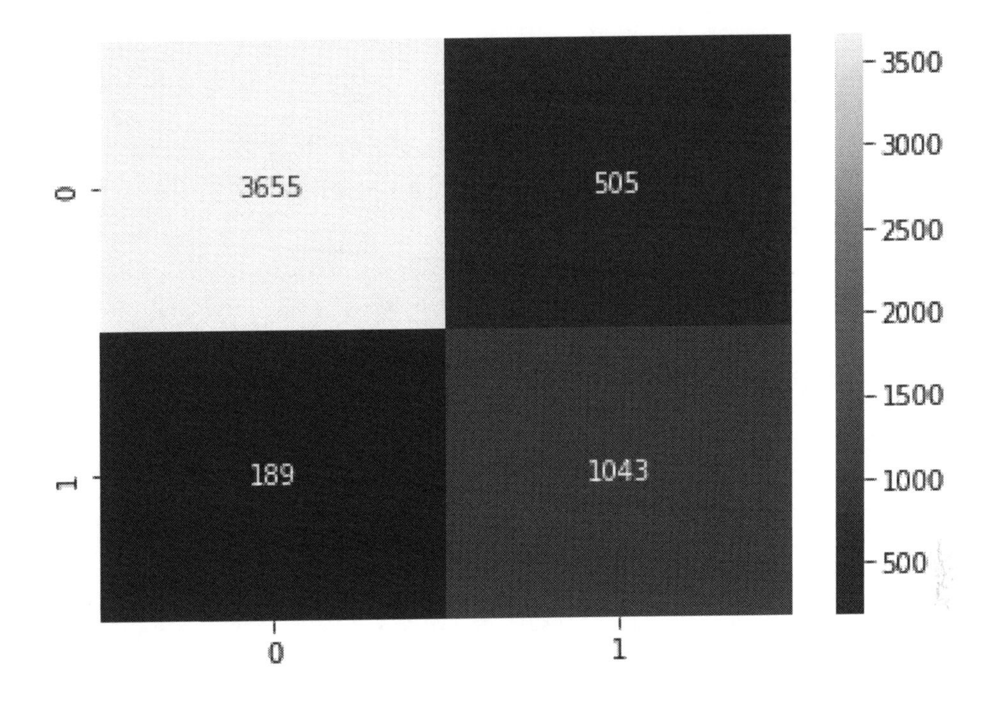

Figure 93:

```
              precision    recall  f1-score   support

         0.0       0.95      0.88      0.91      4160
         1.0       0.67      0.85      0.75      1232

    accuracy                           0.87      5392
   macro avg       0.81      0.86      0.83      5392
weighted avg       0.89      0.87      0.88      5392
```

A jump to 0.75 F1 is a nice one! There's still a lot more to tune and optimize, as well as to train for longer with an LR reduction. EfficientNetV2S is proving to be able to discern between classes capably.

7.7.4 Model Definition - ResNet101

When comparing models, it's worth using models with the same general capabilities. There's no use comparing ResNet50 against Xception and EfficientNetV2S - which are both in a league above it. ResNet101 or ResNet152 is closer, but both can be expected to perform somewhat worse. Let's try ResNet anyways.

Residual Networks (ResNets) are a seminal architecture that popularized an approach used by practically all networks after them - shortcut connections. We'll dive into Residual Learning, blocks and shortcut connections in the next lesson. Let's stay in the ball park of the architecture to hopefully get to exploit it to the fullest:

```
model3 = keras.models.Sequential([
    keras.layers.InputLayer(input_shape=[config['IMG_SIZE'],
        config['IMG_SIZE'], 3]),
    keras.layers.RandomRotation(0.2),
    keras.layers.RandomZoom(0.15),
    keras.layers.RandomFlip("horizontal"),
    keras.applications.ResNet101(weights = 'imagenet', include_top=False),
    keras.layers.GlobalAveragePooling2D(),
    keras.layers.Dense(1, activation = 'sigmoid')
])

model3.summary()

callbacks = [
    tf.keras.callbacks.EarlyStopping(patience=5),
    tf.keras.callbacks.ModelCheckpoint(filepath =
        'breast_cancer_resnet101.h5',  save_best_only=True)
]

model3.compile(loss = "binary_crossentropy",
              optimizer = 'adam',
              metrics=[
                  keras.metrics.BinaryAccuracy(),
                  keras.metrics.Precision(),
                  keras.metrics.Recall(),
                  keras.metrics.AUC()
              ])

history3 = model3.fit(train_set_small,
                      validation_data = valid_set_small,
                      callbacks = callbacks,
                      epochs = 15,
                      class_weight = class_weights)
```

This results in:

```
...
```

```
=====================
Total params: 42,660,225
Trainable params: 42,554,881
Non-trainable params: 105,344
_____________________
Epoch 1/15
2020/2020 [==============================] - 458s 222ms/step - loss: 0.6799
     - binary_accuracy: 0.7913 - precision_2: 0.5342 - recall_2: 0.8198 -
     auc_2: 0.8704 - val_loss: 0.6771 - val_binary_accuracy: 0.8334 -
     val_precision_2: 0.8534 - val_recall_2: 0.3599 - val_auc_2: 0.8354
...
Epoch 8/15
2020/2020 [==============================] - 444s 220ms/step - loss: 0.5091
     - binary_accuracy: 0.8462 - precision_2: 0.6221 - recall_2: 0.8676 -
     auc_2: 0.9248 - val_loss: 0.4817 - val_binary_accuracy: 0.7626 -
     val_precision_2: 0.5005 - val_recall_2: 0.3972 - val_auc_2: 0.7894
```

Let's evaluate it:

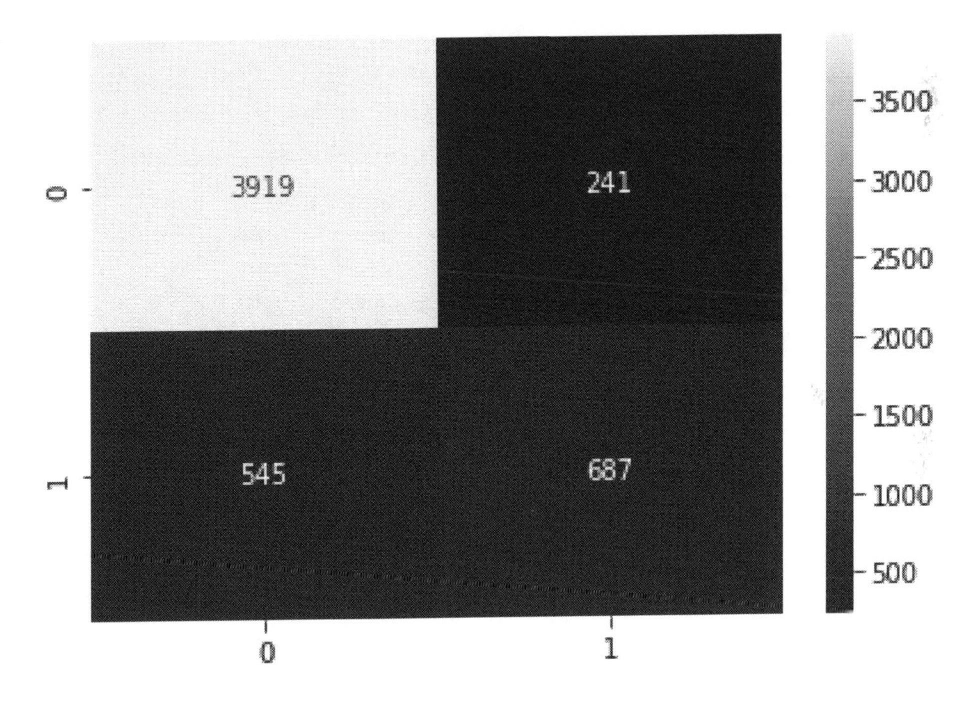

Figure 94:

```
              precision    recall  f1-score   support
```

```
2
3          0.0       0.88      0.94      0.91      4160
4          1.0       0.74      0.56      0.64      1232
5
6     accuracy                           0.85      5392
7    macro avg       0.81      0.75      0.77      5392
8 weighted avg       0.85      0.85      0.85      5392
```

Not that great. Poor recall for class `1`, fairly bad F1 score and 42M parameters! We'll definitely be passing over ResNet for this specific task and dataset.

7.7.5 Model Definition - Xception

Finally, let's try out one last high-performer architecture - Google's Xception, which is a VRAM-hungry, but very powerful architecture that stood the test of time. Standard convolutional layers perform *spatial* computation, while Xception performs *depthwise* computation, through *Depthwise Separable Convolution* layers. More details and a custom implementation are waiting for us in the next chapter.

Again, whether this helps us in our case or not remains to be seen. Xception's head is fairly similar to the one we've seen in ResNet's case, so we'll have the same `GlobalAveragePooling2D` layer, followed by a dense one:

```
1 model4 = keras.models.Sequential([
2     keras.layers.InputLayer(input_shape=[config['IMG_SIZE'],
         config['IMG_SIZE'], 3]),
3     keras.layers.RandomRotation(0.2),
4     keras.layers.RandomZoom(0.15),
5     keras.layers.RandomFlip("horizontal_and_vertical"),
6     keras.applications.Xception(weights = 'imagenet',include_top=False),
7     keras.layers.GlobalAveragePooling2D(),
8     keras.layers.Dense(1, activation = 'sigmoid')
9 ])
10
11 model4.summary()
12
13 callbacks = [
14     tf.keras.callbacks.EarlyStopping(patience=5),
15     tf.keras.callbacks.ModelCheckpoint(filepath =
         'breast_cancer_xception.h5',  save_best_only=True)
16 ]
17
18 model4.compile(loss = "binary_crossentropy",
19               optimizer = 'adam',
20               metrics=[
21                   keras.metrics.BinaryAccuracy(),
22                   keras.metrics.Precision(),
```

```
23                    keras.metrics.Recall(),
24                    keras.metrics.AUC()
25                ])
26
27 history4 = model4.fit(train_set_small,
28                       validation_data = valid_set_small,
29                       callbacks = callbacks,
30                       epochs = 15,
31                       class_weight = class_weights)
```

This results in:

```
1 ...
2 ======================
3 Total params: 20,863,529
4 Trainable params: 20,809,001
5 Non-trainable params: 54,528
6 ________________________
7 Epoch 1/15
8 2020/2020 [==============================] - 339s 166ms/step - loss: 0.6891
      - binary_accuracy: 0.7635 - precision_3: 0.4958 - recall_3: 0.8538 -
      auc_3: 0.8606 - val_loss: 0.3962 - val_binary_accuracy: 0.8479 -
      val_precision_3: 0.6307 - val_recall_3: 0.8687 - val_auc_3: 0.9170
9 ...
10 Epoch 11/15
11 2020/2020 [==============================] - 331s 164ms/step - loss: 0.4427
      - binary_accuracy: 0.8695 - precision_3: 0.6629 - recall_3: 0.8963 -
      auc_3: 0.9425 - val_loss: 0.8295 - val_binary_accuracy: 0.6599 -
      val_precision_3: 0.4056 - val_recall_3: 0.9242 - val_auc_3: 0.8269
```

And, let's evaluate it:

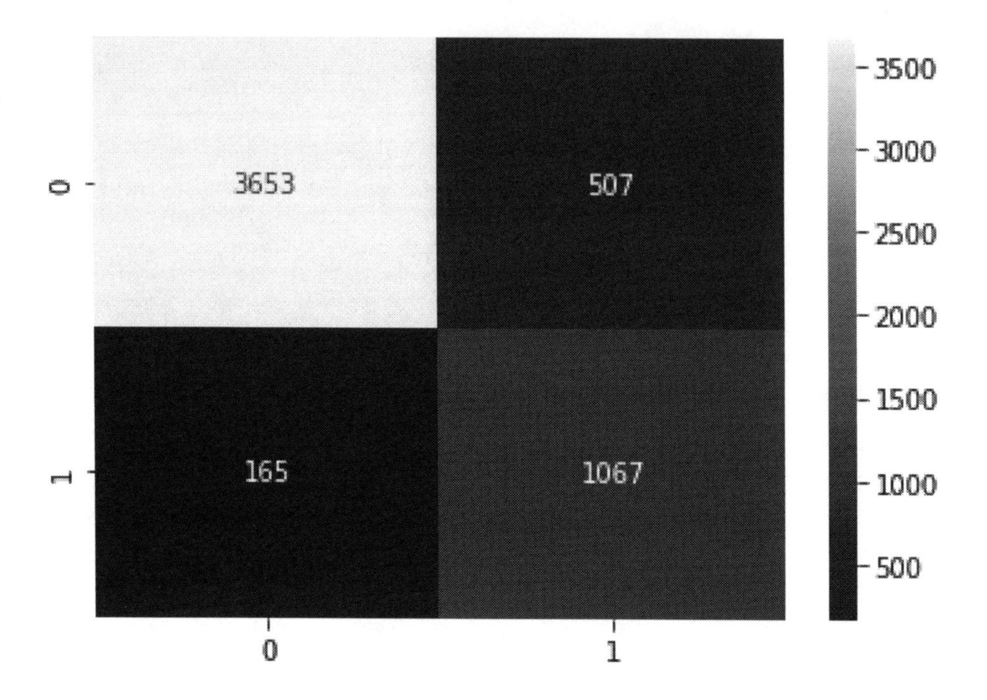

Figure 95:

```
1               precision    recall  f1-score   support
2
3          0.0       0.96      0.88      0.92      4160
4          1.0       0.68      0.87      0.76      1232
5
6     accuracy                           0.88      5392
7    macro avg       0.82      0.87      0.84      5392
8 weighted avg       0.89      0.88      0.88      5392
```

Very similar performance to EfficientNet! Xception did an (e)xceptional job here, outperforming it slightly. Now, the issue is - Xception takes much more VRAM due to its use of `SeparableConv2D` layers, and is fairly wide as a network. Additionally, you can upgrade EfficientNet performance by switching to `EfficientNetV2M` or `EfficientNetV2L`, while Xception is fixed. Since EfficientNets offer more headspace - we'll go with them, regardless of the slightly better performance of Xception in this run (the difference is slight enough to be counted as "luck").

7.7.6 Which Model Performs the Best?

Let's take a step back and take a look at which model is performing the best. This isn't as simple as stacking the accuracies and picking the one with the best score. Picking the best model has more to do with the recall and precision, scalability, how future-proof they are, parameter efficiency, inference speed, etc.

> We want a model with high *recall* but also high *precision*. We won't throw away a good AUC, but it's not as indicative of the performance as recall and precision in our case.

The highest recall a model could get would be when it outputs all true positives and doesn't produce any false negatives. It could do this by outputting a constant `1` for any input. However, its precision would be fairly low then, since there's only ~30% positive samples, making it worse than randomly guessing:

$$Recall = TP/(TP + FN)$$

The highest precision a model could get is when the model doesn't produce any *false positives*, and also outputs true positives:

$$Precision = TP/(TP + FP)$$

The *Precision-Recall* tradeoff is well-known, and covered in most beginner textbooks and courses, so we won't dive deeper into the topic here. They're typically in tension, and oftentimes, maximizing one reduces the other.

That being said, let's plot the relevant metrics for all of our models and check which one has a decent-enough tradeoff. The one with the best scores will be chosen for *hyperparameter tuning* as the best baseline candidate:

```
1 import seaborn as sns
2
3 # Evaluate the models to get performance stats
4 preds_custom = model.evaluate(test_set_small)
5 preds_effnet = model2.evaluate(test_set_small)
6 preds_resnet = model3.evaluate(test_set_small)
7 preds_xception = model4.evaluate(test_set_small)
8
```

```
9 # Extract into relevant model-related stats
10 cnn_recall, cnn_precision, cnn_auc, cnn_params = preds_custom[3],
       preds_custom[2], preds_custom[4], model.count_params()
11 effnet_recall, effnet_precision, effnet_auc, effnet_params =
       preds_effnet[3], preds_effnet[2], preds_effnet[4], model2.count_params()
12 resnet_recall, resnet_precision, resnet_auc, resnet_params =
       preds_resnet[3], preds_resnet[2], preds_resnet[4], model3.count_params()
13 xception_recall, xception_precision, xception_auc, xception_params =
       preds_xception[3], preds_xception[2], preds_xception[4],
       model4.count_params()
14
15 # Create dict to hold values
16 data = {
17     'Custom CNN' : [cnn_recall, cnn_precision, cnn_auc],
18     'EffNetV2S' : [effnet_recall, effnet_precision, effnet_auc],
19     'ResNet101' : [resnet_recall, resnet_precision, resnet_auc],
20     'Xception' : [xception_recall, xception_precision, xception_auc]
21 }
22
23 # Dict to DF
24 df = pd.DataFrame(data, index = ["Recall", "Precision", "AUC"]).T
25
26 print(df)
27
28 fig, ax = plt.subplots(figsize=(12, 8))
29
30 df_bar = df.reset_index().melt(id_vars=["index"])
31 sns.barplot(x = "variable", y = "value", hue = "index", data=df_bar, ax=ax)
```

The relevant metrics are extracted from the evaluations and referenced through indicative variable names. Let's take a look at what the `DataFrame` consists of now:

```
1               Recall  Precision       AUC
2 Custom CNN  0.779041   0.630921  0.910040
3 EffNetV2S   0.846591   0.673338  0.937398
4 ResNet101   0.557630   0.740302  0.896601
5 Xception    0.865963   0.677686  0.944932
```

From the numbers alone - Xception and EfficientNetV2S are standing shoulder to shoulder. Xception has a *slightly* higher precision and recall, but only ever so slightly, and the benefits of scaling outweigh the potentially "lucky" metrics.

Let's plot this data:

```
1 fig, ax = plt.subplots(figsize=(12, 8))
2
3 df_bar = df.reset_index().melt(id_vars=["index"])
4 sns.barplot(x = "variable", y = "value", hue = "index", data=df_bar, ax=ax)
```

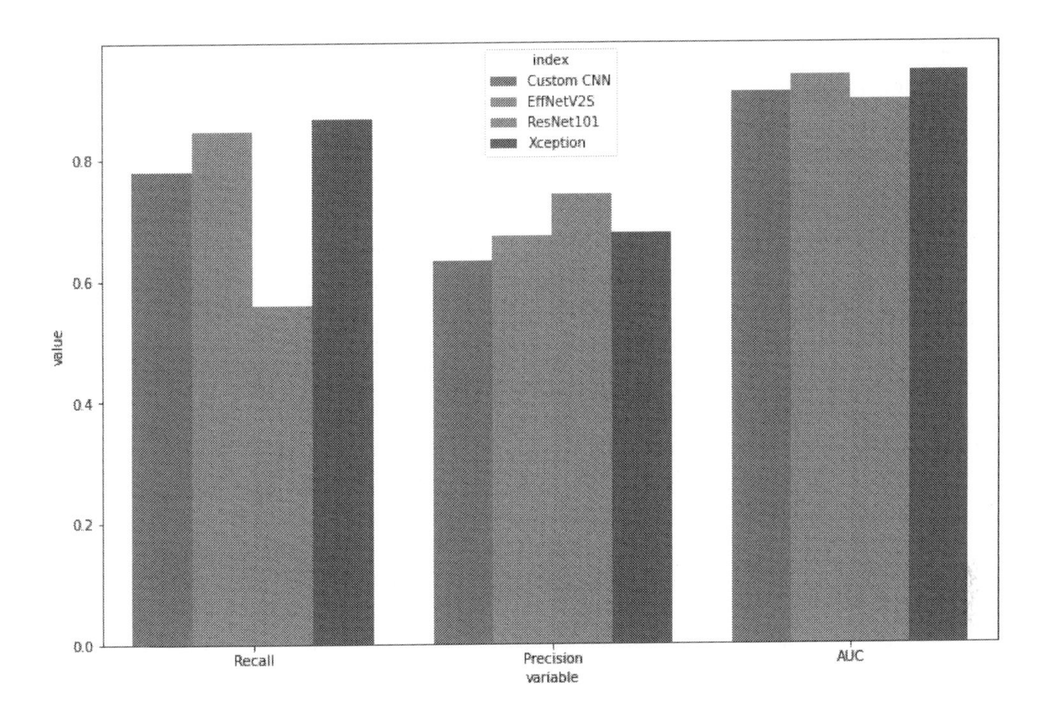

Figure 96:

> EfficientNet's and Xception's stability and high values between the metrics is what makes them a favorable choice here.

It's not super surprising to see EfficientNet beating a plain ResNet or our own custom CNN - and we'll be diving into all of these in an upcoming lesson.

It's worth taking a moment to appreciate how well our custom CNN model is holding up compared to the other architectures! It's not in a whole different league.

7.7.7 Hyperparameter Tuning

Finally, we've decided on an architecture and model. There's no guarantee that we've chosen the best hyperparameters, and oftentimes, choosing the wrong ones can *break* a model, let alone disallow it to perform its best. We've used sensible defaults, guided by educated guessing - but it's improbable (though, not impossible) that we've hit the jackpot straight away. Let's try tuning the hyperparameters of the architecture we chose!

> We'll be using the *KerasTuner* - a great, simplistic library for tuning existing Keras models.

The main hyperparameters we had in our architecture were the augmentation layers, dropout, learning rate and optimizer. We could also try to check out a `decay` for the learning rate, but we'll have a callback to reduce the LR on plateau to somewhat make up for it - but omitting the hyperparameter from the search makes the search faster.

Let's install and import KerasTuner:

```
1 $ pip install keras_tuner
```

```
1 import keras_tuner as kt
```

The `hp` (hyperparameter) module offers `hp.Choice()` stand-ins:

```
1 keras.layers.LayerName(hp.Choice('param_name', [value1, value2]))
```

Any Keras layer will gladly take a `hp.Choice()`, with the name to be referenced in the tuning process and possible values. This lets you set up tests for various parameters, such as the parameters listed earlier. Most importantly - it allows us to perform a hyperparameter search for augmentation parameters as well during tuning. Since there's really not too much we can tweak with the architecture itself (without unraveling it) - let's try to tune our input pipeline and dropout/optimizer. To run the hyperparameter search, we can choose between multiple tuners, including:

- RandomSearch
- BayesianOptimization
- Hyperband
- Sklearn

Random search, well, randomly searches the space and is fairly good at finding good parameters given enough time, just like `RandomizedSearchCV` is good at finding parameters for Scikit-Learn models. Bayesian optimization uses the Gaussian process, and Hyperband is a variation on the Hyperband algorithm, published under *"Hyperband:*

A Novel Bandit-Based Approach to Hyperparameter Optimization"[73]. It rephrases hyperparameter search as a *"pure-exploration non-stochastic infinite-armed bandit problem"* and is designed to be faster than competitor approaches:

```
tuner = kt.Hyperband(
    build_effnet,
    objective = 'val_loss',
    max_epochs=5)
```

It accepts a function that builds a compiled model and passes a `hp` instance to it, which we use to set up parameter choices, the objective metric (if it's a loss metric - the direction is to minimize it and maximize otherwise) and several optional arguments such as`max_epochs` per model (defaults to `100`) and `factor` for calculating brackets (Hyperband delegates the search to several successive brackets). Let's define a method that builds an EfficientNet with open options for some hyperparameters:

```
def build_effnet(hp):
    model = keras.Sequential()
    keras.layers.InputLayer(input_shape=[config['IMG_SIZE'],
        config['IMG_SIZE'], 3]),
    keras.layers.RandomRotation(hp.Choice('random_rot', [0.10, 0.15, 0.20,
        0.3])),
    keras.layers.RandomZoom(hp.Choice('random_zoom', [0.10, 0.15, 0.20,
        0.3])),
    keras.layers.RandomFlip(hp.Choice('flip', ['horizontal', 'vertical',
        'horizontal_and_vertical'])),
    model.add(keras.applications.EfficientNetV2S(weights = 'imagenet',
        include_top=False))
    model.add(keras.layers.GlobalAveragePooling2D())
    model.add(keras.layers.Dropout(hp.Choice('dropout', [0.2, 0.3, 0.4])))
    model.add(keras.layers.Dense(1, activation = 'sigmoid'))

    model.compile(loss = 'binary_crossentropy',
                  optimizer = hp.Choice('optimizer', ['adam', 'sgd',
                      'nadam']),
                  metrics=[
                   keras.metrics.BinaryAccuracy(),
                   keras.metrics.Precision(),
                   keras.metrics.Recall(),
                   keras.metrics.AUC()
                ])

    return model
```

When you run the search, you'll supply the training data, the number of epochs to run, and the validation data by which to evaluate runs (optional but practically required):

[73]https://arxiv.org/abs/1603.06560

```
tuner.search(train_set_small,
             epochs=5,
             validation_data=valid_set_small)
```

Now, kick back and enjoy your hot (or cold) beverage of choice, because this will take its sweet time. If you've followed this Guided Project from start to here, without pausing - it's a great time to get up, stretch a bit, or even go out for a walk in the park! Your body will thank you, and you won't be suspensfully waiting while the numbers crunch. After a while, this results in:

```
Trial X Complete [01h 38m 11s]
val_loss: 0.3385772109031677

Best val_loss So Far: 0.305325448513031
Total elapsed time: 04h 54m 52s
INFO:tensorflow:Oracle triggered exit
```

Note: You can run into an OOM error with KerasTuner for larger models. If you do, try updating the batch size and make it smaller, such as `config['BATCH_SIZE'] = 2`. Sometimes, Jupyter environments continue failing after failing once, so it might be a good choice to restart it and run the code for the tuning stage without re-running previous baseline trainings or to evenn tune in a different notebook.

This wasn't a particularly long search session - they can take much longer than this, depending on the number of hyperparameters you're testing, the networks you're fine tuning, etc. The `val_loss` is lower than what we achieved with our own EffNet, but this doesn't necessarily mean that it has to be a stable train after the initial 5 epochs.

Keras Tuner displays a really nice set of paramaters during training, but doesn't display them once the search is done. Let's take a look at the best runs:

```
tuner.results_summary()
```

This prints out:

```
Results summary
Results in .\untitled_project
Showing 10 best trials
Objective(name = 'val_loss', direction = 'min')
Trial summary
Hyperparameters:
random_rot: 0.2
random_zoom: 0.2
flip: vertical
dropout: 0.3
optimizer: sgd
tuner/epochs: 2
tuner/initial_epoch: 0
tuner/bracket: 1
tuner/round: 0
Score: 0.305325448513031
...
```

Looks like the best values for zooming and rotation were `0.2`, with only vertical flips, a `0.3` dropout rate and an SGD optimizer! This is curious, since it's generally known that SGD takes more tuning to work best, and we haven't even set the momentum or Nesterov acceleration arguments for it, which are pretty common for making SGD optimize a bit better. It looks like it outperformed Adam here though, even despite that. The second best run used `nadam`!

We can extract the best model from the search via:

```
tuned_model = tuner.get_best_models()[0]
```

Let's save the model as a tuned baseline and blank slate. We can run some extra runs with it but saving varied instances under different names, but leaving the baseline intact:

```
tuned_model.save('breast_cancer_tuned_baseline.h5')
```

For future runs, we'll want to keep track of the F1 score, and set up a monitor for the `val_f1` score. As a reminder, F1 is calculated as:

$$F1 = (2 Precision Recall)/(Precision + Recall)$$

We have to calculate precision and recall, based on the number of true positives, false positives and false negatives, and then calculate F1.

Michal Haltuf wrote a great simple F1 Metric and Loss function in a public Kaggle notebook[74], which we'll kindly be using as well:

```
import tensorflow as tf
import keras.backend as K

def f1(y_true, y_pred):
    y_pred = K.round(y_pred)
    # Calculate true positives, true negatives, false positives and false
        negatives
    tp = K.sum(K.cast(y_true*y_pred, 'float'), axis=0)
    tn = K.sum(K.cast((1-y_true)*(1-y_pred), 'float'), axis=0)
    fp = K.sum(K.cast((1-y_true)*y_pred, 'float'), axis=0)
    fn = K.sum(K.cast(y_true*(1-y_pred), 'float'), axis=0)

    # Calculate precision and recall
    # Adding epsilon (small value) to combat potential division by 0
    p = tp / (tp + fp + K.epsilon())
    r = tp / (tp + fn + K.epsilon())

    # Calculate F1
    f1 = 2*p*r / (p+r+K.epsilon())
    f1 = tf.where(tf.math.is_nan(f1), tf.zeros_like(f1), f1)
    return K.mean(f1)

def f1_loss(y_true, y_pred):
    tp = K.sum(K.cast(y_true*y_pred, 'float'), axis=0)
    tn = K.sum(K.cast((1-y_true)*(1-y_pred), 'float'), axis=0)
    fp = K.sum(K.cast((1-y_true)*y_pred, 'float'), axis=0)
    fn = K.sum(K.cast(y_true*(1-y_pred), 'float'), axis=0)

    p = tp / (tp + fp + K.epsilon())
    r = tp / (tp + fn + K.epsilon())

    f1 = 2*p*r / (p+r+K.epsilon())
    f1 = tf.where(tf.math.is_nan(f1), tf.zeros_like(f1), f1)
    # Minimizing 1-F1 is equal to maximizing F1
    return 1 - K.mean(f1)
```

Note: This is an *unweighted* F1 score. It assigns equal weights to Recall and Precision.

Now we can use `f1` as a metric and `f1_loss` as a loss! Let's try using our baseline network with `f1_loss`. When loading models with custom objects such as losses or metrics, you'll have to supply a `custom_objects` dictionary while loading them:

[74] https://www.kaggle.com/rejpalcz/best-loss-function-for-f1-score-metric/notebook

```
# Load model
model_tuned = keras.models.load_model('breast_cancer_tuned_baseline.h5',
    custom_objects={'f1':f1})

# Save under another name to not overwrite baseline
callbacks = [
    keras.callbacks.EarlyStopping(patience=6),
    keras.callbacks.ModelCheckpoint(filepath =
        'breast_cancer_effnet_f1_loss.h5',  save_best_only=True, monitor =
        "val_f1"),
    keras.callbacks.ReduceLROnPlateau(patience=5)
]

model_f1_loss.compile(loss = f1_loss,
              optimizer = 'sgd',
              metrics=[
                  f1,
                  keras.metrics.BinaryAccuracy(),
                  keras.metrics.Precision(),
                  keras.metrics.Recall(),
                  keras.metrics.AUC()
              ])

model_f1_loss_history = model_f1_loss.fit(train_set_small,
                        validation_data=valid_set_small,
                        callbacks=callbacks,
                        epochs=15,
                        class_weight=class_weights)
```

```
Epoch 1/15
8083/8083 [==============================] - 1205s 148ms/step - loss: 0.7980
    - f1: 0.3128 - binary_accuracy: 0.4411 - precision_1: 0.2755 - recall_1:
    0.8570 - auc_1: 0.5868 - val_loss: 0.7013 - val_f1: 0.2987 -
    val_binary_accuracy: 0.2375 - val_precision_1: 0.2375 - val_recall_1:
    1.0000 - val_auc_1: 0.5000 - lr: 0.0010
...
Epoch 12/15
8083/8083 [==============================] - 1193s 148ms/step - loss: 0.8265
    - f1: 0.2930 - binary_accuracy: 0.2332 - precision_1: 0.2332 - recall_1:
    1.0000 - auc_1: 0.5000 - val_loss: 0.6955 - val_f1: 0.3053 -
    val_binary_accuracy: 0.4590 - val_precision_1: 0.2945 - val_recall_1:
    0.9156 - val_auc_1: 0.6424 - lr: 1.0000e-04
```

It's halted at 12 epochs. The validation loss is *higher* than it was in the beginning! The F1 score, precision and accuracy are dismal:

```
              precision    recall  f1-score   support

         0.0       0.71      0.52      0.60      4160
         1.0       0.14      0.27      0.19      1232

    accuracy                           0.46      5392
```

```
7    macro avg       0.42      0.39      0.39      5392
8 weighted avg       0.58      0.46      0.50      5392
```

Looks like our *baseline* model actually outperforms the attempted optimized loss function, as it strikes a good balance between precision and recall.

7.8 Other EfficientNet Models?

You might be tempted to train another EfficientNet model here - `EfficientNetV2M` and `EfficientNetV2L` most notably. Generally speaking, yes, they should outperform `V2S`, and likely will. You'll just need more compute and time. The GPU memory required to train them is rare on home setups, and you'll likely need access to free or paid cloud computational service services, potentially training for a couple of days.

7.9 Training the Selected Model on All Data

Now that we've selected a model to go with - let's process and load in *all* of the data. Let's repeat the rearranging step, for all of the images this time around:

```
1 if not os.path.exists('./hist_images/'):
2     print('Making folders for hist_images')
3     os.mkdir('./hist_images/')
4 
5     os.mkdir('./hist_images/train/')
6     os.mkdir('./hist_images/test/')
7     os.mkdir('./hist_images/valid/')
8 
9     os.mkdir('./hist_images/train/0/')
10    os.mkdir('./hist_images/train/1/')
11    os.mkdir('./hist_images/test/0/')
12    os.mkdir('./hist_images/test/1/')
13 
14    os.mkdir('./hist_images/valid/0/')
15    os.mkdir('./hist_images/valid/1/')
16 
17    print('hist_images not processed, processing now')
18    for batch_num, indices in enumerate(range(1000, len(data), 1000), 1):
19        X = []
20        y = []
21 
22        for i in data[indices-1000:indices]:
23            if i.endswith('.png'):
24                label=i[-5]
25                img = cv2.imread(i)
26                if img.shape == (50, 50, 3):
```

```
27                     X.append(img)
28                     y.append(label)
29
30         X = np.array(X)
31         y = np.array(y)
32
33         print(f'Processing batch {batch_num}, with images from
               {indices-1000} to {indices}', end = '\r')
34
35         X_train, X_test, y_train, y_test = train_test_split(X, y,
               shuffle=True, test_size=0.4, stratify=y)
36
37         for index, img in enumerate(X_train):
38             idc_class = y_train[index]
39             path = os.path.join('hist_images', 'train', str(idc_class),
                   f'batch_{batch_num}_sample_{index}.png')
40             cv2.imwrite(path, img.astype('int'))
41
42         for index, img in enumerate(X_test):
43             if index%2 == 0:
44                 idc_class = y_test[index]
45                 path = os.path.join('hist_images', 'test', str(idc_class),
                       f'batch_{batch_num}_sample_{index}.png')
46                 cv2.imwrite(path, img.astype('int'))
47             else:
48                 idc_class = y_test[index]
49                 path = os.path.join('hist_images', 'valid', str(idc_class),
                       f'batch_{batch_num}_sample_{index}.png')
50                 cv2.imwrite(path, img.astype('int'))
```

Extract the paths:

```
1 train_paths = glob(os.path.join('hist_images', 'train', '*', '*'),
      recursive=True)
2 test_paths = glob(os.path.join('hist_images', 'test', '*', '*'),
      recursive=True)
3 valid_paths = glob(os.path.join('hist_images', 'valid', '*', '*'),
      recursive=True)
```

Make sure that they're all there:

```
1 print(len(train_paths)) # 164759
2 print(len(test_paths))  # 54996
3 print(len(test_paths))  # 54996
```

Extract the labels:

```
1 train_labels = get_labels(train_paths)
2 test_labels = get_labels(test_paths)
3 valid_labels = get_labels(valid_paths)
```

Create the datasets:

```
train_set = create_dataset(train_paths, train_labels)
test_set = create_dataset(test_paths, test_labels)
valid_set = create_dataset(valid_paths, valid_labels)
```

And train the model:

```
model_tuned = keras.models.load_model('breast_cancer_tuned_baseline.h5',
    custom_objects={'f1':f1})

callbacks = [
    tf.keras.callbacks.EarlyStopping(patience=6),
    tf.keras.callbacks.ModelCheckpoint(filepath =
        'breast_cancer_effnet_tuned.h5',  save_best_only=True, monitor =
        "val_f1"),
    tf.keras.callbacks.ReduceLROnPlateau(patience=5)
]

model_tuned.compile(loss = 'binary_crossentropy',
              optimizer = 'sgd',
              metrics=[
                  f1,
                  keras.metrics.BinaryAccuracy(),
                  keras.metrics.Precision(),
                  keras.metrics.Recall(),
                  keras.metrics.AUC()
              ])

model_tuned_history = model_tuned.fit(train_set,
                    validation_data=valid_set,
                    callbacks=callbacks,
                    epochs=15,
                   class_weight=class_weights)
```

This results in:

```
Epoch 1/15
20594/20594 [==============================] - 4137s 200ms/step - loss:
    0.5769 - f1: 0.6968 - binary_accuracy: 0.8300 - precision_1: 0.6524 -
    recall_1: 0.8701 - auc_1: 0.9159 - val_loss: 0.3482 - val_f1: 0.7211 -
    val_binary_accuracy: 0.8539 - val_precision_1: 0.6844 - val_recall_1:
    0.9118 - val_auc_1: 0.9459 - lr: 0.0100
...
Epoch 15/15
20594/20594 [==============================] - 4022s 195ms/step - loss:
    0.2199 - f1: 0.8411 - binary_accuracy: 0.9376 - precision_1: 0.8416 -
    recall_1: 0.9637 - auc_1: 0.9862 - val_loss: 0.2872 - val_f1: 0.7677 -
    val_binary_accuracy: 0.8949 - val_precision_1: 0.7672 - val_recall_1:
    0.9104 - val_auc_1: 0.9603 - lr: 0.0100
```

Let's take a look at the confusion matrix:

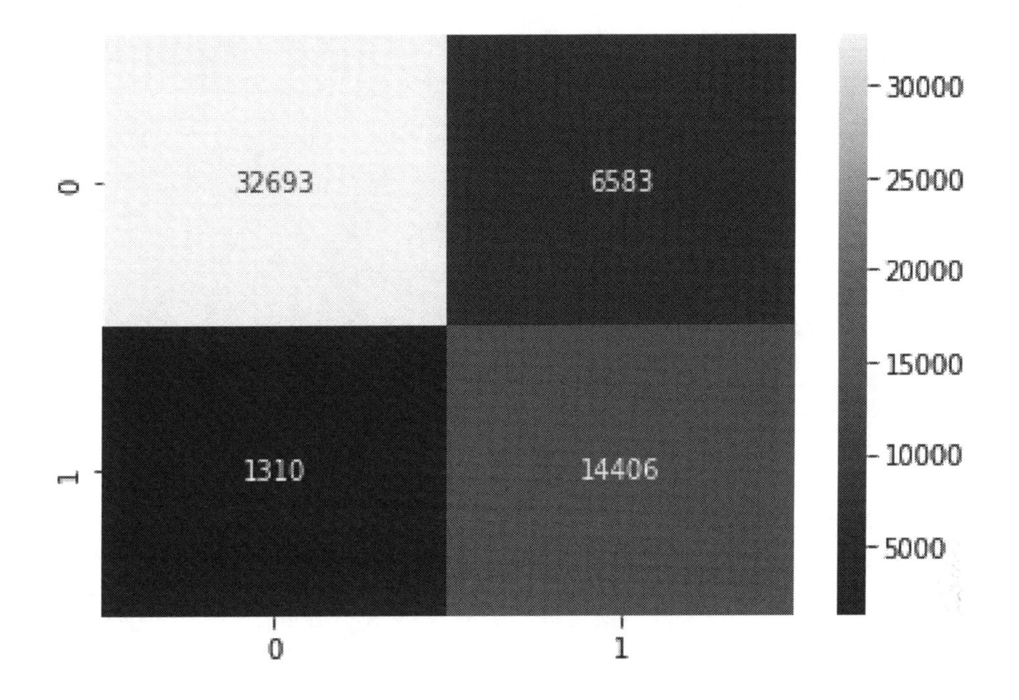

Figure 97:

```
               precision    recall  f1-score   support

         0.0       0.96      0.83      0.89     39276
         1.0       0.69      0.92      0.78     15716

    accuracy                           0.86     54992
   macro avg       0.82      0.87      0.84     54992
weighted avg       0.88      0.86      0.86     54992
```

Finally, let's visualize some of the predictions and images with their true labels:

```
for img_batch, label_batch in test_set.take(1):
    fig = plt.figure(figsize=(10,10))
    for i in range(len(img_batch)):
        ax = fig.add_subplot(4,4,i+1)
        ax.imshow(img_batch[i].numpy().astype('int'))


        image = np.expand_dims(img_batch[i], 0)
        pred = model_tuned(image)
```

```
10         pred = np.squeeze(pred)
11
12         ax.set_title(f'True:{label_batch.numpy()[i]} \n Pred:
               {np.round(pred)} \n Prob: {str(pred*100)[:4]}%')
13 plt.tight_layout()
```

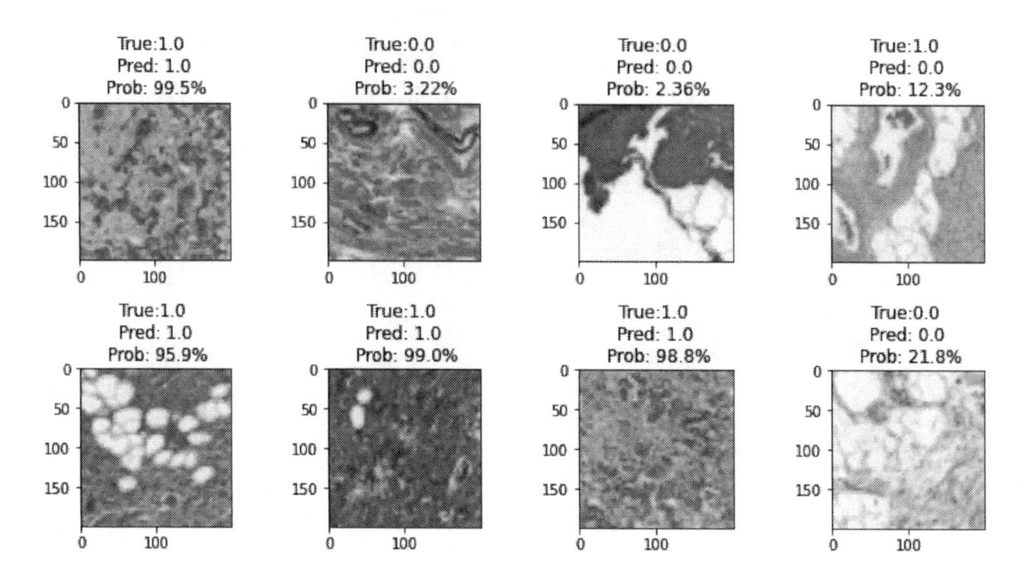

Figure 98:

8 Convolutional Neural Networks - Beyond Basic Architectures

So far, we've been working with a very distinctive, very exemplary architecture. I've noted that it's fairly similar to the VGG architecture that used to reign supreme for a pretty short while, but which is slowly being phased out.

This sort of network is easy to understand because it's practically a 1-to-1 mapping to the most intuitive explanation of how CNNs work - through convolutional layers, pooling layers, flattening layers and a fully-connected layer. It's also the most intuitive to understand with a limited understanding of how the visual cortex works. If you're a neuroscientist - you've likely aggressively cringed at the simplification of the inner-workings of the visual cortex from earlier lessons. The concept of hierarchical representations is there - but that's where our implementation and the cortex part ways.

The architecture used so far is, in a sense, the most natural and gentle introduction to CNNs - conceptually and implementation-wise. It provides fairly decent performance (in terms of accuracy) but bottlenecks with the number of parameters. At this point, you've built multiple classifiers, all of them very capable. You've gotten introduced to the inner-workings of the classifiers, got exposed to latent space visualization, biases, challanged the notion that overfitting is bad, explored the implications of data augmentation and context, implemented a custom loss function and metric, explored class imbalance, and even wrote a research-grade classifier for Invasive Ductal Carcinoma!

In my quest to demystify deep learning for computer vision - another hurdle remains a black box system. I've mentioned various other architectures so far, with a promise that they'll be covered later. It might seem *late* to introduce them now since we've used them both for transfer learning and the breast cancer classification project - but it's exceedingly difficult to really appreciate some of the advancements made with these architectures *without* going through a real project and evaluating the performance of the different architectures. **You don't need to deeply understand an architecture to use it effectively in a product.** You can drive a car without knowing whether the engine has 4 or 8 cylinders and what the placement of the valves within the engine is. However - if you want to *design* and *appreciate* an engine (computer vision model), you'll probably want to go a bit deeper. Even if you don't want to spend time designing architectures and want to build products instead, which is what *most* want to do - you'll still find interesting information in this lesson. If nothing else - you'll get to learn why using outdated architectures like VGGNet will hurt your product and performance, and why you should skip them if you're building *anything* modern, and you'll learn which architectures you can go to for solving practical problems and what the pros and cons are for each. If you're looking to apply computer vision to your field, using the resources from this lesson - you'll be able to find the newest models, understand how they work and by which criteria you can compare them and make a decision on which to use.

Now, it's time to peel back and take a look at how they really work. In this lesson, I'll take you on a bit of time travel - going from 1998 to 2022, highlighting the defining architectures developed throughout the years, what made them unique, what their drawbacks are, and implement the notable ones from scratch. There's nothing better than having some dirt on your hands when it comes to these, and you've come to a point where you can really appreciate these additions and the benefits they give. Some architectures are more complex than others, and it would take a fair bit of theoretical underpinnings to properly implement them with all the quirks, so to stay true to the practical nature of the book we won't implement *all* of them from scratch, but will linger enough to highlight their contributions.

Important: This lesson will serve as a guide through ideas and the progression of "common wisdom". Some architectures are factually more relevant and have left a more significant legacy than others, and I'll spend more time on those. For instance, plain ResNets don't offer cutting-edge performance anymore, but new tweaks, variants and combinations are still relevant today in 2022. Thus - investing more time into ResNets will lower your barrier to entry to newer architectures that leverage the concept of residual learning. I've gone through several dozen research papers to write this lesson (read or re-read 79 of them, to be exact), and many of them will be referenced throughout it. This is also a great time to go through them yourself and practice paper-reading!

Reading papers is a skill in and of itself - they can be complex, full of technical lingo and otherwise hard to follow in some cases if you don't have extensive experience. Throughout the lesson, I'll break down some of the information from them into actionable, easy tasks that we can implement right away. You *don't* have to Google for architectures and their implementations - they're typically very clearly explained in the papers, and frameworks like Keras make these implementations easier than ever. The key takeaway of this lesson is to ***teach you how to find, read, implement and understand architectures*** and papers. No resource in the world will be able to keep up with all of the newest developments and after a few books, you'll want. tostart switching to papers for learning. I've included some of the the newest and relevant papers here - but in a few months, new ones will pop up, and that's inevitable. Knowing where to find credible implementations, compare them to papers and tweak them can give you the competitive edge required for many computer vision products you may want to build.

We won't be implementing all of these in the lesson, since some implementations are fairly long and would necessitate a large time investment in each and every architecture, which would defeat the point. For all implementations - please inspect and play around with the associated Jupyter Notebook.

Besides the notebook - a great place to view concrete implementations is in Keras' `applications`! Through the official GitHub page[75], you can access all of the implemented architectures. There's a necessary amount of software engineering overhead in each class - such as for defining different versions, encapsulating logic, and using optional features such as naming blocks that might make these classes seem super complex. Though, when you focus on the essence - none of these are inherently harder than what we've built so far. These will all use the Functional API from a recent TensorFlow version, since it's much more expressive and most of these architectures aren't sequential, but it's amazing practice to copy the code and "skim off" the non-essential parts to get a good feel for them.

For example, this piece of code might seem much more complex than it is quite literally due to formatting:

```
if input_tensor is None:
        img_input = layers.Input(shape=input_shape)
    else:
        if not backend.is_keras_tensor(input_tensor):
            img_input = layers.Input(tensor=input_tensor, shape=input_shape)
        else:
            img_input = input_tensor
    # Block 1
    x = layers.Conv2D(
        64, (3, 3), activation = "relu", padding = "same", name =
            "block1_conv1"
    )(img_input)
    x = layers.Conv2D(
        64, (3, 3), activation = "relu", padding = "same", name =
            "block1_conv2"
    )(x)
    x = layers.MaxPooling2D((2, 2), strides=(2, 2), name = "block1_pool")(x)
    ...
```

[75]https://github.com/keras-team/keras/tree/master/keras/applications

You can simplify it down to:

```
img_input = layers.Input(shape=input_shape)

x = layers.Conv2D(64, (3, 3), activation = "relu", padding =
    "same")(img_input)
x = layers.Conv2D(64, (3, 3), activation = "relu", padding = "same")(x)
x = layers.MaxPooling2D((2, 2), strides=(2, 2))(x)
...
```

Now - the original wrapper checks for input types and adjusts the code to be compatible with different types. This is the software engineering aspect of model development. In this lesson - we'll mainly be interested in the essence of these models - not the required but oftentimes obfuscating software engineering aspect. Cross-checking these implementations with the papers will allow you to *truly* grasp how an architecture works. Once you've intuitively grasped these - go ahead and add a check for input types and expand the functionality of your model!

Note: As of writing, KerasCV is in the making, and it has a lot of overlap with Keras Applications. As per the roadmap - once KerasCV applications have matured enough (unknown when), a deprecation warning will be added to Keras Applications. This doesn't change the fact that Keras Applications are a really good repository for reading and cross-checking for architectures, but depending on when you're reading this - KerasCV might've already overtaken. You can stay updated by following the documentation and/or the KerasCV GitHub repository[76].

Here's a timeline-spread leaderboard on ImageNet, as per PapersWithCode:

[76]https://github.com/keras-team/keras-cv

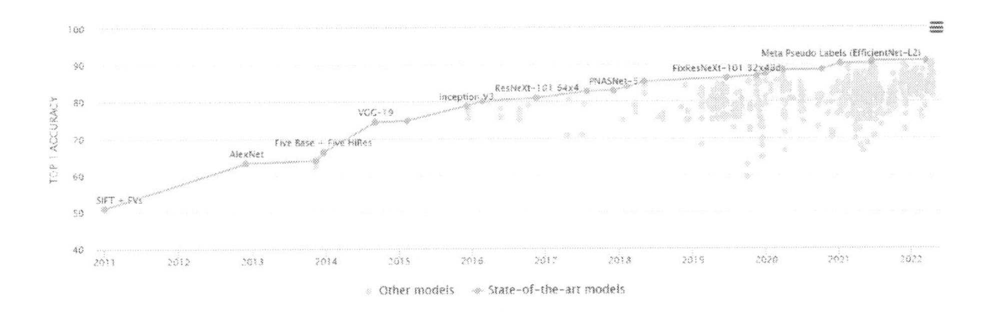

Figure 99:

This leaderboard is measured by *Top-1 Accuracy* - thought, most benchmarks for ImageNet use *Top-5 Error Rate* to gauge network performance instead. The leaderboard is different depending on which metric you look at, and we'll be using the latter when referring to a network outperforming another.

I'll include the outputs of *some* of the `summary()` calls, since the focus of the lesson is on the architectures themselves, and inspecting the summary helps a lot here, but will limit the calls for brevity. For those that are unwieldy for showing in the lesson for formatting reasons - inspect them on your local machine.

Note: Leaderboards change all the time. The "best" image model is "best" only for a short time and many comparisons are outdated. A recent notebook by Jeremy Howard[77] compares various image models with an interactive visualization.

8.1 Datasets for Rapid Testing

All modern architectures are tested on ImageNet, amongst other benchmarks like CIFAR10 and CIFAR100. Most models that are ported and built into libraries like Keras

[77] https://www.kaggle.com/code/jhoward/which-image-models-are-best

are pre-trained on ImageNet as well. Every year, the ImageNet Large Scale Visual Recognition Challenge (ILSVRC) is held, in which teams race to compare their shiniest new models. The tests on ImageNet are so popular that a review paper was made, called *"Do ImageNet Classifiers Generalize to ImageNet?"*[78]. Spoiler alert - they do (but, they're still sensitive to data cleaning and the way the datasets are prepared, which can lead to drops in accuracy).

The main problem is - ImageNet is large. Very large. 14M images to be more precise. The most widely used subset of ImageNet, known as ImageNet-1K (1000 classes, 1.2M images for training, 50k for validation, 100k for testing), takes up roughly 150GB of HDD space. The larger subset, ImageNet-21K contains over a TB of data.

While the average cost per gigabyte has been falling over the years, down to around $0.04/GB today (making a 150GB HDD device cost around $6) - the issue isn't in storing the dataset. The main hurdle remains processing it all. It's a hassle to train networks on so many images, *especially* if you're trying things out, tweaking them a bit here and there and training again while learning. So, what other options do you have?

There are various benchmark datasets you can go with, but they're generally in a different domain than ImageNet, and performance on them doesn't have to translate to ImageNet. While your end goal shouldn't be ImageNet (but generic vision), if it performs well there, there's a higher probability it would perform well on other generic datasets. For rapid testing though - you'll want something smaller. CIFAR10 and CIFAR100 have really small images, which isn't realistic, and they're somewhat synthetic.

8.1.1 Tiny ImageNet-200

A few years ago, Fei-Fei Li, Andrej Karpathy, and Justin Johnson compiled Tiny ImageNet-200! A 200-class version of ImageNet, with downsized images (64x64), where each class has 500 samples for training and 50 samples for testing - so in total, 100k training images, and 10k test images. It's available on Kaggle[79] and Stanford's servers at: http://cs231n.stanford.edu/.

The dataset is a valid alternative to ImageNet, but can still take a fair bit of time to train on if you're training many models while just learning, like we'll be training in this lesson.

---

[78] https://arxiv.org/abs/1902.10811

[79] https://www.kaggle.com/c/tiny-imagenet

8.1.2 ImageNet Resized

ImageNet Resized is similar to Tiny ImageNet-200 in that the images are resized down to 8x8, 16x16, 32x32 and 64x64 - but it contains 1.2M images as per ImageNet-1K! While the labels are jumbled up (you won't be able to use the `decode_predictions()` function to get accurate labels), you can write your own wrapper function for them. Alas - the main downside to this dataset, like the previous one, is that the images are unrealistically small and that it takes even *longer* to train on this dataset since it contains around 12x the data as Tiny ImageNet-200. You're free to follow this lesson with either of these datasets, if you're ready to wait a few hundred hours for all of the models to train on them.

ImageNet Resized is available via TensorFlow Datasets as well, making it a super simple way to load and work with it:

```
(train_set, test_set, valid_set), info = tfds.load("imagenet_resized/64x64",
                                       split=["train[:80%]",
                                              "validation", "train[80%:]"],
                                       as_supervised=True,
                                              with_info=True)

class_names = info.features["label"].names
n_classes = info.features["label"].num_classes
print(f'Class names: {class_names}', ) # ['n02119789', 'n02100735',
      'n02110185', ...]
print('Num of classes:', n_classes) # Num of classes: 1000

print("Train set size:", len(train_set)) # Train set size: 1024934
print("Test set size:", len(test_set)) # Test set size: 50000
print("Valid set size:", len(valid_set)) # Valid set size: 256233
```

The 64x64 version takes up around 13GB of space, 32x32 takes up around 3.5GB, 16x16 takes up a bit less than a GB and 8x8 takes up around 300MB.

```
fig = tfds.visualization.show_examples(train_set, info)
plt.show()
```

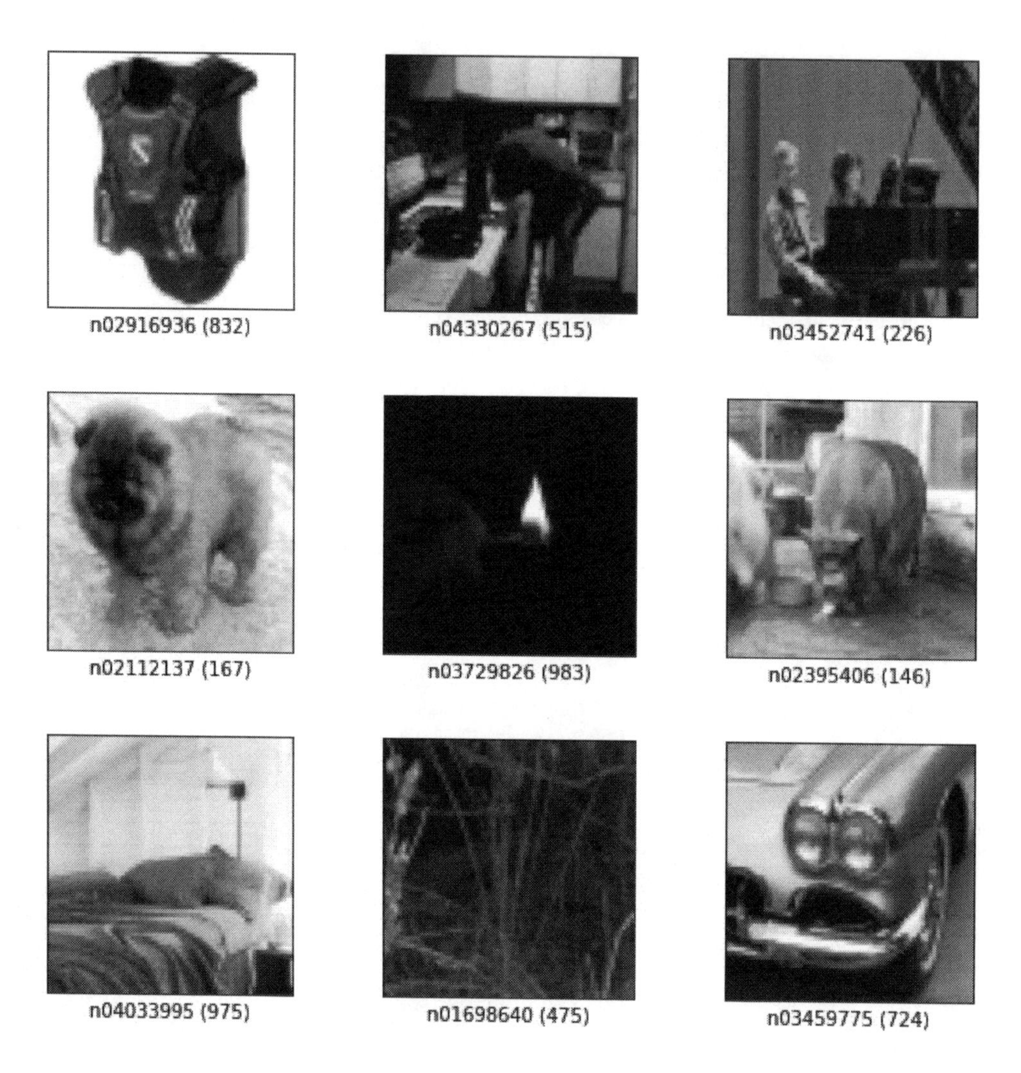

Figure 100:

8.1.3 Imagenette

Prototyping is really important while designing networks, and while learning, you'll benefit from fast training. For this exact reason - Jeremy Howard, the author of fast.ai, created Imagenette! A small version of ImageNet, just 3GB in size (7K for training, 2.3K for testing/validation), with 10 classes. The major upside of this dataset is that it uses native image sizes! They're not awkwardly resized to small unrealistic images.

Note: It's worth noting that in the last couple of years, major strides have been made in speeding up training. It used to take 14 days to train a ResNet50 (which we'll be implementing from scratch shortly) on an M40 GPU, for 90 epochs. Notably, Jeremy Howard, Andrew Shaw and Yaroslav Bulatov managed to train an ImageNet classifier to 93% top-5 accuracy in **18 minutes** using 128 NVIDIA V100 GPUs, via AWS' 16 cloud instances, which cost them only $40. This is possible because we aren't as much limited with hardware anymore - we're more limited algorithmically. The team used several techniques such as - progressive resizing, rectangular image validation, Tencent's weight decay tuning, Google Brain's dynamic batch sizes and gradual learning rate warm-up to make this possible. For more information - you can read Jeremy's blogpost here[80].

If you don't feel like paying, investing a lot of time in optimization from the get-go (don't optimize too early) - you'll probably want to try things out on Imagenette, and only move onto the more time-expensive and resource-expensive endeavor when you think you've got a hit! The point is to minimize the time between testing architectures out and getting to the stage where you'll want to apply several optimization techniques and pay for an instance in the cloud to train your model on.

Let's load Imagenette in through TensorFlow Datasets (makes it so much easier and allows us to prefetch the data seamlessly):

```
1 (train_set, test_set, valid_set), info = tfds.load("imagenette",
2                                               split=["train[:70%]",
                                                   "train[70%:]", "validation"],
3                                               as_supervised=True,
                                                   with_info=True)
4
5 class_names = info.features["label"].names
6 n_classes = info.features["label"].num_classes
```

[80] https://www.fast.ai/2018/08/10/fastai-diu-imagenet/

```
7 print(f'Class names: {class_names}', ) # ['n01440764', 'n02102040',
      'n02979186', 'n03000684', 'n03028079', 'n03394916', 'n03417042',
      'n03425413', 'n03445777', 'n03888257']
8 print('Num of classes:', n_classes) # Num of classes: 10
9
10 print("Train set size:", len(train_set)) # Train set size: 7102
11 print("Test set size:", len(test_set)) # Test set size: 947
12 print("Valid set size:", len(valid_set)) # Valid set size: 1420
```

Since the labels are inherited from ImageNet and aren't very readable - let's create a dictionary of labels to readable names, and a method to fetch the name based on the label:

```
1 labels = {
2     'n01440764' : 'tench',
3     'n02102040' : 'English springer',
4     'n02979186' : 'cassette player',
5     'n03000684' : 'chain saw',
6     'n03028079' : 'church',
7     'n03394916' : 'French horn',
8     'n03417042' : 'garbage truck',
9     'n03425413' : 'gas pump',
10    'n03445777' : 'golf ball',
11    'n03888257' : 'parachute'
12 }
13
14 def label_to_classname(label):
15     return labels[label]
16
17 label_to_classname('n03425413') # 'gas pump'
```

Let's visualize a batch of 25 images:

```
1 fig = plt.figure(figsize=(10, 10))
2
3 for index, entry in enumerate(test_set.take(25), start=1):
4     sample_image = np.squeeze(entry[0].numpy()[0])
5     sample_label = label_to_classname(class_names[entry[1].numpy()[0]])
6
7     ax = fig.add_subplot(5, 5, index)
8     ax.imshow(np.array(sample_image, np.int32))
9     ax.set_title(f"Class: {sample_label}")
10    ax.axis('off')
11
12 plt.tight_layout()
13 plt.show()
```

Figure 101:

Note: There's one downside to using Imagenette. These are easily identifiable classes! There's a pretty big difference between a parachute and a garbage truck. Any network that can at least *kind of* get the difference between these will get a similar score to a network that would be able to also discern between a garbage truck and a cement mixer truck, which the first wouldn't be able to do. Because of this - there's a serious effect of diminishing returns when it comes to accuracy metrics and it can feel like the newer architectures aren't really bringing much to the table.

You can try this same lesson out on the `"food101"` dataset, which contains a much larger set of images, with 101 food categories (some of which are fairly similar), and 101K images, `"imagenet_resized/nxn"`. Though, be weary that this'll probably take much longer than most are willing to invest in training time while learning. Being able to quickly prototype, test things out and observe results in this case trumps a linear sense of progress between implementations.

8.1.4 Keras' Preprocessing Layers

For the preprocessing step - we'll only crop and resize the images since they're not uniform in size. Due to the lack of support for batching and otherwise working with datasets of varying image sizes with TensorFlow, you'll generally want to resize them to the same shape:

```
def preprocess_image(image, label):
    resized_image = tf.image.resize(cropped_image, [224, 224])
    return resized_image, label

train_set =
    train_set.map(preprocess_image).batch(16).prefetch(tf.data.AUTOTUNE)
test_set =
    test_set.map(preprocess_image).batch(16).prefetch(tf.data.AUTOTUNE)
valid_set =
    valid_set.map(preprocess_image).batch(16).prefetch(tf.data.AUTOTUNE)
```

For the augmentation itself - naturally, it'll help, so we'll want to use it. Though, since the `tf.image` API is still fairly limited (fixed angles, for instance), we'll use Keras' augmentation capabilities instead. This marks the *third* TF-Keras option for data augmentation, and that's using *Keras Preprocessing Layers*:

- `Resizing`
- `Rescaling`

- `RandomFlip`
- `RandomRotation`
- etc.

They'll be accessible via `keras.layers.LayerName` or `keras.layers.experimental.preprocessing.LayerName`, if you're using an older vesion of TensorFlow/Keras. The amazing thing about them is - you can use them through a standalone preprocessing step *or* you can make them part of the model itself! That technically makes the latter the *fourth* way to perform data augmentation. So, which one should you use anyway?

The `tf.image` API is hands down the least expressive of the bunch, since it's not built specifically for augmentation. Augmentation through the `ImageDataGenerator` works well with directories, but is a Python generator - not an optimized `tf.data.Dataset` object.

In our case, when working with a `tf.data.Dataset` object (the recommended route), using the preprocessing layers makes a lot of sense - they're expressive (like the `ImageDataGenerator` augmentation options, and more expressive than `tf.image`), and can be both used outside or inside of the model!

If you use them as a distinct part of the model, they'll be saved within the architecture, so you can make it much more robust and general in terms of input. Instead of processing it before feeding into the model for inference, you can simply feed the raw image and have the model work out the rest. It may seem "odd" to have the model "see" the image, and then rotate it before passing it through other layers, but really, the net result is quite literally the same as if you've passed it through a preprocessing step before that. I personally like including layers within the models themselves, because it makes them more robust to input. Additionally, you can tweak the layers instead of the data when trying to optimize the augmentation parameters. You'll have to rebuild the model anyway to not carry over previous training, and this way - the rebuilding is contained in the model - no need to reload the training data.

Additionally - having external preprocessing functions, while technically more flexible, is cumbersome. There shouldn't be a need for users to pass input through dedicated, different functions before using models. This makes it especially annoying if you're serving models in non-Python environments. By bundling as much as you can within a model, more can be done with less code. To create *true* end-to-end models, that genuinely accept raw images (without a bunch of preprocessing on the server *before* it gets passed to the model), you'll want to use preprocessing layers. This builds a strong case for using Keras preprocessing layers as a preferred format for data preprocessing and augmentation.

In KerasCV, over *28 new layers* are being added, as of writing, and this list can also expand in the future! With so many options, it's reasonable to expect Keras preprocessing layers to become much more common in standard pipelines and architectures in the future.

Note: Before applying augmentation - try training without it for a baseline.

8.1.5 KerasCV Preprocessing Layers

KerasCV introduces new preprocessing layers and metrics (amongst other planned additions)! You can find the expanding list of features in the official documentation[81], and naturally, KerasCV layers work just like regular Keras layers. They're separated out to a different package because they were a bit too CV-specific to be included in the main Keras package, but were important enough to warrant being implemented officially as well.

As research progresses, so do training techniques, and KerasCV implements some of the "hot new" techniques in terms of preprocessing and augmentation as well. Instead of manually implementing these - just plug and play a layer such as:

```
1 keras_cv.layers.RandAugment(value_range, augmentations_per_image=3,
      magnitude=0.5, ...)
```

`RandAugment` is meant to be the "holy grail" of augmentation layers. It applies a *random augmentation* on an input image, including other augmentation/preprocessing layers. `CutMix`, `MixUp` and `RandAugment` have recently been catching traction, and you might want to try them out in some of the code samples from this lesson as well. We'll come back to KerasCV in a later lesson.

[81] https://keras.io/api/keras_cv/

8.2 Optimizers, Learning Rate and Batch Size?

Datasets affect learning - nothing new there. All hyperparameters are in for some tuning whenever you change a dataset, and what worked the best in a paper probably won't reflect in a 1:1 mapping to your own dataset. In this lesson, we'll be referencing many papers and their hyperparameters. They probably won't work for you straight out of the box. There are, thankfully, rules of thumb to follow when translating findings to your own local environment.

First off - optimizers. In earlier lessons, I've noted that Adam is a pretty solid default optimizer. Most papers you'll see in this lesson use SGD, with a momentum of 0.9 (and Nesterov acceleration). Some of these papers were released before Adam, so that makes sense, but some were released after Adam and still didn't use it for training. In some cases, you can replace the SGD with Adam and it'll work great. In some cases, you won't be able to, such as with AlexNet and VGG, due to their large parameter counts. Many modern networks have much fewer parameters, so you'll probably be able to use Adam with them. The question is - should you?

The answer isn't clear cut if you read the relevant papers. There's a place for both Adam and SGD... and RMSprop, and other optimizers today. SGD has been observed to generalize better than Adam by the end of training in studies such as *"The Marginal Value of Adaptive Gradient Methods in Machine Learning"*[82]. Adam trains and converges faster than SGD, especially in the initial stages of training, but generalizes worse according to the authors.

In another camp, in *"On Empirical Comparisons of Optimizers for Deep Learning"*[83], the authors note that there is currently no theory that explains which optimizer you'll want to choose, and they've empirically tested widely used optimizers. The takeaway of their research is that *Adam never underperforms SGD*. How can someone make such a confident statement? Adam and RMSprop can simulate SGD with momentum. Thus, SGD with momentum can be seen as a *special case* of Adam. A general optimizer, according to the authors, can perform at least as good as one of its special cases, when tuned to simulate it. The issue is - tuning Adam to simulate SGD can be even more finicky than tuning SGD to perform well, so in those cases, you might as well just use SGD.

[82]https://arxiv.org/abs/1705.08292
[83]https://arxiv.org/abs/1910.05446

> In conclusion - who should you trust? Yourself. Try Adam. Try SGD. Try RMSprop. Compare the results, tune them, then compare the results again. Do this over time, as your data changes and shifts. What's stable once might not be as stable later.

Next - learning rates! When translating learning rates from research papers to your own code, you can follow the linear scaling rule, for non-adaptive optimizers. If someone uses a learning rate of 0.1 on a batch size of 256 - and you use a batch size of 128, your learning rate should be set to 0.05.

$$LR2 = LR1 * (b2/b1)$$

Where your learning rate (`LR2`) is linearly increased or decreased compared to the original learning rate (`LR1`) based on the ratio of your batch size to the original batch size (`b2/b1`).

For Adam, this isn't as important, and you're quite likely going to do just fine with the default learning rate of `1e-3` for most tasks, though, you might want to try going down to steps between `1e-3` and `1e-5` as well.

Finally, batch sizes! I've noted before that you probably don't want to go above 32. Most papers here will use a batch size of 256. Why? Larger batch sizes allow for better parallelization and lead to faster training. But, they also lead to worse generalization and sharper minima, according to *"On Large-Batch Training for Deep Learning: Generalization Gap and Sharp Minima"*[84]. Flat minima is preferable to sharp minima because they're more robust, and a model can be potentially further tuned in that valley, rather than "hitting the walls" around it in a sharp minima point. In *"Practical recommendations for gradient-based training of deep architectures"*[85], Yoshua Bengio notes that any batch size above 10 utilizes at least some of the matrix-matrix product optimizations, and that 32 is a good default batch size.

For all practical purposes - a larger batch size means stronger hardware. You probably won't be able to run large batch sizes on your home computer or even on many cloud-based providers. Using a smaller batch size, between 8 on the lower end and 32 on the higher end is a pretty safe bet. If your computer can't handle a batch size of 32 - most cloud-based providers can, even for larger images and more expensive architectures.

[84]https://arxiv.org/abs/1609.04836
[85]https://arxiv.org/abs/1206.5533

8.3 Performance Metrics

When talking about the performance of a network, the term "performance" is tied to a metric. Depending on which metric you tie it to - one network "outperforms" the other. It's worth noting what metrics people oftentimes take into consideration, since if your conception of the metric is misaligned with the author's, you might be disappointed:

- Computational efficiency
- Parameter efficiency
- Top-K Accuracy Rate
- Top-K Error Rate
- Convergence Speed
- Training Speed
- Inference Speed
- FLOPs

Oftentimes, you'll find "better efficiency" or "faster" attached to an architecture, as compared to another. Are they talking about parameter efficiency? Computational efficiency? Sometimes, it's unclear. Additionally, does better efficiency mean faster training? Not necessarily. It's mainly tied to how efficiently an operation can be done, but many efficient operations might run slower or cost more than a single inefficient one. Finally - efficiency doesn't necessarily mean that a network is lightweight. Even more efficient networks might need more VRAM to work than their inefficient counterparts.

Computational efficiency is concerned with the efficiency with which computation is performed. Parameter efficiency is concerned with how efficiently parameters are being utilized. If many parameters are near-0, they aren't adding much to the network, and could technically be pruned away. As a rule of thumb - the lower the parameter count, and the higher the accuracy is, the better the parameter efficiency. Top-K accuracy and Top-K error rate are not the two faces of the same coin. Top-1 Accuracy leaderboards are typically different from Top-5 Accuracy leaderboards. A network might be better at approximately guessing the class compared to a network that confidently says the class but misses all other classes. Pretty commonly, Top-5 Error Rate is used instead of Top-5 Accuracy. A jump from 94% to 95% in accuracy intuitively feels lesser than a drop from 6% to 5% and it's easier to quantify the progress that way. We're more concerned with what the network got *wrong*, rather than the bulk that it got right, since they're already pretty good at getting things right. Convergence speed is concerned with how many epochs it takes to converge and find an acceptable minima. Even if it takes longer to train an epoch than with another network - if it converges in fewer epochs, it has better convergence speed. Training speed is concerned with training speed per epoch/sample. Inference speed is concerned with how fast a network can perform inference in production (some are too slow to be practical for real-time usage or for mobile devices).

Finally - FLOPs (Floating Point Operations Per Second). The lower you have, the less compute you're using! It is desirable to have fewer FLOPs because why do something in 10 steps if you can do it in 1?

That being said - having a more efficient or faster network can mean various things, depending on which metric you're tying the comparison to. If someone touts their faster and/or more efficient architecture over X, Y and Z - take it with a grain of salt.

8.4 Where to Find Models?

Other than the official implementations - where can you find models? So-called "model zoos" are a good place to take a look at, and TensorFlow Hub[86] is one of the largest hubs to find pre-trained models that you can download and deploy with ease.

You can search for models, collections and/or publishers and some collections contain dozens of models ready for you to download and plug in. For instance, we'll be covering ConvNeXt later in the chaper, and due to it being fairly new, it's not as widely adopted officially as it will be some time in the near future. When a new model gets released - you don't have to wait for an official implementation, nor implement and train it yourself. Hop onto TensorFlow Hub and find it there.

If GUIs aren't your thing - you can download models straight into your project via an internet connection and the `tensorflow_hub` tool:

```
1 $ pip install --upgrade tensorflow_hub
```

Now, downloading a model and instantiating it is as easy as:

```
1 import tensorflow_hub as hub
2 model = hub.KerasLayer("https://tfhub.dev/sayakpaul/convnext_tiny_1k_224/1")
```

[86]https://tfhub.dev/

```
3 model.build([None, 224, 224, 3])
```

8.5 LeNet5 - A Blast from the Past (1998)

LeNet5 was created for recognizing hand-written digits, with a 28x28 size. It used `tanh` activations, and radial basis function for the final activation, instead of a more modern `softmax`, which outputs probabilities of each class. Distinctly, the network was originally written to use the Mean-Squared Error function as a loss function!

Other than these choices - the paper looks like a pretty standard modern deep learning paper. It discusses the data, the preprocessing steps taken, the architecture of the network, hyperparameters, and results. Now, the network itself was *made for* digit recognition, not classifying churches from cassette players, and it was tuned to work well for that dataset. At the time, classifying digits was a daunting task, and we couldn't expect the architecture to perform *too well* on something like Imagenette:

```
1 lenet5 = keras.Sequential([
2     keras.layers.InputLayer(input_shape=(None, None,3)),
3     # Preprocessing made as part of the model itself
4     # 'tanh' didn't do well with data augmentation
5     # Resizing images down to 28, 28, since our input is 224, 224
6     keras.layers.Resizing(28, 28),
7 
8     keras.layers.Conv2D(6, (5,5), padding = 'same', activation = 'tanh'),
9     keras.layers.AveragePooling2D((2,2)),
10
11    keras.layers.Conv2D(16, (5,5), padding = 'same', activation = 'tanh'),
12    keras.layers.AveragePooling2D((2,2)),
13
14    keras.layers.Conv2D(120, (5,5), padding = 'same', activation = 'tanh'),
15    keras.layers.Flatten(),
16    keras.layers.Dense(84, activation = 'tanh'),
17    # LeCunn used Radial Basis Function, which isn't built into Keras
18    # Modern networks use 'softmax', so we'll use that instead to
19    # avoid having to define a custom activation function for now
20    keras.layers.Dense(10, activation = 'softmax')
21 ])
22
23 lenet5.compile(loss = 'sparse_categorical_crossentropy', optimizer =
       keras.optimizers.SGD(), metrics=['accuracy'])
```

The network is fairly simple - a `Conv2D` layer with 6 filters, with a 5x5 kernel size, `'same'` padding and an `'tanh'` activation, followed by `AveragePooling2D()` and another similar block with 16 filters. It's topped off with a 120-filter `Conv2D` layer, before flattening, and a `Dense` extractor/classifier.

I've switched out the original final activation function and loss function, with a plain Stochastic Gradient Descent optimizer. Let's take a look at the complexity of the model:

```
lenet5.summary()
```

```
Model: "sequential"
_______________________
Layer (type)                Output Shape              Param #
======================
resizing (Resizing)         (None, 28, 28, 3)         0
_______________________
conv2d (Conv2D)             (None, 28, 28, 6)         456
_______________________
average_pooling2d (AveragePo (None, 14, 14, 6)        0
_______________________
conv2d_1 (Conv2D)           (None, 14, 14, 16)        2416
_______________________
average_pooling2d_1 (Average (None, 7, 7, 16)         0
_______________________
conv2d_2 (Conv2D)           (None, 7, 7, 120)         48120
_______________________
flatten (Flatten)           (None, 5880)              0
_______________________
dense (Dense)               (None, 84)                494004
_______________________
dense_1 (Dense)             (None, 10)                850
======================
Total params: 545,846
Trainable params: 545,846
Non-trainable params: 0
_______________________
```

550K parameters! Where from? The `Dense` layer, which contributes nearly 500K of that. While 550K isn't a huge number of parameters nowadays - it was back in the day. Keep note of this effect of `Dense` layer as we're progressing through the years! Before that though, let's fit the model, with a `ReduceLROnPlateau` and `EarlyStopping` callback:

```
reduceLr = keras.callbacks.ReduceLROnPlateau(patience=5, monitor =
    'val_accuracy')
early_stopping = keras.callbacks.EarlyStopping(patience=10, monitor =
    'val_accuracy')

lenet5_history = lenet5.fit(train_set,
                            epochs=50,
                            batch_size=32,
                            validation_data=valid_set,
                            callbacks=[reduceLr, early_stopping])
```

```
Epoch 1/50
```

```
2 222/222 [==============================] - 5s 15ms/step - loss: 2.1407 -
      accuracy: 0.2415 - val_loss: 2.0589 - val_accuracy: 0.3106
3 ...
4 Epoch 50/50
5 222/222 [==============================] - 3s 14ms/step - loss: 1.3219 -
      accuracy: 0.5628 - val_loss: 1.4853 - val_accuracy: 0.5070
```

How did the training go? Well - considering the architecture, fairly well! It's gotten 5/10 images right on the validation set. What do the training curves look like?

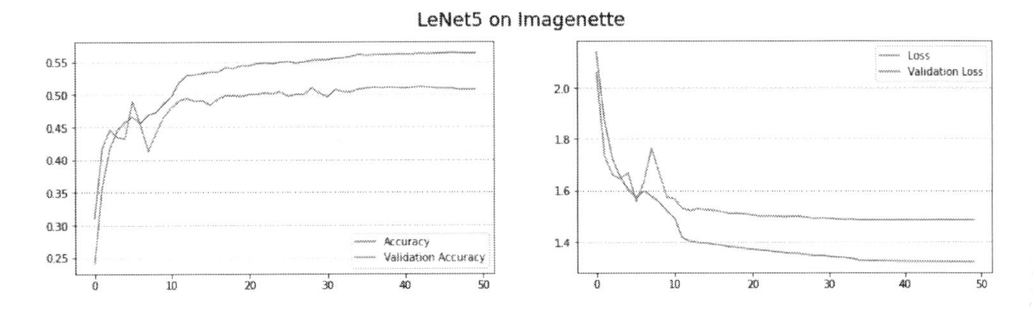

Figure 102:

What if we try to modernize the network with newer activation functions and a newer optimizer?

```
 1 lenet5_relu = keras.Sequential([
 2     keras.layers.InputLayer(input_shape=(224, 224,3)),
 3     keras.layers.Resizing(28, 28),
 4     keras.layers.RandomFlip("horizontal_and_vertical"),
 5     keras.layers.RandomRotation(0.2),
 6
 7     keras.layers.Conv2D(6, (5,5), padding = 'same', activation = 'relu'),
 8     keras.layers.AveragePooling2D((2,2)),
 9
10     keras.layers.Conv2D(16, (5,5), padding = 'same', activation = 'relu'),
11     keras.layers.AveragePooling2D((2,2)),
12
13     keras.layers.Conv2D(120, (5,5), padding = 'same', activation = 'relu'),
14     keras.layers.Flatten(),
15     keras.layers.Dense(84, activation = 'relu'),
16     keras.layers.Dense(10, activation = 'softmax')
17 ])
18
19 lenet5_relu.compile(loss = 'sparse_categorical_crossentropy', optimizer =
      'adam', metrics=['accuracy'])
20
```

```
21 reduceLr = keras.callbacks.ReduceLROnPlateau(patience=5, monitor =
       'val_accuracy')
22 early_stopping = keras.callbacks.EarlyStopping(patience=10, monitor =
       'val_accuracy')
23
24 lenet5_relu_history = lenet5_relu.fit(train_set,
25                                       epochs=50,
26                                       batch_size=32,
27                                       validation_data=valid_set,
28                                       callbacks=[reduceLr, early_stopping])
```

The final validation accuracy is slightly higher - but only slightly, and the curves do imply a closer fit and better utilization of the parameters!

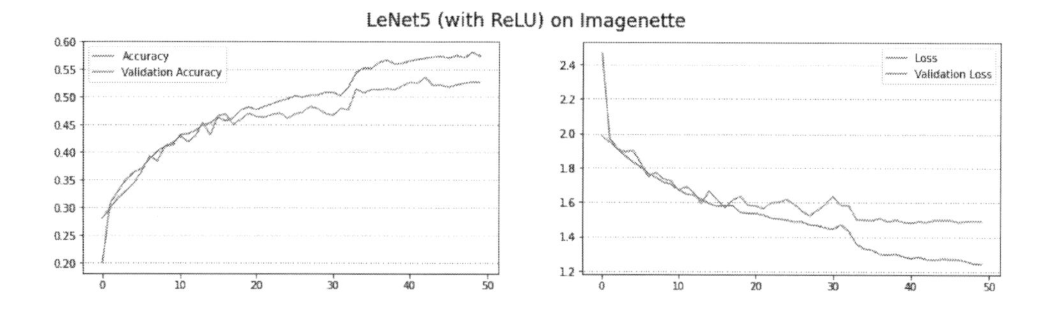

Figure 103:

However, it's not the activation function keeping this network from learning beyond around 50% in accuracy. We're tasking it with something it wasn't built to do. The LeNet5 started modern ConvNets. AlexNet took them from infancy to stardom, and sparked an intense decade of research and development.

8.6 AlexNet - Proving CNNs Can Do It (2012)

AlexNet[87], written by Alex Krizhevsky, Ilya Sutskever and Geoffrey Hinton, was released in 2012. At the time of writing, it's been a full decade since its release! It was successor to LeNet5 and competed in the 2012 ILSVRC challenge, beating the rest of the competitors by more than 10 percentage points in the top-5 error rate! While LeNet5 used a single convolution block, followed by average pooling, AlexNet used multiple

[87]https://proceedings.neurips.cc/paper/2012/file/c399862d3b9d6b76c8436e924a68c45b-Paper.pdf

stacked convolution layers. They highlighted how non-saturating `relu` helps train faster and produces more accurate networks than saturating `tanh`, after which `relu` has been used extensively.

This depth of the network was essential to the performance, at the cost of longer training with more parameters. It starts out with a fairly large kernel size (`11, 11`) and stride size (`4, 4`), and ends up with a much more common (`3, 3`) kernel size with a much smaller stride. The second convolutional block takes a normalized and pooled representation of the first, so we'll add a `MaxPooling2D` and `BatchNormalization` in between them.

The third, fourth and fifth convolutional layers are stacked on top of each other without any normalization or pooling. Finally, the maps are flattened and a dense classifier on top, with large dropouts (0.5) sprinkled in, is used. Since it was written for ImageNet - it has 1000 output classes, but for our dataset, we'll use an output of 10 classes.

Note: The paper references the input size of `224, 224`, however, it's actually `227, 227`. This is reflected in the number of parameters and the feature map produced by the first layer in the figure present in the paper.

```
alexnet = keras.Sequential([
    keras.layers.InputLayer(input_shape=(224, 224, 3)),
    keras.layers.Resizing(227, 227),
    keras.layers.RandomFlip("horizontal"),
    keras.layers.RandomContrast(0.1),

    # No padding on the first Conv2D
    keras.layers.Conv2D(filters=96, kernel_size=(11, 11), strides=(4, 4),
        activation = 'relu'),
    # No padding on MaxPooling layers
    keras.layers.MaxPooling2D((3, 3), strides=(2, 2)),
    keras.layers.BatchNormalization(),

    keras.layers.Conv2D(filters=256, kernel_size=(5, 5), strides=(1, 1),
        padding = 'same', activation = 'relu'),
    keras.layers.MaxPooling2D((3, 3), strides=(2, 2)),
    keras.layers.BatchNormalization(),

    keras.layers.Conv2D(filters=384, kernel_size=(3, 3), strides=(1, 1),
        padding = 'same', activation = 'relu'),
```

```
18      keras.layers.Conv2D(filters=384, kernel_size=(3, 3), strides=(1, 1),
            padding = 'same', activation = 'relu'),
19      keras.layers.Conv2D(filters=256, kernel_size=(3, 3), strides=(1, 1),
            padding = 'same', activation = 'relu'),
20      keras.layers.MaxPooling2D((3, 3), strides=(2, 2)),
21
22      keras.layers.Flatten(),
23
24      keras.layers.Dense(4096, activation = 'relu'),
25      keras.layers.BatchNormalization(),
26      keras.layers.Dropout(0.5),
27
28      keras.layers.Dense(4096, activation = 'relu'),
29      keras.layers.BatchNormalization(),
30      keras.layers.Dropout(0.5),
31
32      keras.layers.Dense(10, activation = 'softmax')
33  ])
34
35  # AlexNet and VGG make adam get a stroke, SGD with manual hyperparameter
        tuning is required
36  alexnet.compile(loss = 'sparse_categorical_crossentropy',
37                  optimizer = keras.optimizers.SGD(nesterov=True,
                        momentum=0.9, learning_rate=1e-4),
38                  metrics=['accuracy'])
```

This network has 58M parameters with 10 output classes, and 62M with 1000 output classes. The jump from 550K to 60M was a *huge* one. The `adam` optimizer doesn't work well with so many parameters, but `SGD` with momentum/Nesterov acceleration does! This unfortunately means that the network's design requires more hyperparameter tuning and hands-on testing to get it to work optimally. It's generally agreed upon that optimizers like Adam require less manual tweaking and testing to converge to a good result so it's a great option to try out as a default optimizer.

The authors did highlight regularization techniques to help the model generalize well, given the parameter number, which was admittedly large. They used data augmentation - horizontal reflections (flipping), and varying the intensities of the RGB channels in the images. Both of these allowed them to have such a huge model and still not overfit too badly. Additionally, high dropout is used in the first two layers of the densely connected top, effectively doubling the convergence time (double the iterations) but allowing the model to not overfit.

A sharp eye might've noticed that both the use of data augmentation and dropout was, in large part, to allow the model to be useful with such a huge number of parameters. They were, in effect, painting over the fact that there are 60M parameters under the hood. This isn't to imply that the authors tried hiding that fact - it was very visibly and explicitly stated in the abstract after all, but regularization was "making up" for the fact that the network was huge. With more modern architectures - you want the model to be able to carry its own weight, and rely on regularization techniques to *boost it*, not *enable it*. Nevertheless, this network was a substantial breakthrough, and was the harbinger of tomorrow. AlexNet matured the approach LeCun took with LeNet5 and set a gold standard at the time. From the Neocognitron, to LeNet to AlexNet - the idea of ConvNets was getting firm ground. From AlexNet and forwards, they've been the defining staple of computer vision until Vision Transformers have been introduced a couple of years ago (after which, another ConvNet became the state-of-the-art).

> AlexNet's paper is sometimes recognized as the most influential computer vision paper of all time, with 107k citations, and is credited with popularizing ConvNets.

Let's train this network:

```
reduceLr = keras.callbacks.ReduceLROnPlateau(patience=3, monitor = 'val_accuracy')
early_stopping = keras.callbacks.EarlyStopping(patience=10, monitor = 'val_accuracy')

alexnet_history = alexnet.fit(train_set,
                              epochs=50,
                              batch_size=32,
                              validation_data=valid_set,
                              callbacks=[reduceLr, early_stopping])
```

Within around 20 epochs, it plateaus at around 72% accuracy on the validation set:

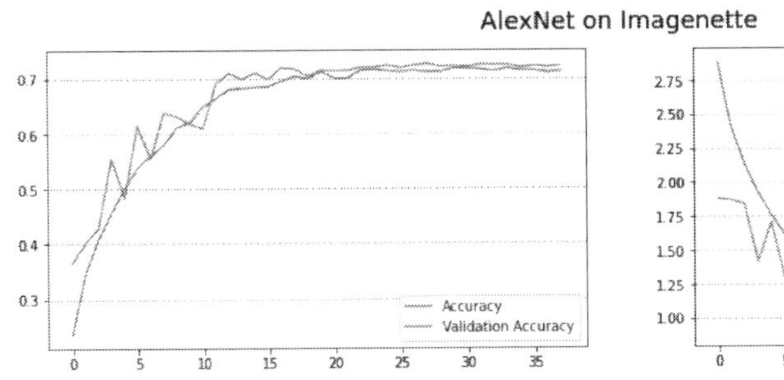

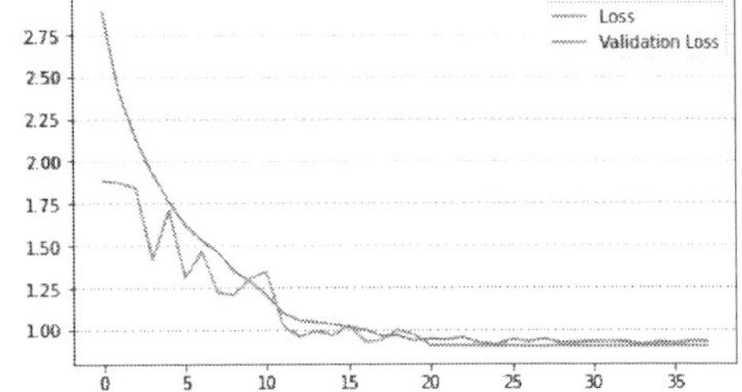

Figure 104:

8.7 VGGNet - Deeeeeeeeep Networks (2014)

LeNet5 had, well, 5 layers. AlexNet had 8 layers. AlexNet was deeper and larger - and it performed better in terms of accuracy. So, which role does depth play with ConvNets? Karen and Andrew at Google DeepMind and Oxford hopped on with their own take on this question, pushing the layer count to 16 and 19.

These were unprecedented depths! With only 8 layers, AlexNet was already sitting at 60M parameters and was difficult to train. How does someone go from there to 19? They fixed some of the hyperparameters in place, and decided to go for depth, using "very small" kernel sizes (`3, 3`). One 7x7 convolutional layer can be replaced with three 3x3 layers, the sum of which introduce *fewer trainable parameters* than the one 7x7 layer. These smaller kernel sizes are what allowed this architecture to push the number of layers up to such a large number at the time.

In *"Very Deep Convolutional Networks for Large-Scale Image Recognition"*[88], a deep model architecture is outlined. An input layer (`224, 224, 3`), followed by a couple of convolutional layers, a max pooling layer, more convolutional layers, a max pooling layer... and so on, until a desired depth is achieved. This is followed by flattening and two fully connected layers, each with `4096` neurons (like AlexNet) and a classification layer with softmax. The paper includes an 11-layer, 13-layer, 16-layer and 19-layer schema, out of which, the 16 and 19-layer schemas are the most well known. They're oftentimes called VGG16 and VGG19. They competed in the 2014 ILSVRC challenge and were the runner up to the *Inception* architecture (covered later in this lesson).

In earlier lessons, we've defined a convolutional neural network from scratch with a very similar architecture to this one - as noted back then as well. The issue with this architecture is that even though it reduced the number of computations *per layer*, it doesn't scale well and ultimately has a lot of parameters. The proposed VGG19 architecture has 144M parameters and VGG16 has 134-138M depending on the number of channels you use. By extension, the compiled models are large (500-600MB) so deployment to servers was slow and annoying. Training times are fairly long too.

The team used a batch size of 256, a mini-batch gradient descent with momentum (of `0.9`). The training was regularized with weight decay and dropout was added to the final dense layers with a large `0.5` dropout (again, like AlexNet). They started out with a large, `1e-2` learning rate, which was decreased by a factor of 10 on each plateau. The team

[88] https://arxiv.org/pdf/1409.1556.pdf

trained with a `1e-2` starting learning rate which is very high. After a bit of tuning after rules of thumb, I've chosen `5e-4` instead of `1e-3` and a reduction factor of 5, not 10.

Note: Even with a batch size of 32, you're quite likely going to see an Out of Memory exception being thrown while training VGG. You can switch to VGG11, as per the paper, or switch to a cloud-based environment such as Google Colab or Kaggle that have much more VRAM. Regular setups don't really appreciate 134M+ parameters. This already raises a couple of red flags and highlights the need for a different paradigm of ConvNet development - but let's bear with it for now. If you see an OOM exception - restarting the Jupyter Notebook is a good idea before you try running anything in it again.

Additionally, it's worth noting that layer weight regularization was used to help combat overfitting with this many parameters - specifically, L2 regularization was used, with a penalty multiplier of `5e-4`. The team notes that during training, they've applied random horizontal flips and brightness fluctuations (just like with AlexNet) and we'll add a few preprocessing layers as well.

8.7.1 Implementing a VGG With Keras

Let's port that into code:

```
1  vgg16 = keras.Sequential([
2      keras.layers.InputLayer(input_shape=(None, None, 3)),
3      keras.layers.Resizing(224, 224),
4      keras.layers.RandomFlip("horizontal"),
5      keras.layers.RandomRotation(0.1),
6      keras.layers.RandomContrast(0.1),
7
8      keras.layers.Conv2D(64, (3, 3), padding = 'same', activation = 'relu',
           kernel_regularizer=keras.regularizers.L2(5e-4)),
9      keras.layers.Conv2D(64, (3, 3), padding = 'same', activation = 'relu',
           kernel_regularizer=keras.regularizers.L2(5e-4)),
10     keras.layers.MaxPooling2D((2, 2), strides=(2, 2), padding = 'same'),
11
12     keras.layers.Conv2D(128, (3, 3), padding = 'same', activation = 'relu',
           kernel_regularizer=keras.regularizers.L2(5e-4)),
```

```
13      keras.layers.Conv2D(128, (3, 3), padding = 'same', activation = 'relu',
            kernel_regularizer=keras.regularizers.L2(5e-4)),
14      keras.layers.MaxPooling2D((3, 3), strides=(2, 2), padding = 'same'),
15
16      keras.layers.Conv2D(256, (3, 3), padding = 'same', activation = 'relu',
            kernel_regularizer=keras.regularizers.L2(5e-4)),
17      keras.layers.Conv2D(256, (3, 3), padding = 'same', activation = 'relu',
            kernel_regularizer=keras.regularizers.L2(5e-4)),
18      keras.layers.Conv2D(256, (3, 3), padding = 'same', activation = 'relu',
            kernel_regularizer=keras.regularizers.L2(5e-4)),
19      # Add next layer for VGG19
20      #keras.layers.Conv2D(256, (3, 3), padding = 'same', activation = 'relu',
            kernel_regularizer=keras.regularizers.L2(5e-4)),
21      keras.layers.MaxPooling2D((2, 2), strides=(2, 2), padding = 'same'),
22
23      keras.layers.Conv2D(512, (3, 3), padding = 'same', activation = 'relu',
            kernel_regularizer=keras.regularizers.L2(5e-4)),
24      keras.layers.Conv2D(512, (3, 3), padding = 'same', activation = 'relu',
            kernel_regularizer=keras.regularizers.L2(5e-4)),
25      keras.layers.Conv2D(512, (3, 3), padding = 'same', activation = 'relu',
            kernel_regularizer=keras.regularizers.L2(5e-4)),
26      # Add next layer for VGG19
27      #keras.layers.Conv2D(512, (3, 3), padding = 'same', activation = 'relu',
            kernel_regularizer=keras.regularizers.L2(5e-4)),
28      keras.layers.MaxPooling2D((2, 2), strides=(2, 2), padding = 'same'),
29
30      keras.layers.Conv2D(512, (3, 3), padding = 'same', activation = 'relu',
            kernel_regularizer=keras.regularizers.L2(5e-4)),
31      keras.layers.Conv2D(512, (3, 3), padding = 'same', activation = 'relu',
            kernel_regularizer=keras.regularizers.L2(5e-4)),
32      keras.layers.Conv2D(512, (3, 3), padding = 'same', activation = 'relu',
            kernel_regularizer=keras.regularizers.L2(5e-4)),
33      # Add next layer for VGG19
34      #keras.layers.Conv2D(512, (3, 3), padding = 'same', activation = 'relu',
            kernel_regularizer=keras.regularizers.L2(5e-4)),
35      keras.layers.MaxPooling2D((2, 2), strides=(2, 2), padding = 'same'),
36
37      keras.layers.Flatten(),
38
39      keras.layers.Dropout(0.5),
40      keras.layers.Dense(1024, activation = 'relu',
            kernel_regularizer=keras.regularizers.L2(5e-4)),
41      keras.layers.Dropout(0.5),
42      keras.layers.Dense(1024, activation = 'relu',
            kernel_regularizer=keras.regularizers.L2(5e-4)),
43      keras.layers.Dense(n_classes, activation = 'softmax')
44  ])
```

Alternatively, to load in the Keras' team's implementation, simply call on the `VGG{LayerNum}` class (16 and 19 are supported):

```
1 vgg16 = keras.applications.VGG16(weights=None, classes=10)
```

Finally, let's compile the network:

```
vgg16.compile(loss = 'sparse_categorical_crossentropy',
              optimizer = keras.optimizers.SGD(momentum=0.9,
                  learning_rate=5e-4),
              metrics=['accuracy'])
```

Let's train it:

```
reduceLr = keras.callbacks.ReduceLROnPlateau(patience=10, monitor =
    'val_accuracy', factor=0.2)
early_stopping = keras.callbacks.EarlyStopping(patience=15, monitor =
    'val_accuracy', restore_best_weights=True)

vgg_history = vgg16.fit(train_set,
                        epochs=100,
                        validation_data=valid_set,
                        callbacks=[reduceLr, early_stopping])
```

This results in:

```
Epoch 1/100
208/208 [==============================] - 176s 815ms/step - loss: 5.7282 -
    accuracy: 0.1153 - val_loss: 5.6941 - val_accuracy: 0.1646 - lr:
    5.0000e-04
...
Epoch 98/100
208/208 [==============================] - 166s 798ms/step - loss: 3.2370 -
    accuracy: 0.9197 - val_loss: 3.8194 - val_accuracy: 0.7964 - lr:
    2.0000e-05
```

VGG16 on Imagenette

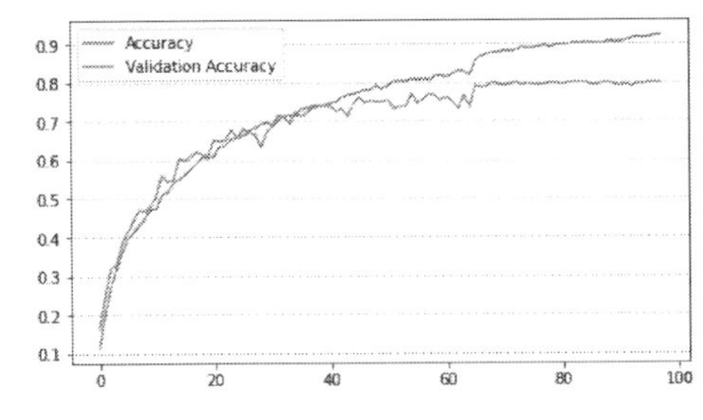

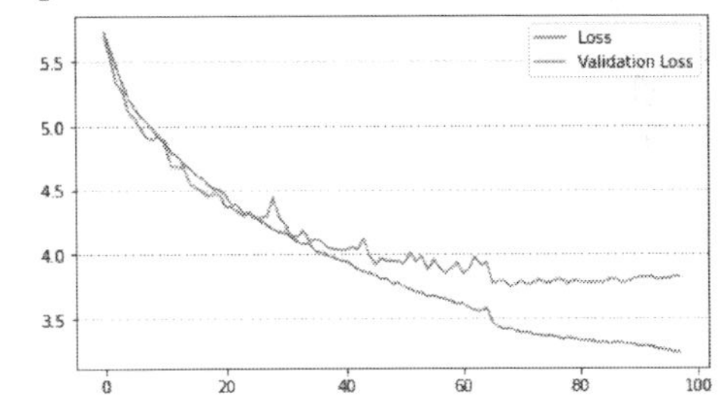

Figure 105:

Note: It might sound like I'm seriously trying to dunk on VGGNets, but these are outdated. As of writing, in 2022, you can still see people online using them, both for introducing other fields with computer vision (medical imagery, for example) but also as backbones for other computer vision applications. Just as I'd advise anyone not to use AlexNet for modern systems, I have to advise anyone not to use VGGNets in modern systems. With the rise of deep learning tools like Keras, not only is it easy enough to implement an architecture like ResNet (coming right up) or much newer ones, but as in the lesson on Transfer Learning shows - it's *dead easy* to load in some of the most performant architectures **in a single line**. They **train faster, utilize parameters better and perform faster inference**. Additionally, most modern architectures **don't have a flattening layer**, as we'll see with ResNets.

If you're a professional from another field and want to apply computer vision to your own domain - please avoid VGGs. While they're hands-down the most intuitive architecture to use if you're new to CNNs - you won't have fun, and neither will your hardware.

8.8 Inception - From Meme to State of the Art (2014)

The Inception network competed in the 2014 ILSVRC challenge and outperformed VGGNets in terms of both accuracy and training speed, winning the number 1 position that year. The first network in the family tree is known as GoogLeNet, followed by InceptionV2, InceptionV3, InceptionV4 and Inception ResNet.

GoogLeNet is also known as InceptionV1. InceptionV2 and InceptionV3 are a redesign of the network and come joint in a single paper and InceptionV4/Inception ResNet come again in a single paper.

The GoogLeNet name is an homage to LeCun's LeNet5. However, the "Inception" name comes from the meme *"We need to go deeper"*, from the movie *"Inception"*, which was viral at the time, reflecting the fact that the network was made to... go deeper than previous networks. The paper that started the Inception tree was aptly named *"Going deeper with convolutions"*[89] by Szegedy et al.

[89]https://arxiv.org/pdf/1409.4842.pdf

The authors noted that the most straightforward way to increase performance is to scale the network up - both in depth and in width. Scaling up means that you'll want to utilize the parameters more efficiently, lest you end up wasting precious compute. The authors of the Inception network note that you can fundamentally solve scaling issues with sparsely connected architectures, rather than densely connected architectures. With this in mind - GoogLeNet had only 6M parameters compared to 60M of AlexNet and 144M of VGGNet, and **had better performance (accuracy, training and parameter)**. This was a nail in the coffin to the previous approach of scaling networks up.

Just as Cobb dreams of dreams in "Inception", the Inception architecture is a set of networks within networks, where multiple kernel sizes are passed over the same feature maps, and which results are aggregated before being passed onto the next network. These networks are known as *Inception modules,* and they're fairly simple in an of themselves - the complexity of the network comes from the connections between modules.

At this point, most networks had some sort of "module" or "block" that could be repeated - and most of them were sequential. GoogLeNet introduced a novel idea with their own modules - they were *wide,* not *deep*. The authors tried addressing the major issues with existing architectures: stacking sequential convolutions can be expensive and wasteful (if parameters are inefficiently used) and that depth leads to overfitting *and* degradation.

The first, "naive", Inception module passed the input through three differently-sized filters and a max pooling layer, concatenating the filters in the end:

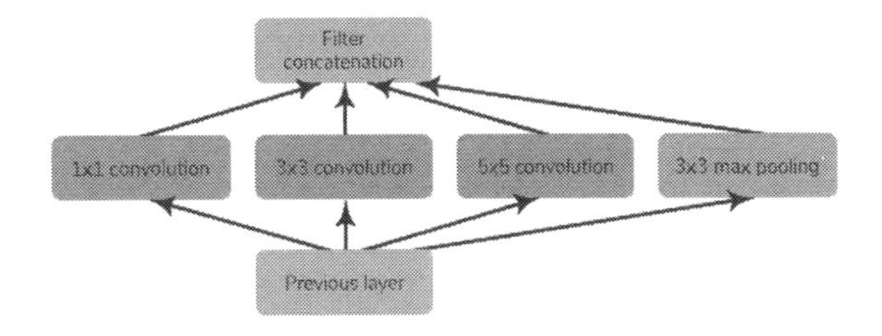

Figure 106:

5x5 convolutions are expensive, so to further limit the dimensions (and thus reduce computational cost) - a dimension-reduction version of the module was made. which used a 1x1 filter to first pass over the input. Low-dimension embeddings oftentimes contain *most* of the relevant data, so this reduction simply allowed the network to work practically:

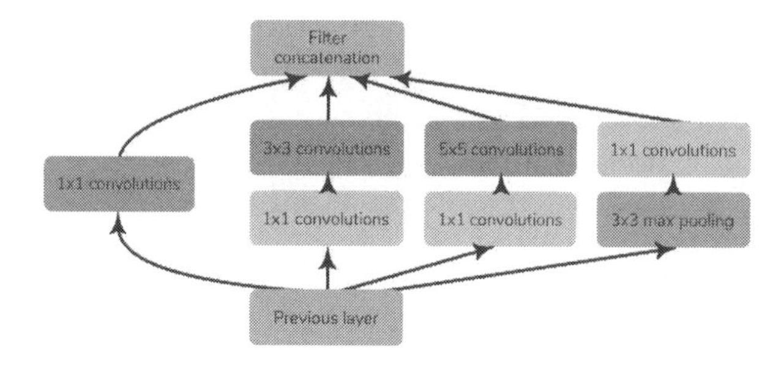

Figure 107:

Inception modules allowed the authors to use many of them without making the number of parameters explode, which meant that they could entertain the idea of deeper networks with limited depth degradation. The authors anticipated an issue with propagating gradients back and had to find a way to fix this issue. Since shallower networks worked well before - it was expected that the middle portion of GoogLeNet had discriminative power (was able to be accurate). The issue was anticipated to come from the lower layers. To boost the ability of lower layers to discern between features, auxiliary classifiers were piped out of the middle of the network. These would perform classification with a `softmax` activation, and a loss would be calculated for the auxiliary classifiers. The loss of each of them would then be combined (weighted to account for only 0.3 of its actual weight) with the loss at the end of the network ("real" loss, which had more weight than auxiliary losses):

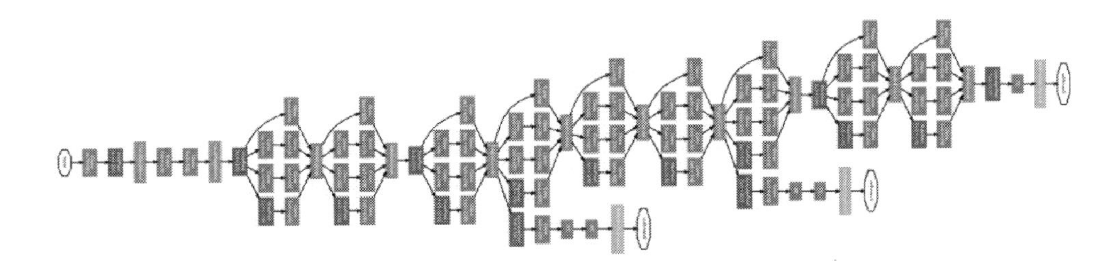

Figure 108:

The network tree is clearly made up of Inception modules, with a few starting convolutions and pooling layers as usual. Again - each Inception module is fairly easy to implement. The difficulty of implementing Inception networks comes from the fact that they're quite cumbersome to write down in a single file.

So - did auxiliary losses actually help? Not quite. A year later (2015), in *"Rethinking the Inception Architecture for Computer Vision"*[90] Szegedy et al. rethink the Inception architecture and propose InceptionV2 and InceptionV3. The main takeaways are considering computational efficiency and representation bottleneck (the fact that you lose data when reshaping input by forcing it to "fit down a bottleneck"). First, the 5x5 filters, which were a sore spot from the beginning (which prompted the dimensionality reduction in the first place) were replaced with two 3x3 filters, since a 5x5 filter is ~2.78 times more expensive than a 3x3 filter (making two of them cheaper than a single 5x5):

[90]https://arxiv.org/pdf/1512.00567v3.pdf

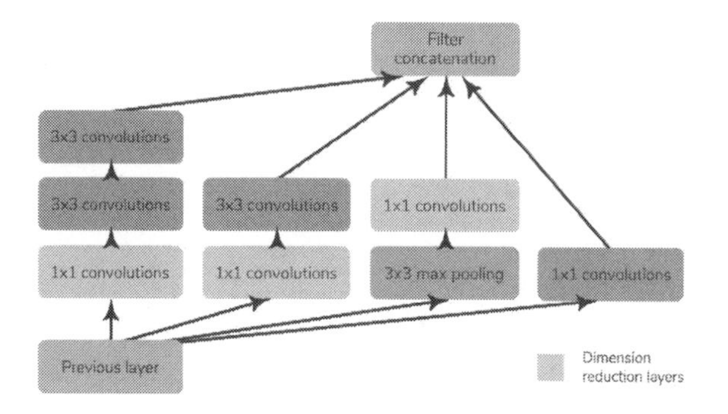

Figure 109:

This was taken further by noting that *any NxN* filter can be replaced by a *1xN* convolution followed by a *Nx1* convolution, which saves computation as *N* increases:

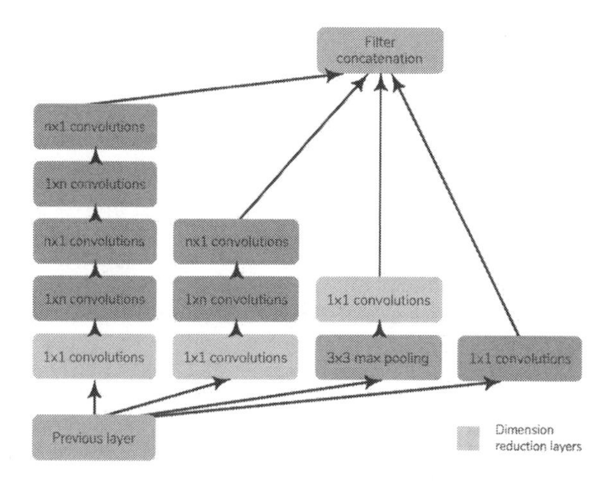

Figure 110:

The utility of auxiliary classifiers was also taken into consideration. It turned out that they didn't really do much until much further into the training, where Inception networks with auxiliary classifiers overtook Inception networks without them, after a while of practically identical training. Furthermore, the second auxiliary classifier, as it turns out, didn't negatively affect the network as initially thought. The authors note that the auxiliary classifiers likely aid in regularization, since the "real" classifier performs better when the side branch of the auxiliary classifier is normalized or has dropout.

To combat bottleneck - width was added to Inception modules to ease the reduction of filter map sizes in a more efficient manner. Thus, InceptionV2 was born and a variation of it got turned into InceptionV3 (V2 + Batch Normalization on auxiliary classifiers)! Yet, even so, ResNets were introduced that same year, which took the cake in the competition, with an exceedingly elegant solution.

While you could implement the modules and then go on a journey of connecting them - you can also easily load in an Inception network via Keras:

```
1 inceptionv3 = keras.applications.InceptionV3(weights=None, classes=n_classes)
```

8.9 ResNet - The Start of a Lineage (2015)

If you ran the VGG model, either on your own local setup or on the cloud - you've definitely noticed how much longer it took to train than AlexNet. VGGNet took more deliberate design as well - pretty precise weight decay on convolutional layers and testing out various SGD hyperparameters, mixed with the longer training times meant it was harder to iteratively improve the model's architecture. Additionally, the architecture suffered from ***depth degradation***. Degradation occurred with deeper networks, which performed *worse* than their shallower counterparts. Similar to how vanishing gradients posed a hurdle for increasing network complexity (including depth), in a similar way, depth degradation posed a hurdle to scale networks in depth. This was a pretty big hurdle, since through the advent of VGGNet and Inception networks, it seemed as if depth is a very desirable property of a network.

Vanishing gradients were relatively easy to fix - normalization between layers and an effective activation function such as ReLU was enough to keep the gradients stable during training, even in more complex networks. On the other hand - what do we do about degradation? The first line of reasoning was that deeper networks, with more layers, lead to more overfitting. However - this was proven to be *false*, because the *training error* went up with network depth as well!

It wasn't a case of overfitting, it was more of a case of the neurons in a network "losing identity". How do we let layers keep their identity? The authors of *"Deep Residual Learning for Image Recognition"*[91] lay out a *residual learning framework*, which changed the way networks learned, and started a new family of models known as ResNets (Residual Networks) and the plain ResNet network won the 2015 ILSVRC challenge. The idea is elegantly simple - if a new stack of layers can lead to a "loss of identity", add a shortcut/skip connection between the start and end of that block, which carries over the identity of the previous block. The input is *added to* the output. Doing so will make sure that the next block is *at least* as good as the previous one. Additionally, if there's a "bad apple" in the line of blocks which would effectively stop other blocks from training properly, through a skip connection, it can be circumvented, allowing other blocks to learn while that block is still figuring things out. This speeds up training significantly.

Finally - valuable information can be lost through pooling and strided convolutions, and skip connections help retain some of that information, injecting it back into the mix.

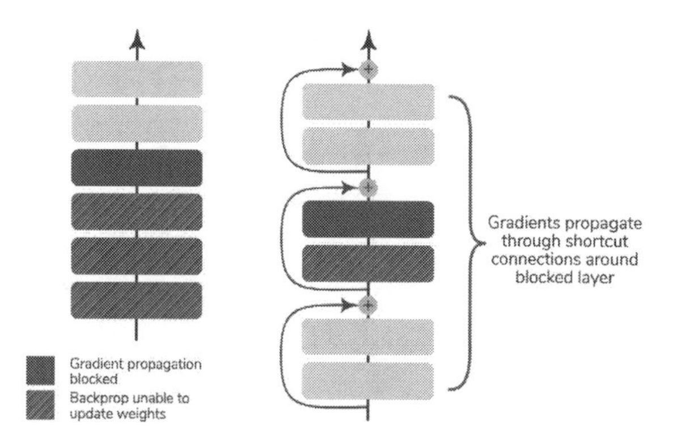

Figure 111:

Note: While it isn't an apparent inspiration noted in the paper - it's curious to note that the neocortex also has skip connections, through which certain layers can "skip" intermediate layers and feed into another one.

---

[91] https://arxiv.org/pdf/1512.03385.pdf

8.9.1 Skip Connections

Skip connections are at the heart of ResNets. Skip connections are a general concept and can be implemented in multiple ways, one of which is outlined in the paper. It's worth noting that they existed before and weren't unknown to the deep learning community! HighwayNets used skip connections before ResNets.

In a great paper by Hao Li, Zheng Xu et al. in 2018. the authors plot the loss landscape of a ResNet56 *with* and *without* skip connections:

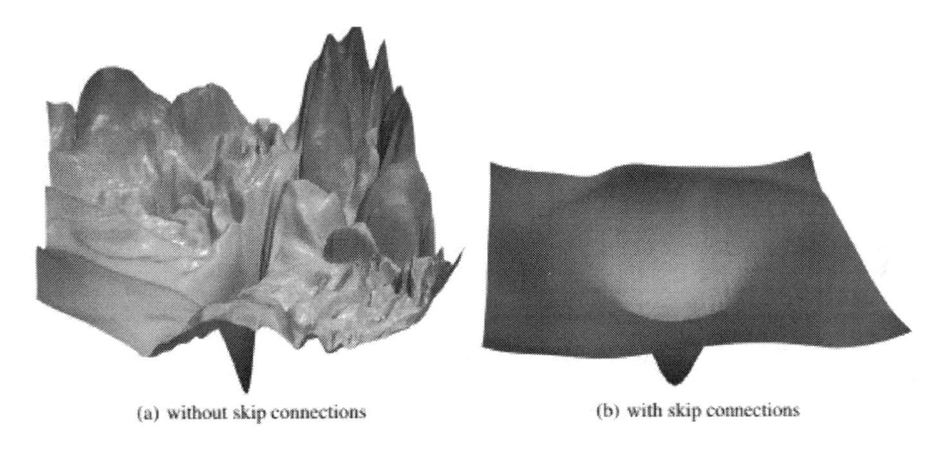

Figure 112:

The path towards the optimized global minimum is significantly smoother and easier with skip connections. If you imagine rolling a boll on both of these landscapes - it would be much more likely to roll into the smoother global minima in the second plot, without bumping into any points that would make learning harder. Conceptually, this is what a skip connection looks like:

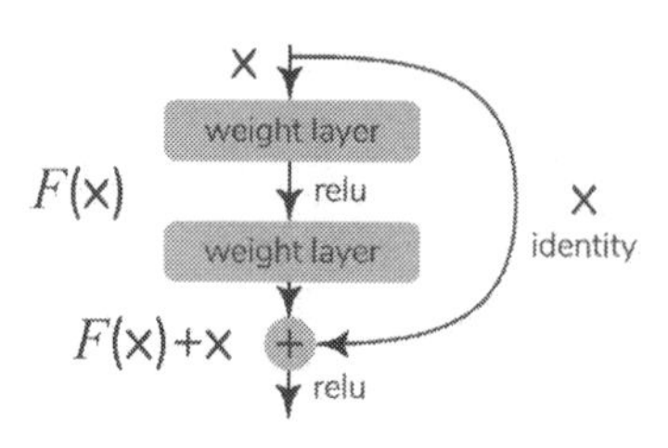

Figure 113:

This elegant mapping between the input and output of a block had profound implications, and negated depth degradation to a large extent. As a matter of fact - the team built a 1202-layer network in the paper! Though, it didn't perform much better (actually, slightly worse) than its 110-layer counterpart. Nevertheless, this just proved that depth degradation is solvable with a single, simple tweak of the architecture. Common ResNet depths are 34, 50, 101 and 152, and models are typically named by their depth - ResNet34, Resnet50, ResNet101 and ResNet152. With these, you'll generally see better performance with more layers, so it's mainly a tradeoff between training time, inference time and accuracy, unless you go to really deep networks with hundreds of layers.

Note: The building blocks of ResNets are known as *Residual Blocks* or *Identity Blocks.*

8.9.2 Implementing Residual Units

Conceptually, a ResNet is a series of residual/identity blocks, each of which has a skip connection from it's input to its output:

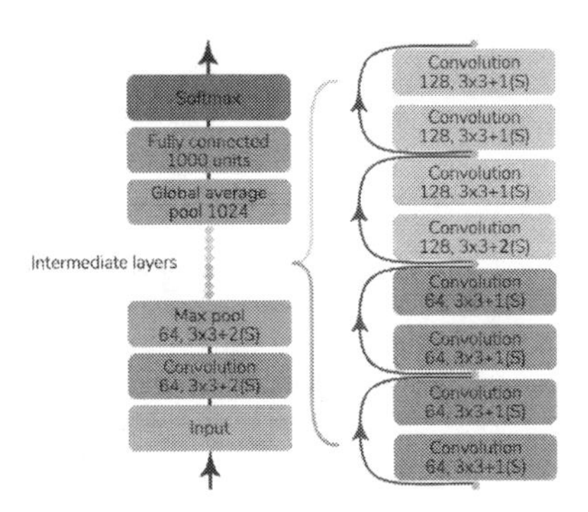

Figure 114:

Periodically, the number of filters (feature maps) is doubled (from 64 to 128, to 256, to 512) while the input itself is halved (vertically and horizontally), through a convolutional layer with `strides=2`. This means that for each increase in filter sizes - the inputs and outputs can't be added since their shapes don't match (the input is downsized within that residual block). While you can resize the input in any way - typically, an altered version of a residual block is used, in which the shortcut connection uses a `1x1` kernel size convolutional block, with `strides=2` to reshape the input to match the output, before it's added together.

So, we have two types of residual blocks - those with a convolutional layer at the skip connection and those without. Let's implement both of these blocks:

```
1 # Also known as a Residual Block
2 def identity_block(layer_in, filter_num):
3     # To stay true to the paper, we'll apply batch norm before the
          activation layer
4     conv1 = keras.layers.Conv2D(filter_num, (1, 1), padding =
          'same')(layer_in)
5     batch_norm = keras.layers.BatchNormalization()(conv1)
6     relu = keras.layers.Activation('relu')(batch_norm)
7
8     conv2 = keras.layers.Conv2D(filter_num, (3, 3), padding = 'same')(relu)
9     batch_norm = keras.layers.BatchNormalization()(conv2)
10    relu = keras.layers.Activation('relu')(batch_norm)
11
12    conv3 = keras.layers.Conv2D(filter_num*4, (1, 1), padding = 'same')(relu)
13    batch_norm = keras.layers.BatchNormalization()(conv3)
14
15    # Add layer_in to the last layer - this is the skip connection!
16    add = keras.layers.Add()([layer_in, batch_norm])
```

```
17      out = keras.layers.Activation('relu')(add)
18      return out
```

Note: This is a good point to mention that batch normalization can be applied before or after the activation layer. Some argue that BN-activation is better, while some argue that activation-BN is better. Bechmarks online exist to prove these points as well, such as Ducha Aiki's benchmark[92] which notes that activation-BN performs better. Others have pointed to a segment in an iconic book, "Deep Learning" by Ian Goodfellow, Yoshua Bengio and Aaron Courville which notes that due to the way ReLU works (turning all negative input into 0 and linearly increasing after that), the skewed distribution to the right isn't amenable to batch normalization, so BN-activation makes more sense. There is debate and you'll find both uses in the wild. The original paper on Batch Normalization (by Christian Szegedy et al.)[93] applies BN *before* activation. Though, in a comment on GitHub[94], François Chollet notes that Christian Szegedy's recent code at the time applied BN *after* activation. Conclusion? You probably shouldn't care too much whether it's applied before or after activation. At the end of the day, try both.

And now let's implement a residual block with a `Conv2D` in the skip connection:

```
1  def conv_identity_block(layer_in, filter_num):
2      conv1 = keras.layers.Conv2D(filter_num, (1, 1), strides=(2, 2), padding
          = 'same')(layer_in)
3      batch_norm = keras.layers.BatchNormalization()(conv1)
4      relu = keras.layers.Activation('relu')(batch_norm)
5
6      conv2 = keras.layers.Conv2D(filter_num, (3, 3), padding = 'same')(relu)
7      batch_norm = keras.layers.BatchNormalization()(conv2)
8      relu = keras.layers.Activation('relu')(batch_norm)
9
10     conv3 = keras.layers.Conv2D(filter_num*4, (1, 1), padding = 'same')(relu)
11     batch_norm = keras.layers.BatchNormalization()(conv3)
12
13     # Before adding layer_in to the last layer
```

[92] https://github.com/ducha-aiki/caffenet-benchmark/blob/master/batchnorm.md
[93] https://arxiv.org/pdf/1502.03167.pdf
[94] https://github.com/keras-team/keras/issues/1802#issuecomment-187966878

```
14      # add a 1x1 kernel size Conv2D with strides=2 to reshape the layer
15      shortcut = keras.layers.Conv2D(filter_num*4, (1, 1),
            strides=(2,2))(layer_in)
16      shortcut = keras.layers.BatchNormalization()(shortcut)
17
18      add = keras.layers.Add()([shortcut, batch_norm])
19      out = keras.layers.Activation('relu')(add)
20      return out
```

These blocks can now be used to build a ResNet! Since ResNets can be very deep, let's build a single-block ResNet and visualize it using Keras' built-in plotting function:

```
1 input_layer = keras.layers.Input(shape=[224, 224, 3])
2 x = conv_identity_block(input_layer, 64)
3 x = keras.layers.GlobalAveragePooling2D()(x)
4 output_layer = keras.layers.Dense(n_classes, activation = 'softmax')(x)
5
6 resnet = keras.Model(inputs=input_layer, outputs=output_layer)
7 tf.keras.utils.plot_model(resnet, to_file = 'resnet_singleblock.png',
      show_shapes=True)
```

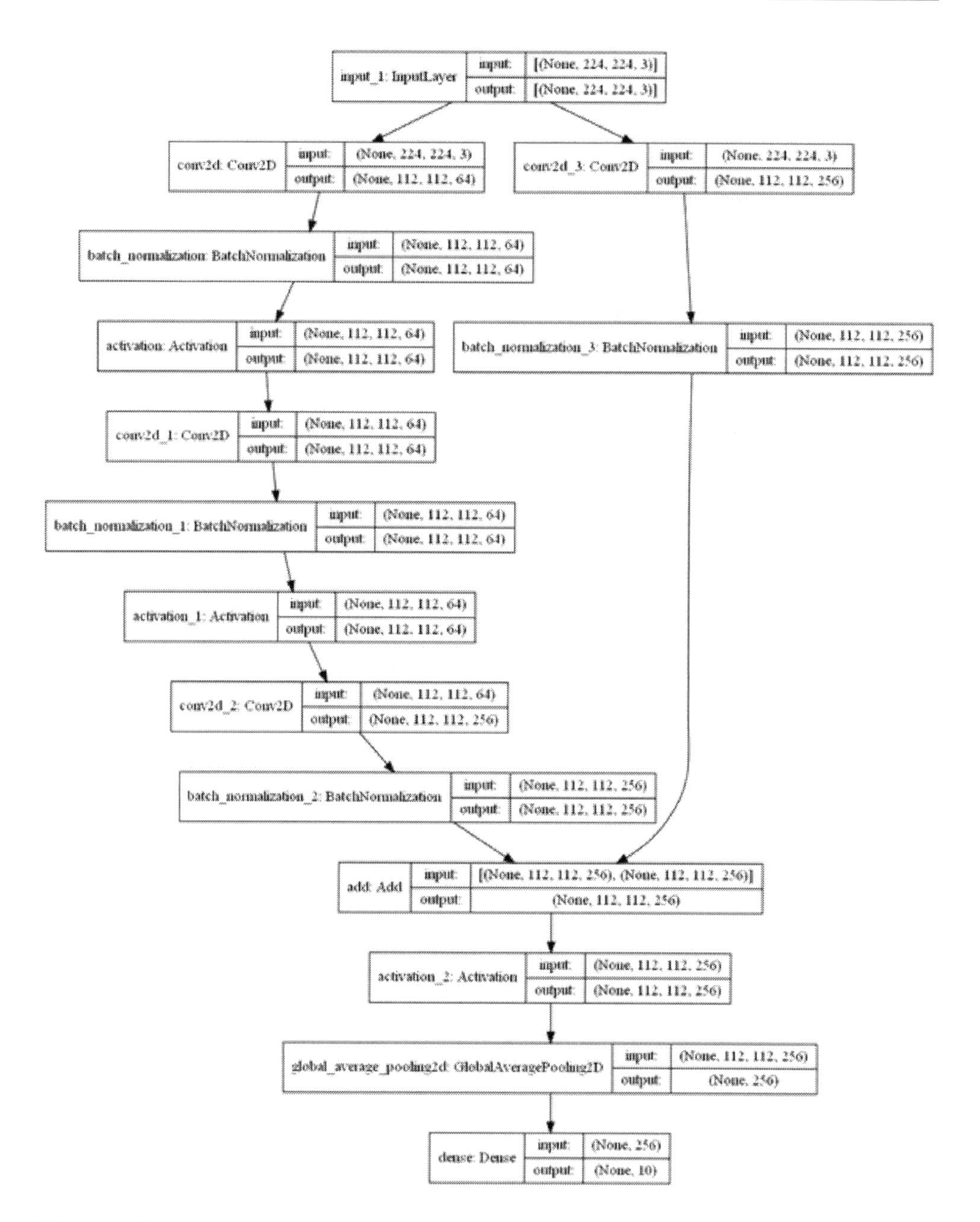
input_1: InputLayer
input: [(None, 224, 224, 3)]
output: [(None, 224, 224, 3)]
conv2d: Conv2D
input: (None, 224, 224, 3)
output: (None, 112, 112, 64)
conv2d_3: Conv2D
input: (None, 224, 224, 3)
output: (None, 112, 112, 256)
batch_normalization: BatchNormalization
input: (None, 112, 112, 64)
output: (None, 112, 112, 64)
activation: Activation
input: (None, 112, 112, 64)
output: (None, 112, 112, 64)
batch_normalization_3: BatchNormalization
input: (None, 112, 112, 256)
output: (None, 112, 112, 256)
conv2d_1: Conv2D
input: (None, 112, 112, 64)
output: (None, 112, 112, 64)
batch_normalization_1: BatchNormalization
input: (None, 112, 112, 64)
output: (None, 112, 112, 64)
activation_1: Activation
input: (None, 112, 112, 64)
output: (None, 112, 112, 64)
conv2d_2: Conv2D
input: (None, 112, 112, 64)
output: (None, 112, 112, 256)
batch_normalization_2: BatchNormalization
input: (None, 112, 112, 256)
output: (None, 112, 112, 256)
add: Add
input: [(None, 112, 112, 256), (None, 112, 112, 256)]
output: (None, 112, 112, 256)
activation_2: Activation
input: (None, 112, 112, 256)
output: (None, 112, 112, 256)
global_average_pooling2d: GlobalAveragePooling2D
input: (None, 112, 112, 256)
output: (None, 256)
dense: Dense
input: (None, 256)
output: (None, 10)

Figure 115:

Awesome! Now, we stack 34 of these for ResNet34, 50 of these for ResNet50, etc.

8.9.3 Implementing a ResNet50 with Keras

Let's build ResNet50! The original paper includes everything you need to know to build different ResNets:

layer name	output size	18-layer	34-layer	50-layer	101-layer	152-layer
conv1	112×112	7×7, 64, stride 2				
conv2_x	56×56	3×3 max pool, stride 2				
		[3×3, 64; 3×3, 64] ×2	[3×3, 64; 3×3, 64] ×3	[1×1, 64; 3×3, 64; 1×1, 256] ×3	[1×1, 64; 3×3, 64; 1×1, 256] ×3	[1×1, 64; 3×3, 64; 1×1, 256] ×3
conv3_x	28×28	[3×3, 128; 3×3, 128] ×2	[3×3, 128; 3×3, 128] ×4	[1×1, 128; 3×3, 128; 1×1, 512] ×4	[1×1, 128; 3×3, 128; 1×1, 512] ×4	[1×1, 128; 3×3, 128; 1×1, 512] ×8
conv4_x	14×14	[3×3, 256; 3×3, 256] ×2	[3×3, 256; 3×3, 256] ×6	[1×1, 256; 3×3, 256; 1×1, 1024] ×6	[1×1, 256; 3×3, 256; 1×1, 1024] ×23	[1×1, 256; 3×3, 256; 1×1, 1024] ×36
conv5_x	7×7	[3×3, 512; 3×3, 512] ×2	[3×3, 512; 3×3, 512] ×3	[1×1, 512; 3×3, 512; 1×1, 2048] ×3	[1×1, 512; 3×3, 512; 1×1, 2048] ×3	[1×1, 512; 3×3, 512; 1×1, 2048] ×3
	1×1	average pool, 1000-d fc, softmax				
FLOPs		1.8×10^9	3.6×10^9	3.8×10^9	7.6×10^9	11.3×10^9

Table 1. Architectures for ImageNet. Building blocks are shown in brackets (see also Fig. 5), with the numbers of blocks stacked. Downsampling is performed by conv3_1, conv4_1, and conv5_1 with a stride of 2.

Figure 116:

To build a 50-layer network, we have a couple of entry layers, and then we stack 3 residual blocks where each residual block has 3 convolutional layers (first one has 64 filters, second one has 64 filters, third one has 256 filters). Between each of these, as per the paper, there's a `BatchNormalization()` and before the activation layer (ReLU). Note the use of `1x1` and `3x3` kernel sizes in each block! On top of these three blocks, we stack another 4, with the detailed filter numbers. On top of that, we stack another 6 and then another 3 blocks.

Given the pretty visible pattern of each block having three convolutional layers of `filter_num, filter_num, filter_num*4` - we can simplify the implementation and only define a single `filter_num` in our `identity_block()` and `conv_block()` functions, where the final `Conv2D` has `filter_num*4`. You could also supply a tuple or list of filters to be used for each block:

```
1 def identity_block(filter_sizes, ...):
2     conv1_filter_num, conv2_filter_num, conv3_filter_num = filter_sizes[0],
          filter_sizes[1], filter_sizes[2]
```

```
3     ...
4
5 x = identity_block(input_layer, [64, 64, 256])
```

This allows for more customization, but we'll stick to the numbers outlined in the paper, which follow the same rule so we can abstract it away and generalize it. It's worth noting that after all of these blocks - **there is no fully connected network**! This makes seriously reduces the number of learnable parameters and without flattening with multiple fully connected layers, we're losing a lot of the parameters introduced in VGGNet!

> VGG19 has 144M parameters with 19 layers. ResNet50 has 23M parameters with 50 layers.

ResNet50 is in the accuracy ballpark of VGG16. However, with so much fewer parameters - it's a clear sign that ResNets utilize their parameters *much* better than VGGNets! This means faster and more stable training, availability to use other optimizers (Adam works with ResNets, which means less manual tweaking and easier testing). There's no need to apply dropout to ResNets, there are already fewer connections between layers than with VGGNets and you generally only apply dropout to fully connected layers (which don't exist in ResNets). ResNets however very liberally use batch normalization for regularization (for every `Conv2D` layer, there's a `BatchNormalization` layer before activation). Though, more importantly - you can't really scale VGGNets up anymore, but can scale ResNets! This means potential for better performance with tweaks.

With this in mind - let's add an input layer for the images, some random rotation/contrast, the entry layers and stack convolutional identity and identity blocks as per the schema in the paper:

```
1  def resnet50():
2      input_layer = keras.layers.Input(shape=[224, 224, 3])
3      preprocess = keras.layers.RandomRotation(0.1)(input_layer)
4      preprocess = keras.layers.RandomFlip("horizontal")(preprocess)
5      preprocess = keras.layers.RandomContrast(0.1)(preprocess)
6
7      x = keras.layers.ZeroPadding2D(padding=(3, 3))(preprocess)
8      x = keras.layers.Conv2D(64, (7, 7), strides=(2, 2), padding = 'valid')(x)
9      x = keras.layers.BatchNormalization()(x)
10     x = keras.layers.Activation('relu')(x)
11     x = keras.layers.ZeroPadding2D(padding=(1, 1))(x)
12     x = keras.layers.MaxPooling2D((3, 3), strides=(2, 2))(x)
13
14     x = conv_identity_block(x, 64)
```

```
15     x = identity_block(x, 64)
16     x = identity_block(x, 64)
17
18     x = conv_identity_block(x, 128)
19     x = identity_block(x, 128)
20     x = identity_block(x, 128)
21     x = identity_block(x, 128)
22
23     x = conv_identity_block(x, 256)
24     x = identity_block(x, 256)
25     x = identity_block(x, 256)
26     x = identity_block(x, 256)
27     x = identity_block(x, 256)
28     x = identity_block(x, 256)
29
30     x = conv_identity_block(x, 512)
31     x = identity_block(x, 512)
32     x = identity_block(x, 512)
33
34     x = keras.layers.GlobalAveragePooling2D()(x)
35     output_layer = keras.layers.Dense(n_classes, activation = 'softmax')(x)
36
37     return keras.Model(inputs=input_layer, outputs=output_layer)
38
39 resnet = resnet50()
```

Alternatively, to load in the Keras' team's implementation, simply call on the `ResNetLayerNum` class (18, 34, 50, 101 and 152 are supported):

```
1 resnet = keras.applications.ResNet50(weights=None, classes=n_classes)
```

Finally, let's compile the network:

```
1 resnet.compile(loss = 'sparse_categorical_crossentropy',
2                optimizer = keras.optimizers.Adam(learning_rate=1e-3),
3                metrics=['accuracy'])
4
5 resnet.summary()
```

Both our custom implementation and Keras' implementation has 23.5M parameters:

```
1 ...
2 activation_100 (Activation)      (None, 4, 4, 2048)  0           add_32[0][0]
3 ________________________________________________________________
4 global_average_pooling2d_2 (Glo (None, 2048)         0
      activation_100[0][0]
5 ________________________________________________________________
6 dense_2 (Dense)                  (None, 10)           20490
      global_average_pooling2d_2[0][0]
7 ================================================================
8 Total params: 23,608,202
9 Trainable params: 23,555,082
```

```
10 Non-trainable params: 53,120
11 _________________________________________________________________
```

```
1 ...
2
3 conv5_block3_out (Activation)   (None, 7, 7, 2048)   0
      conv5_block3_add[0][0]
4 _________________________________________________________________
5 avg_pool (GlobalAveragePooling2 (None, 2048)         0
      conv5_block3_out[0][0]
6 _________________________________________________________________
7 predictions (Dense)             (None, 10)           20490
      avg_pool[0][0]
8 =================================================================
9 Total params: 23,608,202
10 Trainable params: 23,555,082
11 Non-trainable params: 53,120
12 _________________________________________________________________
```

We've followed the paper well then! Time to train the network. The original paper lists out the hyperparameters used to train the network:

- Optimizer: SGD (momentum of 0.9, learning rate of 0.1)
- Batch size: 256
- Learning rate: 0.1
- Reduce learning rate on error plateau (by a factor of 0.1)
- Data augmentation like with VGGNet and AlexNet (horizontal flipping, constrast, etc.)

We'll go with different settings - Adam, with a smaller reduction on plateau and a smaller starting learning rate. Let's train the network:

```
1 reduceLR = keras.callbacks.ReduceLROnPlateau(patience=5, factor=0.7)
2 early_stopping = keras.callbacks.EarlyStopping(patience=15, monitor =
      'val_accuracy', restore_best_weights=True)
3
4 resnet_history = resnet.fit(train_set,
5                             epochs=100,
6                             callbacks=[reduceLR, early_stopping],
7                             validation_data=valid_set)
```

This results in:

```
1 Epoch 1/100
2 208/208 [==============================] - 85s 379ms/step - loss: 2.2217 -
      accuracy: 0.3150 - val_loss: 3.4948 - val_accuracy: 0.1954 - lr: 0.0010
3 ...
4 Epoch 70/100
```

```
5 208/208 [==============================] - 77s 370ms/step - loss: 0.0033 -
      accuracy: 0.9992 - val_loss: 1.4185 - val_accuracy: 0.7783 - lr:
      2.8248e-05
```

Around the same accuracy as VGG16, to be expected - however, it's worth noting how fast it trains! To summarize:

- There was an apparent scaling issue with network depth highlighted by VGGNets.
- ResNets solved network degradation through layers using identity blocks.
- ResNets are made of residual/identity blocks, where each has a skip connection between its input and output.
- When dimensions don't add up (increasing filter numbers and downsizing images via stride) - a residual block with a `1x1` kernel size `Conv2D` at the skip connection is used to resize the input to match the output.
- Much further depths are possible, without degradation, and with better parameter utilization and fewer parameters.
- No dropout - heavy batch normalization regularization is used.
- Lack of flattening and FC layers makes for fewer parameters. This is a trend you'll see taking off around this time - since VGGNets, flattening has become out of fashion (as it should've).
- You can use the Adam optimizer!

8.10 "Bag of Tricks for CNNs"

Although ResNets were outperformed by the Inception network (right up next) - they became a *defining* cornerstone of computer vision, and are quite commonly used even today despite there existing architectures with better parameter utilization, faster training, and higher accuracy. While they are being phased out, their performance is decent, and more importantly, tweaks were made to the original architecture that boosted the performance significantly.

These variations kept ResNets very relevant to this day, and architectures like ResNeXt (which stacks parallely, rather then sequentially, similar to Inception) and variations on ResNeXts have achieve state-of-the art results in 2020!

Some tweaks are pretty small - some are fairly large. Let's take a look at one of the tweaks from *"Bag of Tricks for Image Classification with Convolutional Neural Networks"*[95]

[95]https://arxiv.org/pdf/1812.01187v2.pdf

by Tong He et al. They outline several tricks for training CNNs, and aggregate their results for ResNets, Inception and MobileNet. Their baseline is, naturally, much the same as we've seen it so far - image augmentation (random horizontal flipping, hue/saturation, normalization, etc.), Nesterov-accelerated SGD with a momentum of 0.9, a starting learning rate of 0.1, a factor of 0.1 on reducing the learning rate when the network plateaus and a batch size of 256.

In the following sections, I'll highlight a couple of the easily implementable/actionable takeaways you can start applying *now*. For the rest of the tricks - it's highly advised to read their paper.

8.10.1 Linear Scaling Rule

While exploring the effect of the batch size on the learning rate, they reference Goyal et al.'s work on *"Accurate, Large Minibatch SGD"*[96], noting the **linear scaling rule.**

> Linear Scaling Rule: When the minibatch size is multiplied by k, multiply the learning rate by k.

We've actually been using this exact rule so far when adjusting the learning rate for networks.

8.10.2 Learning Rate Warmup

The idea behind learning rate warmup is simple. In the earliest stages of training - weights are far from their ideal states. This means large updates all across the board, which can be seen as "overcorrections" for each weight - where the drastic update of another may negate the update of some other weight, making initial stages of training more unstable.

These changes iron out, but can be avoided by having a small learning rate to begin with, reaching a more stable suboptimal state, and then applying a larger learning rate. You can sort of ease the network into updates, rather than hit it with them.

[96] https://arxiv.org/pdf/1706.02677.pdf

That's learning rate warmup! Starting with a low (or 0) learning rate and increasing to a starting learning rate (what you'd start with anyway). This increase can follow any function really, but is commonly linear.

> After reaching the initial rate, other schedules such as cosine decay, linear reduction, etc. can be applied to progressively lower the rate down until the end of training. Learning rate warmup is usually part of a two-schedule schedule, where LR warmup is the first, while another schedule takes over after the rate has reached a starting point.

Tong He et al. assume a learning rate warmup for all of their runs, with the warmup lasting 5 epochs, and the learning rate linearly increasing towards the starting rate. In Keras, it's pretty easy to implement a custom learning rate schedule to apply learning rate warmup! By extending the `LearningRateSchedule` class, we can define a custom learning rate scheduler that increases the learning rate linearly for X steps, before either keeping it constant or having it decay over time or reducing it on plateau (decay strategies are again, a different topic).

Typically, in a learning rate warmup schedule - you can delineate the warmup and reduction "parts" of the scheduler.

As a matter of fact, you'll find the exact same piece of code present in many of Keras' example pages, in some form or another:

```
1 class LRSchedule(keras.optimizers.schedules.LearningRateSchedule):
2     def __init__(self, post_warmup_learning_rate, warmup_steps):
3         super().__init__()
4         self.post_warmup_learning_rate = post_warmup_learning_rate
5         self.warmup_steps = warmup_steps
6
7     def __call__(self, step):
8         global_step = tf.cast(step, tf.float32)
9         warmup_steps = tf.cast(self.warmup_steps, tf.float32)
10        warmup_progress = global_step / warmup_steps
11        warmup_learning_rate = self.post_warmup_learning_rate *
              warmup_progress
12        return tf.cond(
13            global_step < warmup_steps,
14            lambda: warmup_learning_rate,
15            lambda: self.post_warmup_learning_rate,
16        )
```

This scheduler can then be supplied to an optimizer, such as `Adam`:

```
model = ...

n_train_steps = len(train_set) * N_EPOCHS
n_warmup_steps = n_train_steps // 20 # Warmup for 1/20 of the training
# post_warmup_learning_rate is the 'initial' learning rate
lr_schedule = LRSchedule(post_warmup_learning_rate=1e-4,
    warmup_steps=n_warmup_steps)

model.compile(optimizer = keras.optimizers.Adam(lr_schedule), loss = ...)
```

Now, this replaces your learning rate *with the scheduler*, so you can't apply callbacks like `ReduceLROnPlateau` anymore, since they expect a floating point learning rate, not an object. Note that this implementation just warms up the learning rate to a certain point and keeps it there. You typically also want to use some decay. While it's easy to add a decay argument to your optimizer, you can also plug in your own decay rule for after the learning rate reaches the target rate.

Using Keras/TensorFlow, we can easily implement a cosine decay LR warmup scheduler as a `keras.optimizers.schedules.LearningRateSchedule` (lower-level) subclass or `keras.callbacks.Callback` callback (higher-level).

8.10.2.1 Learning Rate Warmup with Cosine Decay as a Scheduler In the proceeding code snippet, inspired by the implementation *Chengwei Zhang's "Keras Bag of Tricks" GitHub repository*[97], you can create your own warmup scheduler with cosine decay with:

```
def lr_warmup_cosine_decay(global_step,
                           warmup_steps,
                           hold = 0,
                           total_steps=0,
                           start_lr=0.0,
                           target_lr=1e-3):
    # Cosine decay
    # There is no tf.pi so we wrap np.pi as a TF constant
    learning_rate = 0.5 * target_lr * (1 + tf.cos(tf.constant(np.pi) *
        (global_step - warmup_steps - hold) / float(total_steps -
        warmup_steps - hold)))

    # Target LR * progress of warmup (=1 at the final warmup step)
    warmup_lr = target_lr * (global_step / warmup_steps)

    # Choose between `warmup_lr`, `target_lr` and `learning_rate` based on
        whether `global_step < warmup_steps` and we're still holding.
```

[97]https://github.com/Tony607/Keras_Bag_of_Tricks

```
15      # i.e. warm up if we're still warming up and use cosine decayed lr
            otherwise
16      if hold > 0:
17          learning_rate = tf.where(global_step > warmup_steps + hold,
18                                   learning_rate, target_lr)
19
20      learning_rate = tf.where(global_step < warmup_steps, warmup_lr,
            learning_rate)
21      return learning_rate
22
23
24  class WarmUpCosineDecay(keras.optimizers.schedules.LearningRateSchedule):
25      def __init__(self, start_lr, target_lr, warmup_steps, total_steps, hold):
26          super().__init__()
27          self.start_lr = start_lr
28          self.target_lr = target_lr
29          self.warmup_steps = warmup_steps
30          self.total_steps = total_steps
31          self.hold = hold
32
33      def __call__(self, step):
34          lr = lr_warmup_cosine_decay(global_step=step,
35                                      total_steps=self.total_steps,
36                                      warmup_steps=self.warmup_steps,
37                                      start_lr=self.start_lr,
38                                      target_lr=self.target_lr,
39                                      hold=self.hold)
40
41          return tf.where(
42              step > self.total_steps, 0.0, lr, name = "learning_rate"
43          )
44
45  # If batched
46  total_steps = len(train_set)*config['EPOCHS']
47  # If not batched
48  #total_steps = len(train_set)/config['BATCH_SIZE']*config['EPOCHS']
49  # 5% of the steps
50  warmup_steps = int(0.05*total_steps)
51
52  schedule = WarmUpCosineDecay(start_lr=0.0, target_lr=1e-3,
        warmup_steps=warmup_steps, total_steps=total_steps, hold=warmup_steps)
```

On each step (batch), we calculate the *learning rate* and the *warmup learning rate*, with respects to the `start_lr` and `target_lr`. `start_lr` will usually start at `0.0`, while the `target_lr` depends on your network and optimizer - `1e-3` might not be a good default, so be sure to set your target starting LR when calling the method.

If the `global_step` in the training is higher than the warmup_steps we've set - we use the cosine decay LR. If not, it means that we're still warming up, so the warmup LR is used. If the `hold` argument is set, we'll hold the `target_lr` for that number of steps after warmup and before the cosine decay is applied. `tf.where()` provides a great syntax for this:

```
tf.where(condition, value_if_true, value_if_false)
```

You can visualize the function with:

```
import numpy as np
import matplotlib.pyplot as plt

# Create 1000 arbitrary steps
steps = np.arange(0, 1000, 1)
lrs = []

for step in steps:
  lrs.append(lr_warmup_cosine_decay(step, total_steps=len(steps),
      warmup_steps=100, hold=100))
plt.plot(lrs)
```

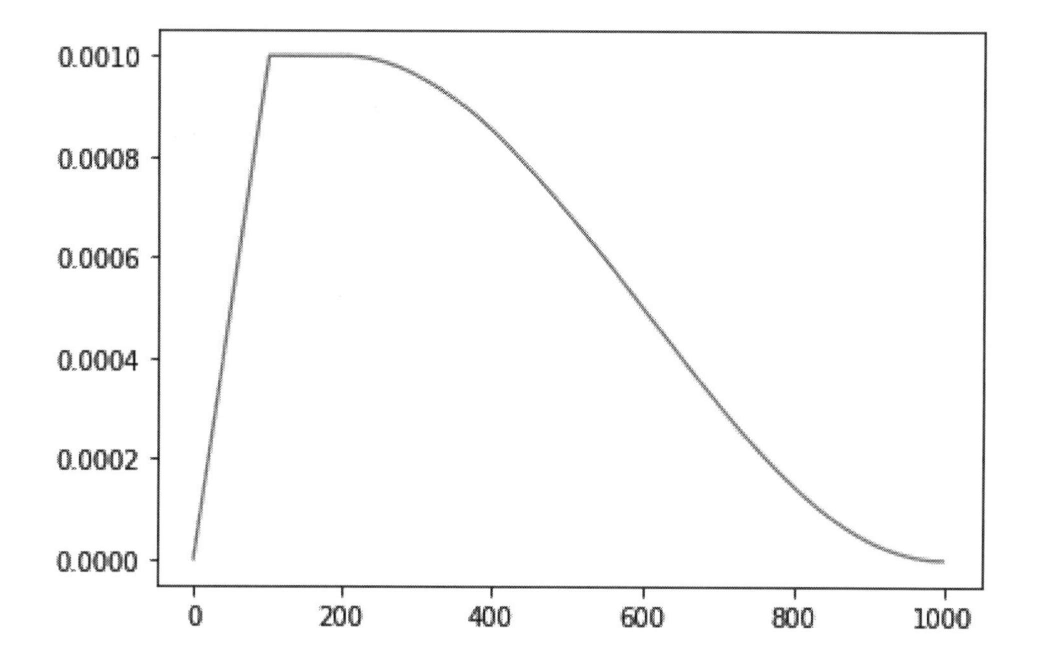

Figure 117:

If you wish to save the warmup scheduler, as it becomes part of the model, you'll have to override the `get_config()` method, to make the object serializable (this applies to all custom objects you want to save as parts of models):

```
    def get_config(self):
        config = {
          'start_lr': self.start_lr,
          'target_lr': self.target_lr,
          'warmup_steps': self.warmup_steps,
          'total_steps': self.total_steps,
          'hold': self.hold
        }
        return config
```

When loading a model in, you'll pass the `WarmupCosineDecay` as a custom object:

```
model = keras.models.load_model('weights.h5',
                                custom_objects={'WarmupCosineDecay',
                                    WarmupCosineDecay})
```

8.10.2.2 Learning Rate Warmup with Cosine Decay as a Callback

You can skip using the low-level `keras.optimizers.schedules.LearningRateSchedule` class and use the `keras.callbacks.LearningRateSchedule` *callback* instead! It accepts a function that serves as your scheduler, which returns a floating point number, so you can use it with other callbacks that expect a float!

```
def func():
    return ...

keras.callbacks.LearningRateScheduler(func)
```

This approach is favorable when if you want to use callbacks like `ReduceLROnPlateau()` since it can only work with a float-based `lr`. However, since we'll want to set parameters of the function, which we can't do by constructing a scheduler like in the previous snippet, we'll implement a `Callback` ourselves, that does accept the parameters we want to be tunable, and which passes them onto our convenience method for calculating the current LR.

We'll re-use the same convenience function from before and apply it on each batch (as counted by our own counter, as we no longer have access to the `step` property):

```
from keras import backend as K

class WarmupCosineDecay(keras.callbacks.Callback):
    def __init__(self, total_steps=0, warmup_steps=0, start_lr=0.0,
         target_lr=1e-3, hold=0):

        super(WarmupCosineDecay, self).__init__()
```

```
        self.start_lr = start_lr
        self.hold = hold
        self.total_steps = total_steps
        self.global_step = 0
        self.target_lr = target_lr
        self.warmup_steps = warmup_steps
        self.lrs = []

    def on_batch_end(self, batch, logs=None):
        self.global_step = self.global_step + 1
        lr = model.optimizer.lr.numpy()
        self.lrs.append(lr)

    def on_batch_begin(self, batch, logs=None):
        lr = lr_warmup_cosine_decay(global_step=self.global_step,
                                    total_steps=self.total_steps,
                                    warmup_steps=self.warmup_steps,
                                    start_lr=self.start_lr,
                                    target_lr=self.target_lr,
                                    hold=self.hold)
        K.set_value(self.model.optimizer.lr, lr)
```

First, we define the constructor for the class and keep track of its fields. On each batch that's ended, we'll increase the global step, take note of the current LR and add it to the list of LRs so far. On each batch's beginning - we'll calculate the LR using the `lr_warmup_cosine_decay()` function and set that LR as the optimizer's current LR. This is done with the backend's `set_value()` method.

Using this approach, you can also obtain the actual LR applied to the model with:

```
lrs = callback.lrs # [...]
plt.plot(lrs)
```

8.10.2.3 Which Learning Rate Warmup + Decay Setup Should I Use?

Is there a benchmark with various schedulers to help you choose which one you'd like to use? Yup. Sebastian Raschka did a test with various common schedules, and hosted the notebooks on GitHub[98]. Here's the concluding plot:

[98] https://github.com/rasbt/machine-learning-notes/tree/main/learning-rates/scheduler-comparison

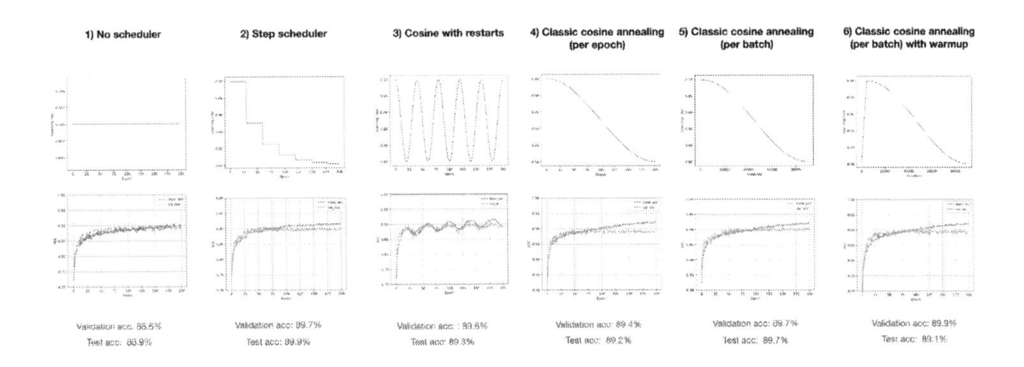

Figure 118:

Step scheduling isn't that bad! Most of these had pretty good results, so you probably won't see much of an accuracy drop if you decide to switch around and find a method you personally like.

8.10.3 ResNet-D

ResNets have popularized skip connections and all eyes were on them. It didn't take long for someone to point out that the strided convolution in the skip connection skips over 3/4 of the input!

> It's a 1x1 Convolution, with a stride of 2x2. It jumps by two to the right, until it reaches the end, and then jumps two down. In a sense, it totally skips every second row and only covers one half of the rows it doesn't skip over.

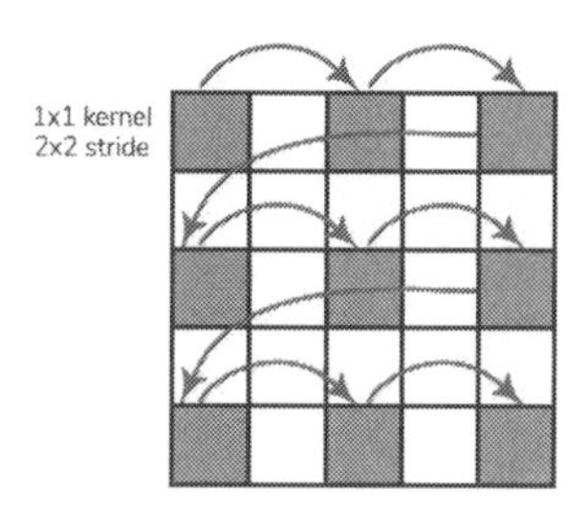

Figure 119:

It really *does* skip 3 out of 4 pixels from the input. Luckily, there's a really easy fix for this. It's labeled the ResNet-D tweak (there are also B and C tweaks in the same paper)! Instead of the regular `Conv2D(filter_num, kernel_size=(1, 1), strides=(2, 2))`, the layer is replaced with a `Conv2D(filter_num, kernel_size=(1, 1), strides=(1, 1))` layer. Now, this doesn't downsample the input, which was the point of the convolutional layer in the first place. However - if you add an `AveragePooling2D` layer right before it, with a stride of 2x2, the input is downsampled, pooled by the average value, and then a `Conv2D` is passed on *all of the (downsized) input*!

```
1  def conv_identity_block_d(layer_in, filter_num):
2      conv1 = keras.layers.Conv2D(filter_num, (1, 1), strides=(1, 1), padding
           = 'same')(layer_in)
3      batch_norm = keras.layers.BatchNormalization()(conv1)
4      relu = keras.layers.Activation('relu')(batch_norm)
5
6      conv2 = keras.layers.Conv2D(filter_num, (3, 3), strides=(2, 2), padding
           = 'same')(relu)
7      batch_norm = keras.layers.BatchNormalization()(conv2)
8      relu = keras.layers.Activation('relu')(batch_norm)
9
10     conv3 = keras.layers.Conv2D(filter_num*4, (1, 1), padding = 'same')(relu)
11     batch_norm = keras.layers.BatchNormalization()(conv3)
12
13     # ResNet-D tweak
14     shortcut = keras.layers.AveragePooling2D((2, 2), strides=2, padding =
           'same')(layer_in)
15     # Change Conv2D strides to `(1, 1)`
16     shortcut = keras.layers.Conv2D(filter_num*4, (1, 1), strides=(1,
           1))(shortcut)
17     shortcut = keras.layers.BatchNormalization()(shortcut)
18
19     add = keras.layers.Add()([shortcut, batch_norm])
20     out = keras.layers.Activation('relu')(add)
21     return out
```

This results in a feature map of the same shape as we had before, but since all of the input from the feature map is pooled and then convolved, we don't lose out so much information, even though some lines are blurred through pooling. This simple tweak increased the accuracy of ResNets by a couple of percentage points!

8.10.4 ResNet-C

Another tweak to the architecture is concerned with the input. The architecture details a 7x7 convolution at the very start. Similar to how VGGNet replaced a larger convolution layer with multiple smaller ones - much the same idea can be applied here. A 7x7 convolution is 5.4 times more expensive than a 3x3 convolution. Thus, using 3 convolutional layers with a 3x3 kernel size is *cheaper* than a single layer with a 7x7 kernel size!

The first two layers have 32 filters with a stride of 2, while the third one has 64 filters:

```
1 input_layer = keras.layers.Input(shape=[224, 224, 3])
2 preprocess = keras.layers.RandomRotation(0.1)(input_layer)
3 preprocess = keras.layers.RandomFlip("horizontal")(preprocess)
4 preprocess = keras.layers..RandomContrast(0.1)(preprocess)
5
6 x = keras.layers.ZeroPadding2D(padding=(3, 3))(preprocess)
7 # Three layers instead of one
8 x = keras.layers.Conv2D(32, (3, 3), strides=(2, 2))(x)
9 x = keras.layers.Conv2D(32, (3, 3), strides=(1, 1))(x)
10 x = keras.layers.Conv2D(64, (3, 3), strides=(1, 1))(x)
11
12 x = keras.layers.BatchNormalization()(x)
13 x = keras.layers.Activation('relu')(x)
14 x = keras.layers.ZeroPadding2D(padding=(1, 1))(x)
15 x = keras.layers.MaxPooling2D((3, 3), strides=(2, 2))(x)
```

8.10.5 Inception ResNet

I've mentioned Inception ResNets before, but it wouldn't make sense to cover them before ResNets. Inception ResNets were proposed alongside InceptionV4 in *"Inception-v4, Inception-ResNet and the Impact of Residual Connections on Learning"*[99] by Szegedy et al. where the Inception modules were tweaked to utilize residual learning:

[99]https://arxiv.org/pdf/1602.07261.pdf

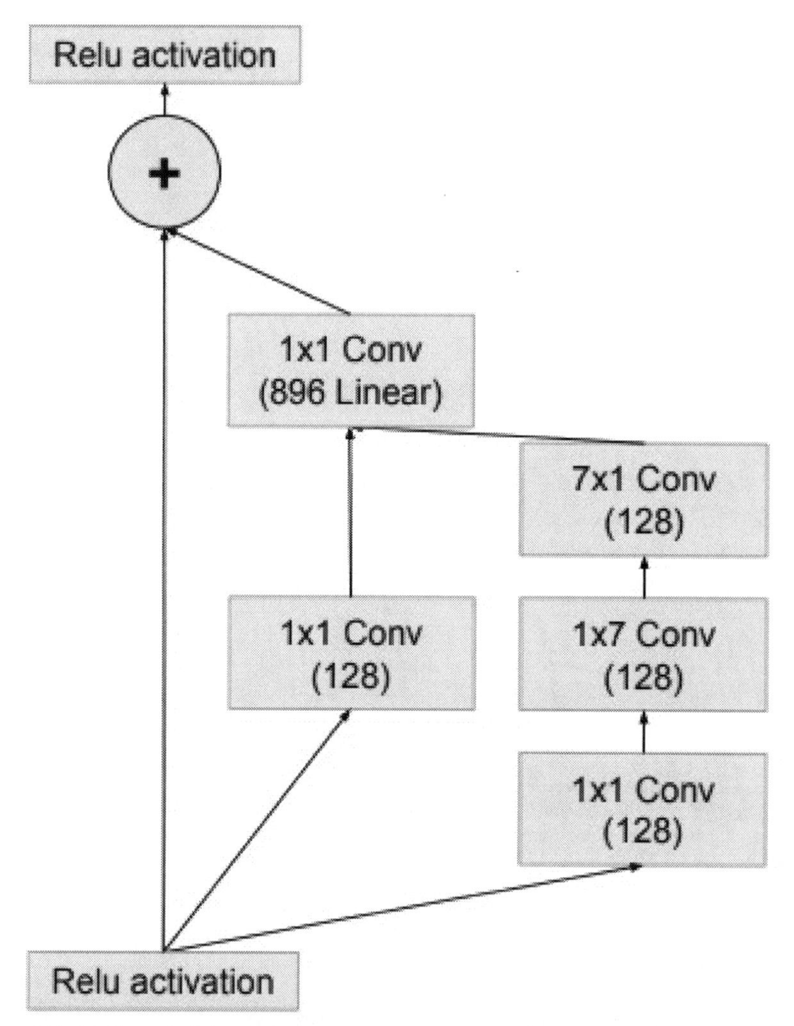

Figure 11. The schema for 17 × 17 grid (Inception-ResNet-B) module of Inception-ResNet-v1 network.

Figure 120:

The paper is full of variations, versions and different combinations - so it's highly encouraged to read the original paper if you're interested in Inception ResNets.

You can load in Inception ResNetV2 in Keras easily:

```
1 inception_resnetv2 = keras.applications.InceptionResNetV2(weights=None,
      classes=n_classes)
```

8.11 Xception - Extreme Inception (2016)

François Chollet, the author of Keras, developed a version of Inception - *Extreme Inception*, shortened to *Xception*. Inception was one of the first networks to not use the conventional model of stacking convolutions on top of each other naively. François notes something that's oftentimes forgot amongst newer practitioners - when we perform convolution on an input, the tensor that gets fed into the `Conv2D` layer is, in fact, 3D. `Conv2D` accepts a 4D tensor `(batch_size, width, height, channels)`, and performs convolutions on `(width, height, channels)`. It's called a `Conv2D`, and not a `Conv3D` because we *only slide it on the X and Y axis* (2D) - but over all the channels (3D). The name arises from the modality of its application, not itself.

In other words - we force a convolutional layer to learn spatial correlations (width and height) *and* cross-channel correlations at the same time. The Inception architecture already offloaded some of this by introducing 1x1 convolutions, which effectively only map cross-channel correlations and perform dimensionality reduction. Building on top of the idea that cross-channel correlations and spatial correlations are decoupled enough for it to make sense for us to process them separately - François entertained the idea that they're decoupled enough that they can be mapped completely separately and called Inception modules that use this principle the "extreme" version of the Inception modules. If you run a 1x1 convolution to map cross-channel correlations, and then completely separately map the spatial correlations on every channel - you get something very similar to depthwise separable convolutions. Let's take a look at them first!

8.11.1 Separable Convolutions - Spatial and Depthwise Separation

Spatial convolutions can be separated into a two-operation process. For instance, imagine a 3x3 filter sliding over an image. You can separate the operation into a 1x3 filter being slid over, followed by a 3x1 filter being slid over. This required fewer parameters than the 3x3 filter in the first place and produces the same result - thus achieving better parameter utilization and less compute (because fewer matrix multiplications are done). This factorization is exactly what the Inception network used to squeeze out more performance! This isn't unique to Inception though - spatially separable convolutions have been in use since 2012, though, in a much more esoteric context as it wasn't a widely accepted practice yet.

In a similar way, depthwise convolutions can also be separated into separate convolutions on each input channel, after which the outputs are concatenated. Being concatenated and separately convolved means that the information between them isn't blended at all. This step is the first step in *depthwise separable convolution.*

- Depthwise convolution can be achieved with Keras' `DepthwiseConv2D` layer and it served as a popularizer of the approach, making it accessible and simple to implement.
- Depthwise separable convolution can be achieved with Keras' `SeparableConv2D` layer - which performs a depthwise convolution followed by a pointwise convolution:

Figure 121:

Note: Spatial convolutions can be separated. Depthwise convolutions can be separated. Both are oftentimes also called "separable convolutions" since the operations are separated, but there's a distinct difference between *spatially separated convolutions* and *depthwise separable convolutions*. The `SeparableConv2D` layer is a **depthwise separable convolution** layer.

In effect - using `SeparableConv2D` practically factorizes a filter and can be used to create "extreme" Inception modules. Other than this, Inception modules introduced non-linearity between operations (`'relu'` to be precise), while Xception doesn't. Additionally - Xception uses residual connections, introduced by He et al. a year earlier!

The beauty of Xception is that it also tackles implementation complexity compared to Inception networks. Since Inception modules are replaced with depthwise separable convolutions, and by using skip connections like with ResNets - Xception *looks* a lot like a ResNet and is fairly linear compared to Inception networks. Also, because of skip connections, no workarounds like auxiliary losses are used. Let's implement it!

Note: `SeparableConv2D` can actually ofentimes be slower than a `Conv2D` layer on GPU-enabled machines, but faster on CPU-enabled machines. In the SqueezeNet paper, Gholami et al.[100] point out that the reason for this inefficiency is that depthwise separable convolution doesn't take advantage of hardware performance and GPUs, which leads to slow training times. Though, they produce significantly smaller models and work better than regular convolutions on CPU-only devices, so they're favored for edge and mobile. MobileNets use depthwise separable convolutions!

8.11.2 Implementing Xception with Keras

Again - Xception can be built fairly similarly to ResNets, through a couple of blocks being called in varying conditions. These blocks will be using `SeparableConv2D` layers within them *except* for the skip blocks, which use `Conv2D` layers instead:

```
1 def conv_batch_relu(x, filters, kernel_size, strides=(1, 1), padding =
      "same"):
2     x = keras.layers.SeparableConv2D(filters=filters,
          kernel_size=kernel_size, strides=strides, padding=padding)(x)
3     x = keras.layers.BatchNormalization()(x)
4     x = keras.layers.Activation("relu")(x)
```

[100]https://arxiv.org/pdf/1803.10615.pdf

```
5     return x
6
7 def conv_batch(x, filters, kernel_size, strides=(1, 1), padding = "same"):
8     x = keras.layers.SeparableConv2D(filters=filters,
          kernel_size=kernel_size, strides=strides, padding=padding)(x)
9     x = keras.layers.BatchNormalization()(x)
10    return x
11
12 def skip_block(x, filters, kernel_size, strides=(1, 1), padding = "same"):
13    x = keras.layers.Conv2D(filters=filters, kernel_size=kernel_size,
          strides=strides, padding=padding)(x)
14    x = keras.layers.BatchNormalization()(x)
15    return x
```

The two main blocks are practically the same - but differ in whether there's a non-linear activation after batch normalization. The default `strides` are `(1, 1)` and the default `padding` is `"same"` - we'll change these for a couple of block calls. The Xception architecture works with an input of `(batch_num, 299, 299, 3)` - which is different from our previous models. You'll want to get the data reshaped right for it when training or add a resizing call within the preprocessing steps:

```
1 def xception():
2     input_layer = keras.layers.Input(shape=[None, None, 3])
3     preprocess = keras.layers.RandomRotation(0.1)(input_layer)
4     preprocess = keras.layers.RandomFlip("horizontal")(preprocess)
5     preprocess = keras.layers.RandomContrast(0.1)(preprocess)
6
7     x = conv_batch_relu(preprocess, 32, (3, 3), strides=(2, 2))
8     x = conv_batch(x, 64, (3, 3))
9     skip_connection = skip_block(x, filters=128, kernel_size=(1, 1),
          strides=(2, 2), padding = "same")
10
11    x = conv_batch_relu(x, 128, (3, 3))
12    x = conv_batch(x, 128, (3, 3))
13
14    x = keras.layers.MaxPooling2D((3, 3), strides=(2, 2), padding =
          "same")(x)
15    x = keras.layers.Add()([x, skip_connection])
16    skip_connection = skip_block(x, filters=256, kernel_size=(1, 1),
          strides=(2, 2), padding = "same")
17
18    x = keras.layers.Activation("relu")(x)
19    x = conv_batch_relu(x, 256, (3, 3))
20    x = conv_batch(x, 256, (3, 3))
21
22    x = keras.layers.MaxPooling2D((3, 3), strides=(2, 2), padding =
          "same")(x)
23    x = keras.layers.Add()([x, skip_connection])
24    skip_connection = skip_block(x, filters=728, kernel_size=(1, 1),
          strides=(2, 2), padding = "same")
25
```

```
26      x = keras.layers.Activation("relu")(x)
27      x = conv_batch_relu(x, 728, (3, 3))
28      x = conv_batch(x, 728, (3, 3))
29
30      x = keras.layers.MaxPooling2D((3, 3), strides=(2, 2), padding =
          "same")(x)
31      x = keras.layers.Add()([x, skip_connection])
32
33      for i in range(8):
34          skip_connection = x
35          x = keras.layers.Activation("relu")(x)
36          x = conv_batch_relu(x, 728, (3, 3))
37          x = conv_batch_relu(x, 728, (3, 3))
38          x = conv_batch(x, 728, (3, 3))
39          x = keras.layers.Add()([x, skip_connection])
40
41      skip_connection = skip_block(x, filters=1024, kernel_size=(1, 1),
          strides=(2, 2), padding = "same")
42
43      x = keras.layers.Activation("relu")(x)
44      x = conv_batch_relu(x, 728, (3, 3))
45      x = conv_batch(x, 1024, (3, 3))
46
47      x = keras.layers.MaxPooling2D((3, 3), strides=(2, 2), padding =
          "same")(x)
48      x = keras.layers.Add()([x, skip_connection])
49
50      x = conv_batch_relu(x, 1536, (3, 3))
51      x = conv_batch_relu(x, 2048, (3, 3))
52
53      x = keras.layers.GlobalAveragePooling2D()(x)
54      output_layer = keras.layers.Dense(n_classes, activation = 'softmax')(x)
55
56      return keras.Model(inputs=input_layer, outputs=output_layer)
57
58  xception = xception()
```

You can also load the official implementation as:

```
1 xception = keras.applications.Xception(weights=None, classes=n_classes)
```

Let's take a look at the summary:

```
1 xception.summary()
```

```
1 ...
2 dense_14 (Dense)              (None, 10)           20490
      ['global_average_pooling2d_4[0][0
3                                                              ]']
4 ======================================================
5 Total params: 20,892,397
6 Trainable params: 20,837,869
```

```
Non-trainable params: 54,528
________________________________________________________
```

On many home systems, you'll get an OOM error when running Xception as it usually take a bit of VRAM to run on larger images. If your system can't handle the VRAM requirements - it's advised to run it on free cloud service providers like Google Colab or Kaggle. Alternatively, as usual, you can lower the batch size.

Xception outperformed InceptionV3 on ImageNet without extensive hyperparameter optimization, and significantly outperformed it on JFT (Google's in-house image classification benchmark). For ImageNet, it was trained with SGD, with a momentum of 0.9, and an initial learning rate of 0.045 with a decay rate of 0.94 (multiplier) every 2 epochs.

Though, you can do away with SGD here, just as you can with ResNets due to a lower parameter count. Adam works well enough and takes a lot of the guesswork out of the equation. When trained with Adam and its default learning rate (0.001), we get up to 86% validation accuracy, which is better than we've seen so far!

```
(train_set_x, test_set_x, valid_set_x), info = tfds.load("imagenette",
                                                         split=["train[:70%]",
                                                              "train[70%:]", "validation"],
                                                         as_supervised=True,
                                                              with_info=True)

def preprocess_image(image, label):
    resized_image = tf.image.resize(image, [299, 299])
    return resized_image, label

# Smaller batch size to avoid OOM
train_set_x =
      train_set_x.map(preprocess_image).batch(8).prefetch(tf.data.AUTOTUNE)
test_set_x =
      test_set_x.map(preprocess_image).batch(8).prefetch(tf.data.AUTOTUNE)
valid_set_x =
      valid_set_x.map(preprocess_image).batch(8).prefetch(tf.data.AUTOTUNE)

reduceLR = keras.callbacks.ReduceLROnPlateau(patience=10)
early_stopping = keras.callbacks.EarlyStopping(patience=15, monitor =
      'val_accuracy', restore_best_weights=True)

xception.compile(loss = 'sparse_categorical_crossentropy',
                 optimizer = keras.optimizers.Adam(),
                 metrics=['accuracy'])

xception_history = xception.fit(train_set,
                               epochs=100,
                               validation_data=valid_set,
```

```
24                    callbacks=[reduceLR, early_stopping])
```

This results in:

```
1 Epoch 1/100
2 829/829 [==============================] - 334s 396ms/step - loss: 2.0984 -
      accuracy: 0.2542 - val_loss: 3.3842 - val_accuracy: 0.2387 - lr: 0.0010
3 ...
4 Epoch 59/100
5 829/829 [==============================] - 334s 403ms/step - loss: 0.0078 -
      accuracy: 0.9979 - val_loss: 0.8138 - val_accuracy: 0.8601 - lr:
      1.0000e-06
```

8.12 DenseNet - Using Collective Knowledge (2016)

By 2016, a paradigm was clear in architectures - many architectures had some sort of short connection between the start and end of layers. Highway Nets, ResNets, FractalNets - they all, in one way or another, had shortcut connections. In *"Densely Connected Convolutional Networks"*[101] Gao Huang, Zhuang Liu et al. proposed another connectivity pattern - connecting *all layers* that could be connected (same feature map sizes). ResNets only had connections within blocks, and *Block_1* only had a shortcut connection within itself. In DenseNets - *Block_1* would also have a short connection to *Block_2*, *Block_3* and *Block_4*. The same would go for *Block_2* which would have a connection to *Block_3* and *Block_4* and so on. Naturally, *Block_1* through *Block_n* would also have standard feedforward connections besides the short connections.

The key difference in the connection process here is that ResNets *add* outputs of layers. The output of a block is a summation of its input *and* the output of the processes within the block. With DenseNets - these connections are *concatenated*, not added. Thus, *Layer N*'s inputs are the outputs of all preceding layers, not their sum. Because of this density - the networks are named *DenseNets*. It's interesting to see teams exploring density in connections, where some teams focus on sparsity in connections with both networks performing great! As a matter of fact - this density doesn't make DenseNets explode with parameters, so it's not going against the common wisdom of avoiding re-learning features and they're actually quite efficient with their parameters. They're actually more efficient than ResNets in terms of parameter usage, since testing ResNets showed that many layers don't add too much value to the predictive power of the network whereas

[101] https://arxiv.org/abs/1608.06993

DenseNets don't suffer from this as much. It turns out that this density allows the network to not learn redundant feature maps, and that there's no need to make them wide. They only add a little bit of narrow "collective knowledge" in each block, since they carry over a lot of previous "collective knowledge". During the implementation, you'll notice how few filters we're actually using.

The concatenation is a bit GPU-heavy, so the reduced parameter count comes at the cost of more VRAM. Ultimately, DenseNets didn't have a much higher accuracy than ResNets, but found a great way to increase parameter efficiency! As usual, DenseNets come in several flavors - DenseNet-121, DenseNet-169, DenseNet-201 and DenseNet-264 and a table that can be referenced to create them is present in the paper:

Layers	Output Size	DenseNet-121	DenseNet-169	DenseNet-201	DenseNet-264
Convolution	112 × 112	7 × 7 conv, stride 2			
Pooling	56 × 56	3 × 3 max pool, stride 2			
Dense Block (1)	56 × 56	[1 × 1 conv, 3 × 3 conv] × 6	[1 × 1 conv, 3 × 3 conv] × 6	[1 × 1 conv, 3 × 3 conv] × 6	[1 × 1 conv, 3 × 3 conv] × 6
Transition Layer (1)	56 × 56	1 × 1 conv			
	28 × 28	2 × 2 average pool, stride 2			
Dense Block (2)	28 × 28	[1 × 1 conv, 3 × 3 conv] × 12	[1 × 1 conv, 3 × 3 conv] × 12	[1 × 1 conv, 3 × 3 conv] × 12	[1 × 1 conv, 3 × 3 conv] × 12
Transition Layer (2)	28 × 28	1 × 1 conv			
	14 × 14	2 × 2 average pool, stride 2			
Dense Block (3)	14 × 14	[1 × 1 conv, 3 × 3 conv] × 24	[1 × 1 conv, 3 × 3 conv] × 32	[1 × 1 conv, 3 × 3 conv] × 48	[1 × 1 conv, 3 × 3 conv] × 64
Transition Layer (3)	14 × 14	1 × 1 conv			
	7 × 7	2 × 2 average pool, stride 2			
Dense Block (4)	7 × 7	[1 × 1 conv, 3 × 3 conv] × 16	[1 × 1 conv, 3 × 3 conv] × 32	[1 × 1 conv, 3 × 3 conv] × 32	[1 × 1 conv, 3 × 3 conv] × 48
Classification Layer	1 × 1	7 × 7 global average pool			
		1000D fully-connected, softmax			

Table 1: DenseNet architectures for ImageNet. The growth rate for all the networks is $k = 32$. Note that each "conv" layer shown in the table corresponds the sequence BN-ReLU-Conv.

Figure 122:

Each convolutional layer is a block with Batch Normalization, followed by ReLU and a convolutional layer. They outline two types of building blocks, a *Dense Block* and a *Transition Layer*. Dense Blocks are just a series of convolution layers (where each layer is connected to all other layers), and several Dense Blocks are stacked on top of each other. A Transition Layer is just a downsizing layer, with a 1x1 convolutional layer, and average pooling. These concepts should already be fairly familiar to you from ResNets and Xception.

8.12.1 Implementing DenseNet Building Blocks with Keras

Okay, let's break down the paper:

> Consider a single image *x0* that is passed through a convolutional network. The network comprises *L* layers, each of which implements a non-linear transformation Hl(·), where *l* indexes the layer. Hl(·) can be a composite function of operations such as Batch Normalization (BN), rectified linear units (ReLU), Pooling, or Convolution (Conv). We denote the output of the *l*th layer as xl.

In simpler terms:

> We pass an image (`img`) through a network of L layers. Each layer has some combination of `Conv2D`, `BatchNormalization` pooling and `Activation('relu')`. We denote the output as `img_layer_num`.

8.12.1.1 Composite Function

Sounds standard so far - you feed an image, and pass it through non-linear transformations. For the composite function, they've opted for:

> **Composite function.** Motivated by [12], we define Hl(·) as a composite function of three consecutive operations: batch normalization (BN), followed by a rectified linear unit (ReLU) and a 3 × 3 convolution (Conv).

Sure! Let's create a function for that:

```
1 def h(input_layer, filters, strides, padding = "same"):
2     x = keras.layers.BatchNormalization()(x)
3     x = keras.layers.Activation("relu")(x)
4     x = keras.layers.Conv2D(filters=filters, kernel_size=(3, 3),
          strides=strides, padding=padding)(x)
5
6     x = keras.layers.Concatenate()([input_layer, x])
7     return x
```

8.12.1.2 Bottleneck Layers

> **Bottleneck layers.** Although each layer only produces *k* output feature-maps, it typically has many more inputs. It has been noted in [37, 11] that a 1×1 convolution can

> be introduced as bottleneck layer before each 3×3 convolution to reduce the number of input feature-maps, and thus to improve computational efficiency. We find this design especially effective for DenseNet and we refer to our network with such a bottleneck layer, i.e., to the BN-ReLU-Conv(1× 1)-BN-ReLU-Conv(3×3) version of Hl, as DenseNet-B. In our experiments, we let each 1×1 convolution produce *4k* feature-maps.

Here, `k` refers to the *growth rate*. Really, it's the number of filters in disguise - but it's useful to think of it as a growth rate between layers for the context of the paper. I'll fall back to using it as `filters` instead for simplicity's sake. In this passage, the authors note that an optional bottleneck layer can be added to further reduce the number of input feature maps. A DenseNet that uses this type of layer before the standard BN-ReLU-Conv block is known as DenseNet-B, and it works well as per the authors. Let's expand the `h()` function:

```
# You can also call these conv_block()
def h(input_layer, filters, strides, padding = "same", bottleneck=True):
    if bottleneck:
        # DenseNet-B addition (Bottleneck)
        x = keras.layers.BatchNormalization()(x)
        x = keras.layers.Activation("relu")(x)
        x = keras.layers.Conv2D(filters=4*filters, kernel_size=(1, 1),
            strides=strides, padding=padding)(x)

    x = keras.layers.BatchNormalization()(x)
    x = keras.layers.Activation("relu")(x)
    x = keras.layers.Conv2D(filters=filters, kernel_size=(3, 3),
        strides=strides, padding=padding)(x)

    # This is where the magic happens! This layer is concatenated
    # onto the previous layer's output, which is concatenated onto
    # the previous layer's output... and so on
    x = keras.layers.Concatenate()([input_layer, x])
    return x
```

You can turn off the bottleneck layer through the `bottleneck` flag, which I've set to `True` by default.

8.12.1.3 Dense Blocks

Now, let's implement the Dense Blocks. They stack several composite function blocks:

```
def dense_block(x, n_blocks, filters=32):
    for i in range(n_blocks):
        x = h(x, filters)
```

```
4     return x
```

While you may feel like you want to connect between these blocks *now* - remember that the output of each `x` in this loop is concatenated to the input of the next layer. *This* is where the dense connections come from. A `dense_block()` function just conveniently calls `h()` several times. Now, between Dense Blocks - there are transition layers. How do we do those?

8.12.1.4 Transition Layers

> **Pooling layers.** The concatenation operation used in Eq. (2) is not viable when the size of feature-maps changes. However, an essential part of convolutional networks is down-sampling layers that change the size of feature-maps. To facilitate down-sampling in our architecture we divide the network into multiple densely connected dense blocks; see Figure 2. We refer to layers between blocks as transition layers, which do convolution and pooling. The transition layers used in our experiments consist of a batch normalization layer and an 1×1 convolutional layer followed by a 2×2 average pooling layer.

Straightforward enough! Let's add a BN-ReLU-Conv-AvgPool layer:

```
1 def transition_layer(input_layer):
2     x = keras.layers.BatchNormalization()(input_layer)
3     x = keras.layers.Activation('relu')(x)
4     x = keras.layers.Conv2D(filters, kernel_size=(1, 1))
5     x = keras.layers.AveragePooling2D(2, strides=(2, 2))(x)
6     return x
```

Though, just as with optional bottlenecks before, there's another useful variant:

> **Compression.** To further improve model compactness, we can reduce the number of feature-maps at transition layers. If a dense block contains m feature-maps, we let the following transition layer generate $\lfloor \theta m \rfloor$ output feature maps, where $0 < \theta \leq 1$ is referred to as the compression factor. When $\theta = 1$, the number of feature-maps across transition layers remains unchanged. We refer the DenseNet with $\theta < 1$ as DenseNet-C, and we set $\theta = 0.5$ in our experiment.

Let's set the default `reduction` to `1` (no reduction), and we'll set it manually later to `0.5` when calling the `transition_layer()`s:

```python
def transition_layer(input_layer, reduction=1):
    x = keras.layers.BatchNormalization()(input_layer)
    x = keras.layers.Activation('relu')(x)

    # Compression - DenseNet-C
    m = input_layer.shape[1]
    compressed = int(reduction*m)
    x = keras.layers.Conv2D(compressed, kernel_size=(1, 1))(x)

    x = keras.layers.AveragePooling2D(2, strides=(2, 2))(x)
    return x
```

8.12.2 Implementing a DenseNet with Keras

> When both the bottleneck and transition layers with $\theta < 1$ are used, we refer to our model as DenseNet-BC.

And with these - we've got the building blocks of DenseNets! With optional bottlenecks and compression, we can build DenseNets, DenseNet-Cs, DenseNet-Bs and DenseNet-BCs with these. Let's put all of this together, with the input pipeline as defined in the paper's table, preprocessing layers and a classifier on top.

There's a 7x7 convolutional layer (don't forget that they assume BN-ReLU-conv when they say "conv"), followed by a 3x3 max pool with a stride of 2. After that, we get `[6, 12, 24, 16]` blocks for DenseNet-121, and other configurations for other flavors. To be nice to our hardware, let's do DenseNet-121 - the implementation for other flavors is the exact same, and just the list of block sizes you pass in differs.

It's worth noting that there's *no* transition layer after the final Dense Block, after which there's a global average pool and a `Dense()` classifier:

```python
# Since we're using both DenseNet-B and DenseNet-C Additions, we're
# effectively building DenseNet-BC here
def get_densenet():
    input_layer = keras.layers.Input(shape=(224, 224, 3))
    preprocess = keras.layers.RandomRotation(0.1)(input_layer)
    preprocess = keras.layers.RandomFlip("horizontal")(preprocess)
    preprocess = keras.layers.RandomContrast(0.1)(preprocess)

    x = keras.layers.BatchNormalization()(preprocess)
    x = keras.layers.Activation('relu')(x)
    x = keras.layers.Conv2D(64, kernel_size=(7, 7), strides=(2, 2))(x)
    x = keras.layers.MaxPooling2D(3, strides=(2, 2))(x)

    blocks = [6, 12, 24, 16]
```

```
15
16     # For all except the last block, there's a dense_block() followed by
           transition_layer()
17     for block in blocks[:-1]:
18         x = dense_block(x, block)
19         x = transition_layer(x, reduction=0.5)
20     # No transition_layer() after this
21     x = dense_block(x, blocks[-1])
22     # Pooling and classification
23     x = keras.layers.GlobalAveragePooling2D()(x)
24     output_layer = keras.layers.Dense(n_classes, activation = 'softmax')(x)
25
26     return keras.Model(inputs=input_layer, outputs=output_layer)
27
28 densenet = get_densenet()
```

You can also load Keras' implementation as:

```
1 densenet = keras.applications.DenseNet121(weights=None, classes=n_classes)
```

Well, that was a concise model! Fewer lines are used for the actual body of the model (the blocks) than for the input pipeline (preprocessing and initial couple of layers). Let's take a look at the summary:

```
1 densenet.summary()
```

```
 1 _________________________________________________________
 2 Layer (type)                    Output Shape          Param #     Connected to
 3 =========================================================
 4 input_24 (InputLayer)           [(None, 224, 224, 3) 0
 5 ...
 6 =========================================================
 7 Total params: 4,376,701
 8 Trainable params: 4,326,191
 9 Non-trainable params: 50,510
10 _________________________________________________________
```

121 layers and just 4.3M parameters! Merely 2 years before this - 19 layers meant 144M parameters. Also, merely a year ago, a 101 layer ResNet would have 44M parameters. By this time - we've already gone through a couple of paradigms. First - networks were made to go deeper. Then, they were made to be more efficient while maintaining that depth. Then - they were made to go even deeper. Finally - we're seeing networks a *fraction* of the size in terms of parameters, but just as deep or even deeper than before! This sort of iterative improvement is at the heart of scientific progress and with each new network, an exciting new door is opened! DenseNets are also fairly narrow. We use a default filter number of `32` with bottleneck layers multiplying it to `128`. Xception uses

2048 in some layers! You can naturally tweak the default number and check how it affects the results.

Let's compile and train this DenseNet:

```
reduceLR = keras.callbacks.ReduceLROnPlateau(patience=10, factor=0.3)
early_stopping = keras.callbacks.EarlyStopping(patience=15, monitor =
    'val_accuracy', restore_best_weights=True)

densenet.compile(loss = 'sparse_categorical_crossentropy',
                 optimizer = keras.optimizers.Adam(),
                 metrics=['accuracy'])

densenet_history = densenet.fit(train_set,
                                epochs=100,
                                validation_data=valid_set,
                                callbacks=[reduceLR, early_stopping])
```

This results in:

```
Epoch 1/100
415/415 [==============================] - 142s 318ms/step - loss: 2.3141 -
    accuracy: 0.2200 - val_loss: 2.0368 - val_accuracy: 0.2746 - lr: 0.0010
...
Epoch 79/100
415/415 [==============================] - 131s 317ms/step - loss: 0.0428 -
    accuracy: 0.9878 - val_loss: 1.7639 - val_accuracy: 0.7310 - lr:
    8.1000e-06
```

8.13 MobileNet - Allowing Mobile Devices to See (2017)

At this point - computer vision was catching quite a bit of wind. Models were getting more and more efficient in terms of parameters, and enough practical experience and theoretical knowledge was spread amongst a large population that further optimizations could take place. Just as computers were bulky and inefficient, so were computer vision networks. As computers became smaller - we put them in our pockets. In 2017, Andrew Howard et al. decided to put computer vision into our pockets as well.

In *"MobileNets: Efficient Convolutional Neural Networks for Mobile Vision Applications"*[102], the authors note that while networks are getting more efficient and powerful, they're also getting larger. While this works great for tasks that aren't time-sensitive, other applications that are time sensitive couldn't rely on fast inference. To address the need to

[102] https://arxiv.org/pdf/1704.04861.pdf

let smaller devices such as mobile phones and embedded devices see - MobileNet was created. The key takeaways are that MobileNet is *small* (easy to upload, download, load into memory and use) and fast (fast inference is required for mobile devices, where every millisecond of delay is felt). In real-time scenarios, being fast trumps being accurate, and "good enough" solutions are much more acceptable.

MobileNet uses depthwise separable convolutions to lower computational cost and increase speed. It applies a single filter to each input channel (depthwise convolution) and the pointwise convolution applies a 1x1 convolution to combine the outputs the depthwise convolution. The authors note that their use of 3x3 depthwise-separable convolutions reduced the computation requirements by 8-9 times with little negative effect on accuracy. Most of the regularization techniques used with larger models aren't required for smaller networks like MobileNet - weight regularization, heavy image augmentation, etc. aren't required to reach a high level of generalization. Additionally, since the term "mobile" and "embedded device" can include anything between a really weak mobile phone and a mobile phone with 12GB of RAM, such as the Google Pixel 6 Pro - it was important to be able to scale this network up and down to suit different devices. Thankfully - there's *one* parameter (called the *width multiplier*) that can be tuned up or down to adjust the *width* of the network, making it larger or smaller, exactly for this purpose.

MobileNet went through a few versions, now known as MobileNetV1 (2017), MobileNetV2 (2018) and MobileNetV3 (2019). MobileNetV3 was created with the help of ***NAS (Neural Architecture Search)*** which has been catching wind recently, and advanced manually from there. The original MobileNet was mainly made up of depthwise-separable convolutional blocks, and the architecture was easy to grasp. With MobileNetV2, the structure was updated to include residual connections - but not the type we've seen so far. They used *inverted residual blocks*, where the skip connections were made between bottleneck layers. Instead of a wide-narrow-wide residual block (such as 3x3, 1x1 for downsizing and then another 3x3) - an inverted residual block has a narrow-wide-narrow structure. It first widens the input and applies a 1x1 convolution, then performs 3x3 depthwise-separable convolution and then another 1x1, squeezing it down in width. This reduces the number of trainable parameters and is more efficient, and because of this, inverted residual blocks are used for efficient CNNs while still exploiting the benefit of shortcut connections. MobileNetV3 builds on top of MobileNetV2 and comes in two fixed flavors - MobileNetV3-Small and MobileNetV3-Large. The large version is actually *faster* but more resource intensive than the small version. The third version includes redesigned expensive layers and optimized non-linearity functions.

It's advised to go with MobiletNetV3 - either small or large if you want to deploy your network within an application for a mobile device. The easiest way to initialize it is via Keras' official implementation:

```
1 mobilenet_small = keras.applications.MobileNetV3Small(weights=None,
      classes=n_classes)
2 mobilenet_large = keras.applications.MobileNetV3Large(weights=None,
      classes=n_classes)
```

8.14 NASNet - Letting Machines Do (Part Of) The Work (2017)

When designing networks, you test a lot of things out. When you try things out a lot, you look for ways to automate it. While you can use tuning frameworks such as Keras Tuner that allow you to input a space of different variations, and have it run them (randomly or guided by an optimization algorithm) - why should you have to create this space yourself? Well, you don't - and this idea is at the heart of *Neural Architecture Search*. NAS is not a new technique, and it's both a very wide and very diverse field, with a lot of research hours going into expanding it. NAS has proven to create state-of-the-art networks, by searching through a search space (network architectures) guided by a strategy (how it navigates the space) after which the found architecture is evaluated with an evaluation strategy and the search continues. Some NAS methods use reinforcement learning, while some use evolutionary algorithms such as genetic algorithms, while others use other classical optimization algorithms. Some believe that the prohibitive time it takes to perform NAS doesn't justify the performance benefits, while some believe it to be the future of architecture design. In any case - the search space is usually constrained. Either possible operations are given, or the search is made to be metric-aware (making sure that, for example, inference/training time doesn't explode into an unpractical range).

In 2017, in *"Learning Transferable Architectures for Scalable Image Recognition"*[103], a Barret Zoph et al. released NASNet. They've used NAS to design "cells" that can be transferrable between datasets, since creating a perfect network for one dataset can lead down a path of hyper optimizing a network for a single, narrow task, with no

[103] https://arxiv.org/abs/1707.07012

generalization capabilities for other tasks. "Cells" were found on CIFAR-10 and then stacked for evaluation on ImageNet. No search is done on ImageNet - but the network is evaluated on ImageNet, which means that the algorithm has to find a *general network architecture* that would work between different tasks. A bunch of possible operations were added to be searched through - factorized 1xn and nx1 convolutions, average and max pooling with different kernel sizes, depthwise-separable convolutions with different kernel sizes, identity blocks, etc. At the end of the search, after 2000 GPU hours, it yielded two types of cells - normal cells and reduction cells:

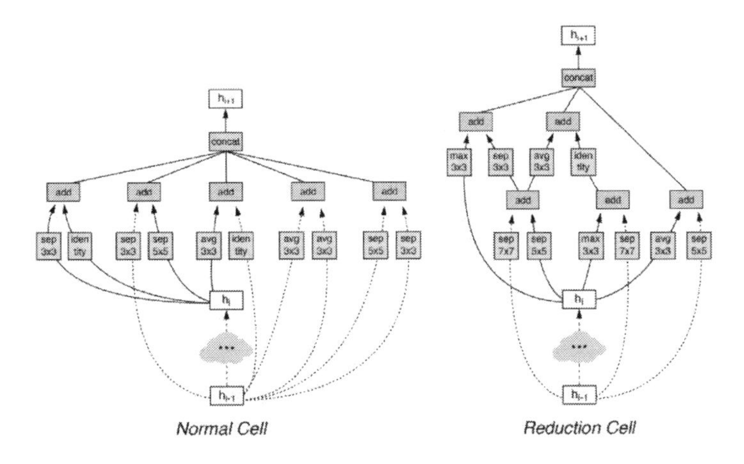

Figure 123:

NASNetMobile is comparable to MobileNetV3, and MNasNet (Mingxing Tan et al.) was specifically built to be platform-aware and to minimize inference time on mobile devices. One of the building blocks used in that search were exactly inverted residual blocks from MobileNetV2.

The easiest way to initialize it is via Keras' official implementation:

```
nas_small = keras.applications.NASNetMobile(weights=None, classes=n_classes)
nas_large = keras.applications.NASNetLarge(weights=None, classes=n_classes)
```

It's worth noting that `NASNetLarge` is, indeed, fairly large. With almost 350MB, almost 90M parameters and fairly slow training and inference time, it's quite bulky, but provides great accuracy. Even though it does provide great accuracy - smaller models that provide the same level exist. Namely - EfficientNets, which also utilized NAS to create a baseline, but are better optimized.

8.15 EfficientNet - Machines Do (Part Of) It Again (2019)

Other than NASNet so far, most networks we've discussed follow a similar designing process. Some common block is made to be more efficient, and the network is scaled up. Scaling is typically done in depth or width. In 2019, Mingxing Tan, who worked on searching for MobileNetV3 and MNASNet paired up with Quoc V. Le to release *"EfficientNet: Rethinking Model Scaling for Convolutional Neural Networks"*[104]. They note that scaling doesn't have to be one-dimensional, and that uniformly scaling depth, width and resolution can be done with a *compound coefficient*. This coefficient has been applied to ResNets and MobileNet as proof of concept, but more notably, the same coefficient is used to scale up a baseline network created by NAS. The scaled-up version of this baseline network resulted in a family of models known as EfficientNets - spanning from EfficientNetB0 to EfficientNetB7. EfficientNetB7 is the largest network of the family, and was 8.4x smaller and 6.1x faster than the second best network (in terms of accuracy) at the time. It's worth noting that larger EfficientNets aren't really meant to be trained on home setups and require *a lot* of VRAM. However, EfficientNetB0 is a decently sized model, sitting at 5.3M parameters, with a fairly fast inference time (about double that of MobileNet, which is already quite fast) and with a great training time, while being only a few dozen megabytes in size!

EfficientNets are available in Keras, B0 through B7. Additionally, since the end of 2021, the EfficientNetV2 (released in 2021) family is built into Keras! The second generation of EfficientNets introduced faster training, smaller models and higher accuracy. If your TensorFlow version allows for it - prefer EfficientNetV2 over the first versions.

There are a few EfficientNet classes in Keras:

- `EfficientNetB0`
- ...
- `EfficientNetB7`
- `EfficientNetBV2B0`
- ...

[104] https://arxiv.org/abs/1905.11946

- `EfficientNetV2B3`
- `EfficientNetV2L` (Large)
- `EfficientNetV2M` (Medium)
- `EfficientNetV2S` (Small)

EfficientNetB0 is in the "same league" (meant to be compared) in terms of accuracy with ResNet50 and DenseNet169. B1 is in the league with ResNet152, Xception, InceptionV3 and DenseNet-264. B3 is in the league with ResNeXt-101. B4 is in the league with NASNet and SENet. Above this, returns were diminishing, and although B7 was cutting-edge, it wasn't much better than B6 or B5. EfficientNetV2S is the equivalent of B5 in terms of performance, V2M is better than B7, V2L and V2-XL were cutting-edge.

The authors note the comparison between these models on the same settings, highlighting the difference between B7 and V2M as:

Table 10. Comparison with the same training settings – Our new EfficientNetV2-M runs faster with less parameters.

	Acc. (%)	Params (M)	FLOPs (B)	TrainTime (h)	InferTime (ms)
V1-B7	85.0	66	38	54	170
V2-M (ours)	85.1	55 (-17%)	24 (-37%)	13 (-76%)	57 (-66%)

Figure 124:

A 17% reduction in parameter count, 37% reduction in FLOPs, 76% reduction in training time and a 66% reduction in inference time! This democratized the power of EfficientNetB7 from training on very expensive equipment to EfficientNetV2M, which can be trained on (powerful) but still home-grade setups, much faster. As a matter of fact - EfficientNetV2B0 networks train about faster than plain ResNets and twice as fast as DenseNet-121.

EfficientNets are great because the tree offers smaller variants that can be trained on most home devices (making it a pretty democratic model), in reasonable time frames (making iterative improvements easier), while being fairly small (allowing it to be deployed more easily). In addition to all of this - they're very accurate and can be the backbone of really strong classifiers. While more accurate networks do exist now, one of which will be covered next, with frameworks like Keras, loading and using an EfficientNet boils down to a single line, making them so accessible that they're more than just a reasonable "go to" family for most classifying needs.

> As of 2022, EfficientNets (especially the second version) are a great family of models to get great performance, training and inference time. Given their adoption and stability over various tasks, as of writing, they're a "standard checkpoint" in ConvNet development. ConvNeXt, covered next, is a new hot take on the way we should steer ConvNet development and introduces new ingredients in the mix.

You'll load them in as either:

```
effnet = keras.applications.EfficientNetB0(weights=None, classes=n_classes)
effnetv2 = keras.applications.EfficientNetV2B0(weights=None,
    classes=n_classes)
```

Or:

```
effnet = keras.applications.efficientnet.EfficientNetB0(weights=None,
    classes=n_classes)
effnetv2 = keras.applications.efficientnet_v2.EfficientNetV2B0(weights=None,
    classes=n_classes)
```

I'll go on record and say that a good portion of research that relies on computer vision to solve practical problems in specialized fields could be improved by switching the model used with an EfficientNet. As of writing, there's still a trend of using older-type networks in classification in medical image diagnosis, and other fields that can benefit from having higher accuracy and faster training times. This is perhaps due to a lack of inter-disciplinary communication, which makes the propagation of new ideas harder, and which makes it harder to appreciate how fast certain areas in computer vision are progressing. I'm taking this opportunity to try and bridge that gap, at least a tiny bit. If you're looking to apply computer vision to your field, using the resources from this lesson - you'll be able to find the newest models, understand how they work and by which criteria you can compare them and make a decision. I'll also take this moment to strongly recommend professionals from other fields to consider training EfficientNets (or even ConvNeXt) rather than older types such as VGGNets and plain ResNets, as the default first network to try out. Do try out other network types, guided by your needs, but these should yield great results. There's no valid argument *not to* use an EfficientNet as it's smaller in size, trains faster, performs inference faster, utilizes parameters better and has a higher level of generalization capability than many other older networks. They're a stable "checkpoint" where most common ConvNet wisdom applies. In the next section - we'll be exploring a new architecture, that introduced some radical changes to the way we do ConvNets.

8.16 ConvNeXt - A ConvNet for the 2020s (2022)

In recent years, Transformers have been "stealing the show" in NLP, but also notably in computer vision. Turns out - so called *Vision Transformers (ViTs)* can be used for computer vision, and they can perform quite well. So well, in fact, that for some time, they've held most of the top spots in ImageNet leaderboards and still do. This is a new paradigm in computer vision and is still young, with much promise for the future. Plain ViTs haven't yet been applied as successfully to other computer vision tasks, such as segmentation or object recognition, in which CNN-based models are clearly in the lead. However, a type of Transformers, known as Swin Transformers, which are hierarchical, *have* been successfully applied as a generic vision backbone. While some practitioners consider themselves as "belonging" to a camp - CNN or Transformer - many are exploring the idea of combining them. Many top-performer architectures are based on a combination of CNNS and Transformers, as of writing. A great example of a combination network is CoAtNet, short for Convolutional Attention Network, which stacks convolutional layers and attention layers, unifying the two paradigms.

ConvNeXt came out in January of 2022 - just as the year started. It is a pure-conv network that was inspired by some of the new advances with ViTs, and appropriated a few concepts that helped it make a leap in CNN-based accuracy. Since then, within only 4 months, **another 35 models** have outperformed it, according to PapersWithCode. It's worth noting that these are Top-1 Accuracy reports - and that the difference between ConvNeXt (87.8%) and CoCa (91%) isn't a huge one. It's also worth noting that ConvNeXt was trained on 14M ImageNet images, while CoCa was trained on 3B images in JFT-3B (internal Google dataset). It's also worth noting that CoCa has a staggering 2.1B parameters (and some other Transformer-based architectures have 7.2B), while ConvNeXt has a "mere" 350M (at least ConvNeXt-XL does - one of the smaller variants has 22M).

ConvNeXt was released alongside the paper dubbed *"A ConvNet for the 2020s"*[105] by Liu et al. and broke a streak of Transformer-based models at the top of the leaderboards:

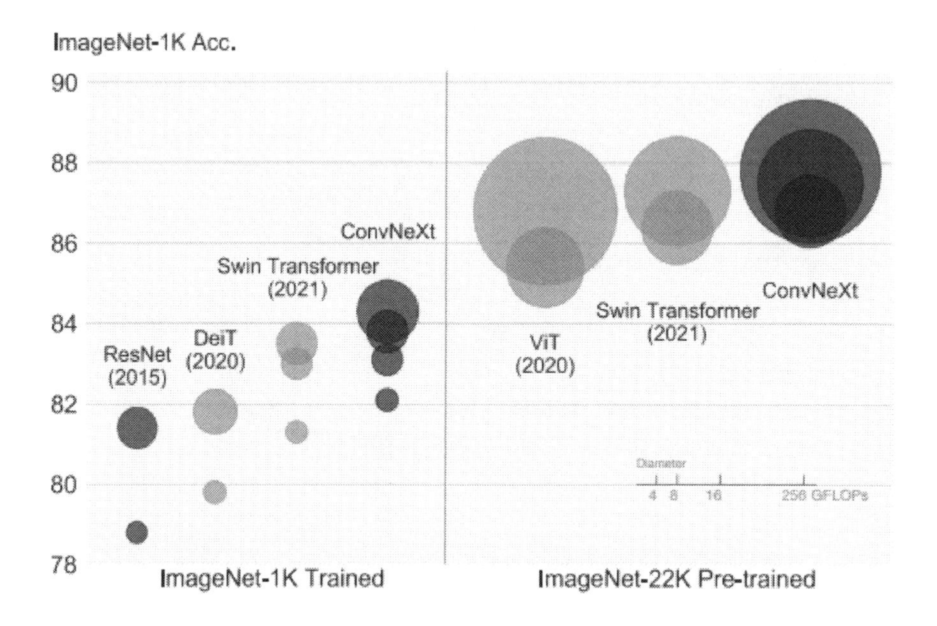

Figure 125:

While this position was short-held (like with all contemporary models), this was a clear reminder that hierarchical representations can get us far in multiple paradigms, and the ConvNeXt paper is an important one in recent years. Hierarchical representations learned through sliding windows are clearly a big part of the mix, which is one of the reasons Swin Transformers have been applied more generically, and why CNNs are still (and will be in the future) highly relevant. The paper provides a great summary of parallel developments between Transformers and ConvNets, and how they suddenly crashed together in 2020. By making Transformers more like ConvNets - Swin Transformers were able to become the best generic vision backbones. By making ConvNets more like Transformers, ConvNeXt was able to outperform Swin Transformers. One clear benefit of Transformers is their ability to scale - they're much

105

easier to scale up, leading to multi-billion parameter models, that are still trainable. This ability stems from a systematic difference between the network types, and at least currently seems to be a pretty tough hurdle for ConvNets to implement, without creating a hybrid solution. An added benefit of having a purely convolutional model is that, well, they're *simpler* to implement. They're intuitively closer to our understanding of our own visual systems, simpler to implement and a large body of CNN-based research can be used to fall back to and discuss ideas, compared to a lot of uncharted territory of hierarchical Transformers. With advancements in both camps, we'll be able to build ever-better generic systems.

The team started with a ResNet-50, a *staple* ConvNet and started modernizing it. They've first changed the training procedure to resemble a Transformer's training. Training epochs were expanded (up to 300), the AdamW optimizer is used, and new data augmentation types are introduced. These include Mixup, CutMix, RandAugment, etc.

Note: These augmentations, alongside various other preprocessing layers are being built into KerasCV, and will be covered in the next lesson.

This was enough to boost ResNet performance, even without any architectural differences. Then, the ratio of blocks was changed from `[3, 4, 6, 3]` to `[3, 3, 9, 3]` to mimic Swin Transformer block ratios. It's worth noting that the idea of creating blocks with ratios was a concept Swin Transformers adopted from ConvNets, and now ConvNets are adopting it back in a slightly different form! The entry of the network which is typically used to downsize the input with a large kernel was changed to mimic the process of patchifying images as Transformers do. Next, the network used depthwise-separable convolutions, popularized by Xception and MobileNets, which turned out to be similar to the spatial and channel separation as seen with ViTs. Next, inverted bottlenecks were added. Transformers have inverted bottlenecks, where a layer outputs more dimensions than it was originally fed. This is also what MobileNetV2 implemented, in the form of inverted residual blocks. Swin Transformers have revisited the idea of smaller local receptive fields, but also have a broad, global receptive field.

While common wisdom since VGGNet was that *smaller* kernel sizes lead to better optimization, ConvNeXt revisits the idea of large kernel sizes within the network. With a couple of tweaks, large kernel sizes were made possible, without increasing the number of FLOPs, and increasing the accuracy! These were *macro design* choices, that visibly change the architecture in a very tangible way.

Next, *micro design* choices were made. ReLU is pretty standard for ConvNets, and Swish (a smoothed ReLU with a small saddle point) has been used to a higher degree in EfficientNets, but hasn't fully replaced ReLU yet. For Transformers, ReLU has been replaced with GeLU (Gaussian Error Linear Unit). ConvNeXt adopted GeLU instead of ReLU and saw no degradation. Furthermore, Transformers use fewer activation functions than ConvNets, so they've reduced the frequency of activation functions overall. At this point - ConvNeXt performed the same as Swin Transformers! Furthermore, Transformers use fewer normalization layers, so they've reduced their number and replaced Batch Normalization with Layer Normalization. In most ConvNets, substituting Batch Normalization with Layer Normalization hurts generalization capabilities. Perhaps, due to the systemic changes in the architecture, Layer Normalization actually had a slightly positive effect on ConvNeXt. The final added change was to introduce separate downsampling layers - instead of having the residual blocks downsize the input, a separate layer with Layer Normalization was used to downsize the input between stages. These can all be summarized in an image, which the authors gracefully created:

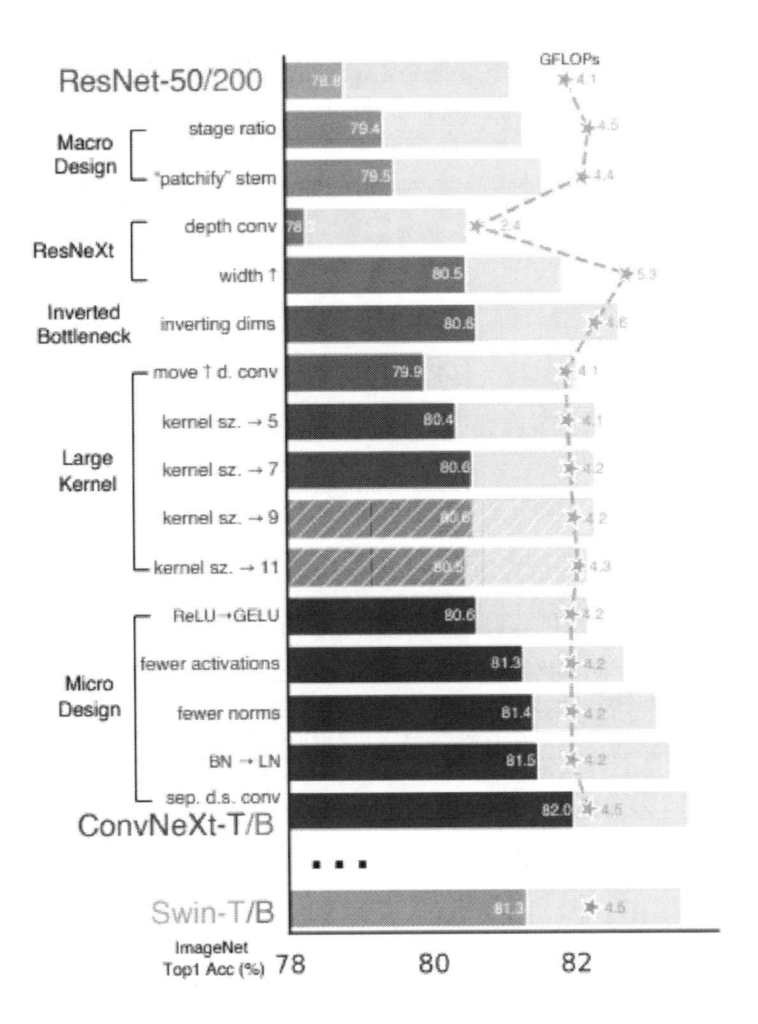

Figure 126:

Each change affected the parameter count, FLOPs and accuracy, and this roadmap provides a great overview of these effects. That's how you rethink the conventions of an entire field and create something truly new! ConvNeXt was fairly quickly ported into various frameworks and languages, and written natively using PyTorch[106].

[106]https://github.com/facebookresearch/ConvNeXt

Unsurprisingly, it's been trained and released for public use in Keras as well! However, it's currently only available in the `tf-nightly` version (experimental version of TensorFlow). It'll likely be released in one of the stable versions after TensorFlow 2.9.1.

If you're using the nightly version, you can load in the variations of ConvNeXt as:

```
1 base = keras.applications.convnext.ConvNeXtBase(weights=None,
      classes=n_classes)
2 large = keras.applications.convnext.ConvNeXtLarge(weights=None,
      classes=n_classes)
3 small = keras.applications.convnext.ConvNeXtSmall(weights=None,
      classes=n_classes)
4 tiny = keras.applications.convnext.ConvNeXtTiny(weights=None,
      classes=n_classes)
5 xlarge = keras.applications.convnext.ConvNeXtXLarge(weights=None,
      classes=n_classes)
```

8.17 Designing Your Own Networks?

Throughout the lesson - we've gone on an adventure of ideas. In many cases, new architectures build on old ones. If you strip away the intricacies and look through a blurred lens - LeNet5 set a baseline. AlexNet was a beefed-up LeNet5. VGGNet was a deeper AlexNet. ResNet utilized a concept already known at the time, skip connections, in a different way. Xception took an existing hypothesis and took it to the extreme. DenseNet is conceptually a dense ResNet. This isn't to devalue the work or improvements of any of these. It is to note that when many people work on stuff, stuff gets better. Fresh perspectives always help and it's not something reserved for the intellectual elite. You can probably help and improve something that already exists. It's not super hard to find small optimization opportunities. For instance, it was fairly clear that the strided 1x1 convolutions in ResNets skip over much of the input, and fixing this wasn't very hard. Several small optimizations later - you have something better than anything before.

> Don't beat yourself into thinking that designing architectures is only for people with doctorates and an academic background. **You can help make a difference.**

Even so, designing networks takes time - most won't want to invest it. With a rapid evolution of networks, as an engineer, you can realistically sit on the sidelines and wait for new architectures to pop up and use them in your own projects without really even reading much into them - as long as they provide more value to you than the previous one.

When architectures aren't ported into frameworks like Keras and its packages like Keras Applications and KerasCV - you'll find community implementations online and will be able to both download them as packaged models or implement them yourself (or more realistically, copy-paste someone else's implementation).

Some time back - I almost reinvented the wheel when trying to build a new architecture. I was reading a Wikipedia page on the visual cortex, trying to learn more about how information flows through it and whether there's something that could be ported into a CNN-based network. Surely enough, something caught my eye:

> *"Visual area V2, or* ***secondary visual cortex****, also called* ***prestriate cortex*** *is the second major area in the visual cortex, and the first region within the* ***visual association area****. It receives strong feedforward connections from V1 (direct and via the pulvinar) and sends strong connections to V3, V4, and V5. It also sends strong feedback connections to V1"*

Strong connections. What if we could model this by making the connections between certain convolutional layers more dense, and also if we connected *all* regions instead of only the successive ones? I started working on an implementation similar to ResNets where different stages of the network were connected. These stages were aptly named V1, V2, V3, V4 and V5 and V1 would connect to all of the proceeding regions, just as V2 would, etc. I was to name it CortexNet! Some time into the implementation, it didn't show super great results, just good results. And then I realized that the architecture already exists, in a similar form, tuned, optimized and scaled up - DenseNets, and they totally flew over my head before that point.

The pain took a few days to fully subside.

But it did serve to teach me a lesson - designing things is for the average-minded as well. Don't curb your ideas and don't be afraid to test things out, no matter how "unexceptional" you might feel.

9 Working with KerasCV

9.1 A Word from the Keras Team

So, why even have KerasCV? Why not just add new layers to Keras, since preprocessing layers already exist? I contacted the Keras team to ask for the motivation behind building KerasCV (and KerasNLP) as a horizontal addition to Keras itself:

> KerasCV and KerasNLP are domain-specific collections of Keras model building blocks, such as layers or metrics. Their purpose is to make it quick and frictionless to assemble computer vision and NLP workflows that are performant and that follow modern best practices. You can think of them as a horizontal extension of the Keras API (`keras.layers`, `keras.metrics`, `keras.losses`, etc.). We could add these APIs in Keras directly, but we believe that using a separate package and namespace makes for greater modularity and increased development velocity. It also improves discoverability! Such building blocks are constantly needed in mainstream CV and NLP workflows. Yet, many of them are hard to implement correctly, because:
>
> - Some implementation details can be subtle, such as the correct way to do causal masking and padding-masking in a Transformer block.
> - Some performance concerns might get overlooked (e.g. performant in-graph COCO metrics is very tricky)
> - Best practices with regard to things like initializers and dropout aren't always well-known; a good API with good defaults guides you towards doing the correct thing.
>
> For these reasons, it is highly beneficial to have one team implement these reusable building blocks once, with best practices baked-in, then have everyone else reuse them rather than implementing their own N times.

In true Keras fashion - new additions are democratized, and reasonable defaults make it harder to mess up. While still in development - you'd be wise to add KerasCV to your toolbelt already, since the layers are already able to boost your workflow. As new features are being released, you'll be able to just plug them in.

There's no need to learn a new API - KerasCV integrates seamlessly into Keras. Using it in your toolbelt is akin to expanding Keras itself, which is why it's called a "horizontal" addition to the package.

9.2 KerasCV Layers and Preprocessing

Let's take a look at some of the new layers, briefly mentioned in earlier lessons. As of July 2022, there are 28 new layers! Again, in true Keras fashion, they can be plugged into your models to create end-to-end predictors, applied to `tf.data.Dataset`s via a simple `map()` call, or used on individual images. This sort of flexibility lets you leverage the augmentations in any working style you personally prefer, or are bounded by via your team.

If you haven't already, install KerasCV:

```
1 $ pip install keras-cv
```

You can import it and use it as:

```
1 import keras_cv
2
3 output = keras_cv.LayerName(args)
```

The expanding list of new layers can be found in the official documentation[107], but let's take a look at a few important ones here:

- `MixUp`
- `CutMix`
- `RandAugment`
- `RandomAugmentationPipeline`

As times change, so do training strategies. In 2019, Yun et al. released *"CutMix: Regularization Strategy to Train Strong Classifiers with Localizable Features"*[108], in which they argue that existing strategies such as MixUp and Cutout can be improved. MixUp would mix up two images, and weigh the labels appropriately, such as overlaying a low-opacity image of a cat over a dog, and assigning 0.5 to 'cat' as well as 0.5 to 'dog'. Cutout would randomly "drop out" spatial data, by either replacing them with black or white pixels. CutMix combines these two - cutting out rectangles from images, and inputting images with other labels in there, weighing the labels by the proportion of the image they take up.

[107]https://keras.io/api/keras_cv/layers/
[108]https://arxiv.org/pdf/1905.04899.pdf

These are easily summarized by applying them to an image and plotting the results. Let's find two images - one of a cat and one of a dog:

```
1 dog = 'dog_pic_url...'
2 cat = 'cat_pic_url...'
```

Let's fetch them and load them in using OpenCV:

```
 1 import urllib
 2 
 3 def url_to_array(url):
 4     req = urllib.request.urlopen(url)
 5     arr = np.array(bytearray(req.read()), dtype=np.int8)
 6     arr = cv2.imdecode(arr, -1)
 7     arr = cv2.cvtColor(arr, cv2.COLOR_BGR2RGB)
 8     arr = cv2.resize(arr, (224, 224))
 9     return arr
10 
11 
12 dog_img = url_to_array(dog)
13 cat_img = url_to_array(cat)
14 
15 fig, ax = plt.subplots(1, 2, figsize=(16, 6))
16 
17 ax[0].imshow(dog_img)
18 ax[1].imshow(cat_img)
```

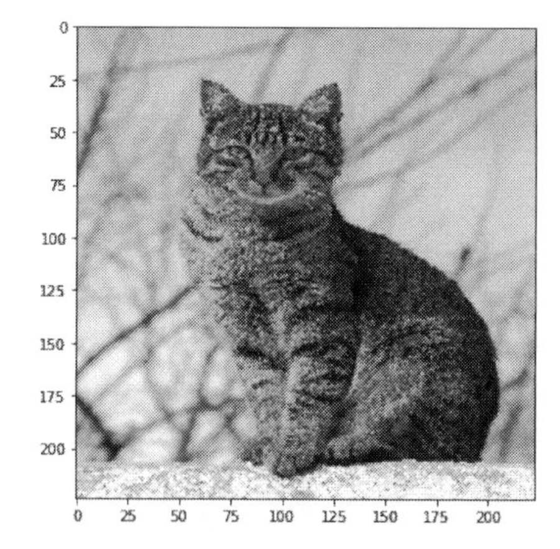

Figure 127:

Great! We've got a cute puppy and a cat. Let's save them as an array of images, and their labels as another:

```
images = np.array([dog_img, cat_img])
labels = np.array([0., 1.])
```

From here, we can define our augmentation layers:

```
rand_augment = keras_cv.layers.RandAugment(value_range=(0, 255))
cutmix = keras_cv.layers.CutMix()
mixup = keras_cv.layers.MixUp()
```

And pass the images in:

```
randaug_imgs = rand_augment(images)
cutmix_imgs = cutmix({"images": images, "labels": labels})
mixup_imgs = mixup({"images": images, "labels": labels})
```

Note: `CutMix` and `MixUp` require a dictionary of `{"images": images, "labels": labels}`, not just an array of images, because they also compute label proportions in an image. Labels will have to be of type `float` as well. Because of this - we'll be applying `CutMix` and `MixUp` during the preprocessing stages - typically on `Dataset` objects, rather than within the model's definition, where the rest of the pipeline can go.

Then, we can visualize them:

```
def visualize(images):
    fig, ax = plt.subplots(1, 2, figsize=(8, 6))
    for index, img in enumerate(images):
        ax[index].imshow(img.numpy().astype('int'))
        ax[index].axis('off')

visualize(randaug_imgs)
visualize(cutmix_imgs["images"])
visualize(mixup_imgs["images"])
```

This results in:

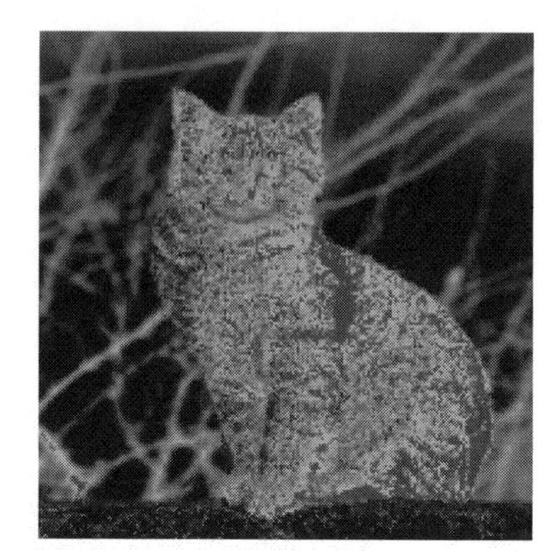

Figure 128:

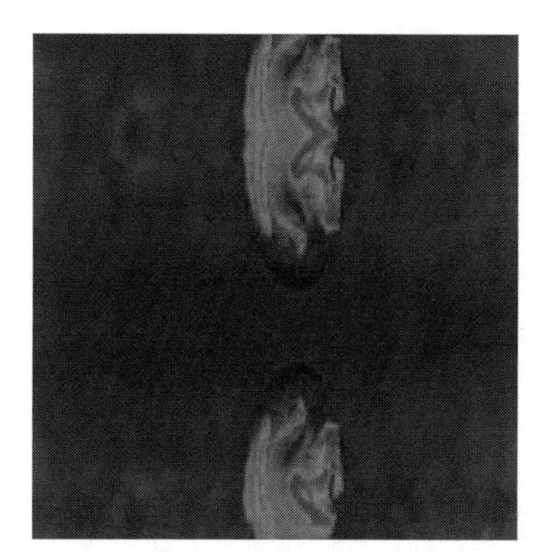
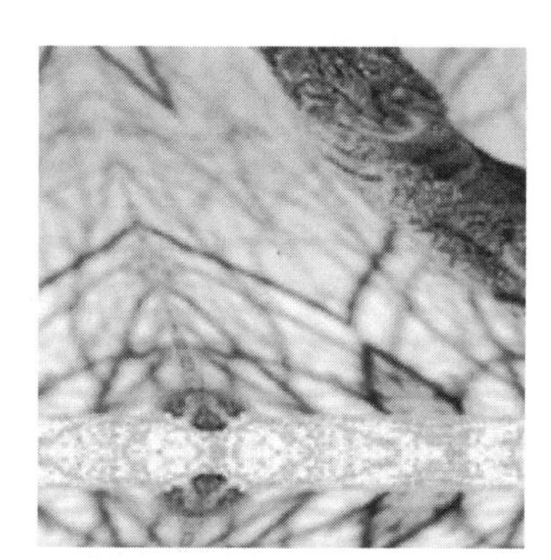

Figure 129:

Figure 130:

The augmentations range from practically none to funky otherworldly images in negative colors. You can set the magnitude of augmentation with the `magnitude` argument, which is a floating point flag set as `0..1`.

Now, alternatively, you can have a `tf.data.Dataset` being fed into a CNN with a couple of preprocessing layers on top. Let's apply a random augmentation, and a CutMix or MixUp augmentation (separately, so we can isolate the effects). When working with `tf.data.Dataset` instances, you can easily apply functions that transform your data with the `map()` function.

Let's create the `Datasets` first:

```
1 def preprocess_img(img, label):
2     img = tf.image.resize(img, (224, 224))
3     img = tf.image.convert_image_dtype(img, tf.float32)
4     img = tf.cast(img, tf.float32)
5     return {"images": img, "labels": label}
6
7 data = tf.data.Dataset.from_tensor_slices((images,
      labels)).map(preprocess_img).batch(2)
```

And let's map the images from `data` to images augmented with the new KerasCV layers, by applying the transformations and returning the images:

```
randaug_imgs = data.map(rand_augment)
cutmix_imgs = data.map(cutmix)
mixup_imgs = data.map(mixup)
```

Finally, we can visualize the effects of the operations:

```
def visualize(dataset):
    fig, ax = plt.subplots(1, 2, figsize=(8, 6))
    for sample in dataset:
        images = sample["images"]
        labels = sample["labels"]
        for index, img in enumerate(images):
            ax[index].imshow(img.numpy().astype('int'))
            ax[index].axis('off')
            ax[index].set_title(labels[index].numpy())

visualize(randaug_imgs)
visualize(cutmix_imgs)
visualize(mixup_imgs)
```

This results in:

Figure 131:

Figure 132:

Figure 133:

The first two images have random augmentations, which were pretty mild here! The second one is CutMix where images from the batch (of only these two) are cut up and mixed. You can see that the returned labels are *0.87 dog* and *0.12 cat*, and *0.78 dog* and *0.21 cat*! Finally, the MixUp images are simply overlaid - with small artefacts added to the image, and with weighted classes as well. The first image, doesn't really look like a mix if you don't know that it is - but it does have underlying "dog" artifacts. Surprisingly enough, ConvNets are pretty sensitive to underlying artifacts, and an entire class of "attacks" on them is based on adding noise to images, which are inperceptible to us, but are very perceptible to ConvNets, making them produce very wrong outputs. You can read more about this in *"Explaining and Harnessing Adversarial Examples"*[109] by Goodfellow et al.

Since we're not really adding noise, but rather, artifacts of other classes, they can still learn the difference between them even in a joined image!

Note: These are known as *inter-class* examples.

These two tricks help with generalization by forcing a model to diversify the features that make up a class. Most modern training pipelines use either a CutMix or MixUp, and rarely are they both applied, so choose the one you prefer, or give it up to chance and augment *some* batches with `MixUp` and *some* batches with `CutMix`! Let's take a look at how you can create an augmentation pipeline that can plug into any network definition or `tf.data.Dataset`. We'll be training an EfficientNet with and without the augmentation pipeline on a small dataset for reference.

9.2.1 Custom RandAugment

`RandAugment` is a special case of `RandomAugmentationPipeline`, in which a random augmentation layer is applied to the input. Internally, `RandomAugmentationPipeline` simply has a list of `layers` that it chooses from.

You can change this list easily by removing or adding `keras_cv.layers.LayerName`, or by simply replacing it with a custom list:

[109] https://arxiv.org/pdf/1412.6572.pdf

```
pipeline = keras_cv.layers.RandomAugmentationPipeline(
    layers=[keras_cv.layers.Grayscale(), keras_cv.layers.AutoContrast()]
)
```

This `pipeline` can then be applied to a `tf.data.Dataset` via `map()`:

```
dataset = dataset.map(pipeline)
```

9.2.2 Creating an Augmentation Pipeline

Let's create an augmentation pipeline! We'll apply several augmentations, using `RandAugment`, and we'll apply `CutMix` or `MixUp` with a 50/50 probability to the dataset we're training on.

We'll make a non-augmented set, a set with only random augmentation and a set with random augmentation *and* CutMix or MixUp and compare how they train.

Now, `CutMix` and `MixUp` require a different format than we'd use for training - it'll need a dictionary with the form `{"images": images, "labels": labels}` as seen before, so we'll have two preparation functions: one for the `CutMix`/`MixUp` augmentations, and one for the model:

```
import random

def preprocess(img, label):
    img = tf.image.resize(img, (224, 224))
    img = tf.image.convert_image_dtype(img, tf.float32)
    img = tf.cast(img, tf.float32)
    label = tf.one_hot(label, n_classes)
    return {"images": img, "labels": label}

def prep_for_model(inputs):
    images, labels = inputs["images"], inputs["labels"]
    images = tf.cast(images, tf.float32)
    return images, labels

def cutmix_or_mixup(samples):
    if tf.random.uniform(()) > 0.5:
        samples = keras_cv.layers.CutMix()(samples)
    else:
        samples = keras_cv.layers.MixUp()(samples)
    return samples
```

`preprocess()` will prepare the data for `cutmix_or_mixup()` and `prep_for_model()` will prepare it for the model. The latter really only extracts the images and labels from the singular `inputs` dictionary into separate returned items.

Furthermore, after the input layer of the model, we'll apply several transformations:

```
# The value_range is concerned with the value range for your images. i.e.
    whether they're normalized to 0..1 or not.
value_range = (0, 255)

data_aug_pipeline = keras.Sequential([
    # magnitude sets how 'aggressive' the augmentations are
    keras_cv.layers.RandAugment(value_range=value_range, magnitude=0.3)
])
```

The pipeline only has one layer, which actually really uses many layers. We'll be applying CutMix/MixUp on the dataset itself. You can replace `RandAugment()` with:

```
keras_cv.layers.RandomAugmentationPipeline(layers=[layer1, layer2, ...])
```

9.2.3 Training a Model with KerasCV Preprocessing Layers

Now, let's load a dataset in using `tfds`, apply these transformations:

```
import tensorflow_datasets as tfds

# Using 0..50% of the data for training for speed
# and to make it more difficult for the network
(train_set, test_set, valid_set), info = tfds.load("imagenette",
                                        split=["train[:50%]",
                                            "validation", "train[70%:]"],
                                        as_supervised=True,
                                            with_info=True)

class_names = info.features["label"].names
n_classes = info.features["label"].num_classes
print(f'Class names: {class_names}')
print('Num of classes:', n_classes) # 10

print("Train set size:", len(train_set)) # 4734
print("Test set size:", len(test_set))   # 2841
print("Valid set size:", len(valid_set)) # 3925
```

We'll create a non-augmented `__set_na` and augmented `__set_aug`:

```
# Chaining calls is less verbose and more readable.
# Calls are separated for book formatting.
train_set_na = train_set.map(preprocess).batch(32)
train_set_na = train_set_na.map(prep_for_model).prefetch(tf.data.AUTOTUNE)

```

```
test_set_na = test_set.map(preprocess).batch(32)
test_set_na = test_set_na.map(prep_for_model).prefetch(tf.data.AUTOTUNE)

valid_set_na = valid_set.map(preprocess).batch(32)
valid_set_na = valid_set_na.map(prep_for_model).prefetch(tf.data.AUTOTUNE)


train_set_aug = train_set.map(preprocess).batch(32)
train_set_aug = train_set_aug.map(cutmix_or_mixup).map(prep_for_model)
train_set_aug = train_set_aug.prefetch(tf.data.AUTOTUNE)

test_set_aug = test_set.map(preprocess).batch(32)
test_set_aug = test_set_aug.map(cutmix_or_mixup).map(prep_for_model)
test_set_aug = test_set_aug.prefetch(tf.data.AUTOTUNE)

valid_set_aug = valid_set.map(preprocess).batch(32)
valid_set_aug = valid_set_aug.map(cutmix_or_mixup).map(prep_for_model)
valid_set_aug = valid_set_aug.prefetch(tf.data.AUTOTUNE)
```

The first model will won't use any augmentation:

```
model = keras.Sequential([
    keras.layers.InputLayer(input_shape=(None, None, 3)),
    keras.applications.EfficientNetV2B0(weights=None, include_top=False),
    keras.layers.GlobalAveragePooling2D(),
    keras.layers.Dropout(0.4),
    keras.layers.Dense(n_classes, activation = 'softmax')
])

model.compile(loss = 'categorical_crossentropy',
              optimizer = keras.optimizers.Adam(learning_rate=1e-4),
              metrics=['accuracy'])

history = model.fit(train_set_na,
                    epochs=100,
                    validation_data=valid_set_na)
```

While the second one will use only `RandAugment()`:

```
model = keras.Sequential([
    keras.layers.InputLayer(input_shape=(None, None, 3)),
    data_aug_pipeline,
    keras.applications.EfficientNetV2B0(weights=None, include_top=False),
    keras.layers.GlobalAveragePooling2D(),
    keras.layers.Dropout(0.4),
    keras.layers.Dense(n_classes, activation = 'softmax')
])

model.compile(loss = 'categorical_crossentropy',
              optimizer = keras.optimizers.Adam(learning_rate=1e-4),
              metrics=['accuracy'])

history2 = model.fit(train_set_na,
```

```
15                          epochs=100,
16                          validation_data=valid_set_na)
```

And the third one will use both the augmentation pipeline and the corresponding CutMix/MixUp sets:

```
1  model = keras.Sequential([
2      keras.layers.InputLayer(input_shape=(None, None, 3)),
3      data_aug_pipeline,
4      keras.applications.EfficientNetV2B0(weights=None, include_top=False),
5      keras.layers.GlobalAveragePooling2D(),
6      keras.layers.Dropout(0.4),
7      keras.layers.Dense(n_classes, activation = 'softmax')
8  ])
9
10 model.compile(loss = 'categorical_crossentropy',
11               optimizer = keras.optimizers.Adam(learning_rate=1e-4),
12               metrics=['accuracy'])
13
14 history3 = model.fit(train_set_aug,
15                          epochs=100,
16                          validation_data=valid_set_aug)
```

Generally speaking - MixUp and/or CutMix with a `RandAugment` of reasonable magnitude (depends on the dataset) will produce better results down the line. They do require a slightly different preprocessing step, and do make the training somewhat slower, but if you're looking to maximize generalization - they're a good bet.

When these three networks train over 100 epochs, here are the validation accurracies:

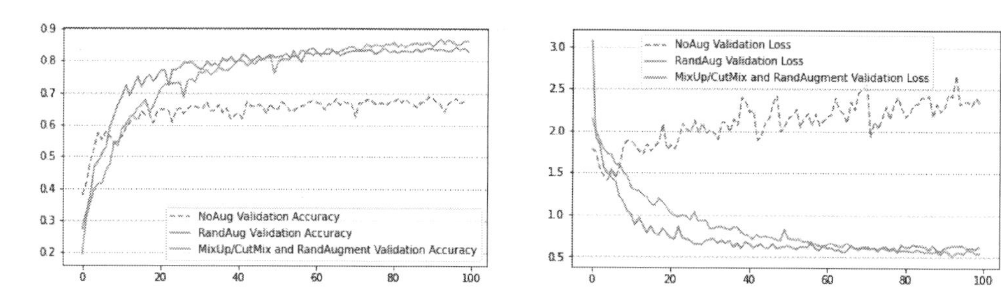

Figure 134:

The MixUp/CutMix pipeline evidently took longer to achieve the higher accuracy - but it eventually overtook the pipeline with just `RandAugment()`, even though it seemed to have been slightly worse in terms of accuracy in the beginning. This makes sense - it was harder to classify these images but the network eventually got the hang of it. Maybe even more importantly - the individual training/validation curves are significantly different:

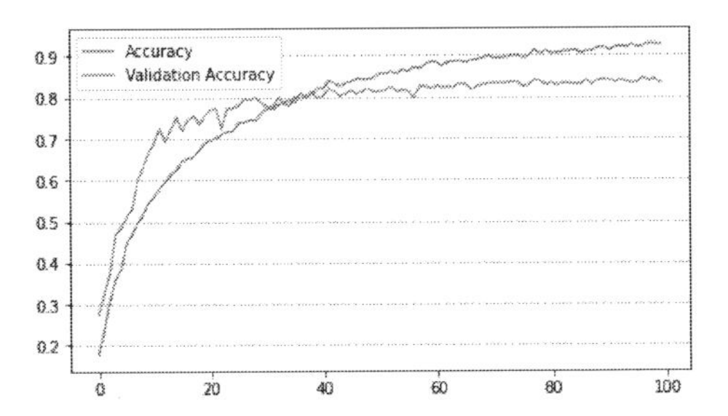

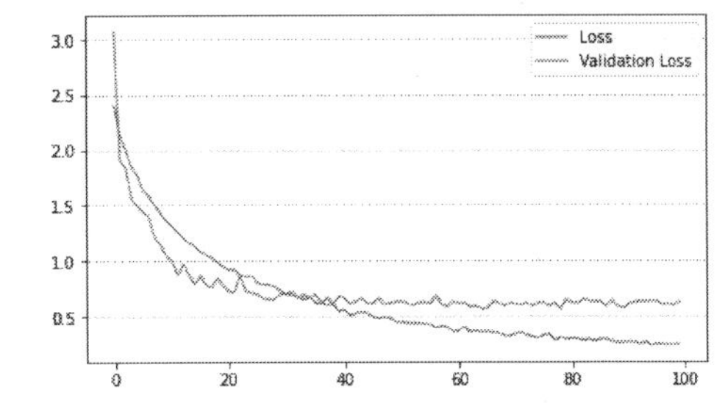

Figure 135:

With just `RandAugment()`, the training and validation curves are fairly similar, until around epoch 40 where the model starts to overfit, and they diverge. Even then, they still follow the same trend. **Gradients are calculated by applying the loss function between training data and the outputs of the network.** This network will only see small gradient updates, as it's correctly classifying most training samples. This makes it difficult to squeeze out the last few percentages and training becomes slower and harder near the end as it's getting better.

On the other hand, the MixUp/CutMix network never gets to see the curves cross:

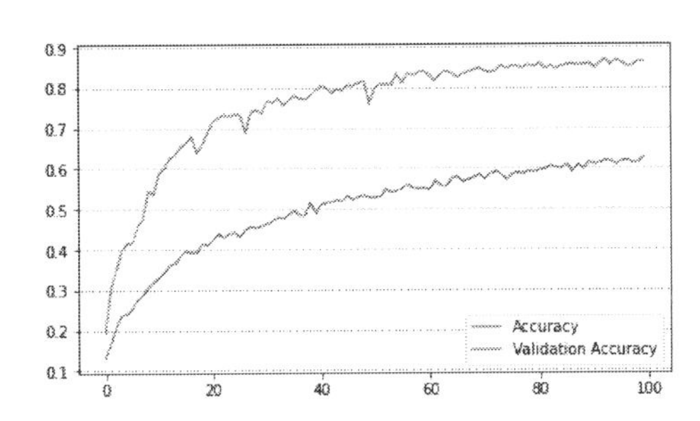

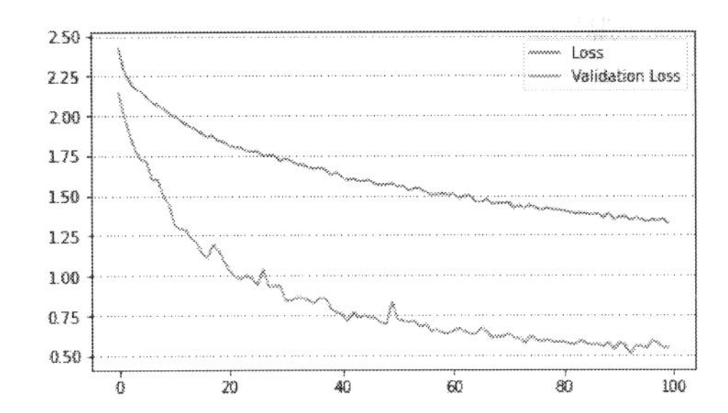

Figure 136:

The training loss, used to update gradients, stays high even though the validation loss and accuracy are high. This almost false belief that the network isn't that accurate might very well be what keeps the validation accuracy rising further than without MixUp/CutMix, as the network isn't settling into place. The training curves are closer to the validation curves at epoch 100, compared to say, epoch 40. Presumably, through more epochs, they'd converge together, as well. The point is - with MixUp/CutMix, we're increasing the potential of the network to learn through an extended period of time, compared to the network that didn't use them.

9.3 KerasCV Metrics, Visualization and Explainability Tools

Besides new layers - KerasCV will also feature new metrics, such as `COCOMeanAveragePrecision` and `COCORecall`, as well as formatting/utility methods for plotting and calculating bounding boxes, and visualization/explainability tools like GradCam++, covered in an earlier chapter through `tf-keras-vis`.

These tools are currently scattered between different projects, and some are rarely updated, so having a centralized repository will undoubtedly bring advanced tools to the average engineer.

All in all - it's a really exciting package to keep track of, especially during development!

9.4 KerasCV Models

As noted earlier - `keras_cv.models` will eventually replace `keras.applications`. When? When they're ready. No hard deadline. Old models are being ported into `keras_cv` via the community's and the team's efforts, and new models are incoming.

Currently, in July of 2022, several models are already ported:

- DenseNet
- MixerMLP
- ResNets V1 and V2
- VGGNet
- DarkNet

And various others, including `EfficientNetV2`, `ConvNeXt`, etc. are currently being worked on. The API is much the same, so you shouldn't have issues porting from one to the other:

```
densenet = keras_cv.models.DenseNet121(include_rescaling=True,
    include_top=True, num_classes=2)
densenet.summary()
```

```
Model: "DenseNet121"
_________________________________________________________________
 Layer (type)                Output Shape         Param #     Connected to
=================================================================
 input_2 (InputLayer)        [(None, None, None,  0           []
                              3)]
...
=================================================================
Total params: 7,039,554
Trainable params: 6,955,906
Non-trainable params: 83,648
_________________________________________________________________
```

The `weights` argument currently doesn't support the `'imagenet'` string - and will presumably be added later. For now, only saved weights can be loaded. For the news - follow the KerasCV GitHub and/or documentation. I'll update the book with new developments!

Object detection is a large field in computer vision, and one of the more important applications of computer vision "in the wild". On one end, it can be used to build autonomous systems that navigate agents through environments - be it robots performing tasks or self-driving cars.

> Naturally - for both of these applications, more than just computer vision is going on. Robotics is oftentimes coupled with Reinforcement Learning (training agents to act within environments), and if you want to give it tasks using natural language, NLP would be required to convert your words into meaningful representations for them to act on.

However, anomaly detection (such as defective products on a line), locating objects within images, facial detection and various other applications of object detection can be done without intersecting other fields.

When talking about certain architectures in previous chapters - I mentioned that some can be used as "generic vision backbones". The backbone of what, exactly? The answer, commonly, is for object detection and instance segmentation. A backbone network (CNN) for feature extraction is used, alongside one of the varying techniques for detecting objects, to localize where instances are.

10 Object Detection and Segmentation - R-CNNs, RetinaNet, SSD, YOLO...

10.1 Object Detection is... Messy and Large

And that's the honest answer. The internet is riddled with contradicting statements, confusing explanations, proprietary undocummented code and high-level explanations that don't really touch the heart of things. Object detection isn't as straightforward as image classfication. Some of the difficulties include:

- **Various approaches:** There are many approaches to perform object detection, while image classification boils down to a similar approach in pretty much all cases.
- **Real-time performance**: Performing object detection should oftentimes be in real-time. While not all appliactions require real-time performance, many do, and this makes it even harder. While networks like MobileNet are fast, they suffer in accuracy.
- **Devices:** The speed-accuracy tradeoff is extremely important for object detection, and you might not be able to know on which devices it'll run on, as well as the processing units that will be running them.
- **Libraries and implementations:** Object detection is less standardized than image classfication, so you'll have a harder time finding compatible implementations that you can just "plug and play".
- **Formats:** Labels for classification are simple - typically a number. For detection - will you be using COCO JSON, YOLO-format, Pascal VOC-format, TensorFlow Detection CSV, TFRecords? Some are in XML, while others are in JSON, Text, CSV or proprietary formats.
- **Utilities:** With classification - you just spit out a number. With detection - you're typically expected to draw a bounding box, plot the label and make it look at least somewhat pretty. This is more difficult than it sounds.

For classification, we've so far become used to a pretty easy workflow:

```
1 1. Load data and preprocess it (resize, encode labels)
2 2. model = ...
3 3. model.fit()
4 4. model.evaluate()
5 5. model.predict()
```

It's a clean, easy, intuitive flow. You won't have that with object detection if you're looking to train networks. Many of the networks you'll download from model zoos will be for inference only - not training. The ones that can be trained usually come from open source projects with utility scripts for training in which you point to images and label maps from which training can be done, unless you define your architectures from scratch.

> With Object Detection - you'll spend more of your time with configurations, rather than models.

This isn't to scare you away from an important task in computer vision - it is to scope the engineering task. Detecting objects in images isn't easy, and we're farther away from solving it than from solving image classification.

> Everything you've learned so far is the **crucial backbone** of object detection, but know that we're moving more towards engineering *around* models, rather than building models. Engineering around models is, at the time of writing, mainly done by individual researchers, maintainers and developers, and isn't standardized.

It's more difficult to compare the progress in object detection than it is to compare progress in image classification - but comparisons can be done (and should be taken with a bit larger grain of salt). What we've been doing so far will typically be abstracted away by more classical software engineering, and behind utility scripts and proprietary training pipelines.

Note: KerasCV aims to change this by making losses, layers and networks in these tasks easier to work with (regular models, rather than the ones you're loading in in an untrainable state), in a much more familiar way - through building blocks, rather than black-box proprietary solutions from model zoos) - such as for image classification.

Advances in image classification models drives advances in their applications. Smaller, faster, more efficient, more accurate architectures have much more impact in this domain, than when just classifying images.

Object detection is a large field, with rapid changes and movements. In this chapter, I'll summarize some of the approaches, tools, architectures and frameworks being used to those ends.

10.2 Object Detection Architecures

Let's start with architectures! At a high-level, you can classify the architectures as two-stage detectors and one-stage detectors. We're moving *away* from two-stage detectors with improvements.

10.2.1 R-CNN, Fast R-CNN, Faster R-CNN

One of the first attempts at solving object detection was with *Regional CNNs*, shortened to R-CNNs. An image would be segmented into regions of interest (2000 of them, to be precise), and each region would be classified by being passed through the CNN for feature extraction and classified with an *SVM (Support Vector Machine) classifier*. Then, the classified regions would be pooled together into a single region in which an object is located. This was a good start but was extremely inefficient and wasn't practical. Additionally, the region proposal algorithm that proposed the regions of interest, called *selective search* wasn't part of the model itself, and wasn't trainable, on top of being inefficient itself.

The author of the paper released an improved version - known as Fast R-CNN shorly after. Instead of passing 2000 regions through a CNN, the entire image was passed only *once* to create a feature map. Only on this feature map was region proposal applied, with a fully-connected classifier top. This made Fast R-CNN faster than the previous approach by an order of magnitude.

Finally, Faster R-CNN replaced the selective search algorithm, and turned region proposal into a task for another network - making it learnable. They were still a two-stage process, but this made Faster R-CNN models faster by another order of magnitude, and actually making them practical, yet still too slow for real-time inference. Even today, you'll see Faster R-CNN architectures around being used, since they're agnostic to the backbone, making them more resiliant to change, but they're enjoying fewer users than some newer methods, and are slowly being phased out in lieu of faster and more accurate networks. Because of this, we won't dedicate too much time to them.

10.2.2 RetinaNet

RetinaNet was released in 2017, after Faster R-CNN, with a totally different approach. Faster R-CNN was a two-stage detector. Some tried to condense object detection into a one-stage process, with success, but trading off accuracy for the speed that comes with one-stage detection. At the time, these were *SSD (Single-Shot Detectors)* and *YOLOv2 (You Only Look Once)*, which were improved over the years, leading to today.

One-stage detectors at the had issues with background-foreground imbalance. Regions to be classified would be more numerous for backgrounds, rather than the "target", which would typically be a smaller region in the image. This imbalance made it hard to get higher accuracies as loss functions would struggle optimizing truly general networks over those who were biased to find backgrounds. RetinaNet addresses this with a new loss - Focal Loss, which attributes higher "weight" to hard-to-classify examples, and lower "weight" to easy-to-classify examples, where backgrounds are easier to classify than the target object(s).

This imbalance, present in our earlier project as well, can make it look like the loss is really low - because non-target-objects are easily classified, making the model steer towards that direction further, and ignoring the actual task at hand. Focal Loss cares more about non-background predictions and relies on that loss to evaluate how the parameters are to be updated.

RetinaNet had two subnetworks on top of the feature extractor (plug-and-play CNN backbone), that predicted the bounding boxes and the classes, packaged as a single trainable network. Even today, RetinaNet provides satisfactory accuracy, but is usually considered too slow for real-time detection on most systems. Since SSD and YOLO-based were improved in the realm of accuracy and speed - they've evened out with RetinaNet in accuracy, but remain significantly faster in 2022. RetinaNet was the leading architecture up until very recently. Nowadays - the main competition is between SSD networks and YOLO-based networks.

10.2.3 Single Shot Detectors and You Only Look Once - SSD and YOLO

SSDs and YOLO are competing approaches, but I've put them together since they're very similar, and the bulk of the explanations are generalizable between them.

Single-Shot Detectors are conceptually simple. They have a backbone and a head. The backbone is typically a regular ConvNet, sans the classifier top, and produces feature maps. The head is another convolutional layer, which produces an output that encodes the bounding boxes and classes.

The network is **fully convolutional**. The extracted features are passed through more convolutions, which produce a feature map that encodes the results of the detection. This is a wholly new way of using feature maps!

The output feature map is a **grid** filled with **grid cells**. For example, a `(7, 7, bbox)` output would be considered a 7x7 grid with `bbox` being a 1D tensor encoding the class, bounding box coordinates and confidence score.

Each grid cell is responsible for some number (oftentimes 5, but this can vary) bounding boxes. These boxes usually overlap, so they're typically compressed and low-confidence boxes are just ignored.

YOLO-based networks have a backbone and head. The network is fully convolutional and outputs an SxS grid. The head outputs a tensor containing all of the bounding boxes for all the objects in the image, as well as their classes, with a shape `(S, S, Bx(5+C)))`, where `S` is the grid size, `B` is the number of bounding boxes (defined by 5 integers - the (x,y) center and the width, height and confidence score) and `C` is the number of classes. So - for each grid, there's a `Bx(5+C)` tensor that describes the bounding boxes tied to that cell.

For a 7x7 grid, with 5 bounding boxes for each cell, and 100 classes - that's an output tensor of `(7, 7, 5x(5+100) -> (7, 7, 525)`, which when flattened is a whopping *25725* predictions!

This turns object detection into an end-to-end regression problem, where the bounding boxes are regressed, alongside the classification of objects. The predicted boxes that overlap are "merged into a box that contains them, and low confidence boxes are ignored. The treshold at which the low confidence boxes are ignored is oftentimes set as a parameter of the model.

The YOLO method was released in 2015 by Redmon et al.[110], and then refined in 2016[111] and 2018[112] - YOLO is a defining method for object detection, and a "family" of models revolving around the method.

Note: YOLO is ultimately a **method** for creating object detection systems. We also call networks that use these methods YOLO networks, usually with a 'vN' suffix, or another suffix to differentiate the application of the method to the method itself. To differentiate, I'll use "YOLO" as the method, and "YOLO-based networks" as the application of it.

These papers correspond to YOLOv1 (model based on the original YOLO method), YOLOv2 (based on the YOLO9000 method) and YOLOv3, written by the same authors, using Darknet - a C-based library for deep learning models. Darknet is not to be confused with DarkNet-N, the backbone used for the first YOLO-based models, where *N* was the number of layers in the backbones which were fairly similar to VGGNets. The naming conventions don't really help, I know.

Since then, the deep learning community took it upon themselves to port YOLOv3 to other libraries, such as Keras and PyTorch, and to build networks such as YOLOv4 and YOLOv5 in 2020. As I was writing this chapter - YOLOv7 was released by an independent contributor.

> As of writing in July of 2022, YOLOv5, built by Ultralytics[a], is probably the most commonly used community-driven YOLO-based repository, with an active team working on improvements around the clock. If any issues arise with the package, you're likely to be able to find a response on their GitHub. Newer models, such as YOLOv7 have a smaller community, which might make the barrier to entry slightly higher if you encounter any bugs. YOLOv5 is written in PyTorch, not Darknet, mak-

[110] https://arxiv.org/abs/1506.02640v5
[111] https://arxiv.org/pdf/1612.08242.pdf
[112] https://arxiv.org/abs/1804.02767v1

> ing it much more intuitive to more people.
>
> [a]https://github.com/ultralytics/yolov5

YOLOv1's process can be summarized as:

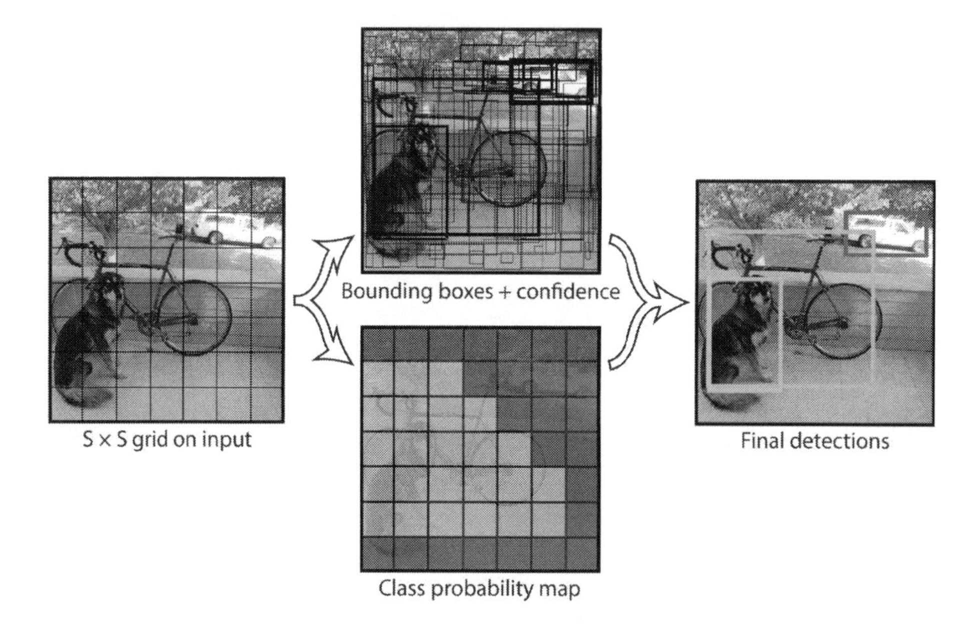

Figure 137:

The output tensor contains the SxS grids, with the class confidences for each cell and the coordinates and sizes of the bounding boxes:

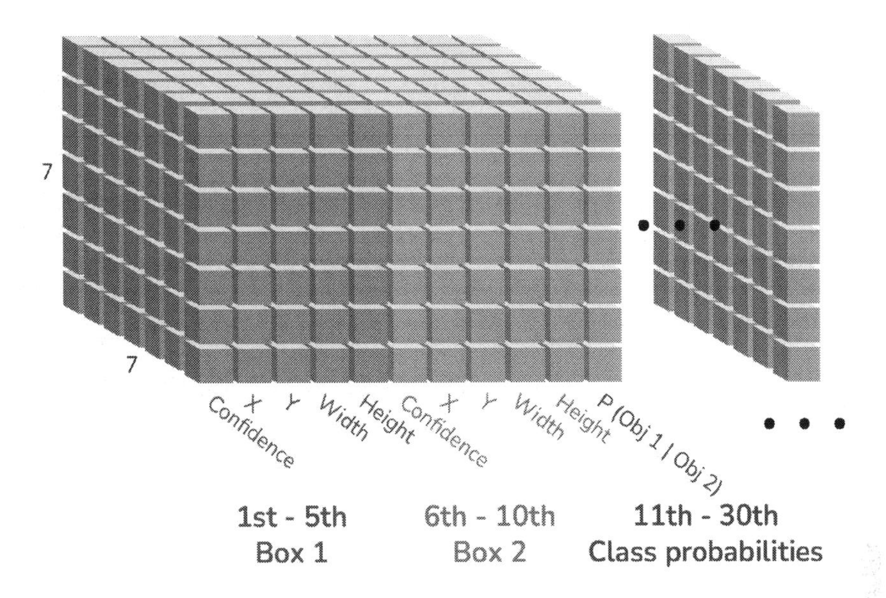

Figure 138:

The main issue with it was that each grid can classify a single class, so if two objects can be found in the same cell - only one will be picked up. This made it difficult to classify small objects in an image. RetinaNet notably didn't have these issues.

Later versions of YOLO-based networks, such as YOLOv3 accounted for this by outputting multiple output tensors with different grid cell sizes, allowing smaller objects to be detected. Additionally, swapping out the VGGNet-like feature extractor with a ResNet-like feature extractor helped a lot.

There's misinformation and shaky explanations to be found about how YOLO works, so to avoid any middlemen - it's highly encouraged to read the original papers. The third one has flair, charm and a refreshing amount of informality.

10.3 Difference Between YOLO and SSD

So, what's the difference between YOLO and SSD? Googling for the answer is oftentimes unfruitful, and the differences are oftentimes scoped as "which is better at which", more commonly than not, using unfair comparisons.

> The entirety of the debate can be boiled down to - SSDs downsample their way down to a prediction. YOLO-based networks upsample.

Matthijs Hollemans did a wonderful job diving into one-staged detectors[113] *without the fluff*, in a conversational, no-nonsense manner on his blog - machinethink.com. The blog remains one of the cleanest overviews of how one-stage detectors work and the comparison of SSDs and YOLO-based networks.

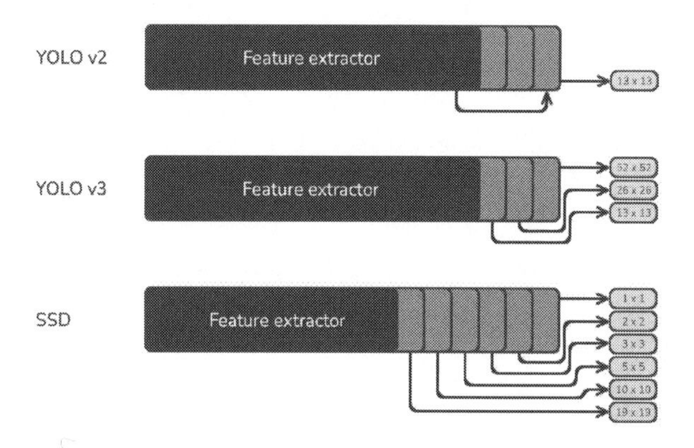

Figure 139:

Originally, YOLO had a single output, which made it sensitive to different-sized objects. The solution proved to be multiple outpus, and one-stage detectors nowadays return several outputs - coarser to finer for YOLO and finer to coarser for SSDs. Besides these - the losses and the way predictions are turned into boxes is somewhat different between the approaches, but these don't have many practical implications for you.

What is relevant for you is that **generally speaking**:

- YOLO is typically faster than SSD, but has a slightly lower map.
- SSD is more likely to find a larger percentage of objects in an image, but is typically slower than YOLO.

[113] https://machinethink.net/blog/object-detection/

- RetinaNet usually has a high mAP and doesn't struggle as much with finding really small objects in images, but has significantly slower speeds. They found great use in Sattelite Imagery where many very small objects may be very close to each other.

This highly depends on what YOLO you use (newer versions are on par with SSDs and RetinaNet in accuracy), which backbones are used, matching strategies, which layers are used for feature extraction at different scales, etc. Point is - it's hard to create an unbiased comparison between them. The best test you can do is to train both on the same dataset, and pick the one that works for you better.

While it is hard to justly compare them, you can use a rough rule of thumb with a pinch of salt - RetinaNet, SSD and YOLO can be seen as if on a scale of accuracy and speed, where the accuracy declines while speed increases from left to right. Before applying this idea - check whether there are any new developments and this changed. Currently, there's a trend of YOLO-based models increasing in accuracy, while retaining their speed.

10.4 How Do You Even Do Object Detection? TensorFlow Object Detection API and torchvision

There is official TensorFlow and PyTorch support for object detection but the support is flimsy. In TensorFlow's case - it's the TensorFlow Object Detection API[114]. In PyTorch's case, it's through `torchvision`[115].

> "The TensorFlow Object Detection API is an open source framework built on top of TensorFlow that makes it easy to construct, train and deploy object detection models."

The API is all fun and games until the official code examples on Google Colab and GitHub don't work. Although the API seems to be really well-built, with dozens of CenterNets, EfficientDets (EfficientNet Object Detection, shortened to EfficientDet) and SSDs in various flavors in their model zoo - the framework is riddled with bugs mainly stemming from issues with dependencies, uncompatible versions, and in some

[114]https://github.com/tensorflow/models/tree/master/research/object_detection
[115]https://pytorch.org/vision/stable/index.html

cases, problems you don't even want to understand. From having to re-install various libraries, to having to run the same installation scripts multiple times (each with a success code, but without actually installing the libs) to creating folder structures, installing even more dependencies and downloading files to them - the official TensorFlow Object Detection API is not user friendly, on top of being difficult to set up and navigate.

To be fully fair - you have to cut them some slack. TensorFlow's ecosystem is so huge, with amazing tools and products in it, distributed over an insanely large team - there had to be one component in the ecosystem that doesn't really work well.

> Because of this, until the framework is either rewritten or fixed, I won't be covering it in the book. It'll cause you way more headaches than you need, and raise the barrier to entry higher than it already is.

10.4.1 Object Detection with PyTorch's torchvision

`torchvision` is PyTorch's Computer Vision project, and aims to make the development of PyTorch-based CV models easier, by providing transformation and augmentation scripts, a model zoo with pre-trained weights, datasets and utilities that can be useful for a practitioner.

While still in beta and very much experimental - `torchvision` offers a relatively simple Object Detection API with a few models to choose from:

- Faster R-CNN
- RetinaNet
- FCOS (Fully convolutional RetinaNet)
- SSD (VGG16 backbone... yikes)
- SSDLite (MobileNetV3 backbone)

While the API isn't as polished or simple as some other third-party APIs, it's a very decent starting point for those who'd still prefer the safety of being in an ecosystem they're familiar with. Before going forward, make sure you install PyTorch and Torchvision:

```
1 $ pip install torch torchvision
```

Let's load in some of the utility functions, such as `read_image()`, `draw_bounding_boxes()` and `to_pil_image()` to make it easier to read, draw on and output images, followed by importing RetinaNet and its pre-trained weights (MS COCO):

```
1 from torchvision.io.image import read_image
2 from torchvision.utils import draw_bounding_boxes
3 from torchvision.transforms.functional import to_pil_image
4 from torchvision.models.detection import retinanet_resnet50_fpn_v2,
      RetinaNet_ResNet50_FPN_V2_Weights
5
6 import matplotlib.pyplot as plt
```

RetinaNet uses a ResNet50 backbone and a Feature Pyramid Network (FPN) on top of it. While the name of the class is verbose, it's indicative of the architecture. Let's fetch an image using the `requests` library and save it as a file on our local drive:

```
1 import requests
2 response =
      requests.get('https://i.ytimg.com/vi/q71MCWAEfL8/maxresdefault.jpg')
3 open("obj_det.jpeg", "wb").write(response.content)
4
5 img = read_image("obj_det.jpeg")
```

With an image in place - we can instantiate our model and weights:

```
1 weights = RetinaNet_ResNet50_FPN_V2_Weights.DEFAULT
2 model = retinanet_resnet50_fpn_v2(weights=weights, score_thresh=0.35)
3 # Put the model in inference mode
4 model.eval()
5 # Get the transforms for the model's weights
6 preprocess = weights.transforms()
```

The `score_thresh` argument defines the threshold at which an object is detected as an object of a class. Intuitively, it's the confidence threshold, and we won't classify an object to belong to a class if the model is less than 35% confident that it belongs to a class.

Let's preprocess the image using the transforms from our weights, create a batch and run inference:

```
1 batch = [preprocess(img)]
2 prediction = model(batch)[0]
```

That's it, our `prediction` dictionary holds the inferred object classes and locations! Now, the results aren't very useful for us in this form - we'll want to extract the labels with respect to the metadata from the weights and draw bounding boxes, which can be done via `draw_bounding_boxes()`:

```
labels = [weights.meta["categories"][i] for i in prediction["labels"]]

box = draw_bounding_boxes(img, boxes=prediction["boxes"],
                          labels=labels,
                          colors = "cyan",
                          width=2,
                          font_size=30,
                          font = 'Arial')

im = to_pil_image(box.detach())

fig, ax = plt.subplots(figsize=(16, 12))
ax.imshow(im)
plt.show()
```

This results in:

Figure 140:

RetinaNet actually classified the person peeking behind the car! That's a pretty difficult classification.

You can switch out RetinaNet to an FCOS (fully convolutional RetinaNet) SSD (VGG backbone), SSDLite, Faster-RCNN (ResNet backbone). Although VGG backbones aren't great, and should be replaced with much newer ones, let's try out an SSD instead of RetinaNet:

```
from torchvision.models.detection import ssd300_vgg16, SSD300_VGG16_Weights

img = read_image("obj_det.jpeg")

weights = SSD300_VGG16_Weights.DEFAULT
model = ssd300_vgg16(weights=weights, score_thresh=0.15)
model.eval()

preprocess = weights.transforms()
batch = [preprocess(img)]
prediction = model(batch)[0]

labels = [weights.meta["categories"][i] for i in prediction["labels"]]
box = draw_bounding_boxes(img, boxes=prediction["boxes"],
                          labels=labels,
                          colors = "cyan",
                          width=2,
                          font_size=30,
                          font = 'Arial')

im = to_pil_image(box.detach())

fig, ax = plt.subplots(figsize=(16, 12))
ax.imshow(im)
plt.show()
```

This results in a similar, yet less detailed view:

Figure 141:

It missed the person in the back, some traffic lights, some of the people near the edges of the image, etc. The bounding boxes don't look super appealing, but they work. We still have to do a bit of extra work compared to `model(inputs)` or `model.predict(inputs)`, but this works just okay.

10.5 Community Packages and Inference Demos

This is where community packages and companies that open-source their work come into play! A fair disclaimer - more of these are built in PyTorch than in TensorFlow. This shouldn't be an obstacle - TensorFlow 2's API was made to mirror PyTorch's, and they're similar enough that transitioning from one to the other isn't hard.

Now - so far, we've been working with TF's high-level API, Keras, which *is* quite different from PyTorch. Nevertheless, a good portion of these packages won't have you work with low-level models, but rather run utilty scripts, so it doesn't really matter which framework they're ultimately lying on. In addition - don't be afraid of diversifying your stack!

Advice: While it's more comfortable to work in a single framework, and we might feel reluctant to spread ourselves on multiple ecosystems - remember that frameworks are tools. A good mechanic has a lot of good tools, and can use different ones when need be. By staying on top of multiple ecosystems, you can reap the benefits of a larger number of human-hours invested in research and development, making your job easier.

Here are a few packages that might be of interest for you. Some of these are naturally more active than others, and I won't limit the list to just the latest and greatest - but will annotate for which purpose they're designed and which ones you'll probably want to use to build deliverables.

10.5.1 Ultralytics' YOLOv5

Ultralytics' YOLOv5[116] is a 30k-star GitHub repository, and arguably one of the largest repos in the community, with wide application and a large community. It's got detailed, no-nonsense documentation and a beautifully simple API, as shown on the repo itself:

```
import torch
# Model
model = torch.hub.load('ultralytics/yolov5', 'yolov5s')  # or yolov5n -
    yolov5x6, custom
# Images
img = 'https://i.ytimg.com/vi/q71MCWAEfL8/maxresdefault.jpg'  # or file,
    Path, PIL, OpenCV, numpy, list
# Inference
results = model(img)
# Results
fig, ax = plt.subplots(figsize=(16, 12))
ax.imshow(results.render()[0]) # or .show(), .save(), .crop(), .pandas(),
    etc.
plt.show()
```

This results in a nicely formatted:

[116]https://github.com/ultralytics/yolov5

Figure 142:

It cannot be overstated how amazingly beautiful and simple the inference API is. Training can be done via their training script:

```
python train.py --data coco.yaml --cfg yolov5n.yaml --weights ''
    --batch-size 128
```

But this naturally requires a bit of preparation for custom datasets. The model supports transfer learning and freezing layers, exports to TensorFlow Lite, CoreML and TensorRT through ONNX (open format built to represent machine learning models which you can use to translate between frameworks).

Note: The exports are only meant for inference and deployment - you can't train them as they are. The training is done in PyTorch, using the associated utility script.

In the next lesson, we'll be using YOLOv5 to perform inference on input images, videos in real time and train an object detection model using their training scripts.

The project is meant to be used for engineers to apply to practical settings and deployed to products, but can be used for applied computer vision research in other fields.

10.5.2 TFDetection

TFDetection[117] is a little-known repository worthy of more usage. It's a toolbox of object detection, semantic segmentation and anomaly detection, built in TensorFlow 2 and Keras.

It's much more along the lines of what we've done so far! The usage examples in the repository itself offer a good demonstration on how the suite works, but as you might have expected - it's pretty verbose.

The toolbox offers various backbones, including the most well known architectures since 2015 to 2022 - ResNets, DenseNets, MobileNets, DarkNets, EfficientNets (including V2), SwinTransformer nets (including V2). Here's a table of components:

Object Detection	Segmentation	Anomaly Detection
Faster R-CNN(2015)	FCN(2015)	SPADE(2020)
RetinaNet(2017)	UNet(2016)	PaDiM(2020)
YoloV3(2018)	PSPNet(2017)	PatchCore(2021)
YoloV3 Tiny(2018)	DeepLab V3(2017)	
Cascade R-CNN(2018)	DeepLab V3+(2018)	
FCOS(2019)	UNet++(2018)	
Hybrid Task Cascade(2019)	UperNet(2018)	
EfficientDet(2019)	Mask R-CNN(2017)	
YoloV4(2020)	Cascade R-CNN(2018)	
YoloV4 Tiny(2020)	Hybrid Task Cascade(2019)	

[117] https://github.com/Burf/TFDetection

Object Detection	Segmentation	Anomaly Detection
EfficientDet Lite(2020)		

I'm excited to see where the toolbox is taken in the future! It's definitely worth a read.

10.5.3 Meta AI's Detectron2 - Object Detection, Instance Segmentation, Panoptic Segmentation and Keypoint Detection

Detectron2[118] is Meta AI (formerly FAIR - Facebook AI Research)'s open source object detection, segmentation and pose estimation package - all in one. Given an input image, it can return the labels, bounding boxes, confidence scores, masks and skeletons of objects. This is well-represented on the repository's page:

Figure 143:

It's meant to be used as a library on the top of which you can build research projects. It offers a model zoo[119] with most implementations relying on Mask R-CNN and R-CNNs in general, alongside RetinaNet. They also have a pretty decent documentation[120]. It's written in PyTorch so if you don't have any experience with it, it might require a bit of getting used to. Regardless of the training, Detectron2 models are exportable to TorchScript, making them easily deployable!

Let's run an examplory inference script. First, we'll install the dependencies:

```
1 $ pip install pyyaml==5.1
2 $ pip install 'git+https://github.com/facebookresearch/detectron2.git'
```

[118]https://github.com/facebookresearch/detectron2

[119]https://github.com/facebookresearch/detectron2/blob/main/MODEL_ZOO.md

[120]https://detectron2.readthedocs.io/en/latest/tutorials/index.html

Next, we'll import the Detectron2 utilities - this is where framework-domain knowledge comes into play. Next, we'll import the Detectron2 utilities - this is where framework-domain knowledge comes into play. You can construct a detector using the `DefaultPredictor` class, by passing in a configuration object that sets it up. The `Visualizer` offers support for visualizing results. `MetadataCatalog` and `DatasetCatalog` belong to Detectron2's data API and offer information on built-in datasets as well as their metadata (we'll be fetching the labels from MS COCO). Unless you plan on using Detectron2, there's no need to dive into how they exactly work but do note that Detectron2 is a pretty powerful project and that you might want to keep it at least in the back of your head.

Let's import the classes we'll be using:

```
1 import torch, detectron2
2 from detectron2.utils.logger import setup_logger
3 setup_logger()
4
5 from detectron2 import model_zoo
6 from detectron2.engine import DefaultPredictor
7 from detectron2.config import get_cfg
8 from detectron2.utils.visualizer import Visualizer
9 from detectron2.data import MetadataCatalog, DatasetCatalog
```

Let's load an image in:

```
1 import matplotlib.pyplot as plt
2 import requests
3 response =
      requests.get('http://images.cocodataset.org/val2017/000000439715.jpg')
4 open("input.jpg", "wb").write(response.content)
5
6 im = cv2.imread("./input.jpg")
7 im = cv2.cvtColor(im, cv2.COLOR_BGR2RGB)
8 fig, ax = plt.subplots(figsize=(18, 8))
9 ax.imshow(im)
```

This results in:

Figure 144:

Now, we load the configuration, enact changes if need be (the models run on GPU by default, so if you don't have a GPU, you'll want to set the device to 'cpu' in the config):

```
cfg = get_cfg()

# Model config file
config_file = "COCO-InstanceSegmentation/mask_rcnn_R_50_FPN_3x.yaml"

cfg.merge_from_file(model_zoo.get_config_file(config_file))
cfg.MODEL.ROI_HEADS.SCORE_THRESH_TEST = 0.5
cfg.MODEL.WEIGHTS = model_zoo.get_checkpoint_url(config_file)
# If you don't have a GPU and CUDA enabled, the next line is required
# cfg.MODEL.DEVICE = "cpu"
```

Finally, we can construct a predictor with this `cfg` and run it on the inputs! The `Visualizer` class is used to draw predictions on the image (in this case, segmented instances, classes and bounding boxes:

```
1 predictor = DefaultPredictor(cfg)
2 outputs = predictor(im)
3
4 v = Visualizer(im[:, :, ::-1], MetadataCatalog.get(cfg.DATASETS.TRAIN[0]),
      scale=1.2)
5 out = v.draw_instance_predictions(outputs["instances"].to("cpu"))
6 fig, ax = plt.subplots(figsize=(18, 8))
7 ax.imshow(out.get_image()[:, :, ::-1])
```

Finally, this image is shown on our local machine in a new window:

Figure 145:

Performing a different task is as easy as fetching a different model from the `model_zoo`. Each model name has an associated task, such as:

- `COCO-Detection/`
- `COCO-InstanceSegmentation/`
- `COCO-Keypoints/`

We've used an instance segmentation model that segmented each instance of each object it was trained to classify. There's a distinct difference between Person 1 and Person 2, and while they belong to the same label, they're different instances.

Segmentation tasks are handled by Mask R-CNNs. Detection can be done via a RetinaNet or Faster R-CNN. Keypoints are done with a Keypoint R-CNN. Additionally, Detectron2 offers support to perform *panoptic segmentation*, which is effectively the product of instance and semantic segmentation together.

10.5.4 Keypoint Detection with Detectron2

Performing different tasks is as easy as switching the model and plotting the results with *the same code*! That being said, you can perform keypoint inference to form body-like skeletons as easily as switching `COCO-InstanceSegmentation/mask_rcnn_R_50_FPN_3x.yaml` to `COCO-Keypoints/keypoint_rcnn_R_50_FPN_3x.yaml`:

```
response = requests.get('pic_url...')
open("input.jpg", "wb").write(response.content)

im = cv2.imread("./input.jpg")
im = cv2.cvtColor(im, cv2.COLOR_BGR2RGB)

cfg = get_cfg()

config_file = "COCO-Keypoints/keypoint_rcnn_R_50_FPN_3x.yaml"
cfg.merge_from_file(model_zoo.get_config_file(config_file))
cfg.MODEL.ROI_HEADS.SCORE_THRESH_TEST = 0.5
cfg.MODEL.WEIGHTS = model_zoo.get_checkpoint_url(config_file)

predictor = DefaultPredictor(cfg)
outputs = predictor(im)

v = Visualizer(im[:, :, ::-1], MetadataCatalog.get(cfg.DATASETS.TRAIN[0]),
    scale=1.2)
out = v.draw_instance_predictions(outputs["instances"].to("cpu"))
fig, ax = plt.subplots(figsize=(18, 8))
ax.imshow(out.get_image()[:, :, ::-1])
```

This results in:

Figure 146:

Detectron2 detects eyes, ears, the nose, shoulders, elbows, hands, hips, knees and feet, making a fairly effective 3D skeleton of a human. High-quality keypoint detection can replace expensive motion capture suits!

Motion capture suits are mainly used in the entertainment industry, to build CGI models around actors in movies, or video games. Though, motion capture can also be used to replace controller-based instructions for robotics. Instead of using a controller - one could use gestures or arm movement to control robotic arms, rovers or give out commands on a computer program such as *Pinch, Zoom,* etc.

Motion capture can also be applied to sports and live events, as well as creating avatars such as for VTubers (Virtual YouTubers/Streamers, who use animated models to represent characters) and metaverse-type characters (such as VRChat - a Virtual Reality game in which you can upload your own 3D models of characters to represent yourself as). Keypoint detection has implications for research, robotics and self-identity.

10.5.5 Other Detectron2 Projects

Detectron2 includes a few other projects built on top of it, including an implementation for TensorMask, ViTDet, Panoptic DeepLab (including DeepLabV3+) and DensePose. These are all research projects that used Detectron2 as the base library, and built functionality on top of it, after which they were featured under `https://github.com/facebookresearch/detectron2/tree/main/projects`.

10.5.6 Matterport's Mask R-CNN

Matterport's Mask R-CNN[121] is a classic, and Matterport's hosted files can be found in various repositories. The company develops 3D image capture technology, turning 2D images into 3D models, mainly for real estate. They've implemented Mask R-CNN (Faster R-CNN that also outputs a mask of the object, performing instance segmentation) in TensorFlow/Keras that delivered great results. Many solutions that took advantage of Mask R-CNNs were built on top of Matterport's implementation, and it's an influential repo with pull requests and issues being opened even today.

Sadly, it hasn't been updated in a few years, since 2018 and thus has compatability issues with newer versions of TensorFlow and Keras. Additionally, it's a bit more involved than Detectron2, but not much more.

10.5.7 Other Packages

Other packages have been popularized and then lost their popularity due to a lack of updates. Darkflow[122] implemented Darknet for TensorFlow 1, and gained traction. As TensorFlow went out of fashion with PyTorch and TensorFlow 2 - those who could've migrated away from TF 1 did. Don't underestimate frustrated developers! Since there were few YOLOv3 implementations in TensorFlow 2, this repository[123], filled with *"I hate tensorflow"* commit messages, provides a TF 2 implementation of YOLOv3.

PaddlePaddle's PaddleDetection[124] offers 30+ model types combined into 250+ pretrained models in their zoo, in the fields of object detection, keypoint estimation (3D

[121] https://github.com/matterport/Mask_RCNN
[122] https://github.com/thtrieu/darkflow
[123] https://github.com/YunYang1994/tensorflow-yolov3
[124] https://github.com/PaddlePaddle/PaddleDetection

skeletons), instance segmentation, face detection, multi-object tracking, etc. Unless you speak Chinese, navigating the documentation might be difficult for you, but the code is readable for English speakers. PaddlePaddle is an independent R&D company, that specializes in open source neural network development, so it comes natural that they've created a large repository for object detection as well!

FacebookResearch's Detr[125] is a Transformer-based object detection model. They have a great demonstration hosted on Google Colab[126] showcasing inference in 50 lines (most of which are boilerplate - the actual inference is similar to YOLOv5's).

10.6 Object Detection Metrics

I've, perhaps surprisingly, left this section for last, and purposefully omitted some technical details from previous writing. Object detection (oftentimes coupled with instance segmentation) can be a bit overwhelming, is scarcely supported officially from popular frameworks and is a much more specialized form of computer vision than what we've done so far.

To that end, I wanted to lower the barrier to entry and give you a holistic view of it first, as well as a few practical inference examples, before drowning you with some technicalities. The metrics used for object detection are different from those used for image classification. Instead of accuracy - we typically use ***average precision (AP)*** and/or ***mean average precision (mAP)***. Some others include recall and precision. To understand *mean average precision*, which sounds a bit... wrong, it helps if we revisit recall and precision, in the context of object detection, as well as an important metric - IoU.

Let's start with IoU as AP and mAP are calculated through the lens of the IoU threshold. The *Intersection over Union (IoU)* is the proportion of the intersection between the predicted bounding box and ground truth box, and the union of the predicted bounding box and ground truth box:

[125]https://github.com/facebookresearch/detr

[126]https://colab.research.google.com/github/facebookresearch/detr/blob/colab/notebooks/detr_attention.ipynb

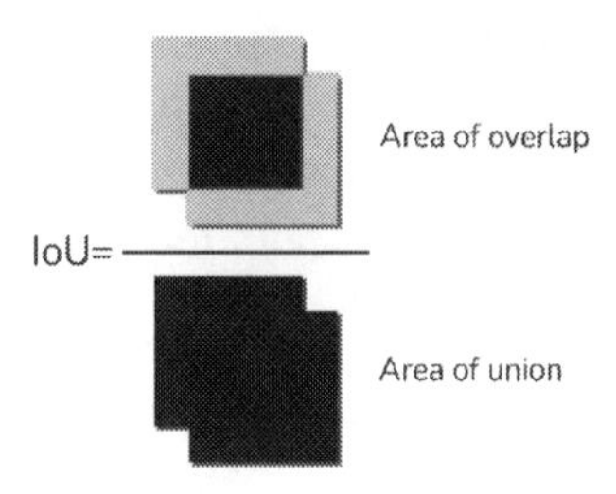

Figure 147:

If the boxes perfectly overlap, the score ends up being 1 (because any number N divided by N will be 1). If the boxes don't overlap, the score will be lower.

An IoU over 0.5 is typically considered a good prediction but this depends on the domain you're working in. Some applications require a more precise IoU to be considered "good".

This score is important because we're not only doing classification! Precision and recall are easy with clear-cut correct or incorrect predictions. However, at which point is the prediction correct with object detection? If the network correctly classifies an object, but places it on the wrong location in the image, we can't really say it's correct. This is why a *threshold* is applied, and we treat low IoU scores as incorrect predictions, even if the label is right.

Precision and recall depend on the IoU, besides the class prediction. Having a lower threshold naturally raises the accepted predictions, and yields higher recall and precision. The IoU threshold is always reported as a parameter when comparing models, and most reports also show the metrics at different IoUs, such as:

- mAP@0.5 = 0.642
- mAP@0.75 = 0.426
- ...

These are read as *"Mean Average Precision at 0.5 IoU threshold"*, etc. So, how do we get Average Precision and Mean Average Precision?

Remember that precision and recall are in a battle of tug-of-war, and an increase in one oftentimes brings about the decrease of the other. You can summarize their relationship in a precision-recall curve, where at Y-Precision, you get X-Recall. There is a point in which you can get the maximum precision and maximum recall for that model - the point closest to the top right corner of the plot:

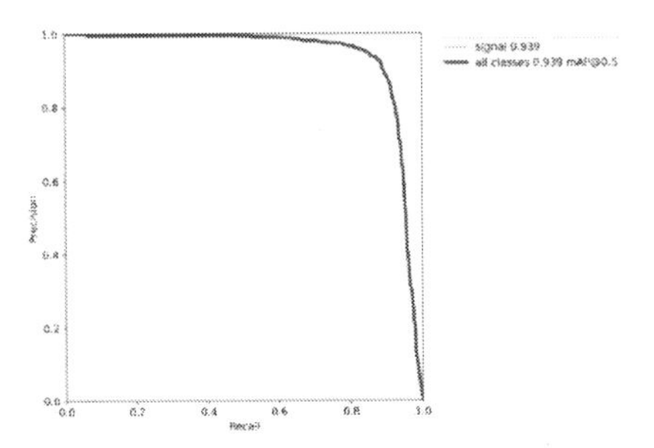

Figure 148:

Though, this curve is, well, a curve. A handy way to assess the precision-recall curve and use it as an actionable metric is by summarizing it into a single number - the area under the curve. This area is the Average Precision, known as AP! When you have more than two classes, you can compute the AP for each class, and the average of these APs is the Mean Average Precision (mAP). While there is a difference between the terms 'average' and 'mean', in this context, it's not too important, and calling something an 'average average precision' wasn't the best idea.

To summarize:

- Average Precision is the area under the precision-recall curve.
- Mean Average Precision is the mean of the APs between classes.
- IoU is the the Area of Intersection divided by the Area of Union - and represents how much a predicted bounding box overlaps with the ground truth, from `0..1`.
- Depending on which IoU we choose as acceptable (threshold for correct predictions), we can compute APs and mAP at that IoU threshold, denoted as ***metric@IoU_threshold*** (such as mAP@0.5).

11 Guided Project: Real-Time Road Sign Detection with YOLOv5

11.1 Real-Time Road Sign Detection

If you drive - there's a chance you enjoy cruising down the road. A responsible driver pays attention to the road signs, and adjusts their speed in accordance to the laws mandating that you follow the speed limit in a given area, amongst other signs that regulate drivers.

Though - what if you miss a sign? Not everyone has a sidekick to also pay attention and to tell them when there's a change in the speed limit or if there's another sign worth acknowledging. Some cars, especially modern ones, are equiped with cameras that *read road signs* in real time and show the current limit on your dashboard. For example, the Citroen C3 has a "Memory" button, which applies the latest noticed speed limit to your cruise control if it's active.

> Wouldn't it be nice to have a system that also watches for road signs and gives you audio cues when it sees one?

Whether it's a speed limit sign, a stop sign, or another sign - having a side passenger that reminds you of the signs can be pretty useful, especially if this side passenger doesn't blink, only watches for the signs, and runs on your phone if your car doesn't already have a system built in. My old car doesn't have this system and I'd love to use my already existing phone to also look out for the signs, with no extra cost. Furthermore, if you're app-savvy, you can integrate the model into an application that plays sounds or audio clips of voices calling the road signs out loud.

> In this guided project, we'll use a mixture of public datasets, and create our own dataset, manually prepare and label it, train and fine-tune a YOLOv5 model with Transfer Learning to detect road signs. We'll then take a look at how PyTorch models are generally deployed to the web with Flask, as well as prepared for deployment to Android and iOS devices. This encapsulates the entire life-cycle of an object detection application.

11.2 YOLOv5 Recap

We've covered YOLO in more detail in the previous lesson and will more be focusing on applying it in a practical setting here, but let's make a quick recap. YOLO is an object detection methodology, upon which a family of models, oftentimes called YOLOv[Version], or other variations.

The methodology works by passing the image through a CNN backbone, and outputing an SxS grid (feature map) which encodes the spatial location of objects of interest, as well as the labels and confidence scores in a single output tensor.

YOLOv1, YOLOv2 and YOLOv3 were created by the same authors, and started the methodology. YOLOv4, YOLOv5 and YOLOv7 were created by individual contributors and companies, and open-sourced. PP-YOLO, YOLOX and YOLOR are some other well-performing models.

> YOLOv7 was released in July of 2022, and the source code and training scripts can be found at the official YOLOv7 GitHub repository[a]. At the time of writing, in July of 2022, it doesn't have a programmatic API that YOLOv5, developed by Ultralytics, does. The previous highest model on the associated PapersWithCode leaderboard was ConvNeXt-XL++, with 9FPS and 55.2 box AP. YOLOv7 had 36FPS with 56.8 box AP. That's real-time!
>
> [a] https://github.com/WongKinYiu/yolov7

Although YOLOv7 does perform better than YOLOv5 by a couple of percentage points in accuracy, the speeds are fairly comparable, and the practicality of YOLOv5's API, export and serving options and rich documentation makes it an easier choice for solving practical problems and deploying solutions.

For inference, the models can easily be loaded on PyTorch's hub:

```
1 import torch
2 model = torch.hub.load('ultralytics/yolov5', 'yolov5n')
3
4 img = '...'
5 model(img).print()
```

Note: PyTorch models accept input and return predictions (outputs) as `model(inputs)`, rather than `model.predict(inputs)`. Keras **also supports the** `model(inputs)` **syntax.** This is actually the recommended syntax for small batch predictions.

For training and inference, you'll want to download the GitHub repository, which includes the entire source code, training and utility scripts:

```
1 $ git clone https://github.com/ultralytics/yolov5
2 $ cd yolov5
3 $ pip install -r requirements.txt
```

Alternatively for inference, you can run the models in the console, like with most other repositories:

```
1 python detect.py --source SOURCE
```

Where the `SOURCE` can be:

- `0` - for your webcam
- `path.jpg/path.png...` - for an image
- `path/` - for a directory
- `path/*.jpg` - for a glob and matching files
- `YouTube link` - for a YouTube video
- HTTP/RTMP/RTSP link - for streaming videos directly into YOLOv5

11.3 YOLOv5 Configurations

You can set various configurations, such as the IoU threshold required for classification, the confidence threshold for displaying detections, number of max detections, automatic mixed precision training (makes training faster and reduces memory requirements with minimal effect on model accuracy/speed, but doesn't work on some GPUs, such as the GTX16xx series), etc.

These are all easily accessible through the `model` instance:

```
1 model.conf = 0.35
2 model.iou = 0.5
```

```
3 model.max_det = 10
4 model.amp = True
```

While loading the model from the hub, you can specify the device you want to run it on:

```
1 model = torch.hub.load('ultralytics/yolov5', 'yolov5n', device = 'gpu')
```

Or, you can set it on the model instance:

```
1 model.cpu()
2 model.gpu()
3 model.to(torch.device(0))
```

Some other optional arguments of the `load()` method include:

- `_verbose=True` - Verbose loading, which displays the version, status, param count, etc. `True` by default.
- `classes=80` - Specifies the number of classes upfront for custom datasets and pre-trained weights. Defaults to `80`.
- `force_reload=False` - Whether you want to re-download the model from the hub again or load it from cache. Helpful in clearing out broken models. Defaults to `False`.

This brings us to the models themselves!

11.4 YOLOv5 Sizes

YOLOv5, like most YOLO-based repositories, offers several sizes of the model, typically going from 'small' to 'large' where there's always a trade off between speed and accuracy.

YOLOv5 classifies the models into 10 categories. The first release had 5:

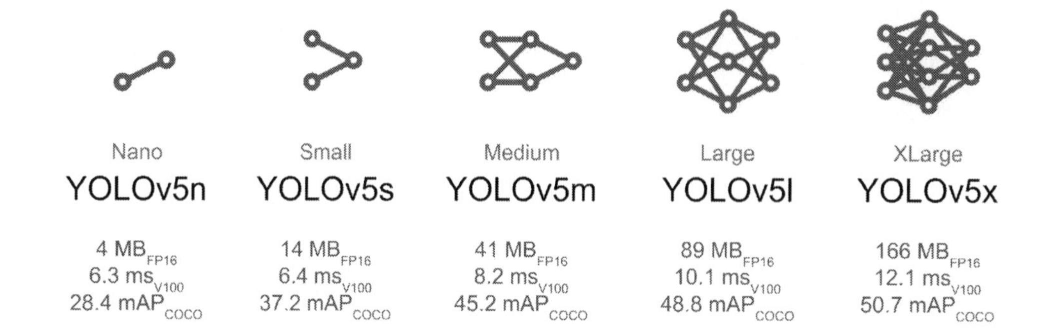

Figure 149:

Though, a new version was released for larger inputs as well, with a suffix of `6` - `YOLOv5n6`, `YOLOv5s6`, ..., `YOLOv5x6`. Generally speaking, YOLOv5 version 6 (version version...) work on bigger input images, provide better accuracy, but are slower than vanilla models.

Depending on the device you'll be running the model on - you'll choose the size that performs real-time enough for you. Running a model on a Raspberry Pi, for example, guarantees similar performance over the same devices. With mobile phones - you can get a wide variety of hardware from $50 to $1500.

> Get to know your users before picking the model size. Better yet, provide multiple models and adjust which one is used automatically based on the hardware, or let the user choose which one they want to use.

11.5 Performing YOLOv5 Object Detection on Videos

Let's do some inference! We've seen examples of inference on images before, so let's do a video. We'll start with the inference script, and then proceed to the programmatic API.

The library relies o `pafy` and `youtube-dl` to download and parse the video, and these might not work all the time. When YouTube introduces new changes to their policies - these libraries might not work for a short time until they're updated. Let's install the dependencies first:

```
1 $ pip install youtube-dl
```

```
2 $ pip install git+https://github.com/Cupcakus/pafy
```

Now, let's run the `detect.py` script:

```
1 $ python detect.py --source 'https://www.youtube.com/watch?v=dQw4w9WgXcQ'
```

This opens up a window next to your console, with the video under inference, outputting the results for each frame:

When the run ends, a message in the terminal lets you know how long it took per image on your device. The example was run on a CPU-based laptop, so the inference time was 194ms per image, which would be more like 6-12ms on a GPU.

Finally, the results are saved in the `runs/detect/expN` directory (each run is one "experiment") under the directory dedicated to YOLOv5 specified while cloning the GitHub repository:

```
1 Speed: 1.3ms pre-process, 194.7ms inference, 1.2ms NMS per image at shape
      (1, 3, 640, 640)
2 Results saved to runs/detect/exp5
```

In the directory - you'll find a video file annotated with the bounding boxes and classes.

Naturally, this can be done with a local file as well, even without the extra dependencies.

Great! Now, how do we do this programatically? Similarly enough - but we'll use OpenCV to read the video, and pass in each frame for inference:

```
# `0` is the webcam
# cap = cv2.VideoCapture(0)
# Alternatively, path to a video
cap = cv2.VideoCapture('tesla.mp4')
while cap.isOpened():
    ret, frame = cap.read()
    results = model(frame)
    cv2.imshow('YOLO', np.squeeze(results.render()))

    if cv2.waitKey(10) & 0xFF == ord('q'):
        break
cap.release()
cv2.destroyAllWindows()
```

Now, this will open a window, and display the results, but won't save the video as an experiment, a screenshot of which can be seen here:

Figure 150:

While we could re-create the logic of saving these frames, combining them back into a video, and saving them under the directory, it loses point and you might as well call the `detect.py` script at that point. This is the basic structure of reading videos and running inference on each frame - you can build on top of this at your leisure.

For instance, you could decide to not save images without any detections, but save the images that have some - such as for say, burglar alarms or security systems that might trigger an alarm if a person is seen on a camera while you're away.

11.6 Export Options

Exporting is dead simple with another utility script. Once a model is trained, as we will train one in the next section - the weights of the model are saved as a `.pt` file. These weights belong to an architecture - and a trained one at that. You can export this file into other formats that can load the weights and run inference.

The `export.py` script accepts a `.pt` file, and exports it into all formats defined after `--include`:

```
1 $ python export.py --weights yolov5s.pt --include onnx tfjs
```

Here, we've exported a hypothetical trained model into ONNX (global model definition language, from which we can export into anything) and also into a TensorFlow JS format, if we for instance know that we'll definitely be using that one soon, keeping an ONNX export for later.

Besides ONNX and TensorFlow JS - the export script accepts pretty much all mainstream formats:

Format	export.py --include	Model
PyTorch	-	yolov5s.pt
TorchScript	torchscript	yolov5s.torchscript
ONNX	onnx	yolov5s.onnx
OpenVINO	openvino	yolov5s_openvino_model/
TensorRT	engine	yolov5s.engine

Format	export.py --include	Model
CoreML	coreml	yolov5s.mlmodel
TensorFlow SavedModel	saved_model	yolov5s_saved_model/
TensorFlow GraphDef	pb	yolov5s.pb
TensorFlow Lite	tflite	yolov5s.tflite
TensorFlow Edge TPU	edgetpu	yolov5s_edgetpu.tflite
TensorFlow.js	tfjs	yolov5s_web_model/

If you're looking for other formats - export to ONNX and then from ONNX to one of the 25 supported formats.

11.7 Freezing and Transfer Learning

You can easily freeze layers and perform transfer learning with frozen layers using a flag while training. The network sizes are defined via `.yaml` files - and each layer has a number associated to it. The backbone layers, are `0..9` for instance, while the entire network (sans the final one) has 24 layers that you can freeze or unfreeze.

The `--freeze` argument of the training script freezes `0..n` layers for the training. To unfreeze the layers, run the script againt without the argument, using the weights of the previous training:

```
1 $ python train.py --freeze 10 --batch 16 --epochs 5 --data data.yaml
      --weights yolov5s.pt
2 ...
3 $ python train.py --batch 16 --epochs 5 --data data.yaml --weights
      path/to/best.pt
```

The default directory has a `yolov5n.pt`, `yolov5s.pt`, and so on as fresh COCO-trained networks to go from, so you can transfer the learning from there to your own network, with frozen layers. Then, you can restart from your fine-tuned frozen network and unfreeze it by loading its weights from the associated `/exp` direcory.

Tip: You can set the floating-point precision to half, using the `--half` argument. This ofentimes brings about significantly lower training times without much loss to the performance.

11.8 Training on Public Roboflow Datasets

Let's start by training the network on some public datasets of road signs. They're fairly universal, but not always identical in the world. YOLOv5 can be instantiated as a blank slate or pre-trained on MS COCO. MS COCO contains images of various objects in context, including traffic lights, cars, buses and trains.

A network pretrained on MS COCO already has a fair bit of knowledge about traffic and objects within traffic, so using Transfer Learning, we can leverage some of that knowledge to make our model more robust and accurate even if we only have small training sets. This is especially helpful since collecting and labelling the data manually takes time and effort and creating a large dataset can be prohibitively expensive, as we'll see in a later section of this project.

> To further decrease reliance on custom-labelled data, and increase the model's robustness, we'll transfer MS COCO weights to a public road sign dataset, and only then fine tune it on our own data.

Let's start with cloning the YOLOv5 repository and installing its dependencies. This is required from training, as the `torch.hub` model is only used for inference:

```
1 $ git clone https://github.com/ultralytics/yolov5
2 $ pip install -r yolov5/requirements.txt
```

This creates a new `yolov5` directory under which the entire source code and utility scripts are.

11.9 Roboflow

We've used Kaggle before - and it's a great source of datasets, but it's not specialized for object detection and you might have issues finding many datasets for it. In addition - the formats are typically fixed, and decided by the uploader. Currently, a large repository of datasets for object detection is hosted by Roboflow - a platform for computer vision. They host datasets, provide labelling software and solutions, support training pipelines and allow you to host your models and interact with their API to send images to it for inference. It works with TensorFlow/Keras, PyTorch, Cloud AutoML Vision, Amazon Rekognition, etc.

While they do host their own datasets - the majority of them are found in the *"Roboflow Universe"*[127], their community where over 90k datasets can be found*.

> Now, not all of these are *really* datasets. If you wish to annotate your dataset using Roboflow, on the free plan, you also have to make the project public.

The Roboflow Universe includes these projects as well, which means that some projects/datasets are 10-image toy sets that someone used while learning about object detection or just playing around to see how it works. Nevertheless, the platform can switch between formats, and lets you export the same dataset for different architectures - in VOC format, YOLO format, etc. This makes it much more agnostic to your use-case than most Kaggle datasets, which are again, typically fixed. Researchers can work in tech X and format Y, upload their dataset, and you can use it with tech Z and format M.

It's exciting to see where Roboflow goes as it grows further! We'll be using Roboflow to find a dataset and download it programatically, taking advantage of their simple API. For custom data collection and preparation, we'll use a free open-source local editor, known as `labelimg` since it's more lightweight, and decouples you from platforms as dependencies.

First, go ahead and open an account on Roboflow Universe. You can peruse and search for datasets there. I've chosen a relatively small dataset, released as part of a paper on applying Mask R-CNNs to detecting traffic signals in Slovenia, TrafficSignals[128]. It only has one class, 'Signal', denoting any sign present in the set. While we'll want to do more than this, it'll be helpful to pre-train the network on more images of traffic signs to etch in the representations into the CNN backbone. We could, naturally, do this with our own custom dataset, but you'll be thankful for less labelling whenever possible.

On the "Download" page of the dataset, you'll be asked to select the version (if applicable) and format (we're using YOLOv5):

[127]https://universe.roboflow.com/

[128]https://universe.roboflow.com/test-cnn/trafficsignals-zgvyv/

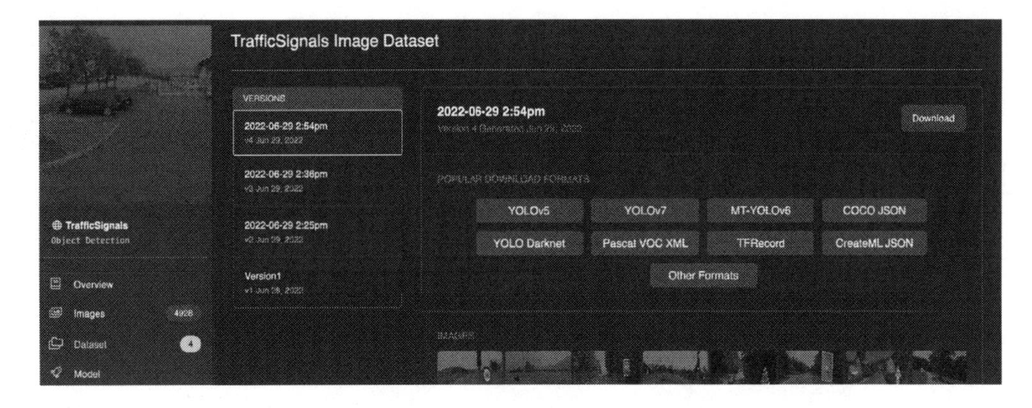

Figure 151:

Then, you'll be prompted to choose between a manual download or a programmatic one:

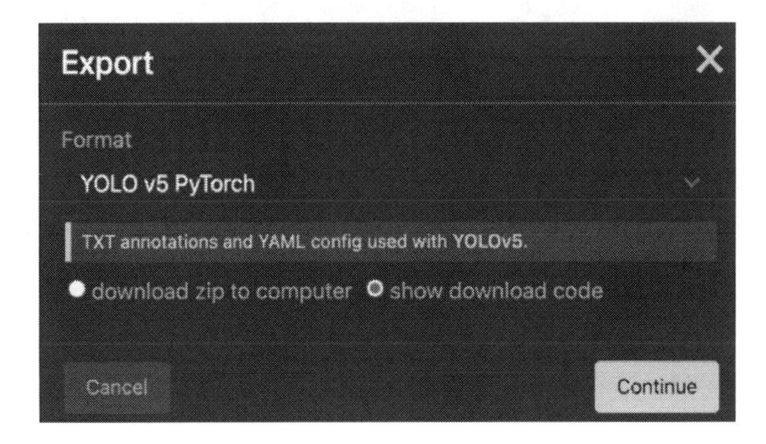

Figure 152:

If programmatic, you can choose between a Jupyter Notebook, the terminal and a raw URL:

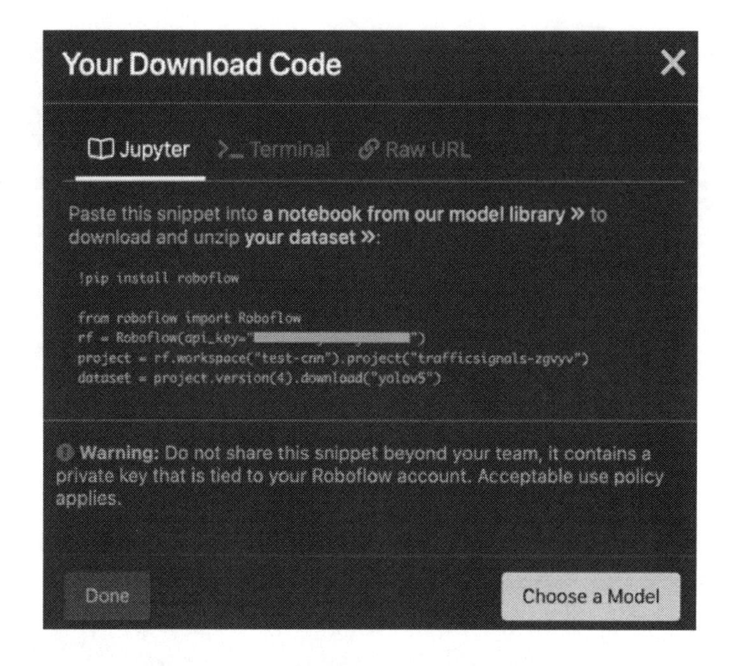

Figure 153:

Let's install the Roboflow package via `pip` and get ahold of the dataset:

```
1 $ pip install opencv-python-headless roboflow
```

Roboflow requires a headless format of OpenCV, which might not be installed on your local machine. On the dataset page, you can get the code for downloading the set, with your API key:

```
1 from roboflow import Roboflow
2 rf = Roboflow(api_key = "[YOUR_KEY_HERE]")
3 project = rf.workspace("test-cnn").project("trafficsignals-zgvyv")
4 dataset = project.version(4).download("yolov5")
```

Quickly enough, the dataset is downloaded:

```
1 loading Roboflow workspace...
2 loading Roboflow project...
3 Downloading Dataset Version Zip in TrafficSignals-4 to yolov5pytorch: 100%
      [145852987 / 145852987] bytes
4 Extracting Dataset Version Zip to TrafficSignals-4 in yolov5pytorch::
      100%|          | 9856/9856 [00:08<00:00, 1198.32it/s]
```

The `dataset` returned is a `roboflow.core.dataset.Dataset` object. You can obtain its location through:

```
dataset.location # /.../TrafficSignals-4
```

11.10 Training YOLOv5 on Roboflow Datasets

Under that location, a `data.yaml` file is served up! YOLOv5 needs this `data.yaml` file as metadata for the training script. It'll define the names of the labels, the number of classes, the location of the images on the disk, etc.:

```
%cat {dataset.location}/data.yaml
# Output:
names: [signal]
nc: 1
train: TrafficSignals-4/train/images
val: TrafficSignals-4/valid/images
```

Please note that the paths are *relative to the root directory,* which by default, isn't mentioned here. Thus, the root directory is considered the directory from which `train.py` is called - the `yolov5` directory.

Our files aren't located there! They're under `/TrafficSignals-4/` not `/yolov5/TrafficSignals-4`. Let's overwrite this file with our own configuration, which does include the root path:

```
import yaml
config = {'path': dataset.location,
          'train': 'train/images',
          'val': 'valid/images',
          'nc': 1,
          'names': ['signal']}

with open(os.path.join(dataset.location, "data.yaml"), "w") as file:
    yaml.dump(config, file, default_flow_style=False)
```

Our root `path` is defined by `dataset.location` so it's no longer inferred to be part of `yolov5`. The `train`, `test` and `val` paths are relative to the root `path`, so we just set `train/images` and `valid/images` instead of the full URLs. Finally, since there's only one class, `'signal'`, we set `nc` to `1` alongside the label supplied as the singular name for the classes. Now, when we inspect `data.yaml`:

```
%cat {dataset.location}/data.yaml
```

```
2 # Output:
3 names:
4 - signal
5 nc: 1
6 path: /content/TrafficSignals-4
7 train: train/images
8 val: valid/images
```

You just need to supply this `data.yaml` file, and a couple of arguments to the `train.py` script, and you're golden!

```
1 $ python3 yolov5/train.py --batch -1 --epochs 10 --data
      {dataset.location}/data.yaml --weights yolov5m.pt
```

:::warn **Advice:** You can also use `%cd yolov5` and run the script from there, but some Jupyter Notebook environments don't 'remember' the changed directory between cells, while some do. To avoid non-cross-compatible notebooks, it's easier to simply include the `yolov5` directory in the script call.

The `--batch -1` argument lets YOLOv5 select the largest batch size your machine can fit, and is a reasonable choice. `--data` should point to the `data.yaml` configuration file, and the optional `--weights` argument corresponds to a `.pt` weights file (PyTorch's saved weight format), from which the training will start. By default, `yolov5n.pt, ... yolov5x.pt` are available in the same directory, under `yolov5`. These are all COCO-pretrained networks and you can use them as a starting checkpoint to train further custom networks. It's always advised to do transfer learning this way. Transfer learning as a concept has been explored in much greater depths in an earlier lesson, so I'm skipping the obvious benefits here.

This script will train a YOLOv5 detector. If verbose, the output will first be populated with the metadata for the detector:

```
1 /content/yolov5
2 train: weights=yolov5m.pt, cfg=, data=/content/TrafficSignals-4/data.yaml,
      hyp=data/hyps/hyp.scratch-low.yaml, ...
3 github: skipping check (Docker image), for updates see
      https://github.com/ultralytics/yolov5
4 YOLOv5   v6.1-344-g0e165c5 Python-3.7.13 torch-1.12.0+cu113 CUDA:0 (Tesla
      T4, 15110MiB)
5
```

```
6 hyperparameters: lr0=0.01, lrf=0.01, momentum=0.937, weight_decay=0.0005,
      warmup_epochs=3.0, ...
7 Weights & Biases: run 'pip install wandb' to automatically track and
      visualize YOLOv5   runs (RECOMMENDED)
8 TensorBoard: Start with 'tensorboard --logdir runs/train', view at
      http://localhost:6006/
9 Overriding model.yaml nc=80 with nc=1
```

And then, with the network definition (the 24 sections that comprise YOLO):

```
1                   from  n    params  module
                          arguments
2  0                  -1  1      5280  models.common.Conv
      [3, 48, 6, 2, 2]
3  1                  -1  1     41664  models.common.Conv
      [48, 96, 3, 2]
4 ...
5 24        [17, 20, 23]  1     24246  models.yolo.Detect
      [1, [[10, 13, 16, 30, 33, 23], ...
6 Model summary: 369 layers, 20871318 parameters, 20871318 gradients, 48.2
      GFLOPs
```

This is followed by checks and configurations that make it easier for you to get ahold of what's going on within the network. It's advised to spend some time reading through the logs to get a better sense of what's going on inside. This is topped off with the number of dataloaders used and the directory in which the results will be logged in:

```
1 Image sizes 640 train, 640 val
2 Using 2 dataloader workers
3 Logging results to runs/train/exp
4 Starting training for 10 epochs...
5
6      Epoch    gpu_mem       box       obj       cls    labels  img_size
7        0/9      12.8G   0.06955   0.02436         0        13       640: 100%
        94/94 [01:45<00:00,  1.13s/it]
8                 Class     Images     Labels          P          R     mAP@.5
                    mAP@.5:.95: 100% 14/14 [00:15<00:00,  1.09s/it]
9                   all       1005       1401       0.48      0.624        0.5
                 0.277
10 ...
11 Epoch    gpu_mem       box       obj       cls    labels  img_size
12        9/9      12.6G   0.01356  0.005207         0         3       640: 100%
        94/94 [01:33<00:00,  1.00it/s]
13                Class     Images     Labels          P          R     mAP@.5
                    mAP@.5:.95: 100% 14/14 [00:14<00:00,  1.01s/it]
14                  all       1005       1401      0.929      0.894      0.951
                 0.781
```

Note: Some machines will throw an error when training on multiple dataloaders. This is easily fixed with `--workers 1` in the `train.py` call. Also, AMP (automatic mixed precision) doesn't seem to work as expected on some GPUs (such as the GTX16xx series). This seems to be an issue with the underlying systems and hardware, not the YOLOv5 project. These bugs are transient and might be fixed or worked around through time. If you're having any issues running the project on your local machine, Google Colab works great with YOLOv5!

11.11 Evaluating a YOLOv5 Model

Great! We've trained an object detection model on a public dataset, using transfer learning. The "experiment" is saved under the `yolov5/runs/train/exp` folder (if it's the first run). For each training run, a new `exp` directory will be made, named `expN` where `N` is the run you're performing.

Within, `exp`, there are several files and a folder:

```
$ ls yolov5/runs/train/exp

confusion_matrix.png                       results.png
events.out.tfevents.1659531782.947dde14df06.280.0  train_batch0.jpg
F1_curve.png                           train_batch1.jpg
hyp.yaml                           train_batch2.jpg
labels_correlogram.jpg                      val_batch0_labels.jpg
labels.jpg                         val_batch0_pred.jpg
opt.yaml                           val_batch1_labels.jpg
P_curve.png                        val_batch1_pred.jpg
PR_curve.png                           val_batch2_labels.jpg
R_curve.png                        val_batch2_pred.jpg
results.csv                        weights
```

The `weights` directory contains `last.py` and `best.pt`, denoting the state of the model at the end of the last epoch, and the state of the model when it had the best validation metrics, considering the `valid` set from the `data.yaml` configuration. You can export these files onto other formats for deployment, or simply use them as a checkpoint for further training like we will.

The hyperparameters used are saved under `hyp.yaml`, to make it easier to inspect and share them (and reproduce configurations for other practitioners), as opposed through going through the verbose output from before:

```
! cat yolov5/runs/train/exp/hyp.yaml
# Output:
lr0: 0.01
lrf: 0.01
momentum: 0.937
weight_decay: 0.0005
warmup_epochs: 3.0
warmup_momentum: 0.8
warmup_bias_lr: 0.1
box: 0.05
cls: 0.5
cls_pw: 1.0
obj: 1.0
obj_pw: 1.0
iou_t: 0.2
...
```

Other than that, you've already got a sleuth of performance graphs plotted, such as the F1, Precision and Recall curves, including the Precision-Recall curve (`PR_curve.png`):

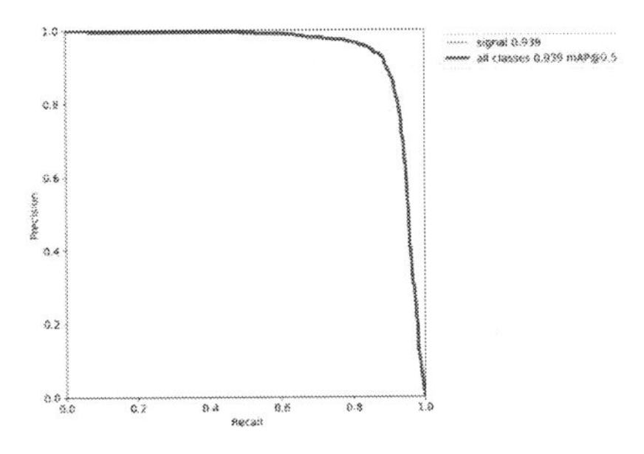

Figure 154:

The results of the "experiment" saved under `results.csv` and plotted under `results.png`:

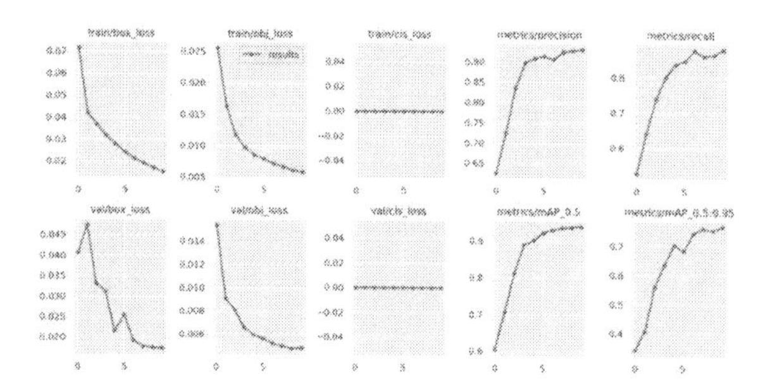

Figure 155:

You can inspect the learning curves for recall, precision and mAP here, with mAP at a fixed 0.5 IoU threshold and the average mAP between 0.5 and 0.95 IoU threshold, with a step size of 0.05 and denoted as `mAP_0.5:0.95` here. In addition, you can inspect the loss curves.

The `box_loss`, `obj_loss` and `cls_loss` are the three losses YOLO uses. `box_loss` is for box regression. `obj_loss` is for classifying whether an object is there or not (also known as objectness). This loss doesn't care what the object is, but only whether something that is an object of interest is present. `cls_loss` is the classification loss. Since we only have one class, it's flat, as the class doesn't really matter for this dataset - as long as there's an object, it'll be of class `signal`.

The bottom plots indicate the losses on the validation set, which are similar to the training losses in our case.

Furthermore, there's a confusion matrix:

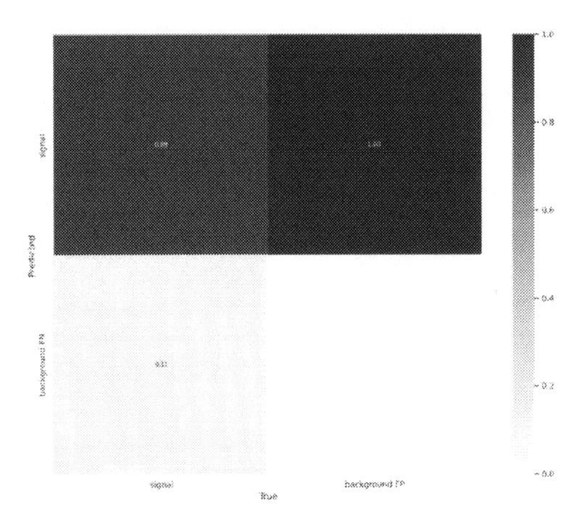

Figure 156:

The information on labels and the count of distinct labels in the set (`labels.png`):

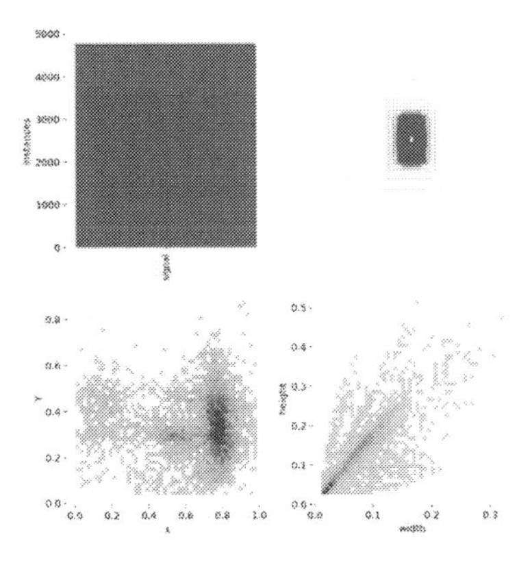

Figure 157:

Here, for example, we can clearly see that most of the signs are located on the right of the image, as can and should be expected from roads in countries where you drive on the right side of the road. Though, this would also mean that we should evaluate our model on examples from countries where cars are driven on the left side of the road, such as the UK, Japan, Australia and India.

The label correlogram gives us a bit more insight into labels:

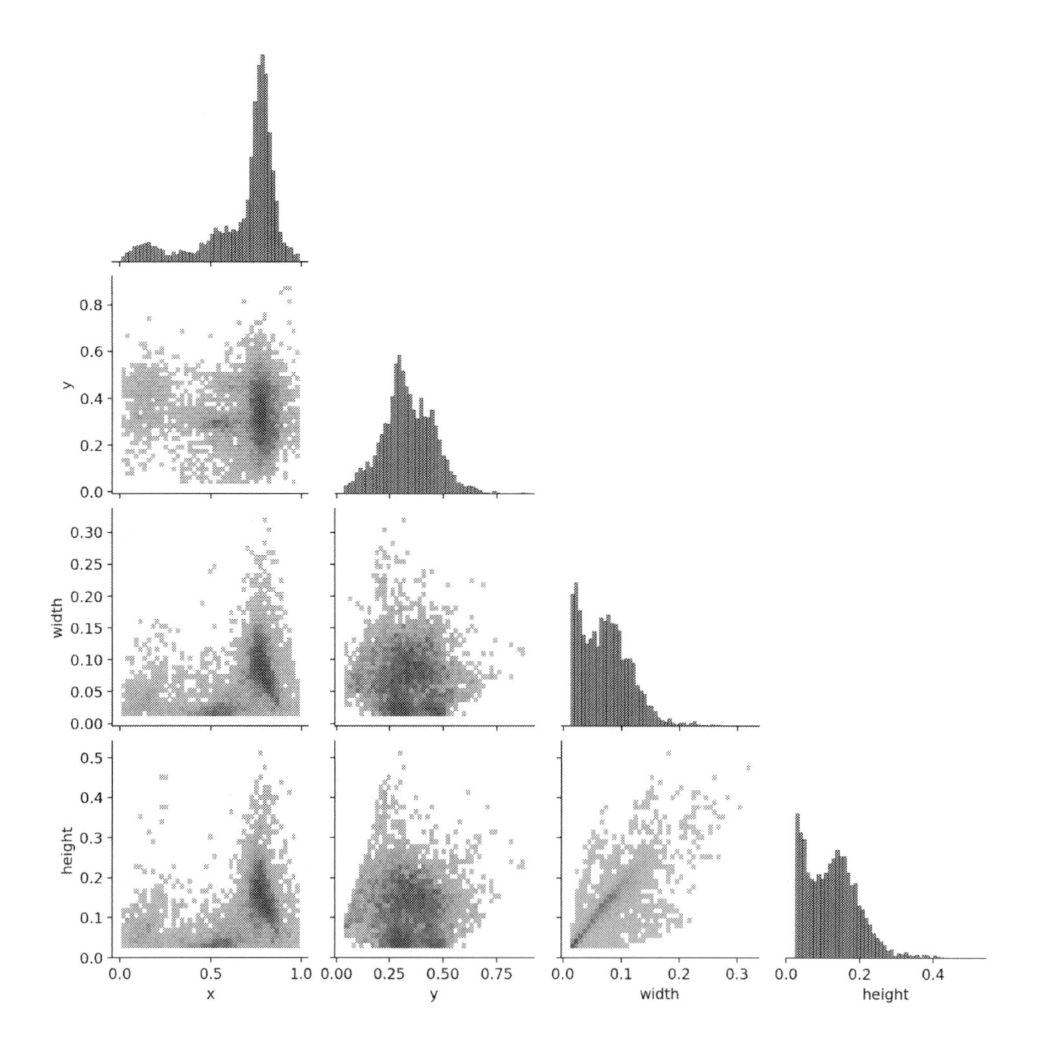

Figure 158:

As well as the training and validation batches (each stiched together into a single image). For example, `val_batch0_labels.png`:

Figure 159:

And the predictions on those batches (for example, `val_batch0_pred`):

Figure 160:

We can see that a pizzeria sign was misclassified as a signal (let's be fair, it's round and in the position to be a traffic sign...), but also that some signs far away are also detected! Take some time to go through all of the exported plots.

Now, let's transfer this network to our own task at hand!

11.12 Data Collection, Labelling and Preprocessing

Let's go ahead and get to the crux of the project. Data collection, labelling and preprocessing.

Object detection is a specialized application of computer vision, and typically, you'll need to detect something specific for a niche you're working in, such as the unique anomalies that can occur in a specific toy factory, on the line 25.

Each dataset will be relatively unique, so it'll be harder to find datasets to pre-train on, but not impossible. Transferring *something* is better than transferring nothing. You might be lucky enough that a team has gone out of their way to label the data for you and provide you with the clean files to work with, so you can call the `train.py` script and everything works!

11.13 Data Collection

More commonly, you'll be collecting your own data and labelling it yourself. Since local traffic signs will always be at least a tiny bit different (their frequency, positions and style) between countries - this is a great time for a little excercise! If you own a car, attach a phone to act as a dash cam, and record a few minutes of representative driving through your neighborhood. If you don't own a car, kindly ask a public bus driver to stand in the front to record. If all else fails, download a dashcam video from the internet.

Depending on the video you take, your labels might be different. For practical purposes, you'll want hours of footage in various terrains, lighting conditions, etc. or at least a good sample size of each sign you want to classify. Since this isn't always feasible, taking a smaller set and augmenting it is a fine substitute.

> We'll make it hard on ourselves and only use a couple of minutes of footage, but we will work with a smaller amount of labels - just 5.

To make it easier for you to reproduce the results, I'll be using a public video[129] rather than a custom one. It's a ~1h long video so there's plenty more to unpack if you so wish. While it's filmed in 4K, you can use smaller resolutions, in anticipation of the device you'll be using the model on, as well as computational efficiency.

[129] https://www.youtube.com/watch?v=C911U_Fo-QU

I've extracted the video between 1:00 and 3:30 minutes, and that will become our data to work with.

Note: We'd ideally want to create a training, testing and validation set from totally different timestamps in the video, or to even have them interlaced. With short timespans, such as 2.5min, there's a high probability that the signs seen in the first minute might not be present at all in the second minute. Segmenting the training, testing and validation sets from here would yield illusory low performance. Only when you can expect a reasonably equal distribution of signs between the sets would that approach be accurate, and this would usually come from larger datasets.

Taking a look at the video - say we want to classify these four signs, plus the traffic light:

```
1 labels = ['crossing',
2           'parking',
3           'wrong way',
4           'no vehicles',
5           'traffic light']
```

We'll want to create a classname/label map, where each classname has an associated label (number) for the model to predict. Additionally, it's useful to create some global locations for the directories in which we'll hold our images and label files (that hold the coordinates for the ground truth bounding boxes):

```
1 IMAGES_PATH = os.path.join('drive-data', 'images') #/data/images
2 LABELS_PATH = os.path.join('drive-data', 'labels') #/data/labels
3
4 classnames = ['crossing',
5               'parking',
6               'wrong way',
7               'no vehicles',
8               'traffic light']
9
10 labels = {
11     'crossing' : 0,
12     'parking' : 1,
13     'wrong way' : 2,
```

```
14     'no vehicles' : 3,
15     'traffic light' : 4
16
17 }
```

Let's create the directory for our dataset, `drive-data`, and the `images` and `labels` directories under it. Since YOLOv5 expects pointers to the `train`, `test` and `valid` directories, we'll create those too:

On Windows:

```
1 $ mkdir drive-data
2 $ mkdir drive-data\images\train
3 $ mkdir drive-data\images\test
4 $ mkdir drive-data\images\valid
5
6 $ mkdir drive-data\labels\train
7 $ mkdir drive-data\labels\test
8 $ mkdir drive-data\labels\valid
```

On Linux/MacOS:

```
1 $ mkdir drive-data
2 $ mkdir drive-data/images
3 $ mkdir drive-data/labels
4
5 $ mkdir drive-data/images/train
6 $ mkdir drive-data/images/test
7 $ mkdir drive-data/images/valid
8
9 $ mkdir drive-data/labels/train
10 $ mkdir drive-data/labels/test
11 $ mkdir drive-data/labels/valid
```

Now - data collection! You could collect data from various sources. It could be a video, a set of images, or even a live collection script. For instance, you could hook up your webcam to collect N images for each name in our `classnames`:

```
1 import time
2 def collect_from_webcam(num_samples):
3     # Webcam capture
4     cap = cv2.VideoCapture(0)
5     # Collect N images for each class
6     for name in classnames:
7         print('Collecting images for {}'.format(name))
8         time.sleep(5)
9
10        for img_num in range(num_samples):
11            print(f"Collecting images for name '{name}', image number
                  {img_num}")
```

```
12            ret, frame = cap.read()
13            imgname = os.path.join(IMAGES_PATH, f"{name}-{img_num}.jpg")
14            cv2.imwrite(imgname, frame)
15            cv2.imshow('Image Collection', frame)
16            time.sleep(2)
17
18            if cv2.waitKey(10) & 0xFF == ord('q'):
19                break
20        cap.release()
21        cv2.destroyAllWindows()
22        cv2.waitKey(1)
```

This is fine for learning purposes, as the specific conditions of the webcam are probably not going to be present in other sets, unless you're creating a product that works from webcams. In that case, bundle this method as a script and forward it to your friends and family to get a decent dataset to work with!

In our case, we'll working with the downloaded video. The flow isn't much different from before, other than that we have no clue what the labels might be. Using OpenCV, we can know the Frames per Second (FPS) and length of the video in frames before starting to work with it. This is a 29.97FPS video, lasting 150s, so we're looking at nearly 4500 images to label.

There are a couple of issues with this:

- 4500 images
- A lot of these images are of the same object in a similar setting. Say that a sign is present in the video for a second - that's 30 images of that sign, in that spot, with those lighting conditions. YOLOv5 does use augmentations on images, so we probably won't overfit badly on it, but it's just redundant and more expensive than it needs to be. Additionally, you don't really want to spend multiple afternoons labeling these! Lowering the number of images to label is crucial.

That being said, we won't extract every frame, but every Nth frame, dictated by the `sampling_rate`. I'll set the default to 30, marking a frame every second. You can decide to go even higher, to 60, 120 or even 300 with significantly longer videos, as long as you produce a dataset of suitable length in the end. Choosing a higher sampling rate means fewer instances of already seen signs, making the detector more robust to other environmental effects.

Let's create a `video_to_frames()` method that accepts a path and extracts a video into frames:

```
1 import cv2
2 video_path = 'madrid_drive.mp4'
3
4 # Path, take every 30th frame (1s),
5 def video_to_frames(path, sampling_rate=30, verbose=True):
6     cap = cv2.VideoCapture(path)
7     # Get FPS, frame count, and calc duration
8     fps = cap.get(cv2.CAP_PROP_FPS)
9     frame_count = int(cap.get(cv2.CAP_PROP_FRAME_COUNT))
10    duration = int(frame_count/fps)
11
12    ret, frame = cap.read()
13    img_num = 0
14    failed = []
15    if verbose:
16        print(f'Processing video {video_path}... \nFPS: {fps}. \nFrame
              Count: {frame_count} \nDuration: {duration}s \nSampling rate:
              {sampling_rate}')
17    for img_num in range(frame_count+1):
18        ret, frame = cap.read()
19        if img_num%30==0:
20            if ret:
21                imgname = os.path.join(IMAGES_PATH,
                      f"{int(img_num/sampling_rate)}.jpg")
22                cv2.imwrite(imgname, frame)
23                if verbose:
24                    print(f'Processed frame
                          {int(img_num/sampling_rate)}/{duration}', end = '\r')
25            else:
26                failed.append(int(img_num/sampling_rate))
27        img_num += 1
28    if verbose:
29        print(f'Failed to process frames: {failed}')
30    print('Processing done.')
31
32    return int(img_num/sampling_rate)-len(failed)
33
34 img_num = video_to_frames(video_path)
```

Since frame reading can sometimes fail, we keep track of a `failed` list, and the frames that OpenCV failed to load.

Advice: When processing data, just printing the output might not be too pretty or readable. You can override the previous `print()` statement with `end = '\r'`! Here, we print the same message, `Processed frame n/m`, so instead of sequentially printing it out, we can contain it to a single line which makes it much more readable, and looks like a progress bar.

Running this code starts with:

```
Processing video madrid_drive.mp4...
FPS: 29.97002997002997.
Frame Count: 4498
Duration: 150s
Sampling rate: 30
Processing frame 1/150
```

And ends with:

```
Processing video madrid_drive.mp4...
FPS: 29.97002997002997.
Frame Count: 4498
Duration: 150s
Sampling rate: 30
Failed to process frames: [147, 148, 149]
Processing done.
```

Great! We've extracted every 30th frame to our `IMAGES_PATH` directory. This directory has `train`, `test` and `valid` folders besides these images. We could've also saved them in a `temp` folder to delete later. We'll now label these images, separate them out into different sets and train our model.

11.14 Data Labelling

Labelling isn't the favorite activity of most, and various tools can be used. Some of the oldschool tools include VGG Image Annotator (VIA)[130], developed by the same group that developed VGGNets.

Nowadays, there are various online services, such as V7, Roboflow, Label-Studio, etc. that let you annotate images in rich environments. The landscape is changing frequently, so I won't recommend any specific product - but you can do your own research and pick one that you personally enjoy.

Note that many of the web-based tools require you to open up an account, and as is the case with Roboflow, to make the dataset public if you're on the free tier. This might be a deal breaker to some, and introduces an extra step that isn't required. Because of this,

[130] https://www.robots.ox.ac.uk/~vgg/software/via/

many prefer working with local environment/offline tools, such as LabelImg, which is an open-source, desktop-based tool for image labeling, with support for VOC, YOLO and CreateML formats.

It's a bit finicky, with a couple of smaller bugs, so it might crash if you don't use it correctly, but if you follow the instructions from this lesson, you shouldn't have any issues.

Let's install it:

```
1 $ pip install labelImg
```

Then, let's save our classnames in a `classes.txt` file in the same directory that'll hold our labels:

```
1 def save_classnames():
2     # Where LabelImg will store labels
3     with open(f'{LABELS_PATH}/classes.txt', 'w+') as f:
4         for name in classnames:
5             f.write(f'{name}\n')
6
7 save_classnames()
```

Now, we can start up `labelimg`:

```
1 $ labelimg
```

This boots up the LabelImg interface:

Figure 161:

First, open the directory to read from - `drive-data/images` by going to "Open Dir" on the left of the interface:

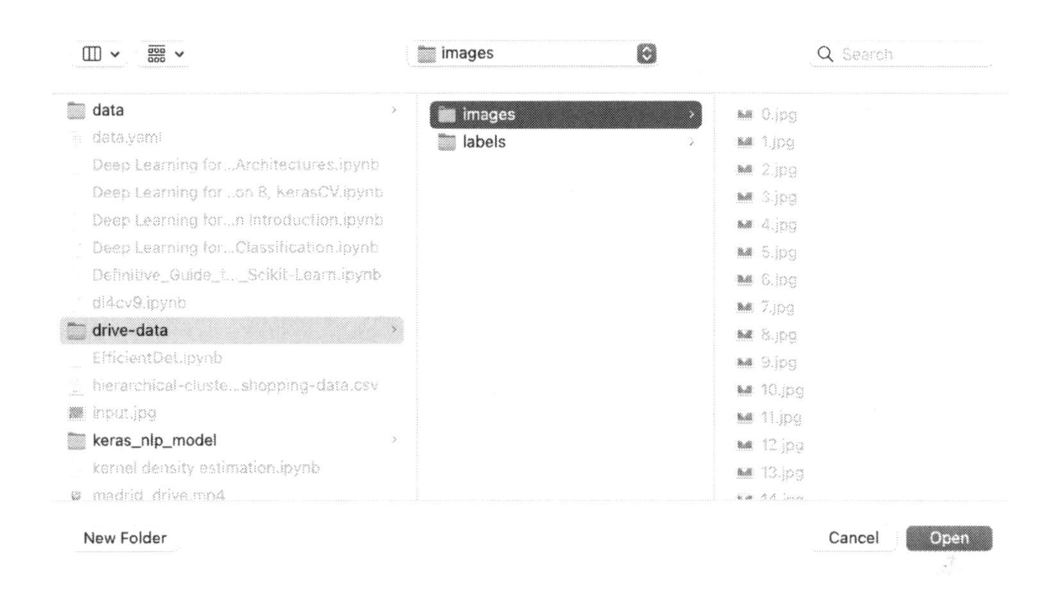

Figure 162:

Once selected, go to *"Change Save Dir"* to set where the labels are to be saved, and choose the `drive-data/labels` directory. Once that's done - you can start annotating! You can draw bounding boxes by clicking *'Create RectBox'* on the bottom of the toolbar on the left:

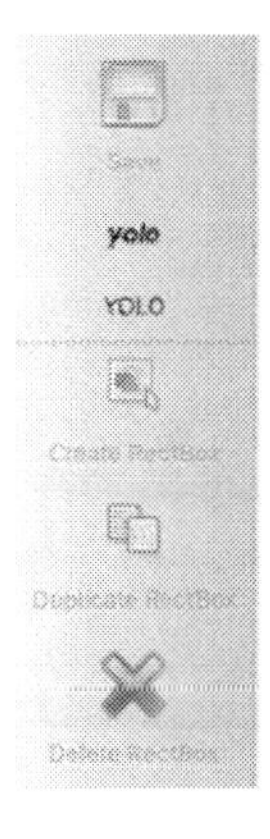

Figure 163:

There, you also select the format for the label - whether you want it to be saved as an XML file for Pascal VOC, as a text file for YOLO or as a JSON file for CreateML. Alternatively, you can use the *'W'* shortcut to create a RectBox:

Figure 164:

Once created, you're prompted to supply a label. Enter the label and click *'OK'*. Repeat this for all objects you'd like to detect in the image:

Figure 165:

Continue this until the last image! Datasets tend to be much larger than this, and may require domain knowledge to label (such as medical images, for example). This is the most laborious and expensive step of the project.

11.15 Labelling Tips

Here are a few labelling tips:

- Encompass the entire object, but minimise the background around it.
- Be consistent with what an object is. For instance, if your objects are hands, and you include all fingers in the first N images, but image N+1 has a hand with a thumb to the other side and including it would include some background - stay consistent. All fingers it should be.
- Label an object even if you can't see it in full.
- Label every object for the given class in the image.
- Many overlapping objects and thus bounding boxes will make it hard for the model to learn.

- Be weary of diagonal objects - to capture a diagonal object, you might have to include a lot of the background.
- You can switch between images using *'A'* and *'D'* - no need to take your left hand off the keyboard.
- LabelImg remembers the last label, and will autofill the box with the last label, which you can apply with *'Enter'*. This makes it easier to label all instances of the same object, in all images, and then go back, for the second label, rather than doing the entire first image, and then the entire second image, etc.
- Use foresight. You can go back and forward in time here - if you're unsure what an object is, go forward in time, check, and go back and annotate it, unless it's so small that the model can't distinguish between it and the background.
- Remember this sequence by rote: ***W -> Mouse -> Enter -> CTRL (CMD) + S -> D***. Once you get the hang of it, you'll be going through each individual image quickly!

Once you've gone through all of the images - close LabelImg. Some images won't have any labels associated with them, as no objects show up. Don't worry about these.

11.16 Train, Test, Validation Splits

Time to get our images and labels assorted into the appropriate folders. Now, they aren't structured currently, and aren't linked. We'll want to create a mapping between images and labels so that we can put the appropriate images with the appropriate labels in the same directory. Since we labelled our files as `0..N.png` and `0..N.txt`, we can create a simple loop that anticipates the filenames for both directories and add them to a dictionary, or more conveniently, a `DataFrame`:

```
1 image_text_mapping = {}
2
3 for label in labels:
4     for n in range(img_num):
5         imgname = os.path.join(IMAGES_PATH, f"{n}.jpg")
6         textname = os.path.join(LABELS_PATH, f"{n}.txt")
7         image_text_mapping[imgname] = textname
8
9 df = pd.DataFrame(image_text_mapping.items(), columns=['Img Path', 'Text
    Path'])
10 df.head(10)
```

This returns:

```
                              Img Path                          Text Path
0  drive-data/images/crossing-0.jpg  drive-data/labels/crossing-0.txt
1  drive-data/images/crossing-1.jpg  drive-data/labels/crossing-1.txt
2  drive-data/images/crossing-2.jpg  drive-data/labels/crossing-2.txt
3  drive-data/images/crossing-3.jpg  drive-data/labels/crossing-3.txt
4  drive-data/images/crossing-4.jpg  drive-data/labels/crossing-4.txt
5  drive-data/images/crossing-5.jpg  drive-data/labels/crossing-5.txt
6  drive-data/images/crossing-6.jpg  drive-data/labels/crossing-6.txt
7  drive-data/images/crossing-7.jpg  drive-data/labels/crossing-7.txt
8  drive-data/images/crossing-8.jpg  drive-data/labels/crossing-8.txt
9  drive-data/images/crossing-9.jpg  drive-data/labels/crossing-9.txt
```

Now, we know that some of these don't exist! Some images didn't load properly via OpenCV and some images don't have any associated labels. You can clear these out with an `os.path.exists()` check before creating the mapping, or while using them in a moment - it makes no difference. Let's split these mappings into a `train`, `test` and `valid` set:

```
from sklearn.datasets import load_iris
from sklearn.model_selection import train_test_split

train_df, test_df = train_test_split(df, train_size=0.8)
train_df, valid_df = train_test_split(train_df, train_size=0.9)
```

This results in:

```
train_df.shape # (104, 2)
test_df.shape. # (30, 2)
valid_df.shape # (12, 2)
```

Finally, once we've assorted our mappings randomly to the sets, we can iterate through them, and move the associated image and label files into the desired directories:

```
import shutil

def df_to_dir(df, set_name):
    for index, row in df.iterrows():
      # Only move if this file exists
      if os.path.exists(row['Img Path']):
           img_name = os.path.split(row['Img Path'])[1]
           shutil.copyfile(row['Img Path'], os.path.join(IMAGES_PATH,
                set_name, img_name))
           os.remove(row['Img Path'])
      # Only move if this file exists
      if os.path.exists(row['Text Path']):
          txt_name = os.path.split(row['Text Path'])[1]
          shutil.copyfile(row['Text Path'], os.path.join(LABELS_PATH,
               set_name, txt_name))
          os.remove(row['Text Path'])
```

We can then use this method to move our files:

```
df_to_dir(train_df, 'train')
df_to_dir(test_df, 'test')
df_to_dir(valid_df, 'valid')
```

Great! Our `images` and `labels` folders aren't full anymore, and the files are neatly assorted into their respective directories. We've got all the info needed to create a `data.yaml` file and train our model.

11.17 Training a YOLOv5 Model on Custom Data

With the images and labels set in their respective folders, we can start training our model! Let's create a `data.yaml` file that encompasses the information required for the `train.py` script:

```
import yaml
config = {'path': os.path.join(os.getcwd(), 'drive-data'),
          'train': 'images/train',
          'test': 'images/test',
          'val': 'images/valid',
          'nc': len(labels),
          'names': labels}

with open(os.path.join("drive-data", "data.yaml"), "w") as file:
    yaml.dump(config, file, default_flow_style=False)
```

11.18 Training

We'll initiate the training script as last time - but with a larger number of epochs, and loading the weights from the previous run, rather than from the network that was just pre-trained on MS COCO:

```
$ python3 yolov5/train.py --batch -1 --epochs 100 --data
    drive-data/data.yaml --weights yolov5/runs/train/exp/weights/best.pt
```

This kicks off a relatively short training session, as our dataset is fairly small:

```
Image sizes 640 train, 640 val
Using 2 dataloader workers
Logging results to yolov5/runs/train/exp2
Starting training for 100 epochs...

```

```
6       Epoch    gpu_mem       box        obj        cls    labels  img_size
7        0/99      7.74G    0.1108    0.02974    0.04983        67       640: 100%
         2/2 [00:08<00:00,  4.20s/it]
8                  Class     Images     Labels          P          R      mAP@.5
                     mAP@.5:.95: 100% 1/1 [00:00<00:00,  1.15it/s]
9                    all         12         17          0          0          0
                         0
10 ...
11 Epoch    gpu_mem       box        obj        cls    labels  img_size
12      99/99      12.9G   0.02097   0.007557    0.01709        88       640: 100%
         2/2 [00:05<00:00,  2.73s/it]
13                 Class     Images     Labels          P          R      mAP@.5
                     mAP@.5:.95: 100% 1/1 [00:00<00:00,  4.51it/s]
14                   all         12         17      0.735      0.611      0.638
                     0.413
15
16 100 epochs completed in 0.182 hours.
17 Optimizer stripped from yolov5/runs/train/exp2/weights/last.pt, 14.4MB
18 Optimizer stripped from yolov5/runs/train/exp2/weights/best.pt, 14.4MB
19
20 Validating yolov5/runs/train/exp2/weights/best.pt...
21 Fusing layers...
22 Model summary: 213 layers, 7023610 parameters, 0 gradients, 15.8 GFLOPs
23 ...
```

As soon as the training is done - you can see the training time, model size and a classification report for the classes from your dataset. Precision, recall, mAP@0.5 and mAP@0.5:.95 are shown for each class:

```
1                  Class     Images     Labels          P          R      mAP@.5
                     mAP@.5:.95: 100% 1/1 [00:00<00:00,  3.89it/s]
2                    all         12         17      0.736      0.631      0.639
                     0.423
3               crossing         12          9      0.894      0.889      0.968
                 0.55
4              wrong way         12          4          1          0       0.19
             0.0772
5            no vehicles         12          3      0.485      0.637      0.403
               0.17
6          traffic light         12          1      0.565          1      0.995
              0.895
7 Results saved to yolov5/runs/train/exp2
```

We clearly have a disbalance in the labels - the short video didn't have a uniform sample between traffic signs. Because of this, some classes have a high recall and lower precision or vice versa. The 'wrong way' sign has a really low mAP, so the model is obviously struggling at recognizing them, but again, consider how small the dataset is. The metrics become much more actionable only on much larger scales.

Nevertheless, let's load the model in from the weights, and do some inference on the test set, and then employ it on a video like before.

11.19 Inference

To load a custom model, we'll use the same `torch.hub.load()` method, but instead of the template, such as `'yolov5n'`, we'll supply `'custom'` and point to our weights file - `yolov5/runs/train/exp2/weights/best.pt`:

```
model = torch.hub.load('ultralytics/yolov5',
                       'custom',
                       path = 'yolov5/runs/train/exp2/weights/best.pt')
```

You can use this model as a regular model now - passing the input to it as `model(input)` and plotting the results as earlier. Let's load some image from the test set and plot it for a quick check:

```
path = os.path.join(IMAGES_PATH, 'test', '15.jpg')
results = model(path)
results.print()
# image 1/1: 720x1280 1 crossing
# Speed: 79.7ms pre-process, 47.2ms inference, 2.4ms NMS per image at shape
    (1, 3, 384, 640)

%matplotlib inline
fig, ax = plt.subplots(figsize=(16, 6))
ax.imshow(results.render()[0])
```

Figure 166:

Awesome! Whether you call this model in a loop, such as loading a video or through the console - it's ready to be deployed. Speaking of which, how could you deploy this model? Deployment can be technical or non-technical, simple or complex.

It really depends on where you want to take the model. Let's take a look at some options.

11.20 Deploying a YOLOv5 Model to Flask, Android and iOS

Hosting platforms that offer **Inference as a Service** are more numerous now than ever before. Roboflow is one of them - and you can upload your model to Roboflow, which will host it and spin up an API that you can send images to and receive predictions from.

This is a low-code solution, but doesn't let you have the good old control over the system. Some prefer deploying the model to their own servers and applications, such as creating a Flask app, and serving an endpoint that acts as an API for your model's inference. Spinning up a Flask REST API takes a minute or so, especially when you consider that the prediction your model will make is essentially a mathematical function call on the input.

Finally - you may decide to totally skip APIs and directly deploy a model to a phone or an edge device such as an Arduino or Raspberry Pi. Platform GUIs and offering's change, so if you want to deploy to a platform to host the model - they usually have a nicely detailed, simple tutorial page.

In this section, I'll focus on spinning up a Flask API and deploying to an iOS/Android device. Mobile development is a very separate skillset, and it out of scope for this book. I'll cover the process of preparing models for mobile phones, and loading them in the respective environments, but will assume experience with Android/iOS development on your part as it is required to make any actual use of the model once it reaches the environment.

11.21 Deploying a Model to a Flask REST API

Flask is a micro-framework that makes web development with Python straightforward and simple, allowing you to build quick prototypes or simple APIs. While it's not fit for larger, enterprise-level applications, at which point Django would be more appropriate (or Spring Boot in the Java ecosystem) - Flask is plenty good enough to serve microservice-level components.

If you don't have it installed already, install Flask with:

```
1 $ pip install flask
```

Then, let's create a directory for the Flask application:

```
1 $ mkdir yolov5-flaskapp
2 $ cd yolov5-flaskapp
3 $ mkdir templates
4 $ mkdir static
```

Into `yolov5-flaskapp`, we'll also copy our best weights as `traffic-yolov5.pt` and create an `app.py`. If you haven't worked with Flask before - this is the standard boilerplate structure. The files and potential CSS we'll want to serve go into the `static` folder. The HTML page templates go into `templates`. The `app.py` contains all the logic:

```
$ ls

app.py          templates
static          traffic-yolov5.pt
```

Within `templates`, we'll create `index.html`:

```
<html style = "background: linear-gradient(#e66465, #9198e5);">
   <body style = "text-align:center">
      <form action = "http://localhost:5000/predict" method = "POST" enctype
          = "multipart/form-data">
         <input type = "file" name = "file"/>
         <input type = "submit"/>
      </form>
      <img src = "{{ image }}" alt = "Returned Image">
   </body>
</html>
```

This is a minimal HTML page, with just a gradient background and a form that aims at the soon-to-be API. If you're deft with web development and front-end development - feel free to go ahead and make the page look a bit nicer! I'll keep it minimal to reduce unnecessary overhead.

Next, let's write out our `app.py`, which will contain the Flask boilerplate, spin up the server, expose an endpoint, handle the incoming request, pass it to the model and return the `index.html` page again - with the `image` injected:

```
# Flask imports
from flask import Flask, request, render_template

# Inference imports
import torch
import cv2
import numpy as np
import os

# Initialize app
app = Flask(__name__)
# Load model
model = torch.hub.load('ultralytics/yolov5', 'custom', path =
     'traffic-yolov5.pt', _verbose=False)
# Define folder to save images
IMG_DIR = os.path.join('static', 'results')

# Default route, page to prompt image upload
@app.route('/')
def home():
    return render_template('index.html')

# Handling form submission
```

```
23 @app.route('/predict', methods=['POST'])
24 def predict():
25     # Get file from the form's POST request
26     file = request.files['file']
27     bytes = np.fromfile(file, np.uint8)
28     # Convert to NumPy array
29     img_array = cv2.imdecode(bytes, cv2.IMREAD_COLOR)
30     # Inference
31     result = model(img_array)
32     # Save results
33     filename = os.path.join(IMG_DIR, file.filename)
34     cv2.imwrite(filename, result.render()[0])
35     # Render page with image
36     return render_template("index.html", image = filename)
37
38 # Start server
39 app.run()
```

You can get the source code for the application on GitHub[131] as well. The application is straightforward - you select an image, and it's displayed with the bounding boxes and classes right below the form:

Figure 167:

This is the general process of using and integrating a model in another application. Once you treat them as functions to be called on input - it becomes clear how to use them.

[131]https://github.com/DavidLandup0/yolov5-flaskapp

Potentially the most difficult aspect is ensuring the same input preprocessing, which itself isn't hard. If you're using scalers - save them, and load them here. If you're using Scikit-Learn pipelines, save them and load them here. You can save most trained Scikit-Learn objects with `joblib` and `pickle` - for example:

```
import joblib

scaler = sklearn.preprocessing.MinMaxScaler()
scaler.fit(X_train)
print('Scaler results:', scaler.transform(X_train)[:1])

joblib.dump(scaler, 'scaler.save')
scaler = joblib.load('scaler.save')
print('Loaded scaler results:', scaler.transform(X_train)[:1])
```

Unless you re-create the environment in which you tested your model - you can't guarantee its performance.

11.22 Preparing a Model for Mobile Phone Deployment

Once you get the model to a mobile phone - again, it's called as a function. The usage possibilities at that point are wide that I'll focus on getting to that stage. Deploying PyTorch models to phones generally follows a blueprint:

```
# Model definition, training, etc.
model = # ...
# Quantize to reduce cost (fp32 -> int8)
model = torch.quantization.convert(model)
# Compile as TorchScript
model = torch.jit.script(model)
# Optimize using a series of optimization scripts
model = torch.mobile_optimizer.optimize_for_mobile(model)
# Save as PTL file (PyTorch Lite)
model._save_for_lite_interpreter('model.ptl')
```

Take hold of this file. In the proceeding section, I'll assume you're familiar with the respectives environments for development in Android and iOS.

11.22.1 Deploy Model to Android

Assuming you work in Android Studio with the standard file structure and practices, in your `build.gradle` file, add:

```
implementation 'org.pytorch:pytorch_android:1.6.0'
implementation 'org.pytorch:pytorch_android_torchvision:1.6.0'
```

Situate the `model.ptl` file in the `/assets` directory. Android code is typically written in Java, and the classes associated with PyTorch are located under `org.pytorch`. You can load a `torch.nn.Module` using `org.pytorch.LiteModuleLoader` (basic PyTorch module for representing networks, from which all networks inherit):

```
Module module = LiteModuleLoader.load(assetFilePath(this, "model.pt"));
```

From here - you'll preprocess input using `org.pytorch` classes and their methods, and call the model:

```
// Load image as bitmap
Bitmap bitmap = BitmapFactory.decodeStream(getAssets().open("file.jpg"));

// Prepare image
final Tensor inputTensor = TensorImageUtils.bitmapToFloat32Tensor(bitmap,
        TensorImageUtils.TORCHVISION_NORM_MEAN_RGB,
        TensorImageUtils.TORCHVISION_NORM_STD_RGB,
            MemoryFormat.CHANNELS_LAST);
// Perform inference
final Tensor outputTensor =
    module.forward(IValue.from(inputTensor)).toTensor();
// Extract scores
final float[] scores = outputTensor.getDataAsFloatArray();
final List<Float> scoresList = new ArrayList<>(Arrays.asList(scores));

// Get max probability and index of that element
float max = Collections.max(scoresList);
int maxId = scoresList.indexOf(max);
```

This way of working with tensors and models is, admittedly, significantly more verbose than working with the Python API, which also provides compatability with general libraries in the ecosystem, such as NumPy. Even so - it's a great way to deliver PyTorch models to Java, the leading ecosystem for enterprise application development.

For a starting application - the official PyTorch GitHub[132] contains a Hello World-style application that can help get you started. It also features a demo application that showcases reading image input from the camera using the CameraX API[133] and running

[132]https://github.com/pytorch/android-demo-app/tree/master/HelloWorldApp/app/src/main/java/org/pytorch/helloworld

[133]https://developer.android.com/training/camerax

a model on the input in another repository[134].

The official JavaDocs[135] can also serve as a starting point in getting familiar with the basics of the Java/Android API of PyTorch.

11.22.2 Deploy Model to iOS

iOS development is typically done in Xcode, using the Swift programming language. If you don't already have a Pod file, in your project directory, run:

```
1 $ pod init
```

And to your Podfile, add:

```
1 pod 'LibTorch', '~>1.6.1'
```

Run:

```
1 $ pod install
```

Situate your `model.ptl` file in the project's directory. To import and use PyTorch using Swift, you'll need to import two files - `TorchModule.n` and `TorchModule.mm`. Xcode will automatically create an Objective-C bridging header for you. You can get the files and take a look at a Hello World-type application of PyTorch with iOS in this GitHub repository[136].

[134]https://github.com/pytorch/android-demo-app/tree/master/PyTorchDemoApp
[135]https://pytorch.org/javadoc/1.9.0/
[136]https://github.com/pytorch/ios-demo-app/tree/master/HelloWorld

12 Guided Project: Image Captioning with CNNs and Transformers

12.1 Image Captioning

In 1974, Ray Kurzweil's company developed the "Kurzweil Reading Machine" - an omni-font OCR machine used to read text out loud. This machine was meant for the blind, who couldn't read visually, but who could now enjoy entire books being read to them without laborious conversion to braille. It opened doors that were closed for many for a long time. Though, what about images?

While giving a diagnosis from X-ray images, doctors also typically document findings such as:

> "The lungs are clear. The heart and pulmonary are normal. Mediastinal contours are normal. Pleural spaces are clear. No acute cardiopulmonary disease."

Websites that catalog images and offer search capabilities can benefit from extracting captions of images and comparing their similarity to the search query. Virtual assistants could parse images as additional input to understand a user's intentions before providing an answer.

> In a sense - Image Captioning can be used to **explain** vision models and their findings.

The major hurdle is that you need caption data. For highly-specialized use cases, you probably won't have access to this data. For instance, in our Breast Cancer project, there were no comments associated with a diagnosis, and we're not particularly quallified to make captions ourselves. Captioning images takes time. Lots of it. Many big datasets that have captions have crowdsourced them, and in most cases, multiple captions are applied to a single image, since various people would describe them in various ways. Realizing the use cases of image captioning and descriptions - more datasets are springing up, but this is still a relatively young field, with more datasets yet to come.

Even today, there are great, large-scale datasets that you can train image captioners on. Some of them include Flickr's compilations, known as Flickr8K and Flickr30K and MS COCO.

MS COCO is large - and contains other metadata that allows us to create object recognition systems with bounding boxes.

> MS COCO is standardized won't require much preprocessing steps to get the caption-image relationships down. We'll purposefully work with a dataset that will require a bit more preprocessing to practice handling different formats and combining multi-file data (text in one file and images in a folder).

So, how do we frame image captioning? Most consider it an example of generative deep learning, because we're teaching a network to generate descriptions. However, I like to look at it as an instance of neural machine translation - we're translating the visual features of an image into words. Through translation, we're generating a new representation of that image, rather than just generating new meaning. Viewing it as translation, and only by extension generation, scopes the task in a different light, and makes it a bit more intuitive. When you experience something visually - it's hard to really convey it into words and a lot of the "magic" of the moment is lost. We translate our experience into a different format that can be conveyed to someone else, and they generate a sort of experience based on our prompts. This is actually the other side of the coin - image generation from textual prompts! Recently, projects like DALL · E have been making waves by creating amazing visual representations from textual prompts.

Recently, a Twitter user shared a generated image of Master Yoda, robbing a store, caught on a CCTV camera:

Figure 168:

Similar examples include Gandalf wrestling John Cena and Peppa the Pig boxing professional athletes. This is also, in a way, translation of an input prompt into visual features, and only by extension is a form of generation.

While it's plain funny to see a character in a situation you wouldn't expect them to be in - prompt-to-image translation can actually have a lot of implications for the way we communicate.

> "Nevermind, you had to be there."

We experience something and lose much in translation into words. Some are exceptional in their ability to stoke your imagination with words, and poets and other authors have been rightfully regarded as artists because of this ability. Since image captioning and prompt-to-image generation are two ends of the same translation process - could we train a network to turn images to text and then that text back into images?

If the mapping can be fairly similar - you could share your experiences and memories more vividly than ever before. You could not only read about the fantastic adventures of Bilbo Baggins, but also experience them visually. While the generated images from your explanations would fall short of *your* subjective experience, they can usher a new age of digital communication.

> Both of these tasks are at the intersection of Computer Vision and Natural Language Processing - both being analogous to important faculties of our own perception.

Framing the problem as one of translation makes it easier to figure out which architecture we'll want to use. Encoder-only Transformers are great at understanding text (sentiment analysis, classification, etc.) because Encoders encode meaningful representations. Decoder-only models are great for generation (such as GPT-3), since decoders are able to infer meaningful representations into another sequence with the same meaning. Translation is typically done by an encoder-decoder architecture, where encoders encode a meaningful representation of a sentence (or image, in our case) and decoders learn to turn this sequence into another meaningful representation that's more interpretable for us (such as a sentence).

If it were seen only as a generation task - we might've applied a decoder-only architecture, which would then miss out on leveraging attended encoded input as well (and would just get ConvNet output as its input).

12.2 KerasNLP

We've talked a fair bit about CV with Keras so far, but not much about NLP. NLP is a huge field. Just as with CV - you can spend your entire life exploring it without discovering everything in that space, putting aside the fact that both fields are growing every day. This isn't the place to build a holistic overview of NLP so I'll condense and compile some of the recent trends in a few paragraphs to help you follow along if you haven't worked much with natural language processing before.

Similar to how KerasCV is a horizontal addition to Keras for CV - KerasNLP is a horizontal addition for NLP. As of writing, it's still very young, at version 0.3, and the documentation is still fairly brief, but the package is more than just usable for our project even at this stage. We'll be making use of some of the layers and metrics from the package, such as `TokenAndPositionEmbedding`, `TransformerEncoder` and `TransformerDecoder` to avoid implementing them from scratch ourselves, similar to how we don't implement our own `Conv2D` layers and optimizers. `Perplexity` is a decent metric to use in our case, and we'll be using BLEU to evaluate our model later on a more widely-accepted/stringent metric. With the classes from KerasNLP, the implementation of our project becomes elegantly simple, streamlined and generic.

The beauty of Transformers is how generically they can be applied to sequential data. You can even build a pure-Transformer image captioning model! This would require more engineering in a different mental framework though, for equal results, and ConvNets are more than just "up to the task" of extracting useful features of images.

To use KerasNLP in our project, you can install it via `pip`:

```
1 $ pip install keras_nlp
```

Once imported into the project, you can use any `keras_nlp` layer as a standard Keras layer:

```
1 import keras_nlp
2
3 input_tensor = keras.Input(shape=[10, 10])
4 output = keras_nlp.layers.TransformerEncoder(intermediate_dim=64,
      num_heads=8)(input_tensor)
5 model = keras.Model(inputs=input_tensor, outputs=output)
6
7 input_data = tf.random.uniform(shape=[1, 10, 10])
8 output = model(input_data)
9 print(output)
```

This results in:

```
1 <tf.Tensor: shape=(1, 10, 10), dtype=float32, numpy=
2 array([[[ 1.6828277 , -1.1304168 , -0.73164904, -0.94957525,
3           0.9806737 ,  0.6721428 ,  0.00995253,  0.16038556,
4           0.83027554, -1.5246162 ], ...
```

Great! For the uninitiated, let's take a look at what Transformers are holistically, without getting into the theoretical nitty gritties, as well as compare them to another network type that used to be applied to language modelling to decent success before them.

Note: If you're not familiar with Transformers - you can still follow this project and I'll briefly cover the architecture. Through KerasNLP, working with Transformers requires only intuitive-level understanding, which we'll build in this project. However, it's highly advised to spend some time studying Transformers as one of the more influential architectures to date, for general use-cases as well.

A great way to start with KerasNLP, besides this lesson is Keras' English-to-Spanish translation[137]. The model we'll be building is fundamentally the same (both are generic transformers), but instead of input sentences, it'll receive input image features.

Another end-to-end guide is my own public guide on 5-Line GPT-Style Text Generation in Python with TensorFlow/Keras[138].

12.3 Transformers and RNNs (LSTM and GRU)

RNNs are used for sequence modelling. Language sentences are sequences! Naturally, RNNs were applied to NLP and proved to be pretty useful for character-level, word-level and sequence-level text generation and translation. To this end, two types of RNN layers were tyically used - Long-Short-Term Memory (LSTM) and Gated Recurrent Units (GRU).

Some of the first image captioning models combined ConvNets and LSTM/GRU networks together, more commonly at the word-level. Typically, these architectures included some form of RNN-based encoder that would be trained on sentence sequences, whose output would be concatenated with image features (extracted with a ConvNet), and fed into a Decoder (typically a fully connected network) that would just choose the next word in the sequence based on the image features and RNN output together.

[137] https://keras.io/examples/nlp/neural_machine_translation_with_keras_nlp/

[138] https://stackabuse.com/gpt-style-text-generation-in-python-with-tensorflowkeras/

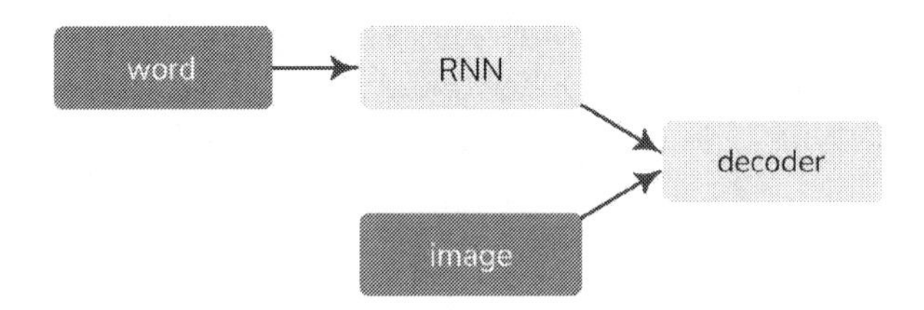

Figure 169:

Some of the major limitations of RNNs was that they were sequential and processed data sequentially, where each state depends on the previous state(s), which was slow, compared to Transformers who process all of the input parallelly.

In RNNs, tokens were embedded in latent space in a fixed manner (word-to-word relationships were clearly defined). With Transformers, the input sentence is also *positionally* embedded besides regular token embedding. Since sentences don't make sense if you switch around words in them, their sequences are encoded to preserve the meaningful relative order of elements, even when input or output sequentially. Most importantly - positional embeddings account for multiple meanings of a word, depending on how the word is used (what the neighbouring words are). Language is much more flexible and context-based than classical RNN encodings were able to capture.

Additionally, in RNN-based encoder-decoder models, the decoder didn't have access to previous states, unlike Transformer encoder-decoder models in which the decoder pays *attention* to past states in the encoder as well as regulates the way embeddings are related to each other. This *attention*, alongside positional token embedding, is at the heart of Transformers, and what allows them to be very powerful and scalable sequence modelling networks.

Attention and positional embedding allow Transformers to figure out what matters and what doesn't, depending on the lens you're looking through. Depending on what your objective is in informational retrieval - some parts of a sentence (or really, any input) are going to be more relevant than others. Pronouns are reference links to people (or objects) and change concrete meaning all the time. "Bat" can be a flying animal. It can also be a metal, wood or carbon stick used to hit inanimate objects. It can also be a verb ("to bat") meaning to "hit something".

> Language is highly contextual and understanding context and the symbolism behind it is what was for a long time seen as a human-only ability. Some languages are much more contextual than English, such as Japanese, while some are less contextual.

Understanding context and encoding it into the heart of data representation is why Transformers have been able to outperform any other architecture on language modelling tasks to date. When explaining images - context also matters. Naturally, we'll be using Transformers to generate captions of images.

KerasNLP abstracts away most of what you need to know about Transformers, but you at least have to know how a Transformer network looks like and what it's made of to be able to supply input and understand output:

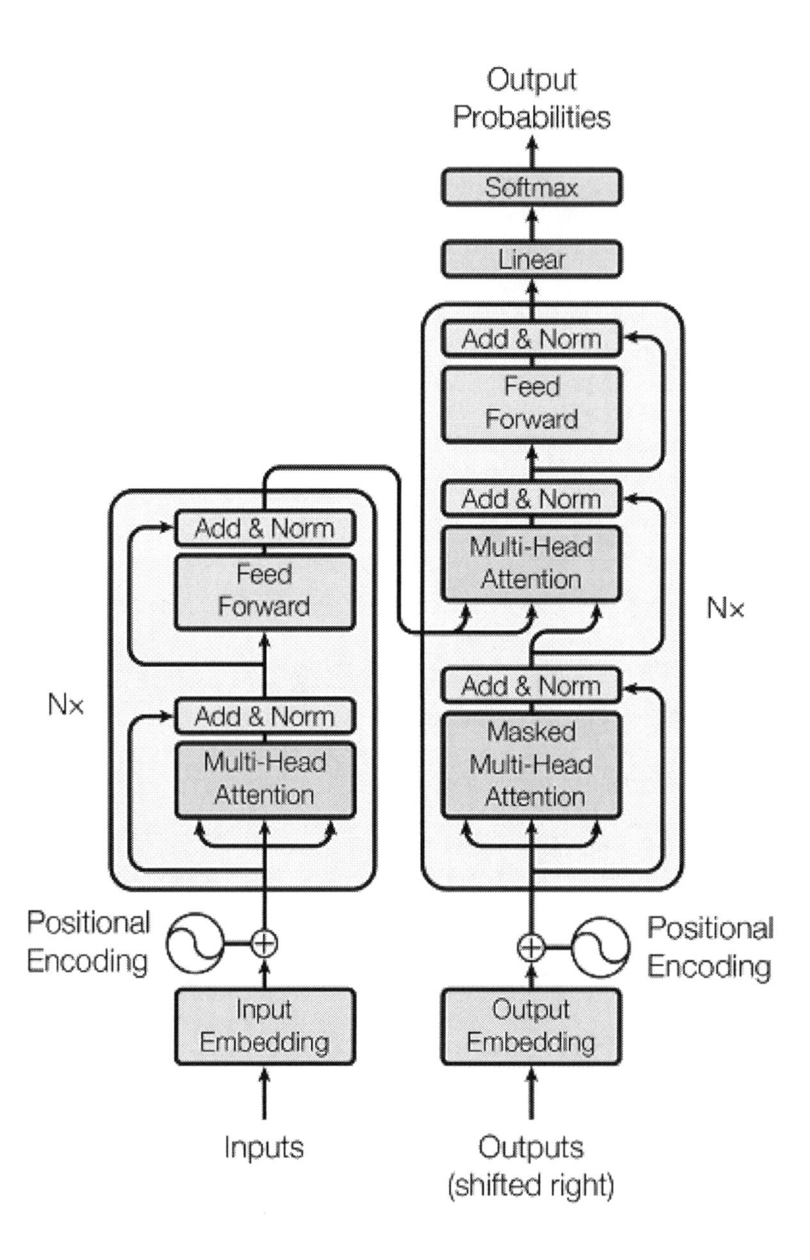
Output
Probabilities
Softmax
Linear
Add & Norm
Feed
Forward
Add & Norm
Multi-Head
Attention
Nx
Add & Norm
Masked
Multi-Head
Attention
Add & Norm
Feed
Forward
Nx
Add & Norm
Multi-Head
Attention
Positional
Encoding
Positional
Encoding
Input
Embedding
Output
Embedding
Inputs
Outputs
(shifted right)

Figure 170:

12.3.1 TokenAndPositionEmbedding

Computers understand numbers, not words. A corpus of words creates a vocabulary, and each word in the vocabulary gets an index. Thus, you can turn a sequence of words into a sequence of indices known as *tokens*:

```
def tokenize(sequence):
    # ...
    return tokenized_sequence

sequence = ['I', 'am', 'Wall-E']
sequence = tokenize(sequence)
print(sequence) # [4, 26, 472]
```

This sequence of tokens can then be embedded into a dense vector that defines the tokens in latent space:

```
[[4], [26], [472]] -> [[0.5, 0.25], [0.73, 0.2], [0.1, -0.75]]
```

This is typically done with the `Embedding` layer in Keras. Transformers don't encode only using a standard `Embedding` layer. They perform `Embedding` and `PositionEmbedding`, and add them together, displacing the regular embeddings by their position in latent space. These are *learnable*.

With KerasNLP - performing `TokenAndPositionEmbedding` is as easy as calling the appropriate layer:

```
input_tensor = keras.Input(shape=[10, 10])
output = keras_nlp.layers.TokenAndPositionEmbedding(vocabulary_size=100,
                                                     sequence_length=10,
                                                     embedding_dim=128)(input_tensor)
model = keras.Model(inputs=input_tensor, outputs=output)

input_data = tf.random.uniform(shape=[1, 10, 10])
output = model(input_data)
print(output.shape) # (1, 10, 10, 128)
```

The data we've passed into the layer is now positionally embedded in a latent space of 128 dimensions:

```
print(output)
```

```
tf.Tensor(
[[[[-0.25513703 -0.05036128 -0.04059875 ... -0.2460355  -0.06487887
    -0.12407114] ...
```

12.3.2 TransformerEncoder

The output of a ConvNet without a top is typically something along the lines of: `(batch_size, n, n, channels)`, and indeed, EfficientNetV2B0 that we'll be using has an output shape of `(batch_size, 7, 7, 1280)` which is pretty standard. We'll apply a reshaping operation to obtain a `(batch_size, 49, 1280)` output vector to act more like a sequence rather than a set of maps. This vector can become the input of our transformer encoder!

The encoder will learn to encode this vector in a new, useful and meaningful way for the image captioning model. In effect - it translates the ConvNet features into useful features for the decoder. The encoder will project the input features onto another dimensionality (depending on what the decoder expects).

Now, the KerasNLP `TransformerEncoder` unfortunately doesn't allow you to set the projection (embedding) dimensions:

```
"""Transformer encoder block implementation based on `keras.layers.Layer`."""

class TransformerEncoder(keras.layers.Layer):
    def __init__(
        self,
        intermediate_dim,
        num_heads,
        dropout=0,
        activation = "relu",
        layer_norm_epsilon=1e-05,
        kernel_initializer = "glorot_uniform",
        bias_initializer = "zeros",
        name=None,
        **kwargs
    ):
    # ...
    def _build(self, input_shape):
        # Create layers based on input shape.
        self._built = True
        feature_size = input_shape[-1]
        # ...
        self._output_dense = keras.layers.Dense(
            feature_size,
            kernel_initializer=self.kernel_initializer,
            bias_initializer=self.bias_initializer,
        )
        self._output_dropout = keras.layers.Dropout(rate=self.dropout)
```

It infers the `feature_size`, which is the size of the output `Dense()` layer based on the `input` (last dimension). So - the input and output dimensionality is essentially the same.

Unless you define your own `TransformerEncoder` (which you totally could, changing the `feature_size` to be equal to an `embed_dim` argument) - you can easily reshape the input (and thus the output) of an encoder by adding another `Dense()` block on top of our input:

```
img_embed = cnn_model(img_input)
img_embed = keras.layers.Dense(embed_dim)(img_embed)
# TransformerEncoder(intermmediate_dims=..., num_heads=...)
img_encoder_outputs = keras_nlp.layers.TransformerEncoder(latent_dims,
    heads)(img_embed)
```

12.3.3 TransformerDecoder

The `TransformerDecoder` works on sequences - it accepts a sequence as input, and produces a sequence as an output. The input sequence can be anything from an encoded sentence in a source language for the decoder to create a sequence in a target language, to sentences it should re-create (text generation), to image features that it should then use to create descriptions of. In any case - decoders accept meaningful representations and generate sequences based on them.

While they generate an entire sequence, typically, the first next output of the decoder is concatenated to the input sequence, and the expanded input sequence is fed again into the decoder to predict the third token. This continued until an end token (or the end of the sequence if you don't use end tokens) is reached. This is known as *autoregressive generation*. Decoders can be called with a single input or two inputs. In the former case, no cross-attention is paid and you can build decoder-only architectures (such as GPT-style models). In the latter case, you'll be providing the decoder inputs, alongside the encoder outputs, and cross-attention is paid to the two inputs.

The class will apply a causal mask (so as not to let the decoder cheat, since it can access elements parallelly rather than sequentially which would physically prevent it from seing beyond the current token). We'll be doing the latter, where we'll feed the caption as the decoder input, and attach the image features (passed through an encoder) as the encoded inputs:

```
decoder = keras_nlp.layers.TransformerDecoder(
        intermediate_dim=64, num_heads=8)

decoder_input = keras.Input(shape=[10, 64])
encoder_input = keras.Input(shape=[10, 64])
```

```
output = decoder(decoder_input, encoder_input)
model = keras.Model(inputs=[decoder_input, encoder_input],
        outputs=output)

decoder_input_data = tf.random.uniform(shape=[2, 10, 64])
encoder_input_data = tf.random.uniform(shape=[2, 10, 64])
decoder_output = model([decoder_input_data, encoder_input_data])

print(output)
```

```
<tf.Tensor: shape=(2, 10, 64), dtype=float32, numpy=
array([[[-0.66880834, -1.4144926 ,  1.4036546 , ...,  0.91013473,
          1.6890937 ,  0.69696546], ...
```

12.4 Perplexity and BLEU Scoring

While accuracy can be used as a proxy of sorts to indicate the performance of a language model - it's not really a good metric. It's great for tracking progress besides loss, but much better metrics are *Perplexity* and *BLEU*.

Perplexity is an intrinsic evaluation metric, testing the model itself, and is essentially, exponential entropy. Due to the exponent, the metric is more sensitive to errors, and a model that's better at predicting a probability distribution will have a lower perplexity. Small improvements in entropy will result in larger improvements of perplexity.

> Lower perplexity indicates a closer prediction to the ground truth. Higher perplexity incidates a farther prediction. Low perplexity = good. High perplexity = bad.

BLEU (BiLingual Evaluation Understudy) is mainly used for translation evaluation, and aims to quantify how close a machine translated some input to a human counterpart. It was one of the earliest attempts at quantifying the quality of computer translations, and has a decent correlation to human translations so it's a popular metric to use for language model comparison. While the "quality compared to human translation" isn't fully objective, it's not the best conceivable metric - but works well enough to be very relevant and used industry-wide.

> BLEU is a score between `[0..1]` where 1 would represent the highest score a model could theoretically achieve. This is, however, a bit misleading! If two people translate a sentence, there's a high probability they won't be the same. This would mean that one of these sentences has a <1 BLEU score compared to the other and vice

> versa, even if they're "equally as good" as translations. As of writing, the best models get around 0.4 BLEU scores on MS COCO.

A BLEU score of 0.4 is actually pretty good! For reference, Google's AutoML documentation[139] offers a grading table for BLEU scores:

- less than 10: Almost useless
- 10 - 19: Hard to get the gist
- 20 - 29: The gist is clear, but has significant grammatical errors
- 30 - 40: Understandable to good translations
- 40 - 50: High quality translations
- 50 - 60: Very high quality, adequate, and fluent translations
- above 60: Quality often better than human

BLEU is run over *decoded sentences*, while Perplexity is an intrinsic metric, which is much cheaper to calculate (since no decoding is being done). To that end, we can use Perplexity during training but it's ill-advised to use BLEU scoring during training as a metric.

KerasNLP has a `keras_nlp.metrics.Perplexity()` and `keras_nlp.metrics.Bleu()`.

12.5 Data Preprocessing

Let's start with importing all of the packages and libraries we'll be using:

```
# tensorflow version
import tensorflow as tf
print('tensorflow: %s' % tf.__version__)
# keras version
from tensorflow import keras
print('keras: %s' % keras.__version__)
import keras_cv
print('keras_cv: %s' % keras_cv.__version__)
import keras_nlp
print('keras_nlp: %s' % keras_nlp.__version__)
import numpy as np
import pandas as pd
import matplotlib.pyplot as plt
import cv2

import os
```

[139] https://cloud.google.com/translate/automl/docs/evaluate#bleu

12.5.1 Downloading the Data

Next up, let's download the dataset we'll be working with - Flickr8k. It was removed from the website publically, but is widely available on Kaggle and other repositories where others are now hosting it. It contains 8K images with 5 human-written captions each. A larger one would be Flickr30K which follows the same format - so you can easily substitute it for a larger one in this project.

Let's use `kaggle datasets` to download the dataset and unzip it:

```
! kaggle datasets download -d adityajn105/flickr8k
! unzip flickr8k.zip -d Flickr8k_Dataset
```

It's unzipped into a `Flickr8k_Dataset` directory, with a text file, named `captions.txt`, and an `Images` directory containing all of the images. Let's save this useful information in a `config` dictionary, alongside the batch size, for global access:

```
config = {
    'IMG_URL': os.path.join('Flickr8k_Dataset', 'Images'),
    'TEXT_URL': os.path.join('Flickr8k_Dataset', 'captions.txt'),
    'BATCH_SIZE' : 32
}
```

Let's take a look at some random image from the lot and verify that we got the path right:

```
from PIL import Image

fil = os.path.join(config['IMG_URL'], '1000268201_693b08cb0e.jpg')
ima = Image.open(fil)

plt.imshow(ima)
```

Figure 171:

12.5.2 Loading and Cleaning the Data

Great! Now, let's load in the text file. It contains a mapping between image paths and captions. We'll rename them to `Path` and `Description` upon loading - and it'll be the most convenient to work with these mappings as a Pandas `DataFrame`, since we can easily perform a train-test split, as well as various other transformations on a `DataFrame` more naturally than on, say, a dictionary:

```
df = pd.read_csv(config['TEXT_URL']).rename(columns={'image': 'Path',
    'caption': 'Description'})
df
```

	Path	Description
0	1000268201_693b08cb0e.jpg	A child in a pink dress is climbing up a set o...
1	1000268201_693b08cb0e.jpg	A girl going into a wooden building .
2	1000268201_693b08cb0e.jpg	A little girl climbing into a wooden playhouse .
3	1000268201_693b08cb0e.jpg	A little girl climbing the stairs to her playh...
4	1000268201_693b08cb0e.jpg	A little girl in a pink dress going into a woo...
...	...	...
40450	997722733_0cb5439472.jpg	A man in a pink shirt climbs a rock face
40451	997722733_0cb5439472.jpg	A man is rock climbing high in the air .
40452	997722733_0cb5439472.jpg	A person in a red shirt climbing up a rock fac...
40453	997722733_0cb5439472.jpg	A rock climber in a red shirt .
40454	997722733_0cb5439472.jpg	A rock climber practices on a rock climbing wa...

40455 rows × 2 columns

Figure 172:

For each image - there are five captions, and the list is flattened - each path is repeated 5 times, once for each caption. If we were to shuffle and split this `DataFrame`, it would be more than likely that a large portion of training images would end up in testing images with different captions. We'll want to bunch them together, grouping by image first.

Besides that, while already processing rows - we can clean the texts (standardize them, remove certain words if need be, add starting and ending tokens, etc.):

```
1 import re
2
3 def clean_descriptions(descriptions):
4     cleaned = []
5     for description in descriptions.split('END'):
6         description = description.lower()
7         description = re.compile(r'\W*\b\w{1}\b').sub('', description)
8         description = description.strip()
```

```
9            description = '<startseq> ' + description + ' <endseq>'
10
11           cleaned.append(description)
12       return list(filter(None, cleaned))
```

The method accepts a string, denoting all of the captions together, splits them and passes through the split list and cleans them up. We've added a specific `END` token, which doesn't exist as a word in the dataset, for an easier delimiter between captions since `.` might be unreliable due to some sentences missing a dot at the end.

We'll want to group the captions by image paths, join the captions together into a string with `'END'` between them, and then apply the `clean_descriptions()` function to each row:

```
1 df['Description'] = df.groupby(['Path'])['Description'].transform(lambda x:
      'END'.join(x)).drop_duplicates().transform(clean_descriptions)
2 df = df.dropna().reset_index(drop=True)
3 df.head()
```

	Path	Description
0	1000268201_693b08cb0e.jpg	[<startseq> child in pink dress is climbing up...
1	1001773457_577c3a7d70.jpg	[<startseq> black dog and spotted dog are figh...
2	1002674143_1b742ab4b8.jpg	[<startseq> little girl covered in paint sits ...
3	1003163366_44323f5815.jpg	[<startseq> man lays on bench while his dog si...
4	1007129816_e794419615.jpg	[<startseq> man in an orange hat starring at s...

Figure 173:

Now - the `DataFrame` contains unique paths with the captions stored as lists, rather than a flat list of paths and descriptions! If we shuffle and split this `DataFrame`, each image will only be present in one set, and all of the captions belonging to an image are anchored to it:

```
1 from sklearn.model_selection import train_test_split
2 train_df, test_df = train_test_split(df, test_size=0.2, random_state=2)
```

Great, we've got a train and test `DataFrame` with captions and a direct line to the images.

12.5.3 Text Vectorization

Again, we'll want to vectorize the text to make it useful for our model to learn from. Traditionally, this was done using a TensorFlow `Tokenizer` and Keras' `pad_sequences()` methods - however, a much handier layer, `TextVectorization`, can be used, which tokenizes *and* pads your input, allowing you to extract the vocabulary and its size, without knowing the vocab upfront!

We'll want to fit the `TextVectorization` layer on a flat list of sentences, so we'll want to flatten them again just for the vectorization layer:

```
from functools import reduce
import operator

def get_flattened_descriptions(nested_descriptions):
    return reduce(operator.concat, nested_descriptions)

flat_desc = get_flattened_descriptions(df['Description'].values)
flat_desc[:5]
```

Verify that the descriptions are flattened correctly:

```
['<startseq> child in pink dress is climbing up set of stairs in an entry
    way . <endseq>',
 '<startseq> girl going into wooden building . <endseq>',
 '<startseq> little girl climbing into wooden playhouse . <endseq>',
 '<startseq> little girl climbing the stairs to her playhouse . <endseq>',
 '<startseq> little girl in pink dress going into wooden cabin . <endseq>']
```

When vectorizing, we'll want to know the maximum length of sequences - as they'll all have to be padded to a uniform shape. This can either be achieved by finding the longest sentence and using its length, or by setting a value manually, based on the distribution of lengths of the sentences:

```
max(flat_desc)
# '<startseq> zaftig woman in tube top and jeans dancing outdoors , with
    guitarist behind her . <endseq>'
max_length = len(max(flat_desc).split(' ')) # 17
```

The 17-token sentence above isn't particularly long, so we'll do just fine by setting the max length to `17`. Let's adapt the `TextVectorization` layer on our flattened descriptions, and get the vocabulary, its size, and create an index lookup (so that we can convert tokens back into words):

```
vectorization = keras.layers.TextVectorization(
    output_mode = "int",
    output_sequence_length=max_length,
)

vectorization.adapt(flat_desc)

vocab = vectorization.get_vocabulary()
vocab_size = len(vocab)
print(vocab_size) # 8847

index_lookup = dict(zip(range(len(vocab)), vocab))
```

We could perform standardization in the `TextVectorization` layer, removing characters that we don't need (such as , and . which count as tokens in the sentence above) or to otherwise clean up the texts, but we've already cleaned them up a bit earlier, so if any additional processing should take place, it should be localized alongside the first processing either to the first step or here.

Let's take a look at a vectorized description and its conversion back to a sequence of words:

```
# Print a caption
print(df.iloc[1]['Description'][1])
# Vectorize it and print it
vec = vectorization(df.iloc[1]['Description'][1])
print(vec)
# Turn vector back into sentence
res = ''
for element in vec.numpy():
    res += f'{index_lookup[element]} '
print(res)
```

This results in:

```
<startseq> black dog and tri-colored dog playing with each other on the road
    . <endseq>

tf.Tensor(
[   2   15    9    8 1560    9   34   10  137   82    6    5  154    3
    0    0    0], shape=(17,), dtype=int64)

startseq black dog and tricolored dog playing with each other on the road
    endseq
```

The `<startseq>` and `<endseq>` tokens are assigned to 2 and 3 respectively. 0 and 1 are dedicated to the padding token `''` and `'UNK'` which denotes a word outside of the vocab. `'tri-colored'` isn't that common, so it's got a higher index! The words in a vocabulary are sorted by how common they are.

12.5.4 Creating tf.data.Datasets

Now that we can call the `vectorization` layer to vectorize any input text - we can create a `tf.data.Dataset` for our model to learn from! Remember, we've got `DataFrames` with image paths and captions. We'll need a method to read images given a path, and to vectorize the input and target sequences:

```
1 # Method to read images, resize them and prepare them for further ingestion
2 # if.image methods deal with *tensors*, not NumPy arrays
3 def read_img(img_path):
4     img = tf.io.read_file(img_path)
5     img = tf.image.decode_jpeg(img, channels=3)
6     img = tf.image.resize(img, (224, 224))
7     img = tf.image.convert_image_dtype(img, tf.float32)
8     return img
9
10 # Read the image, and return it as a tensor as the first input
11 # Return the offset vectorized sequence as the second input
12 # Return the offset vecorized sequence as the target sequence
13 def process_input(path, captions):
14     return (read_img(path), vectorization(captions)[:-1]),
          vectorization(captions)[1:]
```

The sequences are vectorized and offset by one. The model will perform autoregressive prediction - predicting the following tokens of a seed (conveniently, a `<startseq>`). On each prediction, the next word is taken, and put back into the regression loop, so the third word accounts for the starting seed *and* the second word. On each step, `0..n` is used to predict `n+1`.

Now, let's write a convenience method to load our datasets, given a `DataFrame` that contains paths and captions:

```
1 def load_dataset(image_paths, captions, batch_size=config['BATCH_SIZE']):
2     # Add prefix URL so that images can be
3     # located and flatten the paths so we have an
4     # image-caption mapping again (otherwise, we'd have
5     # to write a custom training loop and loop over captions for each image)
6     image_paths = [os.path.join(config['IMG_URL'], x) for x in image_paths
          for i in range(5)]
7     captions = get_flattened_descriptions(captions)
8     # Create dataset from the image paths and captions
```

```
9       dataset = tf.data.Dataset.from_tensor_slices((image_paths, captions))
10      # Apply the `preprocess_input` function (read images, vectrize captions,
            return tuple and target), batch, shuffle and prefetch
11      dataset = dataset.map(process_input).batch(batch_size)
12      dataset = dataset.shuffle(buffer_size = 32).prefetch(tf.data.AUTOTUNE)
13      return dataset
```

Finally, we can load our datasets as:

```
1 train_set = load_dataset(train_df['Path'].to_list(),
        train_df['Description'].to_list())
2 test_set = load_dataset(test_df['Path'].to_list(),
        test_df['Description'].to_list())
```

You can inspect the elements as:

```
1 for entry in train_set.take(1):
2     print(entry)
```

The entry contains a batch of 32 tensors representing images, followed by 32 input sequences and 32 target sequences:

```
1  ((<tf.Tensor: shape=(32, 224, 224, 3), dtype=float32, numpy=
2  array([[[[183.3614   , 160.47748  , 124.803375 ],
3           [182.67459  , 159.60751  , 125.6075   ],
4           [182.44197  , 159.44197  , 126.55804  ],
5           ...
6           [ 78.28219  ,  87.306885 ,  46.88423  ],
7           [105.90339  , 114.279045 ,  61.14154  ],
8           [ 74.19881  ,  85.21777  ,  31.141466 ]]]], dtype=float32)>,
9
10          <tf.Tensor: shape=(32, 16), dtype=int64, numpy=
11 array([[   2,   13,   27,   31,   34,   99,   10,  137,   82,    4,  342,
12            3,    0,    0,    0,    0],
13        ...
14        [   2,   26,   42,   10,   91, 2296,   77,  904,    4,    5,  238,
15            3,    0,    0,    0,    0]], dtype=int64)>),
16
17           <tf.Tensor: shape=(32, 16), dtype=int64, numpy=
18 array([[  13,   27,   31,   34,   99,   10,  137,   82,    4,  342,    3,
19            0,    0,    0,    0,    0],
20        ...
```

You can see that the input sequences all contain a `<startseq>` (2) while none of the target sequences do, as they're offset by one!

12.6 Building a Transformer-Based, CNN-Powered Image Captioning Model

With our datasets primed and ready to go - we can define the model. Using KerasNLP, we can fairly easily implement a transformer from scratch:

```
# Encoder
encoder_inputs = keras.Input(shape=(None,))
x = keras_nlp.layers.TokenAndPositionEmbedding(...)(encoder_inputs)
encoder_outputs = keras_nlp.layers.TransformerEncoder(...)(inputs=x)

encoder = keras.Model(encoder_inputs, encoder_outputs)

# Decoder
decoder_inputs = keras.Input(shape=(None,))
encoded_seq_inputs = keras.Input(shape=(None, EMBED_DIM))
x = keras_nlp.layers.TokenAndPositionEmbedding(...)(decoder_inputs)
x = keras_nlp.layers.TransformerDecoder(...)(decoder_sequence=x,
    encoder_sequence=encoded_seq_inputs)
x = keras.layers.Dropout(0.5)(x)
decoder_outputs = keras.layers.Dense(...)(x)

decoder = keras.Model([decoder_inputs,encoded_seq_inputs], decoder_outputs)
# The output of the transformer is the output of the decoder
transformer_outputs = decoder([decoder_inputs, encoder_outputs])

transformer = keras.Model([encoder_inputs, decoder_inputs],
    transformer_outputs)
```

The input is followed by `TokenAndPositionEmbedding()` and either a `TransformerEncoder` or `TransformerDecoder`. The model is put together by feeding the output of the encoder into the decoder, besides the input it already gets, which is embedded positionally. This architecture is pretty much a perfect reflection of the diagram from the paper. Now, we'll have to make a few tweaks here - transformers work on sequences, and our images aren't sequences, nor are the feature maps output by a ConvNet.

We'll be using `EfficientNetV2B0` so the bottleneck feature maps have a shape of `(7, 7, 1280)`. Typically, a sequence will have a `(seq, n)` shape - so, why don't we just reshape the 7x7 feature maps into a 1D vector of 49 values?

A `(49, 1280)` shape looks a lot more like a sequence! Now, it's a longer sequence (longer than our decoder input) but unless it's *much* longer, it won't make it too hard to learn from. We'll want to condense the `1280` features into something a bit smaller though.

With regular transformer inputs - we'd positionally embed this input sequence. We won't do that here. The feature maps already, to a degree, positionally embed features.

While they are translation invariant, ConvNets do retain a sense of space and order within that space, even if we flatten the feature maps. We could positionally embed these, additionaly, but positional embedding is an expensive operation and doesn't really give us any better performance in my tests. Additionally, it blocks the flow of gradients, so any learnable layers have to be situated *after* embedding, which makes it harder to supply a manageable sequence size to the layer. For instance, if we ran a `GlobalAveragePooling2D` layer over the feature maps, producing a vector of `1280` and then positionally embedded that - we'd have a sequence of `(1280, embed_dim)`, which would be both computationally expensive, and hard to translate to our 17-word sentences!

> Remember - we're effectively doing translation here. Ideally, there would be near-17 tokens in the embedding sequence, that can accurately describe the image, so the decoder can use its 17 tokens to describe it for us.

Let's define the captioning model, using the Functional API, using the general architecture as a guiding blueprint. We'll also have a small augmentation pipeline:

```
1 augmentation_pipeline = keras.Sequential([
2     keras.layers.RandomFlip('horizontal'),
3     keras.layers.RandomRotation(0.3),
4     keras.layers.RandomZoom(0.3)
5 ])
```

With a pipeline that we can plug in to augment input, let's define the model:

```
1 def define_caption_model(vocab_size, max_length, embed_dim, latent_dims,
      heads):
2     effnet = keras.applications.EfficientNetV2B0(weights = 'imagenet',
          include_top=False, input_shape=(224, 224, 3))
3     effnet.trainable = False
4     effnet_out = effnet.output
5     effnet_out = keras.layers.Reshape((-1, effnet_out.shape[-1]))(effnet_out)
6     cnn = keras.models.Model(effnet.input, effnet_out)
7
8     img_input = keras.layers.Input(shape=(224, 224, 3), name = 'Img feature
          input')
9     preprocess_image = augmentation_pipeline(img_input)
10
11     img_embed = cnn(preprocess_image)
12     img_embed = keras.layers.Dense(embed_dim)(img_embed)
13     img_embed = keras.layers.Dropout(0.3)(img_embed)
14
15     img_encoder_outputs = keras_nlp.layers.TransformerEncoder(latent_dims,
          heads)(img_embed)
16
17     decoder_inputs = keras.Input(shape=(max_length-1,), name = 'Decoder
          inputs')
```

```
18        encoded_inputs = keras.Input(shape=(49, embed_dim), name = 'Encoded
              inputs (image features)')
19        x = keras_nlp.layers.TokenAndPositionEmbedding(vocab_size, max_length,
              embed_dim, mask_zero=True)(decoder_inputs)
20        x = keras_nlp.layers.TransformerDecoder(latent_dims, heads, 0.5)(x,
              encoded_inputs)
21        x = keras.layers.Dropout(0.4)(x)
22
23        decoder_outputs = keras.layers.Dense(vocab_size)(x)
24        decoder = keras.Model([decoder_inputs, encoded_inputs], decoder_outputs)
25
26        model_outputs = decoder([decoder_inputs, img_encoder_outputs])
27        model = keras.Model(inputs=[img_input, decoder_inputs], outputs =
              model_outputs)
28
29        model.compile(loss =
              keras.losses.SparseCategoricalCrossentropy(from_logits=True),
30                      optimizer = keras.optimizers.Adam(learning_rate = 0.001),
31                      metrics=['accuracy',
                             keras_nlp.metrics.Perplexity(from_logits=True)])
32        print(model.summary())
33        return model
```

Accuracy is just a proxy metric to track *some* sense of progress here. Perplexity and BLEU are much better metrics for this.

Note: We're not using a `'softmax'` activation in the final `Dense` layer. Because of this, our `SparseCategoricalCrossentropy()` has to use a `from_logits` flag, set to `True`, as does the `Perplexity()` metric. The outputs of the layer aren't normalized so that their sum equals `1`, which is the default expected format for both the metric and loss. This is done because later on, while performing a search for the next tokens, only the top logits will be considered for the SoftMax function, without interference from other possible tokens.

12.6.1 Training

Let's insantiate the model:

```
1 model = define_caption_model(vocab_size=vocab_size, max_length=max_length,
      embed_dim=256, latent_dims=512, heads=8)
```

The summary of this model is:

```
...
==================================================================
Total params: 13,027,295
Trainable params: 7,107,983
Non-trainable params: 5,919,312
__________________________________________________________________
```

The ConvNet is non-trainable, and we've got around 7.1M parameters in our transfomer. Let's visualize it:

```
keras.utils.plot_model(model, to_file = 'model.png', show_shapes=True)
```

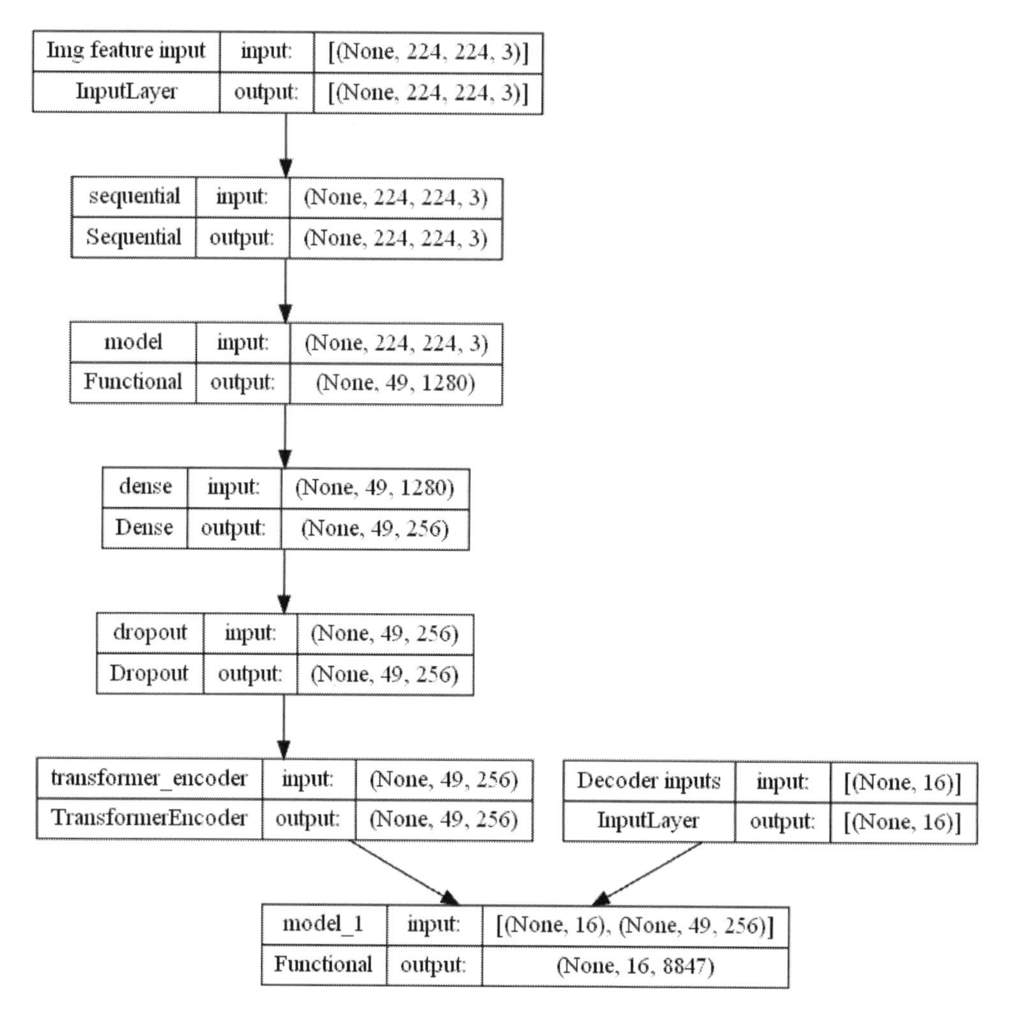

Figure 174:

The image input is fed into the sequential augmentation layer, augmenting the images, before being fed into `EfficientNetV2B0` for feature extraction. These features are then reshaped to act more like a sequence, and encoded using the `TransformerEncoder`. The output of the encoder, alongside the inputs of the decoder (trimmed captions) are fed into the decoder, which produces another sequence, of `max_length` length, with a logit for each word in the vocabulary.

This model can be used greedily (take the highest logit/probability word in each step), but we'll be accounting for how probable a word is and only choose it with that probability. This is why we've been using logits in the first place - we'll take the Top-K logits, run `softmax()` over them, and choose between them, with their respective probabilites. If the network is certain that a word should come next, it'll certainly be chosen. If it's unsure (say, a 50/50 split) - there's an equal chance that either of those will be chosen. In any case - the chosen word is taken into account for the next one, and so on until the end of the sequence length.

Time to train it:

```
1 checkpoint =
      keras.callbacks.ModelCheckpoint('img_cap_generator_model_kerasnlp.h5',
      save_best_only=True)
2 reducelr = keras.callbacks.ReduceLROnPlateau(patience=5, monitor =
      'val_perplexity')
3
4 callbacks = [reducelr, checkpoint]
5
6 history = model.fit(train_set,
7            epochs=35,
8            validation_data=(test_set),
9           callbacks=callbacks)
```

This results in:

```
1 Epoch 1/35
2 1012/1012 [==============================] - 141s 128ms/step - loss: 2.9218
      - accuracy: 0.2938 - perplexity: 69.3980 - val_loss: 2.5077 -
      val_accuracy: 0.3476 - val_perplexity: 38.1548 - lr: 0.0010
3 ...
4 Epoch 35/35
5 1012/1012 [==============================] - 131s 127ms/step - loss: 1.7151
      - accuracy: 0.4362 - perplexity: 12.0400 - val_loss: 2.2738 -
      val_accuracy: 0.4028 - val_perplexity: 27.1195 - lr: 1.0000e-08
```

It got to around 40 in validation accuracy and around 27 in validation perplexity.

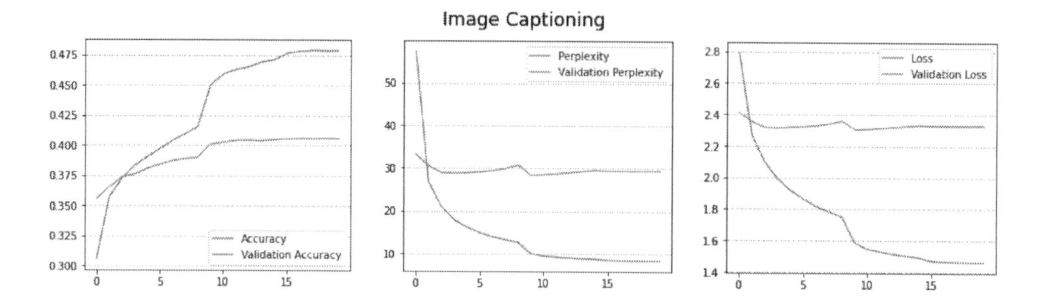

Figure 175:

12.6.2 Model Inference

Let's use the model to generate some captions, given an input image, and a starting seed. We'll use a helper method to find the top K probable tokens and choose one of them, with a probability that we obtain from passing the logits of those tokens through a `softmax` function. Besides that, we'll generate `n` captions for each image since they should be different for any `k>1`:

```
def sample_token(probas, k=2):
    # Find top-k probable tokens
    logits, indices = tf.math.top_k(probas, k=k, sorted=True)
    indices = np.asarray(indices).astype("int32")
    # Pass them through SoftMax to obtain token probabilities
    preds = keras.activations.softmax(tf.expand_dims(logits, 0))[0]
    preds = np.asarray(preds).astype("float32")
    # Choose between tokens, with their own probabilities
    return np.random.choice(indices[-1,:], p=preds[-1,:])

def generate_desc(model, img, max_length, num_captions=1, k=2):
    # Load image and prepare for model
    if type(img) == 'str':
        img = cv2.imread(img)
    img = cv2.resize(img, (224, 224))
    img = cv2.cvtColor(img, cv2.COLOR_BGR2RGB)
    img = np.expand_dims(img, 0)

    # Generate num_captions*captions
    captions = []
    for cap in range(num_captions):
        # Seed the caption with a generic start
        # This is the "sequence so far"
        decoded_caption = "<startseq>"
        # Generate a token for each i in max_length
```

```
26         for i in range(max_length-1):
27             # Vectorize the caption so far
28             tokenized_caption = vectorization([decoded_caption])[:, :-1]
29             # Predict sequence using model
30             predictions = model.predict([img, tokenized_caption], verbose=0)
31             # Sample token using helper method
32             sampled_token_index = sample_token(predictions[0:, i, :], k=k)
33             # Convert token to word
34             sampled_token = index_lookup[sampled_token_index]
35             # End inference is endseq is predicted
36             if sampled_token == "endseq":
37                 break
38             # Add word to caption and run iteration again
39             decoded_caption += " " + sampled_token
40 
41         # Replace start token with empty string
42         decoded_caption = decoded_caption.replace('<startseq>', '')
43         captions.append(decoded_caption)
44 
45     return captions
```

To display our results in a nice fashion, let's create a helper `plot_results()`:

```
1 def plot_results(img, description):
2     fig, ax = plt.subplots(figsize=(12, 6))
3     ax.axis('off')
4     ax.imshow(img)
5     ax.text(img.shape[1]+50, img.shape[0]/2-img.shape[0]/2*0.2, 'Caption for
          image:', fontsize=15, alpha=0.7)
6     for index, desc in enumerate(descriptions):
7         ax.text(img.shape[1]+50, img.shape[0]/2+(30*index), f'{index+1}.
              {desc}', fontsize=20)
8 
9     plt.show()
```

Finally, we've simplified our inference to:

```
1 # Load img
2 img = cv2.imread(os.path.join(config['IMG_URL'], '997722733_0cb5439472.jpg'))
3 img = cv2.cvtColor(img, cv2.COLOR_BGR2RGB)
4 # Run inference
5 descriptions = generate_desc(model, img, max_length, num_captions=3)
6 # Plot results and descriptions
7 plot_results(img, descriptions)
```

Caption for image:
1. man in red jacket is climbing rock
2. man in red shirt is climbing rock
3. man in red jacket is climbing rock

Figure 176:

If you would like to fetch images from hosting services, you can write another helper function to easily convert a URL into a NumPy array describing the image from that URL:

```
import urllib.request
from tensorflow.keras.preprocessing import image

def url_to_array(url):
    req = urllib.request.urlopen(url)
    arr = np.array(bytearray(req.read()), dtype=np.int8)
    arr = cv2.imdecode(arr, -1)
    arr = cv2.cvtColor(arr, cv2.COLOR_BGR2RGB)
    arr = cv2.resize(arr, (224, 224))
    return arr

# Book formatting
url = 'https://www.outsideonline.com/'
url = url + 'wp-content/uploads/2022/01/iStock_89170989_SMALL.jpg'
img = url_to_array(url)

descriptions = generate_desc(model, img, max_length, 3)

plot_results(img, descriptions)
```

Caption for image:

1. woman in black shorts and white shirt walks on the street with stars
2. man in black shirt and shorts is standing on the sidewalk
3. woman wearing black and white shirt is walking on sidewalk

Figure 177:

Let's try another one:

```
url = 'https://live.staticflickr.com/5585/14750945968_b19c7d0e0f_b.jpg'
img = url_to_array(url)
descriptions = generate_desc(model, img, max_length, 3)
plot_results(img, descriptions)
```

Caption for image:

1. brown dog is running through the grass
2. dog running through the grass
3. brown dog is running through field

Figure 178:

```
img = cv2.imread(os.path.join(config['IMG_URL'], test_df['Path'][10]))
img = cv2.cvtColor(img, cv2.COLOR_BGR2RGB)
descriptions = generate_desc(model, img, max_length, 3, 2)
plot_results(img, descriptions)
```

Caption for image:

1. white dog is running in the snow
2. white dog is jumping in the snow
3. dog running through the snow

Figure 179:

Note: As of writing, `keras_nlp.metrics.Bleu()` exists on GitHub but isn't released in a stable version. Until then, NLTK has a great BLEU scoring function!

```
from nltk.translate.bleu_score import sentence_bleu

def evaluate_model(model, img, true_desc, max_length):
    descriptions = generate_desc(model, img, max_length, k=2, num_captions=5)
    descriptions = [desc.split() for desc in descriptions]
    true_desc = [desc.replace('<startseq>', '').replace('<endseq>', '') for
        desc in true_desc]
    scores = []
    for e in zip(descriptions, true_desc):
        score = sentence_bleu(e[0], e[1], weights=(1/2, 1/2))
        scores.append(score)
    return np.array(true_desc, dtype=object), np.array(descriptions,
        dtype=object), np.array(scores, dtype=object)

img = cv2.imread(os.path.join(config['IMG_URL'], train_df['Path'][74]))
img = cv2.cvtColor(img, cv2.COLOR_BGR2RGB)
desc = train_df['Description'][74]

true, preds, score = evaluate_model(model, img, desc, max_length)
```

Now, this isn't a really fair evaluation - since we're testing the first generated caption against the first true caption, and so on. If the first generated caption was equal to the second true caption, the model would get a low score, even though the order is arbitrary, and there's *significant* variance in human captions. Because the captions differ significantly, the "ground truth" is, well, not really a good reference and a low BLEU score doesn't necessarily mean that our model is very wrong.

Let's take a look at the image itself and the true captions for it:

Figure 180:

```
array([' woman dressed in blue jacket and blue jeans rides brown horse near
    frozen lake and snow-covered mountain . ',
       ' woman in blue jacket rides brown pony near water . ',
       ' woman rides horse near frozen lake in the wintertime . ',
       ' young blond woman sitting atop brown draft horse in the snowy
         mountains . ',
       ' woman blue jacket sits on daft horse near frozen lake . '],
      dtype=object)
```

Now, let's write our own caption for it, to get an idea of a baseline BLEU score:

```
sentence_bleu('woman in a blue jacket, on a brown horse, near a frozen
    lake'.split(),
              'woman dressed in blue jacket and blue jeans rides brown horse
                  near frozen lake and snow-covered mountain',
              weights=(1/2, 1/2))
```

This is a BLEU-2 score (easier to achieve than BLEU-3 or BLEU-4) because we simply consider shorter matched phrases as correct as opposed to higher-gram BLEU scoring. This results in a "bad" score of:

```
0.23067585863076587
```

Yikes! Sounds low, but the caption we wrote is fully gramatically correct and explains the image well. With this in mind, let's take a look at the model's predictions:

```
array([list(['woman', 'with', 'brown', 'hair', 'and', 'blue', 'jacket',
    'is', 'riding', 'brown', 'horse']),
       list(['man', 'in', 'blue', 'jacket', 'is', 'riding', 'brown',
           'horse', 'on', 'trail', 'in', 'the', 'snow']),
       list(['woman', 'in', 'blue', 'jacket', 'is', 'walking', 'through',
           'the', 'snow']),
       list(['man', 'in', 'blue', 'jacket', 'is', 'riding', 'brown',
           'horse', 'on', 'snowy', 'ground']),
       list(['man', 'in', 'brown', 'jacket', 'is', 'standing', 'on',
           'snowy', 'hill'])],
      dtype=object)
```

The first one is almost spot on! "Woman with brown hair and blue jacket is riding brown horse" explains the image quite well. The only missing part is that she's near a frozen lake, or that it's winter, that most real captions had. One of the prompts claims she's walking through the snow, which isn't quite right, but you can see how it would make that mistake.

What are the BLEU scores for each of these? Let's take a look:

```
array([0.20274167874526933, 0.3495310368212778, 0.20225995873897265,
       0.25468581598680534, 0.23145502494313785], dtype=object)
```

They're not stellar - but you can evaluate the model's predictions yourself too. If you'd like to see a more general model - train it on MS COCO.

Great! Our model seems to be able to tell apart colors, positions, places, living beings and actions. It gets some things wrong - mainly actions, and can produce weird output, but overall, is describing the images quite well for a training set of only just over 6000 images. This can naturally be scaled up to Flickr30K or even MS COCO!

13 Guided Project: DeepLabV3+ Semantic Segmentation with Keras

13.1 Semantic Segmentation

Semantic and Instance Segmentation is the natural next step of object detection, and uses much the same architectures with new heads to predict masks, rather than bounding boxes. Many object detection architectures can be converted into segmentation architectures, and some projects ship both capabilities such as Detectron2.

We've worked with YOLOv5 by Ultralytics in a previous project, which currently doesn't support segmentation, but it is in the works. When it gets released in a later version, I'll update the book.

13.2 Segmentation Architectures

As with every task - there are various architectures that can be employed to perform segmentation. Some of the defining ones are:

- Mask R-CNN - A Faster R-CNN variant which predicts masks for detected objects. Mask R-CNNs produce pretty good results.
- U-Net - An Encoder-Decoder architecture that downsamples (encodes) and upsamples (decodes) input with skip connections between these steps. The architecture is typically visualized in a way that makes it look like a "U" (with skip connections between the left and right hand side of the "U" letter). While simple, it doesn't provide the best results.
- DeepLabV3+ - An Encoder-Decoder architecture that liberally uses *Atrous Convolutions* and a module named the *Atrous Spatial Pyramid Pooling (ASPP)* module. More on both in a moment. One of the most accurate models to date, and it's surprisingly easy to implement as an end-to-end model for semantic segmentation.

In this lesson - we'll be focusing on DeepLabV3+, as it's not *much* more complicated than U-Net-like architectures, but produces significantly better results. It's worth noting that U-Net-like architectures aren't useless or being replaced - they've found uses in other areas of computer vision as well. For example, Stable Diffusion, mentioned in *"Lesson 2, Introduction to Computer Vision"*, uses a U-Net within the model!

For semantic segmentation, though, it is outperformed by the likes of Mask R-CNN and DeepLab.

13.3 U-Net Implementation with Keras

Given how simple U-Net is to implement, we'll take a look at a quick implementation here, withtout delving into too many details. It's built with downsampling (encoder) and upsampling (decoder) blocks. Let's define a simple `conv_block()` to avoid repetition, and functions to add downsampling and upsampling blocks:

```
1 def conv_block(inputs, filter_num, kernel_size=(3,3), strides=(1,1), padding
      = "same"):
2     x = keras.layers.Conv2D(filter_num, kernel_size, strides=strides,
          padding=padding)(inputs)
3     x = keras.layers.BatchNormalization()(x)
4     x = keras.layers.Activation("relu")(x)
5     return x
6
7 def downsample_block(inputs, filter_num):
8     residual = conv_block(inputs, filter_num)
9     downsampled = keras.layers.MaxPooling2D(2)(residual)
10    return residual, downsampled
11
12 def upsample_block(x, filter_num, residual):
13    x = keras.layers.Conv2DTranspose(filter_num, (3,3), (2,2), padding =
          "same")(x)
14    x = keras.layers.concatenate([x, residual])
15    x = conv_block(x, filter_num)
16    return x
```

These are pretty straightforward - the downsample block applies a `conv_block()` to the input, and saves the result as a `residual`, and returns it alongisde a max-pooled feature map. Upsampling accepts a `residual` and transposes the input (making it larger), concatenating the result to the residual. This is the injection that makes U-net "curl up" into a U-shape!

Once you have the building blocks, you simply

```
1 def unet():
2     inputs = layers.Input(shape=(224,224,3))
3
4     residual1, downsampled1 = downsample_block(inputs, 64)
```

```
    residual2, downsampled2 = downsample_block(downsampled1, 128)
    residual3, downsampled3 = downsample_block(downsampled2, 256)
    residual4, downsampled4 = downsample_block(downsampled3, 512)

    bottleneck = conv_block(downsampled4, 1024)

    upsample1 = upsample_block(bottleneck, 512, residual4)
    upsample2 = upsample_block(upsample1, 256, residual3)
    upsample3 = upsample_block(upsample2, 128, residual2)
    upsample4 = upsample_block(upsample3, 64, residual1)
    outputs = keras.layers.Conv2D(num_classes, kernel_size=(2,2), padding =
        "same", activation = "softmax")(upsample4)
    model = keras.Model(inputs, outputs)
    return model
```

When plotted, it gets it's signature U-shape! At least kind of:

```
keras.utils.plot_model(model, to_file = "unet.png")
```

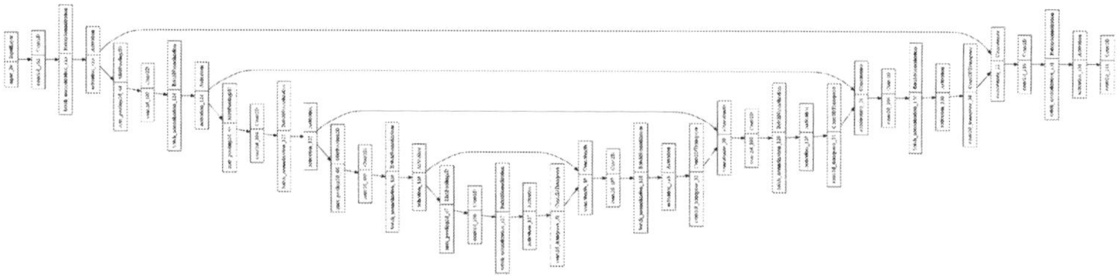

Figure 181:

You can see how the shortcut connections from some of the earlier layers that connect to later layers curl up the model into a U-shape. In the case of `utils.plot_model()`, it's a bit more like a bowl-shape *but* the logic behind the architecture is sound and intuitive.

The first and final layer have the same shape, and it's in effect, symetrical around the bottleneck layer. `Conv2D` with `MaxPooling(2)` is *reverse* from `Conv2DTranspose(strides=(2, 2))`, and both are applied around the middle layer.

13.4 DeepLab Motivations

The main author of DeepLab papers, Liang-Chieh Chen, also contributed to MobileNet, and is a prolific contributor to the landscape. Three papers were released (from 2016 to 2018), associated with the novel technique to perform Semantic Segmentation:

- *"DeepLab: Semantic Image Segmentation with Deep Convolutional Nets, Atrous Convolution, and Fully Connected CRFs"*[140]
- *"Rethinking Atrous Convolution for Semantic Image Segmentation"*[141]
- *"Encoder-Decoder with Atrous Separable Convolution for Semantic Image Segmentation"*[142]

Reading them is encouraged, but as a TL;DR - here are the main takeaways condensed into a short intuitive section.

In 2016, techniques were being proposed mainly for image classification, as it was still significantly less developed than today, while other tasks like object detection, semantic and instance segmentation and so on were getting less spotlight.

13.4.1 Spatial Invariance and Semantic Segmentation

Image classification favors **spatial invariance**, which is horrible for any application that *cares* about spatial relationships in images! Object detection, semantic and instance segmentation don't work even conceptually with spatial invariance.

Use of Max-Pooling and Strided downsampling abstracts away spatial information, which made image classifiers classify a cat leaning towards the right, and to the left - as still a cat. At the time, image classifiers were for the first time being able to go deep (with the foundation ResNets laid down), and this included more spatial abstraction.

To combat this, the first DeepLab version replaced downsampling with *upsampling* near the end of the network, making the feature maps larger, instead of smaller. Upsampling is done via bilinear interpolation. In addition, to expand the filter area without pooling, filters with "spaces between filter cells" are used. This is known as *dilation* and Keras supports filter dilation at different rates via the `dilation_rate` argument of `Conv2D`. Convolution with dilation is, unsurprisingly, known as dilated convolution:

[140] https://arxiv.org/abs/1606.00915
[141] https://arxiv.org/abs/1706.05587
[142] https://arxiv.org/abs/1802.02611

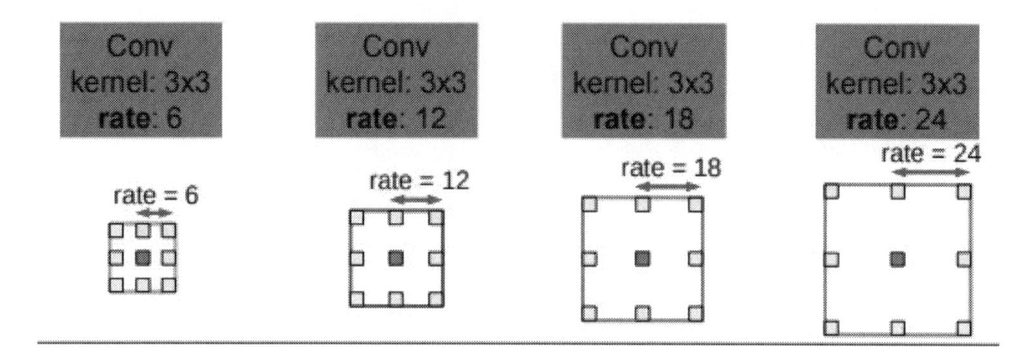

Figure 182:

The `rate` mentioned in the original paper, is known as the `dilation_rate` in Keras.

> Dilation can be imagined as a filter having "holes", and upsampling with dilated filters has been used in signal processing, in a scheme known as "algorithme à trous". "à trous" was shortened to "atrous" and the authors named upsampling convolutions "atrous convolutions", and networks that use the technique "atrous convnets".

DeepLab upsamples the feature maps back to full-resolution of the input. This process is in essence, an encoder-decoder process. First, the input image is encoded, preserving the spatial information into a dense feature map. Then, this feature map is upsampled into a feature map matching the resolution of the input.

This final feature map, in itself, encodes the class of each cell (pixel). Thus, we produce a network that can classify each pixel in an image, according to its semantic class, and ultimately perform semantic segmentation! Really, that's all there is to the essence of semantic segmentation. The feature maps produced in the end are also known as "masks", and they're oftentimes overlaid over the input image to make an intuitive representation of the classifications.

Here's a sneak peak of an input image, the mask used to train it (an `NxN` matrix with class labels for every pixel in the image), an RGB representation of that mask (because it's prettier) and the prediction of the network we'll be training:

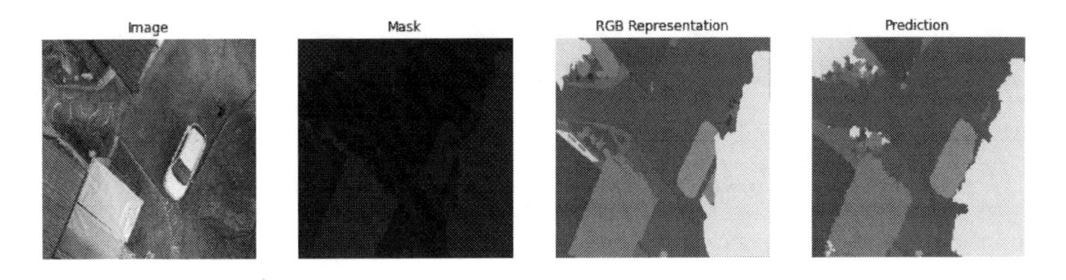

Figure 183:

You can also overlay the predicted maps over the original images:

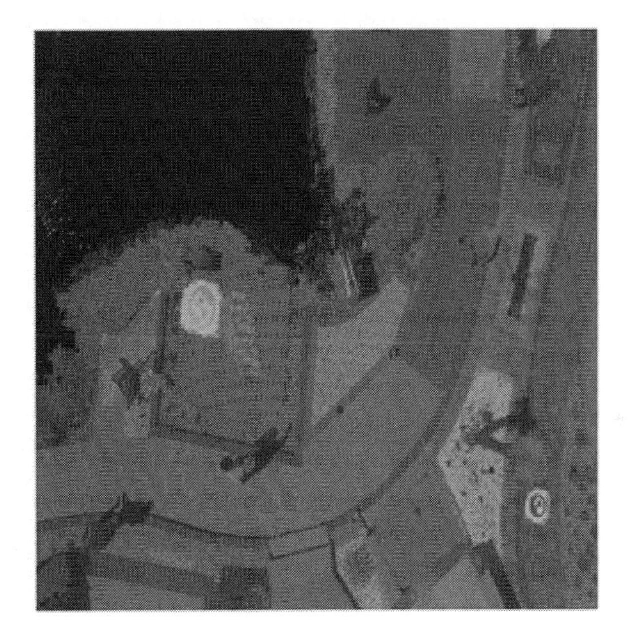

Figure 184:

We could also assign and write textual labels with these, but the issue with semantic segmentation is that it doesn't differentiate between instances of objects. A car is just *"car"* - not *"a car"*. The `image_width*image_height` matrix encodes class labels (`0..n`), and it wouldn't make sense to annotate every pixel. We'd want to annotate every instance if we plotted textual labels. This is what *instance segmentation* does.

13.4.2 Different Object Scales

Another issue that had to be solved was objects of different scales. The same object can be really small or really large in an image. This is typically addressed via image pyramids (rescaling images to different sizes, allowing a network to extract high-level spatial information *and* fine-grain information, based on which size it receives). DeepLab authors use Spatial Pyramid Pooling (pooling layer proposed by He et al.) to capture objects in different scales and context in which they appear. Spatial Pyramid Pooling was adjusted to work with atrous convolutional layers for DeepLab, and was aptly named ***Atrous Spatial Pyramid Pooling (ASPP)***. Intuitively, it encodes global context about the images, and is an essential element of DeepLab.

13.4.3 DeepLab Versions

Put shortly: initial versions of DeepLab used dense *Conditional Random Fields (CRF)* in the final stages, which was later dropped in DeepLabV3. DeepLabV3+ introduced a decoder to the process, which is meant to refine the edges and boundaries of objects, producing a memorable architecture:

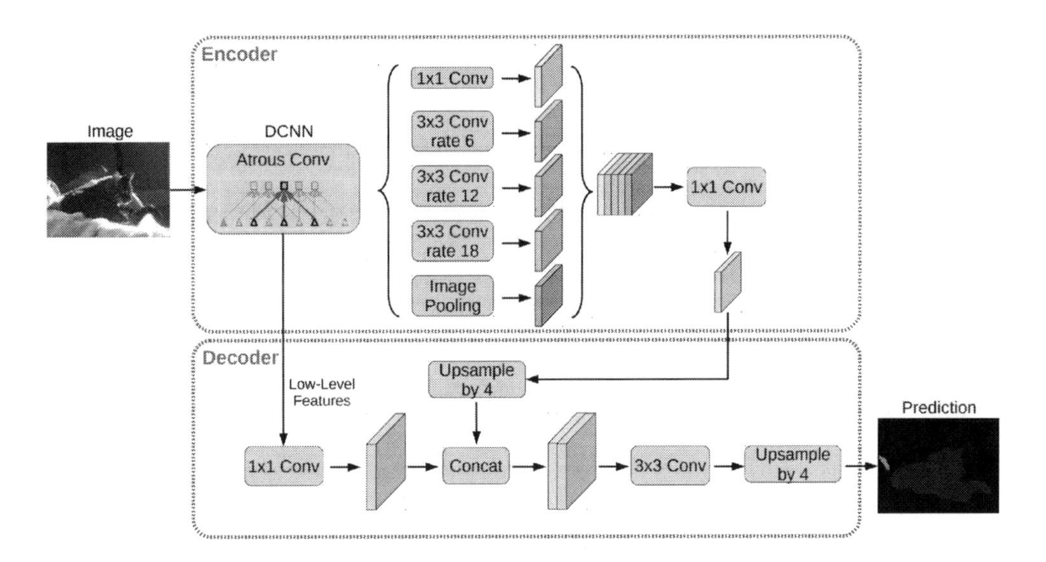

Figure 185:

First, the image is passed through a DCNN (Deep Convolutional Neural Network/CNN/ConvNet) with atrous convolutions. The right-hand side is the ASPP module, which performs atrous convolutions at different scales and pools the results together. These results are convolved with a 1x1 filter and upsampled before being concatenated to the output of the DCNN which was ultimately convolved with a 1x1 filter as well.

The concatenated results are upsampled to produce the full-resolution feature map that encodes the class labels for every pixel. The DCNN in the diagram can be any conv net, and ResNet is a common backbone.

We'll translate this diagram into a working model with Keras in a moment. First, let's take a look at the dataset we'll be working with.

13.5 Data Preprocessing and the Albumentations Library

Segmentation datasets, like object detection datasets, require a large upfront time investment. With segmentation datasets though, you'll typically be annotating everything in an image, instead of just objects of interest, and you'll be doing so more accurately along the borders of the object, instead of a box around it.

Because of this, you're likely going to be working with in-house segmentation datasets, labelled by a team trying to solve a particular problem. Segmentation models are more commonly applied to specific use-cases, and trying to train a *general* segmentation model, without a niche use in mind is rarer. Semantic segmentation models are more sensitive to domain shift than image classification models, in large part because image classification models are blind to many small differences by abstracting them away, while segmentation models pay much more attention to small details. The good thing is - since you're likely going to be making it for a niche problem, you'll have the same type of input during and after training!

Just like with classification and detection - datasets and models are typically single-class or multi-class. Single-class would be detecting "traffic sign" in an image or segmenting it. Multi-class would be detecting "stop sign", "crosswalk" and "wrong way" signs, or segmenting them.

Reducing the number of classes simplifies image annotation. For example, you can create a "background" class and a "human" class, and your network would learn to segment humans and segment everything else as background. One could create an autonomous digital map creation tool, from sattelite imagery, with classes such as "building", "road", "lake", etc. Creating maps is no easy task, and neither is updating them. Could you create a semantic segmentation model, fed labelled data from humans, and generalize to building digital maps of the world?

Yes! Difficulties are obviously present here, including the sheer difference between regions that should be analyzed and digitized. A semantic segmentation model built on data around the Amazon Rainforest will naturally encode different knowledge than the model built around data in the Sahara desert. This can be conceivably be addressed either with a robust, diverse, very large dataset, or with multiple models fit for different regions. Nevertheless, let's apply semantic segmentation to an aerial dataset, with images from the sky!

13.6 Aerial Semantic Segmentation Drone Dataset

A great, relatively small, dataset with 24 classes was released by the Institute of Computer Graphics and Vision. It was later ported to Kaggle under *"Aerial Semantic*

Segmentation Drone Dataset"[143].

> The Semantic Drone Dataset focuses on semantic understanding of urban scenes for increasing the safety of autonomous drone flight and landing procedures. The imagery depicts more than 20 houses from nadir (bird's eye) view acquired at an altitude of 5 to 30 meters above ground. A high resolution camera was used to acquire images at a size of 6000x4000px (24Mpx).

It originally contained bounding boxes for person detection (so drones can learn to steer away from them to avoid hurting anyone), as well as for semantic segmentation of 20 classes, which was expanded to 24 on the Kaggle version. The dataset has a number of images and their semantic masks (label maps):

Figure 186:

> Semantic masks themselves are labels.

Say, `0` represents `dirt`, `1` represents `grass`, etc. A (low-resolution) semantic mask could look like:

```
1 1 1 1 1
0 0 0 1 1
1 1 0 0 0
1 1 1 1 1
1 1 1 1 1
```

[143]https://www.kaggle.com/datasets/bulentsiyah/semantic-drone-dataset

This would, effectively, be a dirt road in some grass. Now, if you want to plot this, sure `0` is black, `1` is white, and you have a black-white image of a small dirt path in a grass field. Though, with more labels than this, such as with labels between `0..23` - the masks don't really look very viewable. They're very dim, because on a spectrum of color values between `0..255`, the 24 labels are all fairly low and you'll see some faint shapes but that's about it. We want the network to learn to predict the labels, not the colors, so this is perfectly fine. Colors are arbitrary, and are only to make it easier for us to view the results.

Thus, we typically don't plot label maps, but RGB representations of those maps! Datasets will usually note the colors used for classes, such as "#00FF00`for`grass`, with a label of`0`. If you're lucky, you'll get a CSV file with the mappings between labels and colors. If you're unlucky, you can just make up colors, and pass the labels through the function (or back) to get RGB representations.

This dataset comes with a handy CSV file that defines the classnames and their RGB values in `class_dict_seg.csv`:

```
1 name        r   g   b
2 unlabeled   0   0   0
3 paved-area  128 64  128
4 ...
```

We'll later take a look at how we can use this file to turn label maps into RGB representations and back. If you don't have a file like this and just have label maps - mark down the colors you want to use, respecting the label order (for this dataset, `0` is `unlabeled`, `1` is `paved-area`, etc.), save them to a `DataFrame`, and you've got a handy data structure with which you can perform label-to-RGB conversions!

13.7 Exploring the Dataset

Let's download the dataset using Kaggle's CLI and unzip the downloaded archive:

```
1 $ kaggle datasets download -d bulentsiyah/semantic-drone-dataset
2 $ unzip semantic-drone-dataset.zip -d sem-drone
```

Then, let's import some of the modules we'll be using in the project:

```
1 import tensorflow as tf
2 from tensorflow import keras
3 from sklearn.model_selection import train_test_split
```

```
4
5 import os
6 from glob import glob
7
8 import cv2
9 import numpy as np
10 import pandas as pd
11 import matplotlib.pyplot as plt
```

First, let's take a look at what's inside the directory:

```
1 dirs = os.listdir("sem-drone")
2 dirs
3 # ['class_dict_seg.csv', 'dataset', 'RGB_color_image_masks']
```

We've got a `class_dict_seg.csv` with our RGB mappings for class labels. The `dataset` directory contains the dataset with the images and masks, while the `RGB_color_image_masks` contains already mapped and exported RGB-mapped label maps. It's only there for convenience so we don't have to convert the masks ourselves which we'll be doing later anyway. We'll use those images for visualization since they're already there, but conversion later is as easy as:

```
1 # Turning a label map into RGB representation
2 representation = rgb_rep[label_map]
```

Let's dig deeper:

```
1 os.listdir(os.path.join('sem-drone', 'RGB_color_image_masks',
      'RGB_color_image_masks'))[:5]
2 # ['000.png', '001.png', '002.png', '003.png', '004.png']
```

The RGB representations are in PNG format. What's in the `dataset` folder?

```
1 os.listdir(os.path.join('sem-drone', 'dataset', 'semantic_drone_dataset'))
2 # ['label_images_semantic', 'original_images']
```

`label_images_semantic` contains images encoded with the labels (pixel values between `[0..23]`), while `original_images` contains the input images:

```
1 os.listdir(os.path.join('sem-drone', 'dataset', 'semantic_drone_dataset',
      'label_images_semantic'))[:5]
2 # ['000.png', '001.png', '002.png', '003.png', '004.png']
3
4 os.listdir(os.path.join('sem-drone', 'dataset', 'semantic_drone_dataset',
      'original_images'))[:5]
5 # ['000.jpg', '001.jpg', '002.jpg', '003.jpg', '004.jpg']
```

Masks are in PNG format, images are in JPG. With these findings, let's define a `config` dictionary to hold some of the general settings in a centralized format that we can reference later:

```
config = {
    'IMG_PATH': os.path.join('sem-drone', 'dataset',
        'semantic_drone_dataset', 'original_images'),
    'LABEL_PATH': os.path.join('sem-drone', 'dataset',
        'semantic_drone_dataset', 'label_images_semantic'),
    'RGB_MASK_PATH': os.path.join('sem-drone', 'RGB_color_image_masks',
        'RGB_color_image_masks'),
    'CLASS_DICT': os.path.join('sem-drone', 'class_dict_seg.csv'),
    'NUM_CLASSES': 24,
    'BATCH_SIZE': 2,
    'IMAGE_SIZE': 512
}
```

Getting paths is always a good idea, especially if you'll be referencing them more than once. We're also simply defining the number of classes, batch size and image size here to make it easier to experiment and change a single knob centrally, instead of updating multiple parts of code later. The batch size and image size are parameters you can play with, depending on your hardware.

Lower-resolution segmentation images will be produced with lower image sizes, but are easier to fit into memory. If you run out of memory, try using a free Google Colab notebook instead.

Let's visualize the image and masks we're working with! Let's visualize the original image, its label map and RGB representation:

```
def visualize_trio(img_num):
    img = cv2.imread(os.path.join(config['IMG_PATH'], f'{img_num}.jpg'))
    img = cv2.cvtColor(img, cv2.COLOR_BGR2RGB)
    mask = cv2.imread(os.path.join(config['LABEL_PATH'], f'{img_num}.png'))
    mask = cv2.cvtColor(mask, cv2.COLOR_BGR2RGB)
    rgb = cv2.imread(os.path.join(config['RGB_MASK_PATH'], f'{img_num}.png'))
    rgb = cv2.cvtColor(rgb, cv2.COLOR_BGR2RGB)

    fig, ax = plt.subplots(1, 3, figsize=(16, 8))
    ax[0].imshow(img)
    ax[1].imshow(mask)
    ax[2].imshow(rgb)

    ax[0].axis('off')
    ax[1].axis('off')
    ax[2].axis('off')
    ax[0].set_title('Image')
    ax[1].set_title('Mask')
```

```
19        ax[2].set_title('RGB Representation')
20        plt.show()
21
22  visualize_trio('408')
```

This'll plot the 408th image, alongside its label mask and RGB Representation of that mask:

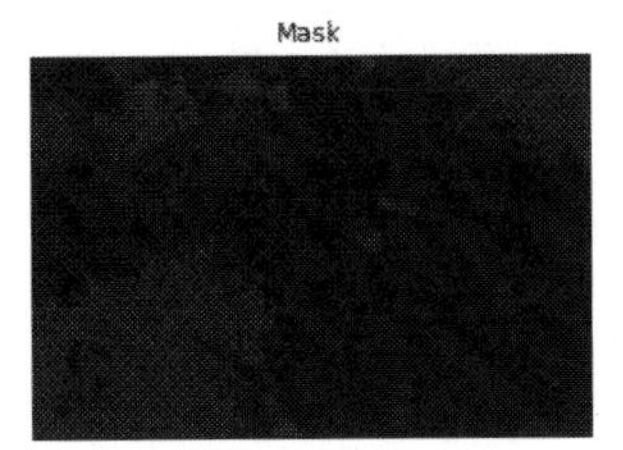

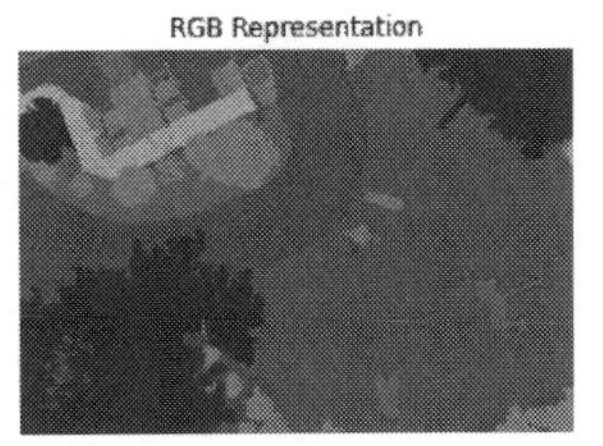

Figure 187:

If you inspect the `mask`:

```
1 mask = cv2.imread(os.path.join(config['LABEL_PATH'], '408.png'))
2 print(mask.shape) # (4000, 6000, 3)
```

It's quite large! We'll be reshaping the images for our model to work with in a moment. Also, observe the values of the mask as you print it:

```
1 [[[10 10 10]
2   [10 10 10]
3   [10 10 10]
4   ...
5   [19 19 19]
6   [19 19 19]
7   [19 19 19]]
```

The first pixels belong to class `10` (`wall`), and some time later, to class `19` (`tree`). Sounds about right. Time to build a dataset using `tf.data`!

13.8 Building a tf.data Dataset

Let's collect all of the available pathnames in the directories for images and labels. This is easily done using `glob`:

```
1 image_paths =  glob(os.path.join(config['IMG_PATH'], '*'), recursive=True)
2 mask_paths =  glob(os.path.join(config['LABEL_PATH'], '*'), recursive=True)
```

Once obtained, we can and will treat images as input, and masks as labels. Using any shuffling technique, such as Scikit-Learn's `train_test_split()`, let's create a training and testing set:

```
1 image_paths_train, image_paths_test, mask_paths_train, mask_paths_test =
      train_test_split(image_paths, mask_paths, shuffle=True)
```

Let's peak at the paths to check whether they're still in sync:

```
1 print(image_paths_train[:5])
2 print(mask_paths_train[:5])
```

```
1 ['sem-drone\\dataset\\semantic_drone_dataset\\original_images\\295.jpg', ...]
2 ['sem-drone\\dataset\\semantic_drone_dataset\\label_images_semantic\\295.png',
      ...]
```

And let's check the sizes:

```
1 print(len(image_paths_train)) # 300
2 print(len(image_paths_test))  # 100
```

Ouch, 300. We're used to dealing with much larger datasets for classification, since labelling for classification is significantly cheaper than for segmentation. Though, one great thing about segmentation is that you can more easily expand the training sets without adversly affecting networks (as much as for classification) in the process. Let's talk augmentation!

Let's save the length as a key in the `config`:

```
1 config['DATASET_LENGTH'] = len(image_paths_train)
```

13.9 Data Augmentation - TensorFlow and Albumentations

Recall *"Lesson 3 - Building Your First Convolutional Neural Network With Keras"*, in which I stated:

> It's not a replacement for a larger dataset - but it does help with increasing variance of the data and thus the robustness of the model. Some regard data augmentation as a *"magic tool"* (not in the sense that it's mystical, but that it helps with generalization as if it's magical).

> Though, data augmentation *also* implies something else. Yes, it's a great way to help a network generalize, by making it learn that a cat is still a cat even if it's slightly rotated. This only makes sense! We wouldn't want a model to forget what a cat is because it's rotated a bit. This might seem like we're giving the model context but don't forget - **machine learning models don't have context** (in the same way that humans do), and data augmentation doesn't help them get it. It, in fact, helps them **become blind to it**. If we show fives images of a cat to a model, slightly altered, and say it's a cat - it'll generalize better that all five images contain a cat.

> It'll learn that even if the image is skewed, flipped or otherwise altered, it's a cat. However - it's won't learn that ***it's a cat in different positions***, it'll learn that ***it's a cat***. Yes, it's a cat, that's true. ***But***, it's a cat *in a slightly different position*. This might sound like just a nuance, but the importance of nuances like this can't be overstated if we're to reach ***real*** computer vision or real intelligent systems.

The issue that arises with augmentation is tied to the fact that for classification, we don't also augment the labels in the same way we augment images. CutMix kind of does this, by providing weight to labels, but the labels themselves don't really encode anything other than "yes class X".

> With label maps for segmentation, this issue can be totally avoided, by treating label maps as images!

First of all - you have to do this. If you rotate an image, you'll have to rotate the target mask as well, or your model won't be able to learn much. But even if you didn't have to do this - it'd be a wasted opportunity to really harness the best of augmentation, with minimal adverse effects! This means that we can relatively aggresively augment our dataset, as long as we balance the augmentations on both images and masks, and combat the lack of images. Let's get to it!

First, we'll have a `preprocess()` function that reads and decodes images:

```
1 def preprocess(image_path, mask_path):
2     img = tf.io.read_file(image_path)
3     img = tf.image.decode_jpeg(img, channels=3)
4     img = tf.image.resize(img, size=[config['IMAGE_SIZE'],
          config['IMAGE_SIZE']])
5     img = tf.cast(img, tf.float32) / 255.0
6
7     mask = tf.io.read_file(mask_path)
8     # Only one channel for masks, denoting the class and NOT image colors
9     mask = tf.image.decode_png(mask, channels=1)
10    mask = tf.image.resize(mask, size=[config['IMAGE_SIZE'],
          config['IMAGE_SIZE']])
11    mask = tf.cast(mask, tf.float32)
12
13    return img, mask
```

First, doing augmentations with TensorFlow's `tf.image` library seems fitting, since we're using the `tf.data` API to create a `Dataset`:

```
1 def augment_dataset_tf(img, mask):
2     # Augmentations should always be performed on both an input image and
          a mask if applied at all
3     if tf.random.uniform(()) > 0.5:
4         img = tf.image.flip_left_right(img)
5         mask = tf.image.flip_left_right(mask)
6     if tf.random.uniform(()) > 0.5:
7         img = tf.image.flip_up_down(img)
8         mask = tf.image.flip_up_down(mask)
9     if tf.random.uniform(()) > 0.5:
10        img = tf.image.rot90(img)
11        mask = tf.image.rot90(mask)
12
13    return img, mask
```

With a probability of 50%, we apply some of the `tf.image` transformation to our images and masks. They always go hand in hand. Then, we can apply both the `preprocess()` function and `augment_dataset_tf()` after creating the a set from image and mask paths:

```
1 def create_dataset_tf(images, masks, augment):
2     dataset = tf.data.Dataset.from_tensor_slices((images,
          masks)).shuffle(len(images))
3     dataset = dataset.map(preprocess, num_parallel_calls = tf.data.AUTOTUNE)
4     if augment:
5         dataset = dataset.map(apply_albumentations, num_parallel_calls =
              tf.data.AUTOTUNE)
6         dataset = dataset.batch(config['BATCH_SIZE'], drop_remainder =
              True).prefetch(tf.data.AUTOTUNE).repeat()
7     else:
8         dataset = dataset.batch(config['BATCH_SIZE'], drop_remainder =
```

```
9         True).prefetch(tf.data.AUTOTUNE)
      return dataset
```

You can then instantiate datasets with:

```
1 train_set = create_dataset(image_paths_train, mask_paths_train, augment=True)
2 test_set = create_dataset(image_paths_test, mask_paths_test, augment=False)
```

Though, this doesn't really scratch the itch. We can list a fair bit of augmentations, but don't really use many of them because the `tf.image` library doesn't really have many options. We could turn to Keras' preprocessing layers and some of the randomized classes from there, but we'd have to impose a seed between images and label maps, which slows down the process and we want to use `tf.data` because it's fast and optimized. Time to introduce Albumentations.

13.9.1 The Albumentations Library

The Albumentations library[144] is an image augmentation library. It provides nearly 50 pixel-level augmentations, and nearly 40 spatial-level augmentations for images. It also has support for different tasks, and differentiates between augmentations for images, segmentation masks, keypoints, etc.

YOLOv5, which we previously used, uses Albumentations extensively, and if you've used PyTorch or `torchvision` before, you're likely familiar with the `A.Compose([])` call used to create a pipeline of augmentations. Industry leaders in applying computer vision to different domains use the Albumentations library.

Note: It addresses a different problem from KerasCV preprocessing layers, and the preprocessing layers that come shipped with KerasCV can be turned into model-level augmentations that help build truly end-to-end systems.

---

[144]https://albumentations.ai/

What's with another way to perform augmentation? TensorFlow and Keras themselves have several ways to perform it, so why should someone dedicate another library to it? The most obvious examples come from object detection and semantic segmentation. As soon as labels get more complex than just numbers, and encode spatial or other data in themselves, augmentation becomes much harder than just rotation, flipping, etc.

Pixel-level augmentations such as making an image brighter or darker doesn't make it harder to make object detection or segmentation models. But if you rotate an image, you should also properly rotate the bounding boxes and masks. If you crop, how do you update these? Also, you might want to be able to control the probability of some augmentations being applied. This is doable, but a bit verbose, such as in the example above.

Additionally, having a consistent API to work with over different tasks - classification, detection, segmentation and pose estimation - is comforting for developers. Albumentations does this for you, with a beautifully simple interface.

Advice: I think that it's important to be flexible, and to switch tools when required. Sometimes, standard Keras and KerasCV preprocessing layers will be your best book for action, sometimes, it'll be Albumentations. You never know whether something new will pop up next year either! Chances are, it will, and you can benefit from testing it out. As of writing, these two are probably your best shot.

Let's install it via `pip`:

```
1 $ pip install albumentations
```

It's typically imported as `A`, after which you can use the global `Compose()` method to define a pipeline of augmentations, and apply it to images:

```
1 import albumentations as A
2
3 transform = A.Compose([
4     A.HorizontalFlip(p=0.5),
5     A.VerticallFlip(p=0.5)
```

```
6 ])
7
8 image = cv2.imread('some_file.jpg')
9 image = cv2.cvtColor(image, cv2.COLOR_BGR2RGB)
10 augmented_image = transform(image=image)['image']
```

The `transform` object can also be a single standalone transform, rather than a composed pipeline, such as:

```
1 transform = A.HorizontalFlip(p=0.5)
```

Whether a pipeline or a single transform, the object itself returns a dictionary from which you obtain your transformed image with the `['image']` key.

13.9.2 Image and Segmentation Mask Augmentation with Albumentations

Let's update our previous augmentation code to use Albumentations instead of `tf.image`. Albumentations integrates with `tf.data` well, but there's a small difference between what we've done so far and what we'll do with the library. So far, we've been defining methods that accept an image and label (`img` and `mask` in this case), augmenting them with TensorFlow methods and returning the results. TensorFlow works with Tensors, which don't always integrate well with other libraries. Albumentations expects NumPy arrays.

We can execute functions that treat input tensors as NumPy arrays via the `tf.numpy_function()` function, so we'll define our `albumentations()` function that accepts our image-mask pairs, and then execute that function via `tf.numpy_function()`. Let's start with the transforms themselves:

```
1 def albumentations(img, mask):
2     # Augmentation pipeline - each of these has an adjustable probability
3     # of being applied, regardless of other transforms
4     transform = A.Compose([
5         A.HorizontalFlip(p=0.5),
6         A.RandomBrightnessContrast(p=0.3),
7         A.Transpose(p=0.5),
8         A.VerticalFlip(p=0.5),
9         A.HorizontalFlip(p=0.5),
10        A.Rotate(limit=70),
11        # CoarseDropout is the new Cutout implementation
12        A.CoarseDropout(p=0.5, max_holes=12, max_height=24, max_width=24)
13    ])
```

```
14
15     # Apply transforms and extract image and mask
16     transformed = transform(image=img, mask=mask)
17     transformed_image = transformed['image']
18     transformed_mask = transformed['mask']
19
20     # Cast to TF Floats and return
21     transformed_image = tf.cast(transformed_image, tf.float32)
22     transformed_mask = tf.cast(transformed_mask, tf.float32)
23     return transformed_image, transformed_mask
```

Albumentations supports segmentation augmentation by passing an `image` and `mask` argument, rather than just the `image` argument. It treats the mask as intrinsically tied to the appropriate `image`, and applies augmentations safe for masks on it. For example, it *won't* apply `CoarseDropout` on masks, as they're labels that should be inferred even with some spatial dropout on the input images.

Now, to apply these augmentations, we'll write another function as a wrapper:

```
1 def apply_albumentations(img, mask):
2     aug_img, aug_mask = tf.numpy_function(func=albumentations, inp=[img,
          mask], Tout=[tf.float32, tf.float32])
3     aug_img = tf.ensure_shape(aug_img, shape=[config['IMAGE_SIZE'],
          config['IMAGE_SIZE'], 3])
4     aug_mask = tf.ensure_shape(aug_mask, shape=[config['IMAGE_SIZE'],
          config['IMAGE_SIZE'], 1])
5     return aug_img, aug_mask
```

If we weren't returning a double output (image and mask) - we'd set `Tout` to just `tf.float32`, not a list with two of them. The official documentation of the Albumentations library has a great page with examples of integrating augmentation pipelines with TensorFlow[145]!

Finally, we can create the `Dataset` objects with:

```
1 train_set = create_dataset(image_paths_train, mask_paths_train, augment=True)
2 test_set = create_dataset(image_paths_test, mask_paths_test, augment=False)
```

Let's take a look at some of the entries in the set with:

```
1 for img_batch, mask_batch in train_set.take(2):
2     for i in range(len(img_batch)):
3         fig, ax = plt.subplots(1, 2)
4         ax[0].imshow(img_batch[i].numpy())
5         ax[1].imshow(mask_batch[i].numpy())
```

[145]https://albumentations.ai/docs/examples/tensorflow-example/

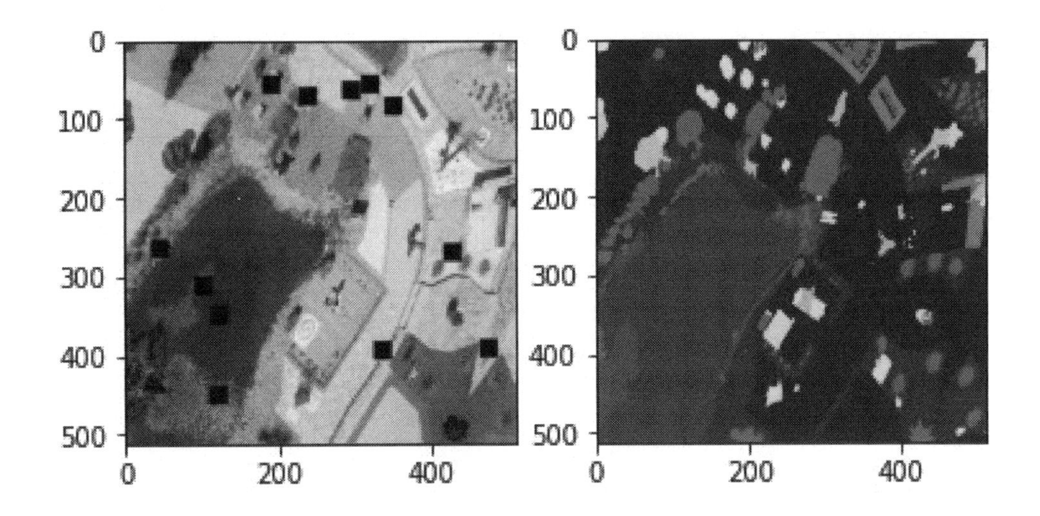

Figure 188:

And:

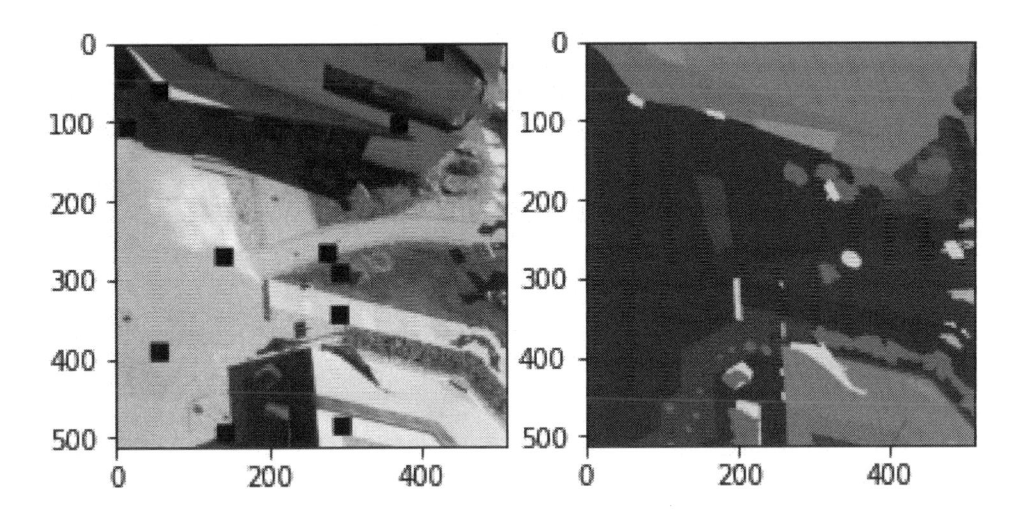

Figure 189:

Looks like our training data is ready! We don't really have the luxury of separating out a validation set from these images, as there's very few of them in total. We'll have to use the `test_set` as our validation set as well, even though it's not ideal.

13.10 Implementing Atrous Convolutional Blocks and Atrous Spatial Pyramid Pooling

With the dataset ready, it's time to create our DeepLabV3+ model. Let's refer back to the diagram and translate it into code:

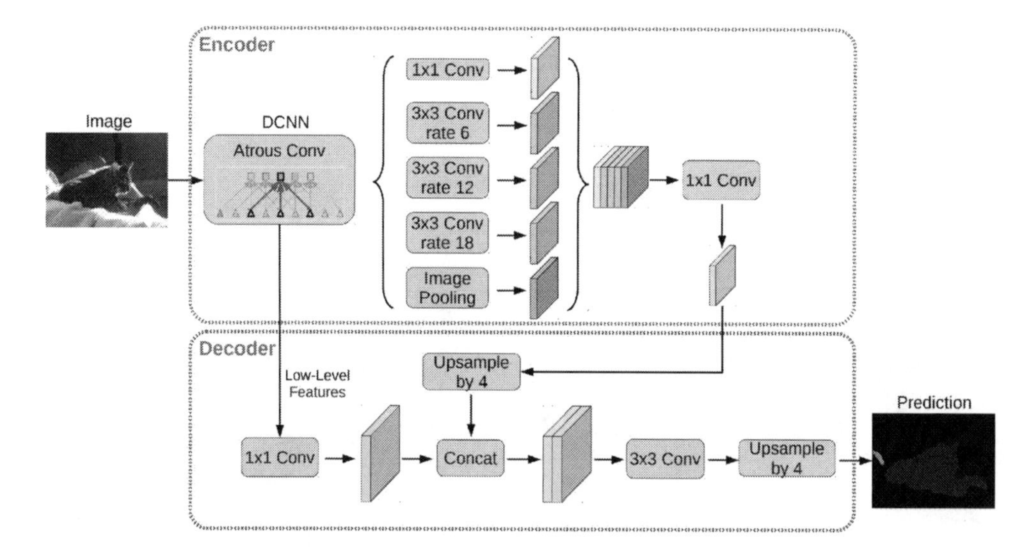

Figure 190:

The network uses several convolutional blocks, with differing dilation rates, both for the Atrous Spatial Pyramid Pooling (ASPP) module, and otherwise. Let's define a `conv_block()` for that first:

```
1 # Turns into atrous_block with dilation_rate > 1
2 def conv_block(block_input, num_filters=256, kernel_size=(3, 3),
      dilation_rate=1, padding = "same"):
3     x = keras.layers.Conv2D(num_filters, kernel_size=kernel_size,
          dilation_rate=dilation_rate, padding = "same")(block_input)
4     x = keras.layers.BatchNormalization()(x)
```

```
5       x = keras.layers.Activation('relu')(x)
6       return x
```

By default, it's a regular convolutional block. By setting the `dilation_rate` to anything above `1` - it becomes an "atrous" convolutional block. This is a pretty standard Conv-BN-ReLU block, with an adjustable `dilation_rate` parameter.

Now, let's define the ASPP module, one of the most important parts of DeepLabV3+. There's a small detail omitted from the diagram above - information on how "Image Pooling" is done.

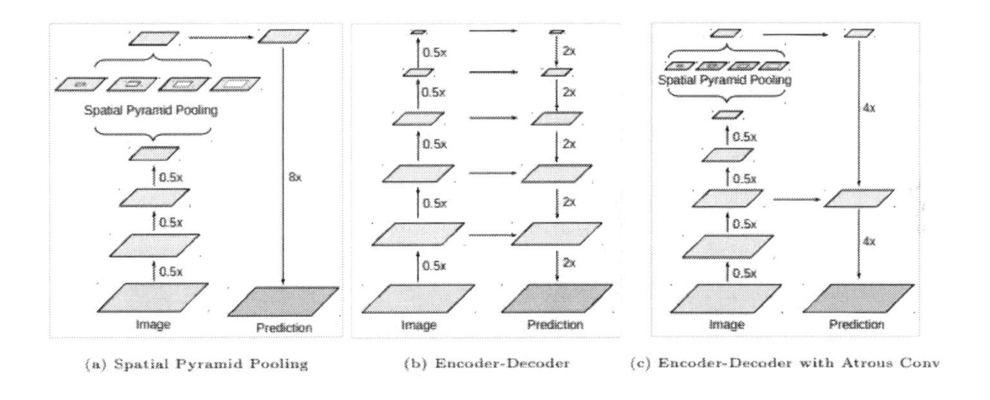

(a) Spatial Pyramid Pooling (b) Encoder-Decoder (c) Encoder-Decoder with Atrous Conv

Figure 191:

Regular Spatial Pyramid Pooling (on the left) downsamples the input and recovers the output from it by upsampling (encodes image into a denser vector and decodes it into a prediction). A U-Net-like encoder-decoder also does this, but injects spatial information on different scales while downsampling into the layers while upsampling (b). DeepLab tries to use the best of both of these approaches and performs Spatial Pyramid Pooling with intermediate shortcut injections of spatial context while upsampling.

Besides this, the input is passed through 4 `conv_block()` layers, with differing filter sizes and dilation rates:

```
1 # Atrous Spatial Pyramid Pooling
2 def ASPP(inputs):
3     # 4 conv blocks with dilation rates at `[1, 6, 12, 18]`
4     conv_1 = conv_block(inputs, kernel_size=(1, 1), dilation_rate=1)
```

```
5      conv_6 = conv_block(inputs, kernel_size=(3, 3), dilation_rate=6)
6      conv_12 = conv_block(inputs, kernel_size=(3, 3), dilation_rate=12)
7      conv_18 = conv_block(inputs, kernel_size=(3, 3), dilation_rate=18)
8
9      dims = inputs.shape
10     # Image Pooling -> (256, 256, 3) -> (1, 1, filter_num) -> (32, 32, 256)
11     x = keras.layers.AveragePooling2D(pool_size=(dims[-3], dims[-2]))(inputs)
12     x = conv_block(x, kernel_size=1)
13     out_pool = keras.layers.UpSampling2D(size=(dims[-3] // x.shape[1],
           dims[-2] // x.shape[2]))(x)
14
15     x = keras.layers.Concatenate()([conv_1, conv_6, conv_12, conv_18,
           out_pool])
16     return conv_block(x, kernel_size=1)
```

The output of each `conv_block()` and image pooling are concatenated (stacked on top of each other), passed through a 1x1 convolutional block and returned. This result is later upsampled by 4 and concatenated to the result of the DCNN. Let's now focus on that part. If you ignore the ASPP module, the network is a linear one, and the result of ASPP is concatenated near the end of the network.

13.11 Implementing DeepLabV3+ with Keras

We can start defining the overall DeepLabV3+ network and inject ASPP within it:

```
1  def define_deeplabv3_plus(image_size, num_classes, backbone):
2      model_input = keras.Input(shape=(image_size, image_size, 3))
3
4      if backbone == 'resnet':
5          resnet101 = keras.applications.ResNet101(
6              weights = "imagenet",
7              include_top=False,
8              input_tensor=model_input)
9          x = resnet101.get_layer("conv4_block6_2_relu").output
10         low_level = resnet101.get_layer("conv2_block3_2_relu").output
11
12     elif backbone == 'effnet':
13         effnet = keras.applications.EfficientNetV2B0(
14             weights = "imagenet",
15              include_top=False,
16              input_tensor=model_input)
17         x = effnet.get_layer("block5e_activation").output
18         low_level = effnet.get_layer("block2a_expand_activation").output
19
20     aspp_result = ASPP(x)
21     upsampled_aspp = keras.layers.UpSampling2D(size=(4, 4))(aspp_result)
22
23     low_level = conv_block(low_level, num_filters=48, kernel_size=1)
24
```

```
25     x = keras.layers.Concatenate()([upsampled_aspp, low_level])
26     x = conv_block(x)
27     x = keras.layers.UpSampling2D(size=(4, 4))(x)
28     model_output = keras.layers.Conv2D(num_classes, kernel_size=(1, 1),
           padding = "same", activation = 'softmax')(x)
29     return keras.Model(inputs=model_input, outputs=model_output)
```

The ability to swap out a backbone adds some optional verbosity, but it's important to note that DeepLab is backbone-agnostic. ResNet is a common backbone, both because it was used in the original paper and has been proven to work well, but also because it's fairly stable during training. Choosing the "right" layers for the high-level and low-level activations takes a fair bit of tweaking, and going with the established flow is easier.

In any case, two layers are extracted from the backbone - a high-level and low-level layer. ASPP is applied to the high-level layer, and the result is upsampled. The low-level features are passed through a 1x1 convolutional layer and concatenated to the upsampled ASPP output. This concatenation is passed through a 3x3 convolutional block and upsampled again to match the original resolution.

Note the `model_output` layer - it's a `Conv2D` with a filter size of `1`, and a `'softmax'` activation. It results in an `(image_size, image_size, num_classes)` shape. In effect, there's a `(image_size, image_size)` output tensor, over the probability distribution of the classes (full-size tensor for every class) in our training set. We'll want to extract the highest probability classes from this output tensor and collapse it into just an `(image_size, image_size)` tensor, which encodes the classes in the same way the label map (mask) does.

Then, using the class dictionary - we can convert these labels into an RGB representation and plot an image of the classes! In my own tests, with the layers selected as in the code example earlier (feel free to change these and play around) - ResNets provide somewhat better performance, train a bit slower and have slightly more stable training curves. Let's instantiate it:

```
1 model = define_deeplabv3_plus(config['IMAGE_SIZE'], config['NUM_CLASSES'],
      'resnet')
2 model.summary()
```

```
1 Model: "model"
2 __________________________________________________________________
3  Layer (type)                   Output Shape         Param #     Connected to
4 ==================================================================
5  input_3 (InputLayer)           [(None, 512, 512, 3  0           []
6                                 )]
```

```
...
conv2d_8 (Conv2D)                (None, 512, 512, 24  6168
    ['up_sampling2d_2[0][0]']
                                 )

====================================================
Total params: 11,269,000
Trainable params: 11,236,776
Non-trainable params: 32,224
____________________________________________________
```

The output shape, as expected, is `(image_size, image_size. num_classes)`. Let's take a brief look at the metrics and loss functions we could be utilizing to train this network.

13.12 Metrics and Loss Functions

Segmentation models can be subjected to an accuracy metric, but it oftentimes isn't the best metric around, and especially suffers from datasets which have masks with lots of background, and small areas of other classes. This is a generally present in medical images where a small area of the image indicates the presence of a disease, injury, etc. Our dataset doesn't suffer much from this issue, since most pixels of an image have a distinct class - and they're distributed enough so that there's not a super large imbalance between classes, though, there are certainly more 'grass' and 'roof' pixels than 'person' pixels.

Because of this imbalance, a network can learn to overemphasize a class which is abundant, and still achieve a high accuracy rating.

The two most common metrics for measuing segmentation performance are the *Jaccard Index* and *Dice Coefficient*. Don't let these fool you! The Jaccard Index is, in fact, just *Intersection over Union (IoU)*. *Mean IoU (MIoU)* is also common. The *Dice Coefficient* (also known as Sørensen–Dice Coefficient or Sørensen–Dice Index) is F1-Score in disguise! You're familiar with both of these metrics from earlier.

What about loss functions? Previously mentioned Focal Loss is one. As a quick reminder, Focal Loss reduces the weight of easily classifiable samples have and makes the network focus on harder-to-classify examples. Crossentropy is a very commonly used metric as well. The Dice Coefficient can be used to calculate a Dice Loss, just as IoU can be turned into an IoU loss. Dice Loss has been generalized into Tversky Loss. You can separate the losses based on what they take into consideration when being calculated:

- **Region-based Loss Functions:** Dice Loss, IoU Loss, Tversky Loss, Focal Tversky Loss
- **Boundary-based Loss Functions:** Boundary Loss
- **Distribution-based Loss Functions:** Crossentropy, Focal Loss

Jun Ma et al. did a great visualization of the loss function landscape and their relationship (in the context of computer vision for medical images) in their paper "Loss Odyssey in Medical Image Segmentation"[146]:

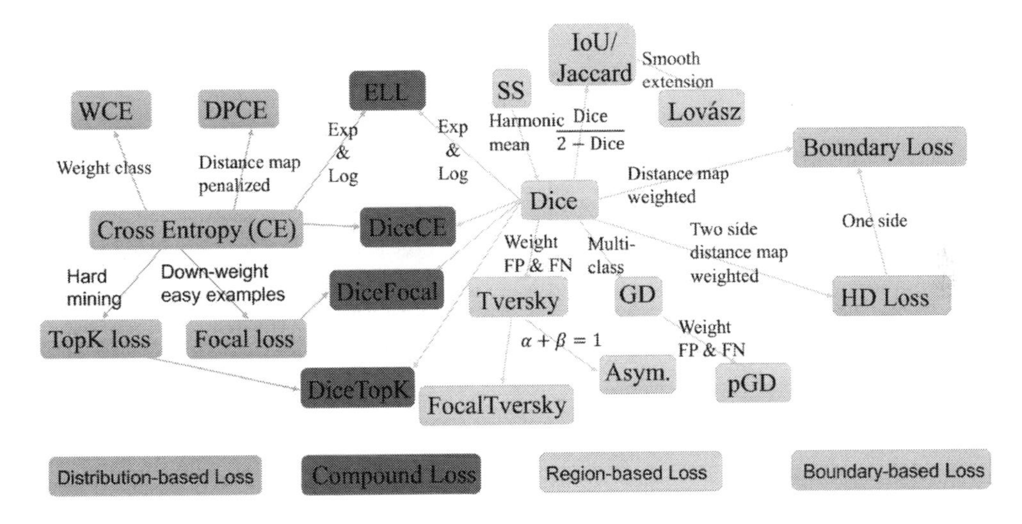

Figure 192:

For practical purposes - it's easiest to use a `SparseCategoricalCrossentropy` or `CategoricalCrossentropy` that ships with Keras. We'll implement the Dice Coefficient as a metric, which can easily be turned into a loss function, but it produced a worse model on this dataset, so we'll focus on the familiar crossentropy loss:

```
1 from keras import backend as K
2
3 def dice_coef(y_true, y_pred, smooth=1e-7):
4     y_true_f = K.flatten(K.one_hot(K.cast(y_true, 'int32'),
          num_classes=config['NUM_CLASSES'])[...,1:])
5     y_pred_f = K.flatten(y_pred[...,1:])
6     intersect = K.sum(y_true_f * y_pred_f, axis=-1)
```

[146]https://www.sciencedirect.com/science/article/abs/pii/S1361841521000815?via%3Dihub

```
7      denom = K.sum(y_true_f + y_pred_f, axis=-1)
8      return K.mean((2. * intersect / (denom + smooth)))
9
10 def dice_loss(y_true, y_pred):
11     return 1 - dice_coef(y_true, y_pred)
```

We'll also want to keep track of MeanIoU. Keras has a built-in `keras.metrics.MeanIoU()` class that accepts a `num_classes` argument. However, it sometimes runs into a bug with Sparse Categorical Crossentropy, due to a casting line in the core of the framework. We can easily implement our own MeanIoU class, and simply delegate the calculation to the TensorFlow/Keras implementation, and override the erroneous line on our end:

```
1 class MeanIoU(tf.keras.metrics.MeanIoU):
2     def __init__(self,
3                  y_true=None,
4                  y_pred=None,
5                  num_classes=None,
6                  name=None,
7                  dtype=None):
8         super(MeanIoU, self).__init__(num_classes = num_classes,name=name,
              dtype=dtype)
9
10    def update_state(self, y_true, y_pred, sample_weight=None):
11        y_pred = tf.math.argmax(y_pred, axis=-1)
12        return super().update_state(y_true, y_pred, sample_weight)
```

Great! We can set up our training callbacks and compile the model:

```
1 reduceLr = keras.callbacks.ReduceLROnPlateau(patience=5, factor=0.3, monitor
      = 'val_sparse_categorical_accuracy')
2 early_stopping = keras.callbacks.EarlyStopping(patience=10, monitor =
      'val_sparse_categorical_accuracy', restore_best_weights=True)
3
4 model.compile(
5     optimizer = keras.optimizers.Adam(learning_rate=5e-5),
6     #loss = soft_dice_loss,
7     loss = "sparse_categorical_crossentropy",
8     metrics=["sparse_categorical_accuracy",
9              MeanIoU(num_classes=config['NUM_CLASSES']),
10             dice_coef])
11
12 steps = int(config['DATASET_LENGTH']/config['BATCH_SIZE'])
13
14 history = model.fit(train_set,
15                     epochs=100,
16                     steps_per_epoch=steps,
17                     validation_data=test_set,
18                     callbacks=[reduceLr, early_stopping])
```

The dataset repeats itself, so we've gone with 150 steps per epoch, calculated as the length of the dataset, divided by the batch size. The training halts after around 80 epochs:

```
Epoch 1/100
100/100 [==============================] - 35s 245ms/step - loss: 2.3580 -
    sparse_categorical_accuracy: 0.4134 - mean_io_u: 0.0549 - dice_coef:
    0.2356 - val_loss: 32.9173 - val_sparse_categorical_accuracy: 0.0144 -
    val_mean_io_u: 0.0039 - val_dice_coef: 0.0146 - lr: 5.0000e-05
...
Epoch 81/100
150/150 [==============================] - 34s 226ms/step - loss: 0.3186 -
    sparse_categorical_accuracy: 0.9002 - mean_io_u: 0.5665 - dice_coef:
    0.8524 - val_loss: 0.4183 - val_sparse_categorical_accuracy: 0.8746 -
    val_mean_io_u: 0.5281 - val_dice_coef: 0.8339 - lr: 1.3500e-06
```

It achieved a validation Dice Coefficient of 0.83. Let's plot the learning curves:

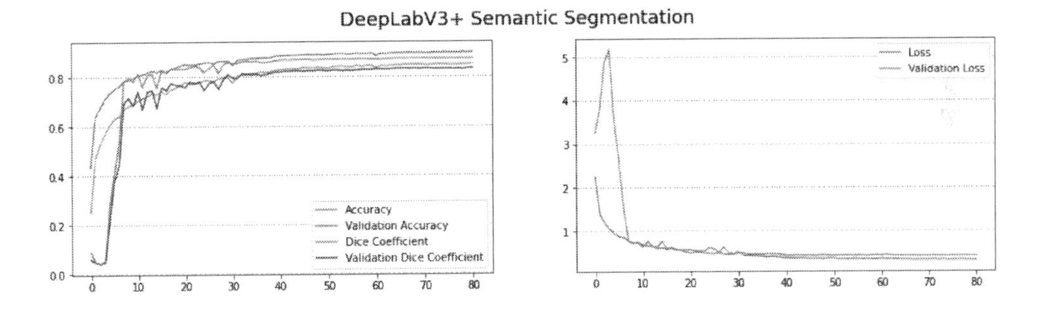

Figure 193:

The training and testing metrics are practically equivalent, so we aren't really seeing much overfitting here. Time to plot some predictions!

13.13 Semantic Segmentation Inference

Let's first read the CSV file that contains the classes and their RGB representations:

```
class_dict_seg = pd.read_csv(config['CLASS_DICT'])
class_dict_seg.head()
```

```
          name    r   g    b
0    unlabeled    0   0    0
1  paved-area   128  64  128
```

```
2        dirt  130   76    0
3       grass    0  102    0
4      gravel  112  103   87
```

You can easily extract a NumPy array from these with:

```
# Note the whitespaces before ' r', ' g' and ' b'
rgb_rep = class_dict_seg[[' r', ' g', ' b']].values
rgb_rep[:10]
```

```
array([[  0,   0,   0],
       [128,  64, 128],
       [130,  76,   0],
       [  0, 102,   0],
       [112, 103,  87],
       [ 28,  42, 168],
       [ 48,  41,  30],
       [  0,  50,  89],
       [107, 142,  35],
       [ 70,  70,  70]], dtype=int64)
```

Conversion between class maps and RGB representations boils down to:

```
rgb_rep[prediction]
```

You can also extract the classnames as:

```
classes = class_dict_seg['name'].values
classes
```

```
array(['unlabeled', 'paved-area', 'dirt', 'grass', 'gravel', 'water',
       'rocks', 'pool', 'vegetation', 'roof', 'wall', 'window', 'door',
       'fence', 'fence-pole', 'person', 'dog', 'car', 'bicycle', 'tree',
       'bald-tree', 'ar-marker', 'obstacle', 'conflicting'], dtype=object)
```

Let's create a convinience function to perform inference and to visualize the input image, the mask, RGB representation and our prediction:

```
def visualize_predictions(img_num):
    if os.path.exists(os.path.join(config['IMG_PATH'], f'{img_num}.jpg')):
        img = cv2.imread(os.path.join(config['IMG_PATH'], f'{img_num}.jpg'))
        img = cv2.cvtColor(img, cv2.COLOR_BGR2RGB)
        img = cv2.resize(img,  [config['IMAGE_SIZE'], config['IMAGE_SIZE']])
        img = img/255.0

        mask = cv2.imread(os.path.join(config['LABEL_PATH'],
            f'{img_num}.png'))
        mask = cv2.cvtColor(mask, cv2.COLOR_BGR2RGB)
        mask = cv2.resize(mask,  [config['IMAGE_SIZE'],
```

```
               config['IMAGE_SIZE']])
11
12          rgb = cv2.imread(os.path.join(config['RGB_MASK_PATH'],
                f'{img_num}.png'))
13          rgb = cv2.cvtColor(rgb, cv2.COLOR_BGR2RGB)
14          rgb = cv2.resize(rgb,  [config['IMAGE_SIZE'], config['IMAGE_SIZE']])
15
16          pred = model.predict(np.expand_dims(img, 0), verbose=0)
17          predictions = np.argmax(pred, axis=-1)
18          representation = rgb_rep[predictions]
19
20          fig, ax = plt.subplots(1, 4, figsize=(16, 8))
21          ax[0].imshow(img)
22          ax[1].imshow(mask)
23          ax[2].imshow(rgb)
24          ax[3].imshow(representation.squeeze())
25
26          ax[0].axis('off')
27          ax[1].axis('off')
28          ax[2].axis('off')
29          ax[3].axis('off')
30          ax[0].set_title('Image')
31          ax[1].set_title('Mask')
32          ax[2].set_title('RGB Representation')
33          ax[3].set_title('Prediction')
34          plt.show()
```

Now, we can call the function on any image from the dataset's directories:

```
1 visualize_predictions('472')
2 visualize_predictions('408')
3 visualize_predictions('109')
```

This results in:

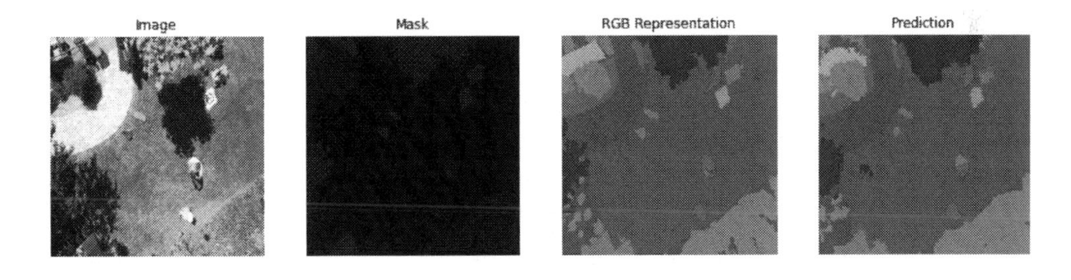

Figure 194:

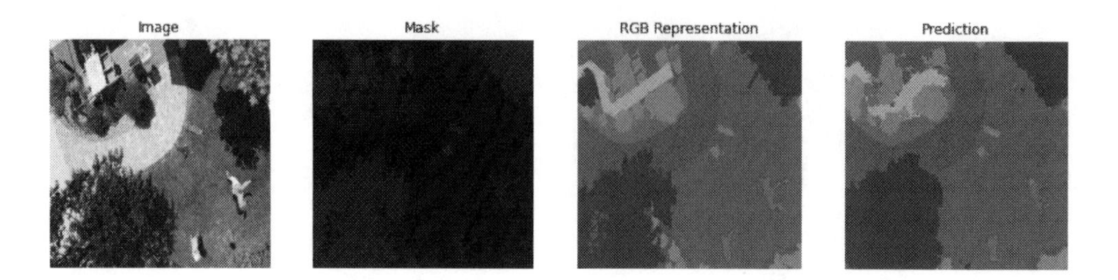

Figure 195:

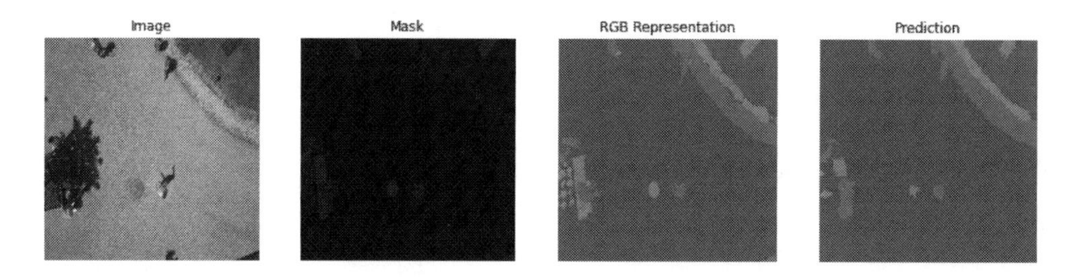

Figure 196:

To display results though, we typically want to overlay the prediction over the input image, effectively coloring each semantic concept in a different color:

```
def predict_and_overlay(img_num):
    if os.path.exists(os.path.join(config['IMG_PATH'], f'{img_num}.jpg')):

        img = cv2.imread(os.path.join(config['IMG_PATH'], f'{img_num}.jpg'))
        img = cv2.cvtColor(img, cv2.COLOR_BGR2RGB)
        img = cv2.resize(img,  [config['IMAGE_SIZE'], config['IMAGE_SIZE']])
        img = img/255.0

        pred = model.predict(np.expand_dims(img, 0), verbose=0)
        predictions = np.argmax(pred, axis=-1)
        representation = rgb_rep[predictions]

        fig, ax = plt.subplots(1, figsize=(16, 8))
        ax.imshow(img)
        ax.imshow(representation.squeeze(), alpha=0.5)
        ax.axis('off')

        plt.show()
```

Let's check it out on another image:

```
1 predict_and_overlay(206)
```

This outputs:

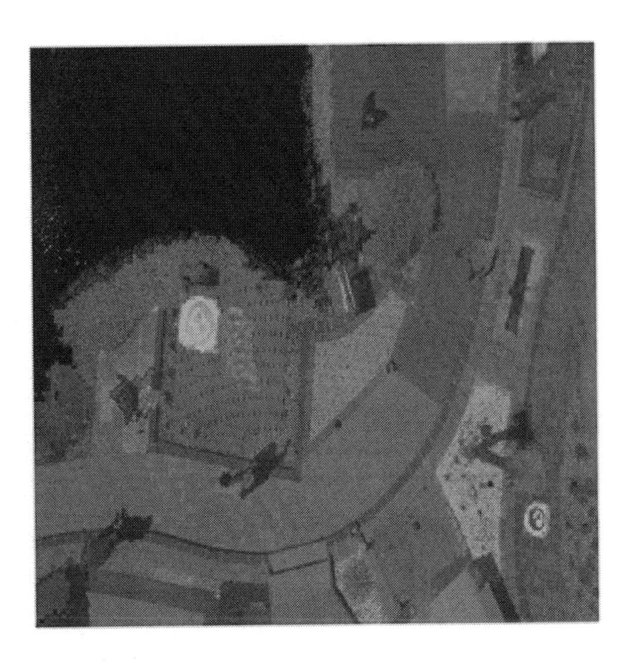

Figure 197:

Can we apply this model to other aerial shots? Semantic segmentation models are more sensitive to domain shift than image classification models, in large part because image classification models are blind to many small differences by abstracting them away, while segmentation models pay much more attention to small details.

It's harder to create a model that generalizes well to data outside of the training and testing sets - because the domain is likely different. Our model fit the data we have, with little overfitting, it generalizes well to the testing set. Though, will it work as well on other aerial shots?

Here are a few things to consider:

- Most of the images were from a single neighborhood, which has its own terrain and urbanism design. Change in urbanism might throw the model off somewhat.
- Most of the shots appear to have been made on the same day. Changes in lighting or weather conditions might throw the model off somewhat.
- Most of the shots were fairly close to the ground. Changes in drone altitude might throw the model off somewhat.
- We only had 300 images to train with, and the model managed to generalize well to 100 images from the testing set. This can be a bit illusory, as some images are very similar to each other. This is minimized by shuffling, but *some* images probably bled through.

When creating an image segmentation model, know that it'll be hard to create a truly general model. We likely won't be able to apply this model to map the world, but we probably could map this neighborhood with new shots on the same altitude and similar weather conditions.

Let's try segmenting an aerial drone image from the internet. We'll make a small helper method to predict and plot an image, overlay and segmentation map:

```
1 def predict_img(img):
2         pred = model.predict(np.expand_dims(img, 0), verbose=0)
3         predictions = np.argmax(pred, axis=-1)
4         representation = rgb_rep[predictions]
5 
6         fig, ax = plt.subplots(1, 3, figsize=(16, 8))
7         ax[0].imshow(img)
8         ax[1].imshow(img, alpha=0.5)
9         ax[1].imshow(representation.squeeze(), alpha=0.5)
10        ax[2].imshow(representation.squeeze())
11        #ax.axis('off')
12
13        plt.show()
```

And now, we can provide the image and take a look at the results:

```
1 import urllib.request
2 from tensorflow.keras.preprocessing import image
3 
4 def url_to_array(url):
5     req = urllib.request.urlopen(url)
6     arr = np.array(bytearray(req.read()), dtype=np.int8)
7     img = cv2.imdecode(arr, -1)
8     img = cv2.cvtColor(img, cv2.COLOR_BGR2RGB)
9     img = cv2.resize(img,  [config['IMAGE_SIZE'], config['IMAGE_SIZE']])
10    img = img/255.0
11    return img
```

```
12
13 # Book formatting
14 url = 'https://wp-tid.zillowstatic.com'
15 url = url+'/8/PARC_Feature_Drones_3200x2134-225fba.png'
16 img = url_to_array(url)
17 predict_img(img)
```

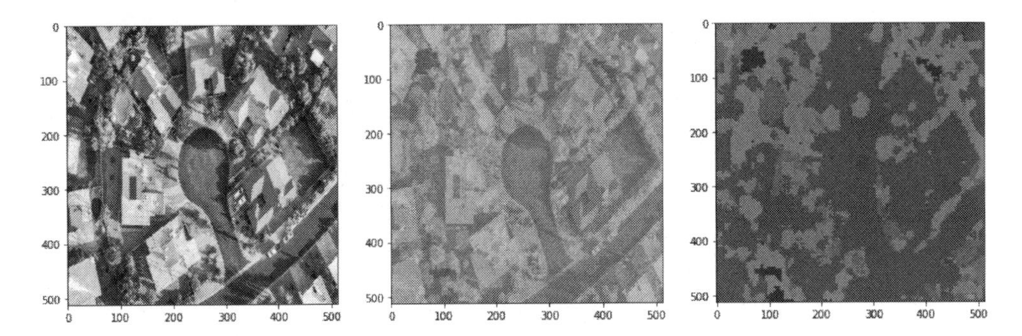

Figure 198:

The image is brighter than most of our training images, shot at a significantly higher altitude and has a lot of trees covering parts of the pavement and driveways. The roofs are quite light, so some of them are misclassified as pavement instead. The trees and grenery are segmented quite well, and it looks like the model is mainly struggling with pavement/roof segmentation. Considering the difference in the conditions - this isn't bad at all! The segmentation map on the right does somewhat look like an old-school RPG game map.

14 DeepDream - Neural Networks That Hallucinate?

Hierarchical abstraction appears to be what our brains do, with increasing support in the field of Neuroscience. While some protest drawing lines between the computation the brain does and silicone computing found in computers, some support the parallels, such as Dana H. Ballard in his book *"Brain Computation as Hierarchical Abstraction"*, who works as a Computer Science professor at the University of Texas, with ties to Psychology, Neuroscience and the Center for Perceptual Systems.

Inspired by hierarchical abstraction of the visual cortex, CNNs are hierarchical, and hierarchical abstraction is what allows them to do what they do. Exploiting exactly this property is what allows us to create a really fun (and practical) algorithm, and the focus of this lesson. It's called *DeepDream*, because we associate odd, almost-there-but-not-there visuals with dreams, and the images are induced by a deep convolutional neural network. Here's a visual created with the code in this lesson:

Figure 199:

In *"Being You"* by British neuroscientist Anil Seth, Anil explains how they used deep dream to create a "hallucination machine". A "hallucination machine" was meant to computationally simulate overreactive perceptual priors. That's a different way to say "emphasize what you expect". Where I'm from, folk wisdom states that *"In fear, eyes are big"*, and it's oftentimes used to explain how you can easily see things that aren't there when you're afraid. You're embedding overreactive perceptual priors in your projection so the shirt you forgot to take off the chair now looks like an intruder in your home during night. In a similar way, you might recognize a cloud as being the shape of a country on a map, or the sequence of lines "-_-" as a face with closed eyes and a flat mouth. This is formally known as *pareidolia*. In 2015, Google engineer Alexander Mordvintsev popularized a way to embed perceptual priors (induce and visualize pareidolia) into CNNs. This algorithm is known as *DeepDream*.

The "hallucination machine" is built on top DeepDream, and in effect, applies it to all input frames of a 360 VR headset, allowing people to experience strong priors that lead to hallucinations in videos around them. It allowed Anil's lab to study perception with enhanced hallucinations, without having to intoxicate participants with hallucinogens! The following image is a screenshot from a demonstration of the hallucination machine, uploaded to YouTube by Keisuke Suzuki[147] (the lead of the project):

Figure 200:

If you follow the link, you can pan around in 360 and observe the effect of embedding

[147] https://www.youtube.com/watch?v=xcg8R1IFm30

priors into vision. The CNN used to produce this was trained on ImageNet, which has lots of images of dogs, birds and other animals. You can see that the network notices patterns that remind it of dogs really frequently. There's an image of two joint cars left of the gate, and a lot of contains that look a bit like coffee brewing containers near the ground.

It's really fun to note that you can go up or down the hierarchy of abstraction and embed high-level or low-level features as priors. With low-level layers being embedded, you'd see the world through geometric shapes. With high-level features, you'd see the world through dog snouts, dogbirds (or whatever those things in the sky look like) and car parts.

In 2021 - a team of researchers showed DeepDream-ified videos to participants[148], and recorded their responses via an *EEG (electroencephalogram)* cap. EEG is a non-invasive method to record high-level brainwaves using an array of electrodes stuck to the scalp. While it's not the most accurate technology for recording brainwaves - it's non-intrusive (just stick pads to your head) and can record patterns that are distinct enough to infer certain emotions, drowsiness, focus, etc. EEG-devices power a new generation of wearables that can learn to discern when you're focused during the day, to help you optimize work and work-life balance. The results of the study indicate that there's a correlation between EEG signals between participants under the effect of psychedelic drugs and participants under the impression of a DeepDream video! This potentially opens a door to using DeepDream-like algorithms to study human perception in general, as well as human perception under the influence of hallucinogens, without actually intoxicating people with substances.

14.1 How Does DeepDream Work?

DeepDream was developed through work on figuring out what networks learn while being trained for classification. One way to do this, as explained by other groups that did so earlier was to start with noise and go *backwards* through a CNN, embedding a prior (telling it what it should expect) and then to update the *image* so that it maximizes the probability of being classified as the prior. This produced hallucinogenic features of classes:

[148] https://www.ncbi.nlm.nih.gov/pmc/articles/PMC8306862/

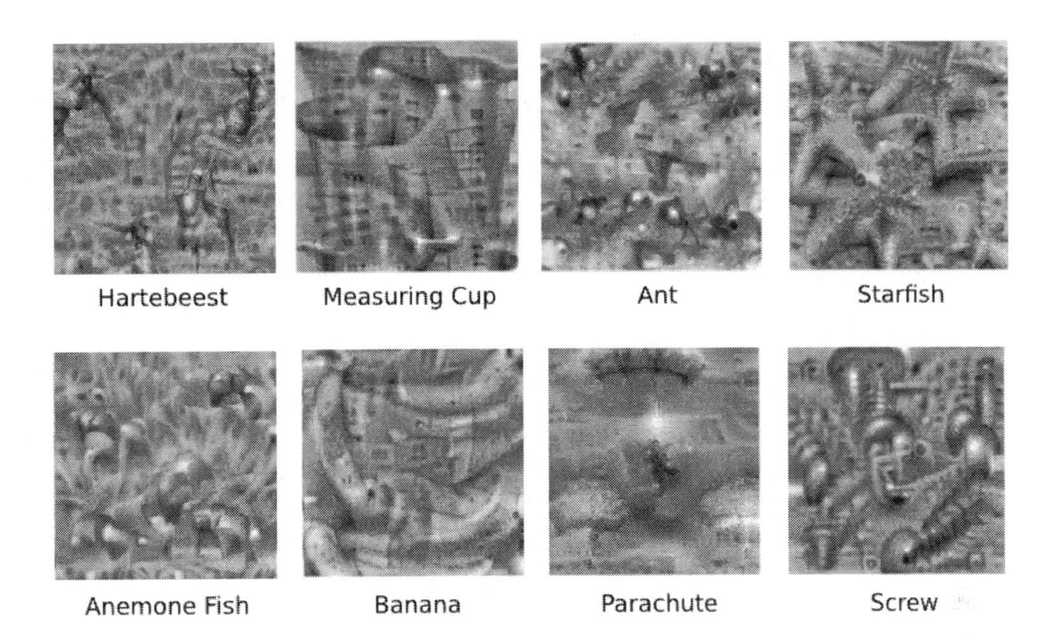

Figure 201:

Though, this is based on us embedding the prior instead of peering into the network's natural activations. You can actually omit the prior and pick out a layer (or a few) and inspect their activations on some given input. Enhancing these activations and injecting them back into the image then enhances the features of the image that led the network to activate some neurons. Depending on the layer, this can be simple lines, or much more complex patterns.

What makes DeepDream fundamentally different from more recent generative models such as DALL-E and Stable Diffusion is that, well, generative models are trained to be generative. They're *trained* to generate images. Here, we're generating images from the innate features that a network learns while it's doing its best to extract meaning from images. In that sense, we're peering into the activations within the network itself, and giving body to them!

A really fun tweak that DeepDream uses is that it employs *gradient ascent*! Instead of function minimization, we're performing function maximization - and maximizing the activations that are triggered on the input, to produce the hallucinogenic visuals.

At the time, Inception was the hot new architecture, and it was used with the original implementations of DeepDream as well. Since then, various other architectures have been used, but "classical" architectures such as ResNets, VGGNets and Inception are very commonly used to produce really nice visuals. The network you use matters, *a lot*, and some simply don't produce satisfying visuals. In addition, the layers you choose to expose is just about everything when it comes to what you visualize, so choosing the "right" layers is important. This is naturally easier in a 16-layer network like VGG16, than a 237-layer network like EfficientNetB0, or 812-layer network like EfficientNetB7, so most don't bother extensively testing layers of a larger network, since how good a visual is is fairly subjective, and there's no strong incentive to test them out other than for curiosity.

In this lesson, we'll implement DeepDream with a couple of supported backbones, that accept a variable list of layers that someone would like to expose. For other open-source implementations of DeepDream - visit Aleksa Gordić's notebook[149], written in PyTorch.

14.2 Imports

Let's start with the imports! We'll mainly be working with low-level TensorFlow in this lesson, and it's a great moment to introduce some of the tensor operations that happen under the hood, as well as to introduce *TensorFlow Addons* - an officially-backed community-driven library that builds on top of TensorFlow to introduce non-standard elements. This is a great time to practice TensorFlow operations, optimizing functions by running them in graph mode, and overall getting used to the low-level API of TensorFlow, which contrary to (oudated) public sentiment, isn't that messy or non-Pythonic.

Note: Spoiler alert - TensorFlow tensor operations are similar to NumPy array operations. So much so, that they're arguably almost identical, and confidence with the NumPy API translated into confidence with the TensorFlow API.

[149]https://github.com/gordicaleksa/pytorch-deepdream

Let's import the libraries we'll be using:

```
import tensorflow as tf
import tensorflow_probability as tfp
import tensorflow_addons as tfa

import numpy as np
import matplotlib.pyplot as plt

import urllib
import cv2
```

As usual, let's set up a `config` dictionary that'll hold some of the global variables we'll be using and to make testing a bit easier and more readable:

```
config = {
    'LR': 0.01,
    'PYRAMID_SIZE': 1.4,
    'DEFAULT_STEPS': 1000,
    'PYRAMID_STEPS': 200,
    'DPI': 300
}
```

You'll see why these are useful in a moment! Naturally, these are also very tweakable parameters, and it's highly encouraged to change the values and observe the results.

14.3 Data Processing

Let's write up a couple of utility scripts to load images from URLs, deprocess them (more on that in a moment) and to display them:

```
def url_to_array(url):
    req = urllib.request.urlopen(url)
    arr = np.array(bytearray(req.read()), dtype=np.int8)
    img = cv2.imdecode(arr, -1)
    img = cv2.cvtColor(img, cv2.COLOR_BGR2RGB)
    return img

def deprocess(img, backbone):
    if backbone == 'inceptionv3':
        return tf.cast(255*(img + 1.0)/2.0, tf.uint8)
    elif backbone == 'resnet50' or backbone == 'vgg19':
        means = np.array([103.939, 116.779, 123.68])
        img = img + means
        img = img[:, :, ::-1]
```

```
15          img = np.clip(img, 0, 255).astype('uint8')
16          return tf.cast(img, tf.uint8)
17
18  def display_img(img):
19      fig, ax = plt.subplots(figsize=(img.shape[0]/config['DPI'],
            img.shape[1]/config['DPI']),
20                             dpi=config['DPI'])
21      ax.imshow(img)
22      ax.axis('off')
23      plt.show()
```

This is the standard `url_to_array()` used so far in the book. The `deprocess()` function will be used to reverse the effects of a `preprocess_input()` call. Note that some `preprocess_input()` calls can be tricky to reverse engineer, and the deprocessing method reverses an InceptionV3 preprocessing stage which is fairly simple. ResNet50 and VGG19 use the same preprocessing step so we have the same deprocessing step as well! In any case, it casts the input as a `tf.uint8`. `tf.cast()` is used to turn a NumPy array into a `tf.Tensor`, and `tf.uint8` is simply the data type we're casting to. This method will be very useful in turning NumPy arrays into `tf.Tensor`s down the line, which will take place multiple times. To make the API of our algorithm a bit more intuitive, it'll accept NumPy array representations of images, and will convert to TensorFlow tensors under the hood. Additionally, it'll make plotting easier to keep track of progress.

Finally - a `display_img()` function is used to display an image, without the axis ticks, and in the image's real size. The real size of the image is calculated as it's shape divided by the *DPI (dots per inch)* that Matplotlib uses to define the resolution of plots on a figure. Since Matplotlib expects a value in *inches* for the `figsize()` argument, we can use the shape of the image divided by the DPI (dots per inch) to get the number of shape of the image in *inches*. The default `dpi` value for Matplotlib is `100`, which is surprisingly low for plotting, but the library allows you to set an arbitrary number, and we've used `300` as a much more fitting DPI for higher-resolution images.

Great, let's load in and display an image:

```
1 # Formatting for the book
2 url = 'https://storage.googleapis.com/download.tensorflow.org/'
3 url = url + 'example_images/YellowLabradorLooking_new.jpg'
4 dog_img = url_to_array(url)
5
6 display_img(dog_img)
```

Figure 202:

14.4 Backbone Model

Time for the backbone! Let's define a general `construct_model()` method that accepts a list of layer names, and a `backbone` argument, setting up an appropriate model for us and exposing the layers in the `layer_names` list:

```
def construct_model(layer_names, backbone):
    if backbone == 'resnet50':
        base_model = tf.keras.applications.ResNet50(include_top=False,
            weights = 'imagenet')
    elif backbone == 'inceptionv3':
        base_model = tf.keras.applications.InceptionV3(include_top=False,
            weights = 'imagenet')
    elif backbone == 'vgg19':
        base_model = tf.keras.applications.VGG19(include_top=False, weights
            = 'imagenet')

    layers = [base_model.get_layer(name).output for name in layer_names]
    return tf.keras.Model(inputs=base_model.input, outputs=layers)

names = ['mixed1']#, 'mixed4', 'mixed5']
dream_model = construct_model(names, 'inceptionv3')
```

Note that VGG19 is very memory-hungry for DeepDream, so you might run into out of memory exceptions with images sufficiently large enough. ResNet50 and InceptionV3 both work well with DeepDream and have pretty intuitive layers for exposing. InceptionV3 in particular has `mixedN` layers - spanning from `mixed1` to `mixed10`, which both produce nice visuals *and* can be understood as a `1..10` knob that you can turn to set the feature levels! Using just `mixed1` will produce geometric images. Using just `mixed10` will produce very high-level features with complex patterns like snouts. Using a mix of layers works great as well - injecting some low-level and some high-level features, that produce more heterogenous images.

Naturally, the weights you use also play a *major* role in the resulting visuals. Low-level features will generally be similar (which is why Transfer Learning works so well), but high-level features from a dataset like ImageNet will naturally be different than weights from datasets like Places365, or your own custom dataset.

14.5 Calculating Loss

DeepDream is generally implemented by inputting an image, taking some activations (exposed layers), calculating a loss for each layer, and performing gradient ascent on these losses. Loss functions are essentially distance metrics between vectors, and we call them "loss functions" or "error function" or "objective function" on the context in which they're used. Typically, we apply a loss function to check how wrong a network is in its predictions (the distance between the prediction and ground truth), with the aim of training it to be better at said predictions. You can get this distance in various ways! We'll still call them *loss functions* as a blanket term.

A simple way is to simply calculate the mean of all activations in a layer. The larger the means, the larger the general activations. Alternatively, you can calculate the given activations against an all-0 tensor with the same shape. Now, with gradient descent that we've used so far - an all-0 tensor would make any activations descend towards 0 as well, since the network would get accurate with all-0 outputs by multiplying the input with all-0s. With gradient ascent, this is reversed, and instead of making these activations fall towards zero, we increase and amplify them in each iteration to create even stronger priors for the next iteration!

Let's create a `calculate_loss()` function, which accepts an input image, the model we're passing it through, and the `loss_func`:

```
1  def calculate_loss(img, model, loss_func):
2      batch = tf.expand_dims(img, axis=0)
3      outputs = model(batch)
4      if len(outputs) == 1:
5          outputs = [outputs]
6
7      losses = []
8      for activation in outputs:
9          if loss_func == 'mean':
10             loss = tf.math.reduce_mean(activation)
```

```
11        elif loss_func == '12':
12            loss = tf.nn.12_loss(activation, tf.zeros_like(activation))
13        elif loss_func == 'mse':
14            loss = tf.keras.losses.MeanSquaredError()(activation,
                  tf.zeros_like(activation))
15        elif loss_func == 'huber':
16            loss = tf.keras.losses.Huber()(activation,
                  tf.zeros_like(activation))
17
18        losses.append(loss)
19
20    return tf.reduce_sum(losses)
```

The model expects a batch, and the input image is a tensor, so we expand the dimensions on the first axis, to create a batch of one image, using `tf.expand_dims()`. This is another NumPy parallel - `np.expand_dims()` and it works in the exact same way, but operates on Tensors instead of NumPy arrays. `tf.math.reduce_mean()` is equivalent to `np.mean()`, and it calculates the mean of all inputs. The `reduce_` part of the method might be confusing for some, and it really just stems from the fact that it performs a *reduction operation* - it accepts a vector (list of values) and returns a scalar (single value, mean of all of the input values). That's a form of reduction, and thus - `reduce_mean()`. TensorFlow methods will generally have a `reduce_operation()` equivalent for NumPy functions, such as:

- `np.std()` and `tf.math.reduce_std()`
- `np.max()` and `tf.math.reduce_max()`
- `np.sum()` and `tf.math.reduce_sum()`.
- etc.

You can use low-level `tf.nn` functions, such as `12_loss()` or high-level Keras functions/classes such as `tf.keras.losses.Huber()`, and pass in the input alongside an all-0 tensor. You can create an all-0 tensor *like another tensor* (having the same shape), using `tf.zeros_like(input_tensor)`. In our case, if we input a `(512, 512, 3)` image, it'll create a:

```
1 <tf.Tensor: shape=(512, 512, 3), dtype=float64, numpy=
2 array([[[0., 0., 0.],
3         [0., 0., 0.],
4         [0., 0., 0.],
5         ...
```

High activations against an all-0 tensor will be favored by gradient ascent! Finally, we simply append the loss of each layer into the `losses` list and sum them all up as the returned value, again, with `tf.reduce_sum()`, which is equivalent to `np.sum()`.

Since we're doing lots of TF operations, it's a great time to introduce `@tf.function`!

14.6 Better Performance with @tf.function

The `@tf.function` decorator works fairly simply, but can have major benefits for your code. A decorator is just a function that changes the execution of another function. Specifically, the `@tf.function` decorator just makes sure that whatever function is decorated with it, runs as a `tf.function()`!

This code snippet:

```
1 def some_func():
2   pass
3
4 result = tf.function(some_func)
```

Is equivalent to:

```
1 @tf.function
2 def some_func():
3   pass
4
5 result = some_func()
```

Why would you use `tf.function()` anyway? TensorFlow can run in two modes - eager mode and graph mode. Eager mode is what you're used to with every day development. Graph mode relies on running an optimized computation graph, consisting of TF operations. Whenever possible, the computation graph creates shortcuts, simplifies computations and parallelizes, so the code usually runs significantly faster, given that you use TF operations that can be turned into the graph. The more of them you use, the higher the optimization benefits!

Whenever you decorate a function with `@tf.function`, the first time it's called, TensorFlow will run it as a regular method, delaying the TF operations, and form the computation graph. This step is known as *tracing*. Then, the graph is run. Next time it's called - the graph already exists, so it can simply be reused, saving computation!

Keep in mind that you can't and shouldn't convert all functions into TF functions. Graph mode is a bit unforgiving when it comes to global variables, standard Python types and methods. Whenever possible, if you're going to annotate the method, use TF-equivalents of NumPy and Python methods, such as `tf.print()` instead of `print()`, etc. Keep in mind that you also won't be able to turn `tf.Tensor`s into NumPy arrays in graph mode, like you usually can in eager mode. Some loops can't be converted correctly either, so it's better to use vectorized operations, such as `tf.reduce_mean(x, axis=0)` rather than a `for` loop that reduces to a mean by row, rather than column. In general, write you function as you would usually, verify that it works, then try to annotate it and adapt if need be.

However, for pure TF-operation functions, you can just apply the decorator without much thought and enjoy performance boosts. How much? The proceeding code has been benchmarked with and without `@tf.function` decorators. The original implementation took ~100s per image. After decorating, it took ~33s per image. That's a huge boost for introducing 3 new lines!

`calculate_loss()` works primarily with TF operations, so we can easily annotate it:

```
1  @tf.function
2  def calculate_loss(img, model, loss_func):
3      batch = tf.expand_dims(img, axis=0)
4      outputs = model(batch)
5      if len(outputs) == 1:
6          outputs = [outputs]
7
8      losses = []
9      for activation in outputs:
10         if loss_func == 'mean':
11             loss = tf.math.reduce_mean(activation)
12         elif loss_func == 'huber':
13             loss = tf.keras.losses.Huber()(activation,
                   tf.zeros_like(activation))
14
15         losses.append(loss)
16
17     return tf.reduce_sum(losses)
```

Unfortunately, using `tf.nn.l2()` here throws an AutoGraph exception - `OperatorNotAllowedInGraphError`, so I've removed it from the pool of possible loss functions here.

14.7 Gradient Smoothing with Gaussian Filter Convolutions

Once the loss is known, you can calculate the gradients that'll lead to higher activations and ascend them:

```
1  # ...
```

```
2 for n in tf.range(steps):
3         with tf.GradientTape() as tape:
4             tape.watch(img)
5             loss = calculate_loss(img, model, loss_func)
6
7         gradients = tape.gradient(loss, img)
8         # ...
```

These gradients are later added to the image, depending on the `lr`:

```
1 img = img + gradients*lr
```

For those with a sharp eye, you'll notice that this looks a lot like:

$$x_{n+1} = x_n - lr * \frac{d}{dx} f(x_n)$$

Which is *gradient descent* for a given weight! However, we're doing:

$$x_{n+1} = x_n + lr * \frac{d}{dx} f(x_n)$$

to perform gradient ascent. In any case - we iterate through a set number of steps, updating the image in each iteration. The image is updated by adding the gradients to the image (more or less depending on the "learning rate"), as they're the same shape. By adding the gradients to the input - we're maximizing the features of the image that lead to those gradients being non-0 in the first place, which in turn makes them produce even higher activations later. This is the essence of both gradient ascent and DeepDream!

Note: The parameter that defines how much of the gradients we effectively apply to the image is denoted as *lr*, because it's parallel to what the *lr* would be in a regular network, even though no learning will be done for DeepDream.

A trick that makes DeepDream produce significantly more intriguing visuals is to smooth out the gradients before applying them. I saw this trick in Aleksa Gordić's notebook. Smoothing can be done in a variety of ways, but a very intuitive one is to apply a gaussian blur to the gradients, which in our case quite literally act like an image. One way to do this is to blur the images through convolution.

This opens up the door to TensorFlow addons!

14.7.1 TensorFlow Addons

You can create your own Gaussian Kernel and apply it to an image via `tf.nn.conv2d()` or `tf.nn.depthwise_conv2d()` which both accept a `filter` argument that can be set to a function such as:

```
def gaussian_kernel(size, mean, std):
    d = tfp.distributions.Normal(mean, std)
    vals = d.prob(tf.range(start = -size, limit = size + 1, dtype =
        tf.float32))
    gauss_kernel = tf.einsum('i,j->ij', vals, vals)
    gauss_kernel = gauss_kernel/tf.reduce_sum(gauss_kernel)
    return gauss_kernel
```

Note: `tfp` is `tensorflow_probability` the officially built and maintained library on top of TensorFlow that provides building blocks for probabilistic models.

Though, this necessitates a decent bit of custom implementations and usage of filters. As always - it's much sweeter when someone else does this for you! TensorFlow Addons has just the function call for us - `tfa.image.gaussian_filter2d()`:

```
@tf.function
tfa.image.gaussian_filter2d(
    image: tfa.types.TensorLike,
    filter_shape: Union[int, Iterable[int]] = (3, 3),
    sigma: Union[List[float], Tuple[float], float] = 1.0,
    padding: str = 'REFLECT',
    constant_values: tfa.types.TensorLike = 0,
    name: Optional[str] = None
) -> tfa.types.TensorLike
```

TensorFlow Addons is a hub of community-built contributions, in the form of activation functions, callbacks, image processing functions, layers, loss functions,metrics, optimizers and building blocks such as transformer encoders and decoders for Seq2Seq tasks. Being a part of TensorFlow, they're usable interchangeably with all other TensorFlow components, and the main page of the library pictures this quite well:

```
model = tf.keras.Sequential([
  tf.keras.layers.Conv2D(filters=10, kernel_size=(3,3),
                         activation=tfa.activations.gelu),
  tfa.layers.GroupNormalization(groups=5, axis=3),
  tf.keras.layers.Flatten(),
  tf.keras.layers.Dense(10, activation = 'softmax')
])

# TFA optimizers, losses and metrics
model.compile(
    optimizer = tfa.optimizers.RectifiedAdam(0.001),
    loss = tfa.losses.TripletSemiHardLoss(),
    metrics=[tfa.metrics.MultiLabelConfusionMatrix(num_classes=10)])
```

A Keras layer, with a `tfa` activation, Keras model with `tfa` layers, as well as seamless compilation with additional optimizers such as `RectifiedAdam` and `AdamW`, losses such as `TripletSemiHardLoss()` and `WeightedKappaLoss()` - the TensorFlow Addons API is fairly extensive, and allows for more flexibility, faster community-driven development, and the same ecosystem you're already used to.

You can easily install `tfa` via `pip`:

```
$ pip install tensorflow_addons
```

We'll be using a `tfa` function to apply Gaussian blur to the input tensor, and thus performing gradient smoothing:

```
@tf.function
def smooth_gradients_tfa(gradients, kernel_size=(9, 9), strides=(1, 1)):
    batch = tf.expand_dims(gradients, axis=0)
    return tf.squeeze(tfa.image.gaussian_filter2d(batch,
        filter_shape=kernel_size, padding = 'REFLECT'), axis=0)
```

Again, `tf.expand_dims()` is used to batch the input tensor into a single-instance batch, and `tf.squeeze()` is used in the same way `np.squeeze()` is. The `padding` argument is set to `REFLECT`, which, well, reflects the row into a padding around the input. A row, such as `[3, 1, 2]` would be padded with a reflected version of itself - `[2, 1, 3]` to create:

```
[1, 3, 3, 1, 2, 2, 1]
```

```
2 [pad] --------- [pad]
```

The number of repetitions depends on how large the padding is. The idea behind the padding is that the padding itself is in essence the data it pads as well, and provides smooth transitions between the input image and the padding. With the gradient smoothing helper function - we can finally get to the crux of the algorithm - and perform gradient ascent, returning the loss at the given step and the image combined with the gradients.

14.8 Gradient Ascent

Gradient ascent is at the core of DeepDream, and given the building blocks we've defined so far - this section should be at least somewhat intuitive. To make testing easier - we'll allow for interchangeable loss functions and a toggle for gradient smoothing. If you haven't worked with low-level TensorFlow earlier - it's useful to know how a `GradientTape` works.

A `GradientTape` is TensorFlow's central class for and calculating gradients (autodifferentiation):

```
1 import tensorflow as tf
2
3 x = tf.constant(5.0)
4 with tf.GradientTape() as tape:
5     tape.watch(x)
6     y = f(x)
7
8 gradients = tape.gradient(y, [x])
```

The `tape` can `watch()` a constant, which we can pass through any function (such as a neural network), and calculate the gradients with respects to the output of that function and the input constant. `GradientTape()` is a key component of underlying TensorFlow components. You'll be working with it for custom training loops and a plethora of custom components and custom layers, if you wish to define them. This will necessarily happen for non-standard architectures and tasks, which don't really fit into the standard use-cases (though, this is relatively rare as you'll be able to fit most problems to existing infrastructure).

Since we're calculating our own loss and performing a relatively "odd" operation with the gradients - we'll be using `GradientTape` to calculate the gradients given the outcome (loss), after passing the input we're watching (`img`) through the `calculate_loss()` function:

```
@tf.function
def gradient_ascent(model, img, steps, lr, loss_func, smooth_gradients=True):
    loss = tf.constant(0.0)
    for n in tf.range(steps):
        with tf.GradientTape() as tape:
            tape.watch(img)
            loss = calculate_loss(img, model, loss_func)

        gradients = tape.gradient(loss, img)
        gradients /= tf.math.reduce_std(gradients) +
            tf.keras.backend.epsilon()
        if smooth_gradients:
            gradients = smooth_gradients_tfa(gradients)

        img = img + gradients*lr
        img = tf.clip_by_value(img, -1, 1)

    return loss, img
```

Once the gradients are calculated, they're added to the input, producing the next input in line to further amplify. The `tf.clip_by_value()` function accepts a tensor and clips all of the values beyond a threshold, which we've set to `[-1...1]` to keep them from exploding.

14.9 The DeepDream Algorithm

With all of these in place - we can finally take some input, and run `gradient_ascent()` on it multiple times, in batches of size `run_steps`. Depending on which network we're using, we'll be preprocessing the input accordingly, and converting the inputs into tensors because they aren't interchangeable data types. The `gradient_ascent()` function is called in incrementing steps of `100`. There are a few optional parameters such as `verbose`, `smooth_gradients` and `plot_results` that we can use to customize the outputs and inner-workings a bit easier as well:

```
def deep_dream(input_img, model, preprocess_mode,
     steps=config['PYRAMID_STEPS'], lr=config['LR'], loss_func = 'mse',
     verbose=2, smooth_gradients=True, plot_results=True):
    if preprocess_mode == 'inceptionv3':
        img = tf.keras.applications.inception_v3.preprocess_input(input_img)
    elif preprocess_mode == 'resnet50' or preprocess_mode == 'vgg19':
        img = tf.keras.applications.resnet50.preprocess_input(input_img)

```

```
7      img = tf.convert_to_tensor(img)
8      lr = tf.convert_to_tensor(lr)
9      steps_remaining = steps
10     step = 0
11
12     while steps_remaining:
13         if steps_remaining > 100:
14             run_steps = tf.constant(100)
15         else:
16             run_steps = tf.constant(steps_remaining)
17         steps_remaining -= run_steps
18         step += run_steps
19
20         loss, img = gradient_ascent(model,
21                                     img,
22                                     run_steps,
23                                     tf.constant(lr),
24                                     loss_func,
25                                     smooth_gradients)
26
27         # Logging and making outputs pretty
28         if verbose == 1:
29             print ("Step {}, loss {}".format(step, loss))
30
31         if verbose == 2:
32             print ("Step {}, loss {}".format(step, loss))
33             fig, ax = plt.subplots(figsize=(img.shape[0]/100,
                   img.shape[1]/100), dpi=100)
34             ax.imshow(deprocess(img, preprocess_mode))
35             ax.axis('off')
36             plt.show()
37
38     if plot_results:
39         fig, ax = plt.subplots(1, 2, figsize=(img.shape[0]/50,
               img.shape[1]/50), dpi=100)
40         ax[0].imshow(input_img)
41         ax[0].set_title('Input Image')
42         ax[0].axis('off')
43         ax[1].imshow(deprocess(img, preprocess_mode))
44         ax[1].set_title('DeepDream Image')
45         ax[1].axis('off')
46         plt.show()
47     return deprocess(img, preprocess_mode)
```

The second half of the function call is simply to print out the status and plot images of the progress. It's put behind a `verbose` argument, which has two levels - just outputting the current loss and steps in the iteration, and plotting the images as well. Let's try out some loss functions and visualize them!

14.10 Testing Out Loss Functions

To run a loss function against the outputs of a model - let's first construct some:

```
# Low-level features
low_level_layers = ['mixed1']
# Mix of lower-level and higher-level features
mix_layers = ['mixed2', 'mixed5']
# High-level features
high_level_layers = ['mixed7']

low_level_dream_model = construct_model(low_level_layers, 'inceptionv3')
mixed_dream_model = construct_model(mix_layers, 'inceptionv3')
high_level_dream_model = construct_model(high_level_layers, 'inceptionv3')
```

These three models have different exposed layers. A low-level layer, a mix of layers and a high-level layer. These will have significantly different results. To avoid running too many expensive iterations - let's try out the loss functions against the `mixed_dream_model`:

```
funcs = ['mean', 'l2', 'mse', 'huber']
for f in funcs:
    print(f'Running DeepDream with loss function: {f}')
    deep_dream(dog_img, model=mixed_dream_model, steps=1000, loss_func=f,
        verbose=1)
```

Figure 203:

Figure 204:

Figure 205:

Figure 206:

Hmm - these aren't really that exciting. Most of the activations applied are relatively small and they're pretty uniform in shape and size. The `'huber'` loss function seems to have the most exciting visual in this case, though. Let's go with `'huber'` for future visuals and figure out a way to make them more vivid. A common issue in computer vision are objects of differing scales and the context in which they appear - and a common fix to these are image pyramids.

14.11 Image Pyramids

Image pyramids are a simple, yet very effective and useful concept, previously briefly covered in lessons. To recap the concept - we can show the same input, at different sizes to the network, with the same filter sizes. This effectively changes the proportion of the image covered with a single filter. When the image is small, more global patterns are captured with the filter. When the image is large, more detailed patterns are captured. If you start with a small image and progress towards a larger image, by multiplying its size via some constant - you can inject global and local context into an image. In the case of DeepDream, you can create and detect larger and smaller patterns, and even make patterns in patterns, by providing an increasing image in multiple iterations:

```
def deep_dream_with_pyramid(img, model, loss_func, preprocess_mode,
        steps=config['PYRAMID_STEPS'], verbose=1, plot_results=True,
        pyramid_range=(-2, 3)):
```

```
2       base_shape = tf.cast(img.shape[:-1], tf.float32)
3       # Go from -2 to 3 image sizes (smaller-than-original to
            larger-than-original)
4       for n in range(*pyramid_range):
5           new_shape = tf.cast(base_shape*(config['PYRAMID_SIZE']**n), tf.int32)
6           img = tf.image.resize(img, new_shape).numpy().astype('int')
7           img = deep_dream(input_img=img,
8                            model=model,
9                            preprocess_mode=preprocess_mode,
10                           steps=steps,
11                           lr=config['LR'],
12                           loss_func=loss_func,
13                           verbose=verbose,
14                           plot_results=plot_results)
15      return img
```

Here, we start with an `n` of `-2` and work out way up to `3`. This first makes the image smaller than it naturally is and creates large patterns in the image. We then progressively increase the image in each iteration, amplifying smaller and smaller patterns (proportionally) within the already existing large-scale patterns. On each iteration, the output of `deep_dream()` is fed back again into the algorithm. This is amongst other reasons, why the `steps` are set to a significantly lower number - by the time the outer loop is finished, we'll have performed quite a bit of steps.

Let's run the input through `deep_dream_with_pyramid()`:

```
1 result = deep_dream_with_pyramid(dog_img, mixed_dream_model, 'huber',
      'inceptionv3')
```

It starts with:

Figure 207:

And ends with:

Figure 208:

Much better! The colors get more and more vibrant, the patterns are much more alive, and it looks like they blend in and out of each other. You can display the final result individually with:

```
1 display_img(result)
```

Figure 209:

If you run the code with the `low_level_dream_model` instead, you'll notice much more geometric shapes enveloping the image:

```
1 result = deep_dream_with_pyramid(dog_img, low_level_dream_model, 'huber',
      'inceptionv3')
```

Figure 210:

The high-level model doesn't produce a very exciting image:

```
1 result = deep_dream_with_pyramid(dog_img, high_level_dream_model, 'huber',
      'inceptionv3')
```

Figure 211:

Let's try another one:

```
url = 'https://upload.wikimedia.org/wikipedia/en/5/5f/Original_Doge_meme.jpg'
doge = url_to_array(url)
result = deep_dream_with_pyramid(doge, mixed_dream_model, 'huber',
     'inceptionv3')
```

Figure 212:

14.12 DeepDream with Zoom - Creating Videos

So, what if we crop to a certain part of the image we just created and run DeepDream again? For example, the top-level dark patch of the image earlier can be used as an input again, and would result in:

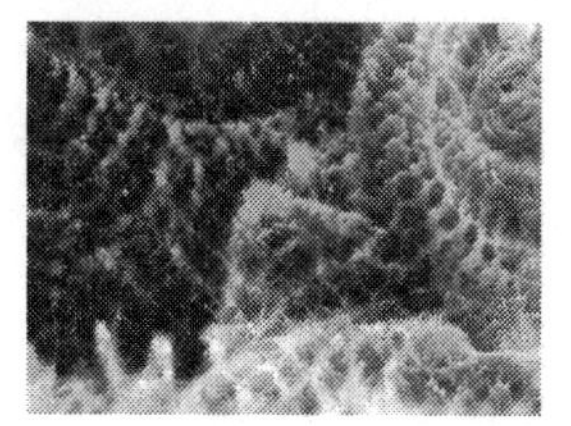

Figure 213:

If we just zoom in - the image itself is fairly blurry, as you'd expect from a relatively small image. However, by feeding it as input again, we get a really nice high-resolution output again. If we do it once more:

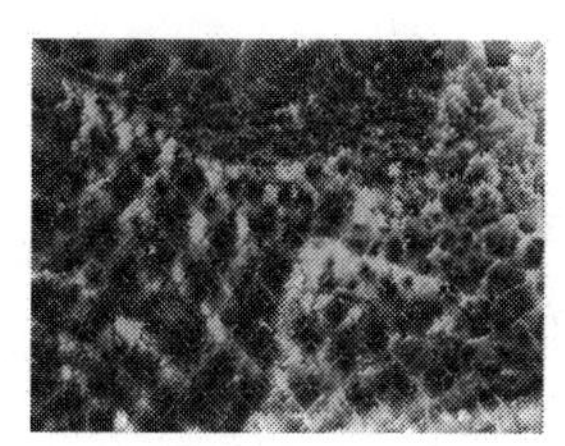

Figure 214:

From the few pixels that are located in this portion of the image, you can create a pretty exciting ecosystem of colorful pixels!

Figure 215:

This creates a really interesting possibility. What if we loop through N-frames, and on each frame, crop the input and dreamify it again? As you might expect, this can create some really trippy, infinitely-zooming and infinitely-dreaming animations and videos! Note that this takes a fair bit of time, because we're calling `deep_dream_with_pyramid()` several times over, each with some number of `steps`, which runs `deep_dream()` many times over again. The longer the animation you wish to create, and the more steps you run in each iteration - the longer it'll take to create. We'll limit ourselves to a relatively reasonable number (even though it is very tempting to let the thing run overnight). These images were created with ~200 steps, which took a decent amount of time to run, and are this intense and compelling because of that.

Going as low as `10` will likely yield unsatisfactory visuals, since it's easy to lose a lot of the activations, especially in the dark top-left area where there isn't much going on. Having a high number will apply the same steps on already dreamified parts, which will make them even more intense, and could make it look like you're frying the image. For this image, I found a good balance between `20` and `100` steps, with a pyramid size of 1.4 and a learning rate of `0.01`. These are all tweakable, and you already have a decent parameter search space to go through! With lower numbers, such as `20` and `30`, the image will get darker through time and repeating patterns will emerge. With larger numbers, the image will get much more saturated as we're repeating the operation on pixels that have already been tweaked many times.

Let's try creating 30 frames with a small step count:

```
results = []
n = 30
for i in range(1, n+1):
    print(f'Generating frame {i}/{n}', end = '\r')
    batch = tf.expand_dims(test_img, 0)
    test_img = tf.image.crop_and_resize(batch,
                                        boxes=[[0.0, 0.0, 0.9, 0.9]],
                                        # Maintain same size after crop
                                        crop_size=[batch.shape[1],
                                             batch.shape[2]],
                                        box_indices=[0])
    test_img = tf.cast(tf.squeeze(test_img), tf.uint8)
    test_img = deep_dream_with_pyramid(test_img,
                                       mixed_dream_model,
                                       'huber',
                                       'inceptionv3',
                                       steps=20,
                                       verbose=0,
                                       plot_results=False)
    test_img = tf.cast(tf.image.resize(test_img, (batch.shape[1],
         batch.shape[2])), tf.uint8)
    results.append(test_img)
```

The `tf.image.crop_and_resize()` function accepts `boxes` - the box(es) that you want to crop out of an image. The coordinates start at the corners. `[0.0, 0.0, ..., ...]` denotes the top left corner and `[..., ..., 1.0, 1.0]` denotes the bottom right corner. With `[0.0, 0.0, 0.9, 0.9]` - we're effectively cropping the right and bottom slices of the image, anchored at the top left corner. The `crop_size` defines the new shape - the method crops and *resizes*. We'll keep the shape the same as the original input's shape, since we've made the image smaller by cropping a box out. Since you can make more than one box crop - you have to supply the `box_indices`, of which we have one.

Note: Try doing this with `central_crop()` instead, which fixes the crop to a central area. Or better yet, try rotating the image by X degrees on each zoom. This can all be achieved with either TensorFlow's or Keras' image processing utilities.

The following line squeezes the batch back into a single image for `deep_dream_with_pyramid()` and runs the image through DeepDream with 20 steps. The plot_results and verbose flags make the output clear, otherwise it would be a bit chaotic. Finally - we resize the final image back to the batch's shape since our pyramid of images creates larger outputs than the inputs, and this could easily explode since we're calling the method 30 times. The couple of tf.cast() calls are required since many methods return tf.float32 types by default, such as tf.image.resize(), so we're just casting them back into tf.uint8.

This code will take some time, depending on the size of the input, your pyramid size, the number of steps used, the model's exposed layers (more layers take more time), etc. This can take anywhere between a couple of minutes to a few dozen. In the end, let's visualize the frames in a small animation and save it as a GIF file:

```
1 # If you're working in a Jupyter Notebok
2 # the animation won't render in the HTML - use a different back-end such as
      Qt
3 %matplotlib qt
4 import matplotlib.animation as animation
5
6 fig = plt.figure()
7 canvas = plt.imshow(results[0], vmin=0, vmax=255)
8
9 def draw_frame(i):
10     canvas.set_array(results[i])
11     return [canvas]
12
13 # Don't forget to assign the return value to a reference variable, such as
      `anim`
14 # Otherwise, Matplotlib might delete the object from memory
15 anim = animation.FuncAnimation(fig, draw_frame, frames=range(len(results)),
      interval=100, blit=True)
```

This opens up a Qt window on your local device and displays the animation. For ease of sharing - let's save the animation as a GIF:

```
1 filename = "doge.gif"
2 writergif = animation.PillowWriter(fps=5)
3 ani.save(filename, writer=writergif)
```

Figure 216:

15 Optimizing Deep Learning Models for Computer Vision

In the lessons so far, I've left various tips and tricks in paragraphs that are behind us. It takes time for some things to "click", and I personally tend to read a resource, do work in that field, and then re-read the resource again once some of the knowledge is really solidified. Usually, I find *gems* sprinkled around that just went over my head the first time I read it.

For those that don't have the luxury of re-reading multiple books from time to time, and for those who are new to the field and want to keep some guiding notes, here's a TL;DR of some of the advice that was given throughout the book.

15.1 Model Design

If you're designing your own network, here are a few *key* elements of performant architectures and notes I gathered while reading through design papers, playing around with the architecures and seeing many architectures being implemented by novices:

- Remember that designing networks isn't limited to PhD owners. Try your hand.
- Skip flattening layers, use global pooling (`GlobalAveragePooling2D()`, `GlobalMaxPooling2D()`).
- Use skip connections (shortcut connections).
- Use multiple layers with smaller filter sizes, rather than one layer with a larger filter size.
- For memory efficiency and smaller models (especially on CPU), use depthwise separable convolutions (`SeparableConv2D()`).
- For training speed and devices with GPUs, use regular convolutions (`Conv2D`).
- Dropout rates are usually good between `0.3` and `0.5`.
- When possible, re-use an existing network and tweak it (usually by adding a new input and top). The EfficientNet family is a great all-round network for most work. Alternatively, try ConvNeXt.

Note: `SeparableConv2D` can actually ofentimes be slower than a `Conv2D` layer on GPU-enabled machines, but faster on CPU-enabled machines. In the SqueezeNet paper, Gholami et al.[150] point out that the reason for this inefficiency is that depthwise separable convolution doesn't take advantage of hardware performance and GPUs, which leads to slow training times. Though, they produce significantly smaller models and work better than regular convolutions on CPU-only devices, so they're favored for edge and mobile.

15.2 Data Preparation and Storage

- Use `tf.data` to create `Datasets`. Please, please use `tf.data` to create `Datasets`. Don't work with NumPy arrays or Python generators (`tf.data` shows an easy ~5x time difference in many cases but not all. At *worst*, it'll perform the same as your custom generator, but has a cleaner implementation).
- Use `tf.data.AUTOTUNE` to let `tf.data` figure out the parameters of the methods used to optimize the data pipeline.
- Prefetch data from a dataset: `dataset.prefetch(tf.data.AUTOTUNE)`
- Parallelize data transformations: `dataset.map(func, num_parallel_calls=tf.data.AUTOTUNE)`.
- Cache data after expensive operations for future calls: `dataset.map(func).cache()`, especially after time-expensive operations so that the results are reused after the first epoch.

Note: The order you apply these in matters. Don't just blindly apply them and hope for the best, as that can actually make your pipeline perform worse. At the end of the day, since optimization depends on your data and hardware - try out different combinations. For example, `cache()` can lead to memory errors, as well as slower execution.

---

[150]https://arxiv.org/pdf/1803.10615.pdf

15.3 Image Augmentation

- Augmentation isn't a magic wand. Consider your data when choosing augmenations.
- Start small and work your way up.
- Keep in touch with new augmentations, such as CutMix.
- KerasCV's `RandAugment` takes a lot of the guesswork out of the equation.
- `RandAugment` works well with `CutMix` in KerasCV.
- You can build augmentation pipelines as parts of your models natively using Keras.
- The previous point lets you tune augmentations as a part of the model.
- The Albumentations library is expressive, effective and efficient and works in a framework-agnostic fashion.
- AugMix is pretty decent in preparing networks for out of distribution data down the line, and can help retain performance on inference data that's different from training data. KerasCV provides `keras_cv.layers.AugMix()`.
- Consider using the `@tf.function` decorator for augmentation pipelines that just use Keras/TensorFlow operations to augment images.

15.4 Training

- Use Transfer Learning. Magic in 99% of the cases, great results in the remaining 1%.
- Overfit on a subset to check your model's entropic capacity.
- Train on subsets, fail fast, update often, scale up.
- Use automatic mixed precision (AMP) - training on `float16` data types, and storing/performing sensitive computations with `float32` for numerical stability. You can see a multiple-fold speed improvement with minimal accuracy deterioration (of no practical significance) using automatic mixed precision training. This is done by setting the global policy: `tf.keras.mixed_precision.set_global_policy('mixed_float16').` or setting a policy for each layer with: `tf.keras.layers.Dense(num_dense, dtype = 'mixed_float16')`. This keeps the model state in `float32` but performs computation in `float16`.
- Larger batch sizes let networks take advantage of hardware computation better. Do note batch sizes larger than 32 can hurt generalization (but are more efficient

computationally), as noted in earlier lessons.

- Try using `jit_compile=True` in your `model.compile()` call. It doesn't work for all models, and can result in a much slower run, but can potentially boost your model's speed *significantly* (multiple fold) by using XLA under the hood, which fuses and optimizes TensorFlow operations.
- Use step-fusing with GPUs and especially TPUs (since they have plenty of memory). You can run multiple batches during training in a single `tf.function` call, instead of running just one and waiting for a sync with the CPU. The number of batches you run is defined by the `steps_per_execution` flag of `model.compile()` and can at most equal to the number of batches in your dataset. Beware of memory consumption though, since this is fairly expensive memory-wise. It can increase your device utilization while keeping batch sizes low.
- Use multiples of eight for hyperparameters - filter sizes, batch sizes, number of steps, etc. Deep learning to a large degree consists of matrix multiplications, and matrices with shapes aligned with multiples of 8 perform perform a bit better due to hardware optimization. This won't always make a difference, though, and it's partly convention rather than a stone-set rule. Sebastian Raschka wrote a good blog post[151] about this.
- Using an LR finder, such as the one implemented in the book can help choosing a good first LR, and reduce the overall number of epochs you need to run a network for for good convergence.
- Try distributed training, if possible. Distribution can happen over multiple GPUs, TPUs or machines, but well, requires access to multiple GPUs, TPUs or machines.
- When referencing existing work, use the linear scaling rule between the batch size and learning rate, explained in *"Lesson 7 - Convolutional Neural Networks, Beyond Basic Architectures"*.
- Try using Cyclical Learning Rates or a learning rate warmup.

Note: Mixed precision works best with GPUs with compute capability over 7.0 and may have minimal effect for GPUs below that capability. Check the official list of Nvidia CUDA-GPUs[152] and their capabilities.

[151] https://sebastianraschka.com/blog/2022/batch-size-2.html
[152] https://developer.nvidia.com/cuda-gpus

15.5 Inference

You'll want to optimize for inference *typically* for mobile and edge devices, as models that need to perform real-time or as fast as possible are oftentimes deployed to non-desktop environments and on-site. A lot of optimization research and techniques are driven by the need to do exactly for these devices.

- Quantize your model.
- Prune your model.
- For extreme reduction, stack quantization and pruning.
- Perform weight clustering.
- If you do have access to distributed environments, try DKeras[153]. It's built on top of Ray and is a one-line modification to existing Keras models (just wrap your model in `dKeras()`.

Some of the advice given in this section require a bit more explanation, so I'll be spinning off quantization, pruning and weight clustering into their own sections. In the following sections, we'll be using the *TensorFlow Model Optimization Toolkit (TFMOT)*:

```
$ pip install tensorflow_model_optimization
```

And import it with:

```
import tensorflow_model_optimization as tfmot
```

15.6 Quantizing TensorFlow Models and Quantization-Aware Training

Similar to how you can use mixed precision data types for *training* and save them in `float32`, you can also *quantize* models for inference. Quantization itself is applied in many aspects of electrical engineering and computer science, and in general, refers to constraining a unbounded signal (such as an analog signal) into a bounded one(such as a digital/discrete signal).

[153]https://github.com/dkeras-project/dkeras

In the context of deep learning models, a *quantized* model is one is represented at lower bitwidths than `float32` - as low as `int8`, which makes them multiple times smaller and faster, at the cost of accuracy in representation. You can perform *Post-Training Quantization* or *Quantization-Aware Training*, referring to training a regular model and then quantizing it, or training it to be aware of quantization up ahead. The latter typically provides slightly better accuracy.

Note You can quantize per (entire) tensor or per axis (channel) of a tensor.

To convert an existing model, the TensorFlow Lite Converter is used, which is naturally part of TensorFlow Lite. Quantization is usually performed for edge and mobile models, since they more often have significantly less memory than desktop devices and laptops. A great free resource for post-training quantization can be found in TensorFlow's guide dedicated to the topic[154], and we'll focus more on quantization-aware training, as it yields better results.

Quantization-aware training boils down to emulating an environment in which a model is quantized, during training. The model is still using `float32` during training but is "aware" of the fact that that won't be the case down the line. Quantization is done later.

It's generally advised to fine-tune models with quantization-aware training, rather than training them from scratch - so you'd be training X-epochs regularly, and only perform quantization-aware training in the end to fine tune. Additionally, if quantization brings your accuracy down significantly, you can try quantizing *some* layers, and to skip quantizing the layers that seriously hurt accuracy.

To fine-tune a model in which all layers are quantized:

```
1 model = ...
2 model.fit(...)
3
```

[154]https://www.tensorflow.org/lite/performance/post_training_quantization

```
4 # Make the model quantization-aware - this doesn't quantize it regardless of
      the method's name
5 quant_aware_model = tfmot.quantization.keras.quantize_model(model)
6 # Recompilation required
7 quant_aware_model.compile(...)
8 # Fine tune a quantization-aware model stemming from a regular Keras model
9 quant_aware_model.fit(...)
```

Alternatively, you can skip all layers of some type, such as `BatchNormalization` for example,

```
 1 model = ...
 2 model.fit(...)
 3
 4 def annotate_quant(layer):
 5     if isinstance(layer, tf.keras.layers.BatchNormalization):
 6         return tfmot.quantization.keras.quantize_annotate_layer(layer)
 7     return layer
 8
 9 quant_annotated = tf.keras.models.clone_model(
10     model,
11     clone_function=annotate_quant,
12 )
13
14 quant_aware_model = tfmot.quantization.keras.quantize_apply(quant_annotated)
15 quant_aware_model.compile(...)
16 quant_aware_model.fit(...)
```

The `quantize_annotate_layer()` function annotates a layer for quantization. To avoid changing the original model, you can clone a model and apply a cloning function, which in this case just annotates all `BatchNormalization` layers and returns each one. The `quant_annotated` model is the same as our regular `model`, but with annotated layers. The `quantize_apply()` method just "activates" the annotated layers to be quantization-aware.

The flexibility here lies in the annotation function - you can annotate layers before training, and then "activate" them layer. For example, while defining your model in the first place:

```
1 model = keras.Sequential([
2     keras.layers.InputLayer(input_shape=(None, None, 3)),
3     tfmot.quantization.keras.quantize_annotate_layer(keras.layers.Conv2D(...)),
4     ...
5 ])
```

During training, this is a regular `Conv2D` layer - and you can turn on quantization-awareness later with:

```
quant_aware_model = tfmot.quantization.keras.quantize_apply(model)
quant_aware_model.compile(...)
```

15.6.1 Quantization-Aware to Quantized Models

In any case - after training a quantization aware model, you'll want to create a quantized model for deployment. This is done via `tf.lite`:

```
converter = tf.lite.TFLiteConverter.from_keras_model(quant_aware_model)
converter.optimizations = [tf.lite.Optimize.DEFAULT]
quantized_tflite_model = converter.convert()
```

15.7 Pruning TensorFlow Models

Pruning is a term that comes from agriculture and refers to the process of removing (typically) branches off of plants, that aren't required for growth, don't yield good products, make it harder for other branches to breathe, or simply aren't visually pleasing. When you trim a plant, it can focus more of its resources to the "good branches" as opposed to the "bad ones" - depending on who sets the criteria.

In the context of deep learning, pruning refers to models in which we enforce further sparsity by assigning some weights (those that don't contribute much) to zero, and removing them from back-propagation. You could remove nodes instead, but this changes the structure of the network, and ignoring nodes during back-prop is practically equal to removing them in terms of performance so weight pruning is more common. You might draw a parallel between pruning and dropout - but these perform a fundamentally different task.

Dropout temporarily turns off some random set of nodes during training, as a regularization technique, to make a network not over-rely on some nodes that carry its weight. In effect, it distributes the knowledge in a network, rather than having some "strong connections" and "weak connections". During inference, **all of them are active** and dropout layers are totally ignored.

Pruning permanently removes a selected set of nodes (those that don't contribute much), as a compression technique, to make a network require less memory both to run and store.

The pruning API is similar to that of quantization. You're also advised to train a network regularly, and then fine-tune it in a pruning mode:

```
model = ...
model.fit(...)

pruning_model = tfmot.sparsity.keras.prune_low_magnitude(model)
# Recompilation required
pruning_model.compile(...)
# Fine tune a model ready for pruning
pruning_model.fit(...)
```

Note: Pruning early layers tends to hurt models more than pruning later layers, as this is the hierarchical point in which foundations are built. The snippet above prunes *all* layers, which will usually result in degraded accuracy. Some layers don't suffer from pruning, while some totally "destroy" the model if you prune them.

You can prune specific layers in the same way as you'd make them quantization-aware. The `clone_model()` function allows us to clone models and apply a mapping function, which can turn some `Layer` into a `tfmot.sparsity.keras.prune_low_magnitude(Layer)`:

```
model = ...
model.fit(...)

def prune(layer):
    if isinstance(layer, tf.keras.layers.Dense):
        return tfmot.sparsity.keras.prune_low_magnitude(layer)
  return layer

pruning_model = tf.keras.models.clone_model(
    model,
    clone_function=prune,
)

pruning_model.compile(...)
pruning_model.fit(...)
```

Also, the same as with quantization-awareness, you can prepare layers for pruning during the model's definition:

```
model = keras.Sequential([
    keras.layers.InputLayer(input_shape=(None, None, 3)),
    tfmot.sparsity.keras.prune_low_magnitude(keras.layers.Conv2D(...)),
    ...
])
```

Marking a layer for pruning doesn't prune it until you train. To prune a layer (or layers) during training, you'll need to supply a `tfmot.sparsity.keras.UpdatePruningStep()` callback to the training loop:

```
callbacks = [
    tfmot.sparsity.keras.UpdatePruningStep(),
    # ... other callbacks
]

pruning_model.fit(train_set, callbacks=callbacks, epochs=EPOCHS)
```

15.7.1 Pruning Parameters

You can tweak the pruning parameters, and pass them in the `prune_low_magnitude()` call. For example, you can set the `pruning_schedule`, `block_size`, etc. A common parameter to tweak is the `pruning_schedule`, which defaults to `ConstantSparsity(0.5, 0)`, which enforces 50% of the weights to be pruned to 0. Another option is the `PolynomialDecay()` scheduler, which starts out with one sparsity, and ends with another sparsity, given a set of steps:

```
tfmot.sparsity.keras.PolynomialDecay(initial_sparsity=0.50,
                                      final_sparsity=0.80,
                                      begin_step=start_step,
                                      end_step=end_step)
```

The easiest way to update multiple parameters is to create a dictionary and destructure it into arguments when you set up a layer for pruning:

```
param_grid  = {
      'pruning_schedule':
          tfmot.sparsity.keras.PolynomialDecay(initial_sparsity=0.50,
                                               final_sparsity=0.80,
                                               begin_step=start_step,
                                               end_step=end_step)
}

pruning_model = tfmot.sparsity.keras.prune_low_magnitude(model, **param_grid)
```

15.8 Weight Clustering with Keras

In a deep network - many weights will end up having similar, or equal weights. Instead of keeping each weight stored as an individual variable that takes up space, you can store only unique values and pointers to where they should be applied. This general idea is applicable in many areas of computer science and is notable in object pools, where commonly used objects are stored in a pool an re-used when equal values are references (such as the string pool in the Java Virtual Machine - JVM).

This technique is simple, but enables you to reduce the size of models with minimal effect on accuracy! The API is very similar to the pruning and quantization APIs, and follows the same guidelines. You should use trained models and fine-tune them to perform weight clustering, instead of training from scratch, and some layers can suffer more from clustering than others, so only clustering the weights in some layers instead of the entire model is generally a good idea.

Clustering is typically performed with the K-Means algorithm (speficially, the K-Means++ variant), with a set number of centroids around which weights are clustered.

To apply clusering to an entire model:

```
1 model = ...
2 model.fit(...)
3
4 params = {
5   'number_of_clusters': 6,
6   'cluster_centroids_init':
        tfmot.clustering.keras.CentroidInitialization.KMEANS_PLUS_PLUS
7 }
8
9 cluster_model = tfmot.clustering.keras.cluster_weights(model, **params)
10 # Recompilation required
11 cluster_model.compile(...)
12 # Fine tune a model ready for weight clustering
13 cluster_model.fit(...)
```

Or to apply it to specific layers:

```
1 model = ...
2 model.fit(...)
3
4 def cluster(layer):
5     if isinstance(layer, tf.keras.layers.Dense):
6         return tfmot.clustering.keras.cluster_weights(layer, **params)
7   return layer
```

```
8
9 cluster_model = tf.keras.models.clone_model(
10     model,
11     clone_function=cluster,
12 )
13
14 cluster_model.compile(...)
15 cluster_model.fit(...)
```

And naturally, you can apply it to a specific individual layer:

```
1 model = keras.Sequential([
2     keras.layers.InputLayer(input_shape=(None, None, 3)),
3     tfmot.clustering.keras.cluster_weights(keras.layers.Conv2D(...),
        **params),
4     ...
5 ])
```

15.9 When to Quantize, Prune and/or Cluster - Collaborative Optimization

Applying multiple optimization techniques to amplify the effect of each step is known as *collaborative optimization*. This is difficult because a step can mess up the previous step. Here are a few tips:

- If you want to cluster weights, you should prune your model first, otherwise you'd be clustering many unecessary weights. Additionally, since pruning creates sparse weights, you should add `'preserve_sparsity': True` to your clustering parameters.
- If you quantize, it's going to be the last thing you do. If you do quantization per axis/channel - you'll want to cluster per axis/channel as well. Additionally, to preserve clusters, you should pass a `Default8BitClusterPreserveQuantizeScheme()` in your `quantize_apply()` call. In a similar way, to preserve sparsity from pruning, you should pass in `Default8BitPrunePreserveQuantizeScheme()` in the `quantize_apply()` call. To apply *both* (if you prune and cluster), use `Default8BitClusterPreserveQuantizeScheme()` with `preserve_sparsity=True` instead. These all belong to the `tfmot.experimental.combine` module.

So, when do you apply these and how much? If your model is large and needs to be reduced - start with pruning. If not enough - prune and cluster. If not enough - prune, cluster and quantize.

A more rich decision tree can be observed in TensorFlow's dedicated guide to collaborative optimization[155]:

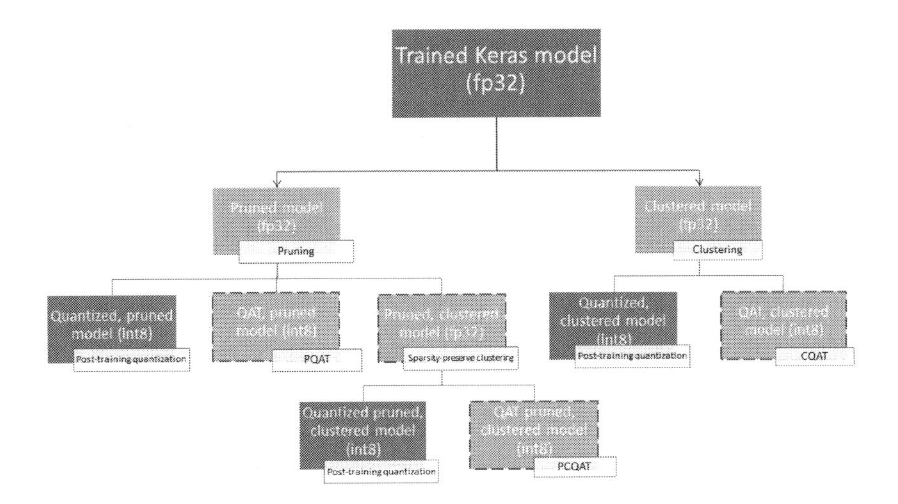

Figure 217:

As soon as your model runs as fast as it needs to, and doesn't degrade in quality beyond the acceptable mark - it's best to stop optimizing.

Optimizing models through pruning, clustering and quantization isn't a small topic, and TensorFlow's official detailed guides[156] are a great place to get into the nitty-gritties of the API.

15.10 Optimizing Keras Models

Let's implement a "naive" model and work out how we can optimize it using the bullet points in this lesson. We'll start out with bad practices - writing our own custom generator for yielding data, flattening feature maps, etc. Then, we'll write an equivalent with better practices and benchmark each step.

[155] https://www.tensorflow.org/model_optimization/guide/combine/collaborative_optimization
[156] https://www.tensorflow.org/model_optimization/guide

15.10.1 Naive Model Implementation

Let's start by revisiting the network we built at the start of the book and the dataset we worked with - updated to use a custom generator. The code samples should be fairly familiar to you, and each element of the implementation has been covered before, so I'll be brief on extra explanations for brevity's sake. First, we'll import the libraries:

```
import tensorflow as tf
from tensorflow import keras
import numpy as np
import matplotlib.pyplot as plt

import albumentations as A

import os
import cv2
import zipfile
from glob import glob
import random
```

Let's download the dataset:

```
! kaggle datasets download -d puneet6060/intel-image-classification
```

Now, let's export the data and set up a `config` dict:

```
if not os.path.exists('./intel-image-classification/'):
    with zipfile.ZipFile("intel-image-classification.zip","r") as zip_ref:
        zip_ref.extractall("intel-image-classification")

ROOT_PATH = 'intel-image-classification'

config = {

    'TRAIN_PATH': os.path.join(ROOT_PATH, 'seg_train', 'seg_train'),
    'TEST_PATH': os.path.join(ROOT_PATH, 'seg_test', 'seg_test'),
    'VALID_PATH': os.path.join(ROOT_PATH, 'seg_pred', 'seg_pred'),
    'BATCH_SIZE' : 16,
    'IMG_SIZE' : 224
}

classnames=['buildings', 'forest', 'glacier', 'mountain', 'sea', 'street']

train_paths =  glob(os.path.join(config['TRAIN_PATH'], '*', '*'),
     recursive=True)
test_paths =  glob(os.path.join(config['TEST_PATH'], '*', '*'),
     recursive=True)

random.shuffle(train_paths)
random.shuffle(test_paths)
```

Once we obtained the paths for the images, we can go ahead and define an `albumentations()` method for augmenting images (NumPy arrays), and a `load_data()` method that'll be the engine for loading the data to be yielded in a generator:

```
def albumentations(img):
    transform = A.Compose([
        A.HorizontalFlip(p=0.5),
        A.RandomBrightnessContrast(p=0.3),
        A.Transpose(p=0.5),
        A.VerticalFlip(p=0.5),
        A.HorizontalFlip(p=0.5),
        A.Rotate(limit=70),
        A.CoarseDropout(p=0.5)
    ])

    transformed_image = transform(image=img)['image']
    return transformed_image

def load_data(pathlist, subset, batch_size=config['BATCH_SIZE'], verbose=0):
    X = list()
    y = list()

    for index, entry in enumerate(pathlist):
        img = cv2.imread(entry)
        img = cv2.cvtColor(img, cv2.COLOR_BGR2RGB)
        img = cv2.resize(img, (config['IMG_SIZE'], config['IMG_SIZE']))
        # Extract label from pathname
        label = entry.split(os.sep)[3]
        # Augment image
        img = albumentations(img.astype('uint8'))

        X.append(img/255.0)
        y.append(classnames.index(label))

    X = np.array(X)
    y = np.array(y)

    return X, y
```

Now, we can use this method to create a simple batch generator:

```
def batch_generator(paths, subset, batch_size = config['BATCH_SIZE']):
    i = 0
    while True:
        if i+batch_size >= len(paths):
            i = 0
        batch = paths[i:i+batch_size]
        i = i+batch_size
        if(len(batch) % batch_size == 0):
            yield load_data(batch, subset, False)
```

Once called on to make a generator - we can call `next(generator)` to create the next batch of images and train on them! We don't have many convenience methods and fields like the size of the data in the generator (it doesn't know this itself), so we'll rely on the length of the input list to calculate the size of the data. Since we trim the data near the end if it's not divisible by the batch size, the actual length is a tiny bit different, but `batch_size-1` images *at most*, so it's not like it makes much of a difference since the epoch will have hundreds of batches.

Let's create the generators:

```
1 train_generator = batch_generator(train_paths, 'train')
2 test_generator = batch_generator(test_paths, 'test')
```

You can all on these and visualize some of the data with:

```
1 batch = next(train_generator) # Entire batch of images
2 # Plotting just the first one
3 plt.imshow(batch[0][0])
4 print(classnames[batch[1][0]])
```

Time to define the network! Let's re-use the same code as before:

```
1 model = keras.models.Sequential([
2     keras.layers.Conv2D(64, (3, 3), activation = 'relu', padding = 'same',
          input_shape=[224, 224, 3]),
3     keras.layers.Conv2D(64, 3, activation = 'relu', padding = 'same'),
4     keras.layers.MaxPooling2D((2, 2), (2, 2)),
5     keras.layers.BatchNormalization(),
6
7     keras.layers.Conv2D(128, 3, activation = 'relu', padding = 'same'),
8     keras.layers.Conv2D(128, 3, activation = 'relu', padding = 'same'),
9     keras.layers.MaxPooling2D(2, 2),
10    keras.layers.BatchNormalization(),
11
12    keras.layers.Conv2D(256, 3, activation = 'relu', padding = 'same'),
13    keras.layers.Conv2D(256, 3, activation = 'relu', padding = 'same'),
14    keras.layers.MaxPooling2D(2, 2),
15    keras.layers.BatchNormalization(),
16
17    keras.layers.Conv2D(256, 3, activation = 'relu', padding = 'same'),
18    keras.layers.Conv2D(256, 3, activation = 'relu', padding = 'same'),
19    keras.layers.MaxPooling2D(2, 2),
20    keras.layers.BatchNormalization(),
21
22    keras.layers.Conv2D(512, 3, activation = 'relu', padding = 'same'),
23    keras.layers.Conv2D(512, 3, activation = 'relu', padding = 'same'),
24    keras.layers.MaxPooling2D(2, 2),
25    keras.layers.BatchNormalization(),
26
27    keras.layers.Flatten(),
28    keras.layers.Dense(64, activation = 'relu'),
```

```
29     keras.layers.BatchNormalization(),
30     keras.layers.Dropout(0.3, seed=2),
31     keras.layers.Dense(6, activation = 'softmax')
32 ])
33
34 model.compile(loss = "sparse_categorical_crossentropy",
35               optimizer = keras.optimizers.Adam(),
36               metrics=['accuracy',
37                        keras.metrics.SparseTopKCategoricalAccuracy(k=2)])
```

Going through all of the lessons, you can hopefully now identify some of the issues with this network. It worked well enough at the start, and was a very natural translation of the concepts covered at the beginning into code, but we can do better, even without creating proprietary blocks, skip connections, etc. This is a pretty shallow network, but let's not deepen it for the sake of comparison with the original.

```
1 model.summary()
```

```
1 ...
2 =====================
3 Total params: 7,476,742
4 Trainable params: 7,474,182
5 Non-trainable params: 2,560
6 _____________________
```

Oof. Let's train it.

```
1 history = model.fit(train_generator,
2                     validation_data = test_generator,
3                     steps_per_epoch = len(train_paths)/config['BATCH_SIZE'],
4                     validation_steps = len(test_paths)/config['BATCH_SIZE'],
5                     epochs = 5)
```

```
1 Epoch 1/20
2 877/877 [==============================] - 397s 447ms/step - loss: 1.4419 -
    accuracy: 0.4390 - sparse_top_k_categorical_accuracy: 0.6705 - val_loss:
    1.2582 - val_accuracy: 0.4987 - val_sparse_top_k_categorical_accuracy:
    0.7204
3 ...
4 Epoch 20/20
5 877/877 [==============================] - 173s 197ms/step - loss: 0.5252 -
    accuracy: 0.8135 - sparse_top_k_categorical_accuracy: 0.9460 - val_loss:
    0.4889 - val_accuracy: 0.8178 - val_sparse_top_k_categorical_accuracy:
    0.9545
```

Now, let's fix some of the glarinng issues with this implementation.

15.10.2 Optimizing the Naive Model

TensorFlow has many of the functionalities that we used in the previous section. While working with Tensors might sound a bit less comfortable than working with NumPy arrays (which is somewhat true), you should get comfortable working with Tensors as well. The last lesson delved into tensor manipulation *in context*, rather than just listing out methods and noting what they do.

Let's import the libaries:

```
import tensorflow as tf
from tensorflow import keras

import numpy as np
import matplotlib.pyplot as plt

import os
import zipfile
from glob import glob
```

The list is much more manageable! Let's download, unzip the data and make a config dict:

```
! kaggle datasets download -d puneet6060/intel-image-classification

if not os.path.exists('./intel-image-classification/'):
    with zipfile.ZipFile("intel-image-classification.zip","r") as zip_ref:
        zip_ref.extractall("intel-image-classification")

ROOT_PATH = 'intel-image-classification'

config = {

    'TRAIN_PATH': os.path.join(ROOT_PATH, 'seg_train', 'seg_train'),
    'TEST_PATH': os.path.join(ROOT_PATH, 'seg_test', 'seg_test'),
    'VALID_PATH': os.path.join(ROOT_PATH, 'seg_pred', 'seg_pred'),
    'BATCH_SIZE' : 16,
    'IMG_SIZE' : 224
}

classnames=['buildings', 'forest', 'glacier', 'mountain', 'sea', 'street']

train_paths =  glob(os.path.join(config['TRAIN_PATH'], '*', '*'),
    recursive=True)
test_paths =  glob(os.path.join(config['TEST_PATH'], '*', '*'),
    recursive=True)
```

No need to shuffle the paths, as we can shuffle the dataset later, unlike in the previous section. Last time, we went around to get the labels from the pathnames, during batching. This will be a bit trickier since as soon as we call `from_tensor_slices()` - the pathnames which are strings, will be turned into Tensors. While we could work with this, it's simply easier to extract the labels upfront:

```
def get_labels(pathlist):
    labels = []
    for path in pathlist:
        labels.append(classnames.index(path.split(os.sep)[3]))
    labels = np.array(labels)
    return labels

train_labels = get_labels(train_paths)
test_labels = get_labels(test_paths)
```

Great! We've got image paths and labels. Let's go ahead and define the augmentation pipeline, using Albumentations as before:

```
import albumentations as A

def preprocess(image_path, label):
    img = tf.io.read_file(image_path)
    img = tf.image.decode_jpeg(img, channels=3)
    img = tf.image.resize(img, size=[config['IMG_SIZE'], config['IMG_SIZE']])
    img = tf.cast(img, tf.float32)

    return img, label

def albumentations(img):
    transform = A.Compose([
        A.HorizontalFlip(p=0.5),
        A.RandomBrightnessContrast(p=0.3),
        A.VerticalFlip(p=0.5),
        A.CoarseDropout(p=0.5)
    ])

    transformed_image = transform(image=img)['image']
    return transformed_image

def apply_albumentations(img, label):
    aug_img = tf.numpy_function(func=albumentations, inp=[img],
        Tout=tf.float32)
    return aug_img, label
```

Great! We can perform augmentations and apply them to a `Dataset`. Let's create a `tf.data.Dataset` and apply the `preprocess()` and `apply_albumentations()` functions:

```
def create_dataset(images, labels):
    dataset = tf.data.Dataset.from_tensor_slices((images,
        labels)).shuffle(len(images))
    dataset = dataset.map(map_func = preprocess, num_parallel_calls =
        tf.data.AUTOTUNE)
```

```
4     dataset = dataset.map(apply_albumentations)
5     dataset = dataset.batch(config['BATCH_SIZE'], drop_remainder=True)
6     dataset = dataset.prefetch(tf.data.AUTOTUNE)
7     return dataset
```

We won't be calling `cache()`, as this isn't a particularly heavy operation, and we'd run out of RAM easily. Note the `tf.data.AUTOTUNE` references, parallel flags and prefetching.

Let's create the datasets:

```
1 train_set = create_dataset(train_paths, train_labels)
2 test_set = create_dataset(test_paths, test_labels)
```

The `make_model()` method will accept a few arguments - `jit`, `separable`, `mixed_precision` and `fuse_steps`. These will turn on JIT compilation, use `SeparableConv2D` instead of `Conv2D` layers, turn on AMP and the number of `steps_per_execution`:

```
1 def make_model(jit=False, separable=False, mixed_precision=False,
      fuse_steps=1):
2     if mixed_precision:
3         tf.keras.mixed_precision.set_global_policy('mixed_float16')
4     elif mixed_precision == False:
5         tf.keras.mixed_precision.set_global_policy('float32')
6
7     if separable:
8         model = keras.models.Sequential([
9           keras.layers.SeparableConv2D(64, (3, 3), activation = 'relu',
                padding = 'same', input_shape=[224, 224, 3]),
10          keras.layers.SeparableConv2D(64, 3, activation = 'relu', padding =
                'same'),
11          keras.layers.MaxPooling2D((2, 2), (2, 2)),
12          keras.layers.BatchNormalization(),
13
14          keras.layers.SeparableConv2D(128, 3, activation = 'relu', padding
                = 'same'),
15          keras.layers.SeparableConv2D(128, 3, activation = 'relu', padding
                = 'same'),
16          keras.layers.MaxPooling2D(2, 2),
17          keras.layers.BatchNormalization(),
18
19          keras.layers.SeparableConv2D(256, 3, activation = 'relu', padding
                = 'same'),
20          keras.layers.SeparableConv2D(256, 3, activation = 'relu', padding
                = 'same'),
21          keras.layers.MaxPooling2D(2, 2),
22          keras.layers.BatchNormalization(),
23
24          keras.layers.SeparableConv2D(256, 3, activation = 'relu', padding
                = 'same'),
25          keras.layers.SeparableConv2D(256, 3, activation = 'relu', padding
                = 'same'),
```

```
        keras.layers.MaxPooling2D(2, 2),
        keras.layers.BatchNormalization(),

        keras.layers.SeparableConv2D(512, 3, activation = 'relu', padding = 'same'),
        keras.layers.SeparableConv2D(512, 3, activation = 'relu', padding = 'same'),
        keras.layers.MaxPooling2D(2, 2),
        keras.layers.BatchNormalization(),

        keras.layers.GlobalAveragePooling2D(),
        keras.layers.Dropout(0.3, seed=2),
        keras.layers.Dense(6, activation = 'softmax')
    ])
    else:
      model = keras.models.Sequential([
        keras.layers.Conv2D(64, (3, 3), activation = 'relu', padding = 'same', input_shape=[224, 224, 3]),
        keras.layers.Conv2D(64, 3, activation = 'relu', padding = 'same'),
        keras.layers.MaxPooling2D((2, 2), (2, 2)),
        keras.layers.BatchNormalization(),

        keras.layers.Conv2D(128, 3, activation = 'relu', padding = 'same'),
        keras.layers.Conv2D(128, 3, activation = 'relu', padding = 'same'),
        keras.layers.MaxPooling2D(2, 2),
        keras.layers.BatchNormalization(),

        keras.layers.Conv2D(256, 3, activation = 'relu', padding = 'same'),
        keras.layers.Conv2D(256, 3, activation = 'relu', padding = 'same'),
        keras.layers.MaxPooling2D(2, 2),
        keras.layers.BatchNormalization(),

        keras.layers.Conv2D(256, 3, activation = 'relu', padding = 'same'),
        keras.layers.Conv2D(256, 3, activation = 'relu', padding = 'same'),
        keras.layers.MaxPooling2D(2, 2),
        keras.layers.BatchNormalization(),

        keras.layers.Conv2D(512, 3, activation = 'relu', padding = 'same'),
        keras.layers.Conv2D(512, 3, activation = 'relu', padding = 'same'),
        keras.layers.MaxPooling2D(2, 2),
        keras.layers.BatchNormalization(),

        keras.layers.GlobalAveragePooling2D(),
        keras.layers.Dropout(0.3, seed=2),
        keras.layers.Dense(6, activation = 'softmax')
    ])


    model.compile(loss = "sparse_categorical_crossentropy",
                  optimizer = keras.optimizers.Adam(),
                  jit_compile=jit,
                  steps_per_execution=fuse_steps,
                  metrics=['accuracy',
                           keras.metrics.SparseTopKCategoricalAccuracy(k=2)])

```

```
78    return model
```

The `mixed_precision` flag, once set, will set the global policy, so when you run a model with AMP, it'll maintain the global state, so keep that in mind in case you want to run more experiments.

Now, we can go ahead and create several models and benchmark them:

```
1 pooling = make_model()
2 pooling.summary()
3 # Total params: 5,873,478
```

```
1 separable = make_model(separable=True)
2 separable.summary()
3 # Total params: 679,137
```

```
1 separable_jit = make_model(separable=True, jit=True)
2 separable_jit.summary()
3 # Total params: 679,137
```

```
1 separable_jit_amp = make_model(separable=True, jit=True,
      mixed_precision=True)
2 separable_jit_amp.summary()
3 # Total params: 679,137
```

```
1 separable_jit_amp_stepf = make_model(separable=True, jit=True,
      mixed_precision=True, fuse_steps=8)
2 separable_jit_amp_stepf.summary()
3 # Total params: 679,137
```

15.10.3 Benchmarking

Trained for 20 epochs each on Google Colab, on a Tesla P100 GPU. I marked down the best validation accuracies over the 20 epochs - this is naturally variable at such early points in training, and the differences will "iron out" over longer training periods, and depend on the dataset.

While not the *most precise* way to compare models in terms of accuracy, you can get a good idea of the performance.

Naive	Pooling	Sep	Sep+JIT	...+AMP	...+Fusing
Parameters	7,476,742	5,873,478	679,137	679,137	679,137
Accuracy	81%	66%	73%	75%	76%
Train time/epoch	82s	77-81s	244s	74s	69-72s
Inference time/step (ms)	51ms/step	40ms/step	54ms/step	42ms/step	39ms/step

The naive implementation has a whopping 7.5M parameters, due to the VGG-like nature.

When introducing pooling, the parameter's dropped to 5.9M, which is already an amazing improvement in network complexity, but is still a network that inefficiently uses parameters. Finally, with separable convolutions - the parameters dropped down to 679K.

> This is a 91% reduction in parameters between the naive and separable model.

So, how does it translate to training times? Separable convolutions, while providing a significant parameter reduction and comparable accuracy, took a lot longer to train - from 82s to 244s. Using the JIT compiler on this network slashes the training time from 244s to 74s. Automatic mixed precision further slashes this down to around 70s (the GPU the model was trained on was a Tesla P100, which has compute capability of 6.0, and thus can't make much use use of AMP), and step fusing takes it further down to 62s.

> This is a 24% reduction in training time.

The inference times are somewhat similar on GPUs, with 51ms/step on the naive implementation, and 39ms/step on the optimized one.

> This is a 24% reduction in inference time.

With CPU-based devices, this effect would be much more noticeable.

When the notebook was re-run on my local machine with a GTX 1660 Super, which has a compute capability of 7.5 and can make use of AMP, these are the results:

Naive	Pooling	Sep	Sep+JIT	...+AMP	...+Fusing
Parameters	7,476,742	5,873,478	679,137	679,137	679,137
Accuracy	82%	65%	74%	76%	74%
Train time/epoch	171s	164s	250s	89s	67s
Inference time/step (ms)	52ms/step	51ms/step	36ms/step	19ms/step	22ms/step

My local machine doesn't have as much VRAM as Google Colab's Tesla P100, so my `steps_per_execution` were set to only 2, which didn't yield much performance boosts, but does have higher compute capability so AMP had more of an effect.

On my home setup, between the naive and final version, there was:

- A 91% reduction in parameters
- A 61% reduction in training time
- A 57% reduction in inference time

My home setup benefit more from optimization than the Google Colab environment! Different setups will note different reductions, but note that even a 20% reduction in training time can really mean a lot if you're training a model for hours on end.

15.11 Conclusion

Optimizing models and pipelines isn't hard. Many of the changes made between a naive pipaline and a more optimized pipeline are one-line changes. This is true because of the massive efforts of the TensorFlow and Keras team to make training models faster and cheaper, making optimization a one-liner for you.

For deployment, collaborative optimization can take a moment to get used to, but is fairly standard and boils down to choosing the right layers to prune, cluster and/or quantize, which is done by simple trial and error.

I hope that this lesson can serve you at your deskside, as a bullet list of actionable items in your early stages of your journey, and as reminders in later stages. These steps can quickly be burned into your memory, but do remember to switch things up and try out different combinations based on your network and dataset. Not all combinations work the same in all cases.

16 Going Further - Resource Recommendations

We've gone far from the first chapter! From the foundations of computer vision, how it can be conceptualized, to building your first CNN classifier, validating and testing it, through several projects, discovering landscapes, building highly performant data and augmentation pipelines, intersecting NLP and CV, reading and implementing papers, applying best practices, etc.

Deep Learning is a large field, and you might want to dive deeper into it, or you might be looking to dive deeper into Machine Learning in general, or Data Science as the parent field to it. This book is intended for a varied audience, as mentioned in the beginning, and with that assumption - I've made choices on what to include and what not to include, to maximize the informational value for everyone involved.

One of the assumptions was that you have at least a basic understanding of ML and DL and that there's no need to cover material such as activation and loss functions, what a neural network is, etc. Condensing it all into a small section at the start of the book wouldn't do it justice, nor would it really help people get a grasp on it, so I've omitted it. This is the section in which I'd love to take a moment to point you to a few resources that could help you deepen your grasp on *data science* in general, as well as other resources on deep learning for computer vision.

Note: I'd also like to formally note that this section is **not** sponsored by any of the publishers or authors of the mentioned resources. I'm including only the resources I've personally had the chance to read and think are useful for practicioners, with small reviews for each.

16.1 Machine and Deep Learning Resources

For those who jumped into this journey without much prior experience:

- *"Hands-On Machine Learning with Scikit-Learn, Keras, and TensorFlow"*, 3rd Edition, by Aurélien Géron (O'Reilly)

- *"Deep Learning with Python, Second Edition"*, by François Chollet (Manning)
- *"Machine Learning with PyTorch and Scikit-Learn"* by Sebastian Raschka, Yuxi (Hayden) Liu and Vahid Mirjalili (Packt)
- *"Deep Learning for Coders with Fastai and PyTorch"* by Jeremy Howard and Sylvain Gugger (O'Reilly)

One of these will generally be enough, as they have many overlapping sections, but if you have the time, energy and finances to obtain more than one - they pair well too.

16.1.1 *"Hands-On Machine Learning with Scikit-Learn, Keras, and TensorFlow"*

Aurélien Géron's book is possibly the best book I've purchased ever. With over a thousand information-rich pages (that you'll *want to* re-read a few times to get the most out of), Aurélien covers everything from the foundations of machine learning with Scikit-Learn to advanced Reinforcement Learning with Keras/TensorFlow. The book is Keras/TF-oriented and teaches you how to work with the libraries themselves, and less so with tools in the ecosystem.

The book is a generalist one, and you'll do everything from employing traditional machine learning methods, to MLPs, Natural Language Processing, Computer Vision, and some generative ML, referencing trends and advancements through the years. At the same time, it provides deeper knowledge than some specialist resources I've seen - with good practices. If you're new to ML, in my opinion, this book is the best place to start, hands down. After that - you can much more easily specialize in any of the other fields.

16.1.2 *"Deep Learning with Python, Second Edition"*

François Chollet is the author of Keras and large contributor to TensorFlow. His book focuses on deep learning as a subset of machine learning, and is widely considered to be one of the best books on the subject. Naturally, it primarily deals with Keras and TensorFlow! It covers the fundamentals of deep learning, as well as its applications to computer vision, time series data, text, generative ML and a set of good practices, as well as some philosophical topics including the limitations of deep learning, going towards more generality, the missing ingredients to implementing intelligence, and staying up-to-date in a fast-paced environment such as this one.

You'll find some goodies in the book such as implementing transformer encoders and decoders from scratch in one of the cleanest/simplest implementations I've seen, and explanations written by an individual with major contributions to the software that powers a huge number of services and devices you use every day, but also its democratization.

16.1.3 *"Machine Learning with PyTorch and Scikit-Learn"*

Sebastian's, Yuxi's and Vahid's book is another generalist book on machine learning with Scikit-Learn and *PyTorch*, and a great introduction to general machine learning with Scikit-Learn and deep learning with PyTorch, delving into the details of how PyTorch and some of its modules work. These sections are followed by PyTorch Lightning, a higher-level API for PyTorch. You'll create and train MLPs, CNNs, RNNs, apply attention to Seq2Seq models for NLP, GANs for generating images, but you'll also get acquainted and work with Graph Neural Networks and graph convolutions. Graphs are a common modality of data, and you can represent most data sources in graphs - especially molecules and the building blocks of life. Finally, the book covers reinforcement learning for training agents in environments.

16.1.4 *"Deep Learning for Coders with Fastai and PyTorch"*

Jeremy Howard is unconventional in all the charming ways. He's trying to make neural networks uncool by making them simple and intuitive enough that they're no longer something only the "cool kids" do. Also, his book and book (from which the book was born) are both free (unless you get the paperback)! He co-founded fast.ai with Dr. Rachel Thomas.

The fast.ai website sums up their motivations well:

> *Being cool is about being exclusive, and that's the opposite of what we want. We want to make deep learning as accessible as possible–including to people using uncool languages like C#, uncool operating systems like Windows (which is used by the majority of the world), uncool datasets (way smaller than anything at Google, and in domain areas you'd consider*

> *obscure), and with uncool backgrounds (maybe you didn' t go to Stanford).*

Fast.ai itself is a research institude focused on research, development and education, but also the name of the framework built on top of PyTorch, that's very high-level and lets anyone with very basic knowledge create neural networks that work. Jeremy also founded Enlitic and for a while served as the Chief Scientist at Kaggle after consequtively winning Kaggle competitions.

Probably most notably - the book also focuses on data ethics and bias, and how you can (try to) avoid bias in your models in one of the first chapters of the book. The overarching theme behind fast.ai and the book is that *deep learning is for everyone*, and it really does break many stereotypes.

In fact, Jeremy Howard himself is a Bachelor of Arts in *philosophy*, with no formal training in machine learning. On the other hand, Sylvain Gugger used to be much more Math/CS-oriented with little practical deep learning experience, and now works as a Senior ML engineer at HuggingFace. The dichotomy between the two authors throughout the book, with frequent notes from both directed at different audience profiles makes for a charming, interesting and widely applicable experience.

16.2 Computer Vision Resources

As mentioned earlier, computer vision is a very large field, and spans well beyond deep learning - though, deep learning is the de facto best approach to solving it so far, and will in all likelihood remain the dominant approach to solving it. Here are some resources that might be useful specifically for computer vision:

- *OpenCV*
- *PyImageSearch*
- *StackAbuse*

16.2.1 OpenCV

Historically, computer vision and pattern recognition was pretty difficult. Vision doesn't conform to blanket rules, and building expert systems for such a large search space wasn't easy or scalable. OpenCV is a general computer vision package that stems from that time period - but has been adopting newer techniques and integrating them into the library, including support for neural networks. Yet - it still remains a repository of techniques used for image processing and computer vision!

The documentation, official OpenCV tutorials, and the community in general offers great learning opportunities.

16.2.2 PyImageSearch

PyImageSearch was founded and is being run by Adrian Rosebrock. Since 2014, Adrian has been publishing long guides, books and courses on computer vision, primarily with OpenCV, Keras and TensorFlow, and has recently been delving into PyTorch as well. To this date, it remains one of the largest computer vision oriented platforms, and a great place to find guides on various topics on building and training deep learning models.

16.2.3 StackAbuse

I've published this book with StackAbuse, and in the book of doing so - had to cut some parts short as to not overwhelm and stray from the point too much. On the platform, I'll keep writing and publishing CV-related guides in the days to come, containing both topics from the book and some which didn't make the cut. While the current list of guides under the "Computer Vision" tag[157] is humbler than some other platforms, I intend to grow it personally, providing a rich set of guides for the wider public.

Additionally - if you have any questions or requests, please feel free to reach out and I might be able to cover it on there!

16.3 MLOps

Machine learning isn't only about building models! Model building is a surprisingly "little" part of it. Much more work and thought goes into design patterns, scalability, preparing models for production (because no model is useful if you can't, well, use it), etc.

[157] https://stackabuse.com/tag/computer-vision/

Taking models into production and maintaining them there is an emerging field, known as MLOps! Similar to how DevOps automates builds and bridges a development environment to the end user, MLOps strives to do the same, but for ML models, rather than standard software. ModelOps refers to DevOps for general AI models (including non-ML ones). MLOps platforms and tools are springing, and it's rapidly expanding, and now's a great time to jump in and get a taste for it. Even with tools - it remains more of a set of practices and things to consider, rather than just preparing scripts for deployment.

16.3.1 *"Designing Machine Learning Systems"*

A recent, but widely accepted and acclaimed book for teaching MLOps principles is Chip Huyen's *"Designing Machine Learning Systems (O'Reilly)"*. The book assumes that you already know at least the basics of machine learning, and focuses on delivering that knowledge as a scalable system.

Chip Huyen is the co-founder of Claypot AI, a real-time machine learning platform, and previously worked at NVIDIA, Netflix, Primer and Snorkel AI. Armed with experience, she teaches the *"CS 329S: Machine Learning Systems Design"* at Stanford University, and has compiled a large portion of her teachings into the book that we can now obtain for $30-40.

16.4 Papers

The most exciting things are hard to encapsulate into fixed-format resources like books and courses, and are best followed through papers. I've updated the first lesson several times in a single month, and just as I finished updating it - 5 new exciting things showed up on my Twitter feed. Namely, text-conditioned video generation models, that create videos good enough to fool me into thinking that they're real, and I have a keen eye for CGI. In fact, several models of this *type* showed up just days apart.

Who knows what happened on the other side of the feed that wasn't personalized for me! Deep learning is accelerating. So much so, in fact, that in *"Predicting the Future of AI with AI"*[158], it's noted that the number of AI papers on arXiv per month grows

[158] https://arxiv.org/abs/2210.00881

exponentially, with a doubling rate of 24 months. If it was hard keeping track of everything in 2020, there's double that amount in 2022:

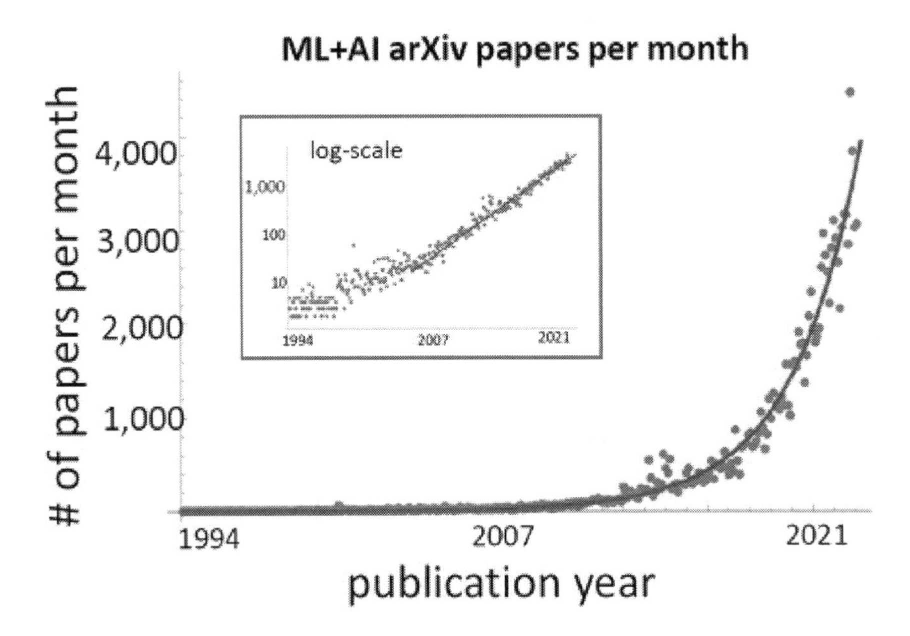

Figure 218:

Even if this process doesn't accelerate at all - you can turn paper-reading into a full-time job and still won't run out of them. Here's how you can distill tangible, workable knowledge from papers:

- **Take the findings with a grain of salt**: It's oftentimes hard to really reproduce these papers.
- **Try your hand in implementing them**: We've had a chapter on reading and implementing CNN architecture papers. Behind the terminology and complex lingo usually lies actionable code. Try using websites like PapersWithCode that connect papers to multiple online implementations of them, as well as the Chrome plugin ResearchCode, which allows you to search for implementations *from the paper PDF.*
- **Read other's implementations:** If you're feeling uncomfortable jumping into

paper implementations, try reading someone else's, and reference the paper while doing so. Creating links between the contents and the concrete implementations can help develop a bridging skill. Just remember that everyone writes code different, just as everyone writes papers different - some will be easier to read and understand than others, depending on your own expression style as well.

- **Take part in Kaggle competitions:** Kaggle competitions are usually difficult to truly solve, and although you can get some score with a reusable pipeline - most competitions have a very different preparation and training pipeline from most others. In high-level notebooks, you'll find implementations of the latest papers (because everyone wants to try using the shiny new thing in a competition to get the edge over others), custom implementations of metrics and layers, as well as all kinds of DIY hacks. Beware of *bad* practices as well, as you'll find them too. It's best to copy a notebook, try tweaking it and running it yourself.

17 Thank you for Supporting Online Education

That concludes this book - *"Practical Deep Learning for Computer Vision with Python"*. Thank you for taking a ride with me!

This book is the result of many nights, coffees, models and research papers, with a sprinkle of love.

> Online education is spreading through the world, and is becoming an increasingly important part of many lives. I believe that accessible, high-quality resources can help empower people that build tomorrow, and remain guided by that goal.

The point of this book is to get you from walking to running, and developing computer vision applications. Whether you want to learn computer vision for sheer curiosity, to apply it to medical images, manufacturing optimization, human workplace risk mitigation, automated robotics and cars, or to study the philosophical implications of computer vision - I hope that you found this book useful and insightful.

Authors have to make tough decisions about what to include, and what not to include, how to portray a concept or tool, identify potential confusing points, assess their work from many angles, and make it digestible, interesting and actionable. Above all, authors have to always remember that the point of writing is to help empower others to act and to make decisions themselves.

There are lots of tradeoffs in the writing process, and I sincerely hope that I made the ones that benefit the majority, and stay aware that I could've made the wrong ones. If I have not - please don't hesitate to contact me and let me know what you think. Of book if you found the book useful as it is - receiving feedback never fails to warm an author up! Additionally, I'd *love* to see and hear what you made while following or after following this book.

For all questions, remarks, discussions or just to share what you made - feel free to send me an email at david@stackabuse.com.

If you purchased the book in paperback format on Amazon or Kindle - please consider leaving an honest review. It can't be overstated how important reviews are, and you'll be helping the next person make a decision as to whether they'll purchase a resource or not.

Thank you for supporting online education, you rock! :)

Made in the USA
Las Vegas, NV
11 November 2023